The Economics of
American Agriculture

Evolution and Global Development

Steven C. Blank

M.E.Sharpe
Armonk, New York
London, England

This book is dedicated to my daughter, Sara. She and her generation will have to live in the world we leave her. Her concern for that future world inspired me to think about it myself. My concern for her made me want to make that world a little better somehow.

Library of Congress Cataloging-in-Publication Data

Blank, Steven C.
The economics of American agriculture : evolution and global development / Steven C. Blank.
    p. cm.
Includes bibliographical references and index.
ISBN 978-0-7656-2228-0 (cloth : alk. paper)
1. Agriculture—Economic aspects—United States. 2. Farm income—United States. I. Title.

HD1761.B564 2008
338.10973—dc22   2008001108

Printed in the United States of America

The paper used in this publication meets the minimum requirements of
American National Standard for Information Sciences
Permanence of Paper for Printed Library Materials,
ANSI Z 39.48-1984.

∞

BM (c)   10   9   8   7   6   5   4   3   2   1

CONTENTS

PREFACE

Sometimes it is not fun being an economist. This is especially true when you have to give good people bad news, which has been the case for agricultural economists for much of the past century. American farmers and ranchers have been doing a great job of expanding their output over that period, providing increasing amounts and types of commodities for consumers here and overseas, but their reward has been a steady decline in real prices for those commodities, thus their profit margins have been squeezed to nearly nothing. During the past three or four decades in particular, the situation has worsened much quicker. As a result, agricultural producers have been seeking help in understanding the challenges they face by asking agricultural economists "What is happening, and why?" Unfortunately, the research of most agricultural economists is, by necessity, narrowly focused on small parts of the very large whole, so few of the answers given could "connect all the dots" to outline the big picture. This book tries to answer the questions by summarizing the big picture.

Another difficult aspect of being an economist is constantly being asked to forecast the economic future. Invariably, after a person asks "What is happening, and why?" he or she then asks, "What does it mean for the future?" American agriculture has not often asked economists this follow-up question because the industry usually expects to be in control of its future. And so it is, on the micro scale of things. However, at the macro scale events are usually beyond the control of independent farmers and ranchers and, instead, create the economic constraints within which producers must operate. This is where economists come in. To help the agricultural sector, agricultural economists need to forecast the future, which is analogous to being asked to describe an iceberg. We can and should describe what little we can see of it above the surface of the water, but we must also use that information, and our imagination, to explain the larger mystery that is under the surface. The challenge being thrown at economists now is to describe what is under the surface, some of it just out of sight, for the economic development of the world. With this book, I try to contribute to that discussion by using existing data on many subjects to identify likely economic trends influencing American agriculture's evolution.

THE PAST

About eight decades ago, Theodore Schultz, the future Nobel laureate, was studying economics so that he could understand the problems being faced at that time by America's farmers and ranchers. However, he developed a different approach to his research than did many of his colleagues. As an empirical economist, Schultz visited farms when he traveled to gain a better understanding of agricultural economics. As a result, he often disagreed with other economists about the nature of the problems he observed. For example, in his book, *Transforming Traditional Agriculture* (1964), Schultz challenged the prevailing view, held by development economists, that farmers in developing countries were irrational in their attitudes toward innovation. He argued that, to the contrary, the farmers were making rational responses to the economic challenges facing them. In that volume and others, Schultz was one of the first to discuss the concept of industrialization as an explanation for the structural and economic changes observed in agriculture at that time. He viewed agricultural development as a precondition for industrialization, thus he saw it all as one continuous evolutionary process.

About three decades ago, industrialization was still being discussed as a threat to American agricultural producers. For example, Plaxico (1979) noted that agricultural industrialization and economic development were likely to cause farmland prices to rise, thus creating economic conditions that would significantly alter the structure of American production agriculture. In explaining his analysis, Plaxico (1979, p. 1099) noted that "scenarios are constructed to identify implications of changing sources of return in agriculture," and in those scenarios, "hobby and subsistence farm units are likely to increase in number but not in terms of market share." Thus, the current structure of agriculture—dominated by small-scale operations—was already an issue. Plaxico went on to describe the changes expected in the sector if farmland prices rose.

> Farmland ownership (control) will be consolidated rapidly due to growth of already large farms with a corresponding decline in the number of medium size (family) farms. The large units will grow as a consequence of financial expertise and leverage with marketing advantages playing a lesser role. Growth will not be due to scale economies in production. Initially large farms will be predominantly owned by individuals and these owners will be the economic elite in the economy—whether they reside in Boston, Zurich, or Gotebo. Large established units will become attractive acquisition targets for large corporations and for pension fund investments as estates are settled. Corporate-owned farmland will generate modest dividends, but stock-holder enchantment will not wane as net worth and stock values rise.
>
> Capital, management, and labor functions will be separated. Initially tenants will farm the land—until a unionized labor force in agriculture emerges. The factor share to land will increase with a concurrent decline in the labor factor share, a continuation of the current trend.... Labor cost rates in agriculture will equal nonfarm wages. Agriculture as a way of life will pass and agriculture will have lost its uniqueness in the American scene. (Plaxico 1979, pp. 1099–1100)

As we know now, farmland prices did rise, and continue rising, so Plaxico was correct in predicting the future in which we now live. Some of the changes he forecast are not yet complete, but the trends are in place. Clearly, the present situation in American agriculture was developing at least three, and maybe eight, decades ago.

The reactions to the problems observed by Ted Schultz and others eight decades ago led to the establishment of agricultural policies by the U.S. government. Those policies included support for research and education programs aimed at agricultural producers. However, three decades ago Plaxico (1979) envisioned a different future with much less support for producers:

> Public support of agricultural research and education will decline. Research will be funded by private agribusiness interests and the results will be proprietary and findings will be guarded—not extended. Land grant institutions will lose their unique advantage as teaching institutions as they decline in importance as agricultural research centers—but those with the leadership, foresight, and desire will adjust to new funding patterns and emerge as the "prestige institutions" of the twenty-first century. The agricultural economics profession may be replaced by systems scientists, applied economists, business managers, accountants, and attorneys. (Plaxico 1979, pp. 1100)

Again, the trends observed by Plaxico are now in place. This is not good news for agriculture, and it points out that the economic trends leading to the difficult situation American agriculture finds itself in at present are not recent. Some agricultural economists have been aware of the many problems facing the production agriculture sector, but the majority of economists apparently have not recognized the implications of those trends.

This all sounds so familiar. Industrialization is still creating problems and agricultural economists are still worrying about what to do for farmers and ranchers. Time has shown that Schultz was correct; agricultural development is a precondition for industrialization. He was correct again when he suggested that industrialization would transform traditional agriculture.

THE PRESENT

For American agriculture it is the best of times and it is the worst of times, depending on which sector you evaluate. Agribusinesses are doing very well; most farmers and ranchers are not doing well at all. As a result, the structures of both sectors are changing. Industrialization is maturing as a process and expanding as an economic phenomenon. This could make forecasting the future of American agriculture impossible, if you look at the micro scale, but it could make forecasts uncomfortably easy on the macro scale. Economic theory is clear about how industries evolve, in general. The strong get stronger and the weak get swallowed, either disappearing or becoming part of the larger beast. The same will be true in American agriculture. Thus, the key to forecasting agriculture's future is to identify who is strong and whose future is at risk.

When attempting to make forecasts about agriculture, economists often err by believing aggregate published data (which is incomplete and estimated) instead of what farmers are saying. We need to listen to farmers and ranchers to know how to correct the data and how to interpret it—a lesson learned by Schultz, but still often forgotten. Ironically, it is micro-level data, such as survey information collected at the farm level, that helps economists understand the real trends in aggregated data. Therefore, much of the research upon which this book is based was conducted using farm-level data.

THE PROPOSITIONS

One of this book's contributions to the discussion of American agriculture's evolution is its use of induction to develop propositions that are consistent with the empirical data from aggregate sources and from farmers and ranchers. These propositions can be developed into theories once sufficient data become available. It is hoped that readers are inspired by these conjectures enough to follow up on them. At present, these propositions are offered to guide the exploration in many of the chapters that follow.

Overall, there is a consistent theme to the propositions scattered throughout this book: all economic/business decisions are *investment decisions.* So, the focus of the book is on who is investing, their investment objective, the risks associated with investment alternatives, and risk attitudes. The same approach is relevant whether the decision is being made at the firm level, industry level, or global level. There are two major points at which decisions might be made: (1) where a person chooses to move to an alternative that is more profitable, and (2) where losses are occurring and a person (or firm or local industry) *must* leave the market. American agriculture's evolution has been full of these decision points and the argument made here is that this is normal and ongoing.

Another theme of this book is that decisions are only truly made at the personal and firm level. Although industry-level decisions are mentioned, they are only the aggregate effects of firm-level investment decisions. In agriculture, farm-level decision making has local and regional effects, which can have national effects, and—because the national activities are repeated in every country—there can be global effects. In essence, this is another lesson Schultz learned: people make decisions, aggregate groups do not. Once again this indicates the importance of using micro-level data in economic research. Aggregate data is nice for summarizing the big picture, but that picture is made up of many small dots and each one has a name.

THE GOAL

The goal of this book is to "connect all the dots," to outline the big picture facing American agriculture as a call to action for those people who do not like the current picture. The current trends documented in this book are carrying America's farmers and ranchers down a particular evolutionary path, but the future is not set in stone. People in and out of the production agriculture sector can have some influence on the actual path followed, but action is needed quickly. The economic currents are flowing strongly at the moment.

This book is written for an audience with some economics background. Nevertheless, it is hoped that a wide audience will wade into this volume and draw from it some inspiration that will lead to action. Sometimes it is not fun being an economist, but one of the good times is when we can open eyes and expand understanding of an important problem. Writing this book has been painful at times because the story here is not the one the author wanted to tell. Yet, it is the data, not the author, telling the story. Economists are translators through whom economic data speak. To serve agriculture and America best, we must give the data a voice and listen to it.

Some of the chapters in this book are, at least in part, revised and expanded versions of papers published in scholarly journals. A few of those papers were co-authored by colleagues who, therefore, deserve recognition here. Thus, co-authorship credit is assigned to the following people: Kenneth Erickson (Economic Research Service, U.S. Department of Agriculture) contributed to Chapters 3, 4, and 18. Charles Moss (University of Florida) contributed to Chapter 3. Richard Nehring and Charles Hallahan (both of the Economic Research Service, U.S. Department of Agriculture) contributed to Chapter 4. Jim Thompson (University of California, Davis) contributed to Chapter 7. Colin Carter (University of California, Davis) and Jeff McDonald (formerly of the University of California, Davis) contributed to Chapter 14. Gary Thompson (University of

Arizona) contributed to Chapter 16. Richard Volpe III (University of California, Davis) contributed to Chapter 18.

Chapter 17 is unique in that it was written almost entirely by Philip Watson (formerly of Colorado State University) and Dawn Thilmany (Colorado State University), with just a very small contribution from Steve Blank. That chapter was prepared specially for this volume from material in Philip Watson's dissertation.

Finally, the real goal of this project is to contribute in some small way to a more prosperous future to be shared by my daughter, Sara, and her generation. For that goal to be realized, the future must involve a prosperous and sustainable food system that is a good citizen in the world. It will take work, but it is achievable.

REFERENCES

Plaxico, James S. 1979. "Implications of Divergence in Sources of Returns in Agriculture." *American Journal of Agricultural Economics* 61, 5: 1098–1102.

Schultz, Theodore W. 1964. *Transforming Traditional Agriculture.* New Haven: Yale University Press.

PART I

AMERICAN AGRICULTURE AND GLOBALIZATION

CHAPTER 1

IS AMERICAN AGRICULTURE SHRINKING?

"Compared to what?"
—Winston Churchill, when once asked, "How's your wife?"

Change is not only inevitable; it is necessary in a dynamic economy. Without change, progress is impossible. However, some changes are so dramatic that it is difficult to think of them as being necessary or progressive. For instance, think of all the American industries that once flourished and now are gone or virtually so. Just a few examples include copper mining in the southwest; gold mining in California, South Dakota, and Alaska; the timber industries of the East Coast; the fishing industries along many parts of both coasts; and the steel industry of the Great Lakes region. Each of these commodity-based industries once was the central force in some local or regional economy. Now each of them has vanished to some degree. All that is left of the copper mining that thrived in Arizona during the late 1800s is a scattering of ghost towns. Gold mining in California has left behind only a few hobbyists and numerous museums. The eastern timber industry has been gone for so long it is not mentioned in most history books. And the steel industry has mostly rusted into memory.

In their heyday, each of these industries caused inward migrations of workers to the regions, triggered large-scale investments in economic activities of many sorts, and fueled the economy of the surrounding region. Each was proud, productive, and profitable . . . in its prime.

Now think of American agriculture. Farms and ranches once numbered over 6 million in this country. Agriculture was the dominant industry in the nation for much of our history. It caused mass migrations and large-scale investments that created and supported the economies of entire regions. It remains proud and may be at its productive prime. But it is no longer very profitable, thus it is slowly disappearing.

Ghost towns are now appearing in parts of the Midwest where agriculture was the economic mainstay. There are a large number of counties that have lost more than 10 percent of their population in the last 20 years. Most of those counties lie in a swath stretching from Texas and New Mexico to Montana and North Dakota. Nationally, hobby farmers and agricultural museums are becoming more numerous. And with each generation, America's rural roots are becoming a smaller part of the nation's collective memory.

This is all part of a normal evolutionary process.

A dictionary provides several definitions of "evolution," the first two of which are: "(1) a process of change in a particular direction, (2) one of a series of prescribed movements (as in a dance or military exercise)." Thus, the evolutionary changes occurring over time in American agriculture must be viewed as being part of a particular process, not a random series of unrelated events. That process is being "prescribed" by the economics of the markets for the commodities produced by American farmers and ranchers. Each movement in the dance toward the future has some rational explanation based on the investment decisions made by agricultural producers as they deal with the evolving markets facing them.

This book offers some insights into the economic explanation for the observed changes occurring in American agriculture. It also offers some possible explanations for what is likely to happen in the future if the current economic "series of prescribed movements" continues to carry the industry in the "particular direction" indicated by the current "process of change."

INTRODUCTION TO THE BIG QUESTIONS

This book is an analysis of American agriculture's profitability and how it is affected by economic and structural changes around the globe. The information here seeks to both describe and explain those changes with an eye on possible future developments. The focus is on profitability because, as the saying goes, "profits are the lifeblood of a firm" (or industry, or economic sector). Without profits, a commercial enterprise cannot survive for long. Some level of profit is needed after all costs of operations are covered to reward the firm's owner-operators for the risks borne. For owners of any business, the incentive to accept some level of risk is the opportunity to earn rewards in the form of profits, which are the source of wealth. Wealth is an accumulation of retained profits. The level of wealth achieved by a family business directly determines the standard of living and, indirectly, the quality of life for the family. Thus, the financial analysis of American agriculture's performance presented in this book is an assessment of the industry's ability to support the owner-operators of the farms and ranches remaining across the country.

A number of big questions are raised in this assessment process. Some of those questions can be answered directly, some can be answered only indirectly, and some can only be speculated about. The process is complicated by the fact that American agriculture is not really one industry, it is a collection of commodity segments. Some of the segments have better prospects for sustainable profits and will survive; many other segments will not survive due to their inability to generate sufficient profits to support the people working in those markets. This book discusses agriculture as a whole and as pieces. Agriculture can be considered as a whole quite often because all of its commodity segments share some common economic circumstances. Most of the material in this book covers agriculture as a whole. In a few places the unique economic circumstances facing some commodity segments are noted. These differences between commodities and their markets are important only when they create significant differences in the potential for sustainable profits for the farmers and/or ranchers involved. In other words, the focus of this book is the profitability of American production agriculture (i.e., farm- and ranch-level producers). The agribusiness sector (i.e., the businesses that provide inputs to, and handle the outputs from, farms and ranches) is dealt with briefly, but only with reference to its role in influencing the profitability of producers.

One big question dealt with is the relationship between American agriculture, the remainder of the American economy, and the global economic development process. In this book it will be argued that global economic development is a *continuous process of change* that never ends. Thus, there are no "developed" nations in the sense that the term implies a country's having completed the process. Therefore, the United States may be more developed than some less-developed nations, but our economy continues to change as it continues to develop with new technical and managerial innovations. The agricultural sector of the American economy is part of that process, thus continuous change must be expected.

Agriculture has gone from being the "initial industry" to a "residual industry" in the U.S. economy. Like most countries, the United States began its economic development with an initial industry of "agriculture" because it was necessary to feed its population with domestic products.

As agriculture became more productive, it required a smaller percentage of the population working in the industry to generate the volumes of food demanded. Resources then began leaving agriculture for other industries that began to develop as technological innovations made profits possible. At this point in American history, resources are now in agriculture as a holding pattern until some nonagricultural use develops that will offer higher profits to the owners of productive resources. In the United States, only 1.3 percent of the population lived and worked on farms in the year 2000. The question arises: how low can farming's share of the population go?

The implications of the change from initial to residual industry are that American agriculture is shrinking and that it is due to economic development at the global level. Such a change is only possible if the relative profitabilities of agriculture and nonagricultural industries have changed in the United States, and if the development processes of countries across the globe are related. This chapter begins a general assessment of both issues as a way to introduce ideas dealt with in more detail in later chapters.

THE PAST IS PROLOGUE

A quick scan of the topics covered in recent professional association presidential addresses given by agricultural economists turns up a recurring issue: changes in agriculture. For example, Antle (1999) begins, "Agriculture in the twentieth century was characterized . . . by technological innovation that . . . made it possible for agricultural production to grow faster than the demand for food despite a rapidly growing world population. The result was a decline in real agricultural commodity prices throughout this era." Gardner (2000) begins, "[D]uring most of the 20th century the U.S. farm economy generated low-average incomes and a higher incidence of poverty than in the non-farm population." A common theme in these and many other papers is the apparent, although reluctant, acceptance of a decline in American agriculture's profitability. This decline is just one signal that the industry may be shrinking in size and/or importance.

Changes discussed in the papers cited above are due to global economic development and the resulting adjustments that trickle down to U.S. agriculture. The scale of the changes to agriculture was significant over the past century and the rate of change is not likely to slow in this new century. The catalyst of this change has been, and will continue to be, technological innovation spurred on by economic opportunities created by changes in consumer demand (e.g., changing tastes, global demographics). In particular, the scale of economic development influences mentioned by Gardner and by Antle make it clear that during this new century, the world will face the possibility that the United States and some other more-developed nations will intentionally allow their production agriculture sectors to shrink. A shrinking agricultural sector, whether the result of intentional or accidental developments, has significant implications for the United States.[1]

In the remainder of this chapter, a test of the hypothesis that American production agriculture is shrinking is proposed. Some empirical data is presented for a brief list of factors to illustrate how the hypothesis test can be constructed and used. Then, observed changes in agriculture and their implications are discussed.

IS AMERICAN AGRICULTURE SHRINKING?

To answer the title question, it is important to first define the measurement scales to be used. The idea that a country's agricultural sector will become relatively less important over time has received much attention (Johnston and Mellor 1961; Johnson 1973; Anderson 1987), but it is only part of the question. In recent years, studies of the economic deterioration of local and regional agricultural sectors have discussed the possibility of failure and absolute shrinkage on those scales (Egan 2001), but the notion that a country's *entire* production agriculture sector might shrink in absolute terms has received little attention. The methodologies used to address each of the two pieces of the question have been very different, thus it is not surprising that the relative and absolute questions have never been considered together.

Anderson (1987), for example, asks the question, Why does a country's agricultural sector decline over time in relative terms, even if the country retains a strong comparative advantage in agriculture? His approach to the problem is typical of those following Johnson (1973) in using a two-sector general equilibrium framework to show that over time agriculture's terms of trade relative to manufacturing will decline with economic growth. This model applies both to an individual country's economy as well as to the entire world economy; therefore, agriculture's international and domestic terms of trade will decline over time. In this type of model, it is easy to show that Engel's Law will be sufficient to ensure that agricultural prices will decline relative to manufacturing prices. Thus agriculture's share of gross domestic product (GDP) declines over time and resources begin to leave the sector. Even if factor productivity growth is biased to agriculture, income-inelastic demand for agricultural output ensures agriculture's terms of trade will still decline along with its share of GDP (Anderson 1987).

Using portfolio theory, Blank (1998a) argued it was possible, and likely, that the investment decisions of individual farmers and ranchers could, in the aggregate, lead to absolute reductions in the size of a country's production agriculture sector. He pointed out there was evidence of this occurring in several highly developed countries, including the United States, Japan, and several countries in Western Europe.

Blank (2001a) developed a theory to show how micro-level decisions of individual producers can eventually lead them to consider diversifying out of agriculture. In particular, cropping choices are viewed as investment decisions constrained by both agronomic and personal economic factors, and these choices have significant impacts on the producer's wealth. When the decision involves only a single asset or some group of investments from which the resulting profits or losses are relatively small compared to the person's total wealth, the expected utility model suits most investors. However, when the scale of possible losses from an investment is significant, risk-averse investors have been shown to adopt "safety-first" decision rules. Safety-first criteria are compatible with the standard utility theory (Robison and Barry 1987, p. 201; Mahul 2000) and several forms of safety-first models have been proposed as alternatives to expected utility maximization (Roy 1952; Telser 1955; Hatch, Atwood, and Segar 1989; Bigman 1996). Therefore, risk-averse farmers and ranchers may quit producing some less profitable commodities voluntarily. In sum, individual agricultural producers are making investment decisions to protect their personal wealth and, in the aggregate, these decisions are causing resources to leave America's agricultural sector.

From the above, it appears both relative and absolute measures of agriculture should be considered. In the following two sections, a multipart test is developed that includes both relative and absolute measures of a country's production agriculture sector, and it is used to test the hypothesis that U.S. agriculture is shrinking.

Tests of a Shrinking Production Agriculture Sector

The proposed methodology for testing the hypothesis is to ask the question in terms of various measures based in economic development and portfolio investment theory. As summarized in Exhibit 1.1, the approach groups different measures together in three test forms. Each group of measures provides a successively stronger assessment of the question.

Exhibit 1.1

Methodology to Test the Hypothesis That American Agriculture Is Shrinking

Weak-form test (agriculture is shrinking in importance, but not necessarily in size)

Relative measures:
- As a percentage of the U.S. economy?
- As a percentage of world agricultural output?

Intermediate-form test (investment attractiveness)

Absolute measures of inputs:
- In number of farms?
- In number of acres?

Relative measure of outputs:
- In relative profit margins?

Strong-form test (economic outputs)

Absolute measures of outputs:
- In total profits?
- In total sales revenues?

A weak-form test is provided by measuring a country's production agriculture sector's size in relative terms. If the sector is shrinking as a percentage of the country's economy or the world's agricultural output, it is shrinking in importance. This is only a weak test because an agricultural sector may be shrinking in importance, yet still growing in absolute scale. As will be discussed later, most developing countries are expected to have an agricultural sector that is shrinking in importance relative to the entire economy, but only highly developed countries are likely to have a shrinking percentage of world agricultural output. This is based on the different rates of growth expected for sectors of a nation's economy (Gemmell, Lloyd, and Mathew 2000). A mature sector of a highly developed country is not expected to grow at the rate of newer sectors that still have significant potential for expansion.

An intermediate-form test shifts focus from the importance of an agricultural sector to indicators of agriculture's attractiveness as an investment. The number of farms is an approximate indicator of the number of people choosing to invest their labor and/or wealth in agriculture. Thus, it indicates the attractiveness of agriculture as an investment, but it also can be viewed as a weak proxy for the degree of political power based in the farm population. However, shrinking farm numbers may be a sign of economies of scale in agricultural production, so a second measure of investment attractiveness is used. The number of acres of land in agriculture is a stronger measure of attractiveness as an investment. Land is the least flexible of resources, so its allocation serves as a slow-moving long-run indicator of agriculture's attractiveness versus alternative uses. Finally, profit margins from agriculture relative to other investments will indicate whether there is incentive for agriculture to expand or shrink. When agricultural profit margins are low relative to alternate investments, farmers begin to shift out of agriculture. Consequently, relative profit margins influence total profit amounts, which is part of a strong-form test.

A strong-form test focuses on the absolute size of the sector's economic outputs: total profits and total sales revenues. Sales revenues measure how the market values aggregate output, and profits measure how well the firm or industry is performing in increasing owners' wealth. For

American agriculture, total sales revenue is an important indicator of the long-running race between falling prices and rising yields. However, Blank (2003) demonstrates that profits lead revenues in the life cycle of a mature product. (The life cycle is discussed in Chapter 2.)

Economic outputs, rather than tangible outputs, are relevant to managers and investors. The fact that the U.S. Department of Agriculture's (USDA) index of aggregate output has risen most years does not help decision makers in their tasks. Aggregate agricultural output is a productivity factor, not an economic factor. Productivity factors affect costs per unit of output, but economic outputs such as profits and sales revenues are decision factors. In commodity markets where demand can be inelastic, increasing aggregate output does not always lead to a positive economic result, and thus is not a strong indicator of economic performance.

The tests described by Exhibit 1.1 can be modified for use at the state or local level to evaluate the size and importance of agriculture. In the cases of many commodities or countries, the answers to the questions will be evident first at local and regional levels before national trends become apparent. Also, the tests can be expanded through the inclusion of additional factors for measuring the importance and absolute size of the national or local agricultural sector. Below, the tests are applied to some sample data from the American agricultural sector to initiate the discussion.

Weak-Form Test Results

Is American agriculture shrinking as measured by its percentage share of the U.S. economy? Yes, the U.S. economy is developing, resulting in other sectors becoming bigger, causing agriculture to represent a smaller percentage of the growing total. U.S. data indicate about 8 percent of gross domestic product GDP came from farms in 1947 versus only 1.1 percent coming from farms in 1997 (Lum and Yuskavage 1997), even though total agricultural sales revenues continued to increase in nominal terms during that period. By 2000, agriculture's share of GDP had fallen to 0.79 percent. As Bardhan and Udry (1999, p. 205) note, this result is expected because "historically, the share of agriculture in national income usually declines with economic growth."

Is American agriculture shrinking as a percentage of the world's agricultural output? In general, the answer is "yes," but the response varies when assessing each commodity separately. For example, as seen from Figure 1.1, over the 1960–2000 period the United States nearly doubled its wheat output, but its share of world production fell dramatically—from about 15 percent to about 10 percent. Obviously, other countries are expanding their agricultural output, thus making the United States a less important player. The situation is similar in other commodity markets. Over the same period, U.S. production of soybeans increased about 400 percent, but America's share of world production decreased from about 75 percent to just under 50 percent. America has done better in some markets, such as corn. In total, however, the growth of commodity production in other countries continues to give us a smaller market share.

Thus, the data support a weak-form test result that American agriculture is shrinking, at least in terms of importance. This result is consistent with the normal process of economic development. To continue the test, next is an intermediate form that combines factors from economic development and investment theory. It begins with two absolute measures of inputs: number of farms and number of acres in production.

Intermediate-Form Test Results

Yes, American agriculture is shrinking in terms of its number of farms. The United States reached its peak of 6.3 million farms in 1935, and has had fewer commercial farms each year since. In

Figure 1.1   **U.S. and World Wheat Production**

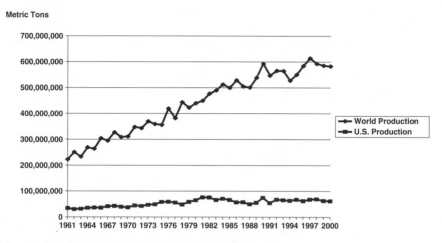

Source: Food and Agriculture Organization of the United Nations.

2005 the Bureau of Labor Statistics forecast that farming and ranching would see the largest decrease of all economic sectors in the United States, losing 250,000 jobs by 2012. Translating farm numbers into farm population reveals the United States is following a typical downward trend.[2]

According to estimates by the United Nations, 65 percent of the world's population was engaged in food production in 1950, and less than 30 percent of the population will be in agriculture in the year 2025. This dramatic shift in human resource allocation is made possible by technological advances in agricultural production (Antle 1999; Johnson 2000). Further, such a shift is known to be an indicator of positive economic development. Shifting labor and other resources into nonagricultural investments is good for America as a whole. Bardhan and Udry (1999, pp. 22–23) state, "as economic growth occurs, the return to skilled labor increases relative to the return to unskilled labor," and, even in America, agriculture is characterized as using primarily unskilled labor. Thus, it is expected that workers leaving agriculture will earn higher wages in nonagricultural jobs and, therefore, will add more value to America's GDP.

Economies of the United States, Japan, and several countries in Western Europe have developed to such an extent that agriculture has become a very small portion of the nation's "portfolio" of investments. In the United States, only 1.3 percent of the population works in agricultural production; the percentage is smaller in Japan, and in the European Union, with a population of about 300 million, the number of people working on farms plummeted to 7.3 million in 1995 from 12.3 million in 1979. For example, French farmers comprise about 2 percent of that country's population and are declining in number by 4.2 percent per year (Reuters 1996). Therefore, these countries are the first to face the questions related to a shrinking agriculture.

A dramatic example of agriculture's role as a holding area for labor is provided by China. A Chinese farm official was quoted in 1997 as saying that many of China's 450 million rural workers were redundant. He said only 200 million were actually needed for farming (Reuters 1997). Also, in 1997, Reuters reported the number of workers in China's agricultural sector would decrease by 2.6 percent each year over the next five years, while the number in manufacturing and the service sector would rise. In the year 2000, employees in China's agricultural sector accounted for only 43 percent of the total labor force, compared to 52 percent in 1990 and 69 percent in 1980.

In U.S. agriculture, labor is not the only major resource leaving the industry. Land is also being reinvested elsewhere. Land is the least mobile of all resources, yet it is leaving agriculture in a steady flow. Total farmland in the United States peaked at 1.2 billion acres in 1954, but has declined every year since. After nearly a half-century of reallocation, there were only 931 million acres of farmland reported in the USDA's *1997 Census of Agriculture* (USDA 1998).

Globally, cropland has been expanding by an average of 0.3 percent per year in recent decades as forest land is cleared and pasture is brought under cultivation (Wiebe 1997). By 1995, cropland represented 11 percent of the world's total land area. Pasture represented 26 percent of total land area, and forest land accounted for 30 percent. Therefore, in absolute and relative terms, America's investment of land in agriculture is shrinking.

The third measure in the intermediate-form test is relative profit margins. When agricultural profit margins are low relative to alternate investments, farmers begin to shift out of agriculture. This factor helps explain the past decline in absolute inputs in agriculture, such as labor and land, and it offers a signal about the potential direction of future investments of inputs. To begin, Figure 1.2 shows the absolute levels of two measures of profitability in U.S. agriculture reported by the USDA over the period 1960–2000: the nominal return on assets and the nominal return on equity.

As observed in Figure 1.2, the national returns have fluctuated around the 2–3 percent range over the past forty years. Return on equity (ROE) was above 3 percent only during seven years and was below zero twice during that period. The trend in ROE is shown in Figure 1.2 to be negatively sloped over the forty-year period. The trend line was estimated using ordinary least squares and has a statistically significant slope of -0.025 percent per year. When evaluating these results, it is important to remember that throughout the period, many of the least profitable producers (and land?) were leaving agriculture. Despite this attrition, the trend in agriculture's profit margins was decreasing, as illustrated in the figure.

In relative terms, these profit margins are low compared to returns from investments available outside of agriculture (Bjornson and Innes 1992). The stock market, for example, averaged about 14 percent nominal returns over the past forty years. Even risk-free investments, like certificates of deposit, have offered profit margins higher than those available from agriculture, on average. Also, returns to agriculture have been low relative to rates needed for farmers to increase their wealth. Some farmers have debt levels of 60–80 percent of the value of their assets, with 16 percent being the current average. This means gross profit margins must be adjusted for borrowing costs to find the real returns to farmers. The USDA (1999) did so and found the average real net return to assets financed by debt has been negative since the late 1980s and was -3.8 percent in 1999. Clearly, some farmers' real net worth has been supported by farmland value improvements, not operating profits over the past decade (USDA 2000a).[3]

Thus, the data support an intermediate-form test result that American agriculture is shrinking in terms of both size and its attractiveness as an investment. Finally, we turn to a strong-form test that looks at two absolute measures of outputs.

Strong-Form Test Results

Total profits in U.S. agriculture are declining. Recent levels of total annual income earned from U.S. agricultural production are presented in nominal terms in Table 1.1. The net farm income

Figure 1.2   **U.S. Agriculture's Profitability, 1960–2000**

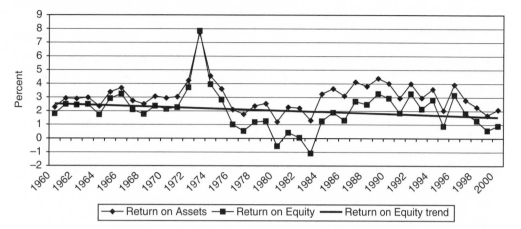

totals reported by the USDA represent one of the most commonly reported measures of absolute profitability. However, they are overstated. Among other things, those totals include direct government payments to agriculture, which have been at record levels in recent years.

In Table 1.1, direct government payments are subtracted from the net farm income totals to obtain adjusted production income for 1996–2003. As observed from these adjusted amounts, the recent decline in profits is much more significant than indicated in reported data. Without government subsidies, it is clear the profits earned from agricultural markets have dropped—from $47.6 billion in 1996 to as low as $24.9 billion in 2000.

While the short period of decline shown in Table 1.1 in nominal dollars is not long enough to provide convincing proof that total profits are falling for good, the eight-year trend is consistent with the hypothesis of a shrinking agriculture. A longer data period is needed to confirm that the past decade was not just a cyclical dip in agricultural profits. Also, to make a relevant long-term analysis, the data must be converted from nominal to real dollars. This was done for the 1949–2000 period, as depicted in Figure 1.3. Clearly, the peak in 1973 and the bottom in 1983 bracket an unusual decade of change in American agriculture. Nevertheless, the fact that net farm income and adjusted production income are both trending downward in the long term is a clear signal American agriculture is less profitable than it used to be.

As shown in Table 1.1, total sales (crop receipts plus livestock receipts) of U.S. agricultural producers have been mixed in recent years. In nominal terms, total sales were $208.9 billion in 1997 and were $21 billion lower two years later. No strong trend, up or down, can be detected in the recent data. This fact is obscured by the reporting of gross cash income and other aggregate "sales" figures including items such as government payments, "other farm income," and "imputed rental value of farm dwellings," which distort true sales results and give the impression sales are trending upward. Also adding to the confusion is the reporting of sales totals in nominal terms. For these reasons, total sales were converted into real dollars for the 1949–2000 period covered by Figure 1.3.

The results reported in Figure 1.3 give rise to a surprising conclusion. It is reasonable to interpret 1973 (or the 1973–1983 period) as a turning point when an uptrend reversed to create a downtrend. Regression analysis shows a positive trend in the real sales data prior to 1973 and

Table 1.1

U.S. Agricultural Nominal Sales and Income, 1996–2003 ($ billion)

	1996	1997	1998	1999	2000	2001	2002	2003
Crop receipts	115.6	112.4	101.7	92.0	92.5	93.4	101.3	106.2
Livestock receipts	92.0	96.5	94.1	95.6	99.6	106.7	93.8	105.5
Total sales	207.6	208.9	195.8	187.6	192.1	200.1	195.1	211.6
Net farm income	54.9	48.6	42.9	46.8	47.9	50.6	37.3	59.2
Direct government payments	7.3	7.5	12.4	21.5	22.9	20.7	11.0	15.9
Adjusted production income*	47.6	41.1	30.5	25.3	25.0	29.9	26.3	43.3

Source: USDA (2000b and 2003).
Note: * This is calculated as net farm income minus direct government payments.

Figure 1.3   **Real U.S. Agricultural Sales and Income, 1949–2002**

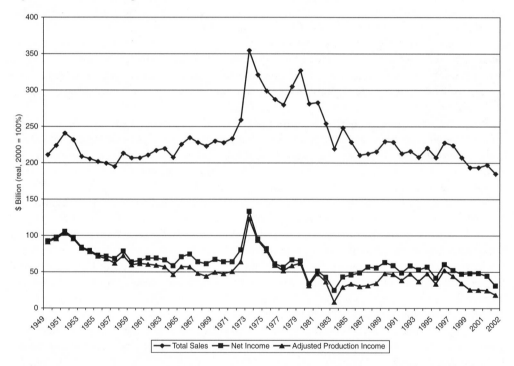

a negative slope in the trend thereafter, whether the data used begin at 1973 or 1983. (The specifics of the regression analysis are presented in the next chapter.)

The results of the three tests presented here are consistent with a shrinking American agricultural sector. The sector is clearly shrinking in relative size and importance, and in absolute size.

SOME IMPLICATIONS OF A SHRINKING AGRICULTURAL SECTOR

The shrinking size of American production agriculture implies that related sectors of the economy will necessarily shrink as well. The current trend of consolidation in agribusiness is expected to continue, meaning there will be fewer firms. The U.S. agribusiness sector will not become less important, however. Economic prospects are very good for firms that add value to agricultural commodities, so those firms will likely grow larger and have ever more power in controlling the world's agricultural resources.

American agribusiness firms will continue to expand their global perspective by using foreign direct investment, strategic alliances, contracting, and other management methods of guaranteeing that American consumers will always have plentiful food supplies available. For example, some American agribusiness firms already have offices in over 100 countries, making them important participants in global commodity markets. In general, this geographic diversification of large American agribusiness firms suggests that a decreasing number of those firms will wield power across the globe.

While the United States becomes a giant processing center for food commodities produced in other countries and destined for consumption domestically, American agribusiness firms will, in effect, be directing a global supply system. As global agribusinesses evolve, the words of Winston Churchill can take on new meaning: "Never has so much been owed by so many [American consumers] to so few [American agribusiness firms]."

With shrinking numbers of farmers and ranchers, shrinking federal and state agencies will be dealing with production issues, although food safety and nutrition regulation could burgeon. Thus, government policies and activities will necessarily shift their focus from production to international trade and resource management issues.

With shrinking numbers of farmers and ranchers, there will be fewer domestic students and colleges of agriculture. However, American research (Land Grant) universities will be called upon to focus increasingly on the needs of foreign students and less-developed producing nations and on agribusiness and trade topics. As Blank (1998b) reports, the number of foreign graduate students in U.S. agricultural economics and other programs has been steadily increasing over the past three decades as other countries increasingly look to the United States as a source of research information.

IS A SHRINKING AMERICAN AGRICULTURE A "BAD" THING?

For individuals, being squeezed out is painful. For farmers or ranchers, the prospect of being squeezed out of the profession they prefer is an unpleasant one. Being squeezed out often means the end of a family business and tradition that has lasted for generations. The personal pain of such an exit is real and significant. Maybe for those (and other) reasons, there are many people calling for the preservation of the "family farm" in America.

In the "big picture," however, letting American production agriculture shrink is allowing comparative advantage to work. The concept of comparative advantage asserts that a country should specialize in the production of whatever products its resources are best suited for, even if it does not have an absolute advantage in the production of any product (Helpman and Krugman 1986). Trade patterns are believed to be determined by comparative advantage, which, in turn, is explained by national differences in technology, factor endowments, and preferences (Peterson and Valluru 2000; Findlay 1995; Treffler 1995; Harrigan 1997; Griffin 1999). It is now understood that "countries may lose industries in which comparative advantage might have been maintained . . . due to changes in comparative advantage and international competition" (Krugman 1998, pp. 98, 101). This is especially true in markets for undifferentiated commodities.

Changes in comparative advantage occur as technological advances create new industries or substantially change existing industries within a country. When those advances result in changes in the relative profitability between industries, they can reduce the attractiveness of investments in existing industries, such as agriculture.

International competition is now relevant to some industries in which comparative advantage once existed, such as U.S. agriculture, because there is an *absolute* limit to how much the world needs of a commodity. Unlike the situation for branded products, undifferentiated agricultural commodities can now be produced in greater quantities than the global market can absorb. This excess supply is due to technological advances and productivity growth. Food commodities, in particular, have an absolute limit to the volume that can be consumed over time because there is a physical limit to how much a person can eat, even if an infinite supply were available free. And because commodities are undifferentiated (i.e., there is no difference between the output from two producers of a standardized commodity), buyers usually make purchases from the lowest-cost supplier. Thus, the "technological treadmill" helps push commodity prices lower (Johnson and Quance 1972).

According to the Heckscher-Ohlin theory of international trade, when a country does not have an absolute advantage in the global market for a product in which it has a comparative advantage, it is forced to compete on the basis of lower input costs (e.g., wages, land prices, etc.) or by adjusting its currency exchange rates. A country can make the price of a product in which it has a comparative advantage competitive in absolute terms by forcing down input costs or lowering the value of its currency. However, this is easier to do in a less-developed country trying to export a limited variety of products, compared to a more-developed country like the United States, which exports many different products. For the less-developed country, the relatively large impact of export sales for a single (or few) important product(s) will be felt in factor markets to a much greater extent than will the effects of export sales of any product from a more diversified, developed country.

For example, when Cuba's economy centered around the production of sugar, export prices of sugar greatly influenced wages and other input costs in that less-developed country. In contrast, sugar produced in Hawaii (although important to the local economy) had insignificant effects on the U.S. wage rate through currency changes because sugar was such a minuscule part of America's total economy. Also, factor prices in Hawaii did not fall sufficiently to lower the production costs of sugar because many alternative uses were available for labor and other resources. As a result, the Hawaiian sugar industry suffered a profit squeeze, forcing much of it out of business. This example is typical of cases where a regional comparative advantage in the production of some commodity is insufficient to overcome the industry's absolute disadvantage in a global market.

Krugman (1998, p. 95) concludes, "if foreigners are willing to sell us high-quality goods cheaply, that is a good thing for most of us, but a bad thing for the domestic industry that competes with the imports." There are many more American consumers benefiting from the growth of global commodity markets than there are agricultural producers being squeezed by the increased competition, so the United States will continue to shift its resources and policies in the direction of increasing agricultural imports.

All of this is bad news for American farmers and ranchers. Global competition in commodity markets will continue to increase as technology changes the comparative advantages of nations, making agriculture more profitable for less-developed countries and less profitable for more-developed countries. Gradually, the highest-cost suppliers will be forced to leave the markets as falling prices reduce profit margins. As noted by Duffy (2001), it is America's less-developed competitors who are increasing their productivity most rapidly, and thus their production costs per unit are falling faster than ours. As a result, the squeeze on U.S. producers will continue (Blank 2001b).

In the "big picture," this reduction in America's production agriculture sector is an improved, more efficient allocation of the nation's and the world's resources, making it a "good thing" from an economic perspective. Thus, many people in government and academia are stuck between wanting to help American agricultural producers and economic theory that says many producers will be squeezed out of business. This will seem like a "bad thing" to some as they deal with the difficult challenges the conflict creates. However, it is "bad" only if they somehow weight producers' interests more heavily than consumers' or taxpayers' interests.

THE PAST IS PROLOGUE, AGAIN

The economic changes affecting American agriculture's profitability and leading to the decreasing size of the industry are not new. Economists have observed and have been evaluating them for decades. In that effort, economists have used various theories to construct partial explanations, called propositions, for specific pieces of the larger processes being observed. This book will do the same. Some of the propositions presented in this volume were inspired by, and are extensions of, propositions presented by economists long ago. For example, Nobel Prize winner Theodore Schultz offered some propositions over three decades ago that are consistent with the results in this book. Using developmental economic theory to derive the propositions, Schultz (1974) foretold such resource shifts as those currently being observed regarding reallocation of land to nonagricultural uses, the rise of environmental concerns and their impacts on agriculture, the tremendous importance of technological advances in keeping American agriculture competitive, the need for continuous investment in agricultural research, and the key role of factors influencing farm household decisions regarding human capital.

Schultz noted the difficulties faced when trying to understand the dynamic changes in America's economy if armed only with standard theory. "Not knowing how to reconcile differences in values and beliefs, the art of economics is to conceal these differences" (Schultz 1974, p. 998). However, he believed that "by going beyond the boundary of standard theory, economic analysis can be extended to deal with some of these developmental changes in the supply of and demand for resources" (p. 1000).

One proposition presented by Schultz is directly related to the question addressed in this chapter. Written in 1974, Schultz's proposition dealt with "new" opportunities "favorable to the reallocation of land to nonagricultural uses and to the decline of the role of the owners of farmland in our economy" (Schultz 1974, p. 1000). He summarized his proposition as follows:

> Urban people are demanding more land for industry, residence, recreation, and for a more satisfying environment. In large part it is the increases in their income that make their demand effective, and the modernization of agriculture contributes to the supply. Our bias, however, is to resist such reallocations of land because of a deep-seated belief that good farmland should never be paved or put to urban uses, as insurance against a shortage of land suitable for agriculture. But the supply effects of agricultural modernization do not support our bias on this issue. The virtually fixed land area suitable for growing crops is not the

critical factor of production in increasing the supply of agricultural products as it was envisioned by Ricardo. The economic importance of cropland declines as a consequence of the modernization of agriculture. (Schultz 1974, pp. 1000–1001)

What Schultz referred to as the "modernization of agriculture" was adoption of technological innovations that expanded productivity. Thus, he essentially argues that productivity improvements from technological innovations are raising Americans' incomes and creating problems for American agriculture, yet the solution to farmers' problems is to continue developing technical innovations that improve their productivity and, therefore, their profitability. This technical treadmill will significantly affect American agriculture's evolution. Schultz (1974, p. 1001) listed some of the major implications of his proposition as the following:

> (1) the value productivity of the original, natural properties of the soil (Ricardian) declines relative to that of the land improvement investments that are made by man; (2) farmland rent declines relative to the other costs incurred in agricultural production and relative to the total retail costs entering into the food and fiber chain serving consumers; (3) real wages rise relative to farmland rent in constant dollars; (4) farmland rent becomes a very small component in our national income; (5) owners of farmland as a class become very small compared to the other economic classes in the economy; and (6) at many margins over space throughout the economy some farmland becomes more valuable for nonagricultural uses than for agricultural production.

These and other propositions are assessed in this book. Data are presented that show these important changes continue to occur in American agriculture. Also, it is argued that the industry's evolution is, indeed, "a process of change in a particular direction." The goal is to identify that direction and to describe the economic implications of that evolutionary path. It will be left to readers to decide whether these changes are "good" or "bad" and to take action to change the course of evolution, if that change is considered to be desirable.

NOTES

Some of this chapter is a revised version of an article published by S. Blank as "The Challenge to Think Big as American Agriculture Shrinks," *Journal of Agricultural and Resource Economics* 26, no. 2 (2001): 309–325.

1. It is important to note that nearly all of the recent literature indicates a very different future for the U.S. agribusiness sector. As will be discussed in Chapter 18, most researchers expect a prosperous future for this sector. The primary reason for the dichotomous expectations for the production versus post-farmgate sectors of American agriculture is that farmers and ranchers sell undifferentiated commodities in competitive global markets, while agribusinesses sell differentiated products and services in less perfectly competitive markets. Thus, U.S. agribusinesses are in a position to influence their profit margins and have been doing so successfully on a global scale for decades. Therefore, the story in this chapter does not apply to the agribusiness sector.

2. Some people are quick to point out that, after about sixty years of decline, the trend in farm numbers leveled off in the 1990s. USDA data document a decline in total farm numbers until 1992, but show these numbers have been fairly stable since 1993. Unfortunately, "total" farm numbers are distorted by the fact that "farms" with annual sales of less than $10,000 have been increasing in numbers since 1992. This size category represented about 48 percent of total farms in 1990 and about 54 percent in 1998. These very small operations have negative profits on average (USDA 1998), and thus cannot

be called "commercial" farms. If these "hobby" farms are excluded, total farm numbers continued to decrease throughout the 1990s.

3. Farm real estate represented about 78 percent of equity in agriculture in 2000. Farmland values are influenced by more than just income-producing potential (USDA 2000a, 2000c). Thus, a farmer's net worth can increase despite weak operating income over time. The role of nonincome factors in determining farmland values will be discussed in more detail later.

REFERENCES

Anderson, Kym. 1987. "On Why Agriculture Declines with Economic Growth." *Agricultural Economics* 1: 195–207.

Antle, John M. 1999. "The New Economics of Agriculture." *American Journal of Agricultural Economics* 81: 993–1010.

Bardhan, P., and C. Udry. 1999. *Development Microeconomics.* Oxford: Oxford University Press.

Bigman, D. 1996. "Safety-First Criteria and Their Measures of Risk." *American Journal of Agricultural Economics* 78 (February): 225–235.

Bjornson, B., and R. Innes. 1992. "Another Look at Returns to Agricultural and Nonagricultural Assets." *American Journal of Agricultural Economics* 74: 109–119.

Blank, Steven C. 1998a. *The End of Agriculture in the American Portfolio.* Westport, CT: Quorum Books.

———. 1998b. "A Decade of Decline and Evolution in Agricultural Economics Enrollments and Programs, 1985–96." *Review of Agricultural Economics* 20 (1): 155–167.

———. 2001a. "Producers Get Squeezed Up the Farming Food Chain: A Theory of Crop Portfolio Composition and Land Use." *Review of Agricultural Economics* 23 (2): 404–422.

———. 2001b. "Globalization, Cropping Choices, and Profitability in American Agriculture." *Journal of Agricultural & Applied Economics* 33 (2): 315–326.

———. 2003. "Where Is American Agriculture in Its 'Life Cycle'?" *Journal of Agricultural and Resource Economics* 28 (3): 396–418.

Duffy, Patricia A. 2001. "Casting Bread upon the Water: Comments on Technology, Globalization, and Agriculture." *Journal of Agricultural & Applied Economics* 33 (2): 341–347.

Egan, Timothy. 2001. "Failing in Style." *Choices* 16 (1): 39–42.

Findlay, R. 1995. *Factor Proportions, Trade and Growth.* Cambridge, MA: MIT Press.

Food and Agriculture Organization of the United Nations. 2001. Rome, Italy. FAO statistics accessed at: http://apps.fao.org, June.

Gardner, Bruce L. 2000. "Economic Growth and Low Incomes in Agriculture." *American Journal of Agricultural Economics* 82: 1059–1074.

Gemmell, N., T. Lloyd, and M. Mathew. 2000. "Agricultural Growth and Inter-Sectoral Linkages in a Developing Economy." *Journal of Agricultural Economics* 51: 353–370.

Griffin, Keith. 1999. *Alternative Strategies for Economic Development.* 2d ed. New York: St. Martin's.

Harrigan, J. 1997. "Technology, Factor Supplies, and International Specialisation: Estimating the Neoclassical Model." *American Economic Review* 87 (4): 475–494.

Hatch, U., J. Atwood, and J. Segar. 1989. "An Application of Safety-First Probability Limits in a Discrete Stochastic Farm Management Programming Model." *Southern Journal of Agricultural Economics* 21 (July): 65–72.

Helpman, E., and P. Krugman. 1986. *Market Structure and Foreign Trade.* Cambridge, MA: MIT Press.

Johnson, D. Gale. 1973. *World Agriculture in Disarray.* London: Fontana.

———. 2000. "Population, Food and Knowledge." *American Economic Review* 90: 1–14.

Johnson, Glenn L., and C. LeRoy Quance, eds. 1972. *The Overproduction Trap in U.S. Agriculture.* Resources for the Future. Baltimore, MD: Johns Hopkins University Press.

Johnston, B., and J. Mellor. 1961. "The Role of Agriculture in Economic Development." *American Economic Review* 51: 566–593.

Krugman, Paul. 1998. *Pop Internationalism*. Cambridge, MA: MIT Press.

Lum, S., and R. Yuskavage. 1997. "Gross Product by Industry, 1947–96." *Survey of Current Business* 77 (November): 20–34.

Mahul, O. 2000. "The Output Decision of a Risk-Neutral Producer Under Risk of Liquidation." *American Journal of Agricultural Economics* 82 (February): 49–58.

Peterson, W., and S. Valluru. 2000. "Agricultural Comparative Advantage and Government Policy Interventions." *Journal of Agricultural Economics* 51 (3): 371–387.

Reuters News Service. 1996. "EU Farm Workforce Slashed." News release, April 18.

———. 1997. "Chinese Workers Increasingly Seen Leaving the Land." News release, January 7.

Robison, L., and P. Barry. 1987. *The Competitive Firm's Response to Risk*. New York: Macmillan.

Roy, A. 1952. "Safety-First and the Holding of Assets." *Econometrica* 20: 431–449.

Schultz, Theodore W. 1974. "Conflicts over Changes in Scarcity: An Economic Approach." *American Journal of Agricultural Economics* 56 (5): 998–1004.

Telser, L. 1955. "Safety-First and Hedging," *Review of Economic Studies* 23: 1–16.

Treffler, D. 1995. "The Case of the Missing Trade and Other Mysteries." *American Economic Review* 85 (5): 1029–1046.

United Nations. 1996. "World Population Prospects: The 1996 Revision." New York: United Nations.

U.S. Department of Agriculture. 1998. *1997 Census of Agriculture*. Washington, DC: National Agricultural Statistics Service.

———. 1999. *Agricultural Income and Finance: Situation and Outlook Report*. Resource Economics Division, Economic Research Service, AIS-72, September.

———. 2000a. "Accumulated Farm Real Estate Value Will Help Farmers and Their Lenders Through Period of Declining Cash Receipts." *Agricultural Income and Finance: Situation and Outlook*. Economic Research Service, AIS-74, February, pp. 30–33.

———. 2000b. "With Low Commodity Prices, Government Payments Support Farm Income." *Agricultural Income and Finance: Situation and Outlook Report*. Resource Economics Division, Economic Research Service, AIS-75, September, pp. 4–13.

———. 2000c. "Farm Households' Incomes Remaining Steady." *Agricultural Income and Finance: Situation and Outlook Report*. Resource Economics Division, Economic Research Service, AIS-75, September, pp. 14–16.

———. 2003. "Farm Income and Costs: Farm Income Forecasts." Economic Research Service "Briefing Room," on web at http://www.ers.usda.gov/Briefing/FarmIncome/fore.htm, September.

Wiebe, K. 1997. "Resources, Sustainability, and Food Security." In *Food Security Assessment*, pp. 36–42. International Agriculture and Trade Report No. GFA-9. Washington, DC: USDA/Economic Research Service, November.

CHAPTER 2

AMERICAN AGRICULTURE'S LIFE CYCLE

"Is that all there is?"
—Peggy Lee, in a song by Leiber and Stoller.

Agriculture was the dominant industry in the nation for much of America's history (Cochrane 1993). But, as shown in Chapter 1, it is slowly shrinking in size and importance due to numerous economic developments over the past century (Anderson 1987; Antle 1999; Blank 2001a; Johnson 1991). Farms and ranches in the United States currently number less than one-third of the 1935 peak of 6.8 million. About one-quarter of the land in agriculture in 1954 has now left the industry (U.S. Department of Agriculture [USDA] 1999). And population is declining in some parts of the Midwest (Goetz and Debertin 1996). Yet, surprisingly, these dramatic structural shifts are typical of those expected as an agricultural sector develops over time (Mundlak 2001). American agriculture seems to be following the path of other industries that have expanded and contracted during their evolution. If that is true, it still comes as a surprise to many people unfamiliar with the economic development literature and others who simply believe that agriculture is unique because its output is food. "People have to eat" is the phrase used by many to try and counter the notion that agriculture is shrinking and may continue to do so.

This raises two questions: (1) What has been learned from studying the evolution of other industries? (2) Are those lessons relevant to American agriculture's decline?

To begin, it has been shown that there are recognized patterns in life, whether the subject is people, products, or industries. Life cycle models identify and describe those patterns, not explain them, yet knowing which stage of the life cycle is being observed provides insight into expected behavior and events as the pattern unfolds. Therefore, identifying where production agriculture is in its economic life could help both business and policy decision makers anticipate important structural changes in the industry as it continues to evolve.

Much research indicates that changes over an economic life span seem to follow a similar pattern. That general pattern includes a series of time periods over which the total sales and profits of an economic unit first increase, peak, and then decline. Klepper (1996) found there are explainable regularities in the evolutionary pattern of industry development. He expanded the extensive life cycle literature by showing how technical innovation, productivity, cost, profitability, and other factors affect an industry's life cycle. He noted that life cycle models have been used successfully in case studies of industries producing branded products ranging from light bulbs to automobiles.

Next, it has been learned that industries can change dramatically. Obviously, the pace of change for an industry is much slower than the pace of change observed at the firm or individual product levels, but the pattern of change appears to be similar (Agarwal 1997; Klepper 1996; Jovanovic and MacDonald 1994). Also, some industries have changed faster than others. As the scale of aggregation increases, from product line to firm to industry, the average life span also increases. However, even entire industries have reached the end of their life spans and disappeared (Chi and Liu 2001; Dunne, Roberts, and Samuelson 1989; Jovanovic 1982).

Finally, economists have learned that industries disappearing from the American economy can be commodity-based. This is somewhat surprising because virtually all of the literature on industry failures has focused on differentiated, branded product markets (Chi and Liu 2001; Jovanovic and MacDonald 1994). Even though commodity industry failures are rare, there is something about the economics of industries with outputs that are undifferentiated between firms that makes it possible for those industries to disappear. Also possible, but rare, is the decline of a commodity-based industry that is national in scale. All of the shrinking industries listed in Chapter 1 were local or regional in scale. Although American agriculture can be viewed as a collection of regional industries or commodity segments, the fact that virtually all agricultural industries are suffering economic hardships (e.g., see USDA 2000b, 2001, 2003) makes it appropriate to discuss the problem in aggregate, national terms.

All of these points are relevant to American agriculture and its apparent decline. They indicate that industries do have a life cycle with explainable regularities and that an analytical framework that evaluates economic performance over time may be useful in analyzing a commodity-based industry.

Therefore, this chapter presents a modification of the standard "product life cycle" model (Lilien and Kotler 1983, pp. 608–613) designed to create a test of general hypotheses identifying where American production agriculture is in its life cycle. Such an empirical application of the life cycle model (LCM) to an industry whose output is undifferentiated commodities is unique. Thus, a theoretical justification for using the LCM with a national commodity-based industry is presented. The justification includes several propositions derived using inductive logic, as well as definitions for the components of the LCM as described in the life cycle literature.

THE LIFE CYCLE MODEL AND INDUSTRY ANALYSIS

The life cycle model offers a description of the relationship between an economic unit and its market as reflected in sales and profit patterns over time. Although the model was originally developed to look at specific products or product lines, it has been extended to firms and to industries because those larger economic units also follow a growth and decline process based in the results of sequential decisions (Agarwal 1997; Bolle 1999).

The success of those decisions in satisfying market demand, relative to the decisions of competitors, influences the competitive position of the product, firm, or industry at each point in time (Anderson and Zeithaml 1984; Rink, Roden, and Fox 1999; Shankar, Carpenter, and Krishnamurthi 1999). However, each group of decision makers has some constraints upon their ability to completely satisfy demand. Some of those constraints include the attributes of the product or service being sold, the selling price, the cost of production, the volume of output per time period, the storage and distribution system available, and many others (Agarwal 1997; Dunne, Roberts, and Samuelson 1989). The net effects of those constrained decisions create a unique life cycle for a firm or industry.

In essence, the LCM shows the effects of the economic unit's comparative and absolute advantages and how they change over time. A theoretical explanation of how these advantages change when an industry faces international competition is presented after the LCM is introduced.

Sales, Profits, and the Life Cycle Model

The standard LCM is shown in Figure 2.1. The model is based on the idea that there are four distinct stages of the life cycle, and these successive stages are each characterized by different patterns in sales and profit performance. The sales and profit patterns are considered to be economic signals indicating the degree of success the unit is having in both satisfying market demand and coping with market competitors (Anderson and Zeithaml 1984), which, for American agriculture, are foreign agricultural industries.

As shown in Figure 2.1, the life cycle begins when the first sale is made. For an industry, this occurs when the first firm to sell a new type of product introduces it into the market—hence the name "Introduction" for the first stage of the life cycle. For the American production agriculture industry, the life cycle began shortly after people arrived on the continent. The introduction stage is characterized by a slow increase in sales over time, and profit levels that are negative initially, but less so over time. The introduction stage ends soon after profits become positive.

The "growth" stage is characterized by an increase in sales at an increasing rate over time, as well as profit levels that increase in absolute amounts over time. While total profits increase during this stage, profit margins may increase at first, but are expected to decrease later in the stage. For an industry, the sales growth comes from both new firms entering the industry and existing firms expanding their output, all in response to rapidly expanding total demand (Shankar, Carpenter, and Krishnamurthi 1999). The growth stage ends when both sales and profits slow in their rate of increase over time. For American agriculture, there was a long growth period as settlers moved west from the Atlantic and expanded the number of farms and the amount of land in production.

The "maturity" stage is characterized by turning points in both profits and sales volumes, with profits leading sales revenues. Sometime early in this stage, profit totals per unit of time peak and begin declining. Late in the stage, total sales volume per time period peaks and slowly begins to decrease. Between the two peaks, profit margins are clearly decreasing rapidly. Industry sales increase early in this stage because new firms are entering and/or existing firms are expanding their output. Profits peak when competition between firms within the industry and competition from other industries becomes significant. More firms may be exiting the industry than are entering. Sales peak later due to competition from other industries and market saturation, which occurs when changes in the industry's demand and supply curves cause marginal revenues to be zero. Industry profits continue decreasing late in the stage because of the costs of competition with other industries and competition between firms within the industry. These costs can be due simply to the industry's lagged response to falling market prices. American agriculture probably entered its maturity stage sometime during the 1900s as the country completed its westward expansion.

The "decline" stage is the final segment of the life cycle. It begins sometime soon after total sales per time period begins decreasing. The sales decrease is usually a result of a decrease in demand brought on by the introduction of an alternative product that is considered "better," or by competitors' ability to provide a similar product at a lower price. Total sales and profits both decrease during the decline stage although, on average, profits remain positive. The life cycle ends when sales end, usually when remaining firms decide to transform into being suppliers for a different market. That decision is triggered by the availability of better profit margins offered by alternative investments; consequently, the decision is usually made before profits fall to zero. For an industry, total sales are the aggregation of sales from all firms within the industry. Therefore, many individual decisions to exit must be made before the industry disappears. Thus, industries

Figure 2.1 **The Product Life Cycle**

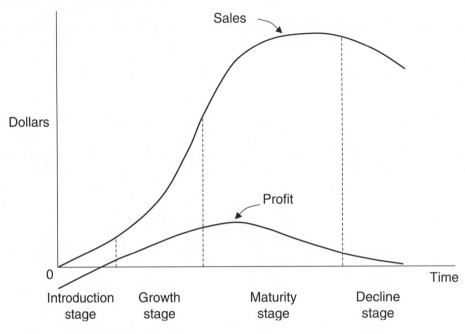

can decline over a lengthy period of time. For American agriculture, the question is whether or not the industry has reached its decline stage.

In summary, the LCM has been modified to describe the expected patterns in the life of an entire industry or economic sector. The general underlying causes of the patterns are comparative and absolute advantage. The model shows that sales and profit totals increase during the introduction and growth stages of the life cycle. This is due to the firm or industry developing, and then exploiting, its comparative advantage in the production of the product(s). Early in the maturity stage, profits level off and sales continue to increase. This is due to the costs of increased competition in the product market as either new firms develop their comparative advantage in that product, or existing firms experience changes in their absolute advantages. In the decline stage, firms exit the market in favor of more profitable alternatives created by changes in comparative and absolute advantages. At some point, absolute disadvantages cause all (or virtually all) firms to exit. Thus, relative profit margins influence total profit amounts. When total profits start to decline, it signals that total revenues are going to follow. For American agriculture, total sales revenue is an important indicator of the race between falling prices and rising yields.

An Economic Explanation of Industry Changes

American production agriculture's size, importance, and profitability are declining because the industry is feeling the effects of two types of ongoing changes: changes in its comparative advantage over the long run, and changes in its absolute advantage over recent decades. The general effects of these changes are illustrated in Figure 2.2.

Changes in comparative advantage occur as technological advances create new industries or substantially change existing industries within a region or country (Acs and Audretsch 1988;

Figure 2.2   **Effects of Changes in Comparative and Absolute Advantages**

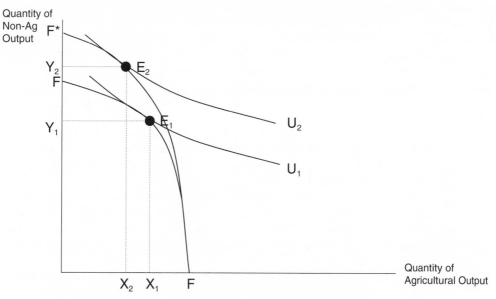

Panel A. Technology changes comparative advantage

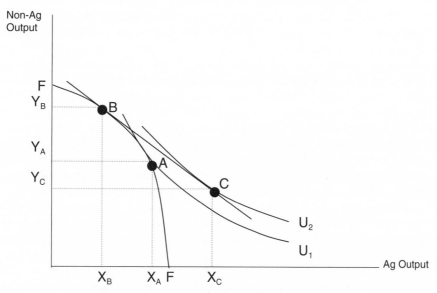

Panel B. Technology changes absolute advantage

Dasgupta and Stiglitz 1980; Shaked and Sutton 1987). When those advances result in changes in the relative profitability between industries, they can reduce the attractiveness of investments in existing industries, such as agriculture, causing resources to be shifted out of the industry (as noted later in Proposition 2.9).

For example, Panel A of Figure 2.2 shows how changes in comparative advantage due to technological advances in the nonagricultural sector of the U.S. economy make declines in the agricultural sector possible. As observed in Panel A, the production possibility frontier, *FF*, shifts upward to *FF** when technical advances lower the marginal costs of production in the non-agricultural sector. In this two-sector model, the result is that the equilibrium output shifts from point E_1 to E_2, which is on a higher indifference curve (U_2 versus U_1), and thus the United States is better off. At that new equilibrium point, nonagricultural output clearly increases from Y_1 to Y_2. Agricultural output is expected to decline from X_1 to X_2 because (as Johnson 1991, Anderson 1987, and others have shown) even if a country retains a strong comparative advantage in agriculture, that industry's terms of trade relative to manufacturing and other nonagricultural industries will decline with economic growth. This is true even if factor productivity growth is biased to agriculture because income-inelastic demand for agricultural output ensures that agriculture's terms of trade will still decline over time (Anderson 1987).

Changes in absolute advantage affect the degree of competition an industry faces. International competition and absolute advantage are now relevant to some industries in which comparative advantage exists, like American agriculture, because a regional comparative advantage in the production of some commodity is insufficient to overcome the industry's absolute disadvantage in a global market.

A global market now exists for a growing number of agricultural commodities due to technological advances in production, storage, and transportation. Technology expanded production output, making it possible to saturate local markets (market saturation is discussed later in this section). As a result, producers were forced to look to more geographically distant consumers to purchase the surplus output. Technological improvements to storage methods enabled even the most perishable commodities to be kept in marketable condition longer, which, when combined with technological improvements to transportation systems, enabled suppliers to cover more distance and reach new markets. It is now routine for perishable agricultural commodities to be traded from one continent to another. This means every producer of a particular commodity is in direct or indirect competition with all other producers of that commodity who sell during the same season, no matter where those producers might be located. This competitive market structure is a symptom of the undifferentiated nature of agricultural commodities.

Panel B of Figure 2.2 illustrates how being a part of a global market affects the terms of trade between America's agricultural and nonagricultural sectors. To begin, assume no international trade of agricultural commodities occurs because it is not technically possible to deliver marketable products to foreign locations. Each country has available to it only the agricultural commodities it can produce. In that situation, the U.S. economy operates at point *A* on the production possibility frontier, *FF*. At point *A,* the domestic price ratio is $-P_x/P_y$, agricultural output is X_A, and nonagricultural output is Y_A. Then, assume a technological advance in product shipping (i.e., storage and/or transportation) makes it possible to deliver commodities to foreign markets. No trade will occur if agricultural prices in the United States (P_x) and the rest of the world (P_{xw}) differ by no more than per unit shipping (transport and storage) costs, *s*. However, if another technical advance in production, storage, or transportation occurs outside of America such that $P_x - s > P_{xw}$, international trade will occur (if trade barriers do not prevent it) and the terms of trade between the U.S. agricultural and nonagricultural sectors will change.

In Panel B, the lower foreign price shifts the inverse price ratio in America to $-P_{x*}/P_{y*}$, which is the slope of the line *BC*. The United States would move to a new equilibrium in which it produced combination *B* and consumed combination *C*. Combination *B* involves the U.S. reducing its agricultural output from X_A to X_B and increasing its nonagricultural output from Y_A to

Y_B. The United States would export $Y_B - Y_C$ to pay for its imports of $X_C - X_B$. (This is consistent with Definition 2.4, presented later.)

In summary, Panel B shows that technological advances in production that reduce commodity prices in other agricultural industries, such as those of less-developed countries, reduce America's absolute advantage in global commodity markets and reduce the terms of trade between our agricultural and nonagricultural sectors. The same result is also caused by technical advances that reduce shipping costs, s. Both of these results cause resources to be shifted out of U.S. agriculture (as expressed later in Proposition 2.6).

Technological advances in U.S. agriculture counteract the effects of technical advances overseas by reducing costs per unit, thus improving U.S. agriculture's terms of trade and absolute advantage. Unfortunately, improvements in production have come with a downside for producers over the last several decades. "Agriculture in the twentieth century was characterized...by technological innovation that...made it possible for agricultural production to grow faster than the demand for food despite a rapidly growing world population. The result was a decline in real agricultural commodity prices throughout this era ..." (Antle 1999, p. 993). The "technological treadmill" of continual productivity improvement expands global supplies, which helps push commodity prices lower when productivity growth outpaces demand for food (Johnson and Quance 1972). American agriculture has been suffering from this treadmill for about a century; Schultz (1932) noted the problem over seventy-five years ago.

It appears that the combined effects of globalization of agricultural markets and the (nearly) perfectly competitive structure of local markets facing individual producers have turned the "treadmill" to a critical point for American agriculture. The problem begins with the different demand curves facing producers versus the industry. For a producer in a perfectly competitive market for an undifferentiated commodity, the demand curve is flat. This creates a marginal revenue curve that is also flat. Marginal revenue (MR) is defined as:

$$(2.1) \qquad MR = \frac{dR}{dQ} = \frac{d(PQ)}{dQ} = P + Q\left(\frac{dP}{dQ}\right)$$

where R is sales revenue, Q is quantity in units, P is the unit price, and d indicates a derivative. As can be seen in Equation 2.1, a flat demand curve has marginal revenues at all price levels of $MR = P$. For a producer, if MR exceeds marginal costs, the producer will expand output. Also, there is an incentive for each producer to adapt any technological advance that reduces marginal costs because it enables profits to be increased by expanding output. In other words, a flat demand curve encourages each producer to push his or her supply curve as far to the right as possible.

Unfortunately, the demand curve facing the entire American production agriculture industry is downward sloping to the right, meaning both prices and marginal revenues will decrease with increased market supplies. As noted by Antle (1999), industry supply has increased faster than demand, thus real prices have fallen for a century. Nominal prices have also fallen in recent decades, as indicated by the USDA's index of prices received by all U.S. farmers. These trends suggest the industry may have saturated its market. The saturation point is where $MR = 0$. As long as $MR > 0$, total sales revenues will increase when output expands. However, when $MR < 0$, sales revenues decrease as output expands. Therefore, it appears that the addition of new foreign supplies to the global market, plus productivity improvements around the globe, has created a new equilibrium where the demand curve facing American producers offers negative marginal revenues at current market prices for many commodities. This partially explains the decreasing real sales revenue totals observed later in this chapter.

Clearly, based on the discussion above, a key issue in a global competitive market is the *relative* rates of productivity increases between competitors because those rates affect marginal cost differences. In less-developed countries, agricultural productivity gains have been relatively higher than those in the United States over the last forty years. Duffy (2001, pp. 344–345) points out that "while the U.S. has out-paced the average of the other industrialized countries in increasing its production, the greatest gains have occurred in the developing nations." She reports Laspeyres indices of productivity for the 1961–2000 period of 2.0 for the United States, 1.6 for other more-developed countries, and 3.5 for less-developed countries. Thus, costs per unit have dropped faster in newly competitive nations, enabling them to remain profitable despite falling world prices. Therefore, the United States is losing the absolute advantage battle created by the advent of global commodity markets.

The Heckscher-Ohlin theory of international trade says when a country does not have an absolute advantage in the global market for a product in which it has a comparative advantage, it must compete on the basis of lower factor prices (e.g., wages, land prices, etc.) or by adjusting its currency exchange rates. A country can make the price of its product in which it has a comparative advantage competitive in absolute terms by enacting policies that reduce factor prices or that lower the value of its currency (Harrigan 1997; Peterson and Valluru 2000).

In America, however, falling agricultural factor prices create incentives to shift resources out of agriculture and into alternative investments. When land, capital, and other factor prices are pushed down by declining agricultural profitability, as they have been in the northern and southern plains over the past two decades (USDA 2000a, 2000b), nonagricultural uses of those factors become more attractive. Thus, agricultural output will decline most quickly in regions where there are the most alternative uses of input factors. In regions with few alternatives, like the grain-producing regions of the Midwest (Weimar and Hallam 1988), agricultural production will continue as long as it offers any profits, but global markets affect the life span.

As Thurow (1996, pp. 44–45) explains, there are other places with both comparative and absolute advantages in grain production that will push global prices so low that American producers will be forced out of the market: "The Ukraine is potentially the best place on earth for growing grain." It has not yet reached its current potential for contributing to global supplies because of capital and other constraints on its ability to fully implement modern production and distribution technologies. When it does get its agriculture up to Western standards, Thurow predicts its "sales will drive millions of less productive grain farmers out of business all around the world."

> In the United States it is clear who goes out of business. Go to the 98th meridian, remembering that about one third of Kansas is east of the 98th meridian, and draw a line from the Canadian border to the Gulf of Mexico; then swing west to the Rocky Mountains. Every grain farmer in that part of the United States goes out of business. The soil is worse, the rainfall is worse, and the transportation system is much, much worse than what is found in the Ukraine. It won't happen tomorrow, but it will happen. (Thurow 1996, p. 45)

A FORMAL MODEL OF AGRICULTURE'S LIFE CYCLE

A simple model of the agricultural industry and of individual firms within it is presented in this section to provide economic insights into the circumstances that create the patterns in sales and profits described in the LCM. Some of those insights are presented here as definitions and propositions from which hypotheses can be derived for testing. The definitions and propositions presented below indicate the two different types of conditions making up the life cycle model of production agriculture developed here. Definitions are derived directly from the literature as the conditions that delineate the specified event. Thus, the definitions presented here are not refutable hypotheses, but necessary conditions against which relevant data are compared when attempting to determine whether the event is in effect. Propositions are refutable hypotheses that are expected to be consistent with the data, based on the relevant theory presented. Propositions are presented and tested in this chapter to provide deeper insights into the structural changes expected in agriculture as it progresses through its life cycle.

For this analysis of the American production agriculture industry, total sales revenues (R) and profits (Π) are defined below. Only revenues from farmers' and ranchers' sales of production output are considered; government transfers and other income sources are excluded so as to get a clearer picture of the economic performance of farmers and ranchers. Therefore, the industry's revenue from all agricultural commodities ($i = 1, 2, \ldots, n$) at time t is given as:

$$(2.2) \qquad R_t = \sum_{i=1}^{n} P_{it}Q_{it},$$

and the industry's profit from all agricultural commodities at time t is

$$(2.3) \qquad \Pi_t = R_t - C_t - K_t$$

where
$$Q_{it} = Y_{it}A_{it},$$
$$C_t = \Sigma_i\Sigma_j c_{jt}x_{ijt},$$
$$K_t = \Sigma_i\Sigma_h k_{ht}z_{iht},$$

and $P_i, c_j, k_h > 0$; $Y_i, A_i, x_j, z_h \geq 0$. The number of commodities produced by the industry is denoted by n. P_{it} is the average unit price of commodity i at time t. Q_{it} is the quantity of commodity i produced at time t; Y_i is the average yield per acre of commodity i; A_i is the total acreage devoted to commodity I; C_t is the total production costs of all commodities at time t; c_j is unit costs of j variable inputs; x_{ij} is quantities of j variable inputs to be applied in the production of commodity I; K_t is the total ownership costs of all commodities at time t; k_h is unit costs of h capital inputs (land, improvements, equipment, etc.); and z_{ih} is quantities of h capital inputs used in the production of commodity i.

Industry sales and profit totals are simply the sum of results from decisions made by the individual firms constituting the industry. In American agriculture, individuals make production decisions based on the goal of maximizing expected profits. However, the analysis in this chapter follows Klepper (1996) in recognizing that results are influenced by both the innovation expertise and capital available within an industry. Thus, expected profit for firm f at time t is specified as:

$$(2.4) \qquad E(\pi_{ft}) = E[R_{ft} - C_{ft} - K_{ft} + (m_f)g(cr_{ft})G - \Delta(cr_{ft})],$$

where R, C, and K are as defined above, but are for firm f only. $E(\bullet)$ is the expected value of $(\bullet)$; m_f denotes the innovation expertise of firm f and m_{max} is the maximum possible innovation expertise (i.e., $m_f = m_{max}$ for the most innovative firm). The distribution of m_f is denoted $W(m)$, and is assumed to be continuous for all $m < m_{max}$ and $W(m_{max}) = 1$ by definition; m_f influences the firm's success at improving productivity. The probability of firm f improving its productivity in period t is $(m_f)g(cr_{ft})$, where cr_{ft} is defined as the firm's cumulative investment in human capital and productive resources through time t, and the function $g(cr_{ft})$ reflects the opportunities for improving productivity. The term cr_{ft} is some function of profits earned in all prior periods. G is the potential increase in profits earned by an innovation that improves productivity. This can result from either reduced input costs per unit (C/Q and/or K/Q) or increased revenue from a higher yield (Y). G is defined to equal $(R_{ft}-C_{ft}-K_{ft})-(R_{ft}^*-C_{ft}^*-K_{ft}^*)$, where the asterisk indicates a value that would have existed for firm f in period t without the innovation. The change in cumulative investment during period t is represented by $\Delta(cr_{ft})$; it equals $cr_{ft} - cr_{ft-1}$, and is constrained to be ≥ 0.

A firm's expected sales revenues are expressed as:

$$(2.5) \qquad E(R_{ft}) = R_{ft-1} + E[(m_f)g(cr_{ft})G + \Delta(cr_{ft})].$$

This specification says that current revenues are expected to equal revenues from the previous year plus expected improvements from a productivity component $[(m_f)g(cr_{ft})G]$ and an investment component $[\Delta(cr_{ft})]$.

In production agriculture, all firms are price takers. It is assumed here that all production is of undifferentiated commodities, thus all firms receive the same average price for a commodity during a period. It is also assumed that the industry clears Q_t at the market price each period. The analysis in this chapter goes beyond previous applications of the LCM (such as Klepper's 1996) by using an open-economy approach. Therefore, the market-clearing price and quantity are influenced by global market conditions.

Several implications can be drawn from the model in Equations 2.2–2.5. First, total agricultural industry sales are the sum of sales from all firms in the industry and depend on the commodities being produced, market prices, productivity, and industry scale. Scale is reflected in the total acreage devoted to production, A, which is controlled by producers. Productivity is indicated by average yield, Y, which is influenced by producers, but not totally controlled. A producer's innovation and capital investments can raise average yields over time, but only within the constraints of agronomics and climate. Market prices are out of producers' control. Thus, uncertain yield and price changes over time make agriculture's total sales highly variable. Industry revenue variability leads to profit variability despite producers' efforts to control production and ownership costs, C and K. Finally, profit risks influence which commodities are being produced (Blank 2001b).

Firm-level implications of the model can be drawn concerning sales and profits. A firm's sales revenue depends on the commodities being produced, market prices, productivity, and firm scale, plus the uncontrollable level of opportunities to improve productivity through innovation, $g(cr_{ft})$. Opportunities will vary across agricultural products and the ability to capitalize on opportunities will vary with m_f across firms within each product market. Therefore, innovation will cause profits to vary across firms, ceteris paribus. This means there are varying levels of incentive for firms to invest in human capital and productive resources, cr_{ft}. These factors, in turn, are expected to influence the industry's life cycle.

At the beginning of the introduction stage of the LCM, there is great uncertainty. Before production begins and the first sale is made, demand is latent, meaning in graphical terms that the supply curve must be above the demand curve at all quantities, so they do not intersect. The first firm must rely on technical and managerial innovation to reduce costs, thereby lowering the supply curve. It can also attempt to raise the demand curve by promoting its future product to potential consumers. In either case, only when the two curves intersect will a sale occur and will long-run production be established. However, in the short run, the first producer will suffer negative profits because (marginal) operating costs, C, are being covered, but not (average) total costs, $C + K$. During the introduction stage of the LCM, the first firm (and all subsequent entrants) is willing to risk short-run losses because profits are expected in the long run. In other words, firms in the industry expect demand to increase and per unit costs to decrease over time. These insights lead to the following definition and proposition:

- DEFINITION 2.1. *At the beginning of the introduction stage of the LCM, industry sales are zero and profits are negative.*
- PROPOSITION 2.1. *During the introduction stage of the LCM, firms enter the industry based on expected profits.*

At the beginning of the growth stage of the LCM, there is great potential. Profits are being earned and expectations are for improvement. This spurs growth in many factors, as noted in the following:

- DEFINITION 2.2. *During the growth stage of the LCM, total industry sales and total industry profits increase.*
- PROPOSITION 2.2. *During the growth stage of the LCM, agricultural commodity prices increase in most cases.*

In a competitive market, commodity prices will rise if demand increases faster than supply. Graphically, this means the demand curve is moving to the right faster than is the supply curve. This condition is expected early in the life cycle of a successful industry because of the constraints slowing output expansion. To begin, in an infant industry, there are relatively few firms contributing to industry supply. To increase output, those firms need to acquire more resources, but their growth rate is constrained by their limited access to profits and borrowed capital. Firms have not accumulated much profit at this early stage and access to agricultural loans is a function of profitability (Thompson and Blank 1994). Demand, on the other hand, can grow as quickly as additional consumers become aware of the product.

While unlikely, it is possible for commodity prices to decrease during the growth stage. For this to occur, technological advances would be required to decrease costs per unit faster than prices are declining. Without the expectation of such an expanding profit margin, commodity producers would not be willing or able to expand output at this stage of the LCM.

Two effects of rising prices on existing firms are (1) the profit margin on each unit sold increases, thus causing total sales revenues and total profits to increase for current sales quantities, and (2) the number of units that can be produced and sold at a profit increases, thus increasing total sales and profits further. This means existing firms move to a new equilibrium point farther to the right on their supply curves.

- PROPOSITION 2.3. *During the growth stage of the LCM, the number of firms in the industry increases.*

Rising prices make it profitable for new firms to enter the industry. As long as demand is expanding faster than supply, prices will increase. An upward price trend tends to raise expectations for the future, thus encouraging firms for which $P > MC$ (marginal cost) to consider entering the market based on a forecast that $P > AC$ (average cost) in the long run.

- PROPOSITION 2.4. *During the growth stage of the LCM, firms in the industry increase their levels of investment.*

Rising profits and opportunities for innovation encourage increased investment by firms in the industry. A firm with increasing profits is financially able to increase its investment, cr_{ft}, and if opportunities for innovation are growing [$g(cr_{ft+1}) > g(cr_{ft})$], expected profits rise with higher cr_{ft}.

The maturity stage of the LCM is characterized by changes brought on by the reversal of several trends. Insights into these changes are offered in the following definition and five propositions:

- DEFINITION 2.3. *During the maturity stage of the LCM, total industry profits peak and then begin decreasing before total industry sales do.*
- PROPOSITION 2.5. *During the maturity stage of the LCM, average commodity prices peak before total industry profits and total industry sales do, and then decrease.*

In a competitive market, commodity prices will fall if supply increases faster than demand. Graphically, this means the supply curve is moving to the right faster than is the demand curve. This condition is expected during the maturity stage because the constraints slowing output expansion in the previous stage are eliminated. At this point, there are relatively many firms contributing to industry supply, and profits earned earlier enable them to acquire additional resources as needed.

The combined pressure of falling prices and rising costs continues to reduce profit margins until total profits peak and then fall, despite increasing numbers of units being sold. In other words, falling prices cause proportionally larger decreases in profit margins in this stage.

Also during this stage, the supply curve is expected to eventually move far enough right that its intersection with the demand curve shifts from the elastic portion to the inelastic portion of demand. Consequently, the increasing unit sales made possible by supply innovations will cause total sales revenues to increase at first, peak, and then decrease as marginal revenues shift from being positive to negative.

- PROPOSITION 2.6. *During the maturity stage of the LCM, firms entering (exiting) the industry are those more (less) able to innovate, ceteris paribus.*

As profit margins on unit sales decrease, it affects which firms (and industries) can compete profitably. As shown in Equation 2.4, firms (and industries) with higher values for m_f will have higher profit margins than other firms, ceteris paribus. Thus, firms with highly skilled managers will be able to capture more of the potential profits from innovations that are causing total supplies to increase, and therefore be able to enter the industry first and exit last because of their higher productivity.

If trade is allowed, foreign firms can enter the industry by selling products in domestic markets. Entering foreign firms may have lower costs, C and K, because they are buying resources from different input markets. Foreign firms may also have more opportunities for innovation, $g(cr_{ft})$, because they may lag behind the American industry in adopting new technologies (Mundlak 2001), thus having unused opportunities still available to them at a time when American producers have no new opportunities. These factors, plus the fact that all firms receive the same global price for an undifferentiated commodity, make foreign firms potentially more profitable than domestic firms.

- PROPOSITION 2.7. *During the maturity stage of the LCM, the average size of firms in the industry increases.*

As shown by Equation 2.4, profits are expected to be higher for firms with larger cumulative investments in human capital and productive resources, cr_{ft}, giving an incentive for firms to grow larger in scale. The higher profits from economies of scale will, over time, enable larger firms to purchase their smaller, less profitable competitors. As this consolidation continues, average firm size must eventually increase.

- PROPOSITION 2.8. *During the maturity stage of the LCM, the number of firms in the industry may initially rise or fall, but by the end of the stage, total firm numbers decrease.*

The combined effects of falling profit margins and the consolidation of firms in the industry both contribute to declining firm numbers during this stage. If trade is allowed, substitution of foreign firms for domestic producers also reduces the number of domestic firms.

- PROPOSITION 2.9. *During the maturity stage of the LCM, firms in the industry may initially increase or decrease their levels of investment, but by the end of the stage, firms decrease their levels of new investment.*

Firms in an industry facing falling prices, profits, and sales revenues have decreasing incentives to invest, especially if the industry faces inelastic demand. On the other hand, firms do have incentives to invest in cost-saving innovations. However, firms with falling profits will have fewer funds to invest over time.

During the decline stage of the LCM, there is no uncertainty about the direction of all economic trends. The only question concerns the amount of time remaining before the life cycle ends. The two scenarios below outline the major trends:

- DEFINITION 2.4. *During the decline stage of the LCM, average commodity prices, total industry profits, total industry sales revenues, and total units sold all decrease.*

Only two general scenarios can result in all of the trends listed in Definition 2.4. First, the usual scenario is for demand to decline as consumers substitute some other product in place of the output of the industry being evaluated. This means the demand curve is moving to the left, causing the market equilibrium point to be farther down the supply curve. That movement down the supply curve continually lowers the market price and profit margin, and firms are forced to exit the industry.

The second scenario involves the substitution of foreign firms for domestic firms. However, this scenario is possible only if trade is allowed. If trade is not allowed in an industry with stable or increasing demand, like that for food, any leftward shift in the domestic supply curve would reduce the total units sold, but would increase prices and, for a market with inelastic demand, would also increase sales revenues and total profits. Such an industry is not declining. On the other hand, trade allows foreign firms to enter a market, expanding market supplies (i.e., pushing the total supply curve to the right) and lowering the market price to the global price level. As that price drops and/or domestic costs increase, domestic firms are forced to exit the industry. There-fore, innovations that increase global supplies cause higher-cost domestic industries to reduce their output, which is replaced in domestic markets by increased imports at the global price. This result pushes higher-cost industries into decline.

- PROPOSITION 2.10. *During the decline stage of the LCM, the number of firms in the industry decreases, but may not reach zero.*

As noted in the discussion of Proposition 2.6, the most innovative firms ($m_f = m_{max}$) are expected to be the most profitable over time, ceteris paribus, and may be able to survive beyond the end of the industry's life cycle. As the national domestic industry declines, it may break into regional and then local fragments. Highly innovative firms may be able to diversify out of the commodity-based industry by differentiating their output through adding value, branding, or some other strategy. By doing so, those firms become part of other industries that may have a much longer life expectancy, thereby enabling small pieces of the original industry to survive as a supply source to a different market. Such survival can occur only for highly innovative firms able to identify opportunities [$g(cr_{ft})$] on which only they can capitalize. This leads to Definition 2.5:

- DEFINITION 2.5. *The life cycle of an industry ends when sales are no longer made in the original market (i.e., to the original type of buyers), even if the remaining firms are making sales in a different market.*

METHODS FOR SORTING THROUGH THE QUESTIONS

A methodology designed to indicate which stage of the life cycle an industry is in at any point in time is proposed here. In general, it is based on the idea that each stage of the LCM pres-ents testable hypotheses derived from changes in the comparative and absolute advantages of an industry and its competition, as expressed in the definitions and propositions above. The hy-potheses for each stage of the life cycle are tested by comparing the expected patterns with data from the time period of interest. The industry is in the stage that offers hypotheses consistent with the data.

There are two groups of hypotheses. The primary hypotheses are derived from the definitions and are the central focus of the empirical analysis in this chapter. The secondary hypotheses are derived from the propositions and are mentioned only in the summary of empirical results.

The primary hypotheses tested here focus on the absolute size of the industry's economic outputs: total sales revenues and total profits. Sales revenues measure how the market values aggregate output, and profits measure how well the industry is performing in increasing owners' wealth. Productivity factors affect costs per unit of output and total output volume; therefore they affect profits and sales revenues, as shown in Equations 2.4 and 2.5.

As summarized in Exhibit 2.1, the approach is to jointly test groups of primary hypotheses to determine which group best fits the data for the time period of interest. The data used are time series because each primary hypothesis expresses a relationship between time and sales and/or profits. For each stage there are two hypotheses. For the introduction stage, accepting hypotheses H_{I1} and H_{I2} are each necessary, and together they are sufficient conditions to determine the industry is in the first stage of its life cycle. The same is true of hypotheses H_{D1} and H_{D2} for the decline stage.

Exhibit 2.1

Methodology to Identify Life Cycle Stage

Introduction stage hypotheses:

H_{I1}: Total sales revenues are increasing ($R_{t+1} > R_t$).
H_{I2}: Total profits are negative but improving ($0 > \Pi_{t+1} > \Pi_t$).

Growth stage hypotheses:

H_{G1}: Total sales revenues are increasing ($R_{t+1} > R_t$).
H_{G2}: Total profits are positive and increasing ($\Pi_{t+1} > \Pi_t > 0$).
A convex sales function is not a necessary, but is a sufficient condition; thus:
H_{G1*}: Total sales revenues are increasing at an increasing rate, $[dR_{t+1}/d(t+1)] > (dR_t/dt) > 0$.

Maturity stage hypotheses:

H_{M1}: Early in the stage, total sales are increasing and profits peak, ($R_{t+1} > R_t$) and $[(d\Pi_t/dt) = 0]$.
H_{M2}: Late in the stage, total profits are decreasing and sales peak, ($\Pi_t > \Pi_{t+1} > 0$) and $[(dR_t/dt) = 0]$.

Decline stage hypotheses:

H_{D1}: Total sales revenues are decreasing ($R_t > R_{t+1}$).
H_{D2}: Total profits are decreasing ($\Pi_t > \Pi_{t+1}$).

Note: These are the primary hypotheses only. They are derived from the definitions. Secondary hypotheses derived from the propositions and involving factors other than sales and profits are not listed due to space constraints.

As noted in Exhibit 2.1, an industry can be identified as being in its growth stage in either of two ways. First, accepting both H_{G1} and H_{G2} is a sufficient condition. Second, accepting only substitute hypothesis H_{G1*} is a sufficient condition. A convex sales function is not a necessary condition, but is a sufficient condition to determine that an industry is in its growth stage because it is a rare situation that could occur only for a relatively new industry experiencing rapid sales growth.

The maturity stage is characterized by two turning points, one for each of the data sets, and so it is evaluated as if it were two different stages. H_{M1} identifies the "early" portion of the stage by testing sales and profit patterns jointly. Each of the two pieces of the hypothesis could be written as separate hypotheses, but for convenience they are written here as one sufficient condition. H_{M2} is treated in the same manner for the "late" portion of the stage. This means H_{M1} and H_{M2} are mutually exclusive; that is, an industry can be in only one portion of the stage or the other, so only one of these hypotheses can be accepted.

The primary hypotheses are tested by estimating regression models of annual total industry profits and sales, and then evaluating the relevant coefficients. As explained by Perron (1989), a Dickey-Fuller type model can be augmented with slope and intercept dummy variables and estimated with ordinary least squares. The dummy variables enable measurement of the slope or, if needed, a change in the level of a trend function between time periods. The general model to measure the slope of a given series, y_t, during some period is specified as:

(2.6) $$y_t = \alpha + \gamma y_{t-1} + \beta T_t + e_t,$$

where α is the intercept (a constant), T_t is a time trend dummy, γ and β are regression coefficients to be estimated, and e_t is an error term at time t specified as an autoregressive-moving average process—ARMA(p, q)—of unknown order. The dummy $T_t = t$ during a period of interest and 0 otherwise. When both slopes and intercepts are to be measured, the model is:

(2.7) $$y_t = \alpha + \gamma y_{t-1} + \beta_T T_t + \beta_D D_t + e_t,$$

where the dummy variable $D_t = 1$ during a period of interest and 0 otherwise, and β_D is its coefficient. Multiple slope and intercept dummy variables may be used in a single regression.

The general industry profit and sales equations estimated, respectively, are derived from Equations 2.4 through 2.7 as:

(2.8) $$\Pi_t = \alpha + \gamma_1 \Pi_{t-1} + \gamma_2 (R_t / A_t) - \gamma_3 [\Delta(cr_t)] + \beta_T T_t + \beta_D D_t + e_t;$$
(2.9) $$R_t = \alpha + \gamma_4 R_{t-1} + \gamma_5 (\Pi_t / R_t) + \gamma_6 [\Delta(cr_t)] + \beta_T T_t + \beta_D D_t + e_t.$$

In Equation 2.8, the lagged profit variable represents the first component of Equation 2.4 ($E[R_t - C_t - K_t]$); the revenue per acre variable represents the productivity component [$(m)g(cr_t)G$]; $\Delta(cr_t)$ represents the total capital invested in agriculture during year t (as reported by USDA [2003]); and γ denotes the relevant regression coefficients.

Equation 2.9 is constructed to represent Equation 2.5, with the average profit margin (i.e., profit as a percentage of sales) variable as the productivity component. The proxy variables representing the productivity component in Equations 2.8 and 2.9 reflect the aggregate results of the industry's innovative efforts. Revenue per acre captures the results of innovations that increase output by raising yield, plus those actions that signal market approval through higher prices. The profit margin reflects market success through higher prices received and/or lower costs per unit (which could enable the industry to expand output and sales while facing falling market prices). The investment component in Equations 2.8 and 2.9 is measured directly using total capital expenditures in agriculture. Multiple trend and intercept variables are used as needed for hypothesis testing. The order of the ARMA(p, q) processes was found using the testing method in Pindyck and Rubinfeld (1976, pp. 490–494) involving R^2 and χ^2 statistics. All combinations of processes were estimated with p and q each ranging from 0 to 3, with only the best-performing combination being reported in the results.

The time-series data should be expressed in real dollars if the problem being investigated spans a long time period. When studying industries, the period will often cover decades. For American agriculture, the partial life cycle has already lasted centuries, so some data aggregation and/or truncation is appropriate. Therefore, the financial data used here are annual real sales and production income for American agriculture from 1949 to 2002. All the data were taken from the Economic Research Service's Web site (USDA 2003).

EMPIRICAL RESULTS FOR AMERICAN AGRICULTURE

The empirical analysis begins by identifying current trends in profits and sales. Then, the definitions and propositions are assessed and the current life cycle stage is identified.

Tests of Profit Hypotheses

Annual (pre-tax) net income for American agriculture over the last half-century is presented in nominal terms in Table 2.1. The net farm income totals reported by the U.S. Department of Agriculture represent one of the most commonly used measures of profitability. However, they are overstated. Among other things, those totals include direct government payments to agriculture.

Table 2.1

U.S. Agricultural Sales and Income, 1950–2002 (Nominal)

Year	Total crop and livestock sales	Net income	Direct government payments	Adjusted production income (API)	Total capital invested	API as percent of sales (%)
1950	31.3	13.6	0.3	13.4	4.0	42.7
1955	31.4	11.3	0.2	11.1	3.6	35.3
1960	35.5	11.2	0.7	10.5	4.0	29.6
1965	41.2	12.9	2.5	10.4	5.6	20.8
1970	51.3	14.4	3.7	10.6	6.8	20.8
1971	54.9	15.0	3.1	11.9	6.8	21.6
1972	62.9	19.5	4.0	15.5	7.5	24.7
1973	91.4	34.4	2.6	31.7	10.2	34.7
1974	92.0	27.3	0.5	26.7	11.4	29.1
1975	93.4	25.5	0.8	24.7	12.4	26.5
1976	95.0	20.2	0.7	19.4	14.0	20.5
1977	98.5	19.9	1.8	18.1	15.0	18.3
1978	115.5	25.2	3.0	22.2	17.9	19.2
1979	137.9	27.4	1.4	26.0	20.1	18.9
1980	134.7	16.1	1.3	14.9	18.0	11.0
1981	149.3	26.9	1.9	24.9	16.8	16.7
1982	142.3	23.8	3.5	20.4	13.3	14.3
1983	126.9	14.2	9.3	5.0	12.7	3.9
1984	149.8	26.0	8.4	17.5	12.5	11.7
1985	142.8	28.6	7.7	20.9	9.2	14.7
1986	134.1	30.9	11.8	19.1	8.5	14.3
1987	140.2	37.4	16.7	20.7	11.2	14.8
1988	147.9	38.0	14.5	23.5	11.5	15.9
1989	165.3	45.3	10.9	34.4	13.1	20.8
1990	173.5	44.6	9.3	35.3	14.1	20.4
1991	168.3	38.5	8.2	30.3	13.1	18.0
1992	176.0	47.7	9.2	38.5	12.6	21.9
1993	174.3	44.3	13.4	30.9	13.9	17.7
1994	190.0	48.8	7.9	40.9	13.9	21.5
1995	183.4	36.9	7.3	29.6	13.8	16.2
1996	207.6	54.9	7.3	47.6	15.4	22.9
1997	208.8	48.6	7.5	41.1	16.5	19.7
1998	196.3	44.6	12.2	32.4	17.8	16.5
1999	187.5	46.2	21.5	24.7	16.2	13.2
2000	192.1	47.9	22.9	25.0	17.3	13.0
2001	200.1	50.6	20.7	29.9	17.1	14.9
2002	195.1	37.3	11.0	36.3	17.1	18.6

Source: USDA (2003).

Note: Data from 1949–69 are presented in condensed form due to space limitations. Data for each year from 1910 to 2002 are available on the web (USDA 2003).

Thus, in Table 2.1, direct government payments are subtracted from the net farm income totals to obtain "adjusted production income" (API), which better reflects profits earned only from agricultural production activities. Those data were converted into real dollars for the 1949–2002 period using the consumer price index (USDA 2003), with 2000 being the base year, generating the results shown in Figure 2.3 (to provide visual context, real data for 1910–1948 are also included).

Table 2.2 presents the results of estimating Equation 2.8 using the real profit (i.e., API) data. To begin, a specification based on Equation 2.6 was used to measure the slope in the profit trend and to test whether that slope changed in 1973, as suggested by inspection of Figure 2.3. As shown by the results in the two columns labeled "Model 1," the trend is negatively sloped and statistically significant for both the 1950–1972 and 1973–2002 time periods. Also, a t-test indicates there is no significant difference in the slopes between the periods. It is noted that all variables in Model 1 (and both of the other profit models) are significant and have the expected sign—positive for lagged income and revenue per acre, negative for capital expenditures.

Next, another Equation 2.6 specification was used to test whether the 1973–1983 period was unique in its profit pattern. Model 2's results show that using three slope dummies, instead of two, provides some improvement in the estimation, but using an Equation 2.7 specification to estimate Model 3 gives the best results. By including an intercept dummy for the 1973–1983 period, the coefficient for the slope dummy T_{73-83} becomes much more negative: from -1.16 to -4.60. So, 1973–1983 does appear to be an unusual period in U.S. agriculture's profit performance, but it does not change the key result that all three slope dummies have significant negative coefficients. This finding indicates the long-run trend in the industry's profit has been negative for over half a century.

Therefore, the real profit data are consistent with hypothesis H_{D2} and the profit portion of H_{M2}, and inconsistent with H_{I2}, H_{G2}, and the profit portion of H_{M1}. These results partially signal that U.S. agriculture is past the introduction, growth, and "early" maturity stages of its life cycle. Whether it is in its "late" maturity stage or its decline stage can be determined only after sales tests.

Tests of Sales Hypotheses

The real sales data (final crop output plus final animal output, as reported by the USDA [2003]) are plotted in Figure 2.3. Those data were used to estimate Equation 2.9. The Cochrane-Orcutt transformation was applied to correct for the ARMA (1, 0) process found during diagnostics checking. In general, the sales models all give consistent results: the profit margin and capital expenditure variables are both significant and have the expected positive signs, while the lagged sales variable is insignificant.

Table 2.3 presents the regression results for five models estimated. Model 1 has negative coefficients on the two slope variables, but neither is statistically significant, thus indicating a flat trend line for the entire period. Model 2 was estimated using an Equation 2.7 specification to test whether 1973 was a turning point. The results indeed indicate some exogenous shift occurred in 1973 that changed an up-trend in sales into a significantly negative trend. Sales Models 3, 4, and 5 repeat the tests in Models 1 and 2, except the 1973–2002 period is broken into two periods for more detailed evaluation. Model 5 shows that 1973–1983 was a dynamic period and appears to have been a turning point in American agriculture. The three slope variables in Model 5 are all different, based on t-tests. The coefficient for T_{50-72} is significantly positive, T_{73-83} is not significantly different than zero, and T_{84-02} is negative and significant. Therefore, agriculture's real sales revenues have trended downward for at least two decades.

Figure 2.3 **Real U.S. Agricultural Sales and Income, 1910–2002**

Table 2.2

Regression results for models of Profits (Real API, 1949–2002)

Variable	Model 1 Coefficient	t stat	Model 2 Coefficient	t stat	Model 3 Coefficient	t stat
Constant	1,378.8	2.76**	2,183.2	4.27**	2,092.3	4.46**
Adj Inc lag	0.58	6.23**	0.55	6.47**	0.42	4.76**
Revenue/acre	0.63	6.32**	0.61	6.76**	0.53	6.05**
Cap expend	−1.77	−5.06**	−1.00	−2.56*	−1.29	−3.48**
T_{50-72}	−0.73	−2.88**	−1.14	−4.41**	−1.01	−4.53**
T_{73-02}	−0.74	−2.97**	– – –	– – –	– – –	– – –
T_{73-83}	– – –	– – –	−1.16	−4.50**	−4.60	−4.12**
T_{84-02}	– – –	– – –	−1.15	−4.48**	−1.09	−4.62**
D_{73-83}	– – –	– – –	– – –	– – –	6930.5	3.15**
Adjusted R^2	.8222		.8543		.8780	
F–Ratio	49.09		51.82		54.46	

Note: ** indicates significance at the 99% confidence level; * indicates significance at the 95% confidence level. All three models have an ARMA(0, 0) process.

Table 2.3

Regression results for models of Real Sales (1949–2002)

Variable	Model 1 Coefficient	t stat	Model 2 Coefficient	t stat	Model 3 Coefficient	t stat	Model 4 Coefficient	t stat	Model 5 Coefficient	t stat
Constant	1,020.5	0.62	−7,063.9	−3.90**	1,539.8	0.85	2,135.3	0.92	−6,396.6	−3.69**
Sales lag	−0.009	−0.14	−0.022	−0.37	−0.003	−0.05	−0.001	−0.01	−0.016	−0.27
API/Sales	3.271	9.35**	3.065	9.06**	3.195	8.66**	3.253	8.22**	3.154	8.12**
Cap expend	2.443	6.09**	2.222	5.92**	2.464	6.08**	2.517	5.97**	2.443	6.03**
T_{50-72}	−0.472	−0.57	3.640	3.95**	−0.736	−0.81	−1.041	−0.89	3.294	3.73**
T_{73-02}	−0.450	−0.54	−1.429	−2.38*	— —	— —	— —	— —	— —	— —
D_{73-02}	— —	— —	10,043.3	4.17**	— —	— —	— —	— —	— —	— —
T_{73-83}	— —	— —	— —	— —	−0.714	−0.79	0.368	0.15	0.368	0.21
T_{84-02}	— —	— —	— —	— —	−0.710	−0.78	−1.010	−0.87	−2.082	−2.83**
D_{73-83}	— —	— —	— —	— —	— —	— —	−2737.9	−0.46	5,810.1	1.41
D_{84-02}	— —	— —	— —	— —	— —	— —	— —	— —	10,672.9	4.68**
rho	0.899		0.710		0.901		0.898		0.677	
Adjusted R^2	.8468		.8713		.8453		.8423		.8748	
F–Ratio	57.39		58.55		47.45		39.91		45.56	

Notes: ** indicates significance at the 99% confidence level. * indicates significance at the 95% confidence level. All five models have an ARMA(1, 0) process.

As noted above, regression analysis shows a positive trend in the real sales data prior to 1973, a flat trend line over the 1973–83 period, and a negative slope in the trend thereafter. Thus, 1973 (or the 1973–1983 period) appears to be a turning point when the historical up-trend reversed to create a down-trend that remains in effect to date.

The sales hypotheses test results indicate the past half-century has been a period of great change for American agriculture. The real sales data for the *entire* 1949–2002 period are not consistent with any of the hypotheses. The data series certainly is not all trending up as required to accept hypotheses H_{I1}, H_{G1}, and the sales portion of H_{M1}. Also, it is not consistent with the flat trend line specified in the sales portion of H_{M2}, even though models 1 and 3 may indicate so. In addition to the different signs on slope coefficients β_{50-72} and β_{84-02} in Model 5, the significant intercept dummy, D_{84-02}, reveals the recent period is different than the 1950–1972 period due to some intervention occurring between 1972 and 1984. The 1973–1983 trend in Model 5 is flat, as required by the sales portion of H_{M2}. The recent real sales data (1984–2002) are trending downward as described in H_{D1}. Overall, the real data have not been consistent with the sales portion of H_{M1} since 1973. Clearly, markets for America's agricultural output have been different since 1973–1983.

Life Cycle Stage Determination

The empirical determination of which life cycle stage American agriculture currently occupies depends on the hypotheses' test results and which definitions and propositions are consistent with the data. A summary of the evidence is presented in Exhibit 2.2. The summary includes expanded definitions for the maturity and decline stages to create more precise hypothesis tests. The need for these expanded definitions became apparent when specifying the hypotheses, as noted earlier in the discussion of Exhibit 2.1.

It is proposed here that the decline stage of the LCM be treated as having an "early" and "late" period, similar to the maturity stage, to facilitate more precise hypothesis tests. The early decline stage is defined to begin when H_{D1} and H_{D2} are supported by real data. The late decline stage begins when total unit sales start trending downward.

Based on the overall results of the analysis in this chapter, American production agriculture has clearly passed its introduction, growth, and early maturity stages, and is probably in the early decline stage of its life cycle. The results are consistent with the argument that 1973 (or the 1973–1983 period) was a turning point signaling the transition from agriculture's late maturity stage into its early decline stage.

CONCLUDING COMMENTS AND OPENING ARGUMENTS

The empirical results in this chapter indicate that American production agriculture appears to be in the early decline stage of its life cycle. The industry's economic output is declining in real terms and the industry faces an increasingly difficult future due to the competitive structure of the expanding global markets for commodities.

The difficulty in reaching conclusions about the economic health of American agriculture and the length of its life span comes from the distortions of government intervention. Direct government payments and other sorts of support that artificially raise total profits have served to slow the flow of resources out of the sector, thereby lengthening its life span. Also, domestic resources stay in the industry longer when trade barriers reduce imports. So, to a great extent, the length of American agriculture's future is a policy decision. Yet the fact that policy interventions have occurred in agriculture since the 1930s is consistent with an industry that reached its late maturity stage long ago.

Exhibit 2.2

Summary of Empirical Results

Definitions and Propositions	Consistent with Data?	Sources
D1: At the beginning of the Introduction Stage, industry sales are zero and profits are negative.	No, H_{I1} and H_{I2} are both rejected	
P1: During the Introduction Stage, firms enter the industry based on expected profits.	No, farm and ranch numbers have declined each year since peaking at 6.8 million in 1935	USDA 1999
D2: During the Growth Stage, total industry sales and total industry profits increase.	No, H_{G1} and H_{G2} are both rejected	
P2: During the Growth Stage of the LCM, agricultural commodity prices increase in most cases.	No, prices are decreasing	USDA 2003
P3: During the Growth Stage, the number of firms in the industry increases.	No, the number of farms and ranches is declining	USDA 1999
P4: During the Growth Stage, firms in the industry increase their levels of investment.	No, total capital expenditures in agriculture peaked in real terms in 1979 and have trended down since	Nominal data in Table 2.1 converted to real dollars
D3: During the Maturity Stage, total industry profits and total industry sales (in that order) peak and then decrease.	Partially observed during the half-century analysis period; more detail needed	
D3a: During the "Early" Maturity Stage, total industry profits peak while total industry sales increase.	No, H_{M1} is rejected; profits trended downward over the entire data period	
D3b: During the "Late" Maturity Stage of the LCM, total industry profits decrease while total industry sales peak.	Not supported by current data– H_{M2} is rejected for the current period (1984–2002); H_{M2} is accepted for the 1973–1983 period	
P5: During the Maturity Stage, average commodity prices peak before total industry profits and total industry sales do, and then decrease.	Not supported by current data– prices, real profit, and real sales all declined in recent decades; USDA's Index of Prices Received for agricultural output decreased in real and nominal terms in recent decades	USDA 2003

Exhibit 2.2 (*continued*)

Summary of Empirical Results

Definitions and Propositions	Consistent with Data?	Sources
P6: During the Maturity Stage, firms entering (exiting) the industry are those more (less) able to innovate.	Inconclusive–average gross profit margins and firm numbers are falling, but firm-level analysis is beyond the scope of this study	USDA 2003, and API as % of sales in Table 2.1
P7: During the Maturity Stage, the average size of firms in the industry increases.	Yes, average farm size has been increasing for decades	USDA 1999
P8: During the Maturity Stage, the number of firms in the industry may initially rise or fall, but decrease by the end of the stage.	Yes, farm and ranch numbers are declining	USDA 1999
P9: During the Maturity Stage, firms in the industry may initially increase or decrease their levels of investment, but by the end of the stage firms decrease their levels of new investment.	Yes, total capital expenditures in agriculture in real terms have trended down since peaking in 1979 at nearly triple the 2002 level	Table 2.1 data converted to real dollars
D4: During the Decline Stage, average commodity prices, total industry profits, total industry sales revenues, and total units sold all decrease.	Partially observed during the half-century analysis period; more detail needed	
D4a: During the "Early" Decline Stage, product prices, total industry profits, and total industry sales revenues all decrease in real terms.	Supported by current data–H_{D1} is accepted for the current period (1984–2002), H_{D2} is accepted for the entire half-century analysis period, and USDA's Index of Prices Received for agricultural output decreased in real and nominal terms in recent decades	USDA 2003
D4b: During the "Late" Decline Stage, total units sold decrease.	No	
P10: During the Decline Stage, the number of firms in the industry decreases, but may not reach zero.	Yes, farm and ranch numbers have declined steadily to less than one-third of the peak in 1935	USDA 1999
D5: The life cycle of an industry ends when sales are no longer made in the original market, even if the remaining firms are making sales in a different market.	No	

The results presented in this chapter raise more questions. Specifically, policymakers and participants in agriculture want to know, "how much of American agriculture will disappear, and when?" The answer is an impossible function of (unpredictable) policies and the (somewhat predictable) reactions of farmers and ranchers to those policies. For example, we cannot know how many acres will be in or out of production at any price level because (1) we do not know the individual costs of each firm, and (2) even if we did, we do not know the profit preferences of agricultural firms' owners. We do know that, on average, people usually leave an investment before profits drop to zero, and they move to alternative investments. This means it is easy to overestimate how many acres might stay in agriculture. If analysts use $0 profit as the condition for exit, rather than some amount greater than $0, forecasts of acres that stay in agriculture will overshoot reality. Thus, profit levels are a key to estimating agriculture's progress through its life cycle.

Despite the declining profit levels reported in this chapter, many people will raise the old argument, "people have to eat," as a sufficient condition to prevent the American production agriculture industry's decline. That argument often continues, "How can American agriculture disappear? Agriculture has never been highly profitable. What is different now?" In essence, this argument says that consumers will always pay for food, so there will always be *some* profit in agriculture.

A response to this argument necessarily centers on an assessment of profits available to farmers and ranchers. It is true that profit margins in agriculture have been low for a long time. The so-called "golden era" of agriculture in America was 1910–1914 (Johnson and Quance 1972). As shown in Figure 2.3, that brief period immediately before World War I had average gross profit margins around 50 percent. As shown in the column on the right hand side of Table 2.1, profit margins have not reached that level during the past half-century and are decreasing. But it is not just the amount of profits or the profit margin that makes agriculture a good investment; it is the *relative* performance of the industry. In 1910–1914, agriculture generated profits that could provide farm households with a relatively prosperous lifestyle (Cochrane 1993). Also, agriculture was highly profitable *relative to the few alternatives* available to farmers in the past. Now, agriculture's profitability is being made relatively less attractive by the *increasing number of improving alternatives* created by America's continuing economic development.

The next chapter provides a general assessment of producers' profitability over time and across the various geographical regions that make up the American industry. It provides an estimate of the answer to the question "How much of American agriculture will disappear?" by focusing on the relative goals of individuals.

NOTE

Some material in this chapter is a revised version of an article published by S. Blank as "Where Is American Agriculture in Its Life Cycle?" *Journal of Agricultural and Resource Economics* 28, no. 3 (2003): 396–418.

REFERENCES

Acs, Z., and D. Audretsch. 1988. "Innovation in Large and Small Firms." *American Economic Review* 78 (4): 678–690.

Agarwal, R. 1997. "Survival of Firms over the Product Life Cycle." *Southern Economics Journal* 63 (3): 571–584.

Anderson, C., and C. Zeithaml. 1984. "Stage of the Product Life Cycle, Business Strategy and Business Performance." *Academy of Management Journal* 27: 5–24.

Anderson, Kym. 1987. "On Why Agriculture Declines with Economic Growth." *Agricultural Economics* 1: 195–207.

Antle, John M. 1999. "The New Economics of Agriculture." *American Journal of Agricultural Economics* 81: 993–1010.

Blank, Steven C. 2001a. "The Challenge to Think Big as American Agriculture Shrinks." *Journal of Agricultural and Resource Economics* 26 (2): 309–325.

———. 2001b. "Producers Get Squeezed Up the Farming Food Chain: A Theory of Crop Portfolio Composition and Land Use." *Review of Agricultural Economics* 23 (2): 404–422.

Bolle, N. 1999. "Real Options and Product Life Cycles." *Management Science* 45 (5): 670–671.

Chi, T., and J. Liu. 2001. "Product Life Cycle and Market Entry and Exit Decisions Under Uncertainty." *IIE Transactions* 33 (9): 695–697.

Cochrane, Willard W. 1993. *The Development of American Agriculture: A Historical Analysis.* 2d ed. Minneapolis: University of Minnesota Press.

Dasgupta, P., and J. Stiglitz. 1980. "Industrial Structure and the Nature of Innovative Activity." *Economic Journal* 90 (358): 266–293.

Duffy, Patricia A. 2001. "Casting Bread upon the Water: Comments on Technology, Globalization, and Agriculture." *Journal of Agricultural & Applied Economics* 33 (2): 341–347.

Dunne, T., M. Roberts, and L. Samuelson. 1989. "The Growth and Failure of U.S. Manufacturing Plants." *Quarterly Journal of Economics* 104 (4): 671–698.

Goetz, S., and D. Debertin. 1996. "Rural Population Decline in the 1980s: Impacts of Farm Structure and Federal Farm Programs." *American Journal of Agricultural Economics* 78: 517–529.

Harrigan, J. 1997. "Technology, Factor Supplies, and International Specialisation: Estimating the Neoclassical Model." *American Economic Review* 87 (4): 475–494.

Johnson, D. Gale. 1991. *World Agriculture in Disarray.* 2d ed. New York: St. Martin's Press.

Johnson, Glenn L., and C. LeRoy Quance, eds. 1972. *The Overproduction Trap in U.S. Agriculture.* Resources for the Future. Baltimore, MD: Johns Hopkins University Press.

Jovanovic, Boyan. 1982. "Selection and the Evolution of Industry." *Econometrica* 50 (2): 649–670.

Jovanovic, B., and G. MacDonald. 1994. "The Life Cycle of a Competitive Industry." *Journal of Political Economy* 102 (2): 322–347.

Klepper, Steven. 1996. "Entry, Exit, Growth, and Innovation over the Product Life Cycle." *American Economic Review* 86 (3): 562–583.

Lilien, G., and P. Kotler. 1983. *Marketing Decision Making: A Model-Building Approach.* New York: Harper & Row.

Mundlak, Yair. 2001. "Explaining Economic Growth." *American Journal of Agricultural Economics* 83: 1154–1167.

Perron, Pierre. 1989. "The Great Crash, the Oil Price Shock, and the Unit Root Hypothesis." *Econometrica* 57 (6): 1361–1401.

Peterson, W., and S. Valluru. 2000. "Agricultural Comparative Advantage and Government Policy Interventions." *Journal of Agricultural Economics* 51 (3): 371–387.

Pindyck, R., and D. Rubinfeld. 1976. *Econometric Models and Economic Forecasts.* New York: McGraw-Hill.

Rink, D., D. Roden, and H. Fox. 1999. "Financial Management and Planning with the Product Life Cycle Concept." *Business Horizons* 42 (5): 65–66.

Schultz, Theodore W. 1932. "Diminishing Returns in View of Progress in Agricultural Production." *Journal of Farm Economics* 14 (4): 640–649.

Shaked, A., and J. Sutton. 1987. "Product Differentiation and Industrial Structure." *Journal of Industrial Economics* 36 (2): 131–146.

Shankar, G., S. Carpenter, and L. Krishnamurthi. 1999. "The Advantages of Entry in the Growth Stage of the Product Life Cycle: An Empirical Analysis." *Journal of Marketing Research* 36 (2): 269–277.

Thompson, R., and S. Blank. 1994. "Ag Loan Analysis." *Journal of Agricultural Lending* 7 (2): 12–14, 16–17.

Thurow, Lester C. 1996. *The Future of Capitalism: How Today's Economic Forces Shape Tomorrow's World.* New York: Penguin Books.

U.S. Department of Agriculture. 1999. *1997 Census of Agriculture.* National Agricultural Statistics Service, no. AC97-A-51, March.

——. 2000a. "Accumulated Farm Real Estate Value Will Help Farmers and Their Lenders Through Period of Declining Cash Receipts." *Agricultural Income and Finance: Situation and Outlook,* pp. 30–33. Economic Research Service, no. AIS-74, February.

——. 2000b. "With Low Commodity Prices, Government Payments Support Farm Income." *Agricultural Income and Finance: Situation and Outlook Report,* pp. 4–13. Resource Economics Division, Economic Research Service, no. AIS-75, September.

——. 2001. "Off-Farm Income Supports Many Farm Households." *Agricultural Income and Finance: Situation and Outlook Report,* pp. 32–34. Resource Economics Division, Economic Research Service, no. AIS-76, February.

——. 2003. "Farm Income and Costs: Farm Income Forecasts." Economic Research Service "Briefing Room," on web at www.ers.usda.gov/Briefing/FarmIncome/fore.htm.

Weimar, M., and A. Hallam. 1988. "Risk, Diversification, and Vegetables as an Alternative Crop for Midwestern Agriculture." *North Central Journal of Agricultural Economics* 10 (January): 75–89.

CHAPTER 3

PROFIT PATTERNS ACROSS AMERICAN AGRICULTURE

"Follow the money."
—Deep Throat to Bob Woodward,
during the reporter's investigation
of the Watergate break-in

The profit performance of American agriculture will ultimately determine its future role in the national economy. This may be even more apparent when considering the viability of agriculture within geographic regions or individual states. To remain viable, agriculture in each location must offer returns (expressed as the rate of return on investments) that are both competitive relative to those from alternative investments and sufficient in absolute amounts to cover producers' financial obligations. In turn, economic theory says that rates of return converge over the long term as resources flow into more profitable industries and out of less profitable industries, causing factor price changes (O'Rourke and Williamson 1994). Much of both traditional growth and trade theory says factor markets will adjust to equalize commodity rates of return over time. For example, Kim (1997, pp 1–2) notes:

> The neoclassical Heckscher-Ohlin trade model argues that incomes of regions vary because of their differing factor endowments and factor prices. Economic integration and trade in goods leads to income convergence through factor price equalization.... Since regions differ in their factor endowments, regions will specialize in different industries.

This implies that if agricultural returns across states and regions have not been equal over time, it is most likely due to different "crop portfolios" being produced across locations (Schott 2003).

Convergence is important because it raises the question of whether the total rate of return to which an area's agricultural markets converge is sufficient to keep agriculture viable. That is, if financial obligations exceed current income in the short run, or if opportunity costs exceed total returns in the long run, off-farm income is needed for producers to avoid leaving agriculture. Returns from current income are a "cash flow" available in the short run to pay financial obligations. Furthermore, returns from capital gains are not liquid, they are gains in wealth fully captured only in the longer term. Therefore, the composition of total returns and its variance influence viability (Plaxico 1979).

Melichar (1979) used the theoretical and empirical relationships among the rate of return on farm assets from current income, capital gains, and asset prices to illustrate several key points about convergence. First, according to asset-pricing theory, a farm economy characterized by rapid growth in the current return to farm assets will tend to experience large annual capital gains and a low rate of return to assets (Melichar 1979, p. 1085). Second, long-run capital market equilibrium requires that the annual rate of increase in the price of an asset equal the growth rate of the annual return, and that the rate of return from current income plus the rate of return from capital gains equal the market interest rate. Since the rate of return from capital gains equals the growth rate of returns, the rate of return from current income is equal to the discount rate (market rate of interest) minus the growth rate of returns. Thus, the market discount rate determines the total rate of return, and the growth rate determines how the total (rate of) return is divided between a capital gain and a current return. Third, the market discount rate used by investors to discount expected returns may vary across farm production regions due to differences in opportunity costs of farm investments and in the ability of investors to manage market (systematic) risk by holding well-diversified portfolios. Therefore, even in the long run, ex post (total) rates of return on farm assets may differ across farm regions.

Furthermore, Melichar (1979) examined (total) rates of return on farm assets over subperiods, based on differences in either the growth rate of the current return, or in the relative importance of capital gains. Consequently, (total) rates of return may be markedly different across farm production regions from those expected from the asset-pricing model. In the short run (over subperiods), when factors like farmland and other farm capital are "quasi-fixed," rates of return typically differ from their long-run equilibrium values.

This chapter examines whether there are spatial relationships in agriculture's profitability over time. Economic theory expects that, in the long run, factor markets adjust to (approximately) equalize agriculture's marginal rates of return over space. This traditional view essentially assumes there is a single, integrated (domestic) network of markets for all commodities. Conversely, it is more likely that differences in profitability between commodity markets have occurred over recent decades due to the presence of global markets for commodities and the effects of an evolving "global comparative advantage" system that has yet to fully integrate all markets (Gutierrez 2000; Schott 2003). Given those differences, marginal factor rates of return will equalize in the short run only to some limited extent because factors are "fixed" to some degree (Davis and Weinstein 2001). Factor immobility and factor price distortions will be reflected in differences in the general level of profitability of states and regions that produce different commodities.

Therefore, the general objective of this chapter is to assess the profitability of American agriculture over space and time so as to identify locations with agricultural sectors most likely to prosper or decline under the pressure of current global economic conditions. Specific objectives are to answer the following research questions: (1) Are there states/regions that have performed especially well or poorly over time? (2) Can a minimum return needed to remain in agriculture be identified for each area? If so, what is it? (3) Are there particular commodities common to the strong or weak states? (4) What are the trends within those strong and weak areas?

PROPOSITIONS TO BE EVALUATED

The objectives are met by evaluating three general propositions that help explain observed aggregate financial results and the farm-level decisions leading to them.

- PROPOSITION 3.1—Convergence. *Convergence in rates of return to American agricultural producers occurs over time and space.*
- PROPOSITION 3.2—Minimum Return to Remain in Agriculture. *There is a minimum rate of return needed to remain in agriculture, and it will be apparent if the data converge to a stable trend over time.*

- PROPOSITION 3.2a. *If there are no off-farm income sources available, the minimum rate of return to production must be at least 0 percent (a break-even operation) and greater than zero if there are opportunity costs for producers to stay in agriculture.*
- PROPOSITION 3.2b. *If there are off-farm income sources available, the minimum rate of return to production can be less than 0 percent (an unprofitable operation), depending on a farmer's willingness and ability to personally subsidize the farm.*
- PROPOSITION 3.2c. *The minimum rate of return needed to remain in agriculture influences the "probability of lost farms" in a state/region.*
- PROPOSITION 3.3—Sources of Returns. *The sources of income/returns are important in determining the economic prospects of agriculture in a state/region over time.*
- PROPOSITION 3.3a. *The farm share of a state's gross state product and that state's farmers' rate of return from current production income will be positively correlated.*
- PROPOSITION 3.3b. *The farm share of a state's gross state product and that state's farmers' rate of return from capital gains will be negatively correlated.*

The rationale for Propositions 3.1 and 3.2 is apparent. Proposition 3.3 is based on expectations derived from the work of Melichar (1979), Plaxico (1979), and others. The relationship stated in Proposition 3.3a is expected due to the need for higher agricultural income in states with relatively fewer opportunities for off-farm income. Proposition 3.3b states a relationship created when nonfarm sectors in states vary in size, and thus have different effects on agricultural asset values.

The economic implications of Propositions 3.1–3.3 are (1) that structural adjustments in the agricultural sector will (continue to) occur in locations (i.e., states, regions) with below-minimum profitability, until average results are reached, if factor markets permit sufficient adjustment; and (2) if factor markets do not permit sufficient adjustment, agriculture will be under pressure to shrink, subject to the willingness and ability of farmers to earn sufficient off-farm income to maintain the required minimum profitability levels.

The literature shows that rates of return to agriculture have been lower than returns to non-agricultural businesses for most of the past century (e.g., Schultz 1932; Bjornson and Innes 1992; Bjornson and Carter 1997). Various explanations for the low rates of return and producers' willingness to accept them have been offered over time in the form of theories: asset fixity, production treadmill, lifestyle considerations. For example, in the 1960s Tweeten (1969) examined three theories advanced to explain persistent low returns to agriculture: (1) the fixed resource theory, (2) increasing returns to farm size, and (3) imperfect competition. He concluded that all three theories could contribute part of the explanation.

Implications of the globalization of commodity markets over the past three decades are that rates of return to commodities may continue to decrease over time (McElroy et al. 2002), depending on American producers' comparative and absolute advantages in each market. Thus, rates of return to commodities—and the states and/or regions in which they are produced—will vary across states/regions unless factor markets can adjust sufficiently over time. If differences are found, as expected, the profitability performance of locations will reflect the relative strength or weakness of each area's agricultural sector. Those areas showing weakness have more economic pressure on the agricultural sector to decline.

ROAD MAP FOR DISCOVERY

The analysis first identifies states that have above- or below-average profit performance, as measured by returns on assets and equity, to fulfill the first specific objective. State-level data are used to identify trends over the 1960–2002 period. From those results, regions with above- or below-average returns are identified.

Economists are increasingly using geographic regions to facilitate analyses of locations sharing common attributes (e.g., Dodson 1994; Isserman 2002; Kim 1997; Quigley 2002). To that end, the U.S. Department of Agriculture aggregated the contiguous 48 states into 10 "farm production regions" based on the dominant agricultural enterprises within each state. This chapter uses those regions: Northeast, Lake States, Corn Belt, Northern Plains, Appalachia, Southeast, Delta, Southern Plains, Mountain, and Pacific (shown in Figure 3.1).

In general, the second specific objective is fulfilled by evaluating the propositions presented earlier. Propositions 3.1 and 3.2 are compared to the data to assess the degree of consistency across time and locations with the proposed convergence to a single, minimum rate of return.[1] Evaluating Propositions 3.3 and 3.2c involves calculating measures that blend returns and risks across time and space. A "safety-first" criterion is applied to evaluate the level of risk facing agricultural producers. This criterion provides results consistent with, but more detailed than, the results generated using standard market risk measures as applied by Daniel and Featherstone (2001) and others. Next, the role of off-farm income, as expressed in Propositions 3.2 and 3.3, is addressed. Finally, the prospects for states'/regions' future performance are discussed with regard to how they are affected by the local convergence of rates of return, or the lack thereof, as expressed in Proposition 3.2c.

Profitability of the agricultural sectors of each state is assessed using data including financial ratios from the balance sheet and income/expenses estimates by state. These data are from the USDA Economic Research Service's Web site (USDA 2003). Issues related to the data and its analysis are discussed in the following sections.

Rates of Return and Profitability

The Economic Research Service (ERS) estimates both the rate of return from current income and the total economic rate of return, including capital gains for the farm business sector, independently of who owns these assets. The rate of return on assets (ROA) from current income is the ratio of residual income to farm assets from current income to the average value of the beginning and end of year's farm assets. The residual income to farm assets is calculated by ERS as income to farm assets less the imputed returns to labor and to management. The rate of return on farm equity (ROE) is the ratio of residual income to farm assets excluding interest paid, to the average value of the beginning and end of year's farm equity. The total economic (ex ante, expected) rate of return to assets (or equity) is divided into two components: current income as a percentage of assets (or equity) and unrealized capital gains/losses as a percentage of assets (or equity):

$$(3.1) \quad \text{Total ROA (or ROE)} = \frac{\text{returns from current income} + \text{returns from capital gains}}{\text{average value of farm assets (or equity)}}$$

The profitability of investments can be described with various financial measures. For example, rate of return may be measured as excluding, or including, capital gains and losses. The rate of return on assets is a widely used indicator of firm or sector profitability. The ROA reflects returns per dollar of owned and borrowed capital and is the ratio of residual income (including interest paid) to total assets. The total rate of return on assets includes the rate of return on real capital gains or losses, as shown in Equation 3.1. In periods of rapidly changing farm income and

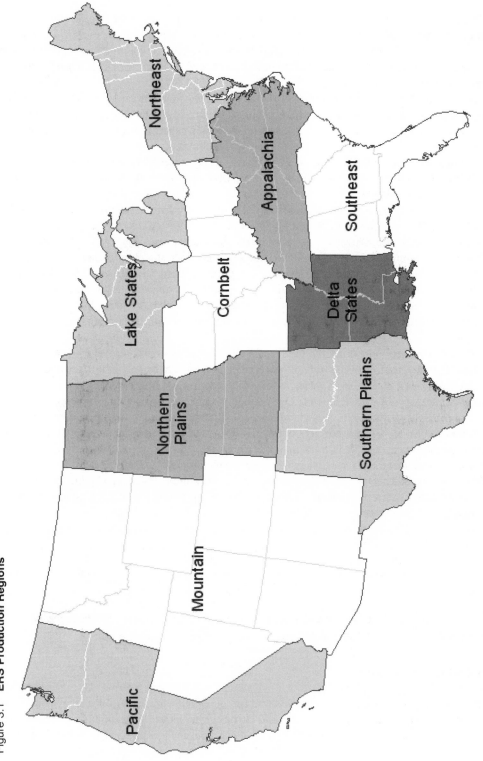

Figure 3.1   ERS Production Regions

land values, such as the 1970s, measures that include capital gains may give better estimates of the farm sector's profitability than those that do not. Therefore, this chapter uses total ROA as its primary measure of profits. Historical ROA data are used in the simple trend analysis needed to evaluate Propositions 3.1 and 3.2. The components of total ROA are assessed when evaluating Proposition 3.3.

One reason for examining returns from both current income and capital appreciation is that farm programs and macroeconomic policy changes affect both the short-term (current) return on farm assets and the wealth of farm asset holders. Changes in expectations about income growth or interest rates can cause large changes in asset values and real capital gains. Also, capital has substituted for both land and labor. This has substantially raised the level of net returns attributable to capital (Ahrendsen 1993; Crisostomo and Featherstone 1990; Hottel and Gardner 1983; Reinsel and Reinsel 1979).

Melichar (1979) examined the relationship between asset values and returns to farm assets. He showed that the rapid growth in real current return to assets led to large annual capital gains and low rates of current return to assets. He pointed out that capital gains could result from a growing stream of net returns. As a result, Melichar argued that since the price of farm assets reflects capital gains due to expected future income growth, those gains should be included in computations of the total returns to farm assets. Dunford (1980) added that although anticipated capital gains are not fully realized until the property is sold, equity increases due to land appreciation can be used to finance other investments, increasing the present value of anticipated (unrealized) capital gains.

Finally, a related issue concerns the distribution of returns across farmland owners and operators. This chapter focuses entirely on the typical case of farm owners who also run their own production operation. However, many farmland owners do not operate farms and, conversely, many farmers do not own farmland. The implications of this ownership structure are not addressed in this book until Parts 4 and 5, but readers ought to be aware of the issue when evaluating total returns. An owner/operator gets both returns: those from current income plus those from capital gains. On the other hand, a tenant farmer gets only returns from current income, which are cash receipts. Some of those receipts must be paid to the farmland owner for use of the land asset. Also, a farmland owner who does not operate a farm gets returns from capital gains, if realized by selling the land, otherwise these are *speculative unrealized gains*. Therefore, total returns can be defined in two new ways:

cash	+	speculative	=	total,
operations	+	ownership	=	total.

It is expected that the relative sizes of each component of total returns influences the nature of total demand for farmland in a geographical area.

Evaluating Convergence

Convergence is assessed using both qualitative and quantitative methods. Both approaches focus on historical returns data. Patterns in the data across locations and time are first identified qualitatively using descriptive statistics. Then, cointegration analysis is used to test for long-run convergence. Finally, a trend model is used to test hypotheses regarding periods of convergence, divergence, and stability in rates of return.

Cointegration Analysis

A typical formulation of convergence (Sala-i-Martin 1996) can be expressed as:

$$(3.2) \qquad \ln\left(\frac{y_{it}}{y_{*t}}\right) = \alpha_0 + \alpha_1 \ln\left(\frac{y_{i,t-1}}{y_{*,t-1}}\right) + \alpha_2 z_{it} + \varepsilon_{it},$$

where $\ln(.)$ denotes the natural logarithm; y_{it} is the level of income per capita in region or state i in time t; y_{*t} is the index income per capita at time t; z_{it} is a vector of other economic variables (such as initial capital) in region or state i at time t; ε_{it} is an error term; and α_0, α_1, and α_2 are estimated coefficients. In this formulation, if α_0 approaches 0, $\alpha_1 < 1$, and $\alpha_2 = 0$, the income in region i converges over time toward the income of the index. Further, this convergence is unconditional, or does not depend on other variables (such as initial capital). The convergence is conditional if α_0 approaches 0, $\alpha_1 < 0$, and α_2 does not equal 0.

Implicit in most discussions of convergence is the assumption that incomes have grown monotonically over time. Empirically, growth implies

$$(3.3) \qquad y_{it} = \gamma_0 + \gamma_1 y_{i,t-1} + v_{it},$$

where γ_0 and γ_1 are estimated parameters and v_{it} is an error term. Monotonic economic growth could imply that γ_1 approaches 1, or that income per capita may be nonstationary. This potential nonstationarity introduces the possibility of spurious regression results (Granger and Newbold 1974). This chapter, however, analyzes whether the rate of return on agricultural assets is converging across regions. Thus, income in Equation 3.3 is replaced with the rate of return on assets, giving

$$(3.4) \qquad r_{it} = \gamma_0 + \gamma_1 r_{i,t-1} + v_{it},$$

where r_{it} is the rate of return on agricultural assets in state i. The Phillips-Perron tests for nonstationarity of the rates of return on agricultural assets are presented in Table 3.1. Note that in 24 of the 48 states, nonstationarity is rejected at the 95 percent confidence level. Further, in 32 of 48 states, nonstationarity is rejected at the 90 percent confidence level. Finally, the returns data are transformed for use in the convergence analysis, as noted below.

Convergence in equation 3.2 is reformulated into

$$(3.5) \qquad \begin{aligned} \ln(y_{it}) - \ln(y_{*t}) &= \alpha_0 + \alpha_1 [\ln(y_{i,t-1}) - \ln(y_{*,t-1})] + \alpha_2 z_{it} + \varepsilon_{it} \\ d_{it} &= \alpha_0 + \alpha_1 d_{i,t-1} + \alpha_2 z_{it} + \varepsilon_{it} \end{aligned}$$

where d_{it} is the logarithmic difference between returns in state i and the index state at time t. Since the rate of return data for agricultural assets in Equation 3.5 are first-differenced, convergence can be estimated directly. Unfortunately, the formulation in Equation 3.5 cannot be directly applied because negative rates of return are sometimes observed in agricultural data. Thus, Equation 3.5 is redefined so that $d_{it} = r_{*t} - r_{it}$, where, for each of ERS's ten regions, r_{*t} is the maximum rate of

Table 3.1

State-Level Phillips-Perron Z_α Statistics for the Rate of Return on Assets

State	α	Z_α	State	α	Z_α
Northeast			**Southeast**		
Connecticut	0.7195	−9.2909	Alabama	0.6124	−13.3791[*]
Delaware	0.6143	−13.9086[**]	Florida	0.7244	−11.0628[*]
Maine	0.3241	−26.8908[***]	Georgia	0.6374	−12.2322[*]
Maryland	0.5421	−16.2135[**]	South Carolina	0.2759	−28.0804[***]
Massachusetts	0.8160	−6.2148	**Delta States**		
New Hampshire	0.2009	−33.9048[***]	Arkansas	0.5273	−19.0899[**]
New Jersey	0.7996	−9.3533	Louisiana	0.6937	−13.0915[*]
New York	0.6833	−10.5786	Mississippi	0.2114	−32.7156[***]
Pennsylvania	0.5274	−16.7369[**]	**Southern Plains**		
Rhode Island	0.8936	−7.5609	Oklahoma	0.6065	−15.7822[**]
Vermont	0.7532	−7.8786	Texas	0.2823	−30.4629[***]
Lake States			**Mountain States**		
Michigan	0.8720	−2.9123	Arizona	0.7945	−7.5593
Minnesota	0.5571	−17.7833[**]	Colorado	0.8282	−8.3992
Wisconsin	0.6932	−8.6551	Idaho	0.7780	−8.5935
Corn Belt			Montana	0.6894	−13.1110[*]
Illinois	0.4204	−24.2368[***]	Nevada	0.5026	−20.7059[***]
Indiana	0.3145	−28.0607[***]	New Mexico	0.6311	−14.3258[**]
Iowa	0.5163	−21.1702[***]	Utah	0.6685	−13.5349[*]
Missouri	0.5178	−17.3323[**]	Wyoming	0.8590	−7.6754
Ohio	0.3967	−26.2823[***]	**Pacific States**		
Northern Plains			California	0.8165	−10.3938
Kansas	0.6425	−15.4928[**]	Oregon	0.8409	−8.5828
Nebraska	0.6714	−11.3804[*]	Washington	0.7269	−12.9085[*]
North Dakota	0.3986	−25.5364[***]			
South Dakota	0.3318	−27.5982[***]			
Appalachia					
Kentucky	−0.1069	−43.9611[***]			
North Carolina	0.9114	−2.8644			
Tennessee	0.7255	−7.2238			
Virginia	0.4531	−21.4534[***]			
West Virginia	0.0511	−39.6884[***]			

[***]Denotes statistical significance at the 99% confidence level.
[**]Denotes statistical significance at the 95% confidence level.
[*]Denotes statistical significance at the 90% confidence level.

return to agricultural assets from one state. Finally, α_0 and α_1 in Equation 3.5 are estimated using maximum likelihood.

Trend Analysis

Cointegration analysis has a weakness relative to the objectives of this chapter that trend analysis can address. This weakness is the inability of standard cointegration methods to provide detailed information about the underlying processes in time series that do not appear to be converging. For example, time series may be diverging or they may have converged previously and are in some stable "equilibrium" during a period of interest. Trend analysis allows these special cases to be identified.

A convergence model derived by Ben-David (1993) is modified here by adding a trend variable. It begins as:

$$(3.6) \qquad R_{i,t} - R_t^* = \omega(R_{i,t-1} - R_{t-1}^*) + T_t,$$

where $R_{i,t}$ is the average return for producers in the states pooled to form region i in year t, R^*_t is the average return for producers in the United States in year t, and T is a time trend variable. Letting $Y_{i,t} = R_{i,t} - R_t^*$ (a first-difference), Equation 3.6 can be rewritten as:

$$(3.7) \qquad \Delta Y_{i,t} = \alpha - \beta Y_{i,t-1} + \gamma T_t + \varepsilon,$$

where $\Delta Y_{i,t} = Y_{i,t} - Y_{i,t-1}$ (a second-difference), α is a constant, β and γ are coefficients to be estimated, and ε is an error term. In this specification, $\beta = -(1-\omega)$, and γ and β jointly indicate whether the region's average returns are converging, diverging, stable, or mixed relative to national average returns.

If the estimated γ is not significantly different from zero over some time period, then location i's returns may be "stable" relative to U.S. average returns, thereby indicating a period of "equilibrium" caused by that location's markets having previously converged to the national average (or some stable amount above or below national average returns). During such a "stable" time period, differences in a location's returns relative to the U.S. average for individual years are expected to occur and are captured by the error term. Thus, the R^2 for an estimate of Equation 3.7 is an indicator of how strongly the location has converged to the national market. In the extremely unlikely case of "perfect" convergence, there is no difference between $R_{i,t}$ and R_t^*, so $Y_{i,t} = 0$ at all times. In the equally unlikely case of "parallel" convergence (defined as two series with a fixed difference between them not equaling zero), $Y_{i,t}$ equals some fixed amount at all times. In both cases, $\gamma = 0$, $\beta = 1$, $\alpha = Y_{i,t}$, $\Delta Y_{i,t} = 0$, and the R^2 is 1.0 (100 percent).

If γ is significantly different than zero over some time period, then location i's rates of return are in the process of either converging to, or diverging from, U.S. average returns. The slope of the trend is indicated by γ, and its sign indicates the direction: a positive sign slopes upward to the right, a negative sign slopes down to the right. Convergence occurs when there is a downward trend in positive $Y_{i,t}$ values or when there is an upward trend in negative $Y_{i,t}$ values (i.e., $|Y_{i,t}|$ decreases). The reverse is true for divergence. Therefore, convergence is indicated by a significant β with an absolute value of one or more (i.e., $|\beta| \geq 1$), and divergence is indicated when a significant β has an absolute value between zero and one (i.e., $1 > |\beta| > 0$).

It is possible for a single trend (a period with a significant γ) to include periods of both convergence and divergence (in that order), thus requiring visual inspection of the data to avoid mislabeling the results. In such a case, the sign of $Y_{i,t}$ changes during the trend period. This means that the values of $|\beta|$ may signal either convergence or divergence, depending upon the relative number of positive and negative $Y_{i,t}$ values, although the result ought to be labeled as a "transition" period with mixed trends.

Safety-First Decision Criteria

Proposition 3.2c is evaluated by inserting the minimum return found while evaluating Proposition 3.2 into a safety-first measure that includes returns and risk levels over some time period.

Safety-first criteria are alternative performance measures (Hagigi and Kluger 1987). They are also widely used tools for decision making under risk (Berck and Hihn 1982; Encarnación 1991; van Kooten, Young, and Krautkraemer 1997) that are compatible with the standard utility theory (Bigman 1996; Pyle and Turnovsky 1970). In agriculture, risk-averse producers have been shown to adopt safety-first decision rules when the scale of possible losses from an investment is significant (Moscardi and de Janvry 1977). In other words, producers will use safety-first rules when down-side risks include bankruptcy or some lesser result that still has a significant negative effect on the household's lifestyle.

Safety-first models create a rank ordering of decision alternatives by placing constraints upon the probability of failing to achieve certain goals of the firm. These orderings also serve as measures of performance relative to the specified goal. Several forms of safety-first models have been proposed as alternatives to expected utility maximization (Hatch, Atwood, and Segar 1989; Bigman 1996). Roy (1952) was the first to suggest that in some situations, such as when the survival of the firm is at stake, decision makers select activities that minimize the probability of failing to achieve a certain goal for income, that is,

$$(3.8) \qquad\qquad \text{minimize } \Pr\{\Pi < \Pi*\},$$

where $\Pr\{.\}$ is the probability of event $\{.\}$, Π is an income random variable, and $\Pi*$ is an income goal often referred to as the "disaster level" or the "safety threshold." Telser's (1955) criterion maximizes expected income subject to probabilistic constraints on failing to achieve income goals:

$$(3.9) \qquad\qquad \text{maximize } E(\Pi)$$

subject to

$$(3.10) \qquad\qquad \Pr\{\Pi < \Pi*\} < \Gamma,$$

where Γ is an upper (acceptable) limit on $\Pr\{\Pi < \Pi*\}$. Telser's approach is a two-step procedure whereby the person first eliminates alternatives that fail to meet the safety requirements for a given level of Γ, and then selects among the remaining alternatives the one(s) that maximizes expected utility. From these two basic models, many researchers have proposed improvements (see Bigman 1996 for a brief review of the literature). What all safety-first models have in common is some safety threshold or minimum income goal that serves as the basis for performance measurements.

Therefore, in an era when decreasing profits threaten the economic viability of many farms, it is reasonable to propose that farmers' decisions are influenced by some safety-first criteria. In such a case, a farmer's objective is to earn a profit that is expected to at least equal some designated minimum level of return, $\Pi*$, with at least the desired level of probability (Mahul 2000). The designated safety threshold, $\Pi*$, is a personal preference based on financial obligations, lifestyle goals, and opportunity costs. Thus it varies across individuals. The desired probability level is also a personal choice, reflecting the individual's degree of risk aversion.

Empirical applications of safety-first models often use a measure called the "Probability of Loss" (PL), or "risk of ruin," that incorporates $\Pi*$. It can be calculated for any market. This measure indicates the chance (in percentage terms) that a producer will generate a return below some critical level. At an aggregate level, this measure can indicate the percentage of farms at risk of failure (hence, it could be called the "probability of lost farms," or PL). The PL is found by calculating a "z" score and finding the relevant probability for that z value in a statistical table. The z for state or region i is calculated here as:

$$(3.11) \qquad\qquad Z_i = \frac{E(R_i) - k}{\sigma_i},$$

where $E(R_i)$ is the expected (average) return (on assets, equity, or some other factor) for state or region i; k is some critical value (such as Π_*); and σ_i is the standard deviation of returns for state or region i. The average return and its standard deviation are calculated for some relevant period (1960–2002 here).

The PL is the chance of earning a return below k; thus, $PL = \Pr\{R_i < \Pi_* = k\}$. The value of k is usually made zero, but it can be made any critical level of return. By making $k = 0$, the PL is the chance of suffering a loss. If some other value is used for k, such as the rate of return needed to cover all financial obligations, the estimated PL represents the probability of earning returns insufficient to cover k; in other words, the PL would indicate the chance of defaulting on some obligations.

In this chapter, PL estimates are calculated with varying values for k to show the sensitivity of production regions to the risks in their agricultural sector. Those estimates also serve as performance measures to rank the regions in terms of their likely decline due to the economic pressures from globalizing commodity markets.

Off-Farm Income Availability

Off-farm income is increasingly important to the survival of many farms and ranches (Ahituv and Kimhi 2002; Betubiza and Leatham 1994; El-Osta and Ahearn 1996; Kimhi 2000; McElroy et al. 2002; Mishra and Sandretto 2002; USDA 2001). In locations where agricultural returns fall below requirements, as expressed in safety-first models, off-farm income can serve as an alternative source (i.e., a good source of diversification) for enabling farms and ranches to remain in business. If off-farm income is readily available, farm profitability can fall with little impact on agricultural output, as implied in Proposition 3.2b. When off-farm income is less easily found, farmers must try harder to increase farming profits so as to meet financial obligations, or face exiting the industry as noted in Proposition 3.2a.[2] Thus, the decline of an agricultural sector can be slowed or reversed by producers' willingness and ability to subsidize their farms and ranches with off-farm income (Blank 2002). However, the availability of off-farm employment varies across locations.

To proxy this important factor affecting the profitability of agricultural sectors, the analysis in this chapter uses data on gross state product (GSP) from the U.S. Commerce Department's Bureau of Economic Analysis (U.S. Department of Commerce 2002). It is expected that the farm share of GSP in a state is inversely related to the availability of off-farm employment and investment opportunities—as the nonagricultural sector of a state's economy grows, more off-farm opportunities develop. Two versions of the data are used, the farm share of GSP and the "location quotient" (LQ), calculated as follows:

$$(3.12) \qquad \text{farm share of GSP} = \frac{\text{farm GSP}_i}{\text{total GSP}_i},$$

$$(3.13) \qquad \text{LQ} = \frac{(\text{farm GSP}_i/\text{total GSP}_i)}{(\text{farm GNP}_{\text{US}}/\text{total GNP}_{\text{US}})},$$

where farm GSP_i is the dollar amount of state i's farm net value added, total GSP_i is the dollar amount of state i's total net value added, and farm GNP_{US} and total GNP_{US} are the same values for the United States. The LQ is an index with a value of 1.0 for a state with exactly the same percentage of total net value added contributed by agriculture as is the case for the nation.

What Is Driving Agricultural Profitability?

The "technology treadmill," the Heckscher-Ohlin trade model, and the "DuPont expansion" of returns to factors of production, taken together, provide some perspective for understanding what is driving the profitability of production agriculture. New technologies including new machines, new genetics, new chemicals, and so forth, have been continuously introduced into the market at an increasing rate. This has been described as a "treadmill" (Cochrane 1993, pp. 427–429)—farmers must repeatedly adopt new technology just to keep up. This affects producers' cost per unit and profitability over time. The Heckscher-Ohlin trade model, mentioned earlier, helps explain how differences in factor endowments and factor prices affect the "crop portfolios" being produced across locations, and thus relative profitability across space and time. The treadmill and trade effects are reflected in the financial results assessed using the DuPont expansion, thus these concepts are applied in this chapter to better understand what is driving profitability in the strong- and weak-performing states.

The DuPont expansion involves decomposing the rate of return on equity into three components. Those components are the relative profitability of each unit of sales measured by the gross margin (operating profit) ratio, the efficiency of asset use indicated by the asset turnover ratio, and a leverage effect represented by the inverse of the solvency ratio. Mathematically, the DuPont expansion for any time period is

$$(3.14) \qquad \frac{\Pi}{E} = \frac{R-C}{R} \frac{R}{FA} \frac{FA}{E}$$

where Π is agricultural profits, E is farm equity, R is the level of sales revenues, C is the cost of production, and FA is farm assets. The operating profit margin ($[R-C]/R$) measures profits earned per dollar of farm production. The asset turnover ratio (R/FA) measures the gross cash income generated per dollar of farm assets. Finally, the ratio of farm business assets to farm business equity (FA/E) measures the leverage effect.

EXPLORATION RESULTS

The empirical results show evidence of patterns in profitability across spatial locations and across time. These patterns and their implications for the propositions and specific objectives are discussed in the following sections so as to fulfill the general objective.

Patterns Across and Within Locations

Table 3.2 shows the average returns on assets and equity earned by agriculture in individual states, the regions, and the entire United States for the 1960–2002 period. Several observations can be made about these results.

First, there is a wide range of returns across states. Thus, the answer to the first research question is "yes." The top five states in terms of profit performance and their ROA (ROE) for the entire period are North Carolina 9.3 percent (10.0 percent), Florida 8.6 percent (9.5 percent), Georgia 8.0 percent (8.6 percent), California 7.7 percent (8.6 percent), and Vermont 7.6 percent (8.4 percent). The five states with the lowest ROA (ROE) results are West Virginia –7.6 percent (−8.9 percent), New Hampshire –2.9 percent (−3.5 percent), New Mexico − 0.4 percent (−1.1 percent), Oregon 0.3 percent (−0.6 percent), and Pennsylvania 0.3 percent (−0.3 percent). These states stand out in their profit performance and are the focus of further analysis below.

Second, there are some patterns in the relative contributions in returns for the top and bottom states. These patterns support Proposition 3.3—Sources of Returns. For the high-performing states, a majority of total ROA usually comes from current income (i.e., agricultural production profits). Vermont is the only one of those five states to obtain a bigger contribution to total ROA from capital gains (ROA_k, i.e., real estate appreciation)[3] than from current income. For the other four states, current income was, by far, the strongest component of total ROA. For Vermont, growth in residential demand for land over the period fueled the nation's highest capital gains to farmland owners. For the least profitable states, the relative source of return weakness varies from East to West. The more densely populated eastern states of New Hampshire, West Virginia, and Pennsylvania all had negative returns from current income and better results from capital gains (although West Virginia had negative returns from capital gains). New Mexico and Oregon both had negative ROA from capital gains, but positive returns from current income. These results appear to illustrate the "urban influence" on farmland values described by the USDA (2000 p. 30):

> Although average agricultural land values nationally are determined primarily by the income earning potential of the land, nonagricultural factors appear to be playing an important role in many local areas. To some extent, the buoying effect of these nonagricultural factors on agricultural land values could be partially offsetting the effect of lower returns from agricultural production.

The third general observation from Table 3.2 reveals that there are some patterns across regions. Six regions' returns have converged around the national average, while two regions have significantly higher rates of return and two regions have significantly lower returns.[4] This result supports Proposition 3.1—Convergence. The average total ROA (ROE) for agriculture in the United States from 1960 through 2002 was 4.3 percent (4.1 percent). Six of the 10 regions had average ROAs (ROEs) for the period in the range of 3.9 percent to 4.8 percent (3.5 percent to 4.6 percent). These results support Proposition 3.2, Minimum Return, suggesting the minimum return required by agricultural producers is in this range. The Southeast and Pacific regions had much higher average total returns (ROA of 7.4 percent and 6.4 percent, respectively), with a large majority of it coming from current income, implying that their agricultural sectors are strong. It is also noted that these two regions were the only ones to have ROEs higher than their ROAs. The Northeast and Southern Plains regions had low returns, each with a total ROA of just under

Table 3.2

Average Returns by State and Region, 1960–2002 (percent)

	ROA from current income	ROA from real capital gains	Total ROA	St. Dev. of total ROA	Total ROE	St. Dev. of total ROE
Connecticut	2.00	2.67	4.67	4.40	4.75	4.83
Delaware	5.07	2.21	7.28	6.52	7.95	7.95
Maine	−0.21	1.47	1.26	5.89	0.73	7.28
Maryland	1.58	1.50	3.07	5.29	2.89	6.16
Massachusetts	0.71	3.44	4.15	4.72	4.21	5.30
New Hampshire	−4.07	1.21	−2.86	9.16	−3.53	10.33
New Jersey	0.96	2.50	3.46	5.30	3.50	5.90
New York	−0.18	3.69	3.51	4.32	3.16	5.35
Pennsylvania	−1.50	1.75	0.25	4.43	−0.34	5.22
Rhode Island	2.38	3.69	6.07	8.25	6.34	9.11
Vermont	0.98	6.63	7.61	5.97	8.35	7.26
NORTHEAST	−0.03	2.56	2.54	3.65	2.24	4.38
Michigan	0.58	2.16	2.74	5.41	2.18	6.91
Minnesota	2.65	1.76	4.41	8.06	4.01	10.51
Wisconsin	1.54	2.59	4.13	5.39	3.79	7.05
LAKE STATES	1.82	2.13	3.95	6.22	3.53	8.15
Illinois	3.61	0.89	4.51	8.19	4.25	9.56
Indiana	2.87	0.88	3.75	8.27	3.30	10.22
Iowa	4.72	0.82	5.54	9.21	5.39	11.83
Missouri	1.30	0.80	2.09	7.01	1.45	8.65
Ohio	1.24	2.32	3.56	6.95	3.26	8.16
CORN BEl T	3.13	1.06	4.18	7.83	3.86	9.57
Kansas	3.51	0.34	3.86	6.90	3.51	8.80
Nebraska	4.56	0.61	5.17	6.89	5.03	8.95
North Dakota	3.23	0.65	3.89	7.64	3.33	9.03
South Dakota	4.43	2.27	6.70	6.61	6.80	8.48
N. PLAINS	3.97	0.83	4.80	6.57	4.57	8.37
Kentucky	2.44	2.05	4.49	4.91	4.35	6.06
North Carolina	8.04	1.24	9.28	6.67	9.96	7.90
Tennessee	0.05	2.11	2.15	5.04	1.74	6.07
Virginia	0.64	1.02	1.66	5.30	1.26	6.09
West Virginia	−5.74	−1.86	−7.60	9.10	−8.89	10.11
APPALACHIA	2.58	1.45	4.04	4.59	3.86	5.52
Alabama	4.28	2.34	6.62	5.20	6.90	6.37
Florida	6.73	1.92	8.64	5.23	9.45	6.25
Georgia	5.72	2.32	8.04	5.80	8.56	7.31
South Carolina	3.07	0.25	3.32	5.43	2.85	6.86
SOUTHEAST	5.50	1.92	7.42	4.48	7.90	5.50
Arkansas	5.58	−0.73	4.84	6.99	4.74	8.76
Louisiana	3.95	0.51	4.45	7.30	4.13	9.18
Mississippi	3.99	0.44	4.42	6.96	4.02	9.08
DELTA	4.62	−0.02	4.60	6.58	4.34	8.42
Oklahoma	1.16	0.05	1.21	5.83	0.38	7.56
Texas	2.07	0.88	2.95	5.18	2.75	6.05
S. PLAINS	1.87	0.71	2.58	4.92	2.27	5.88

(*continued*)

Table 3.2 (*continued*)

	ROA from current income	ROA from real capital gains	Total ROA	St. Dev. of total ROA	Total ROE	St. Dev. of total ROE
Arizona	3.88	2.65	6.54	5.91	6.87	6.96
Colorado	2.85	1.15	4.00	5.96	3.91	7.84
Idaho	3.74	1.67	5.42	6.09	5.48	7.97
Montana	2.28	2.07	4.34	7.07	4.17	8.72
Nevada	1.16	1.99	3.14	6.46	2.99	7.51
New Mexico	2.87	−3.28	−0.41	7.34	−1.08	8.56
Utah	0.81	0.49	1.30	6.59	0.80	7.74
Wyoming	1.16	1.83	2.99	6.25	2.78	7.47
MOUNTAIN	2.67	1.24	3.90	5.51	3.78	6.88
California	6.41	1.27	7.68	5.57	8.51	7.40
Oregon	1.17	−0.85	0.32	5.61	−0.59	7.24
Washington	4.77	1.28	6.05	5.94	6.30	7.47
PACIFIC	5.41	0.97	6.39	4.95	6.84	6.57
Alaska	−0.06	2.67	2.61	12.49	2.50	13.82
Hawaii	3.22	1.85	5.07	5.41	5.17	5.97
AK&HI	2.93	1.92	4.85	5.26	4.92	5.80
U.S.TOTAL	3.04	1.26	4.30	5.26	4.12	6.60

Notes: "ROA" is there turn on assets, "ROE" is there turn on equity, and "St.Dev." is the standard deviation of the time series.

2.6 percent. For the Southern Plains, current income represented a majority of returns, while virtually all of the Northeast's ROA came from capital gains. These results answer "yes" to the second research question but indicate that different factors are affecting the convergence process in each region, as discussed below.

Finally, there are some consistent patterns within regions. Rates of return and sources vary across states within regions in nearly all cases, which supports Proposition 3.3. The only region to have consistent total rates of return across all states is the three-state Delta. The difference between highest and lowest total ROA across the Delta states was just 0.42 percentage point.[5] The Delta also had a fairly consistent pattern across states for one source of returns, with a highest-to-lowest difference of 1.24 percentage points for capital gains.[6] Note that Arkansas had the highest ROA_π and a slightly negative ROA_k. The neighboring Southern Plains region of just two states had an insignificant difference in rates of return from capital gains of 0.83 percentage point ($t = 1.10$). An insignificant difference in ROA_k is found in the Lake States and Corn Belt regions, although Ohio is an outlier in the Corn Belt. The difference across the other four states in that region is only 0.09 percentage point, indicating an amazing degree of convergence in farmland markets. For the regions not yet mentioned, there are no consistent patterns in either ROA source across all states within the region. Patterns appear within some subset of states in some regions, but it is clear that further disaggregation of the data is needed for analysis.

Patterns by Source over Time

Figure 3.2 shows the national average results disaggregated by source over time. Two conclusions can be drawn from the figure. First, as expected, returns from capital gains (which reflect changes in valuations based on expected future income) were much more volatile than returns from current income (which is an historic measure) over the 1960–2002 period: $\sigma_k > \sigma_\pi$. This implies that different economic factors affect each of the two sources of returns, thus necessitating separate assessments of the two data series. Second, the variability of returns, especially from capital gains, σ_k, was higher during the 1970s and 1980s, compared to the 1960s and 1990s. Jointly, these results support Proposition 3.3—that sources of returns are important in determining the economic prospects of agriculture over time; nationally, current income has been a less risky source of returns making states/regions with adequate income more viable than areas with agricultural sectors relying on capital gains.

To facilitate evaluation of the patterns in returns across time by source, Table 3.3 presents data for average ROA aggregated by region and for the country. Several important observations can be made about the results in the table.

First, there is a consistent pattern in total ROA over time, supporting Proposition 3.1, Convergence. At the national level and for every region except the Northeast, total ROA was highest during the 1970s and lowest during the 1980s. Also, only the two most profitable regions, the Southeast and Pacific, had positive total returns during the 1980s.

Second, evaluating the source of returns over time provides mixed results. There is a clear pattern over time in returns from capital gains. For every region, ROA_k was highest during the 1970s and lowest during the 1980s (being negative in each case). No clear pattern holds for ROA_π. This implies capital markets are more integrated than are markets for different commodities.

When comparing the average level of returns for the 1960s and the 1990–2002 period (the decades before and after the boom-recession 1970–1989 period), an interesting pattern emerges for the two sources. Between the 1960s and 1990–2002, ROA_π decreased in three of the regions, with a fourth (Mountain) virtually unchanged, and it increased in six regions.[7] The reverse is seen for ROA_k, which increased in four regions and decreased in six regions. At the national level, ROA_π was surprisingly stable, while ROA_k decreased between the two periods. One interpretation of these patterns is that they are consistent with Melichar's (1979) point that, in equilibrium, the total rate of return on farm assets would equal the market interest rate, thus linking the returns from current income and capital gains in an inverse relationship.

Finally, the profitability performance patterns by region show a distinct shift in American agriculture from the Northeast to the West, a shift that is probably a result of the convergence process. The Northeast region's returns were lower from both sources (ROA_π and ROA_k) in the 1990–2002 period compared to the 1960–1969 period—the only region to have such results—despite efforts to raise profit margins, such as expanding direct marketing and the production of alternative crops. Also, two of the three negative results for ROA_π in Table 3.3 are for the Northeast (i.e., 1970–1979 and 1990–2002). The other negative result for ROA_π is for the Lake States region during 1990–2002. That region and the Corn Belt both had lower returns from current income during the recent decade compared to the 1960s. However, those two regions did have slightly higher levels of capital gains in the 1990–2002 period compared to the 1960–1969 period, probably due to expanding "urban influence" on farmland values. Thus, the only three regions with lower returns from agricultural income during the most recent decade were the three in the north-by-northeast section of the United States.

Figure 3.2 **U.S. Returns on Assets and Equity, 1960–2002**

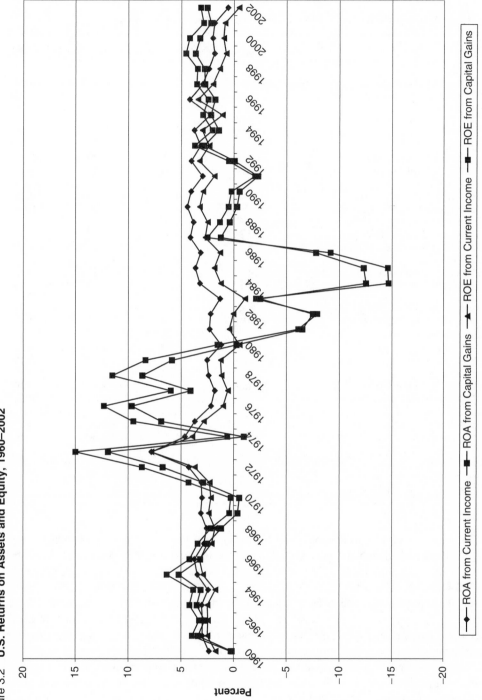

ROA from Current Income ■ ROA from Capital Gains ▲ ROE from Current Income ■ ROE from Capital Gains

Table 3.3

Regional Average Return on Assets over Time, by Source (percent)

	1960–69	1970–79	1980–89	1990–2002
Northeast				
ROA from Current Income	0.44	−0.06	0.78	−0.98
ROA from Real Capital Gains	5.02	5.18	−0.90	1.33
Lake States				
ROA from Current Income	3.03	3.42	2.35	−0.74
ROA from Real Capital Gains	2.77	6.67	−4.60	3.30
Corn Belt				
ROA from Current Income	3.92	3.92	2.86	2.11
ROA from Real Capital Gains	2.05	6.84	−7.49	2.41
Northern Plains				
ROA from Current Income	3.21	4.68	3.76	4.18
ROA from Real Capital Gains	2.52	5.57	−5.35	0.64
Appalachia				
ROA from Current Income	2.39	2.30	2.03	3.38
ROA from Real Capital Gains	3.25	4.79	−3.60	1.39
Southeast				
ROA from Current Income	4.64	4.84	5.53	6.65
ROA from Real Capital Gains	3.34	5.55	−2.46	1.40
Delta				
ROA from Current Income	3.99	5.29	3.72	5.27
ROA from Real Capital Gains	2.50	4.16	−6.81	0.06
Southern Plains				
ROA from Current Income	1.63	2.17	1.64	2.00
ROA from Real Capital Gains	2.70	3.72	−3.57	0.15
Mountain				
ROA from Current Income	2.68	3.05	2.37	2.66
ROA from Real Capital Gains	1.73	5.82	−5.01	2.14
Pacific				
ROA from Current Income	3.84	6.23	6.27	5.33
ROA from Real Capital Gains	0.93	4.21	−2.98	1.56
United States				
ROA from Current Income	2.94	3.54	2.95	2.79
ROA from Real Capital Gains	2.46	5.53	−4.81	1.72

The next five regions to the south and west (Northern Plains, Appalachia, Southeast, Delta, and Southern Plains) all had higher average returns from current income and lower returns from capital gains during the 1990–2002 period, compared to the 1960s. Also, the three lowest results for ROA_k outside of the 1980s occurred in the Northern Plains, Delta, and Southern Plains regions during the most recent decade. Clearly, changes were occurring in that part of the country. During the 1990–2002 period, current income provided the majority of total returns in each of the five regions, whereas during the 1960s the two sources of returns had been mixed in their relative contributions to total returns, with one or the other providing the majority.

The two western regions (Mountain and Pacific) had the most positive pattern in rates of return. Both regions had higher levels of returns from capital gains during the 1990–2002 period, compared to the 1960s, and while the Mountain region's returns from current income were about the same between the two periods, the Pacific region had higher ROA_π in the recent period. Thus, the Pacific was the only region to have higher levels of returns from both sources over the two periods. It is also worth noting that the majority source of returns was always current income for the Pacific region, while the majority source switched for the Mountain region from income to capital gains.

The profit-induced shift in agriculture described above is apparent in data showing changes in aggregate cropland acreage over the 1945–1997 period, as reported by Vesterby and Krupa (2001). Over that period, the Northeast region's total cropland decreased by about 12 million acres, the Southeast lost 9 million acres, Appalachian cropland dropped 7.5 million acres, the Lake States lost about 6 million acres, and the Delta's cropland decreased about 0.5 million acres. These reductions totaled about 35 million acres. Over the same period, however, there were cropland acreage increases in the other regions: the Pacific total grew by about 1.5 million acres, the Southern Plains added 4.5 million acres, the Corn Belt increased by 6.5 million acres, the Northern Plains added 12.5 million acres, and the Mountain region expanded cropland by about 13 million acres. The expansions totaled about 38 million acres. Hence, the cropland increases (predominantly in the western half of the United States) replaced the decreases (mostly in the eastern half of the country). In total, there was a net gain of about 3 million acres of cropland over the period despite a steady decrease in total land in U.S. agriculture after the peak in 1954. The slight expansion of cropland in combination with a drop in total land in agriculture from 1.2 billion acres in 1954 to 931 million acres in 1997 clearly indicates that the composition of American agriculture's portfolio of enterprises is slowly shifting away from livestock grazing and toward higher-value crops and intensive livestock that generate higher returns. This trend can be interpreted as part of the process causing convergence of rates of return.

Overall, total returns increased for only two regions between the 1960s and the 1990–2002 period: the Pacific and Mountain regions. Total returns were virtually unchanged over the two periods for the Southeast region and were lower in all other regions. Thus, while most of the country is following the U.S. trend of lower total returns over time, the agricultural sectors in many western states appear to have converged to a higher rate of returns.

Convergence: Cointegration and Trend Results

The empirical results for the cointegration convergence model in Equation 3.5 are presented in Table 3.4. Based on the data, the rate of return on agricultural assets in Delaware is generally higher than for the remaining states in the Northeast. Thus, Delaware was chosen as the Northeast's index state in Equation 3.5. Following this criterion, Minnesota is used as the index state for the Lake States, Iowa as the index for the Corn Belt, Nebraska as the index for the Northern Plains, North Carolina for Appalachia, Florida for the Southeast, Arkansas for the Delta, Texas for the Southern Plains, Idaho for the Mountain region, and California for the Pacific region.

In general, convergence occurs if α_1 is less than one, implying that the difference between the rates of return for the index and a particular state is declining over time. As indicated by the results reported in Table 3.4, all the rates of return to agricultural assets converge over time within all regions except Appalachia. Within the Appalachian region, the data fail to reject $\alpha_1 = 1$ at the 95 percent confidence level for Kentucky, Tennessee, and Virginia. Overall, the results support at least conditional convergence for the rates of return on agricultural assets within all regions except Appalachia.

To test for unconditional convergence, the convergence between each of the ten index states is examined. The data suggest using North Carolina to normalize the index states for each region. Again, the estimated autoregression coefficient for each region (shown in Table 3.5) is less than

Table 3.4

Estimated Autoregression Coefficients for Difference in Rate of Return on Assets

State	α_1	α_0	State	α_1	α_0
Connecticut	0.42727	0.03915	Kentucky	0.90350	0.06648
	(0.14016)	(0.00781)		(0.06173)	(0.02926)
Maine	0.16453	0.05370	Tennessee	0.94620	0.09253
	(0.15391)	(0.00745)		(0.04424)	(0.04018)
Maryland	0.54789	0.03825	Virginia	0.93138	0.08740
	(0.13075)	(0.00680)		(0.05004)	(0.03171)
Massachusetts	0.66263	0.05027	West Virginia	0.41308	0.15907
	(0.11415)	(0.01331)		(0.14127)	(0.02731)
New Hampshire	0.29933	0.10615			
	(0.15009)	(0.02317)	Alabama	0.33804	0.01761
New Jersey	0.55701	0.04900		(0.14661)	(0.00277)
	(0.12832)	(0.00912)	Georgia	0.48546	0.00171
New York	0.72217	0.05099		(0.13725)	(0.00435)
	(0.10466)	(0.01441)	South Carolina	0.62855	0.02993
Pennsylvania	0.68446	0.07170		(0.13076)	(0.00791)
	(0.11083)	(0.01268)			
Rhode Island	0.62615	0.03835	Louisiana	0.21042	0.01466
	(0.11949)	(0.01378)		(0.15337)	(0.00264)
Vermont	0.67631	0.04426	Mississippi	0.32691	0.01544
	(0.11208)	(0.01393)		(0.14744)	(0.00334)
Michigan	0.19130	0.02966	Oklahoma	0.46637	0.00596
	(0.15320)	(0.00369)		(0.13884)	(0.00248)
Wisconsin	0.44944	0.01419			
	(0.13839)	(0.00477)	Arizona	0.88021	0.00937
				(0.07524)	(0.01653)
Illinois	0.36472	0.01380	Colorado	0.88023	0.01446
	(0.14484)	(0.00294)		(0.08500)	(0.01478)
Indiana	0.29675	0.02256	Montana	0.82381	0.02205
	(0.14939)	(0.00356)		(0.09603)	(0.01359)
Missouri	0.64570	0.04156	Nevada	0.75457	0.03855
	(0.11802)	(0.00593)		(0.10247)	(0.00886)
Ohio	0.35765	0.04471	New Mexico	0.74262	0.01766
	(0.14676)	(0.00415)		(0.10087)	(0.00862)
			Utah	0.85301	0.04053
Kansas	0.57572	0.01151		(0.08231)	(0.01199)
	(0.12687)	(0.00416)	Wyoming	0.87713	0.03504
North Dakota	0.51570	0.01077		(0.07765)	(0.01786)
	(0.13259)	(0.00705)			
South Dakota	0.75043	0.00337	Oregon	0.70482	0.04769
	(0.10322)	(0.00675)		(0.10823)	(0.00505)
			Washington	0.55746	0.01053
				(0.12789)	(0.00429)

Note: Numbers in parenthesis denote standard deviations.

one at any conventional level of statistical significance. It is therefore concluded that the rates of return on agricultural assets across regions are converging.

Table 3.6 shows results of estimates of trends using Equation 3.7 for each region's total ROA and return from agricultural income pooled across the states in that region. In addition to those

Table 3.5

Estimated Autoregression Coefficients Between Regions

State	α_1	α_0
Delaware	0.14355	0.00137
	(0.15523)	(0.00686)
Minnesota	−0.02785	−0.00004
	(0.15611)	(0.00609)
Iowa	0.12998	−0.00164
	(0.15541)	(0.00657)
Nebraska	−0.33293	0.00084
	(0.14674)	(0.00402)
Florida	−0.14876	−0.00047
	(0.15695)	(0.00499)
Arkansas	0.19544	0.00039
	(0.15309)	(0.00778)
Texas	0.26661	−0.00427
	(0.15199)	(0.00933)
Idaho	0.12068	−0.00370
	(0.15599)	(0.00779)
California	0.23690	0.00169
	(0.15307)	(0.00770)

Note: Numbers in parenthesis denote standard deviations.

twenty estimates over the entire 1960–2002 period, the table shows results for subperiods over which a significant trend existed. All other subperiods not listed in the table had no significant trend and, thus, were "stable" in the difference between the location's average returns and U.S. average returns.

In general, the regression results are consistent with the qualitative assessments of profit patterns presented in previous sections: convergence has occurred across the country. All ten equations estimated for total ROA over the entire 1960–2002 period had β's that were significant at the 99 percent confidence level, meaning there is a relationship between the regional and U.S. average returns. In addition, nine of the ten equations have a "stable" relationship ($\gamma = 0$); only the Lake States' equation had a significant time trend. These findings provide strong, consistent support for the argument that convergence of total returns has occurred in U.S. agriculture since 1960. The ten income rates of return equations for 1960–2002 provide mixed evidence of convergence, thereby supporting the hypothesis that the *source* of returns is important in determining the economic prospects for agriculture in a region, as noted below.

Sixteen of the twenty estimates for the 1960–2002 period indicate a stable relationship between regional and national returns, as reported in the last column in Table 3.6. The thirty-two subperiods reported in the table had significant trends which, in general, show that when a region's returns fall below or rise above U.S. average returns for a few years, there is an equilibrating process to bring them back into a fairly narrow range of the average. For example, total ROA in the Northeast region had significant trends over three subperiods. For 1960–1969 there was a positive trend, taking returns from slightly below the U.S. average to slightly above average; this is a mixed trend that begins as convergence and then diverges as regional returns rise above the national average. For 1969–1976 a negative trend reversed the pattern. The pattern reversed again over 1976–1986 as another positive trend carried Northeastern returns from below to far above the U.S. average.

Table 3.6

Regional Returns Convergence/Divergence Regression Results

Region and source	Period	β	t–stat	Trend coefficient	t–stat	R^2	Trend type
Northeast	1960–2002	−0.33	−2.80***	−0.02	−0.71	0.167	S
ROA total	1960–69	−1.22	−3.32**	0.73	3.41**	0.713	M
	1969–76	−1.40	−3.77**	−2.03	−3.41**	0.743	M
	1976–86	−0.81	−2.17*	1.45	2.55*	0.476	M
Northeast	1960–2002	−0.31	−2.67**	−0.01	−0.59	0.155	S
Income	1973–83	−1.35	−4.65***	0.50	4.41***	0.732	C
	1985–95	−0.91	−2.47**	−0.21	−2.35**	0.441	D
Lake States	1960–2002	−0.71	−4.63***	−0.05	−1.70*	0.355	M
ROA total	1960–69	−1.09	−2.82**	0.55	2.08*	0.573	M
	1966–84	−1.07	−4.35***	−0.19	−2.27***	0.567	M
Lake States	1960–2002	−0.50	−3.68***	−0.06	−3.01***	0.258	D
Income	1977–02	−0.69	−3.64***	−0.14	−3.04***	0.367	D
Corn Belt	1960–2002	−0.52	−3.75***	−0.03	−0.80	0.267	S
ROA total	1977–84	−1.30	−4.38***	−1.80	−3.08**	0.799	D
Corn Belt Income	1960–2002	−0.82	−5.25***	−0.04	−3.91***	0.415	M
Northern Plains	1960–2002	−0.64	−4.25***	−0.01	−0.40	0.317	S
ROA total	1987–02	−1.27	−4.93***	−0.29	−3.26***	0.658	C
	1990–02	−1.22	−3.58***	−0.17	−1.96*	0.573	C
Northern Plains	1960–2002	−0.60	−3.93***	0.01	0.86	0.287	S
Income	1960–73	−0.78	−2.04**	0.24	2.56**	0.453	D
	1990–02	−1.20	−4.32***	−0.11	−1.92*	0.687	C
Appalachia	1960–2002	−0.88	−5.58***	0.02	0.77	0.444	S
ROA total	1960–73	−1.11	−2.65**	−0.24	−1.84*	0.450	M
Appalachia	1960–2002	−0.50	−3.65***	0.02	1.68	0.255	S
Income	1960–69	−1.34	−3.93***	−0.23	−2.83**	0.722	M
	1960–73	−1.27	−3.85***	−0.20	−3.94***	0.639	M
	1985–91	−1.05	−4.74***	0.62	5.36***	0.878	M
Southeast	1960–2002	−0.65	−4.33***	0.05	1.44	0.325	S
ROA total	1990–02	−1.21	−6.47***	0.30	3.21***	0.823	D
Southeast	1960–2002	−0.57	−3.92***	0.04	2.91***	0.283	D
Income	1960–73	−1.06	−3.30***	−0.13	−2.82**	0.570	C
	1973–02	−0.83	−4.24***	0.10	3.05***	0.419	D
	1980–02	−0.82	−3.60***	0.09	2.24**	0.402	D
Delta	1960–2002	−0.62	−4.22***	−0.01	−0.42	0.315	S
ROA total	1960–75	−0.77	−3.48***	−0.32	−3.51***	0.579	M
Delta	1960–2002	−0.47	−3.33***	0.01	0.97	0.228	S
Income	1960–78	−1.09	−4.14***	0.07	1.81*	0.533	D
	1990–99	−0.82	−2.18*	0.36	1.91*	0.405	D
	1996–02	−1.22	−3.50**	−0.68	−4.44**	0.834	C
Southern Plains	1960–2002	−0.67	−4.42***	−0.01	−0.20	0.335	S
ROA total	1974–84	−1.26	−3.85***	2.04	3.98***	0.686	M
	1985–02	−1.08	−12.71***	0.30	4.52***	0.925	C
Southern Plains	1960–2002	−0.66	−4.37***	0.01	1.40	0.336	S
Income	1974–83	−1.10	−2.93**	0.26	2.48**	0.553	C
Mountain	1960–2002	−0.95	−5.92***	0.03	1.18	0.479	S
ROA total	1960–71	−0.55	−1.86*	0.26	1.91*	0.409	M
Mountain	1960–2002	−0.80	−4.82***	0.002	0.21	0.378	S
Income	1994–02	−1.16	−4.67***	0.31	3.46**	0.832	M
Pacific	1960–2002	−0.49	−3.59***	0.05	1.26	0.248	S
ROA total	1989–02	−1.02	−3.27**	−0.46	−2.41**	0.493	C
Pacific	1960–2002	−0.39	−3.04***	0.02	1.17	0.193	S
Income	1987–02	−1.05	−3.57***	−0.17	−2.51**	0.497	C

Note: Data are regional average total return on assets or return on assets from farm income. Asterisks indicate significance at the following confidence levels: *** 99%, ** 95%, and * 90%. Trend types: S = stable (γ = 0), C = convergence, D = divergence, M = mixed transition (converge then diverge).

Finally, Northeastern total ROA dropped dramatically in 1987 to slightly below U.S. averages levels and from 1987 to 2002 there was a stable trend at a level below the U.S. average (the stable trend regression results are not reported in the table, but had a trend coefficient of -0.06 with a t-statistic of -0.44 and an R^2 of 0.774).

The four estimates covering the entire 1960–2002 period that do *not* indicate a stable relationship between regional and national average returns support the hypothesis that economic prospects for a region depend greatly on the profitability of the primary commodities produced there. Total ROA and returns from production income in the Lake States region, plus income returns for the Corn Belt region, all have a significant negative trend. Both of these regions depend heavily on grain production and have suffered as world grain markets have become more competitive (i.e., less profitable) over recent decades. In contrast, production income in the Southeast region has a positive trend over the 1960–2002 period, causing regional returns to diverge from the national average (i.e., rising further above the U.S. level). As shown in Table 3.6, this divergence has been especially strong since 1973. This finding implies that the intensive livestock and specialty crops produced in the Southeast make it a much stronger agricultural sector, and consequently the Southeast region is more likely to remain in agriculture after the Lake and Corn Belt regions decline, ceteris paribus.

Probability of Loss Across Regions

There is significant volatility in agricultural returns in all parts of the country. This affects the ability of many producers to meet their financial obligations and/or goals. The sensitivity of each region's agricultural sector to variance in returns is reported in Table 3.7, showing the probability of loss for each region and the United States for different "disaster" levels of total rates of return. Each column of the table shows the probability that average producers in the region would not meet some specified minimum total return, expressed as k in Equation 3.11. For example, the first column (for $k = 0$) shows that average American agricultural producers have a 20.6 percent probability of earning returns that fall below the break-even point (i.e., zero total returns). That probability varies across regions, ranging from a low of 4.8 percent in the Southeast to a high of 30.1 percent in the Southern Plains. Each successive column reports the probability of average producers falling short of a higher return: 1 percent through 4 percent. As shown in the final column, although average American agricultural producers have a 47.6 percent probability of failing to earn a 4 percent total return, the probability ranges as high as 65.5 percent for the Northeast and as low as 22.4 percent for the Southeast.

The results in Table 3.7 reveal that as opportunity costs increase, a significantly higher percentage of agricultural producers must consider diversifying outside of agriculture and, possibly, leaving the sector entirely, as implied in Proposition 3.2c. A risk-averse producer using a safety-first decision criterion is very unlikely to be satisfied with a 47.6 percent chance of failing to reach a 4 percent total return when nonagricultural investments are available.

Off-Farm Income Effects on Returns

The most common nonagricultural investment made by farmers and ranchers is to allocate some family labor to off-farm employment (USDA 2001). The opportunity to make such a labor investment increases as the nonagricultural sector of the economy grows. Thus, the shrinking farm share of gross national product illustrated in Figure 3.3 implies that off-farm employment opportunities have been increasing over time, on average, as the nonfarm sector expands. The relative

Table 3.7

Regional Average Probability of Loss, 1960–2002 (percent)

Probability of loss with k =	0%	1%	2%	3%	4%
Northeast	24.2	33.7	44.0	55.2	65.5
Lake States	26.4	31.9	37.8	44.0	50.4
Corn Belt	29.8	34.1	39.0	44.0	49.2
Northern Plains	23.3	28.1	33.4	39.4	45.2
Appalachia	18.9	25.5	33.0	40.9	49.6
Southeast	4.8	7.6	11.3	16.1	22.4
Delta	24.2	29.1	34.5	40.5	46.4
Southern Plains	30.1	37.4	45.2	53.6	61.4
Mountain	23.9	29.8	36.3	43.3	50.8
Pacific	9.8	13.8	18.7	24.8	31.6
United States	20.6	26.4	33.0	40.1	47.6

Note: These Probability of Loss values were calculated using average Total Return on Assets.

Figure 3.3   **Farm Share of Gross National Product, 1977–2000**

availability of off-farm income in each state is proxied in Table 3.8 using two data series. The second column shows the percentage of gross state product contributed by the farm sector of the state listed in the first column. The third column converts that percentage into the location quotient (LQ), with 1.0 equaling the average farm share for the entire country (i.e., 0.79 percent). The LQ ranges from a low of 0.11 for states with a relatively small agricultural sector, such as

Table 3.8

Farm Share of Gross State Product, 2000

	Farm % of gross product	Location quotient
United States	0.79	1.00
Alabama	1.23	1.55
Alaska	0.09	0.11
Arizona	0.69	0.87
Arkansas	2.57	3.23
California	0.99	1.24
Colorado	0.73	0.92
Connecticut	0.20	0.25
Delaware	0.52	0.65
Florida	0.88	1.11
Georgia	0.81	1.02
Hawaii	0.70	0.88
Idaho	3.88	4.88
Illinois	0.45	0.57
Indiana	0.73	0.92
Iowa	3.45	4.35
Kansas	1.96	2.47
Kentucky	1.68	2.11
Louisiana	0.46	0.58
Maine	0.65	0.81
Maryland	0.32	0.41
Massachusetts	0.08	0.11
Michigan	0.43	0.54
Minnesota	1.33	1.67
Mississippi	1.65	2.08
Missouri	0.91	1.15
Montana	2.91	3.66
Nebraska	3.77	4.74
Nevada	0.26	0.32
New Hampshire	0.17	0.22
New Jersey	0.13	0.17
New Mexico	1.40	1.76
New York	0.18	0.23
North Carolina	1.20	1.51
North Dakota	4.48	5.64
Ohio	0.50	0.62
Oklahoma	1.85	2.32
Oregon	1.40	1.76
Pennsylvania	0.50	0.62
Rhode Island	0.09	0.11
South Carolina	0.64	0.81
South Dakota	6.76	8.50
Tennessee	0.55	0.69
Texas	0.77	0.97
Utah	0.66	0.83
Vermont	1.41	1.78
Virginia	0.41	0.52
Washington	1.11	1.40
West Virginia	0.35	0.45
Wisconsin	1.10	1.38
Wyoming	1.76	2.22

Source: U.S. Department of Commerce, Bureau of Economic Analysis.

Massachusetts and Rhode Island, to a high of 8.50 for South Dakota. In South Dakota, for example, the LQ indicates that the agricultural sector represents 8.5 times as much of the state output as represented by the national agricultural sector. This, in turn, suggests that opportunities for off-farm income are much less common in South Dakota than they are across the country, on average.

At least two implications of the LQ results above can be tested. First, LQ scores and returns from current income are expected to be positively correlated (Proposition 3.3a). This is due to the need for agricultural income to be higher in a state with relatively fewer opportunities for off-farm income (i.e., a higher LQ) compared to a state with more plentiful off-farm opportunities. This would be true no matter what the minimum return level desired by producers using a safety-first decision criterion. Second, it is expected that LQ scores and returns from capital gains will be negatively correlated, as stated in Proposition 3.3b. This is due to the effects of a state's nonfarm sector on agricultural asset values. In a state where the nonfarm sector is relatively large (i.e., a lower LQ), there is more demand for agricultural land and other assets to be converted to non-farm uses, thus asset prices are expected to increase faster than in states with relatively larger agricultural sectors.

Both of these propositions are supported by the data. Simple correlations between the fifty states' LQ values in Table 3.8 and the ROA_π and ROA_k values in Table 3.2 are 0.36 and -0.14, respectively. It also follows that the correlation between LQ values and total ROA is 0.24, indicating higher total returns are required as off-farm income decreases, as stated in Propositions 3.2a and 3.2b.[8]

These results are consistent with the type of substitution between sources of returns that is necessary if producers are using a safety-first criterion with a minimum return level for decision making. Such a minimum return can be composed of returns from three sources: current income from agriculture, capital gains on agricultural assets, and off-farm income (as discussed in the next chapter). When returns from one source are insufficient to meet the minimum return level required for a person to stay in agriculture, returns from another source must be sought to make total returns reach the minimum. As noted often in the literature (e.g., USDA 2001), off-farm income is sought by most agricultural producers because it is a relatively low-risk source of liquid returns. When off-farm income sources are not available to an individual, increased ROA_π must be sought because individuals have little control over the ROA_k available to them and ROA_k is not a liquid cash flow. Thus, in areas with relatively few off-farm opportunities, agricultural producers must pursue higher ROA_π by producing a portfolio of enterprises that are more profitable and risky (this is an expansion of Propositions 3.2a and 3.2b).[9] A person unwilling to take on the higher production risk exposure necessary to achieve the minimum return level over the long run is forced to either leave agriculture or voluntarily accept operating losses like a "hobby farmer."

The results supporting Propositions 3.2a, 3.2b, 3.3a, and 3.3b have ironic implications for American agriculture's development across the country: farms and ranches are more likely to disappear from areas in which agriculture is a relatively more important part of the economy. In areas where agriculture is a relatively small part of the economy, returns from off-farm income and capital gains on agricultural assets are more available, on average, thereby making it more likely that they can adequately substitute for ROA_π in meeting a producer's financial needs. This is the most likely explanation for the Northeast's agricultural sector's convergence to a level below the national average for total returns over the 1960–2002 period. On the other hand, in areas where agriculture is a relatively large part of the economy, such as the Northern Plains (with state LQs of 2.47 to 8.50), total returns converged on the national average because returns from current income rose sufficiently to substitute for the weak capital gains and relatively scarce off-farm income. The average ROA_π levels reported in Table 3.2 for the Northern Plains were likely achieved, in great part, through attrition. Specifically, less profitable farms and ranches left agriculture over time, as expected in areas with relatively few opportunities for off-farm income.

IMPLICATIONS OF THE STRONG/WEAK STATES' RESULTS

Some implications from a more detailed assessment of the five states with the highest average returns and the five states with the lowest average returns over the 1960–2002 period are presented here. The implications are drawn, in part, from the data in Table 3.9.

To begin, the ninth row of Table 3.9 shows the average net income per farm in 2001 (reported in McElroy et al. 2002, appendix table 5) for each of the ten states. Compared to the four other strong states, producers in Vermont have low average income levels. This illustrates that a farm (or state, or region) may on average generate good *returns* while not producing enough *income* to support a family. Vermont's annual average income of $20,613 is less than half of that for the other four strong states. It is also below the poverty level for an American family of four. Thus, it is highly likely that farm households in Vermont supplement this income with off-farm sources of income. This is especially true in recent years, as indicated by the negative average return from farm income in Vermont for the 1990–2002 period. The willingness of farmers to remain in agriculture in Vermont over the long run, if off-farm income enables them to meet their short-run expenses, is increased by the strong capital gains earned in the state (the nation's highest), on average.

New Mexico stands out from the four other states with weak total returns. The average value of New Mexico's production, $53 per acre, is very low due to the dominance of livestock grazing in the state's agricultural output. However, the very large average farm/ranch size of 2,876 acres enables New Mexico to generate average net farm income of $54,643, the fourth highest of any state in the country. Also, careful analysis of the returns data over the 1960–2002 period shows that the New Mexico agricultural sector performed much better than the other four "weak" state sectors. As shown in Table 3.9, New Mexico had positive average returns from current income in each of the four decades. On the other hand, the three eastern states all had negative average returns from income in each of the four periods. New Mexico's average total return was hurt by capital losses in three of the four decades; only during the 1970s did capital gains help New Mexico's producers. Thus, the *source* of returns is important when assessing state profit performance, as stated by Proposition 3.3.

Income versus capital gains patterns over time are mixed. Of the five "weak" states, the two western states, New Mexico and Oregon, both had higher average ROA_π levels during 1990–2002 than they did during the 1960s. For the three eastern states, ROA_π levels went from bad to worse between the two periods. The trend in capital gains was higher between the 1960s and the 1990–2002 period for Oregon, but lower for the other four weak states. For the five "strong" states, the patterns were not very strong. Only California had higher average returns in the 1990–2002 period, compared to the 1960s, from both sources of returns. The three southern strong states all had better ROA_π levels in the later period, but lower levels of capital gains, with Florida suffering an average capital loss in that period. Vermont had positive average ROA_π levels for the first three decades, but the level in the 1990–2002 period was negative and capital gains steadily declined.

Table 3.9

Summary Data from States with Strong or Weak Returns

	NC	Florida	Vermont	Georgia	California	WV	NH	NM	Oregon	Penn
Debt to asset ratio, 2001	14.27	16.19	13.74	14.53	20.41	8.81	10.66	12.74	13.47	12.26
Farm numbers, 2001	56,000	44,000	6,600	50,000	85,000	20,500	3,100	15,000	40,000	59,000
Farms, % drop from 1960 to 2001	73.6	12.0	50.0	55.4	21.3	56.4	55.7	17.6	14.9	44.3
Average farm size, 2001 (acres)	162	232	203	220	315	179	135	2,876	443	130
Value of production, 2001 ($/acre)	1,061	661	455	565	995	144	422	53	218	634
State Rank	4	9	14	11	5	39	16	48	35	10
Net farm income, 2001 ($/acre)	352	212	102	209	136	13	30	19	15	126
State Rank	3	6	13	7	10	47	37	42	45	11
Net farm income, 2001 ($/farm)	57,163	49,230	20,613	45,971	42,827	2,327	4,062	54,643	6,646	16,416
State Rank	3	5	23	7	8	50	48	4	45	30
Probability of Loss, 1960–2001, k=0 (%)	8.5	5.2	10.2	8.7	8.5	79.7	61.0	52.4	47.6	47.2
Probability of Loss, 1960–2001, k=4 (%)	21.8	19.2	27.4	24.8	25.5	89.8	76.4	72.6	73.9	79.7
1960–69 ROA from income (%)	5.03	5.16	1.70	4.91	4.58	-3.43	-0.46	2.76	-0.28	-0.81
1960–69 ROA from capital gains (%)	2.35	2.67	10.55	4.37	0.94	-0.35	1.23	-3.04	-1.28	3.67
1970–79 ROA from income (%)	5.31	6.33	2.17	4.31	7.41	-4.69	-3.75	3.00	1.34	-1.27
1970–79 ROA from capital gains (%)	4.44	6.47	9.24	5.24	4.26	3.08	5.30	1.35	3.36	5.41
1980–89 ROA from income (%)	6.05	7.72	2.32	4.94	7.48	-5.78	-3.19	1.87	2.04	-1.13
1980–89 ROA from capital gains (%)	-4.01	-0.83	4.01	-3.52	-2.22	-9.18	0.54	-8.04	-6.72	-2.70
1990–2002 ROA from income (%)	13.96	7.47	-1.52	8.02	6.22	-8.31	-7.67	3.64	1.48	-2.49
1990–2002 ROA from capital gains (%)	1.97	-0.05	3.64	3.00	1.90	-1.18	-1.43	-3.37	0.76	0.87

Finally, farm numbers decreased much more in the east than in the west over the 1960–2002 period. North Carolina, the state with the highest average total returns over the period, decreased its farm numbers by 73.6 percent. This does not appear due to simply consolidating farms into larger units because North Carolina still has the smallest average farm size (162 acres) of the five strong states. The small average size and high income per acre indicates a significant number of, and contribution by, intensive livestock operations. Consolidation *is* occurring across American agriculture, but there may be more potential for further consolidation in the East compared to the West.[10] Of the ten states in Table 3.9, the three western states are those with the largest average farm sizes. This implies that the high rates of exit from agriculture in eastern states are likely to continue, especially in states with weak profit performance. The actual rates of net farm exits could be as high as the probability of loss levels, if farmers do not subsidize their incomes using off-farm sources (Propositions 3.2b and 3.2c). Of course, off-farm income is common in most parts of the United States and will continue to slow farm exits nationwide in the future. However, in the sparsely populated sections of the country, off-farm employment is not available to many farmers in remote areas. In those places, even low farming exit rates can have significant economic impacts and, as a result, are drawing government efforts to subsidize agriculture. For example, "Sen. Byron Dorgan, D-N.D., and 12 other senators are sponsoring legislation to help counties that have lost more than 10 percent of their population in the last 20 years. Most of those counties lie in a swath stretching from Texas and New Mexico to Montana and North Dakota" (Associated Press 2003). Thus, actual farm exit rates will clearly be lower than called for by agriculture's profit performance.[11] This will inhibit the convergence of agricultural returns across the country.

WHAT DO THE STRONG/WEAK PERFORMING STATES HAVE IN COMMON?

In general, the strong-performing states (especially Florida and California) produce crop portfolios that include a significant amount of high-value fruit and vegetable enterprises, plus North Carolina and Georgia have significant intensive livestock industries (e.g., hogs and poultry). Also, contracting is a common practice (especially in Florida, North Carolina, and California) in the markets for many of these commodities. Forward contracting reduces price (and income) volatility over time, thus reducing producers' risk exposure. That enables more producers to accept the risks inherent in high-value commodity production.

The growth of contracting and contractors as both asset owners and income claimants in production agriculture is causing the USDA-ERS to refine its methods of estimating returns to farm assets and farm sector rates of return. For example, ERS sectorwide estimates of returns to farm assets are to measure the (average) income return to the *owners* of those farm business assets. If others own some of the assets and receive income outside the sector (contractors for example), and these are included (incorrectly) in returns to farm business assets and/or in the value of farm business assets, then farm sector rates of return will be overstated. In the poultry and livestock sectors, contractors' shares of farm assets and of income earned are increasing relative to those of farm operators. Therefore, in "strong-growth" states such as North Carolina, rates of return on farm business assets may be considerably misstated because contractors' share of farm business assets and of income earned on those assets is increasing relative to those of farm operators.[12]

The weak-performing states had less in common with each other except a higher percentage of their cash receipts coming from livestock grazing, rather than intensive crop and livestock en-

Table 3.10

Selected Financial Characteristics: Strong States (averages of each period)

States Time periods	ROE, total (%)	Operating profit margin (%)	Asset turnover ratio (%)	Asset/Equity ratio
California				
1960–1969	5.69	21.69	21.16	1.19
1970–1979	14.56	24.59	29.70	1.29
1980–1989	4.97	29.43	25.15	1.29
1990–2002	8.92	20.50	31.17	1.25
Florida				
1960–1969	8.41	24.91	20.75	1.16
1970–1979	14.87	28.47	22.16	1.19
1980–1989	7.27	33.81	22.52	1.21
1990–2002	7.42	29.45	25.69	1.20
Georgia				
1960–1969	10.21	17.38	28.09	1.20
1970–1979	11.23	18.11	23.31	1.26
1980–1989	−0.25	19.17	24.63	1.34
1990–2002	12.16	27.52	30.15	1.21
North Carolina				
1960–1969	7.68	19.03	26.23	1.12
1970–1979	10.39	21.72	23.98	1.17
1980–1989	1.14	21.26	26.94	1.25
1990–2002	18.39	36.50	39.86	1.19
Vermont				
1960–1969	13.76	6.14	28.31	1.23
1970–1979	13.43	9.11	23.61	1.22
1980–1989	6.68	10.97	21.25	1.19
1990–2002	1.57	−6.21	22.88	1.18

terprises, compared to the strong states. However, other financial characteristics showed common trends in these states. These characteristics show up in the DuPont expansion data, as noted below.

Table 3.10 shows the financial characteristics that make up the DuPont expansion (Equation 3.14) for the strong-performing states, while the same data for the weak-performing states are in Table 3.11. These ratios help decompose the profitability results embedded in the ROE. In general, the data show that one cause of relatively higher profitability in the strong states is higher operating profit margins and asset turnover ratios. The turnover ratio is a measure of how efficiently farm assets are being used to generate income.

The DuPont expansion data for the weak-performing states show that those states have a low operating profit margin and a low asset turnover ratio. New Hampshire, Pennsylvania, and West Virginia all had *negative* operating profit margins in each of the four decades shown, indicating average losses on each dollar of sales. The western states of Oregon and New Mexico had positive profit margins (except for the 1960s in Oregon), indicating that their agriculture sectors suffered more from capital losses than from operating losses. Also, Oregon and Pennsylvania had generally low asset turnover ratios, compared to the strong-performing states, while the asset turnover ratios were especially low in New Hampshire, New Mexico, and West Virginia. Therefore, the

Table 3.11

Selected Financial Characteristics: Weak States (averages of each period)

States Time periods	ROE, total (%)	Operating profit margin (%)	Asset turnover ratio (%)	Asset/equity ratio
New Hampshire				
1960–1969	0.36	−1.49	33.02	1.16
1970–1979	1.65	−17.40	22.29	1.15
1980–1989	−3.26	−20.90	15.20	1.10
1990–2002	−10.23	−40.04	16.61	1.10
New Mexico				
1960–1969	−1.19	17.08	16.06	1.21
1970–1979	4.80	16.30	17.88	1.19
1980–1989	−7.83	13.68	13.08	1.15
1990–2002	−0.40	20.33	17.39	1.13
Oregon				
1960–1969	−2.79	−1.64	17.23	1.22
1970–1979	5.38	7.38	16.23	1.24
1980–1989	−7.42	10.91	17.11	1.29
1990–2002	2.08	7.57	21.45	1.18
Pennsylvania				
1960–1969	2.69	−3.17	25.06	1.16
1970–1979	4.46	−6.90	19.10	1.15
1980–1989	−5.28	−5.87	20.10	1.18
1990–2002	−2.54	−11.20	20.93	1.14
West Virginia				
1960–1969	−4.57	−23.70	15.08	1.20
1970–1979	−1.92	−51.17	9.53	1.11
1980–1989	−17.30	−59.32	10.09	1.14
1990–2002	−11.51	−75.40	11.50	1.12

combination of low operating profit per dollar of sales, low asset turnover (i.e., low efficiency in assets use), and generally more unfavorable solvency ratios (FA/E) have contributed to the relatively low ROE in these "weak" states. The positive operating margins in the two western states indicate that the agricultural sectors there may generate more "normal" returns once the capital asset markets adjust factor prices downward. In the eastern states, nonagricultural demand for agricultural assets (especially land) is unlikely to allow factor prices to decline enough for those agricultural sectors to significantly improve their profitability.

A brief list of general observations about differences between the five strong and five weak states follows. In general, these observations are consistent with the "Farming Food Chain" discussed in Chapter 11. They indicate that the pressures to earn profits are pushing farmers and ranchers to produce more risky enterprises on larger, more efficient operations. This requires more money so as to maintain a reasonably low debt ratio for a safe level of risk exposure. Obviously, the requirement for a larger scale of operation means that fewer people can survive in agriculture. It also means that the current trend of consolidation of small and medium production operations into large-scale operations is inevitable. In short, profit pressures are causing American agriculture to industrialize.

Strong States	Weak States
High-value, intensive crop and livestock	Low-value (e.g., livestock grazing)
Diversified products; contracting	Generally undiversified, bulk products
Larger-scale operations	Generally smaller-scale operations
High debt/asset ratios	Low debt/asset ratios
High asset turnover ratios	Low asset turnover ratios

THE FINAL TALLEY

All the propositions presented in this chapter are consistent with empirical data observed in American agriculture. A summary of the results of this analysis can be found in Exhibit 3.1. In general, the results show temporal and spatial trends toward convergence of returns that are consistent with trade and development theories, but there are constraints unique to state/regional agriculture. Results are summarized here for each of the three general propositions.

Convergence

Most regions converged to the national average for total returns over the 1960–2002 period. Nonfarm sector influences probably kept the Northeast from converging and likely will continue to do so. Conversely, in sparsely populated states with fewer off-farm income opportunities, such as the Northern Plains, convergence of returns did occur, most likely because agricultural factor markets adjusted to declining farm numbers.

Agricultural income is generally higher in regions and states that are able to produce significant amounts of fruit and vegetable crops plus intensive livestock enterprises. Returns are generally lower in areas dominated by livestock grazing, rather than intensive crop and livestock production. This finding supports Schott's (2003) contention that geographic areas with different factor endowments must expect that "price-wage arbitrage may be reduced, or broken, depending on the substitutability of goods" (p. 705) when regions do not produce an identical set of goods. This suggests that convergence of returns is more likely within regions producing similar commodities than across regions specializing in different commodities. Thus, in American agriculture, what Gutierrez (2000) calls "absolute convergence" to a single rate of return is a regional, not a national, phenomenon for total rates of return.

Minimum Return to Remain in Agriculture

Although a "minimum total return" level necessary for continued participation in agriculture appears to be revealed in the data presented here (i.e., an ROA of 3.9 percent to 4.8 percent), no such minimum profit-per-farm amount can be detected. Only two states (Arizona and Delaware) had average net farm incomes per operation that were higher than the 2001 U.S. average household income of $58,208. State average farm incomes per operation for 2001 had totals ranging down to West Virginia's $2,327, with a national average of $21,198. This national amount is below the poverty line for a family of four, thus it is not likely to be considered adequate as a financial goal by most farmers. This affirms the importance of off-farm income to producers and suggests that the necessary "minimum farm income" level is some function of off-farm income.

Exhibit 3.1

Summary of Empirical Results

Propositions	Samples of Supporting Data
P3.1: Convergence in returns to American agricultural producers occurs over time and space.	Six of 10 regions have total ROA near the national average, and 16 of 20 regressions for 1960–2002 indicate a stable relationship between U.S. and regional returns.
	ROA_π within many regions have patterns over time.
	An inverse relationship between ROA_π and ROA_k is observed at the regional level across decades.
P3.2: There is a minimum return and/or profit-per-farm level needed to remain in agriculture and it will be apparent if the data converge to a stable trend over time.	Six of 10 regions have total ROA of 3.9% to 4.8%.
P3.2a: If no off-farm income sources are available, the minimum return to production must be at least 0% and greater than zero if producers face opportunity costs to stay in agriculture.	On-farm and off-farm income are substitutes, as indicated by $r = 0.24$ for LQ scores and total ROA.
P3.2b: If off-farm income sources are available, the minimum return to production can be less than 0%, depending on a farmer's willingness and ability to personally subsidize the farm.	The Northeast region has the highest availability of off-farm income and the lowest average ROA_π (negative for 4 states).
P3.2c: The minimum return needed to remain in agriculture influences the "probability of lost farms" in a state/region.	The U.S. probability of loss goes from 21% to 48% as the minimum ROA goes from 0 to 4%.
P3.3: The sources of income/returns are important in determining the economic prospects of agriculture in a state/region over time.	$ROA_\pi > ROA_k$ for strong states, western weak states.
	There are some ROA patterns across sources in regions.
	$\sigma_k > \sigma_\pi$
P3.3a: The farm share of a state's gross state product and that state's farmers' returns from current production income will be positively correlated.	$r = 0.36$
P3.3b: The farm share of a state's gross state product and that state's farmers' returns from capital gains will be negatively correlated.	$r = -0.14$

In other words, the minimum level of returns can generate the minimum amount of *profit* required to support a family only if the farm is sufficiently large.

Importance of Sources of Returns

The share of a state's output generated by the agricultural sector is positively correlated with returns from current agricultural income, and negatively correlated with returns from capital gains, on average. These results have an ironic implication for U.S. agriculture's development across the country: farms and ranches are more likely to disappear in areas in which agriculture is a relatively more important part of the economy. In areas where agriculture is a relatively small part of the economy, returns from off-farm income and capital gains on agricultural assets are more available, on average, making it more likely they can adequately substitute for ROA_π in meeting a producer's financial needs.

NOTES

Some material in this chapter is a revised and expanded version of an article published by S. Blank, K. Erickson, and C. Moss as "Profit Patterns Across American Agriculture," *Journal of Agricultural and Resource Economics* 30 no. 2 (2005): 205–230. In 2006 it won the Western Agricultural Economics Association's Award for Outstanding Article in the *Journal of Agricultural and Resource Economics.*

1. Farms generating insufficient rates of return will exit over the long run, and farms earning returns significantly above average will face competitive pressures causing decreases in returns over time. Thus, long-run rates of return are expected to cluster around the average for the geographic area if convergence is occurring.

2. Profits per acre from farming can be increased through two general routes: (1) shift to a more profitable (and more risky) portfolio of crops/enterprises, and (2) lower costs per unit of output. The second route, lower costs, may be achieved either through using fewer inputs per unit of output (i.e., a technological and/or managerial advance) or having the cost of inputs fall (i.e., a factor market adjustment). However, there are constraints on both routes. Agronomic constraints may limit which crops can be produced in a location, and factor markets may not adjust to falling demand from agricultural uses when there are nonagricultural sources of demand for particular inputs. In the face of these constraints, many farmers seek to increase total farm profits by expanding the total size of the farm (i.e., producing on more acreage).

3. Real estate appreciation represents about three-quarters of capital gains to agriculture historically (USDA 2000).

4. A paired comparison *t*-test was conducted for each region for the hypothesis that the region's average total ROA equaled the U.S. average total ROA over the 1960–2002 period. The hypothesis could not be rejected for the following six regions (with the calculated *t*-statistics in parentheses): Appalachia (-0.68), Corn Belt (-0.24), Delta (0.70), Lake States (-0.90), Mountain (-1.39), and the Northern Plains (1.39). The hypothesis was rejected for the Southeast (*t*-statistic $= 7.99$), Pacific (3.72), Northeast (-2.93), and Southern Plains (-2.92).

5. Paired comparison *t*-tests for the hypothesis of equal mean total ROA generated the following results: Arkansas versus Louisiana $t = 0.36$, Arkansas versus Mississippi $t = 0.39$, and Louisiana versus Mississippi $t = 0.03$. Thus, the hypothesis could not be rejected in any of the three cases in this region.

6. Comparing the three capital gain rates generated *t*-statistics of 1.29 for Arkansas versus Louisiana, 1.21 for Arkansas versus Mississippi, and 0.07 for Louisiana versus Mississippi, none of which are statistically significant. On the other hand, the rate of return from income for Arkansas was significantly different than that for the two other states (Arkansas versus Louisiana $t = 5.08$, Arkansas versus Mississippi $t = 4.95$). There was no difference in ROA_p between Louisiana and Mississippi ($t = 0.14$).

7. These results are based on *t*-tests comparing mean returns for the two time periods. This is also true for the other results reported in this section.

8. The correlations between LQ and ROA_π and total ROA are statistically significant at the 99 percent and 90 percent confidence levels, respectively. The correlation between LQ and ROA_k was not significant using only the data for 2000 reported in Table 3.8. Thus, further research with expanded data may be needed to resolve questions about whether the size of an area's agricultural sector influences farmers' returns from capital gains. It may be that the very small portion of a state's economy represented by agriculture causes capital markets to ignore that sector.

9. The relationship between off-farm income and the composition of enterprises in a farm's production "portfolio" is discussed in Chapter 12.

10. Consolidation of farms in the central and western sections of the country is difficult because the average farm size is already large, possibly near the size where economies of scale begin to turn negative. For example, some state average sizes in 2001 include Montana, 2,285 acres; South Dakota, 1,338 acres; Colorado, 1,031 acres; and Nevada, 2,208 acres. In the East, farm consolidation is hindered by the "fragmentation" problem created by more dense population levels. This means that contiguous parcels may not often be consolidated, but there still may be economies of scale (e.g., managerial, financial) available to producers in the East. In areas where economies of scale do not exist, consolidation will not occur and average farm size will not increase as farm numbers decrease. That explains why Delaware still had an average farm size of only 228 acres in 2001, despite steadily declining farm numbers that totaled only 2,500, even though the state had the nation's highest average value of agricultural production at $1,646 per acre and was ranked second in both net farm income per acre and net farm income per operation, at $382 and $87,143, respectively.

11. In general, the effects of off-farm income are likely to keep many small farms in operation (Blank 2002), especially in the East and urban West, while small- and mid-size farms will consolidate into larger operations, mostly in the western half of the country.

12. To address this issue, the USDA-ERS is using data from various surveys, including the ARMS (Agricultural Resource Management Survey), to better account for the value of contractors' farm business sector assets and returns.

REFERENCES

Ahituv, A., and A. Kimhi. 2002. "Off-Farm Work and Capital Accumulation Decisions of Farmers over the Life-Cycle: The Role of Heterogeneity and State Dependence." *Journal of Development Economics* 68: 329–353.

Ahrendsen, Bruce L. 1993. "A Structural Approach to Estimating Rate of Return Expectations of Farmers." *Journal of Agricultural and Applied Economics* 25 (2): 56–68.

Associated Press. 2003. "Congress Aims to Slow Depopulation: Plains Counties Losing Residents." April 27.

Ben-David, Dan. 1993. "Equalizing Exchange, Trade Liberalization and Income Convergence." *Quarterly Journal of Economics* 108 (3): 653–679.

Berck, P., and J. Hihn. 1982. "Using the Semivariance to Estimate Safety-First Rules." *American Journal of Agricultural Economics* 64 (2): 298–300.

Betubiza, E., and D. Leatham. 1994. "The Effects of Holding Nonfarm Related Financial Assets on Risk-Adjusted Farm Income." *Journal of Agricultural and Applied Economics* 26 (2): 565–579.

Bigman, D. 1996. "Safety-First Criteria and Their Measures of Risk." *American Journal of Agricultural Economics* 78 (February): 225–235.

Bjornson, B., and C. Carter. 1997. "New Evidence on Agricultural Commodity Return Performance Under Time-Varying Risk." *American Journal of Agricultural Economics* 79: 918–930.

Bjornson, B., and R. Innes. 1992. "Another Look at Returns to Agricultural and Nonagricultural Assets." *American Journal of Agricultural Economics* 74: 109–119.

Blank, Steven C. 2002. "Is Agriculture a 'Way of Life' or a Business?" *Choices* 17 (Summer): 26–30.

Cochrane, Willard W. 1993. *The Development of American Agriculture: A Historical Analysis.* 2d ed. Minneapolis: University of Minnesota Press.

Crisostomo, M., and A. Featherstone. 1990. "A Portfolio Analysis of Returns to Farm Equity and Assets." *North Central Journal of Agricultural Economics* 12: 9–21.

Daniel, S., and A. Featherstone. 2001. "Assessing Agricultural Risk Among States." *Journal of the American Society of Farm Managers and Rural Appraisers* 65: 107–114.

Davis, D., and D. Weinstein. 2001. "An Account of Global Factor Trade." *American Economic Review* 91 (5): 1423–1453.

Dodson, Charles B. 1994. "Profitability of Farm Businesses: A Regional, Farm Type, and Size Analysis." Statistical Bulletin Number 884, Economics Research Service, USDA, Washington, DC, June.

Dunford, Richard W. 1980. "The Value of Unrealized Farm Land Capital Gains: Comment." *American Journal of Agricultural Economics* 62: 260–262.

El-Osta, H., and M. Ahearn. 1996. "Estimating the Opportunity Cost of Unpaid Farm Labor for U.S. Farm Operators." USDA-ERS Technical Bulletin Number 1984, March.

Encarnación, José, Jr. 1991. "Portfolio Choice and Risk." *Journal of Economic Behavior and Organization* 16 (December): 347–353.

Granger, C., and P. Newbold. 1974. "Spurious Regressions in Econometrics." *Journal of Econometrics* 2 (1974): 111–20.

Gutierrez, Luciano. 2000. "Convergence in US and EU Agriculture." *European Review of Agricultural Economics* 27 (2): 187–206.

Hagigi, M., and B. Kluger. 1987. "Safety First: An Alternative Performance Measure." *Journal of Portfolio Management* 13 (Summer): 34–40.

Hatch, U., J. Atwood, and J. Segar. 1989. "An Application of Safety-First Probability Limits in a Discrete Stochastic Farm Management Programming Model." *Southern Journal of Agricultural Economics* 21 (July): 65–72.

Hottel, B., and B. Gardner. 1983. "The Rate of Return to Investment in Agriculture and Measuring Net Farm Income." *American Journal of Agricultural Economics* 65 (1983): 553–557.

Isserman, Andrew M. 2002. "Defining Regions for Rural America." In *The New Power of Regions: A Policy Focus for Rural America,* pp. 35–53. Federal Reserve Bank of Kansas City.

Kim, Sukkoo. 1997. "Economic Integration and Convergence: U.S. Regions, 1840–1987." National Bureau of Economic Research, Working Paper 6335, December.

Kimhi, A. 2000. "Is Part-Time Farming Really a Step in the Way Out of Agriculture?" *American Journal of Agricultural Economics* 82 (February): 38–48.

Mahul, O. 2000. "The Output Decision of a Risk-Neutral Producer Under Risk of Liquidation." *American Journal of Agricultural Economics* 82 (February): 49–58.

McElroy, R., R. Strickland, J. Ryan, C. McGath, R. Green, K. Erickson, and W. McBride. 2002. "Value Added and Net Farm Income Down for 2002." *Agricultural Income and Finance Outlook,* pp. 1–5. USDA Economic Research Service, AIS-79, September.

Melichar, Emanuel. 1979. "Capital Gains Versus Current Income in the Farming Sector." *American Journal of Agricultural Economics* 61: 1085–1092.

Mishra, A., and C. Sandretto. 2002. "Stability of Farm Income and the Role of Nonfarm Income in U.S. Agriculture." *Review of Agricultural Economics* 24 (1): 208–221.

Moscardi, E., and A. de Janvry. 1977. "Attitudes Toward Risk Among Peasants: An Econometric Approach." *American Journal of Agricultural Economics* 59 (4): 710–716.

O'Rourke, K., and J. Williamson. 1994. "Late Nineteenth-Century Anglo-American Factor-Price Convergence: Were Heckscher and Ohlin Right?" *Journal of Economic History* 54 (4): 892–916.

Plaxico, James S. 1979. "Implications of Divergence in Sources of Returns in Agriculture." *American Journal of Agricultural Economics* 61 (5): 1098–1102.

Pyle, D., and S. Turnovsky. 1970. "Safety First and Expected Utility Maximization in Mean-Standard Deviation Portfolio Analysis." *Review of Economics and Statistics* 52: 75–81.

Quigley, John M. 2002. "Rural Policy and the New Regional Economics: Implications for Rural America." In *The New Power of Regions: A Policy Focus for Rural America,* pp. 7–27. Federal Reserve Bank of Kansas City.

Reinsel, R., and E. Reinsel. 1979. "The Economics of Asset Values and Current Income in Farming." *American Journal of Agricultural Economics* 61: 1093–1097.

Roy, A. 1952. "Safety-First and the Holding of Assets." *Econometrica* 20: 431–449.

Sala-i-Martin, Xavier. 1996. "The Classical Approach to Convergence Analysis." *Economic Journal* 106: 1019–1036.

Schott, Peter K. 2003. "One Size Fits All? Heckscher-Ohlin Specialization in Global Production." *American Economic Review* 93 (3): 686–708.

Schultz, Theodore W. 1932. "Diminishing Returns in View of Progress in Agricultural Production." *Journal of Farm Economics* 14 (4): 640–649.

Telser, L. 1955. "Safety-First and Hedging." *Review of Economic Studies* 23: 1–16.

Tweeten, Luther G. 1969. "Theories Explaining the Persistence of Low Resource Returns in a Growing Farm Economy." *American Journal of Agricultural Economics* 51: 798–817.

U.S. Department of Agriculture (USDA). 2000. "Accumulated Farm Real Estate Value Will Help Farmers and Their Lenders Through Period of Declining Cash Receipts." *Agricultural Income and Finance: Situation and Outlook,* pp. 30–33. Economic Research Service, AIS-74, February.

———. 2001. "Off-Farm Income Supports Many Farm Households." *Agricultural Income and Finance: Situation and Outlook,* pp. 32–34. Economic Research Service, AIS-76, February.

———. 2003. "Farm Income and Costs: Farm Income Forecasts." Economic Research Service "Briefing Room," on Web at www.ers.usda.gov/Briefing/FarmIncome/fore.htm, accessed October.

U.S. Department of Commerce. Bureau of Economic Analysis. 2002. Gross state product data reported in press release of June 10, on Web at www.bea.gov/bea/regional/gsp.htm.

van Kooten, G.C., D. Young, and J. Krautkraemer. 1997. "A Safety-First Approach to Dynamic Cropping Decisions." *European Review of Agricultural Economics* 24 (1): 47–63.

Vesterby, M., and K. Krupa. 2001. "Major Land Uses." USDA Economic Research Service, November, on web at www.ers.usda.gov/data/majorlanduses/.

CHAPTER 4

AGRICULTURAL PROFITS
AND FARM HOUSEHOLD WEALTH

"A penny saved is a penny earned."
—Benjamin Franklin

Decreasing production profits, such as those observed in recent decades (especially since 1973), threaten the survival of many mid- and small-sized American farms, as shown in earlier chapters. Normally, the survival of a firm depends on its profitability, in both absolute and relative terms. To remain viable, a firm must offer returns that are both sufficient to cover the owner's financial obligations and competitive with returns from alternative investments. If a firm is profitable, the wealth of its owners can increase over time. An unprofitable firm, on the other hand, reduces owners' wealth until that owner either leaves the industry voluntarily (e.g., in search of more competitive returns) or is forced out (e.g., by bankruptcy). American agriculture, however, is full of firms that routinely earn low or negative returns on equity from production operations (Blank 2002), thus complicating the evaluation of the industry's economic health and prospects. For example, 1996–2002 average rates of return on farm equity in the Lake States, Corn Belt, and Southeast for residential and small family farms (representing about 80 percent of all farms) ranged from -1.96 to -4.51 percent, whereas average returns to large family farms and corporations ranged from 2.10 to 4.51 percent over the same period. This suggests that macro-level forecasts of American agriculture's future structure and performance require a micro-level understanding of the relationship between farm profits and owner wealth. This chapter addresses that relationship.

Assessing financial stress within American agriculture involves identifying which groups are more or less profitable. It also involves assessing farmers' well-being in the context of income, wealth, and consumption at the household level (Mishra et al. 2002). Important questions include: Are there profitability differences across farms when accounting for locations (i.e., regions), farm sizes, or commodities produced? Previous studies (e.g., Dodson 1994) raise expectations of differences due to resources available (and quality) across locations, economies of scale across farm sizes, and supply/demand differences across commodity markets caused by comparative advantage (i.e., competitiveness) issues. However, economic theory says that returns converge over time as resources flow into more-profitable industries and out of less-profitable ones, causing factor price changes (O'Rourke and Williamson 1994; Caselli and Coleman 2001). Both traditional growth and trade theories say factor markets will adjust to equalize commodity returns over time (Andres, Bosca, and Domenech 2004; Ben-David 1993; Gutierrez 2000; Schott 2003). This means an analysis should look across time, locations, and farm sizes. In Chapter 3, spatial and temporal patterns in profits were identified using aggregated data. In this chapter, farm-level data are used to evaluate profit and wealth performance across farm sizes and locations.

Prior research has shown that differences in profit performance can be significant across regions in the United States (as shown in Chapter 3). This is important because relative profit levels indicate which producers are more competitive in a commodity market (i.e., more-profitable producers are said to have a "competitive advantage"). Profit differences across producers lead to some regions' agriculture sectors being financially stronger than other regions' sectors over time. This is most likely due to differences in the crops and livestock being produced in each region. In other words, comparative advantage differences lead to differences in financial performance that, in turn, contribute to differences in the long-run viability of agricultural industries in locations.

Cropping and other decisions are made at the farm level, so the key to assessing a region's agricultural viability is to assess the results of farm-level financial decisions. There is evidence that farm-level decisions are made with an objective of increasing the household's utility by accumulating wealth. An owner-operator household's ability to increase wealth is influenced by the size of the farm, what commodities are being produced, and by its proximity to urban development and opportunity for off-farm employment. Significant differences in income and wealth between households across U.S. agriculture lead to differences in farm exit rates, which, in the worst cases, put some locations at risk of losing their agricultural industries as individuals leave agricultural production for more profitable alternative investments (Goetz and Debertin 1996, 2001).

Farm consolidation and competitive pressures in U.S. agriculture have been unprecedented in recent decades. Where possible, farmers are pursuing off-farm sources of income to support their households, especially when their production operations cannot generate sufficient income. Also, income constraints affect demand for new technologies and new production systems. These changes in agriculture have affected the size and distribution of net value added by farm operators (Mishra et al. 2002) as well as the financial structure of the industry. Such developments indicate the importance of understanding the composition of farm household wealth and its links to profitability and long-run viability.

For example, off-farm income affects how we view efficiency in the farm household. Small farmers have partially adapted to decreasing farming competitiveness by increasing off-farm income, or have adopted an alternative strategy for producing household income that results in lesser farm competitiveness with more certain off-farm income (Nehring, Fernandez-Cornejo, and Banker 2005; Morrison-Paul and Nehring 2005). Additionally, urban proximity, which is associated with higher levels of off-farm income, appears to have raised the costs and decreased the viability of family farms (Nehring et al. 2006).[1] These trends suggest particularly strong competitive pressures on family farms in highly urban areas. As shown in Figure 4.1, population growth during 1996–2004 was strong not only in urban areas in the Northeast, Southeast, and West, but also in many agricultural areas, such as in large swaths of southern Minnesota and Indiana. Also, there are large population centers interspersed in intensive agricultural areas, such as in central and southeastern Iowa, Ohio, all of eastern Texas, parts of western Texas, and western Washington.

Assessing farm owner-operator wealth involves adopting an expanded perspective of farm-level decision making. When estimating inter-sectoral productivity differences, Schmitt (1989, p. 1262) noted that "by analyzing agriculture as an economic activity organized by farm households competing with off-farm and household production, efficient allocation of resources in agriculture can be demonstrated. Therefore, productivity measurements based on the concept of the farm as a firm are misleading."

The financial structure of America's agricultural households has changed in recent decades. In essence, farm households have become more diverse in their sources of income. This change was

84

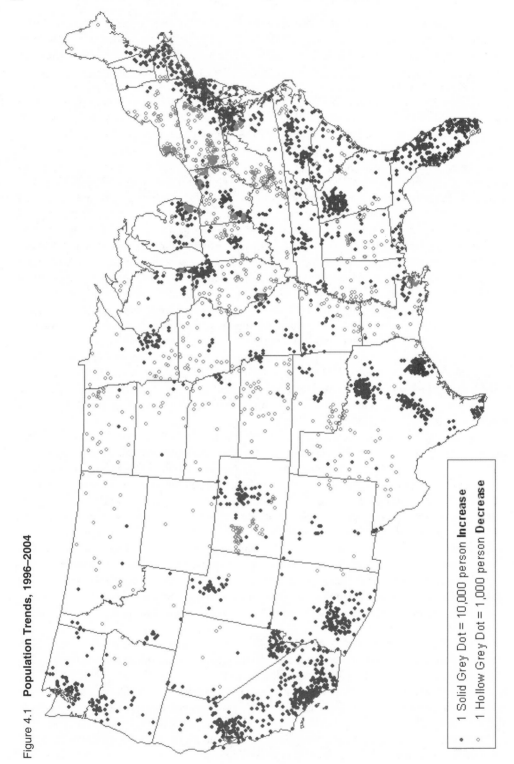

Figure 4.1 **Population Trends, 1996–2004**

• 1 Solid Grey Dot = 10,000 person **Increase**
○ 1 Hollow Grey Dot = 1,000 person **Decrease**

caused by many economic factors, including increased competition in agricultural commodity markets, increased opportunities for off-farm income, and increased non-agricultural sources of demand for farmland. Agricultural households have responded to these factors by expanding the focus of their decision-making. Yet, some household decision factors and their economic implications have received little attention in policy analysis. Existing research has largely focused on the *farm business* as the relevant unit of analysis rather than the *farm household*. However, there is evidence that farmers and ranchers are making consumption decisions based on total household wealth, not just on farm production profitability (Carriker et al. 1993). Most American farms and ranches are family-owned and operated and, as a result, financial decisions are made with an objective of increasing the household's wealth through the allocation of all family resources, not just those allocated to an agricultural production operation (Mishra et al. 2002). Retirement, for example, is a critical financial decision for the owners of a family-operated farm or ranch and that decision must be made based on wealth, not production income levels.

This chapter evaluates wealth patterns across regions and farm sizes in an effort to gain insights into the future financial prospects for American agriculture as a whole, or at least for some agricultural industries. Also, relationships between the components of wealth and farm household decision making are assessed.

There are two general objectives of this chapter. The first objective is to derive a system of equations that explain the inter-linkages between the various components of a farm household's wealth at some point in time. The second objective is to use those equations to empirically assess income and wealth patterns across regions and farm sizes. This will generate implications about future economic performance expected across sectors of U.S. production agriculture.

A FARM HOUSEHOLD MODEL

Most agricultural household decision models assume that producers maximize utility derived from the consumption of goods purchased from income earned on the farm. For example, Chavas and Holt (1990) present a typical model focusing on two points in time (*t-1* and *t*) bracketing a single production period, assumed to be a year ending at time *t*. The only source of income considered in their model is revenues from the production of agricultural commodities (R) and wealth is mentioned but not evaluated. Revenues are described as a risky variable because it is a function of output prices and yields, both of which are unknown at time *t-1* when production decisions are made. The simple model used by Chavas and Holt (1990) is also typical in that its focus on only a single time period (i.e, one year) gives it an unrealistic budget constraint that says all income and wealth could be consumed during that single period. Such an assumption is not important when focusing on annual production decisions (e.g., Chavas and Holt analyze acreage response), but is not appropriate when focusing on multi-period financial issues such as retirement planning. Wealth receives very little direct attention in most applications of household models. For example, Duffy, Shalishali, and Kinnucan (1994) extend the model in Chavas and Holt (1990) by adding the concept of "change in wealth," but only as the compensation needed to keep utility constant at some level. Goodwin and Mishra (2005) add the factors of direct government payments and nonfarm activities to their household model, but only as they influence production decisions. They mention in passing that wealth may influence production decisions. In a more general model, Jorgenson and Lau (2000) include a time constraint and the idea that "leisure" is a desirable residual of a household's labor allocations on and off-farm. Yet, no direct attention is given to household wealth.

This chapter contributes to the literature by developing a household model with a multi-period financial focus. This is done by adding variables to a basic household model to enable direct estimation of the importance of factors affecting changes in wealth over time. Whereas change in wealth is excluded in most other studies because of their one-year focus, it is included here to account for wealth's long term value to agricultural households.

To begin, assume a farm household has preferences represented by a von Neumann-Morgenstern utility function U(Con, L, W) and that the household maximizes expected utility subject to constraints on both its budget and time. The household faces a maximization problem over a period ending at time t that can be expressed as:

$$\text{Max } E_{t-1}U_t \text{ subject to}$$
$$\text{Con}_t = \text{Inc}_t + W_{t-1} - W_t$$
$$T_t = L_t + FL_t + OFL_t \text{ and } L, FL, OFL \geq 0$$

where E is the expectations operator over random variables (such as output prices and yields) and U is utility. The utility function says household members desire consumption of goods (*Con*), leisure time $L = (L_o, L_s)$ for the operator and spouse, and wealth (*W*). The time constraint shows that leisure is part of the time endowments for the owner and spouse $T = (T_o, T_s)$ for the period ending at time t. Other allocations of time include the time spent laboring on the farm (*FL*) and the time spent laboring off-farm (*OFL*).

The budget constraint says the value of consumption during the period ending at time t equals income (*Inc*) for that period, plus accumulated wealth at the beginning of the period (W_{t-1}), minus wealth at the end of the period (W_t). This differs from the one-period budget constraint used by Chavas and Holt (1990) and others (i.e., $\text{Con}_t = \text{Inc}_t + W_{t-1}$) because in this multi-period model the household is concerned about consumption levels in future periods. Including W_t in the budget constraint establishes the substitution between the utility derived from current consumption and expected utility from future consumption. That relationship is expressed as

$$E_t\left(\sum_{m=1}^{j} Con_{t+m}\right) = \lambda(W_t)$$

where j is the uncertain number of years before death, and λ is some function of W_t that equates it with the expected sum of consumption in those years. In essence, this specification defines the consumption decisions facing the household as falling into two periods, the first covering the time between $t-1$ and t, and the second covering household members' remaining lives after t.

At any point in time, accumulated wealth represents savings for future consumption. For any household, wealth serves as a hedge against income uncertainty (Arrondel 2002; Guiso, Jappelli, and Terrlizzese 2002). As Caballero (1991) shows, earnings uncertainty raises the desired level of accumulated wealth. In agriculture, accumulated wealth is especially desirable because of the relatively high degree of income volatility over time and because households often have no other source to fund their retirements (Hamakar and Patrick 1996; Jensen and Pope 2004; Phimister 1995). Thus, agricultural households have an incentive to increase wealth over time by balancing their utility from current consumption with expected utility from wealth accumulated for future consumption.

This chapter focuses on *wealth changes* (ΔW) within the decision period between $t-1$ and t, by including it in the model. Defining changes in wealth as $\Delta W_t = W_t - W_{t-1}$ makes it possible to restate the budget constraint as

$$\text{Con}_t = \text{Inc}_t - \Delta W_t.$$

The income factor in the budget constraint is actually two separate sources of cash flow: income from agricultural production (*FInc*) and income from off-farm sources (*OFInc*). Off-farm income has represented over 90 percent of average farm household income in recent years (Mishra et al. 2002). Off-farm employment is the primary source of non-farm income for a majority of farm and ranch households. That is why the household time constraint specifies separate labor allocations to farm and nonfarm activities.

The multi-period nature of this model enables the inclusion of another type of income into the budget constraint. Capital gains are a taxable form of income and, hence, increase a household's wealth during the period earned (USDA). These gains are simply the change in value of a farmer's capital from one point in time to the next (i.e., $\Delta K_t = K_t - K_{t-1}$). Not all capital gains are liquid (gains on physical capital such as farmland are only realized if the asset is sold)[2] which is why they cannot be included in the typical, one-period household decision model. However, in this model ΔK_t can be captured at time t (or later) and used as part of W_t to fund consumption at a later time, such as during retirement.

Substituting the three sources of income in place of *Inc* in the budget constraint restates that equation into its final form:

$$(4.1) \qquad \text{Con}_t = \text{FInc}_t + \text{OFInc}_t + \Delta K_t - \Delta W_t.$$

With the household's utility maximization problem now fully stated, the model can now be used to derive testable hypotheses about the relationship between agricultural production profits and household wealth.

METHOD TO THE MADNESS

Methods for assessing the components of wealth across locations are described in this section. Next, a system of equations is developed using farm-level data from the USDA's Agricultural Resource Management Survey (ARMS) to help explain the recursive linkages between farm household wealth, income, and productivity (U.S. Department of Agriculture [USDA-ERS] 2004b).[3] A repeated cross-sectional data set is constructed from pooled ARMS data for 1996–2004 over the ten production regions in the United States. The equations are estimated using a fixed effects approach (Baltagi 2001, Chapter 3) to examine factors affecting the change in wealth and factors affecting profitability across these regions and across farm sizes.

Empirically, hypotheses are embedded in a system of four reduced-form equations:

$$(4.2) \qquad \text{FInc}_{ft} = \alpha + \beta_1 \text{Cohort}_f + \beta_2 \text{Year}_t + \beta_3 R_{ft} + \beta_4 \text{GP}_{ft} - \beta_5 \text{PC}_{ft} - \beta_6 \text{Deprec}_{ft} + \varepsilon$$

$$(4.3) \qquad \pi_{ft} = \alpha + \beta_1 \text{Cohort}_f + \beta_2 \text{Year}_t + \beta_3 R_{ft} + \beta_4 \text{GP}_{ft} + \beta_5 \text{Prod}_{ft} + \beta_6 \text{HCap}_{ft} + \varepsilon$$

$$(4.4) \qquad \text{LV}/\text{ac}_{ft} = \alpha + \beta_1 \text{Cohort}_f + \beta_2 \text{Year}_t + \beta_3 R/\text{ac}_{ft} + \beta_4 \text{GP}/\text{ac}_{ft} - \beta_5 \text{CK}_{ft}$$
$$+ \beta_6 \text{Prod}_{ft} + \beta_7 \text{PopD}_{ft} + \varepsilon$$

$$(4.5) \qquad \Delta W_{ft} = \alpha + \beta_1 \text{Cohort}_f + \beta_2 \text{Year}_t + \beta_3 \text{FInc}_{ft} + \beta_4 \text{OFInc}_{ft} + \beta_5 \Delta \text{FK}_{ft}$$
$$+ \beta_6 \Delta \text{NFK}_{ft} - \beta_7 \text{Con}_{ft} + \varepsilon$$

where, for each farm *f* during the period ending at time *t*, *GP* is government payments received, *PC* is production costs, *Deprec* is depreciation, π is a farm's profits defined as the percentage return on farm equity (which is the farm's share of household wealth), *Prod* is an index of productivity of agricultural operations, *HCap* is an index of human capital, *LV/ac* is farmland value per acre, *R/ac* is production revenue per acre operated, *GP/ac* is government payments received per acre operated, *CK* is the average cost of capital, *PopD* is population density (people per square mile in the county), *ΔFK* is a farm household's change in farm capital, and *ΔNFK* is the household's change in non-farm capital. In each equation, α is the intercept, β is a regression coefficient to be estimated, ε is an error term, and a farm size (*Cohort*) and time (*Year*) fixed effects variable is included.

The system of equations above is recursive. Thus, ordinary least squares (OLS) estimation of each equation separately is consistent.[4] The U.S. farm-level data used are from the ARMS Phase III surveys of 1996–2004. This is an annual survey covering a sample of farms in the forty-eight contiguous states, conducted by the National Agricultural Statistics Service, USDA, in cooperation with the Economic Research Service. The data used here cover all ten regions listed in Figure 3.1 and discussed in Chapter 3. There are 95,517 observations in total.

In this chapter, farm income (*FInc* in equation 4.2) is calculated from two ARMS variables: *gross farm income* minus *total farm operating expenses*. A farmer's or rancher's production revenue (*R*) is the cash flow called *gross value of production* in ARMS. Production cost data used are for purchased inputs only, as reported by households, thus inputs such as labor provided by farm household members are not included because those inputs were not "purchased" (*PC* is *total cash expenses* in ARMS). Data for depreciation are used here as a proxy for ownership costs. Government transfers are included as an explanatory variable to enable an assessment of the true sustainability of farm production as an income source. To many farm households, government payments may be significant (Ahearn, El-Osta, and Dewbre 2006; Key and Roberts 2006). Government payments could come from various sources, such as unemployment benefits, pensions or commodity program benefits. However, it is expected that most government payments to agricultural producers come from business activities concerning the household's ownership and/or operation of a farm or ranch. These payments are expected to vary across commodities and locations. Including the *GP* variable enables a test of that hypothesis.

An agricultural household's production profit margin reflects both its market competitiveness and its managerial skills. However, previous research (e.g., Klepper 1996) has shown that results are influenced by both the innovation expertise and capital available within a firm. Thus, equation 4.3 is included in the empirical model to help test for differences across households and across locations. Profits are specified as the rate of return from current farm income divided by the farm's share of total household wealth. Managerial expertise is evaluated using two different indexes. The first index (*Prod*) is calculated using the ARMS variables *gross value of production* divided by *total cash expenses*. In the second, *HCap* is a human capital factor derived from the operator's age and education and multiplied by the *value of farm business assets*.

Equation 4.4 is included in the empirical model to allow tests of several hypotheses about the most important capital asset held by an agricultural household. Farmland has historically represented about 75 percent of assets held by farm households. Also, farmland values vary much more across locations than do the values of other agricultural assets because they are a function of numerous variables (Drozd and Johnson 2004; Huang et al. 2006). Thus, some understanding of the factors influencing farmland prices is critical in understanding agricultural household wealth. In the equation, LV/ac_{ft} is the (average) value per acre of farmland and buildings for farm *f* at time *t*. It is expected to reflect the effects of four variables traditionally included in farmland price analyses (*R/ac*, *GP/ac*, *CK*, and *Prod*). Another variable (*PopD*) is included to capture the effects of urbanization because this factor is becoming increasingly important in rural land markets

(Heimlich and Anderson 2001). CK_{ft} is the farm's average cost of capital at time t. CK_{ft} is calculated as the farm's interest expenses divided by its debt and is expressed as a percentage. $PopD$ is the population density (people per square mile) in the county.

Equation 4.5 was derived by manipulating the budget constraint in equation 4.1. The change in wealth equation captures the behavioral hypotheses of that constraint and the inter-relationships linking the major components of an agricultural household's financial structure. In the empirical model two types of capital gains are included, changes in the total value of farm assets and non-farm assets, to enable evaluation of the significance of recent changes in agricultural household financial structure. National USDA farm-level data indicate that non-farm assets were, on average, one-third as large as farm assets in 2004, a remarkable 50 percent increase in relative size compared to a decade earlier.[5] This shift could have long-run implications for the structure of American production agriculture and for the competitiveness of regional agricultural sectors.

Jackknifing

The rich data available in ARMS make this analysis possible. ARMS is a survey designed to incorporate information from both a list of farmers producing selected commodities and a random sample of farmers based on area (USDA/ERS). Since stratified sampling is used, inferences regarding the means of variables for states and regions are conducted using weighted observations. The USDA's in-house jackknifing procedure is applied here because it is believed to be the most appropriate when analyzing ARMS data (Dubman 2000; Kott 2005; Cohen, Xanthopoulos, and Jones 1988). The farm-level data are used in an innovative way. Nine annual surveys are linked to form a pooled time-series cross-section, assuming that the survey design for each year is comparable. Hence, the annual ARMS data are used to examine structural changes over time.

Incorporating the survey weights, and following the jackknifing procedure described in Kott (2005), assures that regression results are suitable for inference to the population in each of the regions analyzed. The USDA/NASS version of the delete-a-group jackknife divides the sample for each year into 15 nearly equal and mutually exclusive parts. Fifteen estimates of the statistic, called "replicates," are created. One of the 15 parts is eliminated in turn for each replicate estimate with replacement. The replicate and the full sample estimates are placed into the following basic jackknife formula:

$$(4.6) \qquad \text{Standard Error } (\beta) = \left\{ 14/15 \sum_{k=1}^{15} (\beta_k - \beta)^2 \right\}^{1/2}$$

where β is the full sample vector of coefficients from the regression results using the replicated data for the "base" run and β_k is one of the fifteen vectors of regression coefficients for each of the jackknife samples. The t-statistics for each coefficient are simply computed by dividing the "base" run vector of coefficients by the vector of standard errors of the coefficients (Dubman 2000). Each reduced form equation was estimated with year and farm size fixed effects.

Farm Size Issues

One challenge involved in using the repeated cross-section data is that the ARMS design is unique each year, so the economic activity observed is not from the same farms over time. Thus, it is not possible to observe an individual farmer's farm and nonfarm assets and directly compute the change in farm and nonfarm assets from the previous year. As a result, construction of the left-hand side variable, ΔW, and two explanatory variables, ΔFK and ΔNFK, required the ability to (1) define the change in wealth and farm and nonfarm assets from one year to the next for an individual observation, and (2) satisfactorily treat the constructed change in wealth variable as a function of net farm income, earned off-farm income, change in farm and nonfarm assets, and consumption over repeated cross-sections. Therefore, to estimate these equations (the change in wealth equation, in particular) and to construct regional/farm size dummies using repeated cross-sections by year for the period 1996–2004, regional and farm-size groupings were combined (see Appendix Figure A4.1).[6] That is, three size variables were created for each of three Agricultural Statistics District (ASD) groupings by state, assigning to an individual farm the change in farm assets and resulting change in wealth observed in the ARMS data from the nine groupings per state (i.e., three size groups for each of three ASD groupings).[7] This enables an assessment of an individual farmer's change in wealth as a function of his or her income, off-farm income, change in farm assets, change in nonfarm assets, and consumption by assuming that a farmer's change in wealth, change in farm assets, and change in nonfarm assets can be gauged from the year-to-year behavior of his or her group (e.g., change in wealth from 1996 to 1997, etc.), and by assuming that the change in wealth and change in farm and nonfarm assets can be treated as individual observations in the jackknifing procedure, just as land value per acre, net farm income, profits, and other variables are treated. It should be acknowledged that the groupings rely on aggregated data for which some of the variation in explanatory factors has been removed. On the other hand, the aggregated data "true up" within State the measure of change in wealth to the increasingly localized and specialized livestock and crop activity occurring in the United States.[8]

The three size categories follow the USDA's typology for farm types (listed in Appendix Table A4.1; the ASD groupings used are identified in Appendix Figure A4.1). Farm Size 1 corresponds to "limited resource," "retirement," and "residential" farms. Farm Size 2 corresponds to "farm/lower sales" and "farm/higher sales." Farm Size 3 is "large family farms" and "very large farms." The nine-level size/location categories thus formed (i.e., the "cross-section" regional/farm size dummies) are by state and are meant to account for missing variables for similarly sized farms within each state. They are appropriate when estimating the equations by region, for example. Therefore, these "cohort" variables are used as fixed effects in all regional models, along with a year fixed effects variable.[9]

In this assessment of financial performance across farm sizes, three size categories are used, defined above as fixed effects variables. Thus, the farm size models are estimated using a farm-size variable that has three levels. For example, when $FarmSize = 1$ (the smaller farms), the estimation eliminates all observations where $FarmSize = 2$ or 3 (i.e., the middle and larger farms). In that case, the regional/farm-size dummy essentially becomes a state dummy. To unlink this confounding of size the way this analysis across farm sizes does, a new state dummy is created and used for the fixed effects when estimating the various equations for each farm size.

The nominal values of the monetary variables are deflated by the GDP implicit price deflator using the year 1996 as the base. Variables presented in the *Empirical Results* tables (4.1–4.4) are in 1996 dollars.[10] Also, the measure of productivity is refined. Rather than using one measure for all farms (crop and livestock), two alternative measures of productivity are used: one for crop farms and one for livestock farms. The productivity measure for crop farms (*prod_crp*) is calculated as value of crop production per acre; the measure for livestock farms (*prod_liv*) is calculated as value of livestock production per acre. The intent was to allow the data to indicate which index best suited each location. The *value* of output, rather than just the quantity of output, is used to indicate a farm's ability to produce dollars per acre, reflecting a financial goal of the operator. The annual averages of all variables are presented by year in Table 4.1.

Equations 4.2, 4.3, 4.4, and 4.5 are estimated for the ten regions and for the three farm sizes. Reduced forms of the equations are estimated by ordinary least squares (OLS) since these equations constitute a recursive system (Hsiao 2001; Greene 2000, p. 659).

EMPIRICAL RESULTS

The results regarding the system of wealth and income equations have some expected and some surprising implications for American agriculture. Appendix Table A4.2 shows the variables used in estimating these equations. Tables 4.2, 4.3, and 4.4 summarize the regression results. As expected, a diverse pattern of relationships linking farm income, land value, farm household wealth, and profits over time is found. Also, patterns are found when accounting for differences in locations, farm sizes and typologies, and commodity specializations caused by comparative advantage.

Farm Income: Equation 4.2

The results in the top section of Table 4.2 show some differences across regions. One striking result is that revenue and depreciation were generally statistically significant across the country, yet government payments were significant in only three regions in the South and Midwest.[11] *Revenue* was significant in all but two regions, but with varied coefficients indicating varying average profit margins. *Depreciation* was significant in all but three regions, indicating that in most areas farms are capital intensive, which creates high fixed costs. The geographically concentrated significance of government payments implies that those regions (Corn Belt, Southeast, and Northern Plains) specialize in the production of some commodities that may be uncompetitive in global markets.

Farmland Value: Equation 4.4

Economic theory suggests that the price of farmland reflects either its value as an input in agricultural production, or the nonfarm demand for land. The key result here is that the proxy variable for the nonfarm demand for farmland (county population density by year) was significant in all regions (see the bottom section of Table 4.2), especially in the Mountain and Pacific regions, where populations are fast-growing. This is consistent with the growing realization that nonfarm demand for farmland is increasingly affecting farmland values, even in areas such as the Corn Belt and Northern Plains, whose economies were dominated by production agriculture in the last century. The population density variable swamped the effects of the four other variables. This appears to be inconsistent with the traditional theory that farmland value is determined primarily by a parcel's ability to generate agricultural revenues. However, this result is consistent with the "urban influence" on farmland prices found in recent studies (e.g., Livanis et al. 2006; USDA 2000; Shi, Phipps, and Colyer 1997). Thus, the proximity of a farmland parcel relative to non-agricultural development is a key factor in pricing. This implies that no commodity can generate enough revenue to adequately compete with expanding urban development, meaning that land-use ordinances may be needed to preserve farmland in urbanizing areas. However, such policies would be resisted by those farmland owners whose current and/or future wealth would be reduced by land-use restrictions.

Table 4.1

Summary of Average Values ($000s, deflated into 1996 dollars using the GDP implicit price deflator)

Variables	1996	1997	1998	1999	2000	2001	2002	2003	2004
Changewealth	n.a.	117.341	124.184	184.325	27.050	167.937	10.781	471.237	144.795
Netfarmincome	13.663	19.581	14.401	15.722	14.955	16.745	13.962	21.429	28.033
Nonfarmincome[1]	33.391	34.092	39.832	44.098	43.745	45.846	47.830	47.504	50.755
Changefarmcapital	n.a.	67.208	122.656	66.378	76.375	154.623	4.593	412.672	115.218
Changenonfarmcap	n.a.	124.512	−1.875	294.977	−34.651	42.262	72.805	213.363	112.189
Consumption[2]	23.890	53.490	28.716	24.873	27.655	28.925	33.053	41.084	41.173
Profits[3]	−2.932	3.616	−8.445	−5.581	−8.974	−17.309	−8.462	−9.999	−8.475
Grosscashflow	77.910	86.615	83.289	86.397	85.513	94.416	88.034	93.428	106.191
Govtpayments	3.195	3.085	4.137	8.433	9.162	9.150	5.768	6.788	6.347
Prod_crop & livestock[4]	0.998	1.270	0.948	0.917	1.051	1.186	3.728	1.278	1.356
Humancapitaleducation[5]	0.106	0.124	0.141	0.140	0.152	0.157	0.155	0.182	0.207
Totalexpenses	59.759	69.842	64.454	65.800	70.402	75.149	76.050	79.143	89.526
Depreciation	6.652	7.318	7.540	8.137	8.657	9.131	9.712	8.915	10.0169
Landvalueperacre	2.723	3.5308	4.399	3.698	3.701	4.264	4.496	4.980	6.145
Grosscashflowperacre	0.981	1.272	0.945	0.946	1.076	1.231	1.488	1.363	1.426
Govtpayments/ac	0.008	0.006	0.008	0.017	0.018	0.020	0.015	0.017	0.015
Costcapital[6]	8.736	9.230	9.210	8.996	8.996	8.996	8.996	8.996	8.996
Popdensity[7]	116.429	128.235	145.895	134.235	116.727	121.915	140.984	143.020	131.112

[1] Earned income off–farm.

[2] Data for 1997 imputed based on off–farm income.

[3] Estimated as rate of return on equity (percent).

[4] $000s of value of crop or livestock production per acre, deflated into 1996 dollars using the GDP implicit price deflator.

[5] Uses education, and farm physical capital (as a proxy for age); op_educ*atot/10^7, scaled.

[6] Interest on farm debt as percent of farm debt outstanding.

[7] People per square mile (county–level) based on counties in each year's ARMS survey.

Table 4.2

Regression Results for Farm Income and Farmland Value Equations by Region, 1996–2004

Variable	North-east	Lake States	Corn Belt	Appalachia	South-east	Delta	Southern Plains	Northern Plains	Mountain	Pacific
Farm income equation										
Revenue	0.443 (4.09)***	0.314 (0.99)	0.271 (1.77)*	0.248 (3.61)***	0.254 (3.62)***	0.236 (4.01)***	0.108 (1.47)	0.071 (2.62)***	0.450 (2.94)***	0.649 (3.83)***
Govtpayments	0.262 (0.72)	-0.445 (-0.45)	1.245 (2.96)***	0.249 (0.43)	1.001 (3.89)***	0.269 (1.04)	0.465 (1.48)	0.514 (2.08)**	0.512 (1.48)	0.152 (0.81)
Totalexpenses	-0.180 (-1.52)	0.128 (0.28)	-0.197 (-1.42)	0.102 (0.63)	-0.121 (-2.13)**	0.019 (0.25)	0.151 (1.31)	-0.015 (-0.19)	-0.280 (1.85)*	-0.386 (-1.91)*
Depreciation	-1.010 (-4.33)***	-1.315 (-0.95)	-1.423 (-1.91)**	-1.019 (-2.79)***	-0.743 (-3.80)***	-1.127 (-3.89)***	-0.963 (-1.61)	0.512 (1.68)*	-0.240 (-0.49)	-1.27 (-2.42)**
Farmland value equation										
Revenue per acre	0.155 (1.17)	-0.020 (-0.99)	0.221 (1.96)**	0.012 (0.40)	0.018 (0.81)	0.152 (1.90)*	-0.057 (-0.10)	0.298 (0.99)	4.139 (1.023)	0.083 (0.30)
Govtpayments per acre	-7.184 (-1.01)	3.535 (0.32)	33.272 (1.17)	4.378 (1.21)	0.714 (0.92)	-2.455 (-1.77)*	-7.007 (-2.11)**	1.243 (0.17)	-3.934 (-0.46)	0.473 (0.15)
Costcapital	-0.156 (-2.17)**	-0.001 (-0.54)	-0.027 (-1.83)*	-0.004 (-0.34)	-0.028 (-1.32)	-0.008 (-0.86)	0.006 (0.39)	-0.008 (-0.51)	-0.082 (-1.22)	0.054 (0.13)
Productivity	0.037 (0.36)	0.035 (0.31)	-0.052 (-0.44)	0.030 (0.61)	0.188 (3.50)***	-0.146 (-1.82)*	0.067 (0.21)	-0.230 (-0.67)	-3.997 (-1.005)	-0.058 (-0.19)
Popdensity	0.007 (3.99)***	0.004 (5.50)***	0.005 (3.14)***	0.008 (2.15)**	0.009 (5.02)***	0.005 (4.67)***	0.004 (1.66)*	0.008 (3.02)***	0.032 (3.04)***	0.028 (7.20)***

Note: The top value in each box is the variable's regression coefficient and the value in parentheses is its t-statistic.

***, **, and * denote statistical significance at the 99%, 95%, and 90% confidence levels, respectively.

Change in Wealth: Equation 4.5

Wealth consists of both farm and nonfarm capital, although most farm household wealth is held in the form of farmland. As shown in the top section of Table 4.3, both components were significant in eight of the ten regions: the Northeast, Lake States, Appalachia, Southeast, Southern Plains, Northern Plains, Mountains, and Pacific. Clearly, changes in farm and nonfarm capital are important in wealth building. Each of those variables was significant in every region but one. Also, income from either farm or nonfarm sources generally was not significant. This means income, in absolute amounts, was small compared to capital gains. Thus, wealth comes from capital gains, not income, in all parts of the country's agricultural industry.

Both farm and nonfarm capital were significant in most regions but had differential impacts on wealth (top section of Table 4.3). For example, a $1,000 increase in *farm capital* in the Lake States would raise wealth by about $843, compared to $912 in the Delta. Also, a $1,000 increase in *nonfarm capital* would raise wealth by about $387 in the Lake States, for example. In nine of the regions, the lower regression coefficients for *Changes in Nonfarm Capital,* compared to coefficients for *Farm Capital,* imply that there are few economic opportunities for shifting resources out of agriculture and into nonagricultural uses. In general, these results show that holding farmland (which represents about three-quarters of *Farm Capital*) has been a much more profitable investment over the past decade than have nonfarm investment alternatives, on average. The different performance levels of capital asset markets across regions and types of capital may be partly due to differences in the opportunities available off-farm and multiplier effects in different regional economies.

Farm Profits: Equation 4.3

There were weak statistical results across regions for the profits equation (bottom section of Table 4.3) reflecting the common problem of a profit squeeze in the different commodity markets represented by the production specializations across regions. *Productivity* was significant in only two regions. *HCap,* which represents the productivity and investment components of human capital, was significant only in the Corn Belt. No other variable was significant in any region. Combining these results makes it clear how difficult it is to find a significant relationship between profits and any explanatory variables because, on average, profits from agricultural production have been near zero for the past decade. The poor household average profit performance is shown in the data in Table 4.1. As indicated, national average farm profits were negative in most years. These results reinforce the results for the *Change in Wealth* equation, which show that farm income is not significant, indicating that farm owner-operators benefit from the rising value of their farmland, not from producing commodities on that land. Overall, these results support the hypothesis raised by Blank (2002, 2005) that real estate investment, rather than agricultural production, is the true focus of most small-scale farm owners.

Farm Size Results

Results in Table 4.4 show how American farms of different sizes from all ten regions have performed over the last decade. As expected, the size of a farm has significant effects on its financial performance.

In the *Change in Wealth* equation results, it is clear that Size 1 households have been focusing some of their activities off the farm. Gains on farm and nonfarm capital were both significant

Table 4.3

Regression Results for Change in Wealth and Profits Equations by Region, 1996–2004

Variable	Northeast	Lake States	Corn Belt	Appalachia	Southeast	Delta	Southern Plains	Northern Plains	Mountain	Pacific
Change in wealth equation										
Netfarm income	-0.132	0.061	-0.539	0.033	0.153	0.027	-0.089	-0.026	-0.786	-0.212
	(-0.50)	(0.49)	(-0.64)	(1.57)	(0.38)	(0.56)	(-2.01)**	(-0.75)	(-1.07)	(-1.77)*
Nonfarm income	0.308	0.051	-0.203	0.165	0.198	0.083	-0.129	0.124	-0.067	0.630
	(1.43)	(0.47)	(-1.70)*	(1.42)	(1.04)	(0.82)	(-1.76)*	(1.75)*	(-0.25)	(1.76)*
Changefarmcap	0.959	0.843	0.301	0.962	1.102	0.912	1.095	0.893	1.068	1.084
	(6.89)***	(5.46)***	(0.52)	(30.20)***	(44.98)***	(11.70)***	(13.85)***	(31.47)***	(6.08)***	(20.41)***
Changenonfarmcap	0.273	0.387	0.485	0.231	0.356	0.045	0.325	0.191	0.246	0.359
	(6.33)***	(1.80)*	(4.63)***	(10.13)***	(6.06)***	(0.61)	(5.22)***	(5.27)***	(3.70)***	(1.67)*
Consumption	-0.007	0.262	0.368	-0.061	-0.199	0.237	-0.037	0.037	0.541	0.840
	(-0.04)	(0.88)	(0.71)	(-1.11)	(-1.17)	(1.15)	(-0.39)	(0.38)	(0.84)	(0.91)
Profits equation										
Revenue	0.011	-0.004	-0.001	0.001	0.007	-0.017	0.001	-0.001	-0.004	0.006
	(1.41)	(-0.54)	(-0.24)	(0.17)	(1.55)	(-0.16)	(0.18)	(-0.30)	(-0.68)	(0.82)
Govtpayments	0.137	0.113	-0.202	0.009	0.051	-0.884	0.157	0.109	0.085	0.108
	(0.53)	(1.35)	(-0.52)	(0.22)	(0.47)	(-1.23)	(1.35)	(0.83)	(0.41)	(0.94)
Productivity	-0.001	0.244	-0.012	0.111	-0.299	-0.210	-0.065	0.500	1.255	0.198
	(-0.02)	(3.89)***	(-0.08)	(0.28)	(-0.40)	(-0.39)	(-0.02)	(2.68)***	(1.19)	(0.97)
Humancapitaleduc	10.309	25.091	36.473	16.707	-0.868	-565.588	1.187	4.999	2.904	-0.915
	(1.15)	(1.41)	(2.07)**	(0.98)	(-0.94)	(-0.75)	(0.58)	(0.71)	(1.41)	(-0.20)

Note: The top value in each box is the variable's regression coefficient and the value in parentheses is its t-statistic.

***, **, and * denote statistical significance at the 99%, 95%, and 90% confidence levels, respectively.

Table 4.4

Regression Results for Equations by Farm Size, Across Ten Regions, 1996–2004

Variable	Farm Size 1		Farm Size 2		Farm Size 3	
	Estimate	t value	Estimate	t value	Estimate	t value
Change in Wealth Equation						
FarmInc	−0.653	−0.92	−0.039	−1.31	−0.149	−1.08
NonFarmInc	0.009	0.11	0.077	1.54	−0.111	−0.72
ChngFarmCap	1.113	10.09***	1.018	40.74***	1.100	86.85***
ChngNFarmCap	0.318	20.09***	0.100	1.09	0.299	1.64
Consumption	0.516	1.01	−0.089	−1.21	0.313	0.89
Profits Equation						
Revenue (CashFlow)	0.167	0.69	0.075	2.76**	0.002	1.96**
GovtPayments	−1.681	−0.93	−0.112	−0.11	−0.058	−0.24
Productivity	0.782	0.80	−0.312	−0.61	0.170	1.47
HumanCapitalEd	−16.109	−0.40	3.911	0.58	−0.567	−0.28
Farm Income Equation						
Revenue (CashFlow)	0.688	22.75***	0.561	17.95***	0.194	5.63***
GovtPayments	0.246	2.48**	0.260	5.06***	0.479	3.15***
CashExpenses	−0.522	−12.96***	−0.383	−7.58***	0.037	0.84
Depreciation	−0.992	−15.01***	−0.879	−18.50***	−0.808	−1.86*
Farmland Value Equation						
CashFlowPerAcre	0.577	1.79*	0.586	2.81***	0.043	1.12
GovtPayments/ac	−2.552	−0.72	0.684	0.10	0.235	0.13
CostCapital	0.013	0.23	−0.065	−1.43	−0.055	−1.74*
Productivity	0.116	0.46	0.0061	0.06	0.0114	−0.37
PopDensity	0.008	5.99***	0.011	2.87***	0.0208	4.01***

Notes: ***, **, and * denote statistical significance at the 99%, 95%, and 90% confidence levels, respectively. These regressions use state dummy variables for fixed effects.

Farm Size 1 corresponds to limited resource, retirement, and residential farms. Farm Size 2 consists of farm/lower sales and farm/higher sales. Farm Size 3 includes large family farms and very large farms.

sources of wealth for small-sized farms. Medium- and large-sized farms both derive wealth only from gains on their farm capital, which is most likely their land. Neither farm nor off-farm income was significant for any farm size.

The *Profits* equation has interesting statistical results across farm sizes. Profit margins are significantly influenced by cash flows in the form of sales revenue for medium- and large-sized farms only. Small farms have profit near zero, on average, thus making it appear they do not respond to the variables in the profit equation. However, medium- and large-sized farms depend on farm revenue as a significant source of profits. Overall, these results further support Blank's (2005) hypothesis that small-scale farmers focus on real estate more than agricultural production when making financial decisions.

The *Farm Income* equation has excellent results indicating the importance of cash flows. The most interesting result for the *Farm Income* equations is that three of the four explanatory variables have a decreasing absolute value of their regression coefficient as farm size increases. This mostly is explained by the fact that farms often diversify their activities as they grow in size, thus reducing their farm income risk. Also worth noting is that the fourth variable, government payments received, has a *larger* impact on average farm income as farm size increases. This indicates that government payments are going to operators based on criteria other than financial need because larger regression coefficients indicate a larger average amount of those payments are received. Thus, larger farms appear to benefit from government programs that are biased toward making payments per unit of input (i.e., land) or output.

The *Farmland Value* equation results have significant implications for land pricing theory. The revenue per acre generated by farming has no effect on large-sized farms, contrary to traditional theory. Small- and medium-sized farms do get a significant effect from production revenues per acre. Finally, all three farm sizes have significant *Population Density* effects, but the regression coefficient increases with farm size. This implies that a farm's proximity to urban areas is key to its farmland values, as noted by recent studies (e.g., Livanis et al. 2006; Shi, Phipps, and Colyer 1997), but larger farms have more development value per acre.

IMPLICATIONS OF THE RESULTS

These results generally agree with other studies that have used farm-level data to empirically assess wealth and income patterns across states, farm types, and commodity specializations (e.g., Mishra et al. 2002). There are at least three implications of these results.

First, although U.S. farm sector returns are converging over time and across regions, farm profits still vary widely by farm type, farm size, location, and by other factors. However, wealth, income, profits, and productivity are linked. For example, the finding that changes in both farm and nonfarm capital are significant in explaining changes in wealth in most regions suggests that nonfarm capital is a substitute for farm capital. This indicates that farm households have diversified their portfolios.

Second, changes in farm and nonfarm capital have differential impacts on farm wealth across farm locations. In general, the fact that changes in nonfarm capital have smaller impacts than do changes in farm capital across all but one of the regions implies that there are few profitable opportunities to shift resources out of agriculture in most of the country. However, this may also reflect the asset fixity problem faced by most farm households. Or it may indicate simply that urban pressures pushing farmland values up are creating the best investment alternative available to agricultural producers. In other words, farmland has out-performed nonfarm investments over the past decade.

Third, as expected, this analysis found evidence that farm size affects household wealth-building strategies. In Table 4.4, capital gains from farm assets were significant for all farm sizes, but capital gains from nonfarm assets were significant only for small farms. This indicates that owner-operators of small-sized farms are the only group to have made substantial investments off their farms. This off-farm focus of small operators might partly explain the economic hysteresis observed by other studies. Many small-scale farms do not change their cropping choices despite financial losses in most years. Nevertheless, such behavior is understandable if it is assumed that the objective of many small-scale operators is to enjoy their farms while waiting for the value of their farmland to increase.

These results support the long-expressed notion that large-scale farms are more competitive in today's global commodity markets and, therefore, have a higher probability of surviving. They are also consistent with the "big fish eat little fish" story of consolidation long visible in American agriculture. Therefore, the pattern of financial performance observed in the household data indicates that existing trends of decline in small- and medium-sized farms are likely to continue for some time. The unknown is the pace of consolidation because it will depend on how long the "little fish" choose to hang on to their farmland. This analysis implies that this choice will be made based on farm household wealth factors having little to do with agriculture.

APPENDIX

Appendix Table A4.1

The Farm Typology Groups

Typology	USDA definition	Sales ($)
1	Limited resource	<100,000 (assets <150,000, income < 20,000)
2	Retirement	<250,000
3	Residential (other major occupation)	<250,000
4	Farm/lower sales	<100,000
5	Farm/higher sales	<250,000
6	Large family farms	250,000–499,999
7	Very large farms	500,000+

Appendix Table A4.2

Description of Variables

Variable	Equation	Decription	Calculated as:	Source
W_t		Total wealth at time t	Farm plus nonfarm net worth	ARMS
ΔW_t	4.5	Change in total wealth	$W_t - W_{t-1}$	Estimated
FInc	4.2	Net farm income	Total for year	Estimated
OFInc	4.1, 4.5	Off-farm income	Total for year	ARMS
ΔK_t	4.1	Capital gains	$K_t - K_{t-1}$	Calculated
K_t		Capital stock	Farm plus nonfarm capital	ARMS
Con_t	4.1	Household consumption expenditures	Total for year	ARMS
R_t	4.2	Gross value of sales		ARMS
GP_t	4.2	Government payments		ARMS
PC_t	4.2	Production costs		ARMS
$Deprec_t$	4.2	Depreciation		ARMS
Prod	4.3, 4.4	Productivity	Productivity index	Calculated
$PopD_t$	4.4	Population density	People per square mile in county	Bureau of the Census
CK	4.4	Cost of capital	Interest/farm debt x 100	Calculated
LV/ac_t	4.4	Land and building value per acre	Land and0 building value per acre	Estimated
$HCap_t$	4.3	Productivity component and investment component	Uses age, education, and farm physical capital (3 alternatives)	Calculated
π_t	4.3	Profits (%)	Percent rate of return on farm equity	Estimated

Appendix Figure A4.1 **Location of Constructed Cohorts by State and Substate**

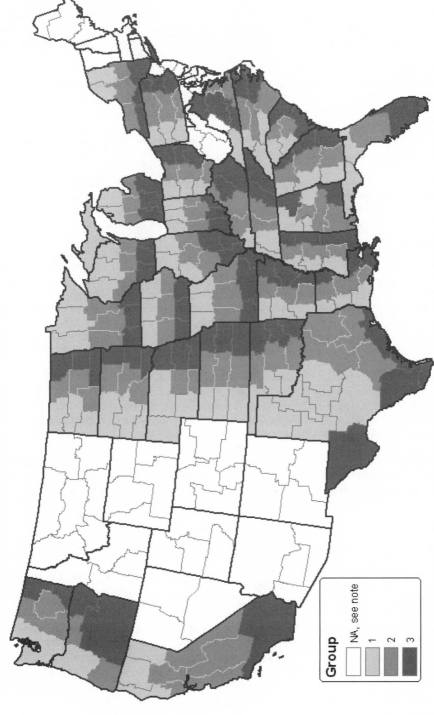

Group

☐ NA, see note
◻ 1
▨ 2
▩ 3

Note: States with three grey shade codes indicate ASD by income grouping; Mountain States were constructed as state averages of farm and nonfarm wealth; and other noncoded states were constructed as state averages of farm and nonfarm wealth by residential, small and large intermediate, and commerical size groupings.

NOTES

Some of the material in this chapter is expanded and revised from an article published by S. Blank, K. Erickson, C. Moss, and R. Nehring as "Agricultural Profits and Farm Household Wealth," *American Journal of Agricultural Economics* 86, no. 5 (2004): 1299–1307, and a paper by S. Blank, K. Erickson, R. Nehring, and C. Hallahan presented at the 2006 American Agricultural Economics Association conference entitled "Agricultural Profits and Farm Household Wealth: A Farm-level and Cross-Sectional Analysis."

1. Nehring et al. (2006) develop an index of urban influence on agricultural activities based on the distance from, and the population of, metropolitan areas relative to the center of each county in the United States. They present a spatial distribution of rural and urban-influenced regions in their study of urban influence on costs of production in the Corn Belt. They find that 30 percent of farms are urban influenced, even in the heavily agricultural Corn Belt, resulting in increased costs and decreases in technical efficiency.

2. It is worth noting that some portion of unrealized capital gains can be converted into liquid assets to improve a farmer's operation through the loan process. In other words, a lender will convert some portion of a farmer's capital gains, for example from the increase in farmland values, into cash in the form of a loan. Thus, a farmer can convert unrealized capital gains into assets, such as more farmland, by borrowing against the assets that have appreciated in value. Lenders will not usually loan a farmer the full value of unrealized capital gains; they will loan up to some specific portion of the market value of the assets. That portion is referred to as a lender's loan-to-value ratio (LTV). The LTV varies with numerous factors specific to the lender, borrower, the assets used as collateral, and the risks involved in the loan (Thompson and Blank 1994). In all cases, $1 > LTV \geq 0$.

Note that this loan process may result in a farmer having more assets under his/her control, but it does not immediately change total wealth, expressed as total equity. The new asset (e.g., the cash or the assets purchased with the cash) is off-set by a new liability (i.e., the loan) on the farmer's balance sheet. However, it is assumed that a farmer will only take out such a loan to acquire assets that will generate additional wealth in future periods. That means the farmer's wealth is expected to grow faster in the future than it would have without the assets funded by the loan. That increased growth in wealth provides the incentive for farmers to take the loan.

When an asset is sold, actual capital gains are realized. The farmer uses the cash received from the buyer to pay off any remaining loan, eliminating the liability on the balance sheet. All cash remaining after the loan is paid off represents the actual realized capital gain. That cash shows as an asset on the balance sheet, raising total equity (and wealth) by an equal amount.

3. This analysis focuses on the principal owner-operator's household wealth and income and excludes nonfamily farms. Nonfamily farms (for which nonfarm wealth information is not collected in the ARMS) are becoming an increasingly important source of agricultural production in many commodity markets and in many locations. For example, in 2004 nonfamily farms accounted for 48 percent of the value of production in Texas, 26 percent in California, 41 percent in Kansas, 32 percent in Arizona, 34 percent in Colorado, and 14 percent in Nebraska.

4. As discussed by Kennedy (2003), if there is no correlation between disturbances in different equations, OLS estimation is consistent and (with no lagged endogenous variables on the right-hand side) unbiased. The ARMS is a complex survey design, therefore jackknifing procedures are used so that inferences to the population can be made.

5. Four regional groupings emerge. Off-farm assets in 2004 were nearly 50 percent as large as farm assets in the Northeast and Southern Plains, 33 to 39 percent as large in Appalachia and the Southeast, 28 to 29 percent as large in the Lake States, Corn Belt, and the Pacific, but only about 25 percent as large in the Northern Plains and Mountain States. All regions also show significant growth in off-farm assets relative to farm assets over time with the ratio of off-farm assets to farm assets doubling in the Northeast and Southern Plains, and growing close to 40 percent in other regions.

6. The other three equations were estimated using farm-level data directly from each cross-section and using secondary cross-section population density data.

7. In states with a limited number of observations, statewide groupings are used by type and size—residential, and small, medium, and large commercial farms—to calculate group change in wealth and farm and nonfarm assets.

8. For example, the ASD groupings in northern Iowa (including hogs, beef, and dairy) and central Iowa (including hogs and chickens) now account for the bulk of highly concentrated livestock production in the state, whereas farming activity in the southern Iowa grouping (including cow/calf operations) is much less concentrated and more dependent on crops. In other words, the trend of local concentrations in enterprise specialization enables the procedures used here to successfully capture the effects of household decisions.

9. For example, nine groups or cohorts are constructed in Texas by identifying "small," "intermediate," and "commercial" farms in six prairie ASDs, three East Texas ASDs, and five Fruitful Rim ASDs. However, a majority of states may simply be divided latitudinally (e.g., Iowa and Minnesota) or longitudinally (e.g., Ohio and Pennsylvania) to form three ASD groupings, each of which is divided by farm size, hence nine groups per state.

10. There is an extraordinary range of farm sizes in this data set. While there is no formal test for heteroscedasticity using repeated cross-section ARMS data, size differences are accounted for using fixed effect dummies. Estimation of the empirical model using slope dummies by size and type of operation (whether crop or livestock) or partitioning the data set by size or type of operation would undoubtedly add more information.

11. As a check for robustness, t-tests were estimated using the Huber-White variance estimator. The H-W results compared very closely to the jackknifing results. The H-W estimator relaxes the IID assumption about the data, adjusting the standard errors for the fixed effects to account for the non-independence within years and across years. Normally, the IID assumption does not hold within years in the case of the ARMS data, and it is compounded by pooling the ARMS data over time. The authors programmed the robust variance commands in SAS. A transparent description of the technique is available in STATA (2005).

REFERENCES

Ahearn, M., H. El-Osta, and J. Dewbre. 2006. "The Impact of Coupled and Decoupled Government Subsidies on Off-Farm Labor Participation of U.S. Farm Operators." *American Journal of Agricultural Economics* 88 (2): 393–408.

Andres, J., J. Bosca, and R. Domenech. 2004. "Convergence in the OECD: Transitional Dynamics or Narrowing Steady-State Differences?" *Economic Inquiry* 42 (1): 141–149.

Arrondel, L., "Risk Management and Wealth Accumulation," *Economics Letters* 74 (2002): 187–194.

Baltagi, Badi H. 2001. *Econometric Analysis of Panel Data.* 2d ed. Chichester, UK: John Wiley & Sons.

Ben-David, D. 1993. "Equalizing Exchange, Trade Liberalization and Income Convergence." *Quarterly Journal of Economics* 106: 407–443.

Blank, Steven C. 2002. "Is Agriculture a 'Way of Life' or a Business?" *Choices* 17 (3): 26–30.

———. 2005. "The Business of an Agricultural 'Way of Life.' " *Choices* 20 (2): 161–166.

Caballero, Ricardo J., "Earnings Uncertainty and Aggregate Wealth Accumulation," *American Economic Review* 81, 4 (1991): 859–871.

Carriker, G., M. Langemeier, T. Schroeder, and A. Featherstone. 1993. "Propensity to Consume Farm Family Income from Separate Sources." *American Journal of Agricultural Economics* 75 (3): 739–744.

Caselli, F., and W. Coleman II. 2001. "The U.S. Structural Transformation and Regional Convergence: A Reinterpretation." *Journal of Political Economy* 109 (3): 584–616.

Chavas, J. and M. Holt, "Acreage Decisions Under Risk: The Case of Corn and Soybeans," *American Journal of Agricultural Economics* 72, 3 (1990): 529–538.

Cohen, S., J. Xanthopoulos, and G. Jones. 1988. "An Evaluation of Available Statistical Software Procedures Appropriate for the Regression Analysis of Complex Survey Data." *Journal of Official Statistics* 4: 17–34.

Dodson, Charles B. 1994. *Profitability of Farm Businesses: A Regional, Farm Type, and Size Analysis,* Statistical Bulletin Number 884, Economic Research Service, United States Department of Agriculture, June.

Drozd, D., and B. Johnson. 2004. "Dynamics of a Rural Land Market Experiencing Farmland Conversion to Acreages: The Case of Saunders County, Nebraska." *Land Economics* 80 (2): 294–311.

Dubman, R.W. 2000. *Variance Estimation with USDA's Farm Costs and Returns Surveys and Agricultural Resource Management Study Surveys.* Washington, DC: U.S. Department of Agriculture, Economic Research Service, Staff Paper AGES 00–01.

Duffy, P., K. Shalishali and H. Kinnucan, "Acreage Response Under Farm Programs for Major Southeastern Field Crops," *Journal of Agricultural and Applied Economics* 26, 2 (1994): 367–378.

Goetz, S., and D. Debertin. 1996. "Rural Population Decline in the 1980s: Impacts of Farm Structure and Federal Farm Programs." *American Journal of Agricultural Economics* 78: 517–529.

———. 2001. "Why Farmers Quit: A County-Level Analysis." *American Journal of Agricultural Economics* 83: 1010–1023.

Goodwin, B. and A. Mishra, "Another Look at Decoupling: Additional Evidence of the Production Effects of Direct Payments," *American Journal of Agricultural Economics* 87, 5 (2005): 1200–1210.

Greene, William H. 2000. *Econometric Analysis.* 4th ed. Upper Saddle River, NJ: Prentice-Hall.

Guiso, L., L. Jappelli, and D. Terlizzese, "Earning Uncertainty and Precautionary Saving," *Journal of Monetary Economics* 74 (2002): 187–194.

Gutierrez, Luciano. 2000. "Convergence in U.S. and EU Agriculture." *European Review of Agricultural Economics* 27 (2): 187–206.

Hamakar, C. and G. Patrick, "Farmers and Alternative Retirement Investment Strategies," *Journal of the American Society of Farm Managers and Rural Appraisers* (1996): 42–51.

Heimlich, R.E., and W.D. Anderson. 2001. *Development at the Urban Fringe and Beyond: Impacts on Agriculture and Rural Land.* Washington, DC: U.S. Department of Agriculture, Economic Research Service, Agricultural Economic Report no. 803.

Hsiao, Cheng. 2001. *Analysis of Panel Data.* 2d ed. Cambridge: Cambridge University Press.

Huang, H., G. Miller, B. Sherrick, and M. Gomez. 2006. "Factors Influencing Illinois Farmland Values." *American Journal of Agricultural Economics* 88 (2): 458–470.

Jensen, F. and R. Pope, "Agricultural Precautionary Wealth," *Journal of Agricultural and Resource Economics* 29, 1 (2004): 17–30.

Jorgenson, D. and L. Lau. 2000. "An Economic Theory of Agricultural Household Behavior," Chapter 3 in D. Jorgenson (ed.), *Econometrics, Volume 1: Econometric Modeling of Producer Behavior,* MIT Press: Cambridge, MA: pp. 97–124.

Kennedy, Peter. 2003. *A Guide to Econometrics.* 5th ed. Cambridge, MA: MIT Press.

Key, N., and M. Roberts. 2006. "Government Payments and Farm Business Survival." *American Journal of Agricultural Economics* 88 (2): 382–392.

Klepper, Steven. 1996. "Entry, Exit, Growth, and Innovation over the Product Life Cycle." *American Economic Review* 86 (3): 562–583.

Kott, P.S. 2005. *Using the Delete-A-Group Jackknife Variance Estimator in NASS Surveys.* U.S. Department of Agriculture, National Agricultural Statistics Service (USDA/NASS), NASS Research Report, RD-98–01, Washington, DC.

Livanis, G., C. Moss, V. Breneman, and R. Nehring. 2006. "Urban Sprawl and Farmland Prices." *American Journal of Agricultural Economics* 88 (4): 915–926.

Mishra, A., H. El-Osta, M. Morehart, J. Johnson, and J. Hopkins. 2002. *Income, Wealth, and the Economic Well-Being of Farm Households.* USDA Economic Research Service, Agricultural Economic Report no. 812, July.

Morrison-Paul, C., and R. Nehring. 2005. "Product Diversification, Production Systems, and Economic Performance in U.S. Agriculture." *Journal of Econometrics* 126 (2005): 525–548.

Nehring, R., C. Barnard, D. Banker, and V. Breneman. 2006. "Urban Influence on Costs of Production in the Corn Belt." *American Journal of Agricultural Economics* 88 (4): 930–946.

Nehring, R., J. Fernandez-Cornejo, and D. Banker. 2005. "Off-Farm Labour and the Structure of US Agriculture: The Case of Corn/Soybean Farms." *Applied Economics* 10: 633–650.

O'Rourke, K., and J. Williamson. 1994. "Late Nineteenth-Century Anglo- American Factor-Price Convergence: Were Heckscher and Ohlin Right?" *Journal of Economic History* 54 (4): 892–916.

Phimister, Euan, "Farm Consumption Behavior in the Presence of Uncertainty and Restrictions on Credit," *American Journal of Agricultural Economics* 77 (1995): 952–959.

Schmitt, Gunther. 1989. "Simon Kuznets' 'Sectoral Shares in Labor Force': A Different Explanation of His (I + S)/A Ratio." *American Economic Review* 79 (5): 1262–1276.

Schott, Peter K. 2003. "One Size Fits All? Heckscher-Ohlin Specialization in Global Production." *American Economic Review* 93 (3): 686–708.

Shi, Y., T. Phipps, and D. Colyer. 1997. "Agricultural Land Values Under Urbanizing Influences." *Land Economics* 73 (1): 90–100.

StataCorp. *Stata Statistical Software*: *Release 9*. College Station, TX StataCorp LP. 2005.

Thompson, R., and S. Blank. 1994. "Ag Loan Analysis." *Journal of Agricultural Lending* 7 (2): 12–14, 16–17.

U.S. Department of Agriculture. 2000. "Accumulated Farm Real Estate Value Will Help Farmers and Their Lenders Through Period of Declining Cash Receipts." *Agricultural Income and Finance: Situation and Outlook,* pp. 30–33. Economic Research Service, AIS-74, February.

U.S. Department of Agriculture, Economic Research Service (USDA-ERS). 2004a. Agricultural Resource Management Survey (ARMS) Briefing Room, www.ers.usda.gov/Briefing/ARMS/._ March.

———. 2004b. Agricultural Resource Management Survey, Phase III, and Farm Costs and Returns Surveys for 1996 through 2004.

U.S. Department of Agriculture, National Agricultural Statistics Service (USDA/NASS). 2000. *Agricultural Prices, 1999 Summary,* Washington, DC: Agricultural Statistics Board. July.

PART II

THE ECONOMICS OF AGRICULTURE AND GLOBAL DEVELOPMENT

CHAPTER 5

THE ECONOMIC FOOD CHAIN
OF GLOBAL DEVELOPMENT

*"It may be that the race is not always to the
swift, nor the battle to the strong—but that's the way to bet."*
—Damon Runyon

The United Nations (1996) estimated that 65 percent of the world's population was engaged in food production in 1950 and predicted that less than 30 percent of the population will be in agriculture in the year 2025. Such a dramatic shift in human resource allocation is made possible by technological advances in agricultural production (Antle 1999; Debertin 1998, Johnson 2000). Also, it is known to be an indicator of positive economic development (Bardhan and Udry 1999). However, when a *declining* trend in an industry is considered a *positive* sign of economic advancement, it implies that the industry is an "inferior good" in the context of national economic development and investment. In other words, agriculture offers returns on investments that apparently are lower than those available from investment of labor (and other resources) in other industries in the economy.

> In the global scale of economic development, farming is an entry-level job. Also, providing raw food products for the population is the first job that must be done by any developing country. Yet, being the *first* job is different than being an *entry-level* job. Agriculture is both. An obvious point that explains why agriculture must be the first job in an economy is that *hungry people do not work very long.* This means that the job must be performed continuously by someone. Being an entry-level job implies that it is something that everyone has to go through, but it is not a highly desirable occupation and is one that, eventually, everyone wants to get out of as they move up. This is true for national economies as well as for individual people.... (Blank 1998, p. 7)

This raises the surprising hypothesis that some countries will leave agriculture entirely as part of their economic development.

The economies of the United States, Japan, and several countries in Western Europe have developed to such an extent that agriculture has become a very small portion of these nations' "portfolios" of investments. In the United States only 1.3 percent of the population is in agricultural production; the percentage is similar in Japan, and in the European Union the number of people working on farms plummeted to 7.3 million in 1995 from 12.3 million in 1979. For example, French farmers comprise about 2 percent of the country's population and are declining in number by 4.2 percent per year. The numbers are very different elsewhere in the world. As shown in Figure 5.1, the United Nations estimated that 46 percent of the world's total population

107

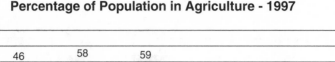

Figure 5.1 **Agricultural Population Shares as an Inverse Indicator of Economic Development**

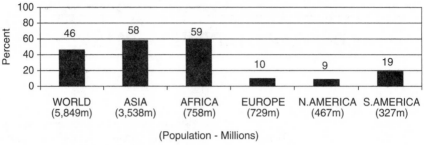

Source: *FAO Production Yearbook*, United Nations (1997).

worked in agriculture in 1997, with the percentage being much higher in Africa and Asia. For individual African countries, the estimates ranged from 84 percent in Ethiopia and 82 percent in Tanzania down to 11 percent for the much more developed South Africa. In Asia, examples include 61 percent for India and 59 percent for Bangladesh down to Japan's 5 percent. In Europe, Russia has the highest percentage of its population still working in agriculture at 11 percent. The average percentage for North America is misleading because the 3 percent for Canada is offset by Mexico's 23 percent and Guatemala's 48 percent, clearly indicating the difference between relatively more and less developed countries. Across the globe this inverse relationship between the share of a country's population in agriculture and its level of economic development is apparent. This reinforces the idea that production agriculture is not a desirable investment, thus it is something a country may want to leave if possible.

Therefore, the United States and a few other highly developed countries are the first to face the questions related to leaving agriculture. The objective of this chapter is to discuss some of those questions, including (1) can the U.S. leave production agriculture entirely? (2) why would a country *want* to leave agriculture? and (3) what about the comparative advantage that a country (or region in a country) may have in the production of agricultural commodities? First, the development process is outlined in simple terms using the logic of portfolio theory. Then, each of the questions above is addressed. The long-run implications of these issues for U.S. and foreign agricultural producers are outlined. Finally, the role of agriculture in a country's economy is used to define an expanded list of development levels that more fully describes a nation's economic progress.

THE ECONOMIC FOOD CHAIN

Countries move up the "food chain" as they develop. This means that countries go through a series of development stages, each with a different focus. Ultimately, nations withdraw their resources invested in lower stages as those resources are needed for new investments in higher stages. Stated more directly, economic development starts by focusing on *food,* then it focuses on freeing labor and other resources from agriculture for use in other, more profitable production as opportunities arise. Food is the entry level, the base industry.

In the beginning, humans spent all of their time trying to keep themselves fed. Hunting and gathering were often risky because people could not always count on finding something to eat. Farming and tending livestock reduced the risk somewhat because people did not have to guess where the food was going to be. Also, as people became better agricultural producers, it took less time for them to generate all the food they could eat. Eventually, everyone did not have to spend every waking moment worrying about food.

At the point where all of a country's population was not needed in agriculture, the base stage of economic development was completed. From then on, a country could begin to devote some resources to other industries and move up through four higher stages of economic development (see Figure 5.2). Each successive stage emphasizes different types of industries because each stage focuses on developing a different combination of the four types of resources: labor, land, capital, and management.[1]

The first stage of development beyond agriculture focuses on exploiting a country's natural or human resources. Industries such as mining and forestry are developed by using surplus unskilled labor from agriculture to "harvest" the natural wealth of the country. The primary resource type used during this development stage (in addition to labor) is land. Countries with more land, like Russia, Canada, and the United States, are more likely to have a wealth of natural resources available for harvesting. Countries with ocean frontage also harvest the seas as part of this development stage. Heavily populated countries, like China and India, may focus on utilizing their large pools of unskilled labor. For the U.S., the first colonies all bordered the Atlantic, so fishing immediately got us into this stage. Forestry and mining followed, with each triggering the settlement and development of various regions of the country. Mining of precious metals, in particular, gave quick boosts to the development of places like California (gold), South Dakota (gold), Arizona (silver and copper), Nevada (silver), Alaska (gold), and New Mexico (uranium). Other parts of the United States are still known for their mining roots, like West Virginia (coal), or their forests, like Oregon and Washington, but in many cases these industries are dead or dying.

Countries enter the second development stage when they begin to produce goods from natural resources. This means that base manufacturing is occurring. An example to illustrate the difference between stage 1 and stage 2 is provided by comparing mining and steel manufacturing. A country in stage 1 only mines the iron ore needed to make steel; a country in stage 2 makes the steel. Countries normally move into stage 2 by using the accumulated wealth (i.e., capital) earned from stage 1 harvesting activities to invest in the necessary hardware of manufacturing. That means stage 2 industries focus on two types of resources (beyond the necessary labor): land and capital. Lots of land is still needed because manufacturing is a "big" business: big factories, big warehouses, big equipment, and big labor pools. Lots of capital is needed because all those big inputs have big price tags. It takes considerable capital to establish base manufacturing industries. Luckily, assets like factories have very long, useful lives so their high set-up costs can be spread over long periods. To facilitate these types of long-term investments, a country must develop capital markets internally or be willing to let foreign capital influence domestic development (Xu 2000; Lele 1991). The United States followed Europe into stage 2 during the industrial revolution of the eighteenth and nineteenth centuries. Most of the remnants from this stage are spread across the eastern half of the United States. For over a decade during the last half of the twentieth century, the region was referred to as the "Rust Belt" because most of the factories were idled. Much of the region is now in economic recovery due to a shift of resources into stage 3 industries.

Figure 5.2 **The Economic Food Chain**

Development stage	Economic activities	Resources emphasized
th	nformation production	apital and management
3rd	igh tech manufacturing	and capital and management
2nd	ase manufacturing	and and capital
st	ploit natural or human resources	and and labor
ase	ood production	and and labor

Source: Blank (1998).

Stage 3 is triggered by the development of a skilled labor force, enabling a country to go into "high-tech" manufacturing. This stage focuses on combinations of land, capital, and management resources. Manufacturing, even high-tech, requires large facilities, so land is needed, although these businesses are much less land-intensive than base manufacturing. Capital is relatively more important in this stage than is land. The cash needs of industries that apply sophisticated technology are high. Nevertheless, it is the application of a third type of resource, management, that enables stage 3 industries to develop. High-tech products are much more complicated than products of base manufacturing, and it takes much more skill to organize the business structures needed to support this type of manufacturing. In other words, more skilled people are needed, both in the factory and in the company office, than was the case in stage 2 base manufacturing firms. The automobile industry was an early example of stage 3 manufacturing, while the computer industry is a more recent case. In fact, it could be argued that the auto industry was a stage 2 industry that transitioned into a stage 3 industry. Cars were originally very basic and easy to understand by today's standards, but the industry kept applying the latest technological advances, thus enabling it to create a modern vehicle that few people now can repair themselves. Computers, on the other hand, started off as magic boxes beyond the technical knowledge of most people.

The United States led Europe and Japan into stage 3 during the twentieth century. Our push began with industries making products like cars and assorted electrical appliances. The emphasis was on consumer goods first because they had the biggest markets, but other products followed. After telephones and phonographs came products like medicines, rocket ships, and nuclear power plants. The high costs of these industries and the fickle nature of the markets for these products make stage 3 industries prone to boom and bust periods. This type of risk makes stage 3 development sustainable only for wealthy nations.

The fourth, and final, stage of development requires a highly educated population because many people get "paid for what they know, not what they do." For industries making up this stage, the focus is on the production of knowledge and information, not of physical products, although products are being developed or services are being provided using the new information. The key resources required are capital and management. Capital is needed to fund the research that generates the new knowledge and information and to create the businesses that make the new products based on the research. Management and problem-solving skills themselves will be valued and marketed between firms. Stage 4 industries include firms engaged in research and problem solving, but may have begun with specialists such as doctors and lawyers. Scientific laboratories, public and private educational entities, and management consulting firms are current examples. The direct output of these companies may be nothing more tangible than patents and reports, but these pieces of information are valuable inputs for stage 3 firms. The United States is leading the way in the creation of this stage of economic development.

Countries move up through the "economic food chain" by shifting some resources from lower-stage industries to higher-stage activities. According to the concept of *comparative advantage*, countries gradually drop lower-level industries as opportunities develop in more profitable higher-level sectors. Comparative advantage involves specializing by investing resources in industries for which they are best suited, as indicated by the fact that they generate the best return, given alternative investments available, and then trading for products in which a comparative advantage is not maintained (Layard and Walters 1978, pp. 113–119; Krugman 1998, pp. 91–98; Thurow 1996, pp. 65–74). This means that given the choice of investing a skilled laborer in a low-level industry that requires mostly unskilled labor, like agriculture, or in a higher-level industry, like those in stage 3 or 4, the country is better off doing the latter to the extent it can; the country's gross national product is higher if the laborer produces a more valuable product. In this sense, agriculture serves as a temporary holding area for land and other resources until a higher-and-better use is available.

A dramatic example of agriculture's role as a holding area for labor is provided by China. A Chinese farm official said in 1997 that many of China's 450 million rural workers were redundant. He said only 200 million were actually needed for farming. Also in 1997, Reuters reported that the number of workers in China's agricultural sector would decrease by 2.6 percent each year over the next five years while the number in manufacturing and the service sector would rise. In the year 2000, employees in China's agricultural sector accounted only for 43 percent of the total labor force, compared to 52 percent in 1990 and 69 percent in 1980.

In American agriculture, labor is not the only major resource that is leaving the industry: land is also being reinvested elsewhere. Land is the most inflexible of all resources, yet it is leaving agriculture in a steady flow. Total farmland in the United States peaked at 1.2 billion acres in 1954, but has declined every year since. After nearly a half-century of reallocation there were only 931 million acres of farmland reported in the USDA's 1997 Census of Agriculture (USDA 1998).

CAN THE UNITED STATES LEAVE AGRICULTURE ENTIRELY?

The United States is moving into stage 4 along with Japan and some European countries. Our increasingly wealthy and educated country now invests much of its resources in stage 3 industries and is poised to make significant strides into stage 4. To reach this point, we have pulled all but 1.3 percent of our population out of farming and ranching for use elsewhere, and we import significant amounts of food. Our stage 1 and 2 industries are slowly shrinking as well.

High-technology jobs are gradually replacing unskilled industry work. What are the implications of this shift in resources?

Figure 5.3 presents a stylized illustration of how the populations of less- and more-developed countries are distributed across industries in the different development stages. The curve on the left shows how a less-developed country might have a high percentage of its population still in agriculture, while smaller percentages of the labor force are in stage 1, 2, and 3 industries. A more-developed country, like the United States, has a labor distribution farther to the right, with few people remaining in agriculture. As a country develops, its labor distribution shifts farther to the right. The extent of the right tail of the distribution is determined by technology available and the country's ability to adopt it. A country's adoption of technology is determined, primarily, by the country's supplies of management and capital (Khanna, Epouhe, and Hornbaker 1999).

From Figure 5.3 it is easy to visualize how a more-developed country with an ongoing rightward shift in its labor distribution may need to pull all remaining labor out of agriculture for use elsewhere. That raises the question: can the United States reduce its current labor allocation from 1.3 percent in agriculture to zero? In other words, can the U.S. depend entirely on imports for the raw commodities that its agribusiness sector needs to feed the nation?

For the United States to leave agriculture entirely, two conditions must be met. First, the world must be able to supply its total population with adequate quantities of food. There is a sizable literature that says total world production of food will not be a problem in the future, despite population projections of up to 12 billion by the end of this century (e.g., Antle 1999; Coyle et al. 1998; Johnson 2000; Rosegrant and Sombilla 1997; Tweeten 1999). How is this possible without a contribution from American farmers? As the United States removes resources from agriculture and stage 1 and 2 industries, the resulting gaps in world output are filled by less-developed countries moving up into those stages of their development.[2] For example, China is expected to shift from being an importer to an exporter of wheat (Rozelle and Huang 1998).

Second, other countries must be willing and able to provide America with agricultural commodities. America has helped some of the world's poorest countries develop their agriculture so that they can progress enough to become customers for our high-tech exports. By helping these countries free up agricultural labor for investment in stage 1 and 2 industries, we help them earn enough wealth to begin buying the products of our stage 3 industries.[3] However, in creating customers for our higher-value industries, we have hastened our departure from agriculture by aiding in the development of competitors. Now those less-developed countries can sell us their new agricultural surpluses and can do so at prices that are often lower than the break-even price for domestic producers. Ultimately, the United States has created a situation of *mutual dependence* that in the future will assure us of a stable supply of agricultural commodities from countries dependent on those sales to us to fund their continued development.

American agribusiness firms, such as food processors and wholesalers, will continue their efforts to assure themselves of adequate supplies of agricultural commodities and, in so doing, will reinforce the mutual dependence between the United States and our foreign suppliers. Our agribusiness firms will accomplish this by continuing their use of contracting and foreign direct investment (Bardhan and Udry 1999, p. 115; Gopinath, Pick, and Vasavada 1998, 1999; McCorriston and Sheldon 1998; Ning and Reed 1995; Swenson 2000). Profits to agribusiness will be comparable with nonagricultural investment returns (Gopinath, Pick, and Vasavada 1999). Therefore, the United States can (theoretically) leave agricultural production entirely because the bright prospects for America's agribusiness sector will provide incentives for that industry to secure America's commodity supplies.

Figure 5.3 **Development and Labor Utilization**

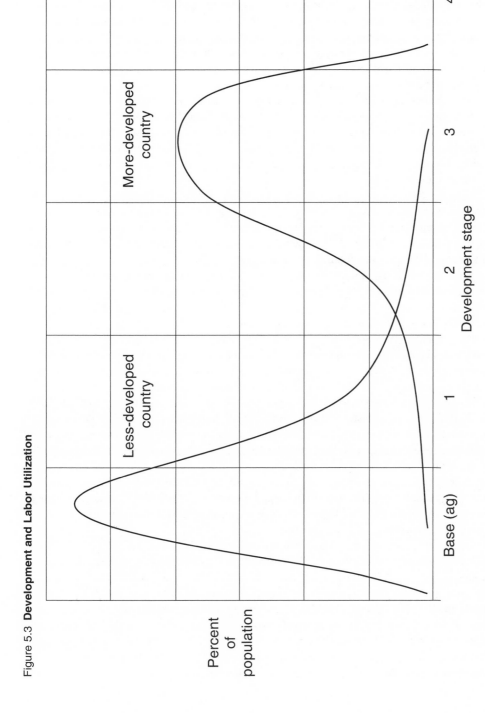

Source: Blank (2005).

WHY WOULD A COUNTRY WANT TO LEAVE AGRICULTURE?

The above discussion leads to the question of why a country would *want* to leave agriculture. The answer? It is an investment decision. U.S. agriculture is still profitable in general, yet the fact that an enterprise is making *some* profit does not make it a good investment. Over the last 20–30 years, agriculture's gross profit margin has been in the 2–3 percent range, on average. That is low relative to investments available outside of agriculture (Bjornson and Innes 1992). From 1960 to 2000, the trend line for average rate of return on equity in American agriculture dropped from 2.5 percent to 1.5 percent (Blank 2001). The average real net returns to assets financed by debt has been negative over the last two decades and was −3.8 percent in 1999 (USDA 1999). Therefore, America's production agriculture may create a deadweight loss to the economy. Much of our labor, capital, and management resources that remain in agriculture are there by choice but could be better invested elsewhere.[4] And these low profit margins should not be a surprise. Agriculture is often described as a close approximation to the theoretical market structure called a "perfectly competitive" industry. Economic theory says that in the long run the average profit margin for such an industry will be zero.

Ironically, it is America's higher level of development, compared to our new less-developed competitors in global commodity markets, causing much of the downward pressure on profits in agriculture. Our production inputs (land, labor, etc.) are higher priced than resources in less-developed countries (Antle 1999). The resulting absolute cost advantage of less-developed countries (many of which adopted our technologies [Griffin 1999, pp. 100–131]) enables them to underprice our agricultural commodities—thus the world's consumers buy agricultural products from other nations' producers rather than from our farmers and ranchers.

WHAT ABOUT COMPARATIVE ADVANTAGE?

In the past, it was believed that "what drives trade is comparative rather than absolute advantage" (Krugman 1998, p. 101). The concept of comparative advantage says that countries should specialize in the production of whatever products its resources are best suited for, even if it does not have an absolute advantage in the production of any product (Layard and Walters 1978, pp. 113–119). It is now understood that "countries may lose industries in which comparative advantage might have been maintained . . . due to changes in comparative advantage and international competition" (Krugman 1998, pp. 98, 101). This is especially likely in markets for undifferentiated commodities.

Changes in comparative advantage occur as technological advances create new industries and/or substantially change existing industries within a country. When those advances result in changes in the relative profitability between industries, it can reduce the attractiveness of investments in existing industries, such as agriculture.

International competition is now relevant to the decision making in some industries in which comparative advantage once dominated, like American agriculture, because there is an *absolute* limit to how much the world needs of a commodity. Unlike the situation for branded products, undifferentiated agricultural commodities can now be produced in greater quantities than the global market can absorb. This is due to technological advances. Food commodities, in particular, have an absolute limit to the volume that can be consumed over time because there is a physical limit to how much a person can eat, even if an infinite supply were available free. And because commodities are undifferentiated (i.e., there is no difference between the output from two producers of a standardized commodity), buyers usually make purchases from the lowest-cost supplier.

Figure 5.4 illustrates the effects of absolute cost advantages in global commodity markets. To begin, assume that there is only one country (such as the United States) supplying the market for a commodity with supply curve S_1. The world demand curve, D, intersects S_1 at point A, resulting in price P_1 being charged for quantity Q_1. Then assume that technological advances in production, storage, and/or transportation enable a new, lower-cost supplier (such as a less-developed country) to enter the market. The new producer has a supply schedule shown as the lower portion of S_2 (that section of the curve becomes almost vertical at Q_2^* because resources limit the production capacity of the new supplier). The new total market supply is found by horizontally summing the supply schedules from the two suppliers, giving S_2, which has a jump at price P_2^*, the lowest price at which the original supplier is willing to participate in the long run. The intersection of the new supply schedule and the world demand schedule is at point B, resulting in price P_2 being charged for quantity Q_2. The introduction of competition from the new supplier will cause the original supplier to scale back its production in response to the lower market price, P_2. Also, depending on the nature of sales in the market (i.e., whether they are made in competitive spot markets, through multiyear contracts, or influenced by personal contacts developed over time between people in the marketing channel), the original supplier may lose additional market share to the new supplier because the new supplier could drop its price to compete for sales and, by dropping its price to P_2^* or slightly less, it could ultimately force the original supplier out of the market. However, in the long run consumers would bid up prices to P_2, leading to total output of Q_2 with the new supplier producing Q_2^* and the original supplier producing the difference $(Q_2 - Q_2^*)$. Finally, as continued adoption of technological advances occurs in less-developed countries, new suppliers become able to enter the market, making S_3 the total supply curve and moving the equilibrium to point C, where P_3 is the unit price for quantity Q_3. In this example, the high-cost original supplier is forced out of the market entirely due to falling prices. The lower-cost suppliers are still profitable at P_3 and consumers benefit because plentiful supplies are available at lower prices. The more inelastic the demand for the commodity, the faster the process leads to the exit of higher-cost suppliers.

Normally, when a country does not have an absolute advantage in the global market for a product in which it has a comparative advantage, it is forced to compete on the basis of lower input costs (e.g., wages, land prices, etc.) or by adjusting its currency exchange rates. A country can make the price of its product in which it has a comparative advantage competitive in absolute terms by forcing down input costs and/or lowering the value of its currency. However, this is easier to do in a less-developed country that is trying to export a limited variety of products, as compared to a more-developed country like the United States, which exports many different products. For the less-developed country, the relatively large impact of export sales for a single (or a few) important product(s) will be felt in factor markets to a much greater extent than will the affects of exports sales of any product from a more diversified, developed country. For example, when Cuba's economy centered around the production of sugar, export prices of sugar greatly influenced wages and other input costs in that less-developed country. On the other hand, sugar produced in Hawaii (although important to the local economy) had insignificant effects on the U.S. wage rate through currency changes because sugar was such a miniscule part of America's total economy. Also, factor prices in Hawaii did not fall sufficiently to lower the production costs of sugar because many alternative uses were available for labor and other resources. As a result, the Hawaiian sugar industry suffered a profit squeeze that forced some of it out of business. This example is typical of cases where a regional comparative advantage in the production of some commodity is insufficient to overcome the industry's absolute disadvantage in a global market.

Figure 5.4   World Market for an Agricultural Commodity: From One Supplier to Competitive Market

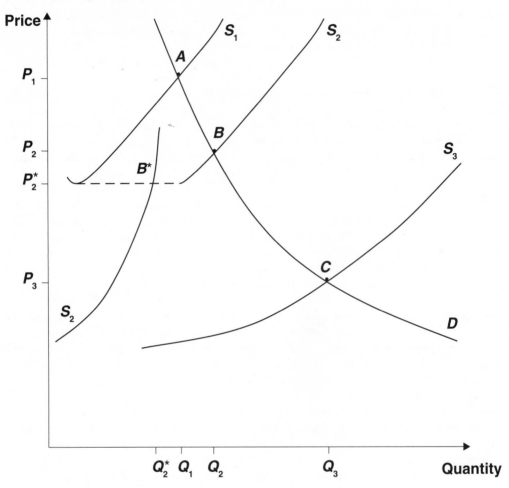

IMPLICATIONS OF IT ALL

Krugman (1998, p. 95) concludes, "if foreigners are willing to sell us high-quality goods cheaply, that is a good thing for most of us, but a bad thing for the domestic industry that competes with the imports." Since there are many more American consumers benefiting from the growth of global commodity markets than there are agricultural producers being squeezed by the increased competition, the United States will continue to shift its resources and policies in the direction of increasing agricultural imports.

Shifting labor and other resources into nonagricultural investments is good for the United States as a whole because, as noted by Bardhan and Udry (1999, pp. 22–23), "as economic growth occurs, the return to skilled labor increases relative to the return to unskilled labor." Agriculture, even in the United States, is characterized as using primarily unskilled labor, thus "historically, the share of agriculture in national income usually declines with economic growth" (Bardhan and Udry 1999, p. 205). This shift is apparent in U.S. gross domestic product (GDP) data that show about 8 percent of GDP coming from farms in 1947, only 1.1 percent coming from farms in 1997 (Lum and Yuskavage 1997), and only 0.7 percent in 2001 even though total agricultural sales revenues continued to increase over that period. The low returns to investments in agriculture are an incentive to continue shifting resources out of the industry.

All of this is bad news for American farmers and ranchers. Global competition in commodity markets will continue to increase as technology changes the comparative advantages of nations, making agriculture more profitable for less-developed countries and less profitable for more-developed countries. Gradually, the highest-cost suppliers will be forced to leave the markets as falling prices reduce profit margins.

As the United States exits agricultural production, profits to remaining agricultural producers will vary, but must eventually settle at a level that makes less-developed countries' comparative advantage in commodity production more acceptable as a permanent investment. The primary factor increasing profits to commodity producers in the future is most likely going to be increases in demand that are created by the increased wealth of countries as they develop. This process will take decades and possibly the remainder of the century.

CONCLUSIONS AND PROPOSITIONS

Agriculture's role in economic development has always been central (Tiffin and Irz 2006). Agriculture is the "entry level"—the starting point—for each country. It is also one of the measuring sticks against which a country's economic progress is evaluated. In general, more-developed countries are those with diversified economies that have relatively little of the nation's resources invested in agricultural production. This is due to production agriculture's "inferior" performance as an investment despite the "superior" performance of agricultural producers in continually raising yields in the United States and other more-developed countries. The economics of undifferentiated commodities will always make farming and ranching less profitable, in terms of return on investment, than investments in agribusiness and elsewhere in the U.S. economy.

As a result, the United States is one of the first countries (along with Japan and a few Western European nations) to reach a new level of economic development. This new level is undefined currently, thus a definition is proposed here. It is based on the degree of national assets (and labor, in particular) that is invested in agricultural production.

Exhibit 5.1 presents an expanded list of development levels that more fully describes a nation's economic progress. It is proposed as a replacement to the current practice of labeling countries as being either "developed" or "less developed." In particular, it eliminates the current misnomer of calling some countries "developed," which implies that economic development is a finite process that concludes after a country achieves some arbitrary level of wealth, as measured by gross domestic product or per capita income. The proposed list acknowledges that development is a continuous process that does not end. The list also includes two new development levels beyond the three levels that have been observed thus far. At this time, most countries are at the "more-developed" or "less-developed" levels, although a few very poor nations still might be described as falling into the "lowest level" of development. The two new levels are labeled "highly developed" and "highest level" of development.

Japan and a few Western European nations may already be described as "highly developed" because their resource limitations forced them to accept being a net importer of agricultural commodities some time ago. Japan, for example, cannot possibly feed its population without imports due

Exhibit 5.1

Proposed Levels of Economic Development

Development Level	Description of a Country's Development Level
Lowest level	Country cannot always feed its population, agriculture is unstable but uses a large majority of the labor force
Less-developed	Large labor investment creates some agricultural surplus for export to fund limited investments in other industries; some substitution of capital for labor in agriculture occurs
More-developed	A higher level of exports, agriculture is still a sizeable exporting industry but uses a small minority of the labor force as capital is increasingly substituted
Highly developed	Begins when a country intentionally shifts from being a net exporter to being a net importer of agricultural commodities to enable both labor and capital resources to be invested in more profitable industries
Highest level	Country is no longer invested in commercial agricultural production

to its limited amount of farmland, so it began developing relationships of mutual dependence with foreign suppliers of commodities immediately after World War II. The United States, with our plentiful agricultural resources, was happy to export commodities to Japan in exchange for Japanese manufactured goods over the decades. Now the U.S. economy has developed to the point where it has more profitable investment alternatives to agricultural production and we are beginning to intentionally shift resources away from agriculture and toward those alternatives. Thus, the United States is becoming "highly developed." And the pace of our economic progress may cause America to reach the "highest level" of development during this century.

How is it possible that one of the world's leading agricultural nations might leave commodity production behind? Absolute limits to comparative advantage change with technological advances, causing countries to develop mature, mutually dependent relationships with suppliers. That enables highly developed countries to leave agriculture entirely when better investments become available. Such a change is a sign of continued growth up the economic food chain.

NOTES

Some of this chapter is a revised and expanded version of an article published by S. Blank as "The Economic Food Chain: America Moves Up by Pushing Agriculture Out," *Current Politics and Economics of the United States* 7, nos. 1/2 (2005): 1–17.

1. Traditionally, economists identify only three types of resources: land, labor, and capital. An economic definition of "management" as a fourth type of resource is proposed in Chapter 8.

2. In markets for agricultural commodities, there are many cases in which the causality of these shifts is reversed. In other words, it is likely that the entrance of new supplies in the global market from less-developed countries is causing the exit of American commodities in some cases, as discussed in the next two sections.

3. The World Bank's managing director has said that Asian economies will contribute about 50 percent of the growth of global gross domestic product in this century (Agence France-Presse 1995).

4. For example, there is a need for skilled workers in U.S. high-tech positions. Ballon (2000) reported that "U.S. companies will have openings for more than 1.6 million information technology workers this year. But more than half of those jobs will go unfilled in the U.S. because of a lack of qualified employees."

REFERENCES

Agence France-Presse. 1995. "Asia-Pacific Economies Grew an Average 7.7% in '94." April 18.

Antle, John. 1999. "The New Economics of Agriculture." *American Journal of Agricultural Economics* 81: 993–1010.

Ballon, Michael. 2000. "U.S. High-Tech Jobs Going Abroad." *Los Angeles Times,* April 24.

Bardhan, P., and C. Udry. 1999. *Development Microeconomics.* Oxford: Oxford University Press.

Bjornson, B., and R. Innes. 1992. "Another Look at Returns to Agricultural and Nonagricultural Assets." *American Journal of Agricultural Economics* 74: 109–119.

Blank, Steven C. 1998. *The End of Agriculture in the American Portfolio.* Westport, CT: Quorum.

———. 2001. "The Challenge to Think Big as American Agriculture Shrinks." *Journal of Agricultural and Resource Economics* 26 (2): 309–325.

———. 2005. "The Economic Food Chain: America Moves Up by Pushing Agriculture Out." *Current Politics and Economics of the United States* 7 (1/2): 1–17.

Coyle, W., M. Gehlhar, T. Hertel, Z. Wang, and W. Yu. 1998. "Understanding the Determinants of Structural Change in World Food Markets." *American Journal of Agricultural Economics* 80: 1051–1061.

Debertin, David. 1998. "Impacts of New Agricultural Technology on Real Growth in the US and KY Farm Economy: 1949–1995." Paper presented at the Southern Agricultural Economics Association meeting, Little Rock.

Gopinath, M., D. Pick, and U. Vasavada. 1998. "Exchange Rate Effects on the Relationship Between FDI and Trade in the U.S. Food Processing Industry." *American Journal of Agricultural Economics* 80: 1073–1079.

———. 1999. "The Economics of Foreign Direct Investment and Trade with an Application to the U.S. Food Processing Industry." *American Journal of Agricultural Economics* 81: 442–452.

Griffin, Keith. 1999. *Alternative Strategies for Economic Development.* 2d ed. New York: St. Martin's.

Johnson, D. Gale. 2000. "Population, Food and Knowledge." *American Economic Review* 90: 1–14.

Khanna, M., O. Epouhe, and R. Hornbaker. 1999. "Site-Specific Crop Management: Adoption Patterns and Incentives." *Review of Agricultural Economics* 21: 455–472.

Krugman, Paul. 1998. *Pop Internationalism.* Cambridge, MA: MIT Press.

Layard, P., and A. Walters. 1978. *Microeconomic Theory.* New York: McGraw-Hill.

Lele, Uma. 1991. "International Capital Markets, Development Performance, and Lessons for the Future." *American Journal of Agricultural Economics* 73: 947–950.

Lum, S., and R. Yuskavage. 1997. "Gross Product by Industry, 1947–96." *Survey of Current Business* 77 (November): 20–34.

McCorriston, S., and I. Sheldon. 1998. "Cross-Border Acquisitions and Foreign Direct Investment in the U.S. Food Industry." *American Journal of Agricultural Economics* 80: 1066–1072.

Ning, Y., and M. Reed. 1995. "Locational Determinants of the Direct Foreign Investment in Food and Kindred Products." *Agribusiness* 11: 77–85.

Reuters. 1997. "Chinese Workers Increasingly Seen Leaving the Land." January 7.

Rosegrant, M., and M. Sombilla. 1997. "Critical Issues Suggested by Trends in Food, Population, and the Environment to the Year 2020." *American Journal of Agricultural Economics* 79: 1467–1470.

Rozelle, S., and J. Huang. 1998. "Wheat in China: Supply, Demand, Marketing, and Trade in the Twenty-First Century." Bozeman: Montana State University, Trade Research Center. Special Report no. 3.

Swenson, Deborah L. 2000. "Firm Outsourcing Decisions: Evidence from U.S. Foreign Trade Zones." *Economic Inquiry* 38: 175–189.

Thurow, Lester C. 1996. *The Future of Capitalism: How Today's Economic Forces Shape Tomorrow's World.* New York: Penguin.

Tiffin, R., and X. Irz. 2006. "Is Agriculture the Engine of Growth?" *Agricultural Economics* 35: 79–89.

Tweeten, Luther. 1999. "The Economics of Global Food Security." *Review of Agricultural Economics* 21: 473–488.

United Nations. 1996. "World Population Prospects: The 1996 Revision." New York: United Nations.

United Nations. 1997. *Production Yearbook.* Rome, Italy: Food and Agriculture Organization.

U.S. Department of Agriculture (USDA). 1998. *1997 Census of Agriculture.* Washington, DC: National Agricultural Statistics Service.

———. 1999. *Agricultural Income and Finance: Situation and Outlook Report.* Resource Economics Division, Economic Research Service, AIS-72, September.

Xu, Zhenhui. 2000. "Financial Development, Investment, and Economic Growth." *Economic Inquiry* 38: 331–344.

CHAPTER 6

COMMODITIES AND THE PROFIT SQUEEZE

"Show me the money!"
—Phrase made popular by
the movie *Jerry Maguire*

American production agriculture is one of the most productive and efficient agricultural industries in the world. So why is it slowly disappearing? In pursuing that question, Blank (1998) identified a large portfolio of threats to U.S. production agriculture including economic, political, social, and environmental issues. Each of the threats, considered separately, seemed manageable because there is at least one well-known solution for each problem identified. However, once he began to take a broader view and tried to consider the interrelationships between and among the threats, he began to see the "big picture" and to realize that *real* solutions are not obvious because, when evaluating agriculture, the solution to one problem often is the source of another problem. The story behind each of the numerous threats, and the interrelationships between them, is fascinating and complicated. However, it is the sum of their parts that matters most because that sum addresses the question of agriculture's decline. This chapter tries to explain the biggest threat to the long-term survival of American farming and ranching, the end result of summing all the threats: there is a profit squeeze in American agriculture.

Economic theory says that, on average, the long-run profit of an industry selling an undifferentiated commodity in a perfectly competitive market is zero. Farms and ranches fit the description of that type of firm. Thus, it should come as no surprise that agricultural production is not a very profitable sector of the economy and never will be. The dismal economics of commodity production are becoming worse in markets that are increasingly global in scale.

The chapters in Part I of this book document the profit squeeze in many ways. Thus, it is taken as given in this chapter that profits in American agriculture have been low and are showing signs of continual decline. The focus here is to offer an explanation for the squeeze.

The explanation involves relatively new changes in U.S. and global agriculture that pose real threats to American producers. In general, the threats to American agriculture are derived from the intersection of global and local scales of decision making. International economic development, personal finance decisions, and political, social, and environmental issues are all part of the portfolio of threats. At the top of the list of threats is the bottom line.

THE BOTTOM LINE

Profits to U.S. agricultural producers are being squeezed because for an increasing number of commodities, *price is global, production cost is local.* That means the markets and prices of commodities have become global in scope, while production costs remain local. Thus, profits vary by location. With a single competitive "world price" ceiling affecting producers of a global commodity, it means that local costs determine the profit per unit for producers dispersed across the globe and, therefore, costs determine which producers will survive in the long run.

What created global markets and prices? Technological advances. As research and innovative managers created new and better machines and methods of producing, storing, transporting, and processing commodities, it became increasingly possible for U.S. and foreign producers to supply commodities to buyers in more distant locations (Antle 1999). First, technologies that expanded output created a surplus in "local" markets, thus creating a need for farmers to look over a wider geographical area to find additional buyers. Next, improvements in storage technologies enabled producers to maintain their output in salable condition for longer periods of time because storage expands the amount of time before spoilage. That extra time enabled sellers to cover more distance, thus more people could be reached as sellers deliver their output to more distant markets. Finally, improved transportation technologies have reduced the costs of covering greater distances between sellers and buyers of commodities. Therefore, improvements in technology increase the number of (possible) producers and expand the geographic reach of each, thus more direct and indirect competition between sellers occurs, creating the "global" market. Within the last three or four decades, science has made it possible for even highly perishable "fresh" produce grown on one continent to be sold to consumers on another. In California, for example, consumers eat fruit from Chile during the winter and many of those consumers do not realize that they are eating imports, rather than the output of California's own fruit industry. Why are American consumers unaware of the increasing amount of imported food in their shopping cart? For one thing, the price, appearance, and quality of the Chilean fruit, and other imports, are about same as that for local produce available during our summer harvest season. Although consumers benefit by having increased supplies available to them, the global effect of technological advances on American farmers is an increase in the competition between them and other suppliers of commodities.

In summary, technological advances have triggered a dynamic change in commodity markets. Roe and Mohtadi (2001, p. 423) argue that "the world economy is in its second wave of globalization, with the first wave ending in the early 1900s, and the second wave beginning in the late 1950s to early 1960s." What is different about this second wave? The first wave could only trade storable commodities, the second wave is increasingly focusing on higher-value perishable commodities. That new focus is possible due to technological and managerial innovations.

Prices for undifferentiated agricultural commodities are now determined by global supply and demand factors, and prices are going down as global output expands. This is part of the dismal economics facing American farmers and ranchers. Producers of raw commodities are price takers, meaning that they must take the price offered by the market—they cannot set their price directly like makers of branded products can. Commodity producers are powerless in this regard because, by definition, commodities are undifferentiated between individual producers. That means the output of one producer (of, say, #2 hard red wheat) is identical to the output of all other producers of that commodity, thus none of those producers has any basis for negotiating a higher price for their output and, therefore, they all must take the market price.

Why local costs? Production costs will always be local because resources are mostly inflexible. Land, obviously, is fixed in location and productivity; labor mobility is low for low-paying jobs in agriculture; and local supplies of other inputs like water, fertilizers, and the like affect the prices of those resources. In other words, a farmer's or rancher's costs per unit of production are dictated largely by the quantity and quality of resources close at hand. Total costs of production are determined by local supply and demand factors for inputs.

What have been recent commodity price and cost trends? World prices, ignoring seasonality, have been trending down in real terms for a century due to increased total supplies and competition between suppliers (USDA 2000c). Also, Blank (1992) shows that nominal prices of a sample of commodities have been variable in recent decades. Hyde, Zilberman, and Chalfant (1994) show that recent prices are just as variable from year to year—that is, risky—as they were decades ago, despite efforts to manage risks. Bankers have noticed the risk in agriculture, relative to other industries, and they remain concerned about these risks relative to the lower rates of return available in agriculture compared to alternative investments (Setala 1998). As Blank (1992) showed, the combination of volatile prices and low average profit margins gives agriculture higher probabilities for losses.

Local costs are rising across the United States as competition for resources expands with alternate uses. Land prices increase with capitalized investments and with pressures from nonagricultural uses such as urban sprawl and environmental programs, especially on the east and west coasts (USDA 2000a). For example, in 1988, the average nominal price for an acre of farmland in the United States was $632. In 1998 that price had increased to $974. By 2006 it was $1,900.[1] Labor prices are being pushed up in the competition with nonagricultural opportunities that are increasingly available to workers. Other input prices also continue to increase.

Production costs per unit of output are also influenced by productivity. The situation faced by Montana wheat farmers is a good example of how U.S. production costs have risen faster than yields, resulting in higher costs per unit of output. Egan (2001) describes how growers in eastern Montana lose money on all wheat produced, but they continue farming because of the government assistance they receive. In less-developed countries, agricultural productivity gains have been relatively higher than those in the United States over the last forty years. Duffy (2001, pp. 344–45) points out, "while the U.S. has out-paced the average of the other industrialized countries in increasing its production, the greatest gains have occurred in the developing nations." She reports Laspeyers indices for the 1961–2000 period of 2.0 for the United States, 1.6 for other more-developed countries, and 3.5 for less-developed countries, meaning costs per unit have dropped faster in newly competitive nations, and this trend is expected to continue. Thus, for a growing list of agricultural commodities, the United States is no longer a low-cost supplier.

In general, two indices illustrate the problem in American agriculture. From 1990 to 2000, the U.S. Department of Agriculture's (USDA 2004) index of prices received by agricultural producers for their output decreased 7 percent. That means nominal (i.e., not adjusted for inflation) prices received by producers when selling their commodities actually *declined* during the decade, on average. Over the same period, the USDA's index of prices paid for inputs by agricultural producers increased 19 percent. That index indicates a large increase in the average level of production costs faced by farmers and ranchers. So, if your prices are flat or declining (without adjusting for inflation), but your costs are continually rising, therein lies the profit squeeze.

DEALING WITH THE SQUEEZE

Total production income at the farm level is low and not significantly improving in American agriculture. Recent levels of total annual income earned from American agricultural production are shown in nominal terms in Table 6.1. The net farm income totals reported by the USDA are one of the most commonly reported measures of absolute profitability. However, they are overstated. Among other things, those totals include direct government payments to agriculture, which have been at record levels in recent years (USDA 2001). In Table 6.1 (which is Table 1.1 duplicated here for readers' convenience), direct government payments are subtracted from the net

Table 6.1

U.S. Agricultural Nominal Sales and Income, 1996–2003 ($ billion)

	1996	1997	1998	1999	2000	2001	2002	2003
Crop receipts	115.6	112.4	101.7	92.0	92.5	93.4	101.3	106.2
Livestock receipts	92.0	96.5	94.1	95.6	99.6	106.7	93.8	105.5
Total sales	207.6	208.9	195.8	187.6	192.1	200.1	195.1	211.6
Net farm income	54.9	48.6	42.9	46.8	47.9	50.6	37.3	59.2
Direct government payments	7.3	7.5	12.4	21.5	22.9	20.7	11.0	15.9
Adjusted production income*	47.6	41.1	30.5	25.3	25.0	29.9	26.3	43.3

Source: USDA (2000b and 2004).
Note: *This is calculated as net farm income minus direct government payments.

farm income totals to get "adjusted production income." The result shows that the decline in profits from production activities is much more significant than indicated in reported figures. Without government subsidies it is clear that the profits earned from agricultural markets are low and volatile, ranging from $47.6 billion in 1996 to $25.0 billion in 2000. Both the low level and the volatility of total profits are arguments used by many in agriculture to justify their strategy of dealing with the sector's profit squeeze by continually asking for government handouts.

The profit squeeze is apparent in other measures of profitability, not just in total income. Profits in U.S. agriculture, as measured by return on assets or return on equity, have been low and declining for decades, as shown in the chapters of Part I. Over the last thirty years, agriculture's gross profit margin has been in the 2–3 percent range, on average (Bjornson and Innes 1992). That is relatively low—most people can do better taking their money to a bank. Once again, therein lies more of the pressure.

At this point, profits from production agriculture alone cannot support most farmers. In response to this profit squeeze, American agricultural producers have long been diversifying into value-added activities and out of agriculture (Blank 2001). Thus, it should not be surprising that the scale of off-farm investments (such as shifting some family labor to nonagricultural pursuits) has steadily increased such that, on average, over 90 percent of farm operator households' income came from off-farm sources over the past decade (USDA 2000b, 2004). For example, in 2002, American farm operator households earned an average of only $3,473 from farming activities, but they earned another $62,285 from off-farm sources. That means the average farm household's total income was $65,757—13.7 percent *above* the U.S. average household income for that year.

Efforts to improve the profit margin for commodities focus both on prices and costs. Strategies that have been successful in raising prices range from adding value to a commodity (through processing, etc.) to using strategic alliances or integration of producers and processors, such as participating in a cooperative. Unfortunately, these and most other price-improving strategies are not often available to most commodity producers. Therefore, farmers and ranchers have focused mostly on strategies to lower costs.

Two general cost strategies have been most successful: (1) reducing cost per unit by increasing the scale of operations, and (2) reducing cost per unit with technological advances in production and/or harvest methods and machines, as well as developments that raise yields. The first strategy is most readily available to producers, so it is used nationally, as indicated by the steadily increasing average size of farms (Table 6.2). The second strategy has been the most successful—technological advances have kept American producers competitive, on average, with other commodity suppliers by greatly expanding yields and reducing costs per unit (e.g., Thompson and Blank 2000). When technological advances occur, early adopters reap the greatest advantages, but those advantages erode over time as other producers adopt the technology and catch up. Thus, U.S. agriculture needs a continual flow of new innovations to remain competitive in global markets (Tweeten 1999). This will require continual investment in research-and-development (R&D) activities related to agricultural products. The United States has made those investments in the past, but Roe and Mohtadi (2001) warn that the recent shift in R&D focus from commodities to value-added products puts some American commodity industries at risk. Finally, the second strategy feeds the first because technological advantages have often come with high price tags (for mechanical harvesters, etc.) that add incentive for producers to expand farm size to fully capture the economies of size in the new technology. Both of these cost strategies have helped to slow the cost squeeze, but they are unable to reverse it permanently. These topics are discussed at length in the next chapter.

LOCAL DECISIONS

Faced with a falling world price ceiling and a steadily rising cost floor, individual American farmers and ranchers are being squeezed out of one commodity after another. When one product becomes unprofitable or simply less attractive relative to alternative investments, producers are forced to look for another crop or livestock enterprise that offers better returns. As a result, low-revenue crops are often being replaced by higher-revenue crops. This process can continue only as long as the local climate and productive resources are suitable for the production of a higher-value commodity.

The aggregate result of these individual decisions is that U.S. agriculture is moving up the "farming food chain" (a detailed explanation of the individual decision process is presented in Chapter 11). There are four general categories of crops in the "chain" and movement from one category to another is virtually always in the upward direction, meaning from lower to higher value crops. At the bottom of the chain are low-value annual crops, like grains, which require relatively low investments per acre and which involve assets that can be shifted into the production of another crop very easily. The second stage of land development involves low-value perennial crops, like alfalfa and other irrigated forages. These crops have a normal economic life of more than one year and require somewhat higher investments per acre, but they involve fairly flexible assets. The third stage requires relatively high investments in inflexible assets to produce high-value annual crops like lettuce and fresh tomatoes. Finally, high-value perennial crops such as tree and vine products lock growers into the highest and least-flexible investments.

High-value perennial crops certainly generate more revenue per acre than low-value annual crops, but there are drawbacks to moving to higher returning crops. First, more money per acre must be invested for longer time periods for higher value crops. For example, it is common for tree or vine crop producers in California to invest $10,000 to $30,000 per acre in improvements to land. Second, that investment goes into assets that are much less flexible than those used for lower-value crops. Thus, higher returning crops are much more risky.

In a particular geographic area, climate and/or agronomic constraints may limit the feasibility of growing some crops. Specifically, growing crops in categories 3 and 4 may not be feasible in

Table 6.2

Census of Agriculture Trends

	1959	1964	1969	1974	1978	1982	1987	1992	1997
Land in farms (million acres)	1,123.5	1,110.2	1,062.9	1,017.0	1,014.8	986.8	964.5	945.5	931.8
Farms (1,000s)	3,710.5	3,157.9	2,730.3	2,314.0	2,257.8	2,241.0	2,087.8	1,925.3	1,911.9
Farms of 1,000 acres or more (number)	136,427	145,292	150,946	154,937	161,101	161,972	168,864	172,912	176,080
Average farm size (acres/farm)	303	352	389	439	449	440	462	491	487
Total real sales ($b, base year = 2000)	206.8	207.4	230.0	321.2	305.0	253.9	212.6	216.1	224.0
Average real sales per farm ($/farm)	55,734	65,677	84,240	138,807	135,087	113,298	101,830	112,242	117,161
Vegetable acreage (million acres)	3.491	3.334	3.352	3.124	3.534	3.331	3.468	3.782	3.773
Orchard acreage (million acres)	4.120	4.251	4.234	4.190	4.464	4.751	4.560	4.771	5.158

Sources: USDA 1998 and earlier censuses. Data from the 2002 Census are not comparable to earlier Census data and, therefore, are not included here. New census methods and definitions have altered the data, but not the trends; farm numbers and land in farms continue to decline.

some locations. In such cases, land moving up the truncated farming food chain of that area will have to leave agriculture to attain the higher level of returns that would normally be available from higher-category crops. Therefore, the number of crop categories available in a geographic area is determined by climate/agronomic conditions and land can leave agriculture from any available category, but it must leave agriculture if it is to generate returns above those of the highest-returning crop available.

Table 6.2 documents America's climb up the farming food chain. Nationwide, acreage of vegetable crop production increased 8 percent between 1959 and 1997 despite the 17 percent decrease in total acreage in agriculture. More impressive, there was a 25 percent increase in orchard crop acreage between 1959 and 1997.[2]

Unfortunately, the nature of tree crop production and markets can cause growers' efforts to backfire. For example, because of the lag between planting and production in tree and vine crops, you often see the problem observed in the California almond industry around the turn of this century. Almonds were very profitable during the 1990s, attracting growers and leading to significant increases in acres planted. In 1999 and 2000, as that new production hit the market, there was not sufficient demand to absorb the record output; hence, market prices for almonds dropped so low that total almond revenue actually *decreased* both years. The result was that new and previously existing acreages were not generating the expected levels of profits, but growers could not afford to pull out productive trees. Thus, the industry was forced to aggressively pursue increased demand to absorb the higher supplies being produced. Their efforts targeted both export and domestic customers. With a falling dollar, relative to other currencies, and a focus on health attributes of the product, the almond industry succeeded beyond its own expectations: between 2001 and 2004 the average price received by farmers increased each year, raising profits in the process (Cline 2004). Sadly, this story is rare in commodity markets around the country. Almonds are a specialty crop with most output coming from central California. That concentrated industry with well-developed marketing organizations was able to differentiate itself sufficiently to have control over its selling price. Most of American agriculture is still in a situation of being a price-taker among numerous competitors, leading to continued pressure on profitability.

For individual farmers and ranchers, profitability pressure creates the *need* to take on more risk (Blank 2001), while government policy creates the *willingness* to take on more risk (Skees 1998). Farmers are moving up the farming food chain and counting on Uncle Sam to be there if disaster strikes. So, the profit squeeze is pushing producers to change the composition of their crop "portfolio" (where possible) by putting a larger share of their land into production of crops that are more risky. This raises their financial needs and their risk exposure.

Eventually, farmers and ranchers are *choosing* to leave agriculture out of personal economic necessity—it is an investment decision based on their new risk-reward tradeoff. The fact that "good" producers are leaving agriculture surprises people because of the following assumption mistakenly believed by many in agriculture: "the most efficient producer will be the last to disappear." That assumption is not true! Being efficient is not sufficient for survival as a farmer or rancher. Consider these three conditions:

1. Being *profitable* is necessary, but not sufficient for survival.
2. Being profitable and able to match or underprice all direct competitors are necessary, but not sufficient for survival in the long-run.
3. Conditions 1 and 2 above, plus a willingness to accept agriculture's low returns on investments, are sufficient conditions for long-run survival.

To illustrate the point, consider the case of a farmer in central Washington State. He might want to grow wheat, just like most farmers in the region did during the decades before the large-scale irrigation projects were built. However, the costs of the irrigation systems and other improvements to land have helped push up his land costs such that he cannot make a profit in wheat despite the high yields that could be produced. He is forced to grow high-value annuals or perennials, like apples, to generate enough revenue to have a reasonable chance of being adequately profitable in the long run. The producer must choose between those risky crops and the nonagricultural investment opportunities available to him. In many parts of America's East and West, urban sprawl is pushing land values up to levels that cannot be matched by any agricultural product. Thus, a farmer may *want* to stay in agriculture, and may choose to hang on as long as he can make some profit in tree and vine crops, but eventually he has to think of his family's wealth. At that point, the best investment of his land and other assets could be outside of agriculture. Therefore, the most efficient producers are not necessarily the last to disappear because those farmers may be quick to find better alternative income sources.

WHY IS AMERICAN AGRICULTURE BEING SQUEEZED?

Ironically, the higher level of development of the United States, compared to its new, less-developed competitors in global commodity markets, is responsible for much of the profit squeeze. U.S. production inputs—land, labor, and so forth—are higher priced than resources in less-developed countries (Antle 1999). The resulting absolute cost advantage of less-developed countries, many of which adopted American technologies (Griffin 1999, pp. 100–131), enables them to underprice American agricultural commodities. In those circumstances, the world's consumers buy commodities from other nations' producers rather than from American farmers and ranchers when they have a choice. Since prices offered by the global market to American farmers are the same as those offered to farmers in less-developed nations, the larger profit margin earned by America's competitors makes them economically stronger over time.

The same economic analysis used to explain international trade explains the patterns of production and trade between regions within the United States over time. For example, Iowa was the sixth largest apple and grape producing state in the 1920s, but it and the other midwestern states are now dominated by the production of grain crops and grain-eating livestock. The change was brought about by technological changes that altered the absolute advantage of those Iowa apple and grape growers. To begin, perishable commodities like apples could not be transported very far during the 1920s because storage and transportation technology was far less effective and more expensive than it is now, so Iowa and other states in the region had to be self-sufficient in those markets. If apples were not grown in the area, consumers would have to go without apples because it was not possible to import them from other apple-producing regions, like Virginia, New York, and Washington. Thus, farmers in Iowa who had a regional comparative advantage in growing apples were the sole source for the local market. However, as technological changes made it possible to ship apples, grapes, and other perishable commodities to Iowa from the East and West Coast regions, absolute cost became relevant. Soon, demand for apples in Iowa and the surrounding region could be met entirely by supplies from outside the region. Midwestern consumers chose to buy the cheaper apples imported from the coasts because the imports were virtually identical to (i.e., undifferentiated from) the local produce. Iowa farmers were forced to shift out of the high-value crops that were not well suited to the midwestern climate and into production of the next-best commodities for which they had a comparative advantage: grains and grain-eating livestock.

The ultimate expansion of cereal production into the semiarid lands of the Great Plains was dictated by least comparative disadvantage. These lands are far less productive in wheat than the fertile and well-watered areas to the east, but cereals are one of the few alternative uses for the dry lands and their production is made economical by an appropriate evaluation of the basic land resource. (Bressler and King 1970, p. 350)

For decades the Midwest had an absolute advantage in the market for grains, so those were profitable industries. In recent decades, however, technology changes have enabled foreign competitors to expand output, pushing global market prices for those commodities down to levels that are often not profitable for midwestern producers. One result is that farmland values in Iowa, Texas, and other states in the Great Plains are lower now in real (and sometimes nominal) terms than they were two decades ago (USDA 2000a). However, this factor price decline is not enough to save much of the domestic industry in the long run.

THE BOTTOM BOTTOM LINE

In general, it appears that if markets are allowed to work and individual and global investment decisions are made without government intervention, production agriculture in the United States will continue its gradual contraction. This trend reflects a normal reaction to an ongoing profit squeeze in agriculture—a result of the increased level of competition in commodity markets. Improvements in production, storage, and transportation technologies have shifted the nature of competition facing U.S. producers from being local to global in scale. That change, in turn, makes U.S. commodity markets closer to being "perfectly competitive." So it should not be surprising that actual profits are approaching the level predicted by economic theory for a perfectly competitive market: zero. It is unfortunate for agriculture that this is occurring simultaneously with other changes in this country. An increasingly urban America has tired of subsidizing farmers and ranchers. Agriculture is losing its appeal as an investment for the nation.

The difficulty American agriculture has in fighting these trends has this bottom line: *everything that is happening in this development of a global market is good for U.S. agribusiness firms and American consumers.* The fact that now both domestic and international producers are willing to provide the United States with products at the same or lower prices means that Americans are eating better and prices are not going up. Politicians do not want to change that. As a result, in the 1990s U.S. farm policy shifted away from agriculture (Bonnen and Schweikhardt 1998). The 1997 farm bill, the "Freedom to Farm Act," clearly signaled that the U.S. government intended to get out of the agriculture business, which, ironically, is what commercial agriculture has been requesting for decades. Farmers have said "let supply and demand set prices, not government policies," and that is what is slowly happening. What that policy meant was that U.S. producers were less protected from the competition of global producers. Unfortunately, there are fewer than 2 million American producers, and in the long run they cannot win any political battles against the 300 million American consumers of the cheap food being provided by the global market.

In 2002 the free-market farm policy was reversed by Congress's reluctance to get out of agriculture "when times are bad." Natural disasters, such as floods and droughts, combine with falling prices to cause economic harm to some regions of the country each year, and Congress responded with huge aid packages. However, the recent high levels of farm aid are not politically or economically sustainable. Now that alternate sources of commodities are increasingly available, Congress must eventually look for a "good time" to wean American agriculture from government aid. The United States needs to continue shifting resources out of agriculture and into new, more profitable industries for us to continue climbing the economic food chain.

None of the trends mentioned in this chapter is likely to diminish in the future. Profits will remain relatively low in agriculture. Thus, U.S. policies aimed at preventing land and other resources from shifting out of American agriculture and into other industries will prove unsustainable in the long run because they create deadweight losses to the U.S. economy.

The discussions in this and the previous chapter explain that a country might *want* to leave agriculture when it becomes a poor investment decision to continue tying up resources in commodity production. American agriculture is still profitable in general; however, the fact that an enterprise or economic sector is making *some* profit does not make it a good investment. Over the last forty years, producers' reluctance to exit, despite agriculture's low gross profit margin, may have already created a deadweight loss to the economy. Much of the labor, capital, and management resources remaining in U.S. agriculture are there by choice, but might be better invested elsewhere.[3] The low average profit margins in production agriculture will not get better. Agriculture is often described as a close approximation to the theoretical market construct called a "perfectly competitive" industry. Microeconomic theory says that in the long run the average profit margin for such an industry will be zero. Thus, the profit squeeze described in this chapter will never end for American producers specializing in undifferentiated commodities. It is a race being run on a treadmill.

NOTES

Some of this chapter is a revised version of an article published by S. Blank as "A Portfolio of Threats to American Agriculture," *Contemporary Economic Policy* 20, no. 4 (2002): 381–393.

1. It is worth remembering that farmland prices are pushed up, in part, due to expectations of income earning potential that are occasionally shown to be overly optimistic. For example, in the mid-1980s farmland prices fell 50–60 percent in some regions. The USDA (2000a, p. 30) reported that after 14 years, "most regions have regained all that they lost during the 1980's," but the Northern and Southern Plains still have nominal land prices below those observed in the early 1980s.

2. Some might argue that the increase in vegetable and orchard acreage is due simply to expanding demand for fruits and vegetables in the diet. However, that argument is inconsistent with the decrease in total acreage in farms. Clearly, expanding demand contributes to the relative profitability of fruit and vegetable crops, but that only partially helps to explain why some acreage is shifted from low-value crops to the higher-value crops (a "substitution effect"); it does not explain why acreage is taken out of agriculture. The *absolute* (low or negative) level of profitability of low-value crops also forces some acreage to shift into higher-value crop production or, if that shift is not possible or desirable, to shift out of agriculture (an "income effect").

3. Governmental intervention that causes profits to be higher than they otherwise would be might be a source of deadweight loss, but interventions can be viewed as an investment decision being made by the U.S. government.

REFERENCES

Antle, John M. 1999. "The New Economics of Agriculture." *American Journal of Agricultural Economics* 81: 993–1010.

Bjornson, B., and R. Innes. 1992. "Another Look at Returns to Agricultural and Nonagricultural Assets." *American Journal of Agricultural Economics* 74: 109–119.

Blank, Steven C. 1992. "Income Risk Varies with What You Grow, Where You Grow It." *California Agriculture* 46 (5): 14–16.

———. 1998. *The End of Agriculture in the American Portfolio.* Westport, CT: Quorum.

———. 2001. "Producers Get Squeezed Up the Farming Food Chain: A Theory of Crop Portfolio Composition and Land Use." *Review of Agricultural Economics* 23 (2): 404–422.

Bonnen, J., and D. Schweikhardt. 1998. "The Future of U.S. Agricultural Policy: Reflections on the Disappearance of the 'Farm Problem.' " *Review of Agricultural Economics* 20: 2–36.

Bressler, R., Jr., and R. King. 1970. *Markets, Prices, and Interregional Trade.* New York: John Wiley & Sons.

Cline, Harry. 2004. "Almonds Defy Ag Economics." *Western Farm Press* 26 (November): 1, 6–7, 9.

Duffy, Patricia A. 2001. "Casting Bread upon the Water: Comments on Technology, Globalization, and Agriculture." *Journal of Agricultural & Applied Economics* 33 (2): 341–347.

Egan, Timothy. 2001. "Failing in Style." *Choices* 16 (2001): 39–42.

Griffin, Keith. 1999. *Alternative Strategies for Economic Development.* 2d ed. New York: St. Martin's.

Hyde, C., D. Zilberman, and J. Chalfant. 1994. "Agricultural Risk: Definition, Assessment, and Management." In *Financing Agriculture in California's New Risk Environment,* ed. S. Blank, pp. 179–210. Davis, CA: Agricultural Issues Center, University of California.

Roe, T., and H. Mohtadi. 2001. "International Trade and Growth: An Overview Using the New Growth Theory." *Review of Agricultural Economics* 23 (2): 423–440.

Setala, J. 1998. "The Future of Ag Lending." *AgriFinance* 2 (2): 1, 6–10.

Skees, J. 1998. "Consequences of Possible Responses to Current Farm Problems." Testimony of Dr. Jerry R. Skees, University of Kentucky, Before the Committee on Agriculture, U.S. House of Representatives, July 30.

Thompson, J., and S. Blank. 2000. "Harvest Mechanization Helps California Agriculture Remain Competitive." *California Agriculture* 54 (3): 51–56.

Tweeten, Luther. 1999. "The Economics of Global Food Security." *Review of Agricultural Economics* 21: 473–488.

U.S. Department of Agriculture (USDA). 1998. *1997 Census of Agriculture.* Washington, DC: National Agricultural Statistics Service.

———. 2000a. "Accumulated Farm Real Estate Value Will Help Farmers and Their Lenders Through Period of Declining Cash Receipts." *Agricultural Income and Finance: Situation and Outlook,* pp. 30–33. Economic Research Service, AIS-74, February.

———. 2000b. "Off-Farm Income Supports Many Farm Households." *Agricultural Income and Finance: Situation and Outlook Report,* pp. 37–39. Resource Economics Division, Economic Research Service, AIS-74, February.

———. 2000c. "With Low Commodity Prices, Government Payments Support Farm Income." *Agricultural Income and Finance: Situation and Outlook Report,* pp. 4–13. Resource Economics Division, Economic Research Service, AIS-75, September.

———. 2001. "Lenders Benefit from the Farm Sector's Receipt of Government Payments." *Agricultural Income and Finance: Situation and Outlook Report,* pp. 5–6. Resource Economics Division, Economic Research Service, AIS-76, February.

———. 2004. "Farm Income and Costs: Farm Income Forecasts." Economic Research Service "Briefing Room," www.ers.usda.gov/Briefing/FarmIncome/fore.htm.

CHAPTER 7

TECHNOLOGY AS CATALYST
AND TREADMILL

"I have not failed. I've simply found 10,000 ways that do not work."
—Thomas Edison

Economists have paid surprisingly little attention to the linkages between the "globalization" of agricultural markets occurring over recent decades and the decisions being made by individual farmers and ranchers in the United States. The two topics have been treated separately in the literature as if there was no linkage between them. Much research has focused on the policy implications of emerging global markets (e.g., Johnson and Martin 1993; Tweeten 1999) while another body of literature has taken the existence of global or world markets as a given and analyzed their operations (e.g., Diakosavvas 1995; Lee and Cramer 1985; Paarlberg and Abbott 1986). Farm-level decision making in the Usnited States has also been the focus of a large body of research, but the portion of that work relevant to this chapter has centered on the "overproduction trap" facing farmers and has dealt with export markets only as a residual outlet for surpluses (e.g., Johnson and Quance 1972). The literature coming closest to directly addressing the linkages includes more recent efforts focusing either on the structure of world resources, markets, and trade (e.g., Coyle et al. 1998; Douglass 1984), or on the "technology treadmill" (e.g., Gallup and Sachs 2000; Levins 2000; Smith 1992). These two topics are part of the story, but more discussion of the direct links between them is needed to understand the profit squeeze described in the previous chapter. Therefore, the objective of this chapter is to contribute to that discussion because the topic will be of increasing importance as global markets become the norm for agricultural commodities.

The central driving force in the linkages is technology. As this chapter hopes to illustrate, technological advances are critical to the survival of American agriculture, and the future holds a continuous battle for farmers and ranchers in this country as they seek those advances. Technology is a two-edged sword for agricultural producers. It is both a catalyst for positive change and a treadmill that prevents them from getting very far ahead in the battle with the profit squeeze.

The story of technology as a catalyst, in brief, involves the linkages that connect technology and profits for commodity producers. To begin, technological advances change (improve) productivity. In other words, improved machines and management methods lead to improvements in output per unit of input, which is a measure of productivity. Such productivity improvements lower production costs per unit of output, which makes the producer more competitive with other suppliers of the product. As Krugman notes with regard to global markets, "our 'competitive' problem is really a domestic productivity problem pure and simple" (1998, p. 16). Finally, competitiveness leads to profits. Thus, technology is a catalyst to generating profits. All of these points will be discussed in this chapter.

Unfortunately, that is not the end of the story. Technology is also a "treadmill" that keeps American commodity producers running for their lives. The agricultural treadmill concept, developed decades ago by Willard Cochrane (1958), describes why technological developments must be sought on a continuous basis to have any chance of remaining competitive. This too will be discussed in this chapter.

TECHNOLOGY IS THE CATALYST

Technological advances make globalization of commodity markets possible. Over time, technological advances make global trade of a product physically possible, economically viable, and then a routine market occurrence. To begin, it is advances in production that create the *need* for global markets. New production methods expand output in a local market by enabling new producers to enter the market and by enabling existing producers to increase their production volume. When surpluses start to occur in the local market, more distant market outlets must be sought if producers are to benefit from their increased output (Bressler and King 1970).

Technology related to storage and transportation is key to expanding the geographic size of commodity markets. Storing an agricultural commodity slows the spoilage process. Improvements in storage methods and machines give market participants even more time before their products perish. Having more time with which to work means that more distance can be covered before spoilage occurs, thus, suppliers of a commodity can reach more places and people. Technical advances in transportation expand the distance that can be covered per unit of time or per dollar of cost. In sum, this means that a market's physical boundaries are potentially expanded by technological advances in storage or transport. To realize a potential market expansion, new technology must be adopted. In today's world, technology can be bought and/or copied, thus it spreads quickly, eventually even to poorer nations (Gallup and Sachs 2000). The rapid spread of technology enables producers to "catch up" with leading competitors over time (Ball, Hallahan, and Nehring 2004).

In summary, a global market is created when it is physically possible and economically feasible for producers to sell their output to buyers in locations across international boundaries. For many agricultural commodities, improved production technology has increased the number of (possible) producers while storage and transportation technology expands the geographic reach of each seller, thus more direct and indirect competition between suppliers occurs as time passes.

Technological advances also make American commodity production possible in this era of global markets. Individual firms, and sometimes entire commodity-based industries, must seek ways to improve their profitability in order to survive in today's markets, as described in the previous chapter. The ongoing profit squeeze brought on by the globalization of commodity market prices puts a premium on the ability to reduce local production costs per unit (Booth 1991). As noted in the previous chapter, two general methods have evolved as the most successful in accomplishing the goal of reducing costs: (1) reducing cost per unit by increasing the scale of operations, and (2) reducing cost per unit with technological advances in production and/or harvest methods and machines, as well as developments that raise yields. The second method involves two categories of technical innovations. The first covers innovations that lead to improved ways to accomplish a specific task. For example, this category of innovation includes ways to produce or harvest a fixed amount of output with a lower total of inputs. The second category includes innovations that lead to higher output totals being produced with a fixed amount of inputs, such as raising yield per acre. In sum, if agricultural producers are able to use either of these strategies to lower their cost per unit of output, the technology involved has improved those producers' chances of being profitable and, therefore, surviving in the competitive market they face.

Two case studies are used below to illustrate how technical innovations have been a catalyst to improve the productivity of two commodity industries over time. The innovations are part of the first category—technical advances that lead to improved ways to accomplish a specific task. The far-reaching effects of the innovations are described as covering long periods of time and having major impacts on the competitiveness and profitability of firms in the industries, such as the ability to expand the scale of operations. These cases are typical of many commodity stories across the United States during the past century.

HARVEST MECHANIZATION HELPS AGRICULTURE REMAIN COMPETITIVE

In the decades since 1940, producers of agricultural commodities have had an increasingly difficult time remaining profitable in those competitive markets. The business strategies available to them were limited to those aimed at raising profits by lowering costs per unit and by increasing the total units of output. American farmers' ability to increase total output has also been impacted by periods, such as World War II and the end of the Bracero Program, in which available farm labor was limited.[1] In the current era of global competition and the resulting squeeze on profit margins, America's farmers need to take advantage of every technological development available to them. Mechanization, in economic terms, involves adopting technical innovations that facilitate substituting capital for labor. Harvesting is one area where technological advances have had significant impact on producers' ability to increase output while lowering costs per unit. Specifically, mechanizing the harvest process greatly improved American farmers' competitive position in agricultural markets over the last half of the twentieth century.

Harvest mechanization offered farmers at least three benefits in their struggle to maintain profitability: it (1) reduced costs per unit, (2) contributed to the ability to expand total production volumes, and (3) provided a cost-effective replacement for manual labor. The net effect of these and other advantages of mechanized harvesting is that profit levels have been maintained such that the United States remains an important supplier in the global market for many agricultural commodities despite increasing competition from foreign producers.

The three benefits of harvest mechanization are illustrated in two case studies from California agriculture. Developments in tomato and rice harvesting technology show the scale of effects that mechanization can have on improving profit margins by both reducing costs per unit and facilitating expanded production. The history of mechanization also provides insight on its effects on labor requirements per ton, total labor use, and the time and variety of technologies needed in the process. The use of mechanization to improve labor productivity was fostered by the adaptation of the internal combustion engine to agricultural operations. Applications began around the turn of the twentieth century, and agriculture is still developing new systems after one hundred years. The mechanization process appears to be slow, involving a great deal of technological development. However, the net effects of mechanization continue to be positive for agriculture. These case studies are relevant to all farmers because other field, fruit, and vegetable crops face similar profit pressures and may have similar levels of potential benefits from technological innovations in the future.

Tomato Harvest

In the late 1940s, the processing tomato industry was concerned that its increasing tomato production could not be harvested with expected shortfalls in farm labor supply. In 1950, Coby

Lorenzen and Jack Hanna of the University of California, Davis, began work to develop a system for mechanically harvesting processing tomatoes. Hanna began development of a tomato that could withstand the stress of mechanical handling, would ripen at one time, and would release from the plant during machine harvest. By 1960 the university was issued a patent for the new tomato and, in conjunction with a local equipment manufacturer, developed a machine that could successfully remove the fruit from the plant. The machine cut the plant at soil level and lifted it to a shaking mechanism that separated the fruit from the vine. The fruit was then sorted by a dozen people to remove green or blemished tomatoes and dirt clods. The harvested product was loaded directly into pallet bins that were transported on a trailer pulled beside the harvester. Commercial use of the new tomato variety as well as the harvester began in 1962. With the end of the Bracero Program in 1964 and the resulting reduced labor supplies, the following harvest season saw 262 harvesters in commercial use, harvesting 25 percent of the state's total crop. Four years later, 95 percent of the processing tomato crop was harvested by machine.

The harvester originally had a labor requirement of 2.9 hours per ton of tomatoes compared with 5.3 hours per ton for hand harvest. These values, and the others presented in the line sloping downward to the right in Figure 7.1 (using the scale on the left axis), were calculated from labor use data reported in a series of production cost studies published over the period by University of California Cooperative Extension Farm Advisors in Yolo County, a major processing tomato production area. As shown by the downward-sloping line with circles, labor hours per ton harvested continued to decline as improvements were made to the harvester over time. Those improvements are described below.

Manual harvesting had been done mainly by men because of the hot, dusty environment and the strength required to carry 50-pound field boxes. Conversely, much of the labor in machine harvest methods involved sorting fruit on the machine, a job that could attract women workers. That immediately expanded the potential labor pool. Also, the machine could operate well at night, allowing two shifts per day versus the single shift available when hand harvesting.

Labor use per ton harvested gradually declined over time as the machinery was developed further and tomato growing was adapted to machine harvest. Growers learned better weed control techniques and improved field preparation and irrigation techniques. Breeders continued to develop tomato varieties better suited to mechanization. Equipment companies improved the reliability of the equipment and reduced time lost to unexpected in-field repairs (Johnson 1999). Some growers began using a night harvest shift. New higher-yielding varieties and better cultural practices also increased yields from 20 tons per acre to 26 tons per acre by 1977. By the mid-1970s, a machine could harvest 220 acres in a season with average labor needs of 1.6 hours per ton. However, the harvesters still used a considerable total amount of labor, each with as many as 20 sorters and a driver.

The next major advancement was an electronic sorter that could automatically remove green fruit. In 1976, 25 percent of the harvesters were equipped with the new sorter and the hand sorting crew was reduced to about 6 people to pick out dirt and moldy fruit. Total labor required for harvest dropped to 1.0 hours per ton. Since then improvements in harvester reliability (particularly because of the brush shaker developed by Henry Studer at UC Davis) and yield increases to 33 tons per acre have reduced labor requirements by another 60 percent to just 0.4 hours per ton. One machine can now harvest about 800 acres in a season.

In 35 years, harvest labor requirements per ton for processing tomatoes dropped by 92 percent. This efficiency was at least partially responsible for the expansion of processing tomato production in California. Total output increased from about 2.5 million tons per year in the early 1960s to over 10 million tons per year by 1997 (the line slopping upward to the right in Figure 7.1

Figure 7.1   **Typical Harvest Labor Use and Annual Production of Processing Tomatoes in California, 1960–1997**

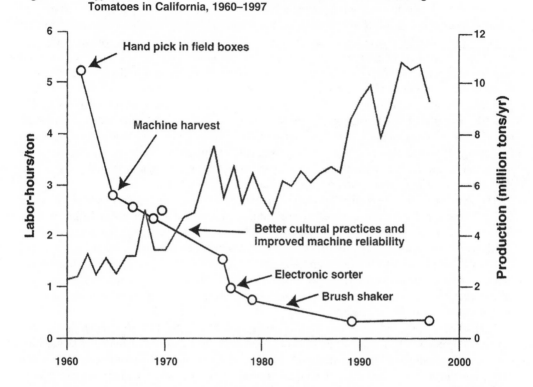

using the scale on the right axis). California produced 94 percent of the processed tomato crop in the United States and 37 percent of total world output in 1997. Exports of California processed tomato products were valued at $226 million and were the state's seventh largest export commodity. Total labor use for the crop dropped from 13.5 million hours in the hand harvest years to about 3.8 million hours per year in 1997.

Hand harvesting of tomatoes was quite costly, accounting for almost 50 percent of total production costs to the grower. Mechanization allowed growers to become more competitive by reducing harvest costs. The first harvester reduced harvest costs to one-third of total costs. After the introduction of the electronic sorter, costs dropped and in 1979 harvest costs were only 16 percent of total costs. Harvest costs have slowly dropped since then, and in 1997, when a new harvester cost nearly $300,000, harvest costs were just 12 percent of the total costs incurred by a typical tomato farmer.

Adoption of harvest machinery fostered the substitution of higher-paying jobs for minimum-wage jobs. The labor productivity improvement allowed farmers to pay workers higher wages. The equipment must be operated by people trained in machine operation and these jobs command more pay in the job market. Processing tomato machinery operators earned 22 percent more than field laborers in 1998—$7.00 versus $5.75 per hour, respectively. Rice harvesting equipment operators earned an additional $1.00 per hour ($8.00 total), making their hourly income 39 percent higher than the minimum wage earned by field workers in many crops and by workers in many nonagricultural jobs.

Rice Harvest

Before 1940, California rice was a labor-intensive operation (Figure 7.2 shows the labor hours per ton harvested, using the scale on the left axis and the downward-sloping line with circles). The plant was cut and tied by machine into 10-inch diameter bundles by a two- or three-man crew. The bundles were stacked in the field in small piles, called shocks, where the grain was allowed to dry, if the weather was suitable. A twenty-man crew then transported the bundles to a central location and separated the grain from the straw with an engine-driven thrasher. The harvested grain was placed in bags for transport, drying, and storage. This harvest method required 4.5 labor-hours per ton of dry rice. This value, and the others presented in Figure 7.2, was calculated from labor use data reported in a series of production cost studies published over the period by the University of California.

During the 1930s, growers began experimental use of harvesters for swathed rice and later began to use combine harvesters. As World War II began, the farm labor supply became tight and burlap bags were in short supply. The rice industry started using a completely mechanized harvest method (Willson 1979). A combine harvester cut the straw and transferred it to a rotating cylinder that detached the grain from the straw. The combine then separated the grain from the straw and chaff. The grain was transferred in bulk to trucks for transport to dryers. The first harvesters were pulled by a track-layer tractor and had a crew of two to four people. With this method, harvest labor requirements dropped to 1.2 hours per ton.

In the 1950s, combines were made self-propelled and only a single operator was needed. Yields also steadily increased from less than 2 tons per acre in the 1940s to 4 tons per acre in 1997, contributing to an increased hourly capacity of combine harvesters. Plant breeders successfully developed earlier maturing varieties, allowing more of the crop to be harvested earlier in the year, when rain and muddy field conditions were less likely to slow the harvest. Manufacturers steadily increased the capacity of machines. In the early 1980s, harvest labor requirements were reduced to 0.40 hours per ton.

In the early 1990s, the stripper header became commercially available. It removed the grain from the straw without cutting the straw. This allowed the separation equipment to operate with greatly increased capacity. In standing grain this device allows a combine to travel two to three times faster than a conventional combine. (A conventional machine is still needed for lodged rice.) By 2000, the average labor requirement for rice harvest was only 0.15 hours per ton.

A 1927 study (Stirniman 1927) indicated that harvest costs ranged from 63 percent to 67 percent of total costs. The early combine harvesters reduced harvest costs to 27 percent of total costs. By the mid-1960s, harvest costs dropped to 18–20 percent of total costs and have remained in that range since then. During this same period, California rice production steadily increased from about 0.2 million tons per year in 1940 to about 2 million tons by 1997 (Figure 7.2).

Assessing the Effects of Harvest Mechanization

Mechanization has reduced harvest cost as a percentage of total costs incurred by farmers and is one of the factors that allowed California farmers to be competitive over the last sixty years. Current harvest costs for processing tomatoes are 75 percent less than they were for hand harvest. The cost of hand harvest was 50 percent of total production costs. The first machine harvesters reduced harvest cost to one-third of total costs, and as machinery and cultural practices improved, harvest costs dropped to the present level of about 12 percent of total costs. Cost savings were

Figure 7.2   **Typical Harvest Labor Use and Annual Production of Rice in California, 1930–1997**

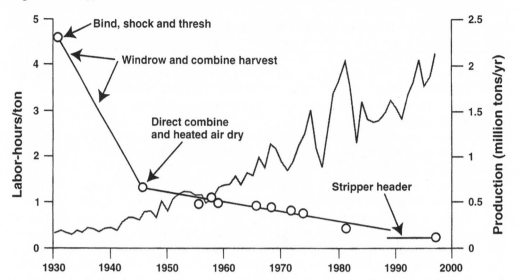

great initially and have only slowly dropped in the past decade. Rice harvest costs have shown the same trends. Hand harvest cost was over 60 percent of total cost and, since 1960, combine harvesting cost has been in the range of 18 percent to 20 percent of total costs.

The value of these cost savings is at least partially responsible for large production increases for both of these crops. In the forty years since tomato harvesters were first used, production has increased by a factor of four. In sixty years of mechanized rice harvest, California production increased tenfold. In the competitive markets for these crops, the expansion in production was possible due partially to the improved profitability created by mechanized harvesting methods.

Harvest mechanization greatly reduces labor-hours per ton of production. Mechanization has reduced labor requirements to 6 percent of that required for hand harvest for processing tomatoes and to only 3 percent for rice. However, total labor needs have not dropped proportionally because of large increases in production. The production increases have also increased employment in tomato and rice processing operations. Mechanization has expanded the worker pool because machine operator jobs are higher paying and less strenuous than hand harvest jobs.

The effect of mechanized harvest has been so significant on these crops that hand harvesting could not be done economically today, nor is it likely that sufficient numbers of workers could be found to accomplish the task in the narrow harvest window. To illustrate this point, the number of additional workers required to hand harvest each crop is estimated. For tomatoes the estimate is: 10 million tons harvested per year needing 5.3 minus 0.4 labor-hours per ton, resulting in 49 million additional labor-hours needed. Dividing by 12-hour per day shifts and dividing again by a 90-day harvest season, gives an estimate of over 45,000 additional workers needed to hand harvest tomatoes. For rice the estimate is: 2 million tons per year times 4.5 minus 0.15 labor-hours per ton is 8.7 million additional labor-hours needed. Dividing by 12-hour per day shifts and dividing again by a 60-day harvest season gives an estimate of over 12,000 workers needed in addition to those working on the crop at present. These estimates of additional workers needed overwhelm the statewide totals for people presently employed in these crops. The California

Employment Development Department (CEDD) reported a total for wage and salary workers in rice production firms of 800–1,800 people (varies by month) for 1996. CEDD (1996) reported only 20,800–40,200 people working in all vegetable and melon production firms within the state in 1996. Thus, hand-harvesting tomatoes would require an *additional* labor force equaling about 112 percent of the current peak total of people working in all vegetable and melon crops. Hand-harvesting rice would require a 667 percent increase in the peak work force for that commodity. Even if farmers could find this huge additional number of workers, they could not pay the $332 million in additional wages that would have been required in 1997 (57.7 million hours times $5.75 per hour) and remain competitive in global markets.

Developing a mechanical harvest system required many years of research and development. The first commercial-scale tomato harvesters were available 12 years after research began. Further machine and plant development over the next 35 years increased machine harvest capacity from 80 to 800 acres per season and reduced labor needs from 2.9 to 0.4 labor-hours per ton. Rice harvester and plant development similarly increased harvester capacity and reduced labor use over a 60-year period.

Mechanized harvest was closely tied to improvements in plant breeding and growing techniques. In fact, mechanical tomato harvesting was probably not possible without these. The old varieties of tomatoes were too delicate for mechanical harvest and did not ripen uniformly enough for a once-over harvest method. New rice varieties allowed greater harvest capacity and fewer problems associated with harvesting in the rain-prone months later in the year.

Mechanization reduces the number of workers needed for a given crop, but the pace of mechanization is usually fairly slow. Even in tomato harvesting (which experienced a fairly rapid transition to mechanical harvest), the industry took seven years to go from the first use of harvesters to 95 percent usage. The Bracero Program ended just as the first commercial harvesters were available, and the reduction in legal migrant worker numbers certainly speeded the adoption of mechanical harvest. The adoption of the combine harvester for rice was similarly stimulated by the onset of World War II and the resulting shortage of labor.

In summary, technology can have significant effects on the profitability, and therefore the competitiveness, of farmers. The two case studies show that the technological and managerial innovations involved in harvest mechanization significantly reduced costs per unit of production compared with hand harvest, and that costs continued to drop after the first introduction of mechanical harvest systems. Lower costs helped growers maintain their competitive advantage and are at least part of the reason that farmers were able to increase total production volume by factors of four to ten over levels achieved during the hand harvest period. Also, the initial introduction of mechanical harvest equipment allowed both crops to be successfully harvested during periods of reduced labor availability. Thus, technology was clearly a catalyst to growth in those agricultural industries.

TECHNOLOGY AS TREADMILL

The concept of technological innovation being a treadmill on which agricultural producers are trapped was developed by Cochrane (1958) half a century ago. Levins and Cochrane (1996, p. 550) summarize the theory as follows.

> The theory was first introduced as a "product price" treadmill in which farmers constantly strive to improve their incomes by adopting new technologies. "Early adopters" make profits for a short while because of their low unit production costs. As more farmers adopt

the technology, however, production goes up, prices go down, and profits are no longer possible even with the lower production costs. Average farmers are nonetheless forced by lower product prices to adopt the technology and lower their production costs if they are to survive at all. The "laggard" farmers who do not adopt new technologies are lost in the price squeeze and leave room for their more successful neighbors to expand.

The theory, as laid out above, makes no mention of the scope of the market involved, but the reference to "neighbors" implies a focus on local markets. That made sense when Cochrane first developed the theory because at that time most commodity markets were local or regional, with only some storable grains being widely traded in international markets. In this new era of global markets for an increasing number of commodities—even highly perishable products—the treadmill concept can be updated to include all markets. That is the goal of the subsections below.

Globalization and Commodity Market Prices

Globalization of markets affects the profitability of commodity production which, in turn, affects the composition of those markets. Recent history has shown that "countries may lose industries in which comparative advantage might have been maintained ... due to changes in comparative advantage and international competition" (Krugman 1998, pp. 98, 101). Significant change in market composition is especially likely for undifferentiated commodities (Liefert 2002). Technological advances can create new industries and substantially change existing industries within a country (Griffith, Redding, and Van Reenen 2004; Jin et al. 2002; Johnson and Evenson 2000; and Luintel and Khan 2004) resulting in changes in the relative profitability and attractiveness of investments in existing industries, such as agriculture. Technological advances have the same effects on international markets as industries in different countries respond to innovations.

Due to technological advances, undifferentiated agricultural commodities can now be produced in greater quantities than the global market can absorb (Antle 1999; Johnson 2000). This means the treadmill is now global in scale, causing global price swings that affect commodity producers everywhere. The effects of technical advances on prices and market composition can be seen using Figure 7.3 (which is Figure 5.4, duplicated here for readers' convenience).

To begin, assume that there is only one country (such as the United States) supplying the market for a commodity with supply curve S_1. The world demand curve, D in the figure, intersects S_1 at point A, resulting in price P_1 being charged for quantity Q_1. As technological advances enable the entry of a new, lower-cost supplier (such as a less-developed country with a supply schedule like the lower portion of S_2), the new total market supply is found by horizontally summing the supply schedules from the two suppliers. The new, increased supply schedule, S_2, has a jump at price P_2^*, the lowest price at which the original supplier is willing to participate in the long run. The intersection of the new supply schedule and the world demand schedule is at point B, resulting in a price drop to P_2 as sales increase to quantity Q_2. Finally, continued adoption of technological advances in less-developed countries enables new suppliers to enter the market, making S_3 the total supply curve and moving the equilibrium to point C, where P_3 is the unit price for quantity Q_3. In this example, the high-cost original supplier may be forced out of the market entirely due to falling prices. In total, this example illustrates how technological advances can increase competition in a commodity market, thus causing (real) prices to fall and less competitive participants to exit.

The market evolution process described above explains why it is absolute advantage, rather than comparative advantage, that is now most relevant to producers of globally traded com-

Figure 7.3 **World Market for an Agriculture Commodity: From One Supplier to Competitive Market**

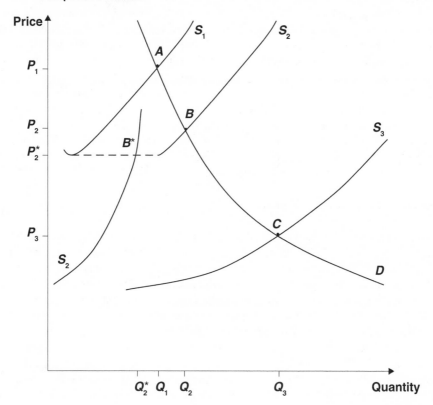

modities. However, this point may be better understood if the story is presented using the more popular term *competitiveness*. Having an absolute advantage in a market makes a firm competitive.

Competitiveness is a concept most economists define using the widely accepted language proposed by the Canadian Task Force on Competitiveness in the Agri-Food Industry: "Competitiveness is the sustained ability to profitably gain and maintain market share" (Agriculture Canada 1991). Clearly, the factors affecting competitiveness are not identical to those affecting comparative advantage. Comparative advantage reflects what products can be produced best (i.e., most efficiently) given the resources available in the location of the firm. Nowhere in the definition of comparative advantage is any mention made of whether the firm makes any profits from the product, nor whether anyone is even willing to buy the product. On the other hand, competitiveness is based entirely on the two questions of profitability and market share.

The basic source of competitiveness is productivity, although several other factors can play a role (Tweeten 1992). Kennedy and Rosson (2002) list domestic agricultural policy, agricultural trade agreements, adding value to products, and technological innovation as issues affecting competitiveness. Nonagricultural domestic policies that affect agriculture, such as environmental regulation, are also relevant to competitiveness (Metcalfe 2002; Rezek and Perrin 2004). Farmers are slow to adopt natural-resource-conserving technologies when profits are not immediately improved (Fuglie and Kascak 2001). Agricultural trade, both domestic and international, has long been linked to productivity (e.g., Gopinath and Kennedy 2000; Dohlman, Osborne, and Lohmar 2003). Also, the link between productivity and comparative advantage is well established (Richardson and Zhang 1999), but it is not sufficient to make a country competitive in a particular market (Ruttan 2002). Competitiveness *is* improved when adding value to a commodity helps differentiate the product from the output of competitors (e.g., Brester 1999). In fact, the ability to add value to a commodity changes the focus of competitive analysis from the commodity to a broader view that also includes downstream processing sectors using the commodity (Hudson and Ethridge 2000). Ultimately, all types of technical innovations affect competitiveness. Thus, competitiveness is influenced by, and analyzed through, the degree of technical efficiency achieved by a firm or industry (Thiam, Bravo-Ureta, and Rivas 2001).

Thus, the story comes back to technology. However, actual decisions are made by individuals managing firms, not by industries or countries. That means the story told thus far must be carried down to the firm level to truly explain the agricultural treadmill.

Technology and Individual Farmers

It has long been understood that individual farmers react to technological advances (Johnson and Quance 1972, pp. 24–25). With the globalization of markets, technological advances affect the profitability of individual crop markets whether or not producers in a local market adopt the new technology. This, in turn, keeps pressure on for (1) new technology to be developed, and (2) changes in cropping choices of individual farmers. Figure 7.4 illustrates these points.

To begin, Panel A in Figure 7.4 shows that there is clearly an incentive for a farmer to adopt some new technology for a single commodity. The farmer's original situation is to produce quantity Q_1 at market price P because that is the profit-maximizing output given the farmer's supply schedule, S_1. When a new technology becomes available, it expands the farmer's productive capacity to S_2, but price P is still available in the short run because the individual farmer's output is not enough to affect prices; the farmer is a price-taker. Therefore, Q_2 is the new profit-maximizing output for that farmer at that time.

Panel B shows the aggregate effect of all production increases from all farmers adopting the new technology for the single commodity. At the global market level, total quantity produced increases from Q_1 to Q_2 over the adoption period and the global market price drops from P_1 to P_2.

Finally, in Panel C is the ultimate effect of a technology advance on an individual farmer, whether or not that farmer adopted the new technology. As shown, demand for that farmer's output, as reflected by the market price being offered to him or her, decreases during the adoption period and settles at some new equilibrium (from D_1 to D_2). Facing a price drop from P_1 to P_2, the farmer must change. In the short run, the change might be to reduce output of the commodity from Q_1 to Q_2. In the long run, the change might be to search for another technological advance that enables his/her production to remain profitable at Q_1. Connecting the short and long run is the need for that farmer to change cropping choices.

Research has shown that technological advances can dramatically lower costs per unit while facilitating large increases in total production volume (e.g., Duffy 2001; Johnson and Quance 1972). However, the key factors in producers' cropping choices are the profitability of the available options (e.g., Isik and Khanna 2003; McBride and El-Osta 2002; Miller and Tolley 1989) and the risks (Ghadim, Pannell, and Burton 2005). Over the last thirty years, falling prices have quickly eliminated much of the increased profit margin created by technological advances in market after market, thus resulting in relatively low and static returns on investments in American agriculture.

Figure 7.4   **Technology's Effect on Individual Farmers**

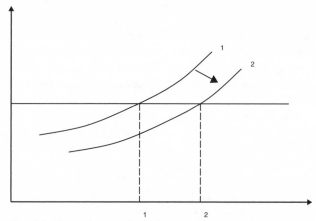

Panel A: Farmer's case: incentive to adopt new technology

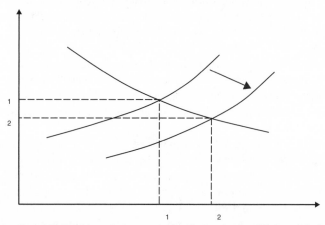

Panel B: World market case: technology adoption lowers global price

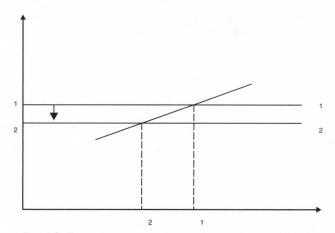

Panel C: Farmer's new case: lower price creates need for change

CONCLUDING COMMENTS: SURFING ON A TSUNAMI

Debertin (2001) asked the question, "are American farmers better off as a result of technological gains?" He looked back over the last half-century and concluded that the answer was "no." That general conclusion indicates that the American production agriculture sector has been able to balance the catalyst and treadmill aspects of technology well enough to survive, but not well enough to make any real economic progress. This result has been masked by the changes in commodity markets as they globalize.

Advances in production technology make market expansion necessary, while advances in storage and transportation technology make market expansion possible. When adoption of a technology becomes economically feasible, market expansion occurs and the profitability of that market is altered. Thus, technological advances are both "industrializing" agriculture and globalizing agricultural commodity markets. The link between these trends is profitability.

All of this is bad news for American farmers and ranchers. Technology adoptions that increase someone's output always make some other groups worse off (Pande 2006). In general, global competition in commodity markets will continue to increase as technology changes the comparative advantages and competitiveness of nations, making agriculture more profitable for less-developed countries and less profitable for more-developed countries. Gradually, the highest-cost suppliers will be forced to leave the markets as falling prices reduce profit margins, thus making those firms uncompetitive.

The fact that profits in U.S. agriculture have declined in real terms for decades, despite farmers' efforts to improve through technical innovations, indicates that prices are falling faster than are costs per unit. Unless future technologies can reverse this trend, U.S. producers will continue being forced to make the investment decision to leave commodity markets and, ultimately, the industry.

Finally, U.S. national policies are not likely to reverse agriculture's trend of declining average returns to investment. Price support and other policies aimed at increasing the profits of freely traded commodities will always fail because they add to the production and price problems that drive the agricultural treadmill (Hudson and Ethridge 2000). One example of this failure is apparent in the wheat market. From 1960 to 2000, the United States approximately doubled its production of wheat. This was spurred on by many policies, including price support programs, and was made possible by technological and managerial innovations. However, total world production of wheat tripled during that period. The U.S. share of the global wheat market dropped from 15 percent to 10 percent because other countries also adopted new technologies and became more competitive (Duffy 2001).

The message of this story is that American farmers and ranchers are like surfers on the face of a giant tsunami. The tsunami is the never-ending wave of technological innovations in global agriculture that carry along surfers who are able to stay up-to-date enough to be competitive. As long as a surfer keeps on the leading edge of the wave, he can survive, but if he falls he will be drowned. So, that is the challenge and the opportunity for American commodity producers: stay ahead of the tsunami and ride it for life.

NOTES

Some of the material in this chapter is revised from articles published by S. Blank as "A Portfolio of Threats to American Agriculture," *Contemporary Economic Policy* 20, no. 4 (2002): 381–393, and "Globalization, Cropping Choices, and Profitability in American Agriculture," *Journal of Agri-*

cultural & Applied Economics 33, no. 2 (2001): 315–326, as well as an article published by J. Thompson and S. Blank, "Harvest Mechanization Helps Agriculture Remain Competitive," *California Agriculture* 54, no. 3 (2000): 51–56.

1. A long-term labor shortage is a phenomenon that can only occur in a highly developed country. In less-developed countries, a higher percentage of the population works in agriculture and, thus, is available when needed for farm work, although local shortages are possible in the short term.

REFERENCES

Agriculture Canada. 1991. "Growing Together: Report to Ministers of Agriculture." Report of the Task Force on Competitiveness in the Agri-Food Industry, Ottawa, Canada.

Antle, John. 1999. "The New Economics of Agriculture." *American Journal of Agricultural Economics* 81: 993–1010.

Ball, E., C. Hallahan, and R. Nehring. 2004. "Convergence of Productivity: An Analysis of the Catch-up Hypothesis Within a Panel of States." *American Journal of Agricultural Economics* 86 (5): 1315–1321.

Booth, Laurence. 1991. "The Influence of Production Technology on Risk and the Cost of Capital." *Journal of Financial and Quantitative Analysis* 26: 109–127.

Bressler, R., Jr., and R. King. 1970. *Markets, Prices, and Interregional Trade.* New York: John Wiley & Sons.

Brester, Gary W. 1999. "Vertical Integration of Production Agriculture into Value-Added Niche Markets: The Case of Wheat Montana Farms and Bakery." *Review of Agricultural Economics* 21 (1): 276–285.

California Employment Development Department. 1996. *Agricultural Bulletin.* Sacramento.

Cochrane, Willard W. 1958. *Farm Prices: Myth and Reality.* St. Paul: University of Minnesota Press.

Coyle, W., M. Gehlhar, T. Hertel, Z. Wang, and W. Yu. 1998. "Understanding the Determinants of Structural Change in World Food Markets." *American Journal of Agricultural Economics* 80: 1051–1061.

Debertin, David. 2001. "Are American Farmers Better Off as a Result of Technology Gains?" *Journal of Agricultural & Applied Economics* 33 (2): 327–339.

Diakosavvas, Dimitris. 1995. "How Integrated Are World Beef Markets? The Case of Australian and U.S. Beef Markets." *Agricultural Economics* 12: 37–53.

Dohlman, E., S. Osborne, and B. Lohmar. 2003. "Dynamics of Agricultural Competitiveness: Policy Lessons from Abroad." *Amber Waves* 1 (April): 14–21.

Douglass, Gordon K., ed. 1984. *Agricultural Sustainability in a Changing World Order.* Boulder, CO: Westview Press.

Duffy, Patricia A. 2001. "Casting Bread upon the Water: Comments on Technology, Globalization, and Agriculture." *Journal of Agricultural & Applied Economics* 33 (2): 341–347.

Fuglie, K., and C. Kascak. 2001. "Adoption and Diffusion of Natural-Resource-Conserving Agricultural Technology." *Review of Agricultural Economics* 23, 2: 386–403.

Gallup, J., and J. Sachs. 2000. "Agriculture, Climate, and Technology: Why Are the Tropics Falling Behind?" *American Journal of Agricultural Economics* 82: 731–737.

Ghadim, A., D. Pannell, and M. Burton. 2005. "Risk, Uncertainty, and Learning in Adoption of a Crop Innovation." *Agricultural Economics* 33: 1–9.

Gopinath, M., and L. Kennedy. 2000. "Agricultural Trade and Productivity Growth: A State-level Analysis." *American Journal of Agricultural Economics* 82: 1213–1218.

Griffith, R., S. Redding, and J. Van Reenen. 2004. "Mapping the Two Faces of R&D: Productivity Growth in a Panel of OECD Industries." *Review of Economics and Statistics* 86 (4): 883–895.

Hudson, D., and D. Ethridge. 2000. "Competitiveness of Agricultural Commodities in the United States: Expanding Our View." *American Journal of Agricultural Economics* 82: 1219–1223.

Isik, M., and M. Khanna. 2003. "Stochastic Technology, Risk Preferences, and Adoption of Site-Specific Technologies." *American Journal of Agricultural Economics* 85 (2): 305–317.

Jin, S., J. Huang, R. Hu, and S. Rozelle. 2002. "The Creation and Spread of Technology and Total Factor Productivity in China's Agriculture." *American Journal of Agricultural Economics* 84 (4): 916–930.

Johnson, D. Gale. 2000. "Population, Food and Knowledge." *American Economic Review* 90: 1–14.

Johnson, D., and R. Evenson. 2000. "How Far Away Is Africa? Technological Spillovers to Agriculture and Productivity." *American Journal of Agricultural Economics* 82 (2000): 743–749.

Johnson, Glenn L., and C. LeRoy Quance, eds. 1972. *The Overproduction Trap in U.S. Agriculture.* Resources for the Future. Baltimore, MD: John Hopkins University Press.

Johnson, H. 1999. Personal communication, president of Johnson Farm Machinery Company.

Johnson, S., and S. Martin, eds. 1993. *Industrial Policy for Agriculture in the Global Economy.* Ames: Iowa State University Press.

Kennedy, L., and P. Rosson III. 2002. "Impacts of Globalization on Agricultural Competitiveness: The Case of NAFTA." *Journal of Agricultural & Applied Economics* 34 (2): 275–288.

Krugman, Paul. 1998. *Pop Internationalism.* Cambridge, MA: MIT Press.

Layard, P., and A. Walters. 1978. *Microeconomic Theory.* New York: McGraw-Hill.

Lee, H., and G. Cramer. 1985. "Causal Relationships Among World Wheat Prices." *Agribusiness: An International Journal* 1: 89–97.

Levins, R. 2000. "A New Generation of Power." *Choices* 15 (2): 43–46.

Levins, R., and W. Cochrane. 1996. "The Treadmill Revisited." *Land Economics* 72 (4): 550–553.

Liefert, William M. 2002. "Comparative (Dis?)Advantage in Russian Agriculture." *American Journal of Agricultural Economics* 84 (3): 762–767.

Luintel, K., and M. Khan. 2004. "Are International R&D Spillovers Costly for the United States?" *Review of Economics and Statistics* 86 (4): 896–910.

McBride, W., and H. El-Osta. 2002. "Impacts of the Adoption of Genetically Engineered Crops on Farm Financial Performance." *Journal of Agricultural & Applied Economics* 34 (1): 175–191.

Metcalfe, Mark R. 2002. "Environmental Regulation and Implications for Competitiveness in International Pork Trade." *Journal of Agricultural and Resource Economics* 27: 222–243.

Miller, T., and G. Tolley. 1989. "Technology Adoption and Agricultural Price Policy." *American Journal of Agricultural Economics* 71: 847–857.

Paarlberg, P., and P. Abbott. 1986. "Oligopolistic Behavior by Public Agencies in International Trade: The World Wheat Market." *American Journal of Agricultural Economics* 68: 528–542.

Pande, Rohini. 2006. "Profits and Politics: Coordinating Technology Adoption in Agriculture." *Journal of Development Economics* 81: 299–315.

Rezek, J., and R. Perrin. 2004. "Environmentally Adjusted Agricultural Productivity in the Great Plains." *Journal of Agricultural and Resource Economics* 29 (2): 346–369.

Richardson, D., and C. Zhang. 1999. "Revealing Comparative Advantage: Chaotic or Coherent Patterns Across Time and Sector and U.S. Trading Partner?" National Bureau of Economic Research Working Paper 7212, July.

Ruttan, Vernon W. 2002. "Productivity Growth in World Agriculture: Sources and Constraints." Staff Paper P02-1(R), Department of Applied Economics, University of Minnesota, April.

Smith, S. 1992. "Farming—It's Declining in the U.S." *Choices* 7 (1): 8–10.

Stirniman, E.J. 1927. "Rice Production Costs." *Transactions of ASAE.* 27: 27–28.

Thiam, A., B. Bravo-Ureta, and T. Rivas. 2001. "Technical Efficiency in Developing Country Agriculture: A Meta Analysis." *Agricultural Economics* 25 (2–3): 235–243.

Tweeten, Luther. 1992. "Productivity, Competitiveness, and the Future of U.S. Agriculture." *Research in Domestic and International Agribusiness Management* 10: 127–147.

———. 1999. "The Economics of Global Food Security." *Review of Agricultural Economics* 21: 473–488.

Willson, J., ed. 1979. *Rice in California.* Butte County Rice Growers Association.

CHAPTER 8

ECONOMIC DEVELOPMENT AND THE IRONY OF AMERICAN AGRICULTURE'S TECHNICAL PROGRESS

"[T]he only thing we have to fear is fear itself..."
—Franklin D. Roosevelt

American agriculture is arguably the most productive, efficient, and technologically advanced production agriculture sector in the world. It can also be argued that the production agriculture sector played a vital role in the economic development of every region in the country. There is no question that the United States has the largest economy in the world and that it generates one of the highest standards of living on the planet. Therefore, during domestic debates about agricultural policy, many people mistakenly argue that a strong agricultural sector is essential to America's continued economic development, and that any decline in agriculture might threaten our economic prospects. That mistaken view indicates a lack of understanding of economic development.

This chapter offers a brief introduction to some of the issues involved in economic development so as to enable readers to understand the general role of development in shaping the future of the American production agriculture sector. Only a few of the many issues are described; no detailed explanation is attempted here. Readers interested in learning more about economic development in general are encouraged to read Bardhan and Udry (1999); in addition, Mundlak (2000) provides a good explanation of agriculture's role in the development process.

To begin, it is important to note that economic development involves more than just agriculture. It involves the entire economy of a country (and smaller entities, such as states, counties, and cities) and all of the resources making up that economy.

> The process of economic development is characterized by a transformation of the technologies used in production. Technological change in the poor countries has often been seen as a process through which techniques of production invented and first used in the rich countries are imported and adapted for local use. (Bardhan and Udry 1999, p. 152)

As the quote above indicates, economic development covers wide-ranging topics from production to the interactions between nations. As will be shown below, development also involves decision making at the firm and individual levels. The creation and dissemination of technologies is a central component of development, as expressed above by Bardhan and Udry. As noted, first a technological innovation has to occur, and that most often is observed in "rich" or more-developed countries. Then, an innovation is used in the country of its origin. That means the more-developed country has access to, and benefits from, the innovation before other countries do. This clearly indicates that more-developed nations are still developing (i.e., they are not "developed"), even if the benefits to the original nation from adopting a new technology are less obvious than what may be significant benefits to a less-developed nation from adopting the same technology. Finally, the dissemination and adoption of technologies are probably the most visible parts of the development process, but that does not eliminate the competitive advantage gained (albeit temporarily) by the nation inventing and first using a technology. As described in the previous chapter, technological innovation reduces costs per unit, thus making users of the technology more competitive in the market for their output. Therefore, this chapter extends that story to point out that even the most developed nations can be competitive in global markets if they maintain a development program that reduces per unit costs because firms in a country inventing new technologies have access to those innovations before firms in other nations. With regard to American agriculture, it is argued in this chapter that economic development has given American farmers and ranchers a competitive edge in the past, but recent conditions have made that advantage narrower and more at risk.

Agriculture is prominent in the development literature because "agriculture is the first industry," as outlined in Chapter 5. In fact, much of the research on economic development issues deals with agriculture as the first of two aggregate sectors (the other sector being "nonagriculture") in a national economic model (e.g., Anderson 1987) and deals with the interchange between the two sectors. Thus, it is appropriate for this chapter to focus on agriculture while describing an economic development process that could be observed in many industries within a national economy.

The second point to be made in this chapter is that it is important to understand the goal being pursued. What is the "goal" of economic development? Most people would say it is to raise the quality of life. To many economists that means the goal of economic development is to increase the quantity and quality of consumption.[1] Increased consumption implies that real incomes are increasing and/or that a rising percentage of the population is earning an income due to increased economic activity. In other words, evaluating economic development involves assessing progress in both raising the mean and reducing the variance in incomes. At present, there is wide variance both between the average incomes across countries (Acemoglu and Ventura 2002) and in the range of incomes across the population within countries. With regard to the agricultural sector only, the implication is that the goal of economic development is to increase the quantity and quality of food available to consumers across the economic spectrum. However, there is an obvious limit to the physical quantity of food a person can consume in a time period, so different consumers pursue different personal goals with regard to development. In the aggregate, less-developed countries are trying to increase the quantity and variety of food available per capita. Conversely, more-developed countries have sufficient quantities of most food products, so they are focusing on raising the quality of food available to their populations. Therefore, different types of economic development activities will be observed across different countries even though a common general goal is being pursued (Macours and Swinnen 2002).

From the points above it is clear that economic development is a never-ending process that is difficult to measure. The idea of raising the "quality of life" implies measuring future progress relative to current conditions, thus no matter how much we have developed, we expect more progress to come. That is one reason why terms like "developed nations," which imply absolute completion of the process, are inappropriate in this discussion. Also, the concept of "quality" is not standardized, thus measures of the quality of life range from "standards of living," often used by analysts to compare the development of entire countries, to personal definitions reported by individuals when asked to describe their own goals. These points certainly apply to development of the agricultural sector. As Gardner (2000) notes, several production and financial variables have been used in different attempts to define and measure the development of agriculture and its contribution to nations, regions, and households. This shows the dynamics and difficulty of the topic. Another part of the difficulty facing American agriculture is that its economic development creates a circular problem, related to the technological treadmill described in the previous chapter. Therefore, the goal of this chapter is to keep things as simple as possible while introducing such a complex story.

ECONOMIC DEVELOPMENT BASICS

Economic development applied to agriculture focuses on growth (pun intended). Part of the reason is that the agricultural sector focuses on feeding the population and that is a moving target. Over time there are more people to feed, so agriculture's output must increase in absolute terms just to keep pace in relative, per capita, terms. As a result, much of the research on development in the agricultural sector focuses on production. In particular, production technologies and their effects on growth in agricultural output over time have been the central issue in much of the discussion.

Different perspectives have been taken in past research on agricultural development and how it occurs. For example, the literature begins with studies of the creation and diffusion of production technologies (e.g., Abdulai and Huffman 2005; Fuglie and Kascak 2001; Luintel and Khan 2004). Then, the focus turns to induced innovation and technological adoption (e.g., Gallup and Sachs 2000; Ghadim, Pannell, and Burton 2005; Gopinath 2003; Lee 2005; Thirtle, Schimmelpfennig, and Townsend 2002) and factors influencing adoption of technologies (e.g., Baerenklau and Knapp 2007; Blackman 2001; Fernandez-Cornejo, Hendricks, and Mishra 2005). Next is the question of how development affects the income of rural (and other) households and the entire agricultural sector (e.g., Binswanger and Townsend 2000; Gardner 2000; Ngarambe, Goetz, and Debertin 1998; Roe and Diao 2004; Saez and Veall 2005). This is followed by questions concerning agriculture's links to other sectors (e.g., Gemmell, Lloyd, and Mathew 2000). Recently, the relationship between globalization of agricultural markets and economic development is being assessed in increasing detail (e.g., Gulati 2002; Reardon and Barrett 2000; Weatherspoon, Cacho, and Christy 2001). Finally, there is continuous interest in how economic development occurs across countries (e.g., Gardner 2005; Gopinath 2003; Rioja and Valev 2004; Schnepf, Dohlman, and Bolling 2001; Self and Grabowski 2007).

What makes agriculture grow as an economic sector? Many researchers have addressed that question, in the whole or in pieces, and over time their results have converged on the summary provided by Gardner (2005 p. 32):

> The story economists are most familiar with is as follows: scientists, engineers, and tinkerers, in both the private and public sectors, apply their knowledge to problems of agriculture; extension services and other sources of information place new knowledge in farmers' hands; and with sufficient property rights and price incentives to call forth the necessary investment, farmers adopt new technology and generate more output and income from their resources. Most of the gains may accrue to buyers of farm products rather than their producers, but nonetheless this is the paradigm of growth.

In other words, assessments of economic development focus on three issues: how technologies are invented, how technologies are disseminated, and who benefits from a technical innovation. This again makes it clear that production technologies are the central focus of agricultural development efforts. However, Gardner (2005) adds a hint as to how the technologies themselves are judged. He notes that "farmers adopt new technology and generate more output and income from their resources." This indicates that an agricultural technology is viewed as some combination of productive resources and its success is measured by how much it increases output and income. Thus, it can be concluded that agriculture grows as an economic sector by accumulating and rearranging its resources in ways that expand output and (presumably) income. This general conclusion readily fits the data from most countries in the world, but it should be regarded as suspect by readers of the earlier chapters in this book in that it clearly needs modification to apply to the agricultural sectors in the United States and possibly other wealthy nations. Nevertheless, it is the usual beginning point for an introduction to economic development in agriculture, so the story starts here.

The Usual Suspects: Land, Labor, and Capital

Economic theory in general and agricultural production theory in particular say there are three types of resources that can generate output when used in some combination: land, labor, and capital. These resources are also referred to as "inputs" or "factors of production" and are the focus of any economic assessment of production. In nonagricultural cases, labor and capital are central. For example, in a standard economic textbook (e.g., Nicholson 1998) there are chapters entitled "Labor Supply" and "Capital," indicating the importance of those resources. There is no chapter with a direct focus on land because, if land is mentioned, it is usually considered to be part of the "capital" of a nonagricultural firm. It is the improvements to land that are considered to have value in production in a nonagricultural firm, hence the usual approach of paying little attention to the dirt underneath the buildings and equipment used in production. However, in agriculture the value of land as a productive resource separate from capital and improvements to land is obvious and land is given significant attention. For example, in a famous book published in 1972 about American agriculture's development, Johnson and Quance (1972) include chapters entitled "Land," "Labor," and "Capital." These three resources remain the focus of recent studies of agricultural development, although many authors (e.g., Mundlak 2000) still have chapters devoted to labor and capital, but not land. Land is usually treated as the palette on which the painter applies his labor and capital resources and, as such, is discussed jointly with the two other resources.

Mundlak's (2000) extensive model of agriculture's role in economic development begins with only labor (L) and capital (K) and adds land (A) later.[2] He shows that some amount of labor is needed to generate any output from a piece of land, and that the productivity of labor is improved by investing some amount of capital. By first focusing on a fixed amount of land, such as an acre, Mundlak is able to explain the effects of the two other standard types of resource in the agricultural production process. Those effects are usually measured by output per unit of land. Then, his model is expanded to show that the total output of the agricultural sector increases when the amount of land used in production is increased. Finally, Mundlak explains how the *quality* of land and labor, and the type of capital used in production, each affect total output. It is a well-told story that introduces the basic concepts of economic development.

Economic development at the national level involves allocation decisions concerning natural endowments of land and population, plus investments in "human capital" and "capital" within each sector and industry in a country's economy. In the simplest sense, this means that a country's potential for economic development depends first on the quantity and quality of land it controls. Land is a necessary, but not sufficient input for agricultural production. Next, the population of a country is both a resource and, possibly, a burden in the development process (Chavas 2000). People have a productive capacity as a supply of labor, but they also represent an immediate demand for food that must be met or the "labor supply" will decrease. This is why agriculture is the world's first and most important business. At the dawn of mankind, agriculture was a business of gathering whatever food grew naturally in a location. In economic terms, this can be described as applying labor to land. The next "development" was the planting of seeds to increase the food supply available in a location. This might be described as applying labor, improved by the learning of a new skill, to land. Another new skill—planting seeds from distant locations—then brought about an increased quantity and variety of food in the original location. The first investment of capital might have been the use of tools, such as pointed sticks to help create the hole or furrow in which the seeds were to be planted. Of course, this also required the new skill of knowing how to use the tools to make the necessary task simpler and/or faster to perform. Eventually, this development process would have progressed to the point where it enabled the people of a location or country to produce enough food to keep them alive all year without having to work all year at the food production task. At that point, some resources could be shifted out of agricultural production and into other uses. Therefore, agriculture can be called a country's "base industry" in the sense that resources are invested there as sort of a "safety first" approach to assuring an adequate food supply for the population, then resources are released for investment in other sectors of the economy as agriculture succeeds in producing or otherwise acquiring sufficient food with fewer inputs.

Taking that perspective makes it clear how "economic development" is driven by improved technologies in agricultural production, at least early in a country's development. If the simple view that technologies are particular combinations of resource inputs is taken, it is easy to see why research efforts have focused on assessing the contributions of each type of resource used in agriculture. The next section summarizes a sampling of the research results related to the marginal and aggregate contributions of the three types of resources discussed in standard models. Then, a fourth type of resource is proposed for inclusion in development studies.

The Usual Results

Globally, farmland prices are not much different today from what they were a century ago (Mundlak 2000, p. 13). This indicates that over the long run, agricultural output has grown at about the same pace as demand for food and other agricultural products. To maintain the necessary growth in agricultural output, different amounts of land, labor, and capital have been used in agriculture. Differences in the degree of success in expanding productivity have been apparent in the resource allocations across countries.

The amount of land and labor used in agriculture has decreased for decades in the United States and other more-developed nations. As noted in earlier chapters, U.S. land in agriculture has decreased each year since 1954, declining about 25 percent over that period. On the other hand, agricultural land and labor have increased in most less-developed countries in recent decades. For example, Mundlak (2000) notes that 65 percent of countries increased their cultivated land during the 1967–1992 period. Labor use is a more complicated story. Total labor used in agriculture increases with population in many less-developed countries, even though the percentage of a country's population working in agriculture may be decreasing over time.

Capital use per acre has increased in the agricultural sectors of most countries across the economic spectrum, but at very different rates across countries and over time (Avila and Evenson 2002). Expanded use of capital per acre, called "capital deepening," raises productivity, but is most effective when it comes from an improvement in technology (Henderson and Russell 2005). For example, adding capital in the form of irrigation raises the productivity of what had been a dry land farm, but doubling or tripling the number of sprinklers per acre does not necessarily raise output and can possibly lower it. A particular combination of resources that succeeds in raising output per unit of inputs is considered a technological improvement because it has improved productivity.

In general, technical change in agriculture benefits the rest of the economy, but in the long run, none of the benefits is captured in agriculture (Mundlak 2000, p. 17). This is because technical advances create tradeoffs between the resources used in current technologies and the resources used in the new technology, and those tradeoffs alter the profit level derived from the costs of inputs. For example, capital deepening increases the labor cost of production of labor-intensive products relative to capital-intensive products. Thus, parts of American agriculture suffer as the United States gets wealthier because increased wealth leads to increased use of capital. So labor-intensive activities, such as fruit and vegetable harvesting, get relatively costlier and profit margins decrease for growers of those commodities. However, in the economy's other sectors, owners of the resources that are valued higher because of the technical progress in agriculture are wealthier.

Changes in the relative amounts of resources used change the price of those inputs. Cultivated area, total capital use, and output all decline when capital costs or production costs rise relative to commodity prices (Mundlak 2000, p. 122). This means as capital costs or production costs rise (usually due to increased demand for inputs in the nonagricultural sectors of our economy), or commodity prices fall, land in production decreases and capital use decreases, at least temporarily. As capital use falls, agriculture may become more labor-intensive, thus again shifting the relative costs of the inputs. Many assets in agriculture are fixed in the short run, thus producers cannot always shift in and out of particular resource allocations, so short-run trends are observed in which resource prices are temporarily distorted from free-market levels (often by government intervention), and individual producer profit margins are affected (Miller and Tolley 1989).

Changes in resource costs directly affect profit margins. Technical advances lower per unit costs of production, thus they improve profit margins in the short run. In turn, a larger profit margin makes agriculture's profit level more robust when the economic environment changes (Mundlak 2000, p. 123). However, with profit margins falling in U.S. agriculture over the past four decades, it should not be surprising that agriculture has been more volatile (weak) in the changing (declining) economic environment of globalizing commodity markets. Profit margins on agricultural commodities are falling in the United States due to increased competition from expanding supplies produced in less-developed countries that have lower production input costs because of the lower level of demand for resources in their national economies (Hudson and Ethridge 2000).

The "competitive position" of agriculture is measured by the factor share of land that makes up the agriculture-specific factor of production (Mundlak 2000, p 127). Farmers on the edge go out of agriculture with economic shocks that move them from being profitable to being unprofitable. In most cases, good land left by exiting farmers is acquired by other farmers, and marginal land leaves agriculture. However, land "at the margin" is identified by the potential profitability of each parcel at each point in time. Thus, the slow decline in average profit margins in American agriculture gradually makes the shrinking agricultural sector more susceptible to unfavorable shocks. Therefore, as land leaves production in a location, agriculture's competitive position weakens, making it more likely that "the end of commercial agriculture" can occur in that location. At this point in the discussion, some people may ask, "the United States is land rich, so why would it leave agriculture?" The decline in agriculture has been seen in the northeastern region of the United States and that area's story illustrates the dynamics of economic development. The transition process occurs in areas with weak demand for farmland due to poor profit margins in local commodity markets, or in areas with strong demand for nonfarm uses of land. In the Northeast, both conditions existed, thus agriculture's competitive position eroded away until most of the agricultural industries of the region lost their critical mass and were replaced by more profitable industries that could out-bid farmers for the land and labor resources.

At present, the rate of growth in productivity is most affected by the rate of acquisition and accumulation of physical *capital* (Mundlak 2000, Chapter 13), although human capital accumulation also has a significant effect (Henderson and Russell 2005). Capital makes land and labor more productive. Growth in total factor productivity elsewhere in the economy increases the costs of economy-wide factors (especially labor), thus decreasing agriculture's domestic and international comparative advantage (Roe and Mohtadi 2001). Land has a total factor "value" as an output (rather than just productivity as an input) for nonagricultural uses now that environmental and recreational uses are being demanded by the public (Roe and Mohtadi 2001). This signals that competition for land is expanding in the United States. That is a dramatic change from the not-so-distant past when land was in agriculture because that residual market was the only use for land in many locations. Now there are alternative uses for land in most locations in the United States. "If resources are free to move, other things being equal, they will move in the direction of higher returns" (Mundlak 2000, p. 239). This means that land can leave agriculture even in the land-intensive midwestern grain regions if alternative uses are competitive in the bidding for the resources (Leatherman, Howard, and Kastens 2002). The trend of resources leaving agriculture has been apparent for decades. As Gardner (2005, p. 36) notes, "although U.S. agricultural productivity . . . has continued to grow at about the same rate of 1.5 to 2 percent annually for the whole 1948–1999 period, since 1980 investment in the sector has turned negative and real agricultural income per farm has declined."

As agriculture's capital share increases with the adoption of new technology, wages in agriculture fall lower than those in nonagriculture industries. In the United States, the current ease with which farm labor can find nonagricultural jobs in most local areas means that agriculture will always face labor shortages as farm laborers pursue higher wages elsewhere in the economy (Tran and Perloff 2002). Those labor shortages create an incentive for agriculture to develop more labor-saving technology (such as the harvest mechanization examples in Chapter 7), thus raising the capital share further. This is part of the development treadmill—the circular dilemma facing American agriculture.

Currently, economy-wide demand for labor is the engine of "growth" in American agriculture. A growing real wage is a sufficient condition for rural household income growth. Gardner (2005) says this is the dominant explanation for the catch-up of farm to urban household income levels observed over recent decades. This means farm households are better off now than they were in the past simply because those households are, on the average, having less to do with production agriculture. This is a significant structural change in American agriculture (which is discussed in more detail in Chapters 15 and 19). A similar result is visible in the development paths of other more-developed countries. There are many implications of this evolutionary change, but two of the most important are (1) that farm households are responsive to alternative returns available when making labor allocation decisions, and (2) the percentage of a country's population working in agriculture can continue to decrease (and approach zero) even when that percentage is already quite small.

In summary, economic growth in American agriculture is driven mostly by two factors: in the short run it is productivity improvements in agricultural production, and in the long run it is off-farm employment. Combining these two results leads to the conclusion that the American agricultural sector must maintain its leadership in technological innovation or it will be swept away by the inevitable economic development process.

One last point needs to be made about resource use in agriculture. Most assessments of the economic development of the sector have indicated that the sum of changes in land, labor, and capital has generally been less than the change in output for most of the last sixty years. The residual difference in total output is usually credited to technical advances. Technology is a vague notion, but all research on the topic refers to it as being separate from land, labor, and capital. Thus, we need to attribute the residual difference in output to something specific other than the three standard resources. It is argued below that a fourth factor responsible for output increases exists and it can be called "management."

MANAGEMENT: THE FOURTH RESOURCE

Peter Drucker (1954) was one of the first people to discuss "management" as a separate concept from labor and to attribute some of the credit for a firm's economic progress to the value being added by managers. Managers were generally described in the early literature as people who knew how to combine resources so as to accomplish specific tasks. Drucker was also one of the first to describe the importance of what he called "knowledge workers." These were people who created knowledge that could be turned into new products or services or improved ways to produce existing products and services. In the corporate world in which Drucker worked as a business consultant, these two groups sometimes overlapped, but were most often made up of separate individuals employed to perform one or the other task. In production agriculture these groups overlap most of the time: the farm owner serves as the business and production manager and as a resident knowledge worker. In the context of agriculture, the functions performed by these people contribute to the development and implementation of "technologies" that enable output to grow over time. Therefore, it is proposed here that technological progress be accounted for as a fourth type of resource to be called "management."

The remainder of this chapter outlines an economic definition of management using the business and economic literature so that the definition can be used in a simple model to demonstrate the situation American agriculture faces at this point in the nation's economic development. The development process, as outlined in Chapter 5, is currently pushing the United States into the fourth stage of development up the economic food chain. In that stage, a country begins to shift significant amounts of resources into economic activities aimed at producing information or "knowledge." The resources emphasized in these activities are "management" and capital. Therefore, we must understand the concept of management in order to understand the economic role it will play in the future of American agriculture.

Three questions are addressed briefly in this section: (1) What is management? (2) What is the *process* of management? (3) What are the economic *effects* of management? Some of the answers to these questions come from the literature and some are proposed here to initiate further discussion.

What Is Management?

In conceptual terms, management is "productive guidance." It is the most important resource because it guides the allocation of all other resources. It is a necessary condition for technical advances. It also serves as a constraint on the portfolio of viable alternatives for a decision maker. The list of alternatives available to a decision maker or a firm can only include decisions that are understandable to that person or the firm's managers. Without the guidance of management, decisions cannot be made in the pursuit of complex goals.

In practical terms, management is a blend of labor and capital. It includes the knowledge, understanding, and skill set embodied in a person or, from a firm's perspective, in the employees of a firm. A person (or firm) invests in creating his/her knowledge base (the knowledge base of a firm's employees), often called "human capital." That investment is made in time and money. Time is invested in learning and money is spent directly to acquire access to information or indirectly in the form of opportunity costs. In each case, the investment is intended to increase the person's awareness and, hopefully, understanding of how something operates or can be done.

Management represents potential, but the actual gains achieved through its application are constrained by the limits of the "labor" component—the fact that there is a physical limit on what a person can do in a given period of time. Thus, to capture as much as possible of a person's potential for adding value to the firm, the firm must give that person access to, and control over, the necessary resources. In other words, a manager must be given an opportunity to apply his/her knowledge base, and the fewer constraints on that opportunity, the more likely it is that the manager's full potential will be achieved (e.g., Stulz 1990). This is true of laborers as well, but the difference between the two groups involves the extent of each person's potential and the scope of the value each can add to the firm.

The extent of a person's potential is some function of his/her human capital. The human or "labor" component of a person's potential performance is constrained to include only what that person can do, such as hammer a nail or drive a tractor. The "capital" component is constrained only by the person's knowledge base. The capital component, rather than the labor component, of management has the highest potential marginal return. This is illustrated by the story of the electrician who, in response to a customer's complaint about his quoted fee for reconnecting some high-voltage power lines to the customer's house, said "you pay me for what I *know,* not what I *do.*" When the electrician offered the customer the chance to reach inside the power box and do the job himself, the customer decided to pay the fee instead.

From the discussion above it should be clear that management is a special form of labor that has been enhanced by the investment of capital. To some people, this might sound like a description of "skilled labor" as described in the economics literature. Indeed there are similarities, but the two concepts are different. It is proposed here there that "labor" and "management" resources are both part of a single continuum. At each point on the continuum there is a different amount of performance potential due to a different amount of human capital having been created. The continuum is summarized by the proposed hierarchy in Exhibit 8.1. An important difference between highly skilled labor and management is the control management has over additional resources other than an individual's own labor. Thus, opportunities to add greater amounts of value to a firm increase for people at higher levels in the hierarchy shown in the exhibit.

What Is the Process of Management?

So, if management is what guides resources in the pursuit of complex goals, how is that task translated into human activities? The process is some function of the human capital of the managers involved. Since each manager possesses unique human capital, business firms are heterogeneous partly due to management. Therefore, no two firms will exhibit the same management process even if they pursue identical goals (Sonka, Hornbaker, and Hudson 1989).

A business firm is an organization that knows how to do something (Murmann et al. 2003). Performing a task involves a collection of activities, called a "routine" in the management literature. "Routines are the building blocks of organizational capability" (Winter 1995, p 148).

Exhibit 8.1

Proposed Hierarchy Relating Labor and Management

Level	Skills	Initiative Potential
1. Unskilled labor	Follow orders; do what they are told	Can show no initiative
2. Skilled labor	Do job trained for	Some initiative shown in problem solving
3. Highly skilled labor	Can do (adapt to) many difficult/ complex jobs	Much initiative shown in finding solutions
4. Management	Can solve any problem by using knowledge of appropriate and/or optimal resource allocations	New knowledge created as needed

The knowledge underlying a routine is embodied or embedded in its associated human, physical, and organizational capital. Resources are requisites of the performance of most routines. This means managers add value to the firm by knowing which routines to execute, when to do so, and how to allocate all necessary resources so that the execution of a routine is successful. It has been found that managers are more likely to be providing idiosyncratic rent-earning resources than are the providers of financial capital (Castanias and Helfat 1991). In other words, standardized capital resources often need unique adjustments before they can be applied in a task and managers are the people who know how to make those adjustments. Firms that invest in the human capital of their management add value in both the short term and the long term. In the short term, deductible investments in assets not showing on the balance sheet, including a manager's initial learning, give rise to new, replicable routines over the long term.

Clearly, there is a temporal dimension to the function of managerial decision making. To survive, a firm must face the dynamic aspect of management: the challenge of leveraging the existing resource position into a more favorable future position. It is improvements in the resource position, usually called gross profits, that pay the wages of the firm's employees and reward the owners for their investments. To accomplish the goal of survival, a firm and its managers must have these components of success:

1. *Speculative component*—a better eye for resource value,
2. *Developmental component*—a superior ability to amplify the contributions of present resources and expand existing lines of activity, and
3. *Creative component*—the ability to combine resources in novel ways and to establish new activities.

These components identify skills that managers want to include in their human capital over time, but the list still leaves a question about what activities managers undertake in the very short term to both acquire these skills and to perform their duties within the firm.

What do managers do? Kotter (1982) says they engage in three primary activities: (1) agenda setting, (2) network building, and (3) execution—getting networks to implement agendas. Thus, just like the electrician in the earlier story, managers are paid for what they know, not what they do in terms of physical activities. Agenda setting involves the creative component of establishing a routine by applying one's knowledge base to the task at hand. Network building involves the speculative component of developing relationships with the best people available for the task at hand. Execution often includes the development component as the task is undertaken. Although successful routines must be repeatable, a good manager keeps experimenting with resource allocations, even when a good fit is found. Thus, a good manager is never satisfied with the status quo. As a result, the correlation between management at time t and at time $t + 1$ is less than one. So, in essence, managers work with ever-changing groups of people over time.

In economic terms, managers function to minimize transaction costs and maximize social, time, and network benefits. This maximizes the value added to the firm by the manager. Transaction costs exist and people "pay" them when they choose to accept an offer other than the lowest cost available. That means managers must continually gather and digest up-to-date information about all of the tasks for which they are responsible so as to avoid unknowingly making costly mistakes. As a result, a manager's knowledge base must grow over time just to maintain the status quo. This indicates the innate value of information to managers and their firms.

Managers have a system of networks. Examples of networks include the buyers of a firm's products and the suppliers of inputs. Networks can include many members or few and the number can depend on the relationship a manager has with each member. Developing and maintaining each contact in a network has a real cost. Therefore, managers would generally prefer to minimize the number of contacts. However, there is a default risk inherent in not having sufficient contacts to meet all needs. The degree of that default risk is a function of the social capital a manager has invested in his contacts. The higher the social capital existing in a relationship, the lower is the need for other sources or contacts in a particular network because there is a lower probability that the trusted contact will fail to perform when needed. As a result, there is often an inverse relationship between the quantity and quality of contacts in a manager's network. Social capital builds trust between people (Fafchamps and Minten 2001). As trust in a member of a network rises, the fewer network members a manager needs, but firms always keep at least two (to assure competition between them) for risk management reasons.

Therefore, the process of management boils down to a manager's efforts to identify a group of people that, when approached in some way by the manager, will work in a systematic fashion that as a whole leads to the successful completion of a specific task. This is true in all types of business, including agriculture.

What Are the Effects of Management?

The economic effects of management include changes in a firm's productivity, profits, and growth. In other words, management is the key factor determining whether a firm or industry or sector survives. This is easily understood if the process is taken one piece at a time. First, *profits* are derived from productivity and efficiency (Valentin, Bernardo, and Kastens 2004). Managers are responsible for the execution of routines and the efficiency of the resource use in those routines (Trip et al. 2002). Also, managers are responsible for adopting new routines when there is a potential improvement in resource use that can improve the productivity of the firm (Fuglie and Kascak 2001; Nivens, Kastens, and Dhuyvetter 2002). If productivity increases, profit margins improve, at least for some time period. Second, *growth* is derived from profits (Baker 2003). It is profits that finance the acquisition of additional resources needed to expand the output of a firm or industry or sector.

In American agriculture, management is the single biggest constraint on the potential growth of the sector. Unlike many less-developed countries, the United States has large amounts of land, labor, and capital available for use in agriculture (Ruttan 2002). However, much of the available land and labor was once in agriculture and left the sector due to poor returns from agricultural use versus alternatives elsewhere in our economy. The available capital is also being invested elsewhere due to agriculture's declining profit margins. Therefore, to grow in the future, American agriculture needs improved management skills to better deal with evolving land (e.g., Alvarez and Arias 2003), labor (e.g., Bitsch and Harsh 2004), and capital (e.g., Gloy and Baker 2002) issues. If technical innovation can keep pace with the evolving economics of input markets, which have been making agriculture a less attractive investment in recent decades, then resources may flow back into the sector (e.g., Knudson et al. 2004).

Toward an Economic Definition of Management

So, how can the effects of management be measured? To begin, we must remember that the key effect is reflected in productivity. An efficient manager keeps output levels over time at the maximum possible for a given technology and budget constraint. Also, managers provide experimentation with routines that can lead to technical advances that increase productivity. Thus, management's effects can be observed in the level and variance of total output for a period of time. Next, we must focus on what causes technical advances. Mundlak (2000, pp. 372–373) says that accumulated knowledge determines the path of research. This means a manager's human capital must be assessed when trying to identify management's effects on technical advances. Unfortunately, when measuring technology, the embodied component (e.g., schooling) can be measured, but the disembodied component cannot be measured directly (Judson 2002). Finally, it has been observed that historically, "the rate of growth of output over time has exceeded the growth rate that can be attributed to the growth in conventionally defined inputs" (Nicholson 1998, p. 312). This means the growth in output can be broken into two components—growth attributed to changes in inputs (capital, labor, and land) and "residual" growth that represents technical progress due to management. Combining these points creates an approach to defining "management" that enables an economic model to be developed for use in trying to measure the contribution of the fourth resource. A definition is proposed in this section, then it is used later in this chapter to assess technology's contribution to American agriculture.

It is proposed here that the quantity of output, q, of some agricultural product for an economic unit (e.g., firm, industry, country) is found using the production function

$$(8.1) \qquad\qquad q = M(t)f(K, L, A)$$

which states that output is a function of capital (K), labor (L), and farmland acreage (A) inputs, plus management (M), which is itself a function of time (t). It is presumed that management improves over time ($dM/dt > 0$) because of the necessity for producers to continually update their practices to keep output increasing with demand. In other words, management grows with human capital and learning over time (Ghadim, Pannell, and Burton 2005; Valentin, Bernardo, and Kastens 2004). The management factor is defined to include all other influences on the quantity of agricultural output, such as technical progress. It is proposed here that management skill is the result of some combination of work experience (W), research (R), and education (E), as noted in the following equations. In the aggregate,

$$(8.2a) \qquad\qquad M = f_m(W, R, E)$$
$$(8.2b) \qquad\qquad W = f_w(E, S_j, B_w)I$$
$$(8.2c) \qquad\qquad R = f_R(E, S_i, B_R)I$$
$$(8.2d) \qquad\qquad E = f_E(V, D, B)Z$$

where S_j is job skills, S_i is intellectual skills, I is inspiration (a residual), V is the total investment in education, D is the distribution of the population receiving education, Z is the intangible ability to retain and apply education received, B_w and B_R are the portions of the population working and doing research (creating knowledge), respectively, and the total population is $B = B_w + B_R + B_x$. A person's job skills include their social capital and personal inventory of routines, and "firm-specific human capital imparted to employees." Also, people have different capacities (Z). Thus, two or more managers with the same land, labor, and capital should not always be expected to get the same results: *management skill* causes differences (Alvarez and Arias 2003).

Management's Contributions in Summary

Management is the most important of the four resources, as indicated by its higher expected marginal returns. A good manager can create ideas (intellectual capital) and organize other resources into a workable technical process to accomplish some goal. In economic terms, a manager can create "better methods of economic organization" or, in management terms, "routines." If successful, these will maintain or raise the firm's productivity, leading to increased profits that can finance the firm's growth over time.

Management is a function of a person's knowledge base. The cost of developing a person's knowledge base pays returns for life (if maintained), but it does not appear on the balance sheet; thus it is a good long-term investment for firms.

The cost of developing and expanding American agriculture's knowledge base is a necessary investment for the long-term survival of the sector. This is demonstrated in the model developed in the next section.

THE IRONY OF AMERICAN AGRICULTURE'S
TECHNICAL PROGRESS

It has often been said that technology is a two-edged sword. In American agriculture this is evident in the effects of new production technologies: they lower costs per unit, enabling our production sector to expand total output and compete in global commodity markets, while at the same time forcing small-scale producers out of business. This reflects the fact that most successful technical advances in American agricultural production over the last century have created economies of scale. The hardware and management practices found to be the most efficient combination of resources have consistently had large price tags that give larger farms an advantage in that they can spread those fixed costs across larger acreages, thus ending up with lower costs per unit of output than would smaller farms. As a result, over time smaller American farms will disappear and be absorbed by their larger, lower-cost neighbors (Morrison et al. 2004). This story is similar to that of other industrial businesses that are concentrating partly due to the nature of their technology (Lambson 1987). Thus, one of the ironies of American agriculture's technical progress is that it is more dangerous to family farms (who are the usual target of programs aiming to "save agriculture") than it is to the large corporate farming operations that are often viewed as "the enemy" by American farm advocates.

Technology is helping the U.S. production agriculture sector survive, but it is helping to reduce the farm population and, in so doing, it is changing the structure of the sector. Farm numbers have fallen much faster than farmland acreage totals, thus average farm sizes have grown steadily over the past half-century. This means the American agricultural industry is concentrating. Yet this structural change has been needed for firms to compete in the globalizing markets for commodities. By becoming larger, American farms have been able to invest more capital and spread those costs across more acres in a process that leads to lower costs per unit when the new technology embodied in the capital increases yields more than costs.

The problem with the current process of technological progress is that the gains from adoption of new technologies are short-lived because technology spreads to foreign competitors in many ways, including "R&D spillovers" (Luintel and Khan 2004).[3] America is the world leader in agricultural research that increases our productivity, keeping us at the highest levels. However, the downside of this leadership position is that the United States is "a net loser in international R&D spillovers" (Luintel and Khan 2004). This means our research and development activities benefit other countries more than their R&D spillovers help us. Currently, we need to continue improving our productivity to reduce our marginal costs because marginal revenues are falling in the global markets created by technical progress in production, storage, and transportation of commodities. In other words, because gains from technology are short lived, we need to stay ahead of competitors in developing new technologies to maintain our competitiveness (Tweeten 1992).

Another irony of American agriculture's technical progress is that American research results are used by firms in less-developed countries, leading those firms to become competitors of the American firms that the research was intended to benefit. Those foreign firms use our technology to reduce their marginal costs, enabling them to expand their output, which, in turn, puts downward pressure on the global prices received by American farmers. The net effect, as Luintel and Khan note, is that "when competitors catch up technologically, they challenge U.S. market shares and investments worldwide" (p. 908, 2004). Ironically, our foreign competitors do not need to develop their own new technologies in order to catch up, they only have to adopt our technologies.

Therefore, our research is a "treadmill" leading us out of agriculture. The great irony is that without our research, the United States would probably already be out of production agriculture. The United States needs a continual flow of new management and technological innovation to keep our production costs per unit low enough to survive in the global market, whereas foreign competitors can invest in (increase) land and capital inputs, as well as technology, to lower their costs. The key point to remember is that the lowest-cost suppliers will survive in a competitive market. This means American production agriculture's competitive advantage is at risk; it depends on the policy decision to continue investing in agricultural research and development. These points are explained in the remainder of this chapter.

Background

At any point in time there are heterogeneous technologies available in the world for the production of a particular agricultural commodity. These technologies can be viewed as falling on a continuum ranging from "old" to "optimal." The optimal technology is the most efficient production system available for that commodity. All other technologies lead to the same output, but with a less efficient process. In this context, a "less efficient" technology is one that requires more resources per unit of output.

Countries choose the best technology they can, given their constraints, such as factor proportions. Across countries, there are differences between "available" and "implemented" technology (Mundlak 2000, p. 218). Technologies in use are "implemented," while other, more efficient, technologies to which a country has access but has not yet implemented are "available" for future adoption. Thus, there are two main reasons why a country might not have implemented the most recent technology. First, that new technology might not be accessible to firms within the country (i.e., it is not yet available). Second, the new technology might not yet be cost-effective for firms in the country due to resource constraints. For example, China uses a labor-intensive production method for rice because that is more cost-effective for its economy than other available rice production technologies that are capital-intensive (Jin et al. 2002). As a country's factor prices and proportions change over time, the cost-effectiveness of a technology may improve enough for that available technology to be adopted. The fact that a country has available technologies means that it can "catch up" some amount simply by implementing a newer (i.e., more efficient) technology as soon as factor markets make it cost-effective.

Highly developed countries have no significant constraints, in the aggregate, on their ability to implement newly available technologies. They can adjust their factors as needed because agriculture is a small part of the economy, so additional supplies of resources are relatively plentiful in their nonagriculture sectors. This means capital and labor can be attracted to agriculture (i.e., shifted from other sectors of the economy) as needed by simply raising the return being offered for capital and/or the wage rate for labor. Of course, the *willingness* of agricultural firms to offer higher returns to attract additional resources depends upon the profitability of that action.

Less-developed countries have binding constraints when considering implementation of a new technology. Agriculture is a big part of their economy, so factors cannot be shifted easily. For example, it was noted earlier that China uses a labor-intensive method of producing rice. The reason for that technology choice is that more capital-intensive methods that are available would require capital that the country may not have in its economy at present, plus replacing labor with capital would idle much farm labor that cannot immediately be absorbed into the nonagricultural sector of the country. In other words, factor markets try to price resources so that all (or nearly all) resources in an economy are utilized at any point in time. Any technological shift that shocks factor markets significantly is not likely to be cost-effective for the country and, as a result, is not likely to occur. In the China rice example, a technical shift that idles large numbers of labors in the short run is not desirable for the Chinese economy, hence they continue to pursue technical advances that can be implemented within existing resource endowments.

The result of differences in resource constraints is that more-developed agricultural sectors operate at, or near, the optimum at all times, while agricultural sectors in less-developed countries often operate below the efficient production frontier (Thiam, Bravo-Ureta, and Rivas 2001). As less-developed countries gain capital and skilled labor, they can adopt more productive technologies that definitely expand output, and possibly enable them to catch up. Therefore, it is the speed of capital deepening and accumulation of human capital that most affect a country's rate of agricultural development (Mundlak 2000, Chapter 13).

The development of the poor parts of the world can be aided by resource transfers. This can have surprising results. The more-developed world can transfer capital (through investments and loans) and skills (through education) to less-developed countries to expand global agricultural output. This has happened for decades through programs such as the U.S. Peace Corps and the Agency for International Development. The improved agricultural output benefits people in those poor countries and it benefits American consumers. The increased economic activity in the less-developed countries spurs the development of their entire economies. In the United States, consumers benefit by having another source of food. The downside of this resource transfer is that it makes it easier for foreign suppliers to replace U.S. commodity producers, thus making it possible for the United States to exit production agriculture.

When technological change occurs, it can augment one or more of the resources, thus altering the rate of substitution between factors. This causes factor price changes, especially for labor and capital. A new technique also affects land use based on the speed of capital adjustment (Mundlak 2000, p. 193). Thus, there are clearly linkages between labor, capital, land, and the fourth resource of technology or "management."

Simple Model for Measuring Technology

It was noted earlier in this chapter that historically, "the rate of growth of output over time has exceeded the growth rate that can be attributed to the growth in conventionally defined inputs" (Nicholson 1998, p. 312). This means the growth in agricultural output can be broken into two components: growth attributed to changes in inputs (capital, labor, and land) and "residual" growth that represents technical progress due to management. With this perspective, a simple model can be created to measure technology and its contribution to economic development.

To begin, the quantity of output, q, of some agricultural product is found using the production function found in Equation 8.1. Differentiating Equation 8.1 with respect to time gives

(8.3)
$$\frac{dq}{dt} = \frac{dM}{dt} \bullet f(K,L,A) + M \bullet \frac{df(K,L,A)}{dt}$$
$$= \frac{dM}{dt} \bullet \frac{q}{M} + \frac{q}{f(K,L,A)} \left[\frac{\partial f}{\partial K} \bullet \frac{dK}{dt} + \frac{\partial f}{\partial L} \bullet \frac{dL}{dt} + \frac{\partial f}{\partial A} \bullet \frac{dA}{dt} \right]$$

Dividing by q gives

(8.4)
$$\frac{dq/dt}{q} = \frac{dM/dt}{M} + \frac{\partial f}{\partial K} \bullet \frac{K}{f(K,L,A)} \bullet \frac{dK/dt}{K} + \frac{\partial f}{\partial L} \bullet \frac{L}{f(K,L,A)} \bullet \frac{dL/dt}{L}$$
$$+ \frac{\partial f}{\partial A} \bullet \frac{A}{f(K,L,A)} \bullet \frac{dA/dt}{A}$$

The growth rate of any variable x is $(dx/dt)/x$, so Equation 8.4 can be written in terms of growth rates (G_x) as

(8.5) $$G_q = G_m + \frac{\partial f}{\partial K} \bullet \frac{K}{f(K,L,A)} \bullet G_K + \frac{\partial f}{\partial L} \bullet \frac{L}{f(K,L,A)} \bullet G_L + \frac{\partial f}{\partial A} \bullet \frac{A}{f(K,L,A)} \bullet G_A$$

However, it is noted that

$$\frac{\partial f}{\partial K} \bullet \frac{K}{f(K,L,A)} = \frac{\partial q}{\partial K} \bullet \frac{K}{q}$$

equals the elasticity of output with respect to capital input, $e_{q,K}$ (and the similar result for the elasticities of output with respect to labor and farmland acreage). Therefore, the growth equation (8.5) can be rewritten as

$$(8.6) \qquad G_q = G_m + e_{q,K}G_K + e_{q,L}G_L + e_{q,A}G_A.$$

This equation can be rearranged to define growth in management (technical progress) as follows.

$$(8.7) \qquad G_m = G_q - e_{q,K}G_K - e_{q,L}G_L - e_{q,A}G_A.$$

In Equation 8.7 it is easily seen that management is specified as the residual once the effects of the three standard resources have been removed. This approach eliminates the need to measure technology directly, yet it enables us to get an exact estimate of the fourth resource's contribution to the output growth of a firm, industry, or country. Given that we have been able to measure changes in the amount of labor, capital, and land resources invested in agriculture within the United States and other countries, several implications can be drawn.

Implications of the Model

Technological progress has been primarily responsible for American agriculture's output growth for half a century. Over the past fifty years in the United States, labor and land used in agriculture have decreased (G_L, $G_A < 0$) because alternative investments of land and labor outside the agricultural sector offer better returns. The declining trends in these two resources are not likely to be reversed because the nonagricultural sector's growth has far outpaced growth in agricultural commodity markets, and is expected to continue doing so. This means that for the United States to maintain its agricultural output level, $G_q = 0$ in Equation 8.6, it must substitute capital and technical progress in the place of the decreases in land and labor. However, over the past three decades, alternative uses of capital have developed elsewhere in the economy such that capital investment in agriculture has decreased since 1980 (Gardner 2005). Therefore, American agriculture will increasingly depend on continued technological progress to maintain its output.

For foreign competitors to maintain their output, fewer technical advances are needed because acreage of farmland is still increasing in many less-developed countries; only their agricultural labor growth rate is negative. Yet, each time the United States develops a new technology, it will be adopted by at least some competitors, causing their output to increase. That, in turn, puts more pressure on the United States: we have to either develop new cost-reducing techniques to remain competitive, or we must reduce our output, which is being replaced in the market by lower-cost supplies from other countries.

Therefore, the cost of developing American agriculture's knowledge base is a necessary, but not sufficient, condition for the long-term survival of the American production agriculture sector. However, American consumers will always benefit from that investment. That means there is a case for arguing in support of investments in research and development programs. Unfortunately, there is another irony in American agriculture: investments made at the national level are directed by Congress and our agricultural policy. That policy has always favored production subsidies and other immediate gratification programs rather than the long-run perspective needed for a research and development investment program. Had the money spent on direct government transfers to individuals been invested instead in research activities over the seventy years of government intervention in agricultural commodity markets, it is quite possible that our agricultural sector would have evolved into a more profitable and sustainable sector of our national economy.

NOTES

1. This view is from the "neoclassical economics" perspective. Alternative perspectives, such as that presented by "ecological economics," exist and are more defensible in the long term. In neoclassical economics, "the market" is the central focus of study and it is assumed that markets will direct resources into their "highest and best use." Unfortunately, not all resources have markets and thus are not included in the decision making of market participants. Also, the neoclassical perspective assumes that resources are available in limitless quantities. Conversely, ecological economics acknowledges that natural resources have fixed limits that may in fact constrain the market allocation of resources and, thus, constrain economic growth. As a result, the neoclassical assumption that everyone can pursue continuous economic growth forever seems silly. Since this book focuses on farm-level decision making in American agriculture, a neoclassical view is presented. However, readers are encouraged to learn more about ecological economics and its implications for economic development by studying texts on the subject, such as that by Daly and Farley (2004).

2. In this book, references to the resource "land" will be abbreviated using A (for "acreage") to avoid confusion with the L used to abbreviate "labor." Thus, A is clearly intended to be a reference to an *amount* of land, just as L and K refer to quantities of labor and capital. The quality of land and its effect on output is a separate issue that is discussed in the next chapter.

3. "Spillover" is a term used to describe the situation in which some research is relevant to firms in countries other than the one that does the research. For example, if research conducted in California on mechanical harvesting of tomatoes can be used by tomato producers in Mexico (by simply purchasing the machine developed from that research), the research and development efforts are said to spill over to those producers in Mexico.

REFERENCES

Abdulai, A., and W. Huffman. 2005. "The Diffusion of New Agricultural Technologies: The Case of Crossbred-Cow Technology in Tanzania." *American Journal of Agricultural Economics* 87 (3): 645–659.

Acemoglu, D., and J. Ventura. 2002. "The World Income Distribution." *Quarterly Journal of Economics* 117 (2): 659–694.

Alvarez, A., and C. Arias. 2003. "Diseconomies of Size with Fixed Managerial Ability." *American Journal of Agricultural Economics* 85 (February): 134–142.

Anderson, Kym. 1987. "On Why Agriculture Declines with Economic Growth." *Agricultural Economics* 1: 195–207.

Avila, A., and R. Evenson. 2002. "Total Factor Productivity Growth in Agriculture: The Role of Technological Capital." Working paper of the Economic Growth Center, Yale University.

Baerenklau, K., and K. Knapp. 2007. "Dynamics of Agricultural Technology Adoption: Age Structure, Reversibility, and Uncertainty." *American Journal of Agricultural Economics* 89, (1): 190–201.

Baker, Gregory A. 2003. "Strategic Planning and Financial Performance in the Food Processing Sector." *Review of Agricultural Economics* 25 (2): 470–482.

Bardhan, P., and C. Udry. 1999. *Development Microeconomics.* Oxford: Oxford University Press.

Binswanger, H., and R. Townsend. 2000. "The Growth Performance of Agriculture in Sub-Saharan Africa." *American Journal of Agricultural Economics* 82: 1075–1086.

Bitsch, V., and S. Harsh. 2004. "Labor Risk Attributes in the Green Industry: Business Owners' and Managers' Perspectives." *Journal of Agricultural & Applied Economics* 36 (3): 731–745.

Blackman, Allen. 2001. "Why Don't Lenders Finance High-Return Technological Change in Developing-Country Agriculture?" *American Journal of Agricultural Economics* 83: 1024–1035.

Castanias, R., and C. Helfat. 1991. "Managerial Resources and Rents." *Journal of Management* 17 (October): 155–171.

Chavas, Jean-Paul. 2000. "On Population Growth and Technological Change: Selectivity Bias in Historical Analysis." *Journal of Agricultural Economics* 51 (3): 333–352.

Daly, H., and J. Farley. 2004. *Ecological Economics: Principles and Applications.* Washington, DC: Island Press.

Drucker, Peter F. 1954. *The Practice of Management.* New York: Harper & Row.

Fafchamps, M., and B. Minten. 2001. "Social Capital and Agricultural Trade." *American Journal of Agricultural Economics* 83: 680–685.

Fernandez-Cornejo, J., C. Hendricks, and A. Mishra. 2005. "Technology Adoption and Off-Farm Household Income: The Case of Herbicide-Tolerant Soybeans." *Journal of Agricultural & Applied Economics* 37 (3): 549–563.

Fuglie, K., and C. Kascak. 2001. "Adoption and Diffusion of Natural-Resource-Conserving Agricultural Technology." *Review of Agricultural Economics* 23 (2): 386–403.

Gallup, J., and J. Sachs. 2000. "Agriculture, Climate, and Technology: Why Are the Tropics Falling Behind?" *American Journal of Agricultural Economics* 82: 731–737.

Gardner, Bruce L. 2000. "Economic Growth and Low Incomes in Agriculture." *American Journal of Agricultural Economics* 82: 1059–1074.

———. 2005. "Causes of Rural Economic Development." *Reshaping Agriculture's Contributions to Society: Proceedings of the Twenty-Fifth International Conference of Agricultural Economists,* pp. 21–41. Malden, MA: Blackwell.

Gemmell, N., T. Lloyd, and M. Mathew. 2000. "Agricultural Growth and Inter-Sectoral Linkages in a Developing Economy." *Journal of Agricultural Economics* 51 (3): 353–370.

Ghadim, A., D. Pannell, and M. Burton. 2005. "Risk, Uncertainty, and Learning in Adoption of a Crop Innovation." *Agricultural Economics* 33: 1–9.

Gloy, B., and T. Baker. 2002. "The Importance of Financial Leverage and Risk Aversion in Risk-Management Strategy Selection." *American Journal of Agricultural Economics* 84 (4): 1130–1143.

Gopinath, Munisamy. 2003. "Cross-Country Differences in Technology: The Case of the Food Processing Industry." *Canadian Journal of Agricultural Economics* 51: 97–107.

Gulati, Ashok. 2002. "Indian Agriculture in a Globalizing World." *American Journal of Agricultural Economics* 84 (3): 754–761.

Henderson, D., and R. Russell. 2005. "Human Capital and Convergence: A Production-Frontier Approach." *International Economic Review* 46 (4): 1167–1205.

Hudson, D., and D. Ethridge. 2000. "Competitiveness of Agricultural Commodities in the United States: Expanding Our View." *American Journal of Agricultural Economics* 82 (5): 1219–1223.

Jin, S., J. Huang, R. Hu, and S. Rozelle. 2002. "The Creation and Spread of Technology and Total Factor Productivity in China's Agriculture." *American Journal of Agricultural Economics* 84 (4): 916–930.

Johnson, G., and L. Quance. 1972. *The Overproduction Trap in U.S. Agriculture: A Study of Resource Allocation from World War I to the Late 1960's.* Washington, DC: Resources for the Future.

Judson, Ruth. 2002. "Measuring Human Capital Like Physical Capital: What Does It Tell Us?" *Bulletin of Economic Research* 54 (3): 209–231.

Knudson, W., A. Wysocki, J. Champagne, and C. Peterson. 2004. "Entrepreneurship and Innovation in the Agri-Food System." *American Journal of Agricultural Economics* 86 (5): 1330–1336.

Kotter, John P. 1982. *The General Managers.* New York: The Free Press, 1982.

Lambson, Val Eugene. 1987. "Is the Concentration-Profit Correlation Partly an Artifact of Lumpy Technology?" *American Economic Review* 77: 731–733.

Leatherman, J., D. Howard, and T. Kastens. 2002. "Improved Prospects for Rural Development: An Industrial Targeting System for the Great Plains." *Review of Agricultural Economics* 24 (1): 59–77.

Lee, Donald R. 2005. "Agricultural Sustainability and Technology Adoption: Issues and Policies for Developing Countries." *American Journal of Agricultural Economics* 87 (5): 1325–1334.

Luintel, K., and M. Khan. 2004. "Are International R&D Spillovers Costly for the United States?" *Review of Economics and Statistics* 86 (4): 896–910.

Macours, K., and J. Swinnen. 2002. "Patterns of Agrarian Transition." *Economic Development and Cultural Change* 50 (2): 365–394.

Miller, T., and G. Tolley. 1989. "Technology Adoption and Agricultural Price Policy." *American Journal of Agricultural Economics* 71: 847–857.

Morrison Paul C., R. Nehring, D. Banker, and A. Somwaru. 2004. "Scale Economics and Efficiency in U.S. Agriculture: Are Traditional Farms History?" *Journal of Productivity Analysis* 22: 185–205.

Mundlak, Yair. 2000. *Agriculture and Economic Growth: Theory and Measurement.* Cambridge, MA: Harvard University Press.

Murmann, J., H. Aldrich, D. Levinthal, and S. Winter. 2003. "Evolutionary Thought in Management and Organization Theory at the Beginning of the New Millennium." *Journal of Management Inquiry* 12 (March): 1–19.

Ngarambe, O., S. Goetz, and D. Debertin. 1998. "Regional Economic Growth and Income Distribution: County-Level Evidence from the U.S. South." *Journal of Agricultural & Applied Economics* 30 (December): 325–337.

Nicholson, Walter. 1998. *Microeconomic Theory: Basic Principles and Extensions.* 7th ed. Fort Worth, TX: Dryden.

Nivens, H., T. Kastens, and K. Dhuyvetter. 2002. "Payoffs to Farm Management: How Important Is Crop Marketing?" *Journal of Agricultural & Applied Economics* 34 (1): 193–204.

Reardon, T., and C. Barrett. 2000. "Agroindustrialization, Globalization, and International Development: An Overview of Issues, Patterns, and Determinants." *Agricultural Economics* 23 (3): 195–205.

Rioja, F., and N. Valev. 2004. "Finance and the Sources of Growth at Various Stages of Economic Development." *Economic Inquiry* 42 (1): 127–140.

Roe, T., and X. Diao. 2004. "Capital Accumulation and Economic Growth: The Case of the Retail Food Industry in Developing Countries." *American Journal of Agricultural Economics* 86 (3): 788–794.

Roe, T., and H. Mohtadi. 2001. "International Trade and Growth: An Overview Using the New Growth Theory." *Review of Agricultural Economics* 23 (2): 423–440.

Ruttan, Vernon W. 2002. "Productivity Growth in World Agriculture: Sources and Constraints." Staff Paper P02–1(R), Department of Applied Economics, University of Minnesota, April.

Saez, E., and M. Veall. 2005. "The Evolution of High Incomes in Northern America: Lessons from Canadian Evidence." *American Economic Review* 95 (3): 831–849.

Self, S., and R. Grabowski. 2007. "Economic Development and the Role of Agricultural Technology." *Agricultural Economics* 36 (3): 395–404.

Schnepf, R., E. Dohlman, and C. Bolling. 2001. "Agriculture in Brazil and Argentina: Developments and Prospects for Major Field Crops." Agriculture and Trade Report WRS-01–3, USDA Economics Research Service, Market and Trade Economics Division, November.

Sonka, S., R. Hornbaker, and M. Hudson. 1989. "Managerial Performance and Income Variability for a Sample of Illinois Cash Grain Producers." *North Central Journal of Agricultural Economics* 11: 39–47.

Stulz, Rene. 1990. "Managerial Discretion and Optimal Financing Policies." *Journal of Financial Economics* 26: 3–28.

Thiam, A., B. Bravo-Ureta, and T. Rivas. 2001. "Technical Efficiency in Developing Country Agriculture: A Meta Analysis." *Agricultural Economics* 25 (2–3): 235–243.

Thirtle, C., D. Schimmelpfennig, and R. Townsend. 2002. "Induced Innovation in United States Agriculture, 1880–1990: Time Series Tests and an Error Correction Model." *American Journal of Agricultural Economics* 84 (3): 598–614.

Tran, L., and J. Perloff. 2002. "Turnover in U.S. Agricultural Labor Markets." *American Journal of Agricultural Economics* 84 (2): 427–437.

Trip, G., G. Thijssen, J. Renkema, and R. Huirne. 2002. "Measuring Managerial Efficiency: The Case of Commercial Greenhouse Growers." *Agricultural Economics* 27 (2002): 175–181.

Tweeten, Luther. 1992. "Productivity, Competitiveness, and the Future of U.S. Agriculture." *Research in Domestic and International Agribusiness Management* 10: 127–147.

Valentin, L., D. Bernardo, and T. Kastens. 2004. "Testing the Empirical Relationship Between Best Management Practice Adoption and Farm Profitability." *Review of Agricultural Economics* 26 (4): 489–504.

Weatherspoon, D., J. Cacho, and R. Christy. 2001. "Linking Globalization, Economic Growth and Poverty: Impacts of Agribusiness Strategies on Sub-Saharan Africa." *American Journal of Agricultural Economics* 83: 722–729.

Winter, Sidney G. 1995. "Four Rs of Profitability: Rents, Resources, Routines, and Replication." In *Resource-based and Evolutionary Theories of the Firm: Towards a Synthesis,* ed. C. Montgomery, pp. 147–177. Boston: Kluwer Academic Publishers.

PART III

GLOBAL AGRICULTURE'S EFFECT ON MARKET EVOLUTION

CHAPTER 9

FARMLAND VALUES AND USES AS INDICATORS OF NATIONAL WEALTH

"I tell you, turning your land into a golf course is the salvation of the farmer. That's the only thing to do with land now is just to play golf on it. Sell your land and caddie."
—Will Rogers, 1928

Land is literally and figuratively the base upon which all economic activity is built. In its literal sense, land is the ground beneath our feet, whereas in its figurative sense land is the tangible resource covering the earth's surface, so it includes the water found in most places. Thus, land has a spatial sense: the "land" found at any two points on the surface of the earth will always differ in location, if not also in its tangible qualities. For example, the dirt found in Iowa obviously differs from the water on the surface of the Indian Ocean, but the Iowa dirt also differs from the dirt found in Ukraine, even though both soils are black in color and similar in productive capacity. Two plots of soil could contain identical organic compositions, but because they differ in their locations there is potential for differences in their agricultural production capacity, market values, and human uses. Differences in location can mean differences in microclimates: temperature, rainfall, and duration of temperature and rainfall combinations. Differences in microclimates between locations create differences in the biological processes that occur at those points, thus affecting which agricultural enterprises can be produced at those locations. This means each plot of land may participate in a unique collection of markets—only those markets for commodities that can be produced at the location. In turn, this means that markets will implicitly value each plot of land differently, to some extent. And ultimately, this means that each plot of land is valued by the economic activity conducted upon it. However, it is not only the current economic activities occurring on a parcel that determine the land's value; activities can change over time, thus current and potential future activities are both considered. This leads to the conclusion that, figuratively, land "moves" from one use to another over time.

This chapter argues that an understanding of how land "moves" over time can provide insights into global and local economic development. It is proposed here that land in general, and farmland in particular, serves as an economic barometer. Farmland values and uses can indicate both national wealth and local economic health.

The wealth of a nation begins with its land endowments. Generally speaking, the more land a nation controls, the wealthier it is because land has a productive capacity, and having more land means that more output can be generated, thus creating more wealth. However, not all land is equal in its productive capacity. Some land is of high quality, in terms of its biological production potential, and other land is of lesser quality. For example, the cropland in Florida has more biological potential than the land in California's Mojave Desert. Thus, land in Florida contributes

171

much more to the wealth of the United States than does the Mojave Desert, even though the Mojave is nearly three times the size of Florida's entire cropland area. Location also affects land's contribution to wealth. This can be seen across the prairies of North America. The quality of soils in northern Canada are similar to those in Kansas, but the revenue per acre generated by Kansas farmland exceeds that of the frozen north simply because of the differences in climate. So, in summary, the agricultural wealth of a nation is a function of the quantity and quality of its land endowments, adjusted for climates. These productive factors must be adjusted into economic terms by producing specific commodities, which are then exchanged for currency. In this sense, a nation "invests" its land into the crops and other uses that are expected to generate the most wealth.

At the local level the story is the same, but the two stories are not always correlated. The wealth of a nation can be increasing as it invests its land and other resources in response to dynamic global market changes, however, those investments may adversely affect the economic health of local areas. This is being observed in many agricultural regions. Land is leaving agriculture in many places, as noted in earlier chapters. To judge whether those developments are indicators of good or bad economic conditions, it is necessary to evaluate the cause of the change. Land leaving agricultural production is a positive indicator when it is due to local developments leading to increased wealth in the area. When people are *choosing* to shift farmland into some other use, it indicates positive economic development of the local area. Conversely, when land is forced out of agricultural production due to global market developments it is usually a bad sign for future prospects in the area. If there are no alternative uses for the land, the lost income from the farmland begins a "ripple effect" through the local economy as the lost dollars are not spent and "multiplied" over time, thus triggering a cycle of decline among other local businesses.

The following sections present a simple explanation of the linkages between the quality of land, the value of land, and the uses of land. It is argued here that the types of use observed indicate national wealth because a nation's wealth influences its willingness and ability to invest land in certain types of land use. The story begins at the intersection of biology and economics.

MARKET MARGINAL LAND

The story of how land quality is part of a nation's natural endowment of wealth and how it influences economic development is presented in more detail by Mundlak (2000). He provides a theoretical basis for the discussion by presenting a model of "market marginal land" (Mundlak 2000, pp. 117–127), which is summarized here.

A date palm oasis in the heart of the Sahara Desert, or a scraggly bush growing out of a crack in the rocky face of a mountain, can serve as examples of how virtually all land can grow *something* if water and other essential resources are brought together. Thus, in absolute terms there is little marginal land: land that cannot produce anything. However, farmers and ranchers live in a relative world and, in those terms, there is a great deal of marginal land: land that cannot produce anything profitably (i.e., relative to the costs of production). Thus, "marginal land" is an expression of quality relative to production capacity in some market.

Mundlak (2000) defines marginal land quality, φ, as a function of market price and/or production costs: $\varphi = f(p, c)$. Given that prices and costs are involved in his definition, he refers to it as a market-driven concept. "Market marginal land" is land of good enough quality (i.e., with adequate physical attributes) to produce a good crop yield, but that output is not profitable due to market price and/or production cost levels. Specifically, market marginal land is the quality level at which the current market for local commodities results in zero profits: $\varphi = f(p, c)$, $\pi_\varphi = 0$. At

Figure 9.1 **Farmland Quality and Rents Earned**

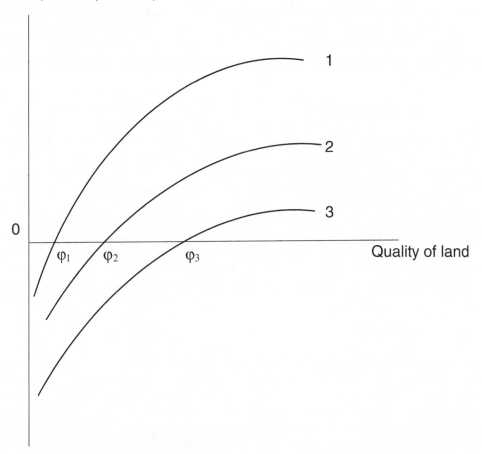

this break-even quality level, there is no incentive for farmers to use the land in production because no economic returns will be earned for the effort.

In Mundlak's model of land use, market marginal land quality, φ, is key. The concepts are illustrated in Figure 9.1. To begin, assume that the concave line labeled "1" is the situation in some agricultural region. The graph shows the relationship between economic "rent" (profit) per acre on the vertical axis and "quality of land" on the horizontal axis. Sloping (concave) line 1 shows that higher-quality land at points farther to the right on the horizontal axis can earn higher profits per acre. The exact location of line 1 is determined by the current market situation for commodities that can be produced in the local area, hence it is an empirical issue. The line's intersection with the horizontal axis, labeled φ_1, shows the current "market marginal land" level. Farmland of qualities below φ_1 will be fallowed in the short-run and, in the long-run, removed entirely from production unless the producer expects prices to recover. Next, assume that the prices of local commodities decline due to increased competition in global markets. The market opportunities available to local producers will shift to reflect the lower profit margins available, such as those along line 2. The point indicating market marginal land moves right with any cost increases or output price decreases (to φ_2 in this case). As a result, good-quality land that was economically viable before the price decrease is no longer in production (this is land of qualities between φ_2 and φ_1). Finally, assume another market price decrease, or cost increase, causes the local situation to shift to that reflected in line 3. As shown in Figure 9.1, very little profit is available and only from the highest-quality land. Land of quality lower than φ_3 will be removed from production.

The explanation of Figure 9.1 presented above is also an alternative way of explaining the profit squeeze discussed in Chapter 6. In other words, Figure 9.1 shows some of the consequences of a profit squeeze: productive land is squeezed out of agriculture. As noted in Chapter 7, the profit squeeze can be combated by technological improvements. Technical innovations and increased use of capital can both reverse the story above. An innovation that lowers costs of production moves the current market marginal land level to the left in Figure 9.1, such as when moving from line 3 to line 2, for example. This would enable some lower-quality land in the local area to enter production.

One assumption built into the model illustrated by Figure 9.1, that there is a positive relationship between land quality and returns per acre, has important implications for farmland values. Since it is usually true that assets which generate higher income streams are valued higher than lower-income-producing assets, it might be assumed that higher-quality farmland would have higher market values than lower-quality farmland. However, this basic piece of theory no longer holds in many places in American agriculture, as discussed next.

FARMLAND VALUES

The traditional theory of farmland valuation said, simply, that the value of farmland was determined directly by the expected income that the land could generate. Essentially, that theory still holds today, but with some significant differences in the way it is applied. The theory was developed long ago, when there was really only one use for farmland: agricultural production. In such circumstances there was no debate about how to value farmland, and some variation of a discounted cash flow method was used with expected profits from production. In recent decades, however, a debate has grown over how farmland should be valued. The debate began when it was realized that the United States has evolved to such an extent that there are multiple potential uses for what is currently "farmland." There have been a few bumps in the road, but farmland valuation theory has come full-circle, back to the idea that the value of land is determined by its income potential. The story is summarized below.

In 1850, the average value of farmland in the United States was $11 per acre, and farmland in California was averaging $1 per acre. The average values in 2006 were $1,900 per acre for the United States and $5,390 for California. Boy, don't we wish our great-great-grandparents had bought a bunch of dirt to leave for us? Well, even if they had, it was not a smooth ride to great wealth. Farmland values have always been a moving target. That was especially true over the last half-century. For example, farmland values developed a speculative bubble during the 1970s that popped in the early 1980s, causing huge losses of wealth for American farmers. The bubble was partially due to lending practices that enabled farmers to act on their inflated income expectations. During the 1970s, grain and other commodity prices rose on unusual global market circumstances. Those high commodity prices translated into unusually high income per acre results for American farmers for a few years, which, unfortunately, were misinterpreted by analysts at the time as being "normal" returns that justified the rising land values (e.g., Melichar 1979). Many farmers began to think the "bull market" would continue indefinitely and they sought to expand their operations. At that time, many banks and other agricultural lenders would give farmers loans to purchase additional farmland based on the equity the borrower had in his or her operation. Most of the equity was in farmland and, as a result, a dangerous feedback loop developed in farmland markets. Farmers eager to expand the size of their operations to capture the expected high incomes from soaring commodity prices found that each year their equity grew because the value of their farmland was increasing, thus they could borrow more money to buy more farmland, thus adding to the demand for farmland that was pushing up farmland prices. The classic speculative bubble pushed average farmland values per acre for the United States from $196 in 1970 up to $737 in 1980: a 376 percent increase in a decade! Of course, the income levels from commodity production could not keep pace, but it did not matter because farmers were making land purchase decisions based both on *expected* income levels (which were inflated by the earlier run-up in commodity prices) and on *expected* equity gains from the bull market for farmland. Even when farmers began suffering losses on their production, land price increases made them wealthier on paper. However, as the speculative bubble grew from year to year, farmers were taking on increased debt, raising their average costs per acre, making it increasingly difficult for them to generate an operating profit. That caused demand for farmland to eventually decline, thus causing farmland prices to quit increasing. At that point, farmers who were suffering oper-ating losses and no longer gaining equity through increased values of their land had no choice but to reduce their expenses, usually by selling some land to reduce interest expenses and to acquire cash needed for living expenses. That started the downward slide as the speculative bubble burst and farmland values began falling. With falling farmland values, farmers' wealth was falling, causing some urgency in the need to eliminate operating losses. Unfortunately, it was too late for thousands of farmers, and loan foreclosures and farm bankruptcies began to soar in many parts of American agriculture, especially in the midwestern states dependent on grain markets. In Iowa, for example, average farm real estate values dropped from $1,999 per acre in 1981 to $786 per acre in 1987: a 61 percent decline in six years! The result of the "farm financial crisis" of the 1980s was a shift in agricultural lending policies. The change involved making loans based on *income* instead of equity. Lenders would loan only amounts that could be repaid from the expected income of the land involved. This was a hugely significant change because it reestablished the direct link between the profitability of production on farmland and the value of that farmland.

However, analysts had difficulties trying to apply the traditional models to farmland price data, thus raising questions about the underlying valuation theory. In 1991, for example, Falk used Iowa farmland value data for the 1922–1986 period and became one of the first to question the traditional reliance on production income as the driver of farmland values. His statistical tests of the present value model found that "although farmland price and rent movements are highly correlated, price movements are not consistent with the implications of this model." Falk and Lee (1998) followed up on Falk (1991) in trying to explain why the present value model failed to explain Iowa farmland values over the 1922–1994 period. They concluded that "fads" cause short-run deviations from the model's predictions, but the model still performs well in the long-run. Next, Lence and Miller (1999) investigated whether the Iowa farmland "constant-discount-rate-present-value-model ... puzzle" was due to transaction costs. Despite using several sophis-ticated models, they got mixed results, indicating that additional factors were still at work in farmland markets. They pointed out that farmland markets often deviate from values indicated by the present value model. While trying to show historical precedence for the speculative bubble of the 1970s and 1980s, Lence and Miller (1999) identified an earlier bubble in Iowa farmland prices

(p. 257): "Land prices rose in every year from 1900 through 1920, for a total cumulative increase of 480% during the boom period.... Land prices fell in every year from 1920 through 1933; in 1933, prices were only about one-fourth of the price level achieved in the price peak of 1920." Clearly, something was missing from the traditional theory of farmland valuation.

Now it is generally accepted that farmland prices are a proxy for expected profit in agriculture (Mundlak 2000, p. 274), *subject to adjustments* for other factors influencing expected returns. Thus, the current debate is over what other factors might be influencing farmland values, and the extent of those influences. In other words, the traditional theory of farmland valuation needs only subtle adjustments to reflect the modern market for farmland in America. In simple terms, most current models of farmland values can be condensed to these essentials:

(9.1)
$$\text{Land Value} = f\left[\pi + PV\left(\sum_{i=1}^{n} E\pi_i w_i\right)\right],$$

subject to:
$$\sum_{i=1}^{n} w_i = 1.0.$$

Equation 9.1 says a parcel of land's value at some point in time is some function of its current profit (π) plus the present value of the weighted sum of expected future profits from all n potential uses of the land.[1] Thus, to estimate farmland's current value, the various potential uses of the land need to be assessed. Also, probability weightings (w), which total 1.0, need to be attached to each alternative future use (i) of the land. If there is no chance of a parcel being shifted out of agriculture in the foreseeable future, then the weighting on expected agricultural use profits is 1.0 and the weighting on other potential uses is zero. As the probability increases that a parcel's use will be changed to a higher-value alternative use, the weighting of that alternative's value is increased in the current value estimation, and the other weightings are adjusted so the total weighting remains one. The fact that agriculture and many other uses can generate profits over multiple time periods is reflected in the present value operator.

Although the ideas in Equation 9.1 are simple in theory, they are complicated empirically because of the many unknowns. In particular, the fact that expectations of which alternative uses might be relevant to a parcel of land, the amount of profits that might result, and the timing of the change in use will all vary between individuals makes the forecasting of farmland values an inexact science, at best. The economics literature is still arguing over which factors influence farmland prices, so at present there is no agreement on which is the "best" detailed model for farmland valuation. For example, the recent reverse migration for lifestyle reasons (i.e., people moving out of cities and into rural areas) counters the trend of labor migration out of agriculture (that out-migration is explained by Mills and Hazarika 2001), complicating the process of estimating demand for farmland. Also, the conflicting trends of rising farmland values (due to urban influences) and falling agricultural profits call for a new theory.

Farmland Values as an Economic Barometer?

A new theory of farmland valuation that can identify the price effects of each source of demand is needed for many reasons, including policy analysis. The traditional theory's presumption of a direct link between production income and farmland values means that those values should serve as an economic barometer for an area. Unfortunately, one shortcoming of relying on the traditional theory is that it can lead analysts to overstate the competitiveness of agriculture in states or local areas. For example, it is easy to misinterpret recent increases in farm real estate values as evidence of strong profitability in the production agriculture sector because (according to the traditional theory) "in rural areas, agricultural land values are primarily determined by the income earning potential of the land, as measured by expected returns from crops and livestock" (U.S. Department of Agriculture [USDA] 2000, p. 30). However, as the discussion below illustrates, a more detailed assessment of the facts related to farmland values gives a much different outlook.

The fact that average farmland values in the United States have risen for two decades masks the fact that long-run performance of farmland values tells a different story. Also, recent changes in the markets for farm real estate and the implications of those changes are often overlooked. Therefore, to provide a long-run perspective illustrating the need for a new theory of farmland valuation, this section presents farmland value data for the past three decades and a summary of the USDA's explanation for the recent increases.

To begin, Table 9.1 presents farm real estate average values per acre in nominal and real dollars for the period of 1980 to 2006, as reported by the USDA. Data are presented for the entire United States, plus separate values for the three states with the highest levels of agricultural sales revenue: California, Texas, and Iowa. The farmland nominal value levels in the four columns on the left are quite different, but in each case the effects of the "farm crisis" of the 1980s is apparent. Values peak in some year during the early/mid-1980s, fall for a few years, and then begin a recovery. As noted earlier, farm real estate values had increased rapidly in the decade prior to the "farm crisis," but the changes in lending practices that followed the crisis were supposed to have reestablished the fundamental link between land values and local commodity market performance across the United States. Variation between the aggregate national values and the values in each of the states calls for a closer look.

For the United States, the nominal price peak of $823 per acre occurred in 1982, the bottom was in 1987, and the recovery was completed in 1995 when values rose above the level of the earlier peak. The recovery was even slower if real values are considered instead of nominal values. Using the Consumer Price Index to convert the average farmland values into *real* terms (in 2006 dollars) gives an early peak of $1,603 per acre in 1981 and a low of $947 in 1987. Thus, the real data show that the decline was steeper than indicated by the nominal data: there was a 41 percent drop in real values and a 23 percent drop in nominal values. Also, the U.S. farmland market, on average, did not completely recover until 2005, when real values passed the early peak of $1,603. In other words, farmland values are now about the same as they were a generation ago. So, in real purchasing power terms, farmers' wealth has not increased over that period.

For the three leading agricultural states, very different pictures emerge from the data in Table 9.1 indicating that agriculture has not completely recovered from the farm crisis of the 1980s. In nominal dollars, California farm real estate peaked later and recovered sooner (in 1984 and 1991, respectively) than did the national average values. Texas farm real estate values peaked at $694 in 1985 and after their 1992 bottom finally rebounded by 2001. In Iowa, nominal farm real estate values peaked at $1,999 in 1981, hit bottom in 1987, and appeared to recover by 2003. However, these values do not reflect the effects of inflation. The real performance of farm real estate in the three states was worse, and it shows the differences in demand for farmland in the three different regions. California's average values recovered to its "pre-crisis" level by 2001, and in 2006 *real* values were about 54 percent above their earlier peak (reached in 1982). Texas farm real estate did not recover to its 1985 peak until 2006, when it was just 9 percent above the previous high. Iowa still has not yet recovered in real terms. Iowa's average value in 2006 was only 74 percent of the real 1980 value. Clearly, the economic performance of the three state agricultural industries has varied over the last three decades.

Table 9.1

Farm Real Estate Average Values, 1980–2006 ($/acre)

	Nominal value				Real value (base is 2006)			
Year	United States	California	Texas	Iowa	United States	California	Texas	Iowa
1980	737	1,424	436	1,840	1,578	3,049	933	3,939
1981	819	1,732	468	1,999	1,603	3,390	916	3,912
1982	823	1,900	539	1,889	1,518	3,505	994	3,484
1983	788	1,918	544	1,684	1,398	3,404	965	2,989
1984	801	1,981	612	1,518	1,370	3,388	1,047	2,596
1985	713	1,841	694	1,091	1,183	3,056	1,152	1,811
1986	640	1,730	594	873	1,039	2,809	965	1,418
1987	599	1,554	546	786	947	2,457	863	1,243
1988	632	1,575	544	947	966	2,408	832	1,448
1989	668	1,742	521	1,095	984	2,566	767	1,613
1990	683	1,884	507	1,090	969	2,672	719	1,546
1991	703	2,077	498	1,139	963	2,846	682	1,561
1992	713	2,157	488	1,153	955	2,889	654	1,544
1993	736	2,213	499	1,212	964	2,897	653	1,587
1994	798	2,210	515	1,280	1,023	2,833	660	1,641
1995	844	2,220	525	1,350	1,060	2,789	660	1,696
1996	887	2,400	540	1,450	1,094	2,959	666	1,788
1997	926	2,500	554	1,600	1,123	3,032	672	1,940
1998	974	2,610	593	1,700	1,168	3,130	711	2,039
1999	1,030	2,800	640	1,760	1,218	3,310	757	2,081
2000	1,090	3,000	680	1,800	1,261	3,471	787	2,083
2001	1,150	3,200	730	1,850	1,299	3,616	825	2,090
2002	1,210	3,400	775	1,920	1,344	3,776	861	2,132
2003	1,270	3,600	810	2,010	1,381	3,915	881	2,186
2004	1,360	3,800	855	2,200	1,438	4,018	904	2,326
2005	1,650	5,090	1,030	2,650	1,693	5,224	1,057	2,720
2006	1,900	5,390	1,250	2,930	1,900	5,390	1,250	2,930

Source: "Land Values" spreadsheets on the web pages of the Economic Research Service, USDA. The real values are calculated using the CPI, adjusted to make 2006 the base year.

Agricultural income has not been strong over the last three decades, as indicated in earlier chapters, so what has been pushing up farmland values in recent years? One answer was provided by the USDA (2000, p. 30):

> Although average agricultural land values nationally are determined primarily by the income earning potential of the land, nonagricultural factors appear to be playing an important role in many local areas. To some extent, the buoying effect of these nonagricultural factors on agricultural land values could be partially offsetting the effect of lower returns from agricultural production.

What the USDA report called "urban influence" affects only about 17 percent of U.S. farm acreage. The USDA classifies only 515 counties in the United States as being both completely rural (contains no part of a city with at least 2,500 residents) and not adjacent to a metro area. In all remaining counties, the USDA says there is some degree of urban influence on land values.

Urban influence has a significant impact on farmland values. The USDA estimated that during 1994–1996 the average value of farmland that was not urban-influenced was $640 per acre, compared to $1,880 for urban-influenced farmland. Thus, they concluded that 66 percent of urban-influenced farmland market value was due to nonagricultural factors. "The market value for undeveloped farmland in these areas often begins to rise above its value based on agricultural returns alone, reflecting anticipation of eventual nonagricultural uses" (USDA 2000, p. 30). That explains why Rhode Island had the nation's highest average farm real estate value during 2006 at $12,500 per acre (see Table 9.2). In densely populated areas along the East and West Coasts, the amount of urban influence on farmland values can be extreme. For example, in 2001 a 35-acre parcel of farmland in California's Ventura County (just north of Los Angeles) was valued at about $300,000 per acre, due almost entirely to its development potential. Such examples can skew the distribution of farmland values within a state and quickly raise the average.

The USDA study results offer two factors as partial explanations for the differences in farmland values observed for the three leading agricultural states. First is the potential profitability of the crops that can be grown on a parcel of land, which is the traditional theory. Second is the potential for nonagricultural uses of a parcel, which is one of the most significant sources of "adjustments" that need to be made to values derived from the traditional theory. For California, the prospects for both factors are better than the prospects for Texas and Iowa, thus farmland values are higher in the Golden State and made a stronger recovery relative to values observed before the farm crisis of the 1980s.

So, in the cases of these three states, farmland values generally do serve as an agricultural economic barometer, although the traditional theory of prices is clearly incomplete because it cannot account for the confounding effects of the modern factors requiring "adjustments" to traditional price estimates. Part of the problem is that there has never been an exhaustive evaluation of the many factors that influence farmland values. Such a task may be impossible because each location will have a unique list of factors, but some general categories of factors are beginning to emerge in the literature. A summary of those follows.

Factors Influencing Farmland Values

The old cliché about real estate says that the three most important factors are location, location, location. When it comes to farmland values, the cliché may be accurate again. Farm owners in the Northeast see their farmland values soaring because of the surrounding urban development. In the Midwest, land values are buoyed by government subsidies from various farm programs. And in the Rocky Mountains, people will pay extra to get a really great view. In sum, where a farm or ranch is located plays a major role in the nature of the local land market because different factors will be more or less important.

The story will differ by location, but the message is the same; there are four categories of influence on farmland values: (1) the productivity of land when in agricultural production, (2) urban influence, (3) policy effects, and (4) amenity effects. The first of these categories, agricultural productivity, is the basis of the traditional theory of valuation. The other three categories are types of "adjustments" to the traditional value.

Productivity of Land

The first category of influence on farmland values was the only category until recently. Productivity and the resulting profitability was the only hypothesis tested in studies such as that by

Table 9.2

Farm Real Estate Average Values by State (nominal $/acre)

State	1980	1985	1990	1995	2000	2006
Alabama	780	797	890	1,260	1,570	2,750
Arizona	267	295	267	840	1,150	3,350
Arkansas	918	907	796	983	1,290	2,050
California	1,424	1,841	1,884	2,220	3,000	5,390
Colorado	387	437	374	520	650	1,090
Connecticut	2,387	3,005	5,033	5,950	7,050	11,400
Delaware	1,798	1,596	2,214	2,440	3,150	10,200
Florida	1,381	1,599	2,070	2,110	2,500	7,280
Georgia	896	886	1,079	1,260	1,750	3,900
Idaho	698	739	658	840	1,150	2,440
Illinois	2,041	1,381	1,405	1,820	2,260	3,800
Indiana	1,863	1,344	1,254	1,620	2,260	3,630
Iowa	1,840	1,091	1,090	1,350	1,800	2,930
Kansas	587	488	450	535	625	930
Kentucky	976	955	978	1,250	1,650	2,750
Louisiana	1,256	1,407	925	1,080	1,310	1,900
Maine	594	774	1,073	1,130	1,400	2,050
Maryland	2,238	2,197	2,563	3,100	3,600	8,900
Massachusetts	1,608	2,377	4,227	5,060	6,500	11,600
Michigan	1,111	1,108	1,005	1,330	2,090	3,500
Minnesota	1,086	898	810	950	1,320	2,400
Mississippi	819	855	736	886	1,200	1,850
Missouri	902	689	701	880	1,230	1,980
Montana	235	243	222	277	330	760
Nebraska	635	485	524	580	710	1,090
Nevada	248	244	207	289	435	1,000
New Hampshire	1,004	1,439	2,269	2,250	2,400	3,700
New Jersey	2,947	2,951	5,494	7,000	7,600	10,900
New Mexico	185	185	185	209	230	520
New York	720	820	1,014	1,280	1,430	2,050
North Carolina	1,219	1,331	1,355	1,750	2,450	4,250
North Dakota	405	373	321	373	405	560
Ohio	1,730	1,215	1,273	1,750	2,330	3,480
Oklahoma	614	597	491	547	640	970
Oregon	587	615	573	844	1,050	1,420
Pennsylvania	1,464	1,427	1,929	2,200	2,800	4,790
Rhode Island	2,523	2,990	5,564	6,500	7,300	12,500
South Carolina	900	898	1,011	1,340	1,700	2,600
South Dakota	292	289	291	302	380	710
Tennessee	976	944	1,067	1,340	2,100	3,070
Texas	436	694	507	525	680	1,250
Utah	530	513	398	710	900	2,070
Vermont	721	947	1,262	1,450	1,700	2,450
Virginia	1,028	1,112	1,665	1,720	2,230	4,900
Washington	736	943	821	1,070	1,250	1,750
West Virginia	669	607	664	920	1,210	2,150
Wisconsin	1,004	944	801	1,040	1,700	3,200
Wyoming	161	181	153	192	255	420
United States	737	713	683	844	1,090	1,900

Source: "Land Values" spreadsheets on the webpages of the Economic Research Service, USDA.

Martin and Jefferies (1966) during the 1960s. That study is typical of traditional analyses in that it expected everything related to ranch values to be explained by the quality of the land resource and its productivity. Forty years later, similar studies begin with the productivity hypothesis and add "adjustments." For example, in 2005 Torell et al. used a hedonic model to study ranch values in New Mexico and found that "ranch buyers maximize utility, not profit." Although ranch income-earning potential was significant, it was a small part of the explanation of land values; "lifestyle amenities" (such as a mountain location and recreational opportunities) explained much more.

Urban Influence

The first category of adjustments recognized in farmland value studies was "urban influence." As cities and other urban areas grow in size, they spread across more land and, in the process, come in direct or indirect contact with land that had been rural in nature and use. That contact had long been understood to change the nature of the valuation process for the farmland affected, but little formal work had been done on the details of what was driving changes in the valuation process and what the level of price effects might be. During the 1990s, research on those questions began to appear in the literature. Typical of the early work is the study by Shi, Phipps, and Colyer (1997). They found that "expected capital gains appear to be more important than current net returns" in determining farmland prices in West Virginia, where farms are small compared to the national average. By the turn of the century, analysts were formally testing hypotheses related to urban sprawl as significant parts of farmland valuation studies. For example, in 2001 Plantinga and Miller argued that "it is the potential influx of new residents to a county that drives up future development rents" (2001, p. 66). They found in New York that "preferential tax assessment is largely ineffective because, in most instances, the returns to development greatly exceed those from agriculture, even with use value assessment," and they note that "on average, increases in agricultural net returns have a relatively small effect on land values because development is perceived as imminent" (p. 66). At present, urban influence is not only an accepted part of farmland valuation models, but is often the central focus. The study by Livanis et al. (2006) illustrates this point. They develop a theoretical model that explicitly accounts for three effects of urban sprawl: conversion of farmland to urban uses, effect on agricultural returns, and speculative effect as represented by farmland conversion risk. Their empirical results show support for all three effects using county-level data from across the nation. Thus, the question is no longer "if," but rather "how much" when it comes to urban effects on farmland values.

Policy Effects

There is also little debate remaining about whether agricultural policies influence farmland values; even the government acknowledges that there is an influence (USDA 2001). However, lots of questions remain about the nature, extent, and direction of the influence. It was easy to see that government policies aimed at increasing returns from farming activities would affect farmland values. For example, Taylor and Brester (2005) use a hedonic regression model and find that the U.S. sugar program's non-cash income transfers to sugar beet producers in Montana have been capitalized into farmland prices. Yet, some policy effects are unintentional "collateral damage" to nearby land values, and some policies are just misguided. Goodwin, Mishra, and Ortalo-Magne (2003) note that "policy drives up land values, . . . transferring benefits toward landowners rather than producers" because 45 to 50 percent of farmland is rented by operators. Some estimates indicate the size of the benefits is substantial. For example, Shaik, Helmers, and Atwood (2005) find that "the share of agricultural land values generated by farm program payments increased up to as much as 30% to 40% of land values during the 1938–1980 period" and has since "declined to levels between 15% and 20%." This explains why it is difficult to reduce or eliminate farm payments: policies positively influence farmland values and the wealth of owners (Moss and Schmitz 2003), so eliminating government transfers would weaken the local economy and reduce the wealth of farmers in regions dominated by the production of "program crops." Thus, midwestern land prices keep going up because of the expectation that federal dollars will continue to roll in. In other parts of the country, where agriculture is no longer dominant, efforts to save farmland using policies such as exclusive agricultural zoning still influence farmland prices (Henneberry and Barrows 1990). Also, zoning policies aimed at maintaining other types of open space directly influence property values (Netusil 2005). Finally, even the effect of federal land acquisitions factor in and are perverse because of the reputation of governmental and nonprofit organizations for paying more than market value for refuges, preserves, open space, and so on. When these sales are factored into a local land market they can reduce factor returns, thus making it *more* difficult for agriculture to remain economically viable in the area. In one case study, Nickerson and Lynch (2001) found that in Maryland there is no price decrease when farmland is preserved from development. They point out that "the results also cast doubt about the ability of PDR/TDR [purchase of development rights, transfer of development rights] programs to support a local farm industry." When farm policies lead to increased land values, that raises ownership costs, lowering profit levels or, at the very least, raising the opportunity costs of remaining in agricultural production.

Amenity Effects

The effects of amenities on land values are parcel-specific and can be measured econometrically only with individual sales data, thus much less empirical research was done on this subject until recently. As sales data began to become available, studies like that by Torell et al. (2005) began to show that "lifestyle amenities" (such as a desirable location and recreational opportunities) explained much more of rural land value than did the productivity of the land in many areas. The range of amenities and the scale of their effects on prices is often surprising. For example, Henderson and Moore (2006) find that wildlife recreation income (e.g., from deer-hunting leases) significantly raises average farmland values in Texas counties. At present, research on new types of amenities is expanding (e.g., Reynolds and Regalado 2002). However, the results are not always positive. This is illustrated by the study of Bin and Polasky (2005). They find that nearby wetlands reduce residential property values in rural areas of North Carolina, whereas other studies had found that the amenity value of wetlands raises property values in urban areas. Such mixed results are proving to be common as the research focus expands from farmland to all types of rural properties. Netusil (2005) uses a hedonic price method to study single-family residential properties and concludes: "the impact of environmental zoning is found to vary with the type of environmental zoning and the property's location. Amenities are found to influence a property's sale price with the effect varying by amenity type and proximity." In general, the types of amenities that have positive effects on property values are those associated with open spaces which, essentially, leave the land unused. Conversely, land being used for agricultural production is considered to have "disamenity," or negative, effects on values, as shown by Ready and Abdalla (2005). They use a hedonic price function for single-family homes in a Pennsylvania county and find that "agriculture has both positive and negative impacts on its neighbors." They report that "open space, including agricultural open space, has a positive impact on house prices within 400m, but that larger-scale animal production facilities . . . have negative impacts on house prices within 1,600m" (2005, p. 324). "A single animal production facility decreases nearby property values by up to 6.4%" (p. 325). That result is supported by Kilpatrick (2001). He shows that property located near a feedlot is negatively impacted by this externality. The degree of impairment depends on proximity and property type and use. Higher-valued properties are impacted more than lower-valued properties. So, people will pay extra to live near water or a park (Cho, Bowker, and Park 2006), but they do not want to see (or smell) any livestock.

The Relative Importance of Pricing Factors

The discussion above indicates that farmland valuation has become much more complicated in the last couple of decades. An increasing number of factors have been shown to influence farmland values, thus adding to the list of "adjustments" to the traditional model. The study by Huang et al. (2006) illustrates how involved price analysis has become. They estimate a hedonic model of Illinois farmland values using county-level cross-section time-series data. Explanatory variables include land productivity, parcel size, improvements, distances to Chicago and other large cities, an urban–rural index, livestock production through swine operation scale and farm density measures, population density, income, and inflation. They note that inclusion of spatial and serial correlation components substantially improves the model fit. They conclude that farmland values decline with parcel size, ruralness, distance to Chicago and large cities, and swine farm density, and increase with soil productivity, population density, and personal income. Clearly, it's not your grandfather's traditional model anymore!

With so many factors to be considered in modeling farmland values, a natural question arises: which one(s) is (are) the most important in today's market? To answer that question, a brief study was conducted. Farm-level survey data from across the continental United States were used to estimate simple equations for farmland values over the 1996–2004 period.[2] To begin, a single equation for the average farmland value was estimated for each of the ten geographic regions of the country. The explanatory variables included are proxies for three of the four categories of influence on farmland values. Productivity of the land is proxied by two variables: revenue per acre and a productivity index. Urban influence is proxied by a county population density measure. Policy effects are proxied by the amount of government payments received per acre. Amenity effects are specific to individual parcels, thus they cannot be estimated using aggregated data and are, therefore, excluded from this analysis. One additional explanatory variable is included: the cost of capital is used to represent the financial factors in a market, as suggested by Moss (1997).

The empirical results of the regressions for each of the ten regions are presented in Table 9.3. The key result is that the proxy variable for the nonfarm demand for farmland (county population density by year) was significant in all regions. This is consistent with the growing realization that nonfarm demand for farmland is increasingly influencing farmland values, even in areas such as the Corn Belt and Northern Plains, whose economies were dominated by production agriculture in the last century. The population density variable swamped the effects of the four other variables. Thus, the proximity of a farmland parcel relative to nonagricultural development is a key factor in pricing. This implies that no commodity can generate enough revenue to adequately compete with expanding urban development, meaning that land-use ordinances may be needed to preserve farmland in urbanizing areas.

Next, the same equation was estimated across three different farm sizes. The results presented in Table 9.4 have significant implications for land-pricing theory. The revenue per acre generated by farming has no effect on large-sized farms, contrary to traditional theory. Small- and medium-sized farms do get a significant effect from production revenues per acre. Finally, all three farm

Table 9.3

Regression Results for Farmland Value Equations by Region, 1996–2004

Variable	North-east	Lake States	Corn Belt	Appa-lachia	South-east	Delta	Southern Plains	Northern Plains	Mountain	Pacific
Revenue per acre	0.155 (1.17)	−0.020 (−0.99)	0.221 (1.96)**	0.012 (0.40)	0.018 (0.81)	0.152 (1.90)*	−0.057 (−0.10)	0.298 (0.99)	4.139 (1.023)	0.083 (0.30)
Govt payments per acre	−7.184 (−1.01)	3.535 (0.32)	33.272 (1.17)	4.378 (1.21)	0.714 (0.92)	−2.455 (−1.77)*	−7.007 (−2.11)**	1.243 (0.17)	−3.934 (−0.46)	0.473 (0.15)
Costcapital	−0.156 (−2.17)**	−0.001 (−0.54)	−0.027 (−1.83)*	−0.004 (−0.34)	−0.028 (−1.32)	−0.008 (−0.86)	0.006 (0.39)	−0.008 (−0.51)	−0.082 (−1.22)	0.054 (0.13)
Productivity	0.037 (0.36)	0.035 (0.31)	−0.052 (−0.44)	0.030 (0.61)	0.188 (3.50)***	−0.146 (−1.82)*	0.067 (0.21)	−0.230 (−0.67)	−3.997 (−1.005)	−0.058 (−0.19)
Popdensity	0.007 (3.99)***	0.004 (5.50)***	0.005 (3.14)***	0.008 (2.15)**	0.009 (5.02)***	0.005 (4.67)***	0.004 (1.66)*	0.008 (3.02)***	0.032 (3.04)***	0.028 (7.20)***

Note: The top value in each pair is the variable's regression coefficient and the value in parentheses is its t-statistic. ***, **, and * denote statistical significance at the 99%, 95%, and 90% confidence levels, respectively.

Table 9.4

Regressions of Farmland Value by Farm Size, Across Ten Regions, 1996–2004

	Farm size 1			Farm size 2			Farm size 3		
Variable	Estimate	t value		Estimate	t value		Estimate	t value	
Cashflowperacre	0.577	1.79	*	0.586	2.81	***	0.043	1.12	
Govtpayments/ac	−2.552	−0.72		0.684	0.10		0.235	0.13	
Costcapital	0.013	0.23		−0.065	−1.43		−0.055	−1.74	*
Productivity	0.116	0.46		0.006	0.06		0.011	−0.37	
Popdensity	0.008	5.99	***	0.011	2.87	***	0.021	4.01	***

Notes: ***, **, and * denote statistical significance at the 99%, 95%, and 90% confidence levels, respectively. These regressions use state dummy variables for fixed effects.

Farm Size 1 corresponds to limited resource, retirement, and residential farms. Farm Size 2 consists of farm/lower sales and farm/higher sales. Farm Size 3 includes large family farms and very large farms.

sizes have significant *Population Density* effects, but the regression coefficient increases with farm size. Again, this implies that a farm's proximity to urban areas is key to its farmland values, but larger farms have more development value per acre.

In summary, the traditional theory that farmland values are influenced primarily by the land's ability to generate profits from agricultural production may still be true for some small- and mid-sized farms in some locations, but for all regions urban influence is the dominant factor in the valuation process. This change in American farmland markets has been caused by the evolution of the national economy. It signals that development is ongoing and more change is coming.

LAND USES

"Buy land, they're not making any more of it!" The old cliché sought to explain why land was such a good investment: a fixed supply in the face of growing demand meant higher prices over time. However, the previous section of this chapter shows that agricultural use of land is not the source of higher prices for farmland; it is potential urban use that is pushing up farmland prices. This might lead some people to incorrectly believe that America is being paved over, replacing pristine pastoral settings with endless urban blight. With only a few exceptions, this is not happening—or at least it is not happening as fast as might be thought. However, there are significant shifts in land use in progress in the United States. Therefore, a few facts are needed to put the farmland story into context.

Historical Data on Land Use in the United States

The United States has a land area of 2.264 billion acres, of which about 2.2 billion acres are categorized as rural and about 60 million acres are categorized as urban (Lubowski et al. 2006). Thus, fears that America is being paved over are greatly exaggerated. Or are they? To make a realistic assessment of the supply of farmland in the United States and any threat from urban development, several adjustments must be made to the basic data.

First, the massive state of Alaska and the tiny Hawaiian islands need to be eliminated from the total land data. Alaska is huge but has virtually no farmland, and Hawaii has only some unique specialty crop agricultural land. Therefore, the remainder of this discussion considers only land in the contiguous forty-eight states. In this case, the total land area is 1.894 billion acres, with some 60 million acres—about 3 percent—in urban use and the remaining 97 percent categorized as rural (Lubowski et al. 2006).

The second adjustment to the basic data that is needed before a clear picture emerges is to distinguish between the different types of "rural" land. There are different methods of doing this, with the National Resources Inventory (NRI) using one set of categories and the U.S. Department of Agriculture using another.[3] The USDA's categories of rural land and their shares of total land in the 48 states include "cropland" 23 percent, "grassland pasture and range" 31 percent, "forest-use land" (exclusive of forested areas in parks and other special uses) 30 percent, "special uses" (parks, wilderness, wildlife, and related uses) 8 percent, and "miscellaneous other land" (deserts, wetlands, and barren land) 5 percent. Trying to identify which of these categories is "farmland" is a bit confusing because there is some overlap. The two categories that are all farmland are "cropland" and "grassland pasture and range," while some forest land is also used for livestock grazing (see Tanaka, Torell, and Rimbey 2005, for example). As a result, totaling the two main agricultural use categories approximates, but is not exactly the same as, the "land in farms" totals given in USDA reports. Table 9.5 reports the "land in farms" totals as well as the totals for cropland and pasture and range over time to show their trends.

As noted in earlier chapters, total land in farms peaked in 1954 at 1.2 billion acres and has decreased in every year since. The 940 million acres reported in the 2002 Census of Agriculture is about half of the total land area of the 48 states, so it seems like the country is still making a huge investment in agriculture. However, it is still only 78 percent of the land investment that had been made in the peak year. Does this reflect the improved productivity of American agriculture over that period—that less land is needed to produce the food we eat? Certainly this could be a factor at the aggregate level, but with our growing population and the growing export markets available to American producers, it would seem that individuals would keep their land in production if it could make a profit. Thus, the declining total for land in farms is an indicator of the shift in the level of market marginal land over time. This is illustrated by Drozd and Johnson (2004), who use a farmland productivity model to show at what point it becomes economically justifiable to convert farmland into acreage tracts. Improvements in agricultural productivity across the globe are pushing lower-quality land out of production. This alters the country's investment in agriculture.

Looking at the simple breakdown of the farmland numbers in Table 9.5 raises some interesting issues. The total "land in farms" and the two primary categories making up the total, "cropland" and "pasture and range," all have declining trends apparent over the last half-century, as shown in the table. However, the trend in total land in farms is more stable than the trends in the two categories. Yet it is clear that land is leaving both categories. Cropland has declined steadily since 1978, losing over 29 million acres during that period, and pasture and range now totals about 52 million acres less than it did in 1964. Comparing the three declining trends leads to the following propositions.

- PROPOSITION 9.1. *Cropland is higher-quality soil and has terrain that is more flexible in its potential for commodity production, compared to pasture and range land, therefore commodity market shocks are less likely to make cropland market marginal.*
- PROPOSITION 9.2. *Over time, cropland will become a larger share of total land in farms because pasture and range land is more likely to be shifted into nonagricultural uses.*

Proposition 9.1 is easy to understand if the two land categories are labeled "improved land" and "unimproved land." Cropland is improved through the investments made in clearing it,

Table 9.5

Land Use, 48 States, Agricultural Census Years 1949–2002

	1949	1954	1959	1964	1969	1974	1978	1982	1987	1992	1997	2002
Land in farms	1,190	1,206	1,179	1,142	1,104	1,080	1,041	1,024	996	979	956	940
Cropland	477,838	465,327	457,483	443,801	471,707	464,702	470,480	468,888	463,580	459,654	454,691	441,273
Irrigated farmland	25,785	29,552	33,022	36,912	38,975	41,100	50,190	48,855	46,235	49,268	56,209	55,244
Pasture and range	631,078	632,417	630,131	636,464	601,004	595,190	584,302	594,252	588,792	589,044	577,977	584,224
Urban land*	18,283	18,561	27,121	29,162	30,840	34,556	44,218	49,649	55,908	57,960	64,292	59,193
Cropland share of farmland	40	39	39	39	43	43	45	46	47	47	48	47
Irrigated share of cropland	5	6	7	8	8	9	11	10	10	11	12	13

Source: USDA, ERS web pages.

Note: The total of crop and pasture land exceeds total land in farms in some years due to double counting of cropland pasture harvested for crops, and grazed forests.

* The data for urban land in 2002 are not directly comparable to earlier years because the definition of "urban" was changed by the USDA beginning in that year.

possibly leveling it, and, in the case of irrigated land, putting in expensive infrastructure. On the other hand, range land has virtually no investments made in changing it from its natural state. Such investments are made by farmers and ranchers only when they expect to receive a return on those improvements. Thus, the higher the amount of investment made in a parcel of land, the higher its agricultural income potential must be, thus indicating the quality of its soil and terrain.

Proposition 9.2 indicates that higher-quality land will remain in agriculture longer, despite the overall decline in total land in farms. This follows directly from Mundlak's (2000) model of market marginal land. If cropland is higher in quality, thus having higher income potential, as argued in Proposition 9.1, then it will remain in agriculture as pasture and range land is shifted out of production, hence altering the relative shares of land-use categories. On the surface of the data in Table 9.5, the proposition appears to be supported. The row labeled "cropland share of farmland" indicates that cropland has grown from 39–40 percent to 47–48 percent of total land in farms over the last half-century. However, the issue is confused by the fact that the total of cropland and pasture/range land exceeds total land in farms in some years due to double counting of cropland pasture harvested for crops, and forest land that is grazed by livestock.

To eliminate some of this confusion, a third adjustment must be made to the basic data. Lubowski et al. (2006) note that the "cropland" category includes five components: cropland harvested, crop failure, cultivated summer fallow, cropland pasture, and idle cropland. They explain (p. 12):

> Cropland harvested, crop failure, and cultivated summer fallow comprise the total amount of cropland used for crops, or the acreage devoted to crop production in any year. Cropland pastured and idle cropland are not directly involved in crop production in a given year, but may rotate into production in another year.

This means the data for cropland in Table 9.5 are the total of these five components. In other words, those data overstate the amount of cropland truly in production. To see how much land America is actually investing in crop production, the cropland voluntarily idled completely or partially must be subtracted.

Table 9.6 shows America's real investment in crop production. Two things jump out from the numbers. First, the amounts of both cropland harvested and total cropland are currently about the same as they were a century ago. Second, only about 70 percent of total cropland is harvested. The relatively stable amounts of cropland over time indicate how significant the advances in productivity have been: the country's population has tripled over the past century and yet about the same amount of land produced enough crop output to not only feed the expanding population, but to generate quantities sufficient to lower food prices after adjusting for inflation. Also important is the point that between 85 million and 139 million acres of cropland have been voluntarily removed from crop production each year, signaling how much land is questionable in its ability to generate production profits. Another way to view these numbers is that the 300–335 million acres of total cropland that have been harvested consistently over the past century are probably a good estimate of the country's amount of highest quality cropland—land that is competitive with the best cropland in other parts of the world. The voluntarily sidelined cropland acreage is probably land of slightly lesser quality, while land in the "pasture and range" category is poorer still. Thus, it makes sense that land leaving agriculture is more likely to come from those categories in reverse order, based on their relative levels of profitability (Wolverton 2004).

In summary, shifts in global commodity markets have, in general, made cropland more profitable than pasture and range land and, as a result, acreage of cropland harvested is relatively

Table 9.6

Cropland Harvested and Total for the 48 States, Selected Years, 1910–2005 (million acres)

Year	Cropland harvested*	Crop failure	Cultivated summer fallow	Total
1910	317	9	4	330
1915	332	11	5	348
1920	351	12	5	368
1925	351	12	7	370
1930	360	11	11	382
1935	336	25	16	377
1940	331	16	21	368
1945	345	9	18	372
1950	336	12	29	377
1955	333	16	29	378
1960	317	6	32	355
1965	292	6	38	336
1970	289	5	38	332
1975	330	6	31	367
1980	341	11	30	382
1985	334	7	31	372
1990	310	6	25	341
1995	302	8	22	332
2000	314	11	20	345
2005	314	7	16	337

Source: USDA web pages.
* Land from which one or more crops were harvested.

stable while grassland pasture and range has been on what Lubowski et al. (2006) call a "steady downward trend since the 1940s." However, the story varies in different regions of the country.

Table 9.7 shows how total cropland has varied over time in each of the 10 regions in the 48 contiguous states. A clear theme seems to appear in the divergent results. In 3 of the 10 regions cropland decreased significantly over the 1949–2002 period. Those regions are the easternmost three, along the Atlantic coast, where there has been the most urban growth: the Northeast, Appalachia, and the Southeast. Three other regions have had slight declines in total cropland: the Lake States, Delta States, and the Pacific. Those regions also had urban pressures on limited agricultural areas. On the other hand, the two regions with the largest cropland areas, the Corn Belt and the Northern Plains, had virtually no change in acreage over the long period (although acreage did expand during the 1970s), most likely because there was little urban pressure in those areas. Finally, the Southern Plains had a slight increase in cropland acreage and the Mountain region had a significant expansion, in each case due to conversion of pasture and range to cropland over the decades. In these two livestock-dominated regions, population growth appears to have expanded markets for crops (possibly such as fruits and vegetables) enough to make the land conversion profitable. In Wyoming, for example, Inman, McLeod, and Menkhaus (2002) identified three types of agricultural land, each with unique supply and demand factors that can trigger conversions. Therefore, it appears that in the absence of population growth and related urban development, no changes in cropland acreage are likely, yet in sparsely populated areas some urban growth can push acreage into a higher-developed use category and, finally, land will

Table 9.7

Total Cropland by Regions, Agricultural Census Years 1949–2002 (1,000 acres)

Region	1949	1954	1959	1964	1969	1974	1978	1982	1987	1992	1997	2002
Northeast	24,557	22,830	20,973	19,173	17,853	17,334	17,501	16,954	15,707	14,337	13,402	13,700
Lake States	46,410	45,897	45,495	44,970	44,332	44,117	45,147	45,041	42,393	42,519	40,704	42,102
Corn Belt	95,956	95,268	95,090	94,750	101,969	100,464	101,761	100,421	99,636	99,608	98,565	95,728
Northern Plains	100,666	101,043	101,054	98,843	107,237	105,013	102,903	106,969	109,613	106,602	107,846	101,978
Appalachian	37,363	33,722	29,990	28,883	31,630	30,656	31,259	30,369	29,451	29,136	27,992	26,011
Southeast	27,919	24,824	21,071	18,880	20,424	20,708	21,150	20,338	18,290	18,053	17,982	14,824
Delta States	24,283	22,162	20,808	20,238	24,558	25,054	25,950	24,978	23,888	23,739	22,031	21,046
Southern Plains	53,986	52,120	53,916	49,446	56,043	53,769	55,842	54,566	52,337	55,073	56,377	55,670
Mountain	39,675	41,218	42,952	43,167	43,359	42,801	43,589	43,849	47,029	46,659	45,426	46,265
Pacific	27,023	26,243	26,134	25,451	24,302	24,786	25,378	25,403	25,236	23,928	24,367	23,949
48 States	477,838	465,327	457,483	443,801	471,707	464,702	470,480	468,888	463,580	459,654	454,691	441,273

Source: USDA, ERS web pages.

leave agriculture as population density grows, even when agriculture is relatively profitable (such as in the Southeast and Pacific regions).

This discussion gives the impression that land leaving agricultural production is becoming urban. As shown in earlier chapters, American agriculture is shrinking. This is a sign of economic development at the global level. It is *not* just a shift of farmland to urban uses. From 1949 to 2002, urban land use increased steadily from 18.3 million to over 60 million acres (see Table 9.5), yet urban expansion is not the primary threat to agriculture in total. About 270 million acres left American agriculture between 1954 and 2005, thus most land leaving agriculture is going into some use other than urban development.

Urban growth is having many effects on agricultural land. For example, Table 9.5 contains data on total acreage of irrigated farmland, which is a subset of cropland. As shown in the table, irrigated acreage more than doubled over the 1949–2002 period. The expansion of irrigated acreage—most often for use in the production of high-value fruit and vegetable crops—is even more pronounced when expressed as a share of total cropland. The bottom row of the table shows that irrigated land has grown from 5 to 13 percent of total cropland over the period. The similar amounts of increase in the two series raises the hypothesis that urban growth is driving the expansion of markets for commodities produced on irrigated acreage. The data in Table 9.5 support that hypothesis. The correlation between urban acreage and irrigated farmland acreage data is very high: $r = 0.95$.

Ironically, one of the most threatening aspects of population growth is not urban development directly, but the related trend of rapidly expanding rural residential development. "Rural residential land" is a new land-use category introduced by the USDA in 1997. It was created in recognition of the significant impacts of the recent trend of a "reverse migration" of people moving out of cities and into nearby rural areas (Vesterby and Krupa 2002). First the migration was thought to be limited to exurban areas outside large metropolitan areas (see Berube et al. 2006 for a discussion of exurbia), then the growth of rural residential development was finally identified as a national trend. When the USDA first created the land-use category and began collecting the data, people realized how significant the category had become. The first estimates, made in 1997, were startling. The USDA used housing data from other sources to calculate that in 1980 rural residential land totaled 56 million acres nationally, compared to 29 million acres of urban residential land (in addition to 18 million acres of nonresidential urban land use). The 1997 estimate of rural residential land was 83 million acres, while urban land totaled only 36 million acres for residential and about 30 million acres for nonresidential use (Vesterby and Krupa 2002). By 2002, rural residential land totaled 94 million acres—an area more than 150 percent the size of all urban uses of land! This means that the combined total of urban and rural residence land was about 154 million acres: approximately half the size of all cropland harvested that year. Suddenly, the threat to America's farmland from economic development becomes very real.

There is an ironic twist in the threat to agriculture from rural residential growth: it creates a development loop. The people moving to rural areas want a lifestyle that is full of pastoral beauty and free of the congestion of urban life (Deller et al. 2001). Yet, over time those people provide the economic incentive for businesses that support life (like grocery stores and gas stations) to follow them into the rural locations. Gradually, other support businesses and their employees move to the area, thus fueling a gradual development process that creates the type of sprawl from which the original rural residents were trying to escape, thereby creating an incentive for those pioneers to move again.[4] Carrion-Flores and Irwin (2004) define sprawl as "a term that is often used to describe perceived inefficiencies of development, including disproportionate growth of urban areas and excessive leapfrog development" (p. 889). They explain (p. 902):

Empirical findings from the land-use conversion model show that there are several factors that influence residential land conversion that are hypothesized to contribute to a sprawl pattern of development. Preferences for low-density areas that are outside of established urban places, limited agglomeration economies around the central city, and heterogeneity among local jurisdictions are found to be important determinants of residential land conversion.

They also note, "new residential development is more likely to occur next to existing development" (p. 902), creating a clustering effect. Sprawl can be efficient or inefficient as a pattern of development, depending on whether externalities are involved. The development pattern is determined by profits, as noted by Isakson and Ecker (2001, p. 41):

> One might reasonably expect that subdivision profitability would evolve spatially and temporally because risk differs from site to site through time. Thus, the temporal component is potentially driven by expectations for future urban growth. The spatial component may be driven by proximity to centers of economic activity.

In other words, residential and other types of urban development follow the lead of rural residential pioneers. This gives a new meaning to the famous movie line: "if you build it, they will come."

Efforts to keep them from coming are only partially successful, at best. Hardie et al. (2000) studied the responsiveness of land uses in the American south to see if economic incentives could be used in policy efforts to direct land use in some desired direction. They found that (p. 671) "one can draw few universal conclusions about the response of land use to change in the determinants of land rent." They concluded that the varied results of their modeling efforts made it easy to see "why uniform policies have different results in different localities, and why targeted policies can be more efficient in inducing land use change." A rare example of a targeted policy that succeeded was presented by Cho et al. (2006), who found that an "urban growth boundary" aided in reducing urban sprawl by directing development into urban areas of Knoxville, Tennessee. In general, policies aimed at guiding land into particular uses have succeeded completely only when alternative uses are prohibited. Such prohibitive policies are always unpopular with the owners of land that is prevented from reaching some higher level of development because the use prohibition reduces the value of the land, thus reducing the wealth of the owners. That problem has created some situations in the United States that could only happen in a wealthy country.

Land Use as an Indicator of Economic Development

Farmland and, to a lesser extent, forest land are the least developed forms of private use, thus they offer the most flexibility in present and future uses.[5] Pasture and range land, in particular, has usually had the least amount of investment made in its condition. Thus, farmland serves as a residual use until more profitable alternative uses become available (Hardie et al. 2000).

In less-developed countries a larger share of the total land area is used in agricultural production, compared to wealthy countries like the United States, Japan, and most of Western Europe. This is because hunger is a real threat in poor countries. As a result, policies in less-developed countries are most often aimed at maximizing the output of food and other agricultural commodities. This leads to land-use policies and production management practices that facilitate maximizing the yield of each acre of land, given the economic constraints of the landowners. It is only after the threat of hunger has been lifted from the entire population that a country can afford to shift land out of agricultural production. It does not matter whether food sufficiency has been achieved by self-sufficiency in production or by purchasing food imports paid for with earnings from other sectors of the economy; feeding the population is a government's first job. Thus, the relative share of agriculture in a country's economy and the shares of agriculture and forests in its land-use patterns are indicators of that country's degree of economic development. When land-use patterns show either significantly decreasing amounts of farmland or even marginal increases in forest land, it indicates the country has achieved a high degree of wealth.

Only in a wealthy country can certain types of land use be observed on a wide scale. Viewing land use as a type of investment being made by a country, or a person, leads to the following general observation.

- PROPOSITION 9.3. *A wealthy nation (or person) can afford to "waste" agricultural land by allocating it to leisure activity (e.g., hobby farms) and/or focus on the quality of output rather than the quantity of output, as poor countries must do.*

This proposition can be translated into simple economic terms. It states that wealthy investors seek to maximize utility, whereas poor investors seek to maximize output. A poor farmer, for example, will use every possible meter of land in production of food to eat or sell. A wealthy landowner is not afraid of going hungry, so he or she can afford to use some or all available land in the pursuit of other goals. The United States is a wealthy landowner.

As shown in Table 9.8, the United States is both reducing its farmland and increasing its forest land that is not used in agricultural production. The cropland acreages listed in the table are smaller than those reported by the USDA because NRI estimates remove pasture land from cropland and report them separately, thus more accurately reflecting the country's investment in crop production.

More telling is the fact that the United States *pays* to idle cropland. The Conservation Reserve Program (CRP) idles over 30 million acres each year. As Feng et al. (2005) note, the CRP "was introduced with the dual goals of controlling supply and reducing soil erosion" (p. 1231). With the program begun in 1985, "over $15 billion was spent in the first fifteen years and resulted in the retirement of about 10% of the total cropland across the country from active production" (p. 1231). Currently, the CRP pays farmers about $2 billion per year to retire cropland under ten- to fifteen-year contracts (Roberts and Bucholz 2006). Typical of most land-use programs, the CRP is less effective than it appears to be with regard to both of the goals noted above. Wu (2000) found that slippage—an unintended stimulus of new plantings—offsets some of CRP's environmental benefits. He estimated that for each 100 acres removed from production in the CRP, 20 acres of non-cropland are converted to cropland in a substitution effect. This converted non-cropland is likely to be of lesser quality (otherwise it would have been in crop production to begin with) and potentially more susceptible to erosion than the original cropland, thus reducing the aggregate efficiency and sustainability of the country's agricultural production.

In total, between 19 million and 68 million acres of cropland have been idled each year since World War II in federal acreage reduction programs such as the CRP and the Acreage Reduction Program. Even more cropland is underutilized, such as being used only for pasture. Each year since 1949, between 57 million and 88 million acres have been used in this way (Daugherty 1998; Vesterby et al. 1997). Therefore, the country is paying both direct and indirect costs to intentionally reduce total agricultural output. The direct costs are the billions of dollars paid out each

Table 9.8

Land Use in the 48 States: National Resources Inventory Estimates of Cropland and Land Removed from Production (million acres)

	1982	1987	1992	1997	2002
Cropland	419.6	406.2	381.2	376.4	368.4
Conservation Reserve Program	0.0	13.8	34.0	32.7	31.6
Forest land ungrazed	338.4	341.7	342.3	346.5	349.8
Water and Federal areas	447.7	449.3	450.9	451.6	452.3

Source: USDA, National Resources and Conservation Service.

year by the government for programs such as the CRP. The indirect costs incurred are the opportunity costs to farmers and ranchers who underutilize their productive land. These indirect costs could also be considered a deadweight loss to the national economy.

Reduced-output uses of land, which result in lower-than-maximum yields, are an option for a rich country; poor countries, however, must maximize output. One example of reduced-output land use that is growing in the United States and Europe is "organic" farming (Greene 2006). It usually results in lower yields per acre. In Chapter 16, organic agriculture is described as a quality niche because farmers are voluntarily using production practices that yield less but are believed to generate a higher-quality output. Quality niches can be pursued by wealthy countries, but are a less efficient use of some resources that wealthy buyers must value enough to pay more for, to at least cover producers' extra costs, or the niche results in a financial loss to the farmer. Another example of reduced-output land uses are those in which ecological practices are applied, causing lowered yields and/or higher costs per unit of output (Moon et al. 2002).

Zero-output uses of land, such as conservation or recreation uses, can be voluntary or involuntary. "Voluntary" means that the landowner can afford to make productive-profitable use of the land, but chooses not to do so. This is an option for a wealthy owner. "Involuntary" means that the owner cannot afford to use land productively (it is market marginal land), hence it is fallow. This happens in rich and poor countries.

An example of a voluntary zero-output use of land could include forests that are not harvested, such as those in wilderness areas and government parks. Forests that serve a demand for recreation have been recognized in recent decades as falling into the "reduced-use" category, thus partially justifying their "idle" status in wealthy countries. However, a new perspective on forests and their use status is beginning to demonstrate how differently rich and poor countries view land use. In Europe, forestry's capacity to sequester carbon has been officially recognized by the Kyoto Protocol. This has prompted much interest in the European Union in forestry as a land use competing with traditional agricultural production (Behan, McQuinn, and Roche 2006). In other words, in the wealthy parts of Europe, governments are considering paying farmers to replace productive fields with forests, while in poor parts of the world, rainforests are being ripped out by farmers desperate to expand their land so they can increase their limited income (Lopez and Galinato 2005).

Americans do not have to look oversees to find contradictory land-use policies. In addition to its policies aimed at taking some land out of agricultural use, the United States also has policies aimed at keeping land in agriculture. For example, in a study of wetlands, Claassen et al. (1998)

found that "up to 82.7 million wetland acres would be exempted under the proposed delineation changes, of which as many as 12 million acres could be profitably converted to crop production" (p. 390). That is a lot of dirt! Only 10 states had more than 12 million acres of cropland in production in 2002. Are these programs that pay to take land out of production a good deal? Kirwan, Lubowski, and Roberts (2005) observed that the CRP "offers annual rental payments to farm operators who voluntarily retire environmentally sensitive cropland under ten- to fifteen-year contracts" (p. 1239). They "estimated the premiums received by CRP participants above their reservation rents. Estimated premiums have generally increased over time and constitute 10–40% of the program's rental pay-outs," thus there have been large transfers of wealth from taxpayers to farmers (p. 1245). At the same time, money is being spent to keep farmland in production. Hellerstein et al. (2002) report: "Measures used to protect farmland include zoning, preferential tax assessments, agricultural districts, right-to-farm laws, and purchase of development rights (PDR) programs. Currently, 19 states and 41 local jurisdictions operate PDR programs, which pay farmers to give up rights to develop their land." Duke and Lynch (2006) surveyed the literature and found twenty-eight techniques for retaining farmland, which they classified into four types. Retention programs can have significant financial effects on many types of people. For example, King and Anderson (2004) explain one type of farmland retention program (p. 919): "Conservation easements establish a private tax incentive for private individuals to provide a public good"; landowners keeping land in farming, forestry, or open space do so without being taxed on the component of the land's value attributable to future development opportunities, while towns can preserve their rural character. Results in Vermont show that "conservation easements are tax-neutral or tax-diminishing in the long run, but increase taxes in the very short run" (p. 930). The long-run effect comes from the increased values of surrounding lands. These property-value increases raise the property taxes of the owners. Thus, "in addition to guaranteeing open space amenities, landowners entering into conservation easements increase the wealth of their neighbors" (pp. 930–931). Therefore, it should not be surprising that Lynch and Musser (2001) concluded that farmland preservation programs are not always efficient in achieving one or more of the four standard goals used to justify the programs: "local and national food security, employment in the agricultural industry, efficient development of urban and rural land, and the protection of rural and environmental amenities." So, it seems that when it comes right down to creating programs aimed at keeping land in or out of American agriculture, it's all about somebody's wealth.

IDLE FARMLAND AND GLOBAL CAPACITY

This chapter began by showing that, in theory, the land in use for agricultural production is a function of productive quality, location, and relative profitability. The discussion showed it is entirely possible for the conditions to exist that lead all land within a local or regional market area to leave agriculture. Next, this chapter explained that the first step an individual parcel of farmland would take on its way out of agriculture is to be left idle for some period of time. Farmland does not need to have an immediate use in some other economic sector for it to be taken out of agricultural production and left idle. However, it is well understood that once an alternative use for a parcel of farmland becomes available, it is unlikely that the parcel will remain in agriculture indefinitely unless some land-use policy intervention occurs. It is also well understood that once land is developed into some higher-value use, it virtually never returns to use in agricultural production. As a result, every time some farmland is developed out of agriculture, the globe's capacity to produce food is reduced by some amount.

At this point in the book, it should be clear that two significant trends are on a collision course: (1) the United States and most other more-developed countries are reducing the amount of land they use for agriculture, and (2) the world's population is increasing. Putting these trends together creates a huge problem when considering that there is a fixed land area in the world; at some point, global capacity to produce food might be insufficient given the population. Global economic development is causing the first trend and may be facilitating the second. So, does this mean that global economic development is leading the world to increased levels of hunger, just like Malthus warned hundreds of years ago? This question and its relevance to America are briefly addressed below by breaking it into three questions.

Can Vast Tracts of American Farmland Go Idle?

The United States is such a large country that most Americans never give any thought to the idea that large chunks of it could leave agriculture, especially given the dominance of agriculture in the local economies of many parts of the country. Yet, it has been a fact for decades that land is leaving the American industry as global markets develop foreign competitors and local domestic economies develop alternative uses for that land. As explained in this chapter, it is global competition, not local development, that is having the biggest impact on American agriculture and poses the biggest threat. This has been understood by a few people for a long time, but it remains a mystery to most. The reason it is inconceivable to uninformed observers is, again, because of the dominance of agriculture in the local economies of many parts of the country. In the grain-dominated Midwest, the fact that nothing else seems to be able to compete with grain production misleads people into thinking grain production is the only viable agricultural use of the land. That may be true, using the concept of comparative advantage, but it ignores the fact that another use of the land is to leave it idle. People forget that absolute advantage overrules comparative advantage when markets are global. Thus, if land is being used to produce its most profitable agricultural enterprise and that output becomes unprofitable due to changes in the global commodity market, the land will have to be left idle to reduce farmers' operating losses. This is the sad truth facing large chunks of American land.

As Thurow explained in 1996, there are other places with both comparative and absolute advantages in grain production that will push global prices so low that American producers will be forced out of the market: "The Ukraine is potentially the best place on earth for growing grain" (Thurow 1996, pp. 44–45). It has not yet reached its current potential for contributing to global supplies because of capital and other constraints on its ability to fully implement modern production and distribution technologies. When it does get its agriculture up to Western standards, continues Thurow (p. 45), its "sales will drive millions of less productive grain farmers out of business all around the world."

> In the United States it is clear who goes out of business. Go to the 98th meridian, remembering that about one third of Kansas is east of the 98th meridian, and draw a line from the Canadian border to the Gulf of Mexico; then swing west to the Rocky Mountains. Every grain farmer in that part of the United States goes out of business. The soil is worse, the rainfall is worse, and the transportation system is much, much worse than what is found in the Ukraine. It won't happen tomorrow, but it will happen. (Thurow 1996, p. 45)

In that large chunk of the country, residential and recreational uses of land are developing slowly, so it is likely that vast tracts of land will go idle after it becomes market marginal. This is a disastrous prospect for the owners of the idled land, but it will happen slowly, giving markets time to adjust. Land prices will be pushed down as the potential production income from the land is reduced by declining profits from increasingly competitive global commodity markets for grains. The story will be repeated for smaller tracts of American farmland currently invested in the production of other commodities whose markets are being changed by increased participation of farmers or ranchers in less-developed countries. All of these lower land prices will make alternative uses look more promising but, in the meantime, the wealth of affected landowners will be declining.

What Is the Global Capacity for Agricultural Production?

One reason uninformed analysts find it impossible to believe that the United States might substantially reduce its land invested in agriculture in the future is that over one billion people are hungry in the world now (Senauer and Sur 2001), and therefore, the reasoning is that American agriculture is needed to help feed the world. The truth is an entirely different story. The world is currently in an oversupply situation for many commodities (indicated by falling real prices), based on current wealth and income distributions around the globe. In other words, more food is being produced than can be purchased by the current population. However, that misleading fact is based on the uneven distribution of land resources across the countries of the world. In places with less land per person, the ability to produce food is often insufficient, necessitating trade between nations. Unfortunately, less-developed nations usually lack other resources, as well as land, and may not be able to generate the income needed to purchase food on international markets, thus leading to local and regional pockets of hunger in the face of global food surpluses. Therefore, global capacity for agricultural production and the ability of the population to buy food are two different stories. The sad story of hunger due to poverty is about resource distribution imbalances, not about total global capacity. Resource imbalance issues are addressed in the next section; here, the focus is global capacity for agricultural production.

The first issue is to determine how much agricultural land there is on the planet. Various methods have been used by many different organizations to get an estimate of the total agricultural land resource base. As an example, the Center for Sustainability and the Global Environment at the University of Wisconsin, Madison, uses a combination of satellite images and historical records, such as census and tax records. Their estimate is that between 1.5 and 1.8 billion hectares (an area about the size of South America) are used for crops, and roughly 3.2 to 3.6 billion hectares are used for pasture and range land. That means between 4.7 and 5.4 billion hectares are available at present.

The second issue is to identify what the trend in total agricultural land has been in recent years. As shown in Table 9.9, total agricultural area has decreased in most more-developed countries and increased in most less-developed countries over the past four decades. It is interesting to note that among the forty-four countries listed in the table (representing about half the world's total agricultural area), the largest percentage decrease in agricultural area over the 1965–2005 period occurred in Japan (33 percent decline) and the two largest decreases in area occurred in Australia (27 million hectares) and the United States (21 million hectares). These three countries are all high on the development scale, with Japan and the United States being two of the wealthiest countries in the world. In turn, the largest percentage increase in agricultural area occurred in the small, less-developed country of Papua New Guinea (98 percent increase) and the two largest increases in area were found in Brazil (93 million hectares) and Sudan (25 million hectares). Thus, in simple terms, the land that left American agriculture over the last forty years was more than replaced by

Table 9.9

Agricultural Area, Selected Countries (1,000 Hectares)

	1965	1975	1985	1995	2005		% Change 1965–2005
United States	435,873	430,158	431,399	420,139	414,778		−4.8
Western Europe							
France	34,001	32,357	31,442	30,059	29,569		−13.0
Germany	19,534	18,792	18,244	17,343	17,030		−12.8
Poland	19,946	19,224	18,914	18,622	15,906		−20.3
United Kingdom	19,585	18,583	18,168	17,379	16,956		−13.4
Eastern Europe							
Russian Federation				216,400	215,680	*	−0.3
Belarus				9,339	8,860	*	−5.1
Ukraine				41,853	41,304	*	−1.3
USSR	544,818	550,240	557,911			*	2.4
Asia							
Bangladesh	9,637	9,729	9,735	8,748	9,015		−6.5
Cambodia	3,627	2,500	3,190	5,320	5,356		47.7
India	177,243	180,858	180,949	180,780	180,180		1.7
Japan	7,004	6,273	5,879	5,443	4,692		−33.0
Korea, Republic of	2,278	2,272	2,220	2,048	1,893		−16.9
Pakistan	24,263	24,830	25,610	26,550	27,070		11.6
Austral–Asia							
Australia	472,976	486,837	472,960	463,348	445,149		−5.9
Indonesia	38,500	38,256	39,679	42,187	47,800		24.2
Malaysia	4,409	4,927	5,963	7,885	7,870	*	78.5
New Zealand	16,346	17,030	17,551	16,578	17,235	*	5.4
Papua New Guinea	530	714	808	944	1,050	*	98.1
Philippines	8,132	9,192	10,910	11,230	12,200	*	50.0
North Africa							
Algeria	44,167	43,753	39,051	39,649	39,956	*	−9.5
Chad	47,900	48,000	48,155	48,450	48,630	*	1.5
Egypt	2,672	2,825	2,497	3,283	3,520		31.7
Libya	11,995	14,055	15,427	15,515	15,450	*	28.8
Morocco	24,420	26,917	29,398	30,749	30,376	*	24.4
Sudan	109,242	110,215	112,790	130,412	134,600		23.2
Tunisia	8,648	8,964	8,822	9,348	9,784		13.1
Central & Southern Africa							
Angola	57,270	57,400	57,400	57,500	57,590	*	0.6
Botswana	26,001	26,002	26,008	25,946	25,980	*	−0.1
Congo, Republic of	10,543	10,562	10,568	10,520	10,547	*	0.0
Kenya	25,220	25,572	25,790	26,130	26,512	*	5.1
Niger	31,500	29,780	30,780	36,500	38,500	*	22.2
Nigeria	69,210	70,000	71,035	72,830	72,600	*	4.9
Rwanda	1,355	1,612	1,819	1,485	1,935	*	42.8
South Africa	97,262	95,132	94,547	99,525	99,640	*	2.4
Zambia	34,860	35,000	35,188	35,282	35,289	*	1.2
Zimbabwe	19,265	19,665	19,905	20,410	20,550	*	6.7
South America							
Argentina	131,780	128,650	128,391	127,938	128,747	*	−2.3
Brazil	170,395	213,416	231,041	258,472	263,600	*	54.7
Chile	14,069	16,550	16,472	15,330	15,242	*	8.3
Colombia	43,008	45,115	45,375	44,513	42,557		−1.0
Ecuador	4,730	5,385	7,420	8,108	7,552		59.7
Venezuela	19,514	20,298	21,640	21,620	21,640	*	10.9

Source: FAO Stat web pages.

* Indicates a data period covering the dates shown, for the former Soviet states, and for all other countries designated, a data period ending in 2003, rather than 2005.

increased agricultural land in Sudan. Or, even more startling, the combined land reductions in the United States and Australia total just over half the total expansion in Brazilian agricultural area during the period. This roughly illustrates the "substitution" process occurring in global agriculture: more-developed countries are reducing their investments in agriculture and are being replaced by new agricultural investments in less-developed countries. In a sense, farmland is "moving." In total, the agricultural area of the forty countries in Table 9.9 for which there are data over the entire four-decade period (this excludes the USSR and the former Soviet states) increased by 4.6 percent between 1965 and 2005. So, even though agricultural area decreased in 13 of the 40 countries, it was unchanged in 1 country and increased in 26 countries, leading to the net increase.

How are countries increasing their agricultural land totals? Barbier (2004) explains (p. 1352):

> Many low- and middle-income economies are rapidly changing land use, by converting forests, woodlands and other natural habitat to agriculture and other land-based development activities. In all tropical regions of the world, deforestation is occurring at around 12 million ha per year, mainly the result of agricultural land expansion.

Barbier continues, "if a developing economy has a sizable 'reserve' or 'frontier' of potential cropland available, increased conversion of this frontier land will occur as agricultural development proceeds in the economy." However, Barbier (2002) found that "effective institutional constraints on land clearing reduce the rate of deforestation due to agricultural land expansion" (p. 517). This implies that land-use decisions are controllable within a country. Unfortunately, there are many economic incentives for less-developed countries to convert forests into agricultural land. Therefore, when land leaves agriculture in a more-developed country, it is ultimately replaced by converted forest land in a less-developed country.

The direction of causality of this substitution process has not been researched, but it is probably the reverse of general expectations; it is most likely to flow from less-developed countries to more-developed countries. Economic incentives such as reducing domestic hunger, raising employment levels, and raising wealth all serve to encourage less-developed countries to pursue (or at least allow) expansion of land used in agricultural production. Therefore, such land conversions are likely to occur without regard to global market effects. Conversely, the landowners in more-developed countries who decide to remove their land from agriculture and use it in some other way are very likely to be reacting to the effects of global market changes, such as price decreases, caused by the increases in aggregate supplies flowing from less-developed countries. Thus, increased land use in the agriculture sectors of less-developed countries ultimately pushes land out of agriculture in more-developed countries. Of course, the pace of this land-use change is determined by the flow of alternative uses for agricultural land made available by economic development in more-developed countries.

The third issue is to quantify the long-run potential for global production capacity. In that effort, Cohen (1995) found 60 studies showing that the earth can support 4–16 billion people. This estimate was made assuming existing technologies or foreseeable increases in current production techniques. Differences in the estimated population that could be supported were partly due to differences in the quantity of food per person assumed to be necessary by each study (e.g., 2,500 calories per day). A more recent assessment of agricultural productivity growth concluded, "if the world fails to meet its food demands in the next half century, the failure will be at least as much in the area of institutional innovation as in the area of technical change" (Ruttan 2002, p. 30). Institutional innovation will be needed because a number of the world's poorest countries are expected to face constraints on their agricultural production growth. Thus, aggregate production capacity and distribution of capacity will remain two different problems.

The fourth issue is to assess how global production capacity compares with global demand for agricultural production in the long run. Obviously, the demand for agricultural output comes from people, thus it is a function of population. So, long-run forecasts of global population proxy for aggregate demand for agriculture. The most accepted source of population forecasts is the United Nations (2001). Research by that organization indicates that total global population is expected to increase from its current 6.1 billion to about 9.3 billion in 2050 and then gradually peak and level off at between 9 and 12 billion people sometime late in this century. Combining this estimate of future aggregate demand with the estimated production capacity of up to 16 billion people indicates that current agricultural production technology and the resource base is sufficient to feed everyone.

As noted earlier, related to total global agricultural capacity is the issue of resource distribution imbalances that lead to hunger due to poverty. Senauer and Sur (2001) evaluated the trends in economic development, income distribution, and population change to see if "food insecurity" could be reduced. They noted that the United Nations Food and Agricultural Organization estimates that there are currently over one billion people who are food insecure, with over 800 million of them being chronically undernourished. They made forecasts for the years 2025 and 2050 and found that hunger is expected to decline. They estimated the number of food insecure people to drop from over one billion to 830 million by 2025. They concluded (p. 68), "with pro-poor growth and a decline in real food prices, this number could be reduced to 380 million by 2025. Ending chronic, mass hunger in this century is an achievable goal."

The fifth and final issue is to identify any risks to the estimate of production capacity noted above. There are two: one overestimated and a second nearly unknown. Conventional wisdom suggests that the first risk to global production capacity comes from urban development. The good news is that the total area likely to be developed out of agriculture into urban uses is relatively small, as discussed earlier in this chapter. The bad news is that much of the land that is shifted from agriculture to urban use contains high-quality soil. The unfortunate history of much of economic development is that people usually settled first in areas well suited to food production. That means cities of today are often expanding to cover up some of the best soil in the area. Thus, urban growth has a disproportionate impact on the globe's inventory of high-quality farmland, whereas lower-quality land is not developed into urban uses at nearly as fast a rate. In total, this means that urban development does tend to reduce the average quality of available agricultural land, thus adversely affecting the average productivity of the resource base. This certainly could be a significant issue in the future as pressures from population growth require growth in yields in some parts of the world.

The second risk to current estimates of global capacity is virtually unknown to the general public. "Desertification" is a real, long-term threat to global agricultural capacity. The United Nations Convention to Combat Desertification reports that desertification has been happening at an increasing rate since the 1950s, although it has been occurring for thousands of years (Hawley 2004). The UN designated 2006 as the International Year of Deserts and Desertification and established a UN Secretariat for Combating Desertification in Bonn, Germany. There is also a European initiative to expand research on desertification, led by groups from Germany, France, and Belgium, with members from several other European countries.

When asked why the United Nations declared 2006 as the International Year of Deserts and Desertification, Miriam Akhtar-Schuster, chairwoman of the German Desert*Net, responded (*ZEF News* 2006):

Over 250 million people in more than 110 countries are directly affected by desertification, and the lives of over a billion people are threatened by it. Furthermore, there is an increasing danger of desertification in all arid lands bordering desert lands. This has a negative impact not only on soil fertility, water availability, vegetation, and biodiversity, but also on the livelihoods of people living in these affected areas, and leads to migration into cities.

She notes that research results indicate a large degree of misunderstanding about desertification. For example, in one report, "scientists were not able to confirm the previous common assessment that 70% of arid lands worldwide are directly affected by decreasing productivity of agricultural lands and pastures. Their calculations indicate a mere 10 to 20%." This means the problem can be dealt with if policymakers give it proper attention. Just like global warming, the scale of the desertification problem and its economic impact justifies global attention, but the multinational nature of the problem complicates the effort.

World Agriculture Without America?

Thus, some ironic conclusions come from this brief assessment of America's trend of idling farmland and the globe's capacity to feed an expanding population. First, the world's agricultural sector could feed everyone without any contribution from American producers. Second, less-developed countries would generally be better off if the United States quit competing with them in many agricultural commodity markets.

The first conclusion—that America's agricultural production is not needed in the long-run effort to feed the population—is essentially based on the idea that America's farmland can be replaced by new farmland in other countries. Depending on which estimate is used, America has between 306 and 414 million hectares of land in agriculture. That represents 6 to 8 percent of the global total agricultural area, which seems like a big slice of the pie. However, if using the U.S. Department of Agriculture's estimate of 940 million acres (306 million hectares) of land in farms (Table 9.5), and remembering that only about one-third of that total is harvested cropland (Table 9.6), then only about 126 million hectares of new cropland needs to be brought into production in other countries to completely replace America's contribution to crop markets, ceteris paribus. That is an easily achieved total, given the scale of increases in some countries shown in Table 9.9. As reported by Mundlak (2000, p. 7), 65 percent of countries increased their cultivated area during 1967–1992. In the foreseeable future, less-developed countries will continue to expand their land investments in agriculture.

The uncertainty in this global land substitution process comes from differences in land qualities and productivities over locations. If the productivity of American land exiting agriculture is higher than the productivity of land entering production in another country, then the substitution rate will require more than one acre elsewhere for each American acre. Productivity is a function of both land quality and production technology applied. Over time, technologies will improve, thus differences in productivities between American farmland and "replacement" farmland will decrease, causing the land substitution ratio to approach one. In the long run, progress in economic development in less-wealthy countries could virtually eliminate differences in technologies applied, thus reducing the land substitution ratio to a pure indicator of differences in land qualities between two locations. That would mean an acre of American farmland could be replaced by less than an acre of higher-quality farmland in another country. This is part of the reason American grain-producing regions are expected to be replaced by places such as Ukraine.

A final factor influencing America's ability to leave agriculture is the world's ability to replace America's contribution in each commodity market. It is quite likely that the United States can gradually exit at least some commodity markets without a significant price effect. For example, America's share of global wheat production has fallen to below 10 percent in recent decades, so the many other countries that grow wheat would be able to fill in if the United States leaves that market. However, if America tries to leave or downsize significantly in some specific commodity markets in which there are few potential replacements, there could be supply effects that lead to global price effects that create profit incentives for some American producers to remain in those markets. In other words, a "new equilibrium" would be found in each global market if America reduced its output of specific commodities and that equilibrium could include American producers.

It is impossible to know how many acres of American farmland will be in or out of production of any commodity at any price level for two reasons. First, it would require knowing the individual production costs of each firm. Those costs are needed to compare against market prices to calculate profit levels for each commodity. Second, even if those costs were known, the profit preferences of each firm's owner would also be required. It is known that, on average, people leave an investment before profits drop to zero—they move to other alternative investments that are expected to generate higher profits. This means it is easy to *overestimate* how many acres might stay in production of a particular agricultural commodity if the condition for exit is assumed to be the zero profit level. The acreage estimate is complicated even more by the presence of "hobby farmers" who stay in agriculture despite losses year after year.

The second conclusion—that less-developed countries would generally be better off if the United States quit competing with them in commodity markets—stems from the fact that those countries would be able to expand their economies faster if America were their customer instead of their competitor. This point is easy to understand. As an example, if the United States quit subsidizing wheat production in places ill suited to it, like Montana (Egan 2001), we could buy wheat from farmers in poor countries and, thus, give those producers a stable market that would facilitate quick improvements in their quality of life. Conversely, as long as we produce wheat, some poor farmers in less-developed countries will be unable to compete in the global wheat market and will be forced to grow some crop not as well suited to the land available.

A final note on the world's capacity to feed people puts a new spin on the famous line attributed to Marie Antoinette: let them eat fish. The estimates of global food production capacity reported in the previous section did not include the potential contribution of the oceans, which could be substantial. The *Economist* (2003) reported that fish farming holds much promise, plus fishery management practices are improving as marine biologists learn more about the sustainability of fish species. Science continues to learn more ways to "farm" the surface of the earth. The technological tsunami may sweep us all out to sea, but we are assured of something to eat.

GLOBAL CAPACITY AND LAND USE AS A NATIONAL AND LOCAL RESPONSIBILITY

This chapter began by stating that, figuratively speaking, land "moves" over time. In particular, it was described how farmland is moving from more-developed to less-developed countries through a type of substitution process driven by economic development. That trend is creating a new type of responsibility for the United States and other more-developed countries: protecting the global capacity for production of food.

What is the nature of this responsibility? The task can be called risk management. The potential risk is that the world's ability to generate food may be pressed by its future population's demand for food. As explained earlier, the world's agricultural capacity is a function of land available and the productivity of that land. Given that land virtually never returns to agricultural production once it is developed into some higher-valued use, the best way to manage the risk of not having enough farmland is to never allow the global inventory of farmland to fall below the maximum amount needed in the future, especially in the face of uncertain population estimates for the distant future. This is similar to the risk management strategy called "precautionary savings" employed by farm households (Jensen and Pope 2004).

This new responsibility falls on more-developed countries because of the resource imbalances between wealthy and poor countries. Only more-developed countries have the wealth necessary to pay the significant costs involved in preserving farmland. Less-developed countries are usually resource poor and, as a result, have fewer viable options for investing their limited resources. More-developed nations have usually benefited from having more land from which to derive wealth over time. Given that there is a fixed amount of land in the world, landownership brings both wealth and responsibility. Both the wealth and the responsibility come from how an owner uses his or her land, especially if the land is currently in agriculture. Wealthy nations are not at risk of suffering from hunger, whereas many poor countries face a significant risk. As a result, poor nations must use all available land in the current production of food. Conversely, a wealthy nation does not need to use all available land for food production. Even though individual farmers in a wealthy country may not be able to afford idling land for long periods of time, the country can spread the cost of doing so among its wealthy population, thus creating a public good that would benefit the world's populace of the future. The idea is summarized by the following proposition.

- PROPOSITION 9.4. *A wealthy nation can afford to preserve agricultural capacity, even though individual farmers cannot afford to do so.*

This new responsibility has not received much attention. In the United States it comes up occasionally as part of the "food security" debate (Davis, Thomas, and Amponsah 2001), but has never been discussed as being the nation's responsibility as a global citizen. Accepting such a responsibility first requires recognition of the externalities coming from land-use decisions of every country. Next, a wealthy nation must be willing to pay part of the costs of those externalities, viewing it as an investment in global social welfare.

How can the responsibility to protect the global capacity for production of food be fulfilled? Although the resource base is global in scale, national policies are required and those are implemented at the local level. Therefore, widespread acceptance of the responsibility is needed in order for it to be met successfully. The action necessary is a change in our approach to land investment. Given that there is a fixed amount of "good" agricultural land, some thought ought to be given to its use. At present, land use decisions in the United States are often made by individual developers who build houses for sale. That usually results in the "good" land near cities and towns being developed out of agriculture. A better, more responsible long-run approach would be to follow the example of a poor, small-scale farmer. That farmer, with a very limited amount of land, would be keenly aware of the need to maximize output so as to feed her expanding family in the future. Therefore, that farmer would build her house on the poorest piece of her land so as to leave as much good land as possible for cultivation. Such a simple idea. Sometimes all that is needed is for a wealthy nation to act like a poor farmer.

NOTES

1. Time subscripts are not included here to avoid confusion.

2. See Chapter 4 for a detailed discussion of the model and its estimation procedures. The data used are from the USDA's annual surveys of agricultural producers across the contiguous forty-eight states for the years 1996 through 2004.

3. Trying to reconcile the two systems of accounting for land use between the USDA and the NRI is impossible because they do not even come up with the same total land area for the forty-eight states: the USDA reports 1.894 billion acres and the NRI reports 1.938 billion acres. The confusion gets worse when comparing the different numbers of categories used by the two systems. The only category name that appears to be the same in the two lists is "cropland," but different total acres are reported for that category by each system. Thus, the USDA data will be used here to reduce confusion.

4. It is not just farmland that is threatened by this process. For example, Vesterby et al. (1997) report that nationally, 8.0 million acres of farmland and 5.2 million acres of forest land were converted to urban or suburban use between 1982 and 1992. Thus, both types of "rural" land are being consumed.

5. Forest land could be labeled as undeveloped or developed, depending on the nature of its use. "Old growth" forests on land that has never been harvested is usually called "undeveloped." Conversely, forest land that has been harvested and replanted to forests is "developed" in the sense that specific investments have been made to establish the productive condition of the land.

REFERENCES

Barbier, Edward B. 2002. "Institutional Constraints and Deforestation: An Application to Mexico." *Economic Inquiry* 40 (3): 508–519.

———. 2004. "Explaining Agricultural Land Expansion and Deforestation in Developing Countries." *American Journal of Agricultural Economics* 86 (5): 1347–1353.

Behan, J., K. McQuinn, and M. Roche. 2006. "Rural Land Use: Traditional Agriculture or Forestry?" *Land Economics* 82 (1): 112–123.

Berube, A., A. Singer, J. Wilson, and W. Frey. 2006. *Finding Exurbia: America's Fast-Growing Communities at the Metropolitan Fringe*. Washington, DC: The Living Cities Census Series, The Brookings Institution, October.

Bin, O., and S. Polasky. 2005. "Evidence on the Amenity Value of Wetlands in a Rural Setting," *Journal of Agricultural & Applied Economics* 37 (3): 589–602.

Carrion-Flores, C., and E. Irwin. 2004. "Determinants of Residential Land-Use Conversion and Sprawl at the Rural-Urban Fringe." *American Journal of Agricultural Economics* 86 (4): 889–904.

Cho, S-H., J. Bowker, and W. Park. 2006. "Measuring the Contribution of Water and Green Space Amenities to Housing Values: An Application and Comparison of Spatially Weighted Hedonic Models." *Journal of Agricultural and Resource Economics* 31 (3): 485–507.

Cho, S-H., Z. Chen, S. Yen, and D. Eastwood. 2006. "Estimating Effects of an Urban Growth Boundary on Land Development." *Journal of Agricultural & Applied Economics* 38 (2): 287–298.

Claassen, R., R. Heimlich, R. House, and K. Wiebe. 1998. "Estimating the Effects of Relaxing Agricultural Land Use Restrictions: Wetland Delineation in the Swampbuster Program." *Review of Agricultural Economics* 20 (2): 390–405.

Cohen, Joel. 1995. *How Many People Can the Earth Support?* London: W.W. Norton.

Daugherty, Arthur. 1998. "Land Use." *Agricultural Resources and Environmental Indicators, 1996–97*, ed. M. Anderson and R. Magleby. Washington, DC: USDA/ERS, Agricultural Handbook no. 712.

Davis, C., C. Thomas, and W. Amponsah. 2001. "Globalization and Poverty: Lessons from the Theory and Practice of Food Security." *American Journal of Agricultural Economics* 83: 714–721.

Deller, S., T. Tsai, D. Marcouiller, and D. English. 2001. "The Role of Amenities and Quality of Life in Rural Economic Growth." *American Journal of Agricultural Economics* 83: 352–365.

Drozd, D., and B. Johnson. 2004. "Dynamics of a Rural Land Market Experiencing Farmland Conversion to Acreages: The Case of Saunders County, Nebraska." *Land Economics* 80 (2): 294–311.

Duke, J., and L. Lynch. 2006. "Farmland Retention Techniques: Property Rights Implications and Comparative Evaluation." *Land Economics* 82 (2): 189–213.

Economist. 2003. "A New Way to Feed the World: Fish Farming Is a Good and Promising Thing, Despite the Environmental Worries." August 9, 9.

Egan, Timothy. 2001. "Failing in Style." *Choices* 16 (1): 39–42.

Falk, Barry. 1991. "Formally Testing the Present Value Model of Farmland Prices." *American Journal of Agricultural Economics* 73 (1): 1–10.

Falk, B., and B. Lee. 1998. "Fads Versus Fundamentals in Farmland Prices." *American Journal of Agricultural Economics* 80 (4): 696–707.

Feng, H., C. Cling, L. Kurkalova, S. Secchi, and P. Gassman. 2005. "The Conservation Reserve Program in the Presence of a Working Land Alternative: Implications for Environmental Quality, Program Participation, and Income Transfer." *American Journal of Agricultural Economics* 87 (5): 1231–1238.

Goodwin, B., A. Mishra, and F. Ortalo-Magne. 2003. "What's Wrong with Our Models of Agricultural Land Values?" *American Journal of Agricultural Economics* 85 (3): 744–752.

Greene, Catherine. 2006. "U.S. Organic Farm Sector Continues to Expand." USDA/ERS *Amber Waves* 4, Special Issue (July): 13.

Hardie, I., P. Parks, P. Gottleib, and D. Wear. 2000. "Responsiveness of Rural and Urban Land Uses to Land Rent Determinants in the U.S. South." *Land Economics* 76 (4): 659–673.

Hawley, Chris. 2004. "World's Land Turning to Desert at Alarming Speed, United Nations Warns." Associated Press, June 16.

Hellerstein, D., C. Nickerson, J. Cooper, P. Feather, D. Gadsby, D. Mullarkey, A. Tegene, and C. Barnard. 2002. *Farmland Protection: The Role of Public Preferences for Rural Amenities.* USDA/ERS, AER-815, November.

Henderson, J., and S. Moore. 2006. "The Capitalization of Wildlife Recreation Income into Farmland Values." *Journal of Agricultural & Applied Economics* 38 (3): 597–610.

Henneberry, D., and R. Barrows. 1990. "Capitalization of Exclusive Agricultural Zoning into Farmland Prices." *Land Economics* 66: 249–258.

Huang, H., G. Miller, B. Sherrick, and M. Gomez. 2006. "Factors Influencing Illinois Farmland Values." *American Journal of Agricultural Economics* 88 (2): 458–470.

Inman, K., D. McLeod, and D. Menkhaus. 2002. "Rural Land Use and Sale Preferences in a Wyoming County." *Land Economics* 78: 72–87.

Isakson, H., and M. Ecker. 2001. "An Analysis of the Influence of Location in the Market for Undeveloped Urban Fringe Land." *Land Economics* 77 (1): 30–41.

Jensen, F., and R. Pope. 2004. "Agricultural Precautionary Wealth." *Journal of Agricultural and Resource Economics* 29 (1): 17–30.

Kilpatrick, John A. 2001. "Concentrated Animal Feed Operations and Proximate Property Values." *The Appraisal Journal* (July): 301–306.

King, J., and C. Anderson. 2004. "Marginal Property Tax Effects of Conversion Easements: A Vermont Case Study." *American Journal of Agricultural Economics* 86 (4): 919–932.

Kirwan, B., R. Lubowski, and M. Roberts. 2005. "How Cost-Effective Are Land Retirement Auctions? Estimating the Difference Between Payments and Willingness to Accept in the Conservation Reserve Program." *American Journal of Agricultural Economics* 87 (5): 1239–1247.

Lence, S., and D. Miller. 1999. "Transaction Costs and the Present Value Model of Farmland: Iowa 1900–1994." *American Journal of Agricultural Economics* 81 (2): 257–272.

Livanis, G., C. Moss, V. Breneman, and R. Nehring. 2006. "Urban Sprawl and Farmland Prices." *American Journal of Agricultural Economics* 88 (4): 915–929.

Lopez, R., and G. Galinato. 2005. "Trade Policies, Economic Growth, and the Direct Causes of Deforestation." *Land Economics* 81 (2): 145–169.

Lubowski, R., M. Vesterby, S. Bucholtz, A. Baez, and M. Roberts. 2006. "Major Uses of Land in the United States, 2002." Economic Information Bulletin *EIB*-14, Economic Research Service, USDA, May.

Lynch, L., and W. Musser. 2001. "A Relative Efficiency Analysis of Farmland Preservation Programs." *Land Economics* 77 (4): 577–594.

Martin, W., and G. Jefferies. 1966. "Relating Ranch Prices and Grazing Permit Values to Ranch Productivity." *Journal of Farm Economics* 48: 223–240.

Melichar, Emanuel. 1979. "Capital Gains Versus Current Income in the Farming Sector." *American Journal of Agricultural Economics* 61 (5): 1085–1092.

Mills, B., and G. Hazarika. 2001. "The Migration of Young Adults from Non-Metropolitan Counties." *American Journal of Agricultural Economics* 83 (2): 329–340.

Moon, W., W. Florkowski, B. Bruckner, and I. Schonhof. 2002. "Willingness to Pay for Environmental Practices: Implications for Eco-Labeling." *Land Economics* 78: 88–102.

Moss, Charles B. 1997. "Returns, Interest Rates, and Inflation: How They Explain Changes in Farmland Values." *American Journal of Agricultural Economics* 79 (5): 1311–1318.

Moss, C., and A. Schmitz. 2003. *Government Policy and Farmland Markets: The Maintenance of Farmer Wealth.* Ames: Iowa State Press.

Mundlak, Yair. 2000. *Agriculture and Economic Growth: Theory and Measurement.* Cambridge, MA: Harvard University Press.

Netusil, Noelwah R. 2005. "The Effect of Environmental Zoning and Amenities on Property Values: Portland, Oregon." *Land Economics* 81 (2): 227–246.

Nickerson, C., and L. Lynch. 2001. "The Effect of Farmland Preservation Programs on Farmland Prices." *American Journal of Agricultural Economics* 83 (2): 341–351.

Plantinga, A., and D. Miller. 2001. "Agricultural Land Values and the Value of Rights to Future Land Development." *Land Economics* 77 (1): 56–67.

Ready, R., and C. Abdalla. 2005. "The Amenity and Disamenity Impacts of Agriculture: Estimates from a Hedonic Pricing Model." *American Journal of Agricultural Economics* 87 (2): 314–326.

Reynolds, J., and A. Regalado. 2002. "The Effects of Wetlands and Other Factors on Rural Land Values." *The Appraisal Journal* 70 (April): 182–190.

Roberts, M., and S. Bucholz. 2006. "Slippage in the Conservation Reserve Program or Spurious Correlation? A Rejoinder." *American Journal of Agricultural Economics* 88 (2): 512–514.

Ruttan, Vernon W. 2002. "Productivity Growth in World Agriculture: Sources and Constraints." Staff Paper P02–1(R), Department of Applied Economics, University of Minnesota, April.

Senauer, B., and M. Sur. 2001. "Ending Global Hunger in the 21st Century: Projections of the Number of Food Insecure People." *Review of Agricultural Economics* 23 (1): 68–81.

Shaik, S., G. Helmers, and J. Atwood. 2005. "The Evolution of Farm Programs and Their Contribution to Agricultural Land Values." *American Journal of Agricultural Economics* 87 (5): 1190–1197.

Shi, Y., T. Phipps, and D. Colyer. 1997. "Agricultural Land Values Under Urbanizing Influences." *Land Economics* 73 (1): 90–100.

Tanaka, J., A. Torell, and N. Rimbey. 2005. "Who Are Public Land Ranchers and Why Are They Out There?" *Western Economics Forum* 4 (2): 14–20.

Taylor, M., and G. Brester. 2005. "Noncash Income Transfers and Agricultural Land Values." *Review of Agricultural Economics* 27 (4): 526–541.

Thurow, Lester C. 1996. *The Future of Capitalism: How Today's Economic Forces Shape Tomorrow's World.* New York: Penguin Books,.

Torell, A., N. Rimbey, O. Ramirez, and D. McCollum. 2005. "Income Earning Potential Versus Consumptive Amenities in Determining Ranchland Values." *Journal of Agricultural and Resource Economics* 30 (3): 537–560.

United Nations. 2001. "World Population Prospects: The 2000 Revision." Population Division, Department of Economic and Social Affairs, New York, February.

U.S. Department of Agriculture (USDA). 2000. "Accumulated Farm Real Estate Value Will Help Farmers and Their Lenders Through Period of Declining Cash Receipts," pp. 30–33. *Agricultural Income and Finance: Situation and Outlook,* Economic Research Service, AIS-74, February.

———. 2001. "Lenders Benefit from the Farm Sector's Receipt of Government Payments," pp. 5–6. *Agricultural Income and Finance: Situation and Outlook,* Economic Research Service, AIS-76, February.

USDA, Natural Resources and Conservation Service. 2004. *National Resources Inventory: 2002 Annual NRI.* Washington, DC.

Vesterby, M., and K. Krupa. 2002. "Rural Residential Land Use: Tracking Its Growth." Economic Research Service, USDA, *Agricultural Outlook* (August): 14–17.

Vesterby, M., A. Daugherty, R. Heimlick, and R. Claassen. 1997. "Major Land Use Changes in the Contiguous 48 States." *AREI Updates* 3.

Wolverton, Marvin L. 2004. "Highest and Best Use: The von Thunen Connection." *The Appraisal Journal* (Fall): 318–323.

Wu, JunJie. 2000. "Slippage Effects of the Conservation Reserve Program." *American Journal of Agricultural Economics* 82 (4): 979–992.

ZEF News. 2006. "Desertification: Half-Time for the IYDD." Center for Development Research, University of Bonn, no. 19 (July): 10.

CHAPTER 10

INTERNATIONAL MUTUAL DEPENDENCE

"Can't we all just get along?"
—Rodney King, *during the 1992 Los Angeles riots following his arrest*

Global agriculture's influence on market evolution has been widespread and circular: the evolution of some markets helped create global agriculture, which, in turn, helped other markets evolve. At this point in global economic development, most agricultural commodities have markets spreading across many countries and continents. These "global" markets are relatively new additions to the world's economy, but they have already had major impacts on the course of economic development. For example, the trend of farmland substitution between more-developed countries and less-developed countries described in the previous chapter is made possible by international trade. In turn, international trade is necessary, by definition, for a "global market" to exist. Without international trade, each country must be self-sufficient in food production. Since resource limits prevent many countries from achieving food self-sufficiency, trade will occur. The existence of trade signals awareness on the part of each person or nation involved in trading that they and their trade partners are mutually dependent to some degree. As this awareness turns to acceptance of mutual dependence, global agriculture's role in economic development will mature into its fullest form, facilitating market evolution that will raise the quality of life for people everywhere.

The people of the world are slowly realizing that all countries are mutually dependent to some degree. The primary reason for this dependence is that the world's natural resources are scattered unevenly across the globe. A secondary reason is the constraints put on people's access to resources due to artificial barriers created by political borders. Combined, these issues lead to differences in wealth per capita between countries. As noted in the previous chapter, much of wealth is derived from land. With a world of countries differing in physical size, population, and other resources, it is to be expected that some countries will be able to feed themselves easier and better than will others. The resource imbalances between countries create differences in the comparative advantage of each country (Vollrath 2007), thus giving people in each location easy access to the food and other products that are most efficiently produced at that locale, but reducing their access to products for which no local comparative advantage exists. Giving everyone access to products not produced locally requires resources, or the outputs from them, to be traded. Recognizing this mutual dependence makes it more likely to be embraced.

The goal of this chapter is to briefly describe international mutual dependence and its role as a driving force behind economic development in the world as it now exists. Mutual dependence is a consequence of resource imbalances and it involves a blending of comparative advantages and the ability to trade, as will be described in this chapter. Just as two or more people can be mutually dependent, international mutual dependence involves two or more countries. What brings the trade partners together is the desire to reduce their own shortages of some product, thus the process is driven by a focus on selfish interests, which makes it a sustainable arrangement. In a mature world, mutual dependence will continue to facilitate dramatic changes in the way resources are used, thus leading to improvements in the lives of people living in countries that are participating in the evolving networks of cooperation.

SHORT SUPPLIES CREATED INTERNATIONAL TRADE

In the beginning, trade was motivated by supply shortfalls of desired products. When a person realized that he or she did not have enough of some product, and resources available were insufficient to make the product, the solution quickly became apparent: trade with another person for the desired product. What was given away in the trade was any product or resource that was plentiful to the person and needed by another. In other words, one of the first economic lessons learned by humans in their evolution was to trade away local surpluses in order to acquire additional supplies of things in shortage. This is the origin of what we call a "market": a process of trade, or exchange, between two or more people.[1] Thus, it is shortages that drive trade and surpluses that enable trade.

Trade improves the economic position of both traders. Each trade involves two or more people who differ in their shortages and surpluses. In each case, the people have a surplus of a product that is in shortage to the other party. Each gets their desired product by trading away some of their surplus product.

The story is the same at the global level. Roe, Somwaru, and Diao (2006, p. 406) found that "persistently poor countries can gain from globalization but trade and institutional reform is required. Since poor countries are largely exporters of primary commodities, access to developed country agricultural markets seems crucial." It is well known that international trade, especially of agricultural products, stimulates the growth of poor countries (Dawson 2005; Roe and Mohtadi 2001; Senauer and Sur 2001; Senauer 2002). For example, research results suggest that

> ... a move to free merchandise trade would increase farm employment, the real value of agricultural output and exports, real returns to farm land and unskilled labor, and real net farm incomes in developing countries. This would occur despite the decline in international terms of trade for some developing countries that are net food importers or are enjoying preferential access to agricultural markets of high-income countries. (Anderson, Martin, and van der Mensbrugghe 2006, p. 168)

In general, it has been shown that international trade leads to a stable world income distribution (Acemoglu and Ventura 2002). Country-to-country variations in economic policies, savings, and technology translate into country-to-country variation in incomes. World income distribution is determined by the degree of openness to international trade and the extent of specialization.

Specialization in production is an efficiency gain derived from trade (Schott 2004). This, in turn, leads to productivity improvements. For example, Alcala and Ciccone (2004) show that international trade has an economically significant positive effect on productivity in manufactured product markets. In agriculture, being able to focus on the production of what grows well in an area, and trading for commodities that do not grow as well locally, enables producers to specialize their capital and operations, thus gaining economies of scale and other types of production efficiencies.

The relationship between trade and productivity is circular. In addition to the productivity gains from trade that come from the ability to specialize operations, there are the gains to trade that come from technological advances. Trade in agricultural products was made increasingly viable by technological advances in production, storage, and transportation of commodities. First, improvements in production expanded output, generating the surpluses that can be traded. Next, improvements in storage technologies made it possible for agricultural commodities, even perishables, to be stored for longer periods of time with lower spoilage rates. Finally, with more time available, more distance can be covered, so improvements in transportation technologies made ever more distant markets reachable. The ultimate result is that for the past two or three decades it has been economically feasible for even highly perishable commodities to be traded between almost any two points on the globe. Thus, productivity improvements created the need for trade, and trade created a global market that enables participants to specialize their production in the limited number of products for which they have the highest level of productivity.

Barriers to Free Trade

A nation's transition from trying to be self-sufficient in food production to being dependent on trade for some share of food supplies is rarely smooth. The same resource imbalances that create the need for trade create difficulties in finding a trade partner that is willing and able to exchange the quantities of the desired product at the desired time. The problem is complicated by the fact that at the national level there are usually many products being exported and imported at any given time. Thus, resource imbalances often lead to trade imbalances: unequal amounts of imports and exports during a time period. Therefore, smooth trade operations are virtually impossible if all trades have to be made in kind—that is, requiring the actual exchange of two or more products. Instead, timely trades require the use of an exchange medium: money. However, trade imbalances can lead to other economic imbalances, causing shifts in markets, such as shifts in currency exchange rates, which can adversely affect national economies and trade between specific countries (Orden 2002). For example, Cho, Sheldon, and McCorriston (2002) found that exchange rate uncertainty had a significant negative effect on agricultural trade over the 1974–1995 period. The negative effect was greater on agriculture than on any other sector in national economies. To avoid these adverse market effects, countries often take action to interfere with free trade.

Barriers to free trade are usually erected as part of a temporary balancing act. Barriers are used by countries that cannot balance the shifts in resources (i.e., they are losing the balance in their trade) and want to slow the trading process. Using trade barriers is an inexact process, as shown by Gulati (2002). He describes how India has trouble balancing tariffs with volatile world prices, often raising tariffs too much, thus hindering markets. Tariffs are a surcharge used when attempting to balance the prices of a single commodity originating from two or more countries in order to make the commodity from the higher-priced country more competitive in domestic markets. The price of the import is thus raised so as to discourage domestic consumers from demanding cheap imports that compete with domestic sources for the commodity. Gibson et al. (2001) note that "high protection for agricultural commodities in the form of tariffs continues to be the major factor restricting world trade." Other technical barriers to trade ultimately have similar effects on import or export markets: they raise the price to domestic consumers (Yue, Beghin, and Jensen 2006). Whereas tariffs are usually aimed at protecting domestic markets from import competition, another barrier to free trade—the export subsidy—is aimed at making exports cheaper for consumers in foreign markets. In the United States, some government policies seek to expand export markets of domestically produced commodities. The usual justification for such policies is that the subsidies aid domestic producers by lowering the effective price of their output on the global market, thus increasing aggregate demand from foreign buyers. However, Leathers

(2001) found that arguments in support of export subsidies are not supported by economic analysis. Schmitz, Schmitz, and Rossi (2006) argue that without decoupling, it is difficult to assess the affects of export subsidy policies. Using U.S. cotton as an example, they show how some groups are helped while others are hurt by the policy. Unfortunately, what is clear is that less-developed countries cannot compete with wealthier nations in providing export subsidies (Brandon 2002).

Another type of barrier to free trade is collusive behavior by commodity sellers. It is well known that market power can exist in global commodity markets (Rakotoarisoa and Shapouri 2001). Thus, many nations have tried to improve the profitability of their export sales by forming cartels and other imperfect market arrangements in an attempt to balance their trade flows (e.g., Paarlberg and Abbott 1986, 1987; Filson et al. 2001). These collusive arrangements can be especially damaging to free trade when the natural resources involved are highly imbalanced in their distribution around the globe. The resulting higher market price causes poorer countries to reduce their consumption of the product, thus potentially lowering the standard of living of their population.

One effective means of reducing barriers to free trade has been to create trade agreements involving more than one product. The most common type of arrangement is a bilateral trade agreement between two countries that can exchange numerous products. Recently, multilateral agreements have become even more effective in reducing trade barriers. For example, Burfisher, Robinson, and Thierfelder (2002) found that when a regional trade agreement forces a developing country to reform its domestic market distortions that are linked to trade restrictions, it becomes a building block toward multilateralism, thus moving all nations involved toward free trade.

Tools of Trade

There are many tools used to facilitate international trade: organizations, agreements, and vertical integration of firms across borders. These tools are making trade more common and safer, thus facilitating mutual dependence and recognizing its role in future economic development around the globe.

By far, the most important institution is now the World Trade Organization (WTO). It has replaced earlier trade institutions, such as the General Agreement on Tariffs and Trade (GATT), to become the "United Nations" of trade negotiations and the single accepted "high court" of trade disputes between countries. Most nations in the world are now WTO members and, as a result, the WTO will grow in importance and sway in creating global trade rules, regulations, and patterns. In particular, it is already becoming central in global efforts aimed at resolving trade disputes between nations. In that role, it is making an increasing contribution in shaping international trade policies. This includes applying pressure to countries that are causing slow-downs in the global efforts to facilitate trade so that resource imbalances can be reduced and economic growth enhanced. For example, Diao, Roe, and Somwaru (2002) argue that since developing countries' agricultural export markets are in the northern hemisphere, and since most distortions in world agricultural markets are due to a few of those northern countries, all trading nations would benefit from the opening of markets in the European Union and the United States, although the effects would be regional. In other words, the WTO is not afraid to confront the United States or European countries over policies that inhibit free trade. This was illustrated in December 2005 when the WTO agreed to eliminate agricultural export subsidies by 2013. As a result of this institutional pressure, agricultural trade liberalization is expected to occur despite decades of disputes (McCalla 2003). However, the WTO is still an evolving institution needing changes as new types of trade disputes arise, as described by Smith (2007), thus the transition toward free trade will be a slow, negotiated one.

Trade agreements between countries have existed for centuries, but since the Second World War the number and types of agreements have increased rapidly. For example, Koo, Kennedy, and Skripnitchenko (2006) note the growth in regional preferential trade agreements (RPTA). They report that GATT and the WTO "have been notified of 254 preferential trade agreements since 1948, with nearly half occurring after 1995" (p. 408). They explain the trend by concluding (p. 415):

> Although the benefits of RPTAs are greater for member countries than for nonmembers, the results of this analysis indicate that RPTAs are not harmful to nonmember countries. This suggests that RPTAs improve global welfare by increasing agricultural trade volume among member countries and, to a lesser degree, among nonmember countries.

Zahniser et al. (2002) add support to this conclusion by assessing U.S. agricultural trade deals and showing that bilateral trade agreements have benefited the United States and our trade partners (such as Mexico), although those effects differ by commodity.

Vertical integration of agricultural firms is the newest tool being used to facilitate trade across international borders. American agribusiness firms, in particular, have recognized that creating vertical supply chains using foreign direct investment and contracting is an effective way to stabilize mutually dependent relationships across countries (e.g., Skripnitchenko and Woo 2005; Sheldon, Pick, and McCorriston 2001). This trend is discussed at length in Chapter 18.

Other tools of trade have been tried successfully in various agricultural markets over time (e.g., Rosson, Hammig, and Jones 1986), but the bottom line is always the same: trade is all about the people involved. As Fafchamps and Minten (2001) note, social capital boosts the productivity of agricultural traders, thus creating an economic incentive for trade to continue. Thus, mutual dependence can bring people together and, as those people see the willingness of their trade partners to maintain the mutually beneficial relationship, the relationship becomes even more mutually beneficial over time.

CONFLICT BETWEEN LOCAL AND GLOBAL COMPARATIVE ADVANTAGE

> *"Stocks have reached what looks like a permanent high plateau."*
> Irving Fisher, Professor of Economics, Yale University, 1929

Looks can be deceiving. Fisher's statement, that "stocks have reached what looks like a permanent high plateau," was made just months before the stock market crash of October 1929 that began the American economy's slide into the Great Depression. Obviously, Professor Fisher was wrong. Why was he so wrong? In a sense, he made the same mistake that is being made by many analysts of today's situation in American agriculture: not being able to see past the local market, thus missing the global picture. To use a mathematical analogy, the mistake is in believing that calculating the local minimum (or maximum) of some function is sufficient when, in fact, there is a global minimum (or maximum) that dominates the local value. Currently, too many analysts of

American agriculture are focused on domestic production and marketing statistics and are unable or unwilling to look around for the big picture.

Global economic development, especially in the agricultural sector, has changed the nature of international trade. As a result, there is now a conflict between local and global comparative advantage. Having a local comparative advantage in the production of some commodity is now a necessary, but not sufficient, condition for the profitable production of that commodity. Failing to recognize this point can cause much economic harm, but it will not prevent mutual dependence from developing over the long run.

The key change we must understand in dealing with the modern world is that, when discussing agricultural commodities, the global situation has reversed—trade was once driven by local and global shortages of commodities, whereas now there are global surpluses of many commodities. This is a result of technological advances and economic development that led to global commodity markets. Before global trade of perishable commodities was possible, each location was limited to consuming only what could be produced locally. Also, many areas were unable to trade for some commodities because those goods could not be shipped to the location due to spoilage. Nevertheless, people in every location could always use their local surplus production to pay for whatever it was that they sought through trade. That is no longer true. Technology increased both the volume of each commodity that could be produced per acre and also the distances that could be covered before product spoilage occurred. Now, virtually all locations can acquire the quantities desired of virtually any commodity, but their local surplus output is not always of value.[2] Global surpluses exist in many agricultural markets, as indicated by falling real commodity prices, so holders of "excess" quantities of a commodity cannot always find a willing trade partner. What's going on here?

Economic theory says that domestic (regional) production is determined by spatial comparative advantage. In other words, the resources available in a location are used to produce whatever commodities are best suited to those resource inputs. That was fine when technology and the world's resource imbalances led to shortages of commodities in most locations. Letting comparative advantage determine which commodities were produced in an area worked well, enabling economic development to occur in an explainable fashion. As Gopinath and Kennedy (2000, p. 1217) conclude,

> productivity growth and factor accumulation explain U.S. agricultural export patterns and performance at the state level. That is, the sources of comparative advantage in the context of open economies include cumulative factors such as knowledge, human and physical capital. Thus, comparative advantage is dynamic and can be brought about by conscious efforts directed toward the accumulation of these factors.

Using comparative advantage as a development guide worked in all parts of the world. For example, Liefert (2002) concluded that after Russia moved to a market economy it changed its agricultural sector in response to its disadvantage in agricultural outputs compared with its agricultural inputs, as illustrated by Russia's severe contraction of its livestock sector and its greatly increased meat imports. However, this action indicates that comparative disadvantage also exists and raises a related concept: absolute advantage.

Absolute advantage is a concept that has been neglected in the agricultural literature because it is only truly relevant when there exists a surplus of a traded commodity. However, surplus situations are routinely created in global markets today. As a result, the concept now guides much of global agricultural trade. The term refers to which trader has a lower cost of production for a commodity and, thus, is able to exchange that commodity for the lowest absolute price. When a buyer has multiple potential sellers offering amounts of a commodity that, in total, exceed his needs, that buyer will usually make purchases from the lowest-cost source, ceteris paribus. That means higher-cost sellers may be unable to find markets for their output during periods of global surplus.

In a global market for a commodity, the Law of One Price holds, thereby establishing the potential for absolute advantage to exist. The economic theory behind the Law of One Price says that a "commodity" is an undifferentiated product—there are no differences in the tangible attributes of the output of two or more suppliers, by definition—thus there is no justification for a price difference between sellers. As a result, a single price exists in a commodity market, with adjustments observed only to account for differences in the commodity's location and product form over time. This theoretical relationship has been found to exist in commodity prices in many empirical studies (e.g., Ardeni 1989; Baffes 1991; Goodwin 1992; Goodwin, Grennes, and Wohlgenant 1990; Yang, Bessler, and Leatham 2000). This means that all countries wishing to trade their surplus of some commodity must essentially do so at the same absolute price, adjusted for transportation and storage costs. As a result, least-cost suppliers prevail in the long run when there is a global "surplus" situation (which is indicated by the falling real prices observed in current markets). This is due to the absolute advantage of least-cost suppliers; they can make a profit at lower world prices than can higher-cost suppliers and, therefore, have a better chance of surviving in a free trade market.

The bottom line in this issue is that international trade has significant effects on local and global production (see Marsh 2001, for example). Specifically, trade narrows the list of commodities produced locally to those with the highest yields and lowest costs relative to the output of competitors in a global market. Thus, international trade is now causing commodity production to be concentrated in locations with global absolute advantage (Dollar and Wolff 1995). This is an ongoing transition process that is reordering the world's resource utilization distribution. The net effect is to make more efficient use of the resources scattered around the globe. However, progress in that effort is hindered by political boundaries and the willingness of countries to take the necessary long-run view of social welfare while facing their short-run requirements of trying to balance trade, national budgets, and the economic demands of their diverse populations.

There are hugely important implications of the transition process. Ball et al. (2001) show evidence of convergence in international farm sector productivity from 1973 to 1993, consistent with the "catch-up" hypothesis that poor countries will catch up to wealthy nations, or at least narrow the gap between the two groups. Ball et al. (2001) show a positive relationship between capital accumulation and productivity growth. This indicates that agricultural development is indeed improving the lives of people across the globe. However, this is not always good news to people in the United States. Hudson and Ethridge (2000) argue that both the commodity and its processing sector must be considered when judging the true competitiveness of a country's commodity in global markets. "Policies such as export subsidies, which have a positive impact on the competitiveness (at least in the short run) of the commodity sector, may ultimately have a detrimental impact on the industry as a whole" (p. 1223). That is why mutual dependence will not be quickly embraced by many people in the United States, but in the long run, it will prove to be a good investment.

MUTUAL DEPENDENCE AS A REVOLVING DOOR

A revolving door is a barrier to the elements outside, yet it is in constant motion, allowing traffic to flow both in and out simultaneously. International mutual dependence operates in much the same manner. It is a mechanism that protects those inside a country from the commodity shortages that would occur due to resource limitations, and it does so by allowing constant flows of products both into and out of the country.

For the United States, international mutual dependence and trade will make it possible for us to leave agriculture—if not entirely, then at least to the extent that our resources put us at an absolute disadvantage in some commodity markets. International mutual dependence will be recognized and pursued because the United States, like virtually all countries, does not have adequate resources to be self-sufficient in all things. Nevertheless, with a network of cooperation between nations that recognize the benefits of trade in a system of international mutual dependence, America and its trading partners will have access to a wider variety of agricultural commodities than could ever be produced with the limited resources within our borders. Plus, the prices paid by consumers for those commodities may be lower than current prices. In essence, this all means that Americans do not have to fear the current trend of our becoming uncompetitive in global agricultural commodity markets; we will still have sources for food.

Most economists define competitiveness using the widely accepted language proposed by the Canadian Task Force on Competitiveness in the Agri-Food Industry: "Competitiveness is the sustained ability to profitably gain and maintain market share" (Agriculture Canada 1991). Clearly, the factors affecting competitiveness are not identical to those affecting comparative advantage. Comparative advantage reflects which products *can* be produced best (i.e., most efficiently) given the resources available in the location of the firm. Nowhere in the definition of comparative advantage is any mention made of whether the firm makes any profits from a product, nor whether anyone is even willing to buy the product. On the other hand, competitiveness is based entirely on the two questions of profitability and market share.

The new absolute advantage situation created by market globalization creates the possibility that some U.S. regions with strong comparative advantages in a narrow range of crops will be under greater pressure from global competitors, thus economic performance of the regions will suffer. Conversely, regions such as the Southeast and West that have more diverse cropping due to their broader comparative advantages are expected to have stronger financial performance longer into the future (for areas where urban pressure is not significant). For example, wheat, corn, soybeans, hogs, and cattle are produced in the Midwest, but what are recent trends in America's share of the global markets for those commodities? America's share is falling, implying that other countries are developing their regional comparative advantage in the production of those commodities and also expanding their market share due to an absolute advantage (i.e., lower output cost per unit). For example, American wheat output approximately doubled during the 1960–2000 period, but the U.S. share of global market supplies fell from 15 percent to 10 percent during that period (Duffy 2001). That means wheat producing regions in other countries are a competitive threat to American wheat producers in the long run, even though it appears that our domestic industry's output is growing in the short run. The story is similar for many commodities. There are many less-developed countries becoming more competitive with American agricultural producers every year (Dohlman, Osborne, and Lohmar 2003; Kennedy and Rosson 2002; Pan et al. 2007). The effects of absolute advantage mean that as global (real) prices fall, and American production costs rise, and at some point profits will fall to the level needed to effectively shut down a production region.

This brings us to the big question: "Will America leave agriculture (or at least some commodity markets)?" There are three possible answers to this question. (1) The first answer will be used by those who underestimate the power of technological innovation: "*Can't.*" They will argue that other countries cannot fill the supply gap if we leave the market, and therefore foreign sources cannot (or will refuse to) supply us with adequate product quantities and/or qualities. This argument is based on concerns over global supply and trade issues. (2) The second answer is related to the first: *"Won't."* It is based on fears that trade barriers may be used against us by foreign suppliers, leading to "food as a blackmail weapon." That argument will be used by those who do not want to depend on imports for food—calling it a national security issue—because they do not understand the reality of global food markets. (3) The correct answer is *"Yes."* It will be used by those who understand the economics of international mutual dependence.

The first answer is invalidated by the massive amount of potential growth already forecast to occur in less-developed countries. For example, even the U.S. Department of Agriculture acknowledges that Brazil's agricultural expansion potential is underrated (2003). Both Brazil and Argentina have already begun development efforts that will generate huge increases in output of the same field crops currently produced in the American Midwest (Schnepf, Dohlman, and Bolling 2001). The same is true of Ukraine and other countries in Eastern Europe. Also, China's ongoing move to specialized family farms will greatly increase its output and trade of food products, ultimately turning that food importer into a food-exporting nation (Carter and Rozelle 2001).

The second answer is invalidated simply by the fact that it is backward; it is more likely that the United States will use its power as a food importer as a weapon against suppliers than the reverse. "Food" is not one product; there are hundreds of products that can be eaten. If supplies of one commodity are short, we can eat something else for a while. Plus, it is virtually impossible to imagine all suppliers of *all* food products trying to cut off America's supplies at the same time. But if they tried? It would hurt them more than it would hurt us. America is the world's biggest market, so losing us as a customer for any reason could devastate a less-developed country, whereas no single food supplier is big enough to significantly affect America's calorie intake. The old cliché, "the customer is always right," acknowledges that sellers must respond to buyers' wishes because the risk of losing one's market means risking one's economic life. No other country, especially the less-developed nations that will be producing most of the world's food, can afford to lose us as a customer. Finally, American agribusiness firms will ensure America gets the food it needs by establishing vertical supply chains across the globe (as discussed in Chapter 18). International trade issues will become increasingly important, however, and the geographical diversification of American agribusiness firms will enable them to put pressure on foreign nations' trade policies so as to make it more certain that the United States will have secure food supplies.

The third answer is the correct one for so many reasons. In addition to the economic arguments already highlighted in this chapter, there is the surprising idea that becoming more of a food importer than we already are might actually *improve* the quality of the products available to American consumers. For example, Hummels and Skiba (2004) find, for manufactured products, that the Alchian-Allen Theorem is right: higher-quality products are exported, leaving lower-quality products for domestic sale. This implies that buying our TV dinners from foreign contract suppliers, rather than eating what is made here, might actually give us more choices, forcing the suppliers to compete on the basis of quality. Nevertheless, the third answer is the best choice because it indicates that international mutual dependence is the path most likely to lead to economic growth across the globe while establishing bonds of cooperation between countries and, thereby, reducing the potential for immature conflicts of all types.

MUTUAL DEPENDENCE IS THE GAME OF LIFE

International mutual dependence has the potential to be an infinitely repeated game in which the cooperative outcome is best for each player. However, it will require a mature and practical view of economic development to achieve that successful outcome. That outcome will occur, but the dynamic process of global economic development makes it impossible to predict when. The good news is that the process has already begun; global trade models indicate that more people are moving toward a cooperative outcome (van Tongeren, van Meijl, and Surry 2001).

A game theoretic approach is increasingly being used to assess international trade (e.g., Lee and Kennedy 2007) and a similar approach can be applied in a theoretical assessment of international mutual dependence. A simple assessment here can provide insights into global agriculture's future effect on market evolution. To begin, the typical 2-player game (i.e., the United States versus the Rest of the World) is insufficient; a 3-player game is needed. The real players are the United States (US), other more-developed countries (OMDC), and less-developed countries (LDC). The goal is to see what sort of mutually dependent system is possible. It is assumed for simplicity that there are only two types of output possible from each country: agricultural products and manufactured goods. The relevant data for this example can be condensed from the literature and international sources to the following:

$$\text{Agricultural marginal costs}: \text{OMDC} > \text{US} > \text{LDC}$$
$$\text{Goods marginal costs}: \text{LDC} > \text{US} \geq \text{OMDC}$$

This means that at present, average marginal costs for agricultural output are lowest for less-developed countries and highest for more-developed countries. Conversely, LDCs have the highest average marginal costs for manufactured goods. In the infinitely repeated game of life, the short-run and long-run outcomes in a fair trade world can easily be seen. In the short run (defined as the period over which LDCs do not have the capacity to supply the world's total food needs), LDCs produce only food while OMDCs and the US produce food and goods. Gradually, LDCs will expand their output, thus increasing their competitiveness with higher-cost agricultural suppliers in OMDCs and the US, until finally reaching the point where the highest-cost agricultural producers will be forced to exit the market. Given the global cost structures, OMDCs (such as Japan and small countries in Western Europe) will leave agriculture first, and may continue to buy food from the US during the interim period. That interim ends when LDCs expand their agricultural output capacity to the level needed to supply the entire world. At that point, the "long-run" outcome begins when OMDCs and the US produce no food, only manufactured goods. Of course, this simple assessment must be repeated for each commodity to get a more detailed view of which products are best produced by each of the three players in this game. Even though OMDCs are likely to leave virtually all agricultural commodity markets, there will probably be some small local comparative advantages that survive as absolute advantages due to the imbalance of resource distributions around the globe. The same is probable in the United States, as assessed in Chapter 17. However, the general result here is that agricultural production will gradually be shifted to LDCs as America and other more-developed countries focus on value-added manufactured goods. Hence, free trade will lead to production specialization in all three of the "players" in the mutual dependence game.

How will this outcome play out? America's "trigger strategy" for the game is already operating: establish trade relationships using trade agreements. A trade agreement is a form of explicit collusion between countries. This type of cooperation can be a "subgame perfect equilibrium." Also, there may be a Nash equilibrium in this game, but only in the "short run." In the very long run, any particular equilibrium will not be stable because economic development will gradually shift the trade positions of countries around the globe, thus causing adjustments to be made in response. Ultimately, the cooperative outcome is superior to all others if a long-run view of global social welfare is taken.

NOTES

1. It is important to remember that many people (non-economists) use the term "market" in a literal sense to refer to a place, such as "the local market," but to economists the term actually means a process of trade or exchange. Locations called a "market" are places where trading occurs.

2. The use of currency as a trade good eliminates the need for local areas to "pay" for their imports by trading some physical amount of a commodity that is in local surplus. Therefore, a local area can continue producing a commodity that has no export demand as long as there is some domestic demand for that commodity. If domestic demand also falls short of local supplies, the government can subsidize the local economy by purchasing the area's surplus commodity output. This is done often in the American wheat market, for example.

REFERENCES

Acemoglu, D., and J. Ventura. 2002. "The World Income Distribution." *Quarterly Journal of Economics* 117: 659–694.

Agriculture Canada. 1991. "Growing Together: Report to Ministers of Agriculture." Report of the Task Force on Competitiveness in the Agri-Food Industry, Ottawa, Ontario, Canada.

Alcala, F., and A. Ciccone. 2004. "Trade and Productivity." *Quarterly Journal of Economics* 119: 613–646.

Anderson, K., W. Martin, and D. van der Mensbrugghe. 2006. "Distortions to World Trade: Impacts on Agricultural Markets and Farm Incomes." *Review of Agricultural Economics* 28 (2): 168–194.

Ardeni, Pier G. 1989. "Does the Law of One Price Really Hold for Commodity Prices?" *American Journal of Agricultural Economics* 71: 661–669.

Baffes, John. 1991. "Some Further Evidence on the Law of One Price: The Law of One Price Still Holds." *American Journal of Agricultural Economics* 73 (5): 1264–1273.

Ball, E., J. Bureau, J. Butault, and R. Nehring. 2001. "Levels of Farm Sector Productivity: An International Comparison." *Journal of Productivity Analysis* 15: 5–29.

Brandon, Hembree. 2002. "Developing Nations Not Able to Compete: World Food Summit Delegates Urge Ag Subsidies End." *Western Farm Press*, July 6, 5.

Burfisher, M., S. Robinson, and K. Thierfelder. 2002. "Developing Countries and the Gains from Regionalism: Links Between Trade and Farm Policy Reforms in Mexico." *American Journal of Agricultural Economics* 84 (3): 736–748.

Carter, C., and S. Rozelle. 2001. "Will China Become a Market Force in World Food Markets?" *Review of Agricultural Economics* 23 (2): 319–331.

Cho, G., I. Sheldon, and S. McCorriston. 2002. "Exchange Rate Uncertainty and Agricultural Trade." *American Journal of Agricultural Economics* 84 (4): 931–942.

Dawson, P.J. 2005. "Agricultural Exports and Economic Growth in Less Developed Countries." *Agricultural Economics* 33: 145–152.

Diao, X., T. Roe, and A. Somwaru. 2002. "Developing Country Interests in Agricultural Reforms Under the World Trade Organization." *American Journal of Agricultural Economics* 84 (3): 782–790.

Dohlman, E., S. Osborne, and B. Lohmar. 2003. "Dynamics of Agricultural Competitiveness: Policy Lessons from Abroad." *Amber Waves* 1 (April): 14–21.

Dollar, D., and E. Wolff. 1995. *Competitiveness, Convergence, and International Specialization.* Cambridge, MA: MIT Press 1995.

Duffy, Patricia A. 2001. "Casting Bread upon the Water: Comments on Technology, Globalization, and Agriculture." *Journal of Agricultural & Applied Economics* 33 (2): 341–347.

Fafchamps, M., and B. Minten. 2001. "Social Capital and Agricultural Trade." *American Journal of Agricultural Economics* 83: 680–685.

Filson, D., E. Keen, E. Fruits, and T. Borcherding. 2001. "Market Power and Cartel Formation: Theory and Empirical Test." *Journal of Law and Economics* 44: 465–480.

Gibson, P., J. Wainio, D. Whitley, and M. Bohman. 2001. *Profiles of Tariffs in Global Agricultural Markets.* Economic Research Service, USDA, Agricultural Economic Report no. 796, January.

Goodwin, Barry K. 1992. "Multivariate Cointegration Tests and the Law of One Price in International Wheat Markets." *Review of Agricultural Economics* 14: 117–124.

Goodwin, B., T. Grennes, and M. Wohlgenant. 1990. "A Revised Test of the Law of One Price Using Rational Price Expectations." *American Journal of Agricultural Economics* 72: 682–693.

Gopinath, M., and L. Kennedy. 2000. "Agricultural Trade and Productivity Growth: A State-level Analysis." *American Journal of Agricultural Economics* 82 (5): 1213–1218.

Gulati, Ashok. 2002. "Indian Agriculture in a Globalizing World." *American Journal of Agricultural Economics* 84 (3): 754–761.

Hudson, D., and D. Ethridge. 2000. "Competitiveness of Agricultural Commodities in the United States: Expanding Our View." *American Journal of Agricultural Economics* 82: 1219–1223.

Hummels, D., and A. Skiba. 2004. "Shipping the Good Apples Out? An Empirical Confirmation of the Alchian-Allen Conjecture." *Journal of Political Economy* 112 (6): 1384–1402.

Kennedy, L., and P. Rosson III. 2002. "Impacts of Globalization on Agricultural Competitiveness: The Case of NAFTA." *Journal of Agricultural & Applied Economics* 34 (2): 275–288.

Koo, W., L. Kennedy, and A. Skripnitchenko. 2006. "Regional Preferential Trade Agreements: Trade Creation and Diversion Effects." *Review of Agricultural Economics* 28 (3): 408–415.

Leathers, Howard D. 2001. "Agricultural Export Subsidies as a Tool of Trade Strategy: Before and After the Federal Agricultural Improvement and Reform Act of 1996." *American Journal of Agricultural Economics* 83: 209–221.

Lee, D., and L. Kennedy. 2007. "A Political Economic Analysis of U.S. Rice Export Programs to Japan and South Korea: A Game Theoretic Approach." *American Journal of Agricultural Economics* 89 (1): 104–115.

Liefert, William M. 2002. "Comparative (Dis?)Advantage in Russian Agriculture." *American Journal of Agricultural Economics* 84 (3): 762–767.

Marsh, John M. 2001. "U.S. Feeder Cattle Prices: Effects of Finance and Risk, Cow-Calf and Feedlot Technologies, and Mexican Feeder Imports." *Journal of Agricultural and Resource Economics* 26 (2): 463–477.

McCalla, Alex F. 2003. "Liberalizing Agricultural Trade: Will It Ever Be a Reality?" *Journal of Agricultural and Resource Economics* 28 (3): 419–434.

Orden, David. 2002. "Exchange Rate Effects on Agricultural Trade." *Journal of Agricultural & Applied Economics* 34 (2): 303–312.

Paarlberg, P., and P. Abbott. 1987. "Collusive Behavior by Exporting Countries in World Wheat Trade." *North Central Journal of Agricultural Economics* 9: 13–27.

———. 1986. "Oligopolistic Behavior by Public Agencies in International Trade: The World Wheat Market." *American Journal of Agricultural Economics* 68: 528–542.

Pan, S., M. Fadiga, S. Mohanty, and M. Welch. 2007. "Cotton in a Free Trade World." *Economic Inquiry* 45 (1): 188–197.

Rakotoarisoa, M., and S. Shapouri. 2001. "Market Power and the Pricing of Commodities Imported from Developing Countries: The Case of US Vanilla Bean Imports." *Agricultural Economics* 25 (2–3): 285–294.

Roe, T., and H. Mohtadi. 2001. "International Trade and Growth: An Overview Using the New Growth Theory." *Review of Agricultural Economics* 23 (2): 423–440.

Roe, T., A. Somwaru, and X. Diao. 2006. "Globalization: Welfare Distribution and Costs Among Developed and Developing Countries." *Review of Agricultural Economics* 28 (3): 399–407.

Rosson, C., III, M. Hammig, and J. Jones. 1986. "Foreign Market Promotion Programs: An Analysis of Promotion Response for Apples, Poultry, and Tobacco." *Agribusiness: An International Journal* 2: 33–42.

Schmitz A., T. Schmitz, and F. Rossi. 2006. "Agricultural Subsidies in Developed Countries: Impact on Global Welfare." *Review of Agricultural Economics* 28 (3): 416–425.

Schnepf, R., E. Dohlman, and C. Bolling. 2001. "Agriculture in Brazil and Argentina: Developments and Prospects for Major Field Crops." Agriculture and Trade Report WRS-01-3, USDA Economics Research Service, Market and Trade Economics Division, November.

Schott, Peter K. 2004. "Across-Product Versus Within-Product Specialization in International Trade." *Quarterly Journal of Economics* 119: 647–677.

Senauer, Ben. 2002. "A Pro–Poor Growth Strategy to End Hunger." *American Journal of Agricultural Economics* 84 (3): 826–831.

Senauer, B., and M. Sur. 2001. "Ending Global Hunger in the 21st Century: Projections of the Number of Food Insecure People." *Review of Agricultural Economics* 23 (1): 68–81.

Sheldon, I., D. Pick, and S. McCorriston. 2001. "Export Subsidies and Profit-Shifting in Vertical Markets." *Journal of Agricultural and Resource Economics* 26: 125–141.

Skripnitchenko, A., and W. Woo. 2005. "U.S. Foreign Direct Investment in Food Processing Industries of Latin American Countries: A Dynamic Approach." *Review of Agricultural Economics* 27 (3): 394–401.

Smith, Vincent H. 2007. "Regulating State Trading Enterprises in the World Trade Organization: An Urgent Need for Change? Evidence from the 2003–2004 U.S.–Canada Grain Dispute." *Review of Agricultural Economics* 29 (2): 187–200.

U.S. Department of Agriculture. 2003. "Brazil: Future Agricultural Expansion Potential Underrated." Foreign Agricultural Service, Production Estimates and Crop Assessment Division, January 21. Available at: www.fas.usda.gov/pecad/highlights/2003/01/Ag_expansion/index2.htm.

van Tongeren, F., H. van Meijl, and Y. Surry. 2001. "Global Models Applied to Agricultural and Trade Policies: A Review and Assessment." *Agricultural Economics* 26 (2): 149–172.

Vollrath, Dietrich. 2007. "Distribution and International Agricultural Productivity." *American Journal of Agricultural Economics* 89 (1): 202–216.

Yang, J., D. Bessler, and D. Leatham. 2000. "The Law of One Price: Developed and Developing Country Market Integration." *Journal of Agricultural & Applied Economics* 32 (3): 429–440.

Yue, C., J. Beghin, and H. Jensen. 2006. "Tariff Equivalent of Technical Barriers to Trade with Imperfect Substitution and Trade Costs." *American Journal of Agricultural Economics* 88 (4): 947–960.

Zahniser, S., D. Pick, G. Pompelli, and M. Gehlhar. 2002. "Regionalism in the Western Hemisphere and Its Impacts on U.S. Agricultural Exports: A Gravity-Model Analysis." *American Journal of Agricultural Economics* 84 (3): 791–797.

PART IV

AMERICAN PRODUCTION AGRICULTURE'S RESPONSE

CHAPTER 11

PRODUCERS AS INVESTORS AND PORTFOLIO MANAGERS

"Why not go out on a limb? Isn't that where the fruit is?"
—Frank Scully

There are a number of seemingly contradictory trends in the structure of American agriculture. For example, total revenues for agriculture in the United States increased nearly every year until this century began, yet both the total number of farmers and the total acreage of land in farms steadily decrease. A casual observer might attribute the combined rise in revenues and decline in farm numbers to a successful concentration process that is clearly apparent in some agricultural production sectors, such as the hog industry. Indeed, the number of farms of 1,000 acres or more has increased steadily, totaling 168,864 in 1987 and 176,080 in the 1997 Census of Agriculture (USDA 1998). However, the trend of higher sales revenues is not consistent with *falling* acreage totals. Even if an observer wanted to explain higher revenue totals by pointing to increasing productivity rates in agriculture, it does not explain why people are taking land out of agriculture, instead of bringing more into production so as to take advantage of technological advances. And the decrease in total farmland has been significant, dropping from the peak of 1.2 billion acres reported in 1954 to 931.8 million acres in 1997. Also, rising revenue totals are not consistent with recent downward price trends such as those observed in grain and other commodity markets.

Close examination of the aggregate trends in American agriculture offers only one general explanation that is consistent with both the trends and the rational behavior of individual producers: farmers must produce higher-value crops over time to remain economically viable, and, at some point, nonagricultural investments must be considered, thus causing land to leave agriculture. The objective of this chapter is to present that explanation as a simple theory of crop portfolio composition and land use. A portfolio model constrained by a safety-first criterion is used to evaluate the investment decisions facing individual producers, leading to some general conclusions presented in the form of propositions.

In brief, the theory is that whenever changing market conditions result in decreased profits from the existing mix of enterprises in production, a farmer will be forced to change the composition of his/her "crop portfolio" to a new mix that is expected to generate sufficient profits to meet his/her financial requirements. Over time, the crop and livestock enterprises added to the production mix in response to profit pressures will generate more revenue per acre, but will be more risky, making the farmer's crop portfolio more risky, thus adding incentive for the farmer to begin diversifying outside of agriculture, even if he/she does not want to do so. Therefore, a "profit squeeze" forces changes in cropping patterns that are visible to even casual observers.

The theory is presented in stages. To begin, decision rules used when making cropping choices are discussed. Then, the first stage of the theory shows the base case of a farmer who wants to be fully invested in agricultural production. Next, it is shown how external shocks will create conditions that require the farmer to change the composition of his/her crop portfolio and, eventually, to consider diversifying out of agriculture. The next section explains the situation facing a farmer when assets must leave agriculture. Finally, spatial land-use patterns are explained in the context of the crop portfolio composition.

DECISION RULES IN AGRICULTURE

Agricultural producers face many types of business decisions, just like all managers. Those decisions, in general, are investment choices. For example, a prospective farmer must first decide what piece of property to acquire (i.e., invest in). That choice depends upon the farmer's long-run expectations of what crops can be grown profitably on that property. Then, each year the farmer must select the actual crops to produce. That choice depends on the short-run prospects offered by the market for each product. Thus, a farmer operates like any other investor: alternatives are assessed over the long- and short-run and resources (i.e., cash, labor, and land) are invested with the goal of acquiring (i.e., producing) some asset (i.e., output) that is expected to have a market value exceeding the investment costs, thus resulting in a profit when the asset is sold. An investor with more than one asset (i.e., agricultural enterprise) is said to have a portfolio. In that case the person makes decisions about each asset with an eye on the effects on total returns from the portfolio of investments. In other words, the agricultural producer is a portfolio manager. He or she invests a portfolio of inputs (i.e., land, labor, and capital) in an effort to acquire a portfolio of outputs that can be sold profitably. Therefore, the logic behind a farmer's business decisions is the same portfolio theory that is used to explain any investor's actions.

In portfolio theory, utility maximization is assumed to be a person's objective. Therefore, the focus of decision making is the certainty equivalent of expected profits, which Freund (1956), Levy and Markowitz (1979), Meyer (1987), and others have shown is

$$(11.1) \qquad E(U_\phi) = E(\Pi_\phi) - (\Lambda/2)(\sigma^2 \Pi_\phi)$$

where $E(\cdot)$ is the expected value of $(\cdot)$, U is utility, Π_ϕ is profit per acre from crop portfolio ϕ, Λ is a risk-aversion parameter which is zero for risk-neutral farmers and positive for risk-averse producers, and $\sigma^2(\Pi_\phi)$ is risk defined as the historical variance of average profits per acre for portfolio ϕ. In general, "the expected utility model is the premier indexing rule for ordering choices under uncertainty" (Robison and Barry 1987, p. 20). When the decision involves only a single asset or some group of investments from which the resulting profits or losses are relatively small compared to the person's total wealth, the expected utility model suits most investors. However, when the scale of possible losses from an investment is significant, risk-averse investors have been shown to adopt "safety-first" decision rules. Safety-first criteria are compatible with the standard utility theory (Robison and Barry 1987, p. 201; Bigman 1996; Pyle and Turnovsky 1970).

Safety-first models place constraints upon the probability of failing to achieve certain goals of the firm. Several forms of safety-first models have been proposed as alternatives to expected utility maximization (Hatch, Atwood, and Segar 1989; Bigman 1996). Roy (1952) was the first to suggest that in some situations, such as when the survival of the firm is at stake, decision makers select activities that minimize the probability of failing to achieve a certain goal for income, that is,

(11.2) $$\text{minimize } \Pr\{\Pi < \Pi*\},$$

where $\Pr\{.\}$ is the probability of event (.), Π is an income-random variable, and $\Pi*$ is an income goal often referred to as the "disaster level" or the "safety threshold." Telser's (1955) criterion maximizes expected income subject to probabilistic constraints on failing to achieve income goals:

(11.3) $$\text{maximize } E(\Pi)$$

(11.4) $$\text{subject to } \Pr\{\Pi < \Pi*\} < \Gamma,$$

where Γ is an upper (acceptable) limit on $\Pr\{\Pi \leq \Pi*\}$. Telser's (1955) approach is a two-step procedure whereby the person first eliminates alternatives that fail to meet the safety requirements for a given level of Γ, and then selects among the remaining alternatives the one(s) that maximizes expected utility. From these two basic models, many researchers have proposed improvements (see Bigman 1996 for a brief review of the literature). What all safety-first models have in common is some safety threshold or income goal.

Therefore, in an era of decreasing profits that threaten the survival of many farms, it is reasonable to propose that farmers' decisions are influenced by some safety-first criteria (van Kooten, Young, and Krautkraemer 1997). In such a case, a farmer's objective is to earn a profit that is expected to at least equal some designated minimum level of return,[1] $\Pi*$ (Mahul 2000). The designated safety threshold, $\Pi*$, is a personal preference based on financial obligations and lifestyle goals, thus it will vary across individuals.

WHEN ALL ASSETS ARE IN AGRICULTURE

When only agricultural investments are being considered, a farmer's objective is to earn a profit from all production efforts, Π_ϕ, that is expected to at least equal some minimum level of return, $\Pi*$, thus: $E(\Pi_\phi) \geq \Pi*$. In effect, this self-imposed constraint serves as a necessary, but not sufficient, condition in the farmer's decision to produce crop portfolio ϕ.

In this first stage of the model, a farmer is assumed to prefer having all of his/her tangible and financial assets engaged in agricultural production. Thus, the farmer's sole source of income is profits derived from his/her production efforts. In this case the farmer's return is:

(11.5) $$\Pi_\phi \equiv \sum_{i=1}^{n} w_i \pi_i$$

$$\text{where}: \pi_i = R_i - C_i - OC_i$$
$$R_i = P_i Y_i$$
$$C_i = \Sigma_j c_j x_{ij}$$
$$K_i = \Sigma_h k_h z_{ih}$$

and $\Sigma w_i = 1.0$; P_i, c_j, $k_h > 0$; and Y_i, x_j, $z_h \geq 0$. π_i is profit per acre from crop i. R_i is revenue per acre from crop i. P_i is the unit price of crop i. Y_i is the yield per acre of crop i. C_i is the total production costs per acre of crop i. c_j is a vector of unit costs of j variable inputs. x_{ij} is a vector of quantities per acre of j variable inputs to be applied in the production of crop i. OC_i is the total ownership costs per acre of crop i. k_h is a vector of unit costs of h capital inputs (land, improvements, equipment, etc.). z_{ih} is a vector of quantities per acre of h capital inputs used in the production of crop i. w_i is the weight of crop i in the farmer's crop portfolio, and n is the number of crops in the farmer's crop portfolio.

In this model, the total return per acre received by a farmer equals the share-weighted sum of the returns from each commodity produced. If the farmer produces more than one crop ($n>1$), then he/she is described here as producing a "portfolio" of crops.

The financial risk faced by a farmer is defined to be the variance in returns from all income sources. For a producer of only a single crop, that risk is $\sigma^2(\pi_i)$, the historical variance of profits per acre for crop i. For a producer of a crop portfolio, risk is $\sigma^2(\Pi_\phi)$, the historical variance of average profits per acre for portfolio ϕ.

When producing a crop portfolio, the degree of a farmer's total risk exposure depends on the covariance (Cov) between returns from the crops. For example, for a portfolio containing three crops, risk is:

$$\sigma^2(\Pi_\phi) = w_1^2\sigma^2(\pi_1) + w_2^2\sigma^2(\pi_2) + w_3^2\sigma^2(\pi_3) + 2w_1w_2\text{Cov}(\pi_1, \pi_2)$$
$$+ 2w_1w_3\text{Cov}(\pi_1, \pi_3) + 2w_2w_3\text{Cov}(\pi_2, \pi_3)$$

where: $\text{Cov} = \rho_{ij}(\sigma\pi_i)(\sigma\pi_j)$

$\rho_{ij} =$ the correlation between the returns from crops i and j.

As noted earlier, utility maximization is assumed to be a person's general objective. Therefore, the focus of decision making is the certainty equivalent of $E(\Pi_\phi)$, which is expressed in Equation 11.1. As specified, it is clear that for a risk-neutral or risk-averse farmer to meet his/her financial objective, it must be true that: $E(\Pi_\phi) \geq E(U_\phi) \geq \Pi*$.

To begin the crop selection process, a farmer in a particular market must first identify the opportunities available in that market. Those opportunities can be plotted on an expected return-variance (EV) graph to facilitate analysis. This is done for a hypothetical market in Figure 11.1. The concave line labeled EV_1 represents the initial opportunity set available to crop producers within some geographic market. Each point on EV_1 is a crop or portfolio of crops that is efficient in terms of its return/risk relationship. The location and shape of any EV is determined by the data used to calculate expected returns for all portfolios.

A farmer would choose to produce the portfolio represented by the point on the EV that is tangent to one of his/her indifference curves (not shown here). Thus, even if two farmers in the same market had identical expectations about cropping opportunities (i.e., they identify identical EV curves), they will produce different crop portfolios if they have different risk attitudes. For example, assume that one farmer's indifference curve is tangent to EV_1 in Figure 11.1 at point A. That farmer would produce the crop portfolio represented by point A on EV_1 and would expect returns of $\Pi_{\phi A}$ with variance of $\sigma^2\Pi_{\phi A}$, as shown. Also, extending the linear tangent line from point A to the vertical axis identifies the certainty equivalent of the expected returns from portfolio A (hence, it is called the "certainty equivalent line," Robison and Barry 1987, p. 73). As it is drawn in Figure 11.1, $E(U_{\phi A}) = \Pi_{*A}$, so the farmer would be willing to produce portfolio A because its returns are adequate. On the other hand, a second farmer with a lower degree of risk aversion would have an indifference curve tangent to EV_1 at some point to the right of point A. The crop portfolio identified by that point would have higher expected returns, higher variance,

Figure 11.1   **Cropping Opportunities in a Declining Market**

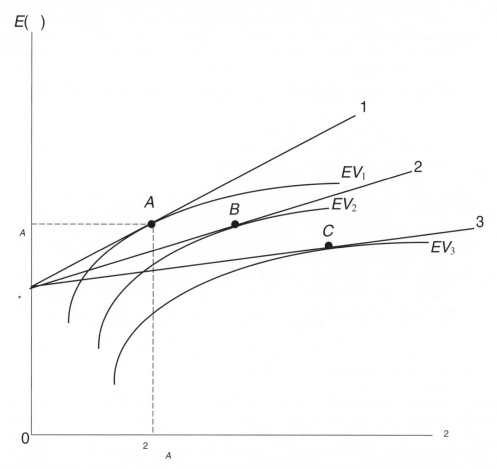

and a higher certainty equivalent. Assuming that the second farmer has the same $\Pi*$, he/she would clearly be willing to produce that crop portfolio because its returns are more than adequate to meet his/her financial objective.

If a risk-free investment exists, the opportunity set available to farmers is altered. In this chapter, a risk-free return (R_f) to land is defined as the return from cash leasing it to others.[2] During the period covered by a cash lease, the landowner is guaranteed a specific return that will not vary. Such a risk-free return is available only if an active market exists for cash leases on land (Robison and Barry 1987). Leasing out land is analogous to investing in a risk-free asset, which has a return of R_f, and would be plotted as a point on the vertical axis of an EV graph.

When leasing is possible, the separation theorem indicates that all landowners who have the same returns expectations will produce the same crops, although the composition of their selected portfolios will still vary with their risk attitudes; producers who are more risk averse will lease out a larger portion of their land (Blank 1993; Johnson 1967; Turvey, Baker, and Weersink 1992). Using the risk-free return, a single optimal risky portfolio and a farmer's cropping opportunities line (*COL*) can be identified. The *COL* represents the opportunity set available to landowners in a market (given some returns expectations). It is plotted as a straight line that passes through the point representing the risk-free return and is tangent to the *EV*. The *COL* dominates the *EV* at all points except where the two frontiers are tangent. The point of tangency represents the market's "optimal" portfolio. The portfolio selected by each farmer is found at the point of tangency between this linear *COL* and an indifference curve for that person. The selected portfolio is a mix of the market portfolio of crops and the risk-free asset. The only difference in composition of selected portfolios between farmers will be the relative proportions of land each chooses to lease in or out, which is calculated using the first-order conditions for Equation 11.1. This result comes from the separation theorem that suggests that the selection of the crop mix does not depend upon the decision maker's risk preferences, since it is constant along the straight *COL*. Instead, the amount of land leased in or out is the variable influenced by risk preferences. (The *COL* and its use are explained in Chapter 13.)

The inclusion of a minimum return, $\Pi*$, adds a constraint to utility maximization (as noted by Telser 1955). If $\Pi* < R_f$, then the farmer may lease out some portion of his/her land. If $\Pi* \geq R_f$, then the farmer will produce on all available land. Taken together, these constraints lead to Proposition 11.1.

- PROPOSITION 11.1. *In a market area with a single leasing rate, farmers who only consider agricultural investments and have higher financial obligations (i.e., higher $\Pi*$) are more likely to be active producers (i.e., use all available land for crop production) than are farmers with lower debt levels and other financial obligations.*

WHEN CROP PORTFOLIO CHANGES ARE NEEDED

When a farmer has all assets invested in agriculture, external shocks may cause production adjustments. For a farmer to meet his/her profit objective in the future, a change in that farmer's crop portfolio composition is needed immediately whenever $E(\Pi_\phi) < \Pi*$. Also, for risk-averse farmers, a change is needed when in the long run $E(U_\phi) < \Pi*$. In other words, when the returns from a planned crop portfolio are not expected to reach the level necessary for the farmer to meet his/her financial obligations (i.e., safety threshold), the farmer has no choice but to change the composition of the planned portfolio. In cases where expected returns meet financial obligations, but not a farmer's utility requirements $[E(\Pi_\phi) \geq \Pi* > E(U_\phi)]$, that farmer might choose not to make changes in the crop portfolio in the short run but must in the longer term to derive the desired degree of personal satisfaction. And when $\Pi* > E(U_\phi)$ is expected only for the short run, farmers without liquid assets could still be forced to change their portfolio composition because they would be unable to pay any resulting shortfalls (i.e., $\Pi* - \Pi_\phi$); for those farmers, $\Pr\{\Pi_\phi < \Pi*\} = 0 = \Gamma$ so as to eliminate default risk.

Numerous factors, such as market price and/or production cost changes, cause portfolio changes. In recent years, most of the observed external shocks to agriculture have triggered the need for a change in farmers' crop portfolio composition, as shown in Table 11.1. In general, real output prices continue to fall and input costs rise to reduce the return from many crops to below farmers' desired/needed level, creating a "profit squeeze." This forces a farmer to shift acreage into higher-returning crops. New portfolios made up of crop and/or livestock enterprises with relatively higher return and higher risk raise a farmer's total risk exposure, thus necessitating adjustments, as described below.

Table 11.1

The Effect of Recent Trends on a Farmer's Profit

Recent trends in agriculture	Effect on crop portfolio's profit (Π_ϕ)	
Yield increase	$\Pi_\phi > \Pi_\cdot$	
Price (real) decrease	$\Pi_\phi < \Pi_\cdot$	
Input cost increase	$\Pi_\phi < \Pi_\cdot$	
Land price increase	$\Pi_\phi \square \Pi_\cdot$	[opportunity cost increase]
Capital/technology increase	$\Pi_\phi < \Pi_\cdot$	[although may increase yield]
Cash leasing rate increase	$\Pi_\phi < \Pi_\cdot$	[opportunity cost increase]
Recent general trends		
Management (off-farm) wages increase	$\Pi_\phi < \Pi_\cdot$	[opportunity cost increase]
		[increase in risk-free rate and production
Interest rates rise	$\Pi_\phi < \Pi_\cdot$	costs
		[opportunity cost increase if not investing
Stock market rises	$\Pi_\phi < \Pi_\cdot$	in π_v]

The available crop and livestock enterprises in which a farmer might invest can be grouped into four categories, shown in Figure 11.2 (assuming that all four types of crops can be produced in the farmer's location).[3] Crop category 1 (low-value annuals) includes crops with expected returns per acre ranging from a low of $E(\pi_{1L})$ to a high of $E(\pi_{1H})$, with an average of $E(\pi_{1A})$. Crop categories 2, 3, and 4 also each have an identifiable range of returns from individual crops. Empirical results by Blank (1992), summarized in Table 11.2, show that, although they sometimes overlap, the ranges are successively higher such that

$$E(\pi_{1L}) < E(\pi_{2L}) < E(\pi_{3L}) < E(\pi_{4L}),$$
$$E(\pi_{1H}) < E(\pi_{2H}) < E(\pi_{3H}) < E(\pi_{4H}), \text{ and}$$
$$E(\pi_{1A}) < E(\pi_{2A}) < E(\pi_{3A}) < E(\pi_{4A}).$$

Based on Blank's (1992) results, it is expected that risk levels increase also at higher stages of the farming food chain:

$$E(\sigma^2\pi_{1A}) < E(\sigma^2\pi_{2A}) < E(\sigma^2\pi_{3A}) < E(\sigma^2\pi_{4A}).$$

Therefore, agricultural producers seeking a higher-returning crop must normally accept higher-risk exposure when adding the new crop to their production portfolio to restore the portfolio's total return to the desired level. Thus, producers may resist investing in higher-category crops. Nevertheless, continuing market shocks will eventually force producers to add higher-return/higher-risk crops to their crop portfolio and, ultimately, to shift assets out of agriculture.

To illustrate the point, assume a farmer's minimum desired return, Π_*, is low enough that it can be achieved initially with a crop portfolio composed entirely of category 1 crops. Then, market shocks cause portfolio returns to decline, making necessary a change in the current portfolio composition. If $\Pi_* < E(\pi_{1H})$, then the farmer's new portfolio may contain crops from

Figure 11.2 **The Farming Food Chain**

Development stage	rop t pe	nvestment asset i it
4th	High-value perennial	Very high, highly fixed
3rd	High-value annual	High, inflexible
2nd	Low-value perennial	Moderate, flexible
1st	Low-value annual	Low, very flexible

Source: Blank (1998, p.76).

Table 11.2

The Returns and Risk from a Sample of Crops Across Categories

Category 1 crops	Average gross profit/acre ($)	Coefficient of variation
Corn	51–147	0.92–1.90
Cotton	258	1.09
Rice	187–201	1.03–1.10
Category 2 crops		
Alfalfa hay	61–88	1.48–2.34
Category 3 crops		
Broccoli	337–891	1.77–4.07
Carrots	233–1,675	0.38–7.70
Lettuce	545–860	0.95–1.11
Category 4 crops		
Almonds	170	8.14
Grapes (table)	1,342	0.49
Oranges	566–911	0.68–1.24
Peaches	247–1,681	0.37–3.00
Walnuts	97–262	5.08–6.67

Source: Blank (1992). These data are for crops grown in specific counties in California over the 1958–86 period and are adjusted into 1986 dollars. The ranges show the lowest–highest values observed from different counties.

category 1. If $\Pi_* > E(\pi_{1H})$, the farmer's new portfolio *must* contain some higher-category crop(s). Likewise, if $\Pi_* > E(\pi_{2H})$ or $\Pi_* > E(\pi_{3H})$, then the farmer must produce some successively higher-category crop(s). And if $\Pi_* > E(\pi_{4H})$, then some acreage (and/or possibly some other assets) must leave agriculture in order for the person to receive total returns that are adequate to meet his/her financial objective as constrained by the safety threshold.

In summary, all recent trends in agriculture, except expanding yields, exert pressure on producers to move up the "farming food chain" (the hierarchy of crops in Figure 11.2) when selecting which crops to produce over time. A yield increase from new technology is the only type of external shock to increase profit per acre over recent decades, ceteris paribus. All other types of external shocks being observed recently gradually reduce profits per unit, necessitating a change in farmers' crop portfolio composition and an increase in farmers' total risk exposure.

As a farmer moves his/her land up the farming food chain, additional leasing out of land may be desired in that farmer's efforts to rebalance his/her risk exposure, but it may not be a viable option.[4] Eventually, however, when $\Pi_* > E(\pi_{4H})$, and possibly long before that time, some of that farmer's acreage (and/or some other assets) must leave agriculture to enable him/her to meet the financial objective embodied in $\Pi*$.

The effects of external shocks are illustrated in Figure 11.1. Assume that the original situation has three neighboring producers with identical expectations about market returns (Farmer 1, Farmer 2, and Farmer 3), each producing some unique portfolio of crops represented by a different point on EV_1. All three producers are assumed to have the same minimum financial objective, so $\Pi_{*1} = \Pi_{*2} = \Pi_{*3}$, however they have different risk preferences: $\Lambda_1 > \Lambda_2 > \Lambda_3$. Originally, Farmer 1 is producing the crops in the portfolio at point A, and $E(U_A) = \Pi_{*1}$. Thus, the tangent line labeled "1" in Figure 11.1 is the certainty equivalent line (CEL) for Farmer 1. The slope of an individual's CEL is $\Lambda/2$ (Robison and Barry 1987), so line 1 has a slope of $\Lambda_1/2$. Farmers 2 and 3 both are less risk averse than Farmer 1, so they would originally be producing portfolios of crops at different points on EV_1 to the right of point A. That means for both Farmers 2 and 3, the returns and risks of their original crop portfolios are higher than that for portfolio A, yet they are quite willing to produce those portfolios because the certainty equivalent of their returns exceeds the farmers' minimum objective (i.e., $E(U_2) > \Pi_{*2}$ and $E(U_3) > \Pi_{*3}$). Then, some external shocks (e.g., commodity price decreases and/or production cost increases) reduce the profitability of crops in the local market, making EV_2 the opportunity set available to the three farmers. Now Farmer 2 finds that his CEL is line 2 (with slope $\Lambda_2/2$) in the figure and point B represents his new crop portfolio. At this point, even though all three farmers have the same absolute level of financial obligations, their reactions to the new market opportunities are quite different because $E(U_1) < \Pi_{*1}$, $E(U_2) = \Pi_{*2}$ and $E(U_3) > \Pi_{*3}$. Farmer 2 is less happy, but still willing to produce (although a more risky portfolio); Farmer 3 is also less happy, but quite satisfied with the more than adequate returns of his new, more risky portfolio (at some point to the right of B); Farmer 1 is in the uncomfortable position of deciding whether or not to remain in agriculture. For Farmer 1, his preferred new crop portfolio would be found at the point (to the left of B) where a line (approximately) parallel to his CEL (which is line 1) is tangent to EV_2.[5] As Figure 11.1 is drawn, Farmer 1's new (more risky) portfolio will generate profits such that $E(\Pi_{\phi 1}) \geq \Pi_{*1} > E(U_{\phi 1})$. This forces Farmer 1 to choose one of these courses of action: (1) produce the new portfolio in the hopes that future external shocks will increase returns to at least the original level, (2) produce the portfolio represented by point B and live with more risk than is comfortable for that person, or (3) seek higher returns by shifting at least some assets out of agriculture. Finally, assume another round of external shocks further erodes the profits offered in agricultural markets and EV_3 represents the choices available to the three farmers. Now it is assumed that line 3 is the CEL (with slope $\Lambda_3/2$) for Farmer 3 who adjusts into the production of the crops in portfolio C. Portfolio C is less profitable and more risky than Farmer 3's previous crop portfolio, but it still generates returns that are adequate to meet his financial objective. As Figure 11.1 is drawn, Farmers 2 and 3 are not happy about the prospects available to them in the current market (based on where lines approximately parallel to their CELs would be tangent to EV_3—to the left of C). Farmer 2 is now in the difficult position that Farmer 1 was in after the shift to EV_2 and Farmer 1 now faces a situation $[E(\Pi_{\phi 1}) < \Pi_{*1}]$ that is forcing him to consider

Table 11.3

U.S. Census of Agriculture Trends

	1987	1992	1997
Land in farms (million acres)	964.5	945.5	931.8
Farms (1,000s)	2,087.8	1,925.3	1,911.9
Farms of 1,000 acres or more (number)	168,864	172,912	176,080
Vegetable acreage (million acres)	3.468	3.782	3.773
Orchard acreage (million acres)	4.560	4.771	5.158

Sources: USDA 1998 and earlier censuses. Data from the 2002 Census is not comparable to earlier Census data and, therefore, is not included here. New census methods and definitions have altered the data, but not the trends; farm numbers and land in farms continue to decline.

immediately shifting some or all of his assets out of agriculture in search of higher returns. In general, this example illustrates two propositions:

- PROPOSITION 11.2. *External shocks that reduce agricultural profitability cause all farmers to shift into the production of more risky crop and/or livestock enterprises.*
- PROPOSITION 11.3. *Farmers who are relatively more risk averse will be the first to diversify out of agriculture, ceteris paribus.*

Proposition 11.2 is consistent with observed national trends. Profits in agriculture have declined for decades, as shown in Chapters 2 and 3. The profit squeeze has been widespread and significant: for example, from 1990 to 2000 the U.S. Department of Agriculture's (USDA's) index of prices paid by all farmers for inputs increased about 19 percent while the index of prices received for outputs dropped 7 percent. As shown in Table 11.3, total acreages of vegetables (crop category 3) and orchards (crop category 4) have increased despite the decrease in total land in farms.[6] Many regions not known for production of these crops are adding them to their portfolios (Weimar and Hallam 1988). Also, the decreasing numbers of farms and full-time farms show that people continue to diversify out of agriculture, first partially then entirely, as suggested in Proposition 11.3.

WHEN ASSETS MUST LEAVE AGRICULTURE

When a farmer is willing to consider both agricultural and nonagricultural investments, his/her total return, $\Pi_{\phi'}$, includes profit from all productive efforts plus profits from other assets owned. The farmer's profit function shifts from that in Equation 11.5 to the expanded form in Equation 11.6,

$$(11.6) \qquad \Pi_{\phi'} \equiv \sum_{i=1}^{n} w_i \pi_i + \sum_{v=1}^{m} w_v \pi_v$$

where $\pi_v = f(\lambda_v)$ and $\sum w_i + \sum w_v = 1.0$. In this equation, π_v is the profit (or return on investment) of nonagricultural investment v and is a function of a vector of exogenous factors (λ_v),

w_v is the weight (percentage of asset values) of investment v in the farmer's total portfolio, m is the number of nonagricultural investments in the farmer's total portfolio, and other variables are as defined previously. The variance of returns to the portfolio in Equation 11.6 is

$$(11.7) \qquad \sigma^2(\Pi_{\phi'}) \equiv \sum_{i=1}^{n} \sum_{v=1}^{m} Cov(\pi_i \pi_v) w_i w_v.$$

When nonagricultural investments are considered along with production options, there are more incentives to move up the farming food chain and to diversify out of agriculture. These new incentives are based in both expanded returns opportunities and expanded risk management opportunities. Empirical work has found that, on average, returns on nonagricultural assets are higher than returns to farmer-operators (Bjornson and Innes 1992; Irwin, Forster, and Sherrick 1988). Thus, a farmer can increase his/her level of profitability by diversifying out of agriculture. This is obvious in the case where the expected return on a nonagricultural investment exceeds the expected return on the highest-returning crop opportunity, $E(\pi_v) > E(\pi_{4H})$. Also, the fact that a farmer's portfolio risk can be more easily reduced and/or managed with the inclusion of non-agricultural investments creates incentives to diversify, as will be discussed later.

Opportunity costs (OK) become key in decision-making when crop production and non-agricultural investments are being considered. In this regard, the designated minimum level of return is more fully described as:

$$\Pi_* = \text{fixed financial obligations} + \text{lifestyle costs} + \text{OK}.$$

This means that a farmer's desired return is the sum of financial obligations and living costs plus some function of opportunity costs. The nature of an individual's response to opportunity costs will vary with his/her sensitivity to foregone opportunities. Thus, the OK component of Π_* is analogous to a risk premium—it is a minimum amount desired above the person's bare financial requirements—although in this case it is some desired contribution to wealth. It has long been hypothesized that farmers willingly accept lower returns than other investors because of the lifestyle benefits derived from farming (Brewster 1961). That hypothesis implies that farmers are not sensitive to foregone opportunities off the farm. It explains why some farmers might exclude nonagricultural investments from their opportunity set, limiting themselves to production op-portunities as described in Equation 11.5. On the other hand, the large percentage of farmers who are part-timers (USDA 2001) indicates that farmers are indeed sensitive to off-farm opportunities and will respond if able (Kimhi 2000).[7] Like all investors, farmers also have a desire to build wealth at or above some minimum rate. As a result, opportunity costs provide the first incentive to pull assets out of agriculture, although absolute profitability is the final blow.

This discussion of opportunity costs and profitability raises the question: At what point do farmers decide to not produce? This refers to the point at which they prefer to lease out or sell all of their land. In the portfolio model presented in this chapter, it is argued that any potential grower will decide to not produce when the certainty equivalent of expected returns from the selected portfolio is less than or equal to the sum of all opportunity costs faced in the long run, as explained below.

As noted earlier, farmers are concerned about the certainty equivalent of expected gross returns when deciding to produce crops. The opportunity costs incurred by farmers involve their land, labor, and financial assets. For a landowner, the foregone opportunity when investing land in crop production is the chance to collect cash lease payments, valued at R_f per acre. It was shown earlier that, in the short run, farmers will lease out their land if $E(U_\phi) < R_f$. If a grower invests his own labor in crop production, he foregoes the opportunity to invest it off the farm where it would be valued at least at the equivalent of $c_L L$ (the wage rate, c_L, times the quantity of labor "sold" off farm, L, equals some number of dollars per acre). Both leasing out land and working for a wage off the farm are considered to be riskless investments. Also, some riskless off-farm investment (π_{vf}) is always available for financial assets. Thus, it is clear why a necessary condition for crop production in the long run on the part of a risk-averse farmer is

(11.8) $$E(U_\phi) > (R_f + c_L L + \pi_{vf}),$$

where the factors on the right side are the opportunity costs. If this condition is not expected to be met over the long run, the farmer must consider diversifying out of agriculture and, possibly, selling all agricultural assets. However, the farmer's degree of sensitivity to these opportunity costs will influence the speed at which such actions will be undertaken. This leads to Proposition 11.4.

- PROPOSITION 11.4. *Farmers who desire to build wealth fastest will consider diversifying out of agriculture before farmers who are willing to accept slower growth in their wealth, ceteris paribus.*

Ironically, diversification off-farm postpones the final blow of inadequate profits bringing a halt to crop production. The results of Bjornson and Innes (1992) imply that there are nonagricultural investments offering returns higher than anything available in farming, such that $E(\pi_v) > E(\pi_{4H})$. Therefore, in cases such as where $E(U_{\phi'}) \geq \Pi_* > E(U_\phi)$, adding nonagricultural investment(s) v to the farmer's portfolio is a necessary condition for continued production. In other words, combining a high-returning investment with lower-returning crops can result in adequate profits to meet financial objectives, even when no crop can do so alone [i.e., $\Pi_* > E(\pi_{4H})$]. Thus, it should not be surprising that the scale of off-farm investments has increased such that, on average, about 95 percent of farm operator households' income came from off-farm sources in 2002 (USDA 2003). (This is discussed in detail in Chapter 18.)

- PROPOSITION 11.5. *Adding nonagricultural investments to a farmer's portfolio of assets enables that person to remain in agricultural production longer.*

In addition to the profit motive noted above, there are risk incentives for farmers to diversify using nonagricultural investments. First of all, a farmer's total risk exposure can be reduced when combining crops and other investments. Bjornson and Carter (1997, p. 918) found that "commodities provide a natural hedge against business cycles" because crop returns are not generally correlated with the returns of nonagricultural assets. Robison and Barry (1987, p. 148) show that a portfolio's total risk is reduced when returns on individual assets have a correlation of zero or less. Given how a diversified farmer's risk is defined in Equation 11.7, off-farm investments can significantly improve the risk efficiency of a person's portfolio as well as alter the crop mix of that portfolio, as noted in Proposition 11.6.

- PROPOSITION 11.6. *The use of nonagricultural investments with returns that are inversely correlated or uncorrelated [$(0 \geq \rho_{iv} \geq -1)$] with agricultural returns reduces the total risk exposure of farmers, thus making it possible to include more high-risk/high-return crops in a farmer's portfolio than his/her risk preferences would permit normally.*

One type of investment whose returns are uncorrelated with crop returns is the risk-free opportunity, because, by definition, such investments have no variance. As a result, they appeal to highly risk-averse farmers seeking to manage their risk exposure. Drawing from Propositions 11.3 and 11.5, it follows that having more risk-free opportunities available enables those farmers to postpone their exit from farming, as noted in Proposition 11.7.

- PROPOSITION 11.7. *The number of risk-free nonagricultural investment opportunities available to farmers who are willing to consider diversifying out of agriculture slows the departure of highly risk averse farmers.*

In summary, the willingness to consider diversifying into nonagricultural investments has three general effects on the opportunity set available to a farmer. In a portfolio context, all three effects are positive and can be illustrated with an *EV* graph. The effects were described in the arguments above supporting Propositions 11.5–11.7. First, the expanded profit opportunities, discussed in support of Proposition 11.5, move the opportunity set upward. This means that for each level of risk, a higher return is available than would be available without nonagricultural opportunities. Next, the *EV* moves to the left with the effects of actions noted in Proposition 11.6. Using inversely or uncorrelated returns from off-farm investments directly improves the risk efficiency of the entire opportunity set. This means less total risk must be accepted for each level of returns. Finally, the wide availability of risk-free investments, noted in Proposition 11.7, means that each person's opportunity set (*EV*) intersects the vertical axis at some point. Therefore, all three of these effects serve to counter the influences of a declining market (like that illustrated in Figure 11.1).

LAND-USE PATTERNS

The farming food chain causes rough patterns in agricultural land use. These patterns are most visible in regions that are capable of producing crops in all four of the categories, but they exist everywhere. In a spatial sense, the patterns are areas that are dominated by the production of crops from one crop category, such as a region covered mostly with tree or vine crops or another area dominated by field crops. These cropping patterns are not random—there are spatial market factors helping to shape them, as explained below.

Each area in a pattern may be regional in scope or quite local. In other words, taking a national view, the Midwest would have large areas dominated by low-value crops, such as grains, while the East and West Coast regions will have more variability in cropping patterns with more areas in high-value crops. Taking a local view, a city in California's Central Valley, for example, is most likely surrounded by a "ring" of land dominated by high-value perennial crops (category 4), with a contiguous ring of category 3 high-value annual crops surrounding that, and farther outside of town are rings of land planted predominately with low-value category 2 and/or 1 crops. Within each "ring," any type of crop might be observed, but the distribution of crops is concentrated in one category type. For example, in a ring of category 3 crops, high-value annuals make up the bulk of the acreage, but some amount of category 1, 2, or 4 crops may be observed. It is expected, however, that over time the distribution will have declining percentages of acreage in lower-category crops (except for that used in crop rotations for agronomic reasons) and increasing percentages in the dominant and higher-category crops (categories 3 and 4, in this example).

The idea of "production zones" dates back to 1826 when Von Thunen (1966) laid out the basic economic logic that Bressler and King brought up to date in 1970. However, different market forces have developed over the last three decades to create the spatial cropping patterns observed now. As explained by Bressler and King (1970), the maximum return per unit of land, called the "site rent," was primarily a function of transfer costs between the site and the nearest market (with land-quality constraints on production alternatives):

> Each potential use for this agricultural land will then generate a conelike structure of site rents centered on the city and decreasing with distance from market. These rents represent the ability of the particular use to compete for the land and, in a perfect market, will give rise to concentric zones of optimum product uses. (Bressler and King 1970, p. 336)

From Von Thunen's era through the 1960s, transportation costs were highly significant when estimating the potential profits for a parcel of land and, thus, in determining the optimal pattern of land use. In the last thirty years, however, technological advances in our ability to transport, store, and process food have made the bulkiness and/or perishability of a product less important in land-use decision making. Now it is the relationship between site rents and opportunity costs that determines land use. Bressler and King (1970, pp. 347–349) discussed the role of opportunity costs in determining regional production, but there are now new opportunity costs and constraints that lead to the rings of the farming food chain, as explained below.

At present, site rents are buffeted about much more often than in the past. Not only do output prices and input costs change more often in our dynamic markets, but new sources of variance in production profits develop over time. For example, technology and production management methods change more often due to both scientific advances affecting products and consumer demands for increasingly processed foods. Additional opportunities available to farmers, especially those brought about by the growth of nearby cities and towns, all add to the list of opportunity costs facing those farmers.

The biggest change in the opportunity set available to farmers is the ability to diversify into nonagricultural investments and the expanded ability to shift assets into uses other than farming. This has enabled farmers to choose a desired minimum return, $\Pi*$, rather than being forced to accept what agriculture offered in their location.

An example will serve to illustrate how shocks affect the relationship between site rents, opportunity costs, a person's desired minimum return and the resulting cropping patterns. To begin, assume a small town is located in a region with climate and land qualities enabling the production of crops from all four of the categories. Also assume an efficient, unrestricted market with rapid dissemination of information regarding land's productive potential. At the urban fringe, land prices are highest because the potential for development is added to the demand from farmers wanting to produce crops on a parcel (Shonkwiler and Reynolds 1986). The opportunity costs associated with this valuable land will force up each owner's desired return, $\Pi*$, making only high-category crops competitive when deciding on a use for that parcel. The opportunity costs to farmers on the urban fringe include not only the higher potential land value from development, but also the opportunity of earning a wage in the town. For farmers located farther outside of town, the development potential drops off quickly and the net off-farm wages (adjusted for commuting costs and time) decline more slowly. As a result, more distant farmers have lower opportunity costs, making it more likely that lower-category crops may be able to generate adequate profits to meet their financial objectives. Now assume that a farmer on the urban fringe decides that leaving farming is the only way to meet his/her desired level of returns and, therefore, sells to a land developer. This sudden shock to the equilibrium brought on by the shift to the new urban fringe will create "ripples" of reactions that radiate outward from the town. A neighboring farmer who was some distance "out of town" is now on the new urban fringe. This increases the potential for development of the second farmer's land, thus increasing the total opportunity costs faced by that farmer. To resist the urge to capture some of the newly available opportunity costs, the farmer may need to adjust his/her crop mix to a higher-returning portfolio. More distant farmers also need to adjust their estimates of opportunity costs faced in the new market environment. Such a readjustment process occurs each time there is any shock to the equilibrium.

It is noted that such an adjustment process can occur far from towns; other sources of shocks trigger "ripples" as well. Market price changes (which make crops more or less profitable) and changes in the crop portfolio of a single farmer are two of many shocks that can affect the spatial pattern of cropping in regions that are far from any city.

The variety and frequency of shocks felt in particular locations have implications for cropping patterns. In general, sites that have more shocks and added opportunity costs are expected to adjust more quickly. This leads to:

- PROPOSITION 11.8. *Land closest to cities, land with greater development opportunities (residential, commercial, and/or recreational), and land on which higher-category crops can be produced all will move up the farming food chain faster than other land.*

Proposition 11.8 captures the affects of location relative to development opportunities on a parcel's cropping patterns. A second result concerning land use from the model presented here specifies the straightforward effects of a parcel's soil quality and/or climate on cropping patterns.

- PROPOSITION 11.9. *Land on which higher-category crops can be grown will stay in agricultural production longer than land limited to lower-category crops, ceteris paribus.*

To illustrate the point in Proposition 11.9, consider the case of two parcels of land in an area with a climate that makes possible the production of crops from any of the four categories. One parcel has high-quality soil that suits all crop categories, while the other parcel has poorer soil types that prevent the profitable production of category 4 (tree and vine) crops. In this example, as shocks to the profitability of available alternatives push the owners of the two parcels up the farming food chain, the owner of the poorer-quality land is expected to be the first to reach the point that $\Pi_* > E(U_\phi)$, ceteris paribus, because his/her potential crop returns ceiling is lower than that of the owner of the higher-quality land. Thus, when profit pressures cause the farmer with the good land to begin considering which tree or vine crop to add to his/her portfolio, the other farmer will be forced to begin considering diversifying out of agriculture. Evidence of this situation is readily visible in many places. In California's San Joaquin Valley, for example, it is common to see orchards and fallow parcels in close proximity to one another along the edge of the valley, where the flat land meets the foothills. Land left fallow for extended periods of time is out of agriculture currently (i.e., being fallow is a transition state) and will be out permanently as soon as viable alternative uses develop. Many of California's fallow parcels noted above were in field crop production only a few years ago.

It is important to note that a parcel of land can exit agriculture at any time; it does not have to work its way up the entire farming food chain. Landowners can decide at any time to shift out of agricultural production. This means that land capable of producing tree and vine crops profitably may leave production before the owner tries a category 4 crop. However, it is also important to note that when the owner of a parcel has shifted into the crop capable of generating the highest possible profits per acre, if that profit is insufficient to meet the owner's financial objectives, the owner is forced to consider nonagricultural uses or selling the land.

CONCLUDING COMMENTS

This chapter offers an explanation for the seemingly contradictory national trends of rising total sales revenues and falling acreage and farm numbers. The explanation takes the form of a simple theory of cropping decisions and land use. A model is presented using the logic of portfolio theory that leads to some conclusions presented in the form of propositions. The model shows the importance of a person's designated minimum return (a safety-first criterion) and opportunity costs when making cropping decisions. In summary, the farming food chain describes a micro-level response (of farmers) that shows the relevance of portfolio theory in explaining the macro-level (national) trends.

The continuing profit squeeze in agricultural production is having a significant effect on the cropping choices of America's farmers. In general, that effect has been to cause acreage to be shifted out of low-revenue-generating crops and into higher-revenue-generating crops. This shift makes crop portfolios more risky over time, thus encouraging risk-averse farmers to consider diversifying out of agriculture. Such diversification has the ironic effect of making it possible for individual farmers to remain in agricultural production longer than would otherwise be the case.

The results of the model presented here have implications for land prices and the spatial distribution of crop production. First, the long-observed correlation between land prices and crop profits (Robison, Lins, and VenKataraman 1985) will be expanded to include crop profits, current and potential. In other words, a parcel's price will more closely reflect the potential maximum profit a parcel is capable of generating with the highest category crop that is suitable in that location (i.e., the site rent), not just its current crop returns. As information about site rents becomes more prominent in land sales, the prices of land in less flexible/desirable areas will be under increasing pressure to decline in response to other market shocks that reduce potential profits from agricultural production.

Finally, the spatial distribution of crop production will continue to reflect the relationship between farmers' designated minimum return and opportunity costs. "Production zones" similar to the concentric circles radiating out from a town as described by Von Thunen (1966) and Bressler and King (1970) now exist for different reasons. Instead of transportation costs being a key determinant in the location of specific crop production, it is now the capability of a parcel to generate returns and the compatibility of those returns with the landowner's financial objectives that determine what types of crops are grown where.

NOTES

Some of this chapter is a revised version of an article published by S. Blank as "Producers Get Squeezed Up the Farming Food Chain: A Theory of Crop Portfolio Composition and Land Use," *Review of Agricultural Economics* 23, no. 2 (2001): 404–422.

1. This return can be expressed as either profit per acre or return on investment (ROI), and is discussed in both ways in this chapter. To begin, the model presents profit per acre because that is the context most relevant to farmers. Later, ROI is used because it facilitates comparisons between agricultural and nonagricultural investments.

2. In this book, a "return" is a gross profit, not net profit, on some investment. This means that directly related costs have been subtracted from an investment's revenue to get its "return." To get

net profit, indirect costs must be subtracted as well. Those include fixed costs, such as ownership expenses. In the case of a "risk-free return" from cash leasing out farmland, it is a return, and not a net profit, because only direct costs related to the lease have been subtracted from the revenues that a landowner receives from the lease. Thus, it is symbolized using R_f as is done in the finance literature, rather than π_f.

3. Figure 11.2 illustrates the "farming food chain" and the relationship between crop types, investment amounts, and the flexibility of production assets. At the bottom of the chain are low-value annual crops, like grains, which require relatively low investments per acre and involve assets that can be shifted into the production of another crop very easily. The second stage of land development involves low-value perennial crops, like alfalfa and other irrigated forages, and livestock grazing. These crops have a normal economic life of more than one year and require somewhat higher investments per acre, but they involve fairly flexible assets. The third stage requires relatively high investments in inflexible assets to produce high-value annual crops like lettuce and fresh tomatoes. Finally, high-value perennial crops, such as tree and vine products, and intensive livestock enterprises like hogs and poultry, lock growers into the highest and least flexible investments. In general, the risks and potential returns involved increase with each step up the chain.

In a particular geographic area, climate and/or agronomic constraints might limit the feasibility of growing some crops. In particular, crops in categories 3 and 4 may not be feasible. In such cases, land moving up the truncated farming food chain of that area will have to leave agriculture to attain the higher level of returns that would normally be available from higher-category crops. Therefore, the number of crop categories available in a geographic area is determined by climate/agronomic conditions, and land can leave agriculture from any available category, but it must leave agriculture if it is to generate returns above those of the highest returning crop available.

4. Leasing out land can occur only if a farmer is willing and able. Shocks reducing crop profitability also reduce π_f, the rate tenants are willing to pay based on their expectations of the returns to the highest value use. Thus, shocks to profitability make it more likely that $\Pi* > R_f$, meaning that farmers will be less willing to lease out land.

5. Indifference curves are convex, so a major change in the location of the concave EV may cause the new point of tangency between the EV and an indifference curve to identify a new CEL that is not perfectly parallel to the original, but for small changes in the EV the old and new CELs will be nearly parallel.

6. Some might argue that the increase in vegetable and orchard acreage is due simply to expanding demand for fruits and vegetables in the diet. However, that argument is inconsistent with the decrease in total acreage in farms. Clearly expanding demand contributes to the relative profitability of fruit and vegetable crops, but that only helps partially explain why some acreage is shifted from low-value crops to the higher-value crops (a "substitution effect"); it does not explain why acreage is taken out of agriculture. The *absolute* (low or negative) level of profitability of low-value crops also forces some acreage to shift into higher-value crop production or, if that shift is not possible or desirable, to shift out of agriculture.

7. An alternative to Brewster's (1961) hypothesis is that farmers "accept" lower returns because they are unable to respond to nonagricultural investment opportunities. For example, a farmer living in a remote region might not have off-farm employment opportunities and, like most farmers, might have all available capital invested in land acquisition and/or production technology, leaving no capital available for nonagricultural investments. A second alternative hypothesis is that farmers generally and repeatedly overestimate expected returns from agricultural production. This could be called the "eternal optimist" hypothesis, or it could be a function of government subsidies.

REFERENCES

Bigman, D. 1996. "Safety-First Criteria and Their Measures of Risk." *American Journal of Agricultural Economics* 78 (1): 225–235.

Bjornson, B., and C. Carter. 1997. "New Evidence on Agricultural Commodity Return Performance Under Time-Varying Risk." *American Journal of Agricultural Economics* 79 (3): 918–930.

Bjornson, B., and R. Innes. 1992. "Another Look at Returns to Agricultural and Nonagricultural Assets." *American Journal of Agricultural Economics* 74 (1): 109–119.

Blank, S. 1992. "Income Risk Varies with What You Grow, Where You Grow It." *California Agriculture* 46 (5): 14–16.

———. 1993. "Effects of Farmland Cash Leasing Rates on Crop Selections: A Portfolio Analysis." *Agricultural Finance Review* 53: 1–14.

———. 1998. *The End of Agriculture in the American Portfolio.* Westport, CT: Quorum Books.

Bressler, R., Jr., and R. King. 1970. *Markets, Prices, and Interregional Trade.* New York: John Wiley & Sons.

Brewster, J. 1961. "Society Values and Goals in Respect to Agriculture." In *Goals and Values in Agricultural Policy,* pp. 114–137. Ames: Iowa State University Press.

Freund, R. 1956. "The Introduction of Risk into a Programming Model." *Econometrica* 24: 253–263.

Hatch, U., J. Atwood, and J. Segar. 1989. "An Application of Safety-First Probability Limits in a Discrete Stochastic Farm Management Programming Model." *Southern Journal of Agricultural Economics* 21 (1): 65–72.

Irwin, S., L. Forster, and B. Sherrick. 1988. "Returns to Farm Real Estate Revisited." *American Journal of Agricultural Economics* 70 (3): 580–587.

Johnson, S. 1967. "A Re-Examination of the Farm Diversification Problem." *Journal of Farm Economics* 49: 610–621.

Kimhi, A. 2000. "Is Part-Time Farming Really a Step in the Way Out of Agriculture?" *American Journal of Agricultural Economics* 82 (1): 38–48.

Levy, H., and H. Markowitz. 1979. "Approximating Expected Utility by a Function of Mean and Variance." *American Economic Review* 69: 308–317.

Mahul, O. 2000. "The Output Decision of a Risk-Neutral Producer Under Risk of Liquidation." *American Journal of Agricultural Economics* 82 (1): 49–58.

Meyer, J. 1987. "Two Moment Decision Models and Expected Utility Maximization." *American Economic Review* 77: 421–430.

Pyle, D., and S. Turnovsky. 1970. "Safety First and Expected Utility Maximization in Mean-Standard Deviation Portfolio Analysis." *Review of Economics and Statistics* 52: 75–81.

Robison, L., and P. Barry. 1987. *The Competitive Firm's Response to Risk.* New York: Macmillan.

Robison, L., D. Lins, and R. VenKataraman. 1985. "Cash Rents and Land Values in U.S. Agriculture." *American Journal of Agricultural Economics* 67 (4): 794–805.

Roy, A. 1952. "Safety-First and the Holding of Assets." *Econometrica* 20: 431–449.

Shonkwiler, J., and J. Reynolds. 1986. "A Note on the Use of Hedonic Price Models in the Analysis of Land Prices at the Urban Fringe." *Land Economics* 62: 58–63.

Telser, L. 1955. "Safety-First and Hedging." *Review of Economic Studies* 23: 1–16.

Turvey, C., T. Baker, and A. Weersink. 1992. "Farm Operating Risk and Cash Rent Determination." *Journal of Agricultural and Resource Economics* 17 (1): 186–194.

U.S. Department of Agriculture. 1998. *1997 Census of Agriculture.* National Agricultural Statistics Service.

———. 2001. "Off-Farm Income Supports Many Farm Households." *Agricultural Income and Finance: Situation and Outlook Report,* pp. 32–34. Resource Economics Division, Economic Research Service, AIS-76, February.

———. 2003. "Farm Income and Costs: Farm Income Forecasts." Economic Research Service "Briefing Room," on web at www.ers.usda.gov/Briefing/FarmIncome/fore.htm, September.

van Kooten, G.C., D. Young, and J. Krautkraemer. 1997. "A Safety-First Approach to Dynamic Cropping Decisions." *European Review of Agricultural Economics* 24 (1): 47–63.

Von Thunen, J. 1966. *Von Thunen's Isolated State: An English Edition of Der Isolierte Staat,* trans. by C. Wartenberg and ed. P. Hall. New York: Pergamon Press. (*Der Isolierte Staat,* originally published 1826.)

Weimar, M., and A. Hallam. 1988. "Risk, Diversification, and Vegetables as an Alternative Crop for Midwestern Agriculture." *North Central Journal of Agricultural Economics* 10 (1): 75–89.

CHAPTER 12

MEASURING RISK FOR DECISION MAKING

"If I'd known I was going to live this long I would've taken better care of myself."
—Mickey Mantle

Selecting which crop and livestock enterprises to produce is one of the most important decisions faced by agricultural producers, yet many of those managers do not understand the risks associated with that decision. Too often their analysis of market opportunities stops once a market window has been identified. However, the fact that a particular crop market appears to offer profit potential is not sufficient reason to produce that crop. Other enterprises may offer better opportunities (Burton et al. 1996; Walker and Lin 1978; Weimar and Hallam 1988). Hundreds of different agricultural products are produced and marketed profitably by American farmers and ranchers, and previous research indicates that each enterprise is different from all others in its profit performance relative to its inherent risks. The difficulty faced by producers when assessing market opportunities comes from a lack of both understanding and information about risks involved.

Business risks faced by agricultural producers vary widely in type (Just and Pope 2002; Robison and Barry 1987; Harwood et al. 1999). For example, Harwood et al. (1999) list numerous sources of risk ranging from volatile output prices to family health concerns. However, surveys of farmers and ranchers have found that concerns for all other types of risk are assessed relative to the effects of those risks on income. In other words, income variability is arguably the most important source of risk for agricultural producers. Income is the ultimate goal of production (assuming that utility is derived from income) because income is necessary for wealth building. Therefore, prospective producers must know how to select the crop and livestock enterprises that best suit their financial needs. That selection process is influenced by risk management strategies.

Risk management involves selecting methods for countering business risks. However, methods that lower income generally reduce expected net returns. Thus, it is important to account for the risk/return tradeoff when designing risk management strategies. The first step in that process involves measuring risk so that it can be evaluated during decision making.

The objective of this chapter is to provide some basic information about how to assess income risk and how to manage that risk while selecting enterprises to be produced. Specifically, quantitative estimates of income variability resulting from price and yield fluctuation over time are generated. Also, descriptions of how to account for the risk/return tradeoff when designing income risk management strategies are offered using case studies from a sample of California counties that produce a variety of crops. This is only a brief introduction; readers interested in a detailed presentation of topics on risk are encouraged to see the book by Just and Pope (2002).

INCOME RISK AND ITS COMPONENTS

In this book, "risk" is defined as "volatility" or "fluctuation" following the example of Carter and Dean (1960). The basic measures of risk are the standard deviation (σ), variance (σ^2), and coefficient of variation (CV) for a data series. A CV is usually calculated by dividing a data series' standard deviation by its mean and multiplying by 100 to express the result in percentage terms. All three of these standard measures can be quickly calculated using a computer spreadsheet. McSweeny, Kenyon, and Kramer (1987) compare methods of calculating measures of uncertainty and conclude that a mean-squared forecast error (MSFE) method is better than variate difference and regression methods for risk programming. Therefore, in addition to the usual CV, a MSFE version of the CV is calculated for use in this chapter's analysis. Other risk measures based in portfolio theory are also introduced later in the chapter.

Income risks are a function of (1) production and yield risks, (2) market and price risks, and (3) forecasting risks. Production risk has many sources, both exogenous and endogenous to the firm, all of which combine to create variation in yields per acre across time. In this chapter, a crop's yield risk is measured using average annual yields per acre (in tons) within a single area, such as a county, rather than across locations. Price risk is generated by market sources exogenous to a firm (Seale and Shonkwiler 1987; Hueth and Ligon 1999). Price risk is measured here using a crop's average annual price per ton within a single market, thus it too is a temporal, rather than spatial, form of risk. Since nominal prices include the influence of any inflationary trend existing over a data period, the series are adjusted into "real" terms using the Consumer Price Index (Ford and Musser 1995). The production and price data are combined to generate measures of sales revenue. Then, year-by-year estimates of sales revenues per acre are compared with average cost estimates to calculate average net returns per acre for each product. Sales revenue per acre is calculated by multiplying price (P) times yield (Y). Costs per acre (C) include total variable costs of production. Therefore, for each crop i, expected average returns per acre at time t is

$$(12.1) \qquad E(R_{it}) = (PY)_{it} - C_{it}$$

where $E(\cdot)$ is the expectations operator.

Note that "returns" are defined in this chapter as gross profits or income, rather than net profits, because fixed costs are not subtracted in Equation 12.1 (whereas they are subtracted in net profit equations such as 2.3). This is due to the fact that fixed (i.e., ownership) costs are specific to each firm and, thus, are unknown in aggregate analyses. This definition of returns is common, but can be confusing because R is used for both revenues and returns in the literature. In this chapter, R indicates returns, which are revenues minus production costs.

Forecasting risks faced by agricultural producers are often overlooked, but can be significant in their impact on decision making (Lence and Hayes 1995). Forecast risks are replacements for the usual risks measured ex post in that forecast values, rather than historical values, are used in calculating risk measures (Karolyi 1992). For example, both price and yield are unknown at the time that a producer must make a cropping decision, so both must be forecast to estimate expected returns for each crop. This means that income risk measures calculated using only historical data misrepresent the level of uncertainty faced by a producer by an amount equal to the error in forecasts made.

Producer expectations concerning both price and yield are based upon historical data, in most cases. Producers often forecast expected prices and yields by using some filter rule with recent data. A typical filter rule is a moving average approach. McSweeny, Kenyon, and Kramer (1987) argue that such a scheme should be used to better reflect current trends in variables. To illustrate this process, this chapter uses a three-year moving average. Therefore, at time t, the amount of real gross income a producer expects to receive for product i at the end of the next crop year (time $t+1$) is calculated:

$$(12.2) \qquad E_t(R_{i,t+1}) = \left[\left(\sum_{k=0}^{2} P_{t-k} Y_{t-k} \right) \div 3 \right] - C_t,$$

but since $R = PY - C$, the expression can be simplified by forecasting net returns directly as:

$$(12.3) \qquad E_t(R_{i,t+1}) = \left(\sum_{k=0}^{2} R_{t-k} \right) \div 3.$$

Forecasting risk is measured in the same way as the usual coefficient of variation, except that a mean-squared forecast error (at time t) version of the equation is used for each product:

$$(12.4) \qquad \text{MSFE} = \frac{\sqrt{\frac{\sum [R_t - E(R_t)]^2}{N-k-1}}}{\bar{R}}$$

where $k = 3$ (the number of lags), $\bar{R}$ is average returns, and N is the number of annual observations (Oviatt and Bauerschmidt 1991; Ruefli and Wiggins 1994). The result from Equation 12.4 is multiplied by 100 to convert it into percentage terms. This measure more truly reflects the level of income risk faced by a producer at the time a cropping decision must be made.

METHODS OF REDUCING INCOME RISK

After measures of risk and return have been estimated for individual products, they can be used in a "portfolio approach" to crop selection. This strategy, enterprise diversification, is one of many general types of risk-reducing strategies to develop in agriculture. However, it is one of only two methods available for use in managing income risk directly. The other method is allocating some household labor to earning off-farm income (addressed in detail in Chapter 18).

Harwood et al. (1999) summarize the other major risk management strategies in agriculture as including vertical integration, production contracts, marketing contracts, hedging using futures and/or options, using crop (and other) insurance, maintaining financial reserves, liquidity, leasing inputs, adopting risk-reducing production technologies, and more. All of these strategies focus on managing one type of risk, usually either price or yield risk, and have some limitations (Blank 1995).

Diversification into a portfolio of products, on the other hand, is a very flexible strategy available to all crop producers and can be used to manage income risk directly. The economics of a portfolio model with a risk-free asset are similar to those of hedging, as noted in papers by Feder, Just, and Schmitz (1980) and Meyer and Robison (1988). Diversification does not restrict a grower's ability to negotiate prices or contract at any time. Also, being in multiple markets increases opportunities to spread cash flows across seasons, possibly reducing borrowing requirements.

Restrictions on a grower's use of the portfolio approach to crop selection are mostly internal, rather than external. Internal restrictions are those specific to an individual producer, such as a grower's knowledge of production techniques, scale economies of production, and financial requirements. First, a successful portfolio can include only crops that a grower is proficient in producing. Second, the list of crops from which a grower can choose may be reduced further if noncompetitive cost levels are incurred when diversification limits the scale of production for any particular crop. Finally, capital requirements may grow along with the number of crops produced, forcing a grower to restrict the level of diversification achieved to the degree that can be financed. For example, some crops may require special equipment that cannot be used in producing other crops, thus increasing the total capital requirements beyond the borrowing capacity of the operation. The only significant external restrictions faced by growers considering enterprise diversification are agronomic limitations on the list of crops that can be chosen. These limitations concern the productive capabilities of the resources at the location—specifically, what crops can be grown efficiently and what crops must be grown to maintain resource productivity. For example, crops such as alfalfa are often included in traditional rotations (portfolios) because alfalfa has positive effects on soil quality.

The flexibility of applying a diversification strategy has helped make it the most commonly used risk management method in American agriculture (Blank 1995; Harwood et al. 1999). Nevertheless, the other strategies listed above are used as well by many producers (e.g., Bosch and Johnson 1992; Burton et al. 1996; Held and Helmers 1991; Mahul 2001; Martin 1997; Nartea and Barry 1994). In surveys of agricultural producers it is apparent that most farm and ranch operations have formal or informal strategies for managing most of the numerous sources of risk faced and those plans include using varied risk tools (Blank 1995). In general, risk management strategies are usually "layered" on a farm and decision makers may have a priority system for deciding which strategy "dominates" (this is a form of the safety-first model). The leading concern of producers is usually income, so it is not surprising that the only risk management strategy to deal directly with income risk from production operations should become the most often used.

Therefore, the following section presents portfolio theory concepts as well as examples of how to create a successful "portfolio" of crops and how to compare different portfolios. Strategies that can be used by crop producers to reduce total variability of returns (risk) through diversification are described.

PORTFOLIO APPROACH TO RISK REDUCTION

The standard Markowitz (1959) mean-variance approach to developing portfolios implies that adding more crops to the production mix reduces risk. Portfolio risk is measured using the full covariance model of returns for n products below:

(12.5)
$$\sigma^2(R_p) = \sum_{i=1}^{n} x_i^2 [\sigma(R_i)]^2 + \sum_{i=1}^{n}\sum_{j=1}^{n} x_i x_j \mathrm{Cov}(R_i, R_j), \ i \neq j$$
$$= \sum_{i=1}^{n}\sum_{j=1}^{n} x_i x_j \mathrm{Cov}(R_i, R_j)$$

where $\sigma^2(R_p)$ is the variance in returns from portfolio p, x_i, and x_j are the proportion of the portfolio in products i and j, and $\mathrm{Cov}(R_i, R_j)$ is the covariance between products (Jacob and Pettit 1988, p. 201).[1]

The expected return of a portfolio equals the sum of the weighted expected returns from the crops included in the portfolio:

$$E(R_p) = x_1 E(R_1) + x_2 E(R_2) + \ldots + x_n E(R_n)$$

(12.6)
$$= \sum_{i=1}^{n} x_i E(R_i)$$

In this chapter, gross income is expressed in real dollars per acre, but it can also be presented in rate-of-return form where

(12.7)
$$E(R_p) = \frac{(PY - C)_p}{C_p}.$$

Correlation between (crop) returns is the key to risk reduction through diversification. Portfolio risk is reduced most by inclusion of an individual product that has perfect negative correlation with the portfolio's returns (MacMinn 1984). Therefore, a common strategy for portfolio creation is to start with the highest-returning crop, then continue to add crops that have the greatest amount of negative correlation with the first product and/or the portfolio.

The efficient frontier (EF) of crop portfolios for a market area is generated when short selling is not possible. The EF identifies the portfolio with the lowest level of risk for each level of return available under current market conditions. The restriction on short selling means that all crops considered for inclusion in a portfolio have non-negative proportions: $x_{i,j} \geq 0$. Graphically, the curvilinear EF is usually presented by plotting mean returns of possible portfolios on the vertical axis and some measure of risk on the horizontal axis, such as the standard deviation, variance, or beta of returns. Beta, β, is a standard measure used in the finance literature to indicate the relationship between product or portfolio i and the "market." It is defined as the ratio of a security's covariance with the market to the market's variance,

(12.8)
$$\beta_i \equiv \frac{Cov(R_i, R_m)}{\sigma(R_m)^2},$$

thus it is a regression coefficient. Beta is also referred to as a measure of a security's systematic risk relative to the market index (Siegel 1995).

If a risk-free investment exists, borrowing and lending can occur and the EF is altered. An investment with a positive return and no volatility over time is considered to be risk free. A typical risk-free financial investment is a T-bill; the government guarantees that a specific return will be paid to the holder of a T-bill and that returns will not vary over the holding period. In this chapter, the investor (crop producer) is not choosing how to allocate cash across the range of available financial securities, but how to "invest" agricultural land (Lence and Hayes 1995). Therefore, a risk-free return (R_f) to land is defined as the return from cash leasing it to others (as suggested by Collins and Barry 1986). During the period covered by a cash lease, the landowner is guaranteed a specific return that will not vary. Such a risk-free return is available only if an active market exists for leases on land.

Using the risk-free return and the optimal risky portfolio from the EF of a market, that market's capital market line (CML) can be identified. The CML represents the equilibrium opportunity set available in a market.[2] It is plotted by drawing a straight line through the points representing the risk-free return and optimal portfolio, with risk (σ) on the horizontal axis and expected returns on the vertical axis. The slope of the CML,

$$(12.9) \qquad\qquad \Delta CML \equiv \frac{E(R_m) - R_f}{\sigma(R_m)},$$

is literally the reward for bearing risk, per unit of such risk, offered by the optimal portfolio for the market.

Risk-free lending and borrowing of land—that is, expressing risk in terms of β, instead of $\sigma(R_m)$—transforms the linear CML into a security market line (SML) of possible portfolios that are combinations of the optimal crop portfolio and the risk-free asset (leasing). Lending occurs when land is leased to others, borrowing occurs when land is leased from others. Lending land is analogous to investing in a risk-free asset, which has a return of R_f. Borrowing land implies that a producer chooses to invest more than 100 percent of land owned in some crop portfolio p that is expected to generate returns exceeding the leasing rate

$$(12.10) \qquad\qquad E(R_p) - R_f > 0.$$

The SML created by combining these possible investments with the optimal crop portfolio is the new EF available to individual decision makers. It is graphed just as was the CML except that risk is measured in terms of beta, not σ. The slope of the SML is

$$(12.11) \qquad\qquad E(R_m) - R_f$$

because the market portfolio has a beta of one by definition.

Allowing short selling of crops makes possible the creation of a zero-beta portfolio. Although the zero-beta portfolio is on the EF (at the point where the parabola has a slope of infinity), it is inefficient and would never be held alone, but it serves a useful purpose. Since $\beta = 0$ indicates there is no correlation in returns for this portfolio relative to returns for the optimal market portfolio, the two portfolios can be combined in different ways to form any portfolio on the EF. The zero-beta portfolio expected return, $E(R_z)$, calculated from actual market data, will equal the risk-free return in an efficient market that is in equilibrium. In the Capital Asset Pricing Model (CAPM), expected equilibrium return on an asset or a portfolio of assets is

$$(12.12) \qquad\qquad E(R_i) = R_f + \beta_i[E(R_m) - R_f],$$

where R_i is the return on asset i and R_m is the return on an index portfolio representing all assets in the market. Therefore, substituting $\beta = 0$ into Equation 12.12 gives the zero-beta portfolio result:

$$(12.13) \qquad\qquad E(R_z) = R_f,$$

assuming a single rate for borrowing and lending (Jacob and Pettit 1988, p. 244). R_z is inefficient because it is *not* risk-free, thus a rational investor would always choose R_f over R_z.

Figure 12.1 illustrates the relationship between the EF, R_f, optimal portfolio (p_o), zero-beta portfolio (p_z), and the borrowing and lending sections of the SML. The point of tangency between the EF and SML identifies the optimal portfolio (point p_o), which has expected returns of

Figure 12.1   **The Efficient Frontier and the Security Market Line**

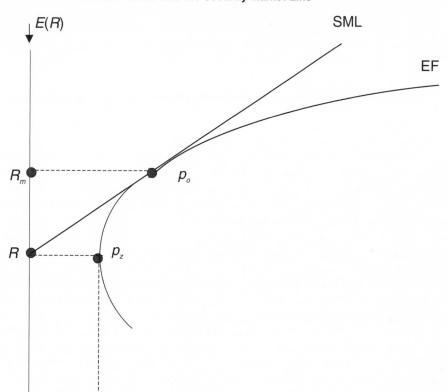

R_m. The lending section of the SML is left of point p_o, and the borrowing section is to the right of point p_o.

The Single Index Model (SIM) developed by Sharpe (1963) as an application of the CAPM generates a measure of risk for each enterprise being considered for inclusion in a portfolio. That measure closely approximates a full variance-covariance matrix, which makes it a good alternative to the Markowitz (1959) approach to portfolio choice (Collins and Barry 1986). The SIM most often used is

(12.14) $$R_i = \alpha_i + \beta_i R_m + \varepsilon_i$$

where the return to enterprise i (R_i) is linearly related to the market's return (R_m), β is the risk measure (as defined in Equation 12.8), α is a constant, and ε is an error term. The variance of returns for an enterprise is

(12.15) $$\sigma^2(R_i) = [\beta_i \sigma(R_m)]^2 + \sigma^2(\varepsilon_i).$$

The SIM assumes that part of variance is due to the single factor of "the market," and a second component of variance comes from random factors unique to the enterprise (Turvey, Driver, and

Baker 1988). The β coefficient reflects the "systematic" risk from the market. The $\sigma^2(\varepsilon_i)$ portion of variance is "nonsystematic" or diversifiable risk that can be eliminated by diversifying totally.

In this chapter, the β coefficients are adjusted to reflect risk in expected returns, above the level required to justify producing a crop, by subtracting the risk-free rate (R_f) from Equation 12.14 to give

$$(12.16) \qquad \begin{aligned} E(R_i) - R_f &= \alpha_i + \beta_i[E(R_m) - R_f] + \varepsilon_i \\ E(R_i) &= \alpha_i + R_f + \beta_i[E(R_m) - R_f] + \varepsilon_i. \end{aligned}$$

The expected values of α_i and ε_i are zero. As noted by Collins (1988), the SIM in Equation 12.16 appears similar to, but is quite different than, the standard CAPM in Equation 12.12.

Single index portfolio models have been used since the 1980s to assess diversification in agriculture. For example, Turvey and Driver (1987) used gross revenue data to conclude that opportunities for diversification in Canada are limited due to the large degree of systematic risk within agriculture in that country. Yet Collins and Barry (1986) found a large degree of non-systematic risk in California markets using net returns data. Gempesaw et al. (1988) show that such contrasting results indicate the significance of data measurement and estimating techniques. The SIM is used below to derive some performance measures that can help decision makers evaluate diversified portfolios.

The rewards to diversification, reflected in the relationship between absolute risk levels and the number of crops included in a portfolio, are expected to be similar to those for stock market portfolios (Featherstone and Moss 1990). For stocks, risk (measured as standard deviations in annual returns) is reduced significantly at first as additional securities are added to a portfolio, but the rate of decline in risk levels constantly diminishes as the portfolio grows (Jacob and Pettit 1988, p. 188). In other words, a majority of possible risk reduction is achieved with relatively few products being included in a portfolio. This raises the question of whether there is an optimal number of crops to be included in an agricultural producer's portfolio.

By definition, the goal of diversification is risk reduction. However, it is expected that absolute levels of risk and return are positively related, so diversification reduces returns as well as risk (Moss, Weldon, and Featherstone 1991). Therefore, crops included in a portfolio because of their low level of absolute risk or their negative correlation with returns of another crop must be evaluated in terms of their effects on relative risk and return levels of the portfolio as well (Ramirez and Somarriba 2000). In this effort, the coefficient of variation for gross income per acre is calculated for portfolios of crops to show the relative levels of risk and return facing producers in a sample of counties.

Measures in addition to the CV are needed to more fully assess the risk/return relationship and the effects of diversification on that relationship. The CV is a limited, aggregate measure that reflects risk and returns over the entire data series for a single crop or portfolio. A temporal measure may be more appropriate for evaluating the relative return/risk tradeoffs for diversification. Therefore, along with the CV, four different indexes are calculated, two from the finance literature and two derived for agriculture by Blank (1990).

The first index is the slope of a market's CML, defined in Equation 12.9. It is the equilibrium return to risk for the market. It represents the reciprocal of a risk-adjusted CV for a fully diversified portfolio, one including all crops grown profitably in the market weighted according to each crop's percentage of total acreage in the area.

The second index to be calculated is the commonly used Treynor-Black (Treynor and Black 1972) appraisal ratio. It is a performance measure that divides the alphas by the residual standard deviations (nonsystematic risk),

(12.17)
$$\frac{\alpha}{\sigma(\varepsilon)},$$

from the temporal Jensen (1968) Performance Index equation,

(12.18)
$$R_{it} - R_{ft} = \alpha_i + \beta_i(R_{It} - R_{ft}) + \varepsilon_{it}.$$

In the appraisal ratio, α is a measure of an individual crop or portfolio's abnormal performance (positive or negative) relative to the CAPM, as expressed in the SIM specified in Equation 12.16. The term R_{It} in Equation 12.18 is the return at time t on an index portfolio reflecting the entire market. The index portfolio is created such that $R_I = R_m$. Dividing alpha by $\sigma(\varepsilon)$ enables relative performance ranking of crops or portfolios (assuming constant-absolute-risk-aversion) (Lehmann and Modest 1987).

Two measures of agricultural diversification performance derived by Blank (1990) are used here. Blank's first index, Ω, is derived using Equation 12.16 and assuming $R_I = R_m$. The marginal abnormal return to risk (β) that results from shifting from a fully diversified market portfolio to a specific portfolio p can be measured by comparing returns from the two portfolios. The market index portfolio has expected returns calculated using Equation 12.6, where n is the number of crops grown in the county. By definition, this SIM market reference portfolio is fully diversified (it includes all crops grown in the market region) and has no nonsystematic risk remaining; its total risk equals its systematic risk. Any portfolio p that does not include all the crops in the market portfolio is not fully diversified and its producer is exposed to some diversifiable risk. This means β_p (portfolio p's risk relative to the market index portfolio) will not precisely measure that portfolio's total risk. An adjustment to account for this voluntary change in risk is to divide beta by the correlation coefficient between returns for portfolio p and the market index portfolio, ρ_{pm} (Jacob and Petit 1988, pp. 674–675). This makes the portfolio's total risk-adjusted expected returns

(12.19)
$$E(R_p) = R_f + \left(\frac{\beta_p}{\rho_{pm}}\right)\left[E(R_m) - R_f\right].$$

Blank's Ω index is derived from the difference in expected portfolio returns,

$$E(R_p) - E(R_m) = \left\{ R_f + \left(\frac{\beta_p}{\rho_{pm}}\right)\left[E(R_m) - R_f\right] \right\} - \left\{ R_f + \beta_m\left[E(R_m) - R_f\right] \right\}$$

$$E(R_p) - E(R_m) = \left\{ \left(\frac{\beta_p}{\rho_{pm}}\right)\left[E(R_m) - R_f\right] \right\} - \left\{ \beta_m\left[E(R_m) - R_f\right] \right\}$$

$$E(R_p) - E(R_m) = \left\{ \left(\frac{\beta_p}{\rho_{pm}}\right) - \beta_m \right\}\left[E(R_m) - R_f\right]$$

$$\frac{E(R_p - R_m)}{\left[\left(\frac{\beta_p}{\rho_{pm}}\right) - \beta_m\right]} = \left[E(R_m) - R_f\right]$$

and with $\beta_m = 1$ by definition,

(12.20)
$$\Omega_p \equiv \frac{E(R_p - R_m)}{\left[\left(\frac{\beta_p}{\rho_{pm}}\right) - 1\right]} - \left[E(R_m) - R_f\right].$$

By design, Ω_p tests whether portfolio p conforms to theoretical expectations concerning a market's risk/return tradeoff. If so, $\Omega_p = 0$; if not, it measures the deviations. However, it does not distinguish between the two sources of any deviations: (1) abnormal returns earned by portfolio p, and (2) changing between the total risk levels of β_m and β_p/ρ_{mp}, that is, accepting some diversifiable risk.

Blank's second index specifies the sources of deviations from expected returns by evaluating the risk/return tradeoffs faced when considering crop diversification. By evaluating abnormal returns in more detail, this index makes it easier to both (1) detect returns due to risk changes between portfolios of crops, and (2) rank portfolios. The index, π_D, measures "returns to limited diversification." For any portfolio p, these returns are expected to be a function of three factors.

The first factor is the cost of limited diversification (CLD). As expressed in Equation 12.19, a portfolio's risk measure needs to be adjusted when not fully diversified. The cost of limiting the degree of diversification, therefore, is the difference between the total risk-adjusted and the unadjusted equations:

(12.21) $$\text{CLD} = \left\{ R_f + \left(\frac{\beta_p}{\rho_{pm}}\right)\left[E(R_m) - R_f\right] \right\} - \left\{ R_f + \beta_p\left[E(R_m) - R_f\right] \right\}.$$

The second factor is the revenue from limited diversification (RLD). A portfolio's returns are expected to change (increase) when its contents become more selective (i.e., not all crops are included). This means the revenue from limiting the degree of diversification equals the difference between actual returns on portfolio p and the total risk-adjusted expected returns:

(12.22) $$\text{RLD} = Rp - \left\{ R_f + \left(\frac{\beta_p}{\rho_{pm}}\right)\left[E(R_m) - R_f\right] \right\}.$$

By subtracting the expected revenues calculated with a total risk-adjusted beta from actual returns, RLD more accurately measures the benefits portion of a portfolio's performance.

The third factor expected to affect the benefits of diversifying crop portfolios is scale costs (SC). It is expected that economies of scale in production and marketing will be lost as a grower includes additional crops in the product mix. For portfolio p,

(12.23) $$SC_p = \sum_{i=1}^{k} \left(AVC_{ip} - AVC_i^*\right) + \sum_{i=1}^{k} \left(MTC_{ip} - MTC_i^*\right)$$

where AVC_{ip} is the average variable costs of product i in portfolio p, AVC_i^* is the average variable costs if product i is a one-product portfolio, MTC_{ip} is the marketing transaction costs of product i in portfolio p, MTC_i^* is the marketing transaction costs if product i is a one-product portfolio, k is the number of crops in portfolio p, and $k \leq n$. If k equals one, SC_p will equal zero by definition. SC_p will also equal zero if there are no benefits to specialization at the scale of operations observed in a market. SC_p cannot be estimated without detailed data from a cross section of farmers, therefore, it is assumed in this chapter that $SC_p = 0$ for all portfolios.

Subtracting the two costs from the revenue gives the returns to limited diversification: $\pi_{Dp} = RLD_p - CLD_p - SC_p$.[3] Risk preference parameters (exponents) can be placed on each of the three factors (RLD, CLD, SC). In this analysis, all preference parameters are assumed to be one and, hence, are excluded. Substituting Equations 12.21 and 12.22 gives

$$\pi_{Dp} = (R_p - \{R_f + (\beta_p/\rho_{pm})[E(R_m) - R_f]\})$$
$$- (\{R_f + (\beta_p/\rho_{pm})[E(R_m) - R_f]\} - \{R_f + \beta_p[E(R_m) - R_f]\}) - SC_p.$$

Combining terms gives

$$(12.24) \qquad \pi_{Dp} \equiv R_p - R_f - 2\left(\frac{\beta_p}{\rho_{pm}}\right)\left[E(R_m) - R_f\right] + \beta_p[E(R_m) - R_f] - SC_p.$$

The decision criterion normally is to select the portfolio with the highest π_D. Gains from diversification equal the difference between any portfolio p (which has more than one crop) and the single-product portfolio, $\pi_{Dp} - \pi_{D1}$, or the difference between any two portfolios. Any number of portfolios can be ranked relative to their π_D values. This facilitates comparisons among portfolios of different size that have large differences in their absolute levels of return and risk.

EMPIRICAL METHODS AND RESULTS

This discussion of portfolio performance raises the possibility that there might be an optimal number of crops to be included in a crop rotation. If this is true, it helps a producer narrow the choices to be made when selecting the desired portfolio.

Portfolio selections made by individual investors depend upon their attitudes toward risk and return (Buschena and Zilberman 1994; Harper et al. 1991). Various models of the selection process have been developed based on assumptions ranging from safety first to utility maximization (Pyle and Turnovsky 1970; Levy 1992; McCarl 1990). In theory, the preferred portfolio is identified easily on a mean-variance graph as the point where a decision maker's indifference curve is tangent to the SML. In practice, the difficulties in estimating risk preferences noted by Antle (1987), Bard and Barry (2001), Pennings and Garcia (2001), and many others have been avoided in most previous studies by using linear or nonlinear (quadratic) programming procedures to identify optimal crop portfolios for a particular case (e.g., Coyle 1999; Crisostomo et al. 1993; Turvey, Driver, and Baker 1988). Although risk programming approaches lead to theoretically optimal portfolios, there are practical limitations to the use of these methods by agricultural producers. For example, many farmers cannot do this kind of analysis due to time, skill, and data requirements, as described by Collins and Barry (1986). Thus, a SIM was suggested as a computationally simpler technique. However, applications of the SIM in agriculture have not overcome two limitations facing producers when using the method to select a portfolio of enterprises. The first problem is the SIM's reliance on an enterprise risk measure, beta, which is unstable over time, creating potential measurement error in portfolio risk and return forecasts. Second, no decision criterion has been specified for the SIM to aid in evaluating the risk/return tradeoff among portfolios. On the other hand, Blank's (1990) index of returns to limited diversification (augmented by his first index, Ω) has none of these shortcomings while providing an answer to the question of the optimal number of crops to include in a crop rotation. As a result, the empirical analysis in this chapter illustrates the benefits of Blank's approach to using the SIM by highlighting three issues: the value of a simple alternative to quadratic programming analysis, the ability to reduce problems caused by unstable crop betas, and the robustness of π_D as a performance measure.

The analysis conducted by Blank (1990) reported here differs from earlier efforts in its approach to crop portfolio creation. No portfolios were specified a priori. Portfolios were created based on marketing, rather than production, concerns only. This means that products were chosen so as to create the best portfolios based upon risk-adjusted profitability.[4] Also, this analysis is done on a per-acre basis. This method facilitates assessments of simultaneous production of any number of different crops on portions of total farm acreage, without being bound by a particular farm size. This assumes that economies of scale in production will not vary significantly over the range of possible acreages allocated to any crop in a portfolio. Rotation of crops among particular fields on a farm between years is still possible, although the pattern need not be specified in this analysis.

The list of crops for any market, such as a county, can be divided into two groups: trees and vines (those crops requiring a long-term commitment), and field and horticultural crops (those requiring a commitment of one year or less). Separate portfolios can be developed for each group of crops. In this way, an individual grower can limit his choices to one group or can combine the two by developing a portfolio of the two group portfolios.

Risks Faced by Crop Producers

When making decisions, one type of risk faced by crop producers is forecasting risk, defined earlier as income risk adjusted for expectations based on forecasts. Tables 12.1 through 12.3 present a comparison of CV and MSFE measures of risk in sales revenues for three counties. These counties were arbitrarily selected to represent different agricultural regions of California: Yolo County—northern valley/delta, Fresno County—southern valley, and Imperial County— southern desert. The results for these counties illustrate the sensitivity of both risk measures and the relative rankings of crops to the method of calculating risk.

In Tables 12.1 through 12.3, there are often quite significant differences between CV and MSFE measures of risk for particular crops. In general, there is an absolute reduction in reported levels of risk for each county when a forecasting filter is used to transform the standard CV into a MSFE. Also, relative risk levels change, as indicated by changes in the two rank orderings. For example, in Fresno County (Table 12.1), even though plums have a smaller absolute level of risk when measured with a MSFE, their relative ranking deteriorates from seventh to twentieth out of twenty-nine crops.

Differences in the two risk measures noted above have significant implications for growers concerning the importance of forecasting in crop production and marketing strategies. The somewhat surprising absolute improvement (reduction) in risk reported across counties when using the MSFE indicates that agricultural products, in general, have trends and/or cycles in their revenues. If these trends or cycles can be identified and used in forecasting for specific crops, the resource allocation decisions of farmers can be improved. For the crops that had lower MSFEs than CVs in Tables 12.1 through 12.3, the simple moving average filter used led to better estimates of risk because it was able to detect trends in the data. Better forecasting filters may be able to generate more precise risk measures that give needed precision in relative risk rankings. The relative rankings of crops are important because they influence crop selection decisions.

Table 12.1

Forecasting Risk for Revenues per Acre from Selected Crops: Fresno County

Crop	CV	CV rank	MSFE	MSFE rank
Barley	17	1	19	6
Rice	20	2	23	11
Corn, field	21	3	17	3
Silage, corn	21	4	16	2
Cotton	23	5	19	5
Alfalfa hay	24	6	17	4
Plums	24	7	22	20
Wheat	24	8	16	1
Strawberries	25	9	21	8
Grapes, wine	25	10	24	13
Alfalfa seed	26	11	22	9
Grain sorghum	26	12	28	21
Beans, dry	27	13	26	18
Peaches	29	14	19	7
Figs	30	15	25	17
Safflower	30	16	23	12
Tomatoes, fresh	33	17	25	16
Oranges	34	18	24	15
Grapes, raisin	34	19	27	20
Almonds	34	20	38	26
Grapes, table	34	21	24	14
Sugar beets	38	22	35	24
Honeydew	38	23	40	28
Onions, dry	39	24	35	25
Walnuts	40	25	26	19
Lemons	40	26	34	22
Lettuce	41	27	38	27
Olives	46	28	51	29
Apricots	74	29	35	23

Note: The mean squared forecast error was calculated using Equation 12.4.

Profit, rather than revenue, data should be used when developing portfolios. Therefore, crop production cost data was used to generate gross income series in real dollars for the three selected counties to illustrate the range of risks faced by agricultural producers. As expected, the CV for these series shows a much higher level of risk than that for revenues (examples are presented in Tables 12.4 through 12.6). The CVs in Table 12.4 are often higher than those reported by Carter and Dean (1960), Reid and Tew (1987), and Walker and Lin (1978) because considerably more annual observations were used in the calculations here (29) compared to the other studies (5–7).

The high absolute levels of risk evident in the profit data imply a need for, and potential gains from, diversifying into a variety of crops. Figure 12.2 illustrates this potential by presenting the average relationship between the number of crops in a portfolio and the level of risk for all California counties. The portfolios used in the calculations were derived as examples only by starting with the single most profitable crop in each county and adding the second most profitable crop to form an equally weighted two-product portfolio, then adding the next most profitable crop, and so forth. Standard deviations of each portfolio from each county were converted into percentage terms with the one-product value being 100. The standard deviations from all portfolios

Table 12.2

Forecasting Risk for Revenues per Acre from Selected Crops: Imperial County

Crop	CV	CV rank	MSFE	MSFE rank
Grain sorghum	18	1	15	1
Cantaloupes	18	2	18	2
Barley	24	3	20	4
Cotton	24	4	24	6
Asparagus	27	5	22	5
Sugar beets	27	6	31	8
Alfalfa hay	27	7	18	3
Watermelons	28	8	34	9
Alfalfa seed	30	9	26	7
Lettuce	34	10	40	10
Tomatoes, fresh	35	11	45	13
Onions, dry	39	12	42	12
Carrots	41	13	41	11
Grapefruit	81	14	69	14
Oranges	105	15	96	15

Note: The mean squared forecast error was calculated using Equation 12.4.

Table 12.3

Forecasting Risk for Revenues per Acre from Selected Crops: Yolo County

Crop	CV	CV rank	MSFE	MSFE rank
Pasture, irrigated	8	1	6	1
Barley	16	2	18	5
Alfalfa hay	17	3	18	4
Prunes	17	4	17	3
Tomatoes, processing	18	5	16	2
Rice	19	6	20	8
Grain sorghum	25	7	18	6
Sugar beets	26	8	28	10
Almonds	28	9	30	13
Wheat	28	10	24	9
Beans, dry	30	11	33	15
Walnuts	30	12	28	11
Safflower	30	13	31	14
Grain hay	31	14	29	12
Corn, field	33	15	19	7
Pears	51	16	44	16
Asparagus	56	17	45	17
Apricots	68	18	69	18
Peaches	70	19	79	19

Note: The mean squared forecast error was calculated using Equation 12.4.

Table 12.4

Gross Income Mean, Standard Deviation, and Coefficient of Variation for Crops Grown Profitably in Fresno County

Crop	Mean ($/acre)	St Dev ($/acre)	CV (%)
Alfalfa hay	61.31	142.61	232.6
Alfalfa seed	46.81	190.99	408.0
Apricots	1,041.11	1,135.70	109.1
Beans, dry	27.94	165.01	590.6
Corn, field	50.78	97.05	191.1
Cotton	258.24	282.17	109.3
Grapes, raisin	209.01	555.53	265.8
Grapes, table	1,341.51	659.03	49.1
Grapes, wine	439.67	559.21	127.2
Lemons	1,507.14	837.11	55.5
Lettuce	860.44	814.18	94.6
Olives	60.53	694.28	1,147.0
Onions, dry	1,934.83	1,127.21	58.3
Oranges	911.39	616.02	67.6
Peaches	1,680.71	628.80	37.4
Plums	2,500.21	991.97	39.7
Rice	187.35	191.94	102.4
Silage, corn	145.14	61.85	42.6
Strawberries	2,910.55	5,145.49	176.8
Sugar beets	228.49	225.94	98.9
Tomatoes, fresh	5,280.24	2,970.69	56.3

Note: Gross income is defined in Equation 12.1. All amounts are in real 1986 dollars. Crops listed in Table 12.1 which are not listed here had negative mean returns for the data period.

Table 12.5

Gross Income Mean, Standard Deviation, and Coefficient of Variation for Crops Grown Profitably in Imperial County

Crop	Mean ($/acre)	St Dev ($/acre)	CV (%)
Alfalfa hay	88.32	129.99	147.2
Alfalfa seed	91.23	79.77	87.4
Asparagus	159.53	715.41	448.4
Barley	73.01	78.32	107.3
Cantaloupes	718.42	555.92	77.4
Carrots	617.92	1,138.42	184.2
Cotton	354.88	469.68	132.3
Onions, dry	469.70	909.80	193.7
Oranges	565.91	703.87	124.4
Sugar beets	818.74	1,535.03	187.5

Note: Gross income is defined in Equation 12.1. All amounts are in real 1986 dollars. Crops listed in Table 12.2 which are not listed here had negative mean returns for the data period.

Table 12.6

Gross Income Mean, Standard Deviation, and Coefficient of Variation for Crops Grown Profitably in Yolo County

Crop	Mean ($/ac)	St Dev ($/ac)	CV (%)
Alfalfa hay	73.94	139.79	189.1
Beans, dry	49.50	192.84	389.6
Corn, field	147.25	135.34	91.9
Grain sorghum	39.65	160.96	406.0
Pears	497.45	1,885.13	379.0
Rice	201.34	221.01	109.8
Safflower	71.61	94.46	131.9
Sugar beets	234.52	263.72	112.5
Tomatoes, processing	582.22	483.21	83.0
Wheat	111.33	54.58	49.0

Note: Gross income is defined in Equation 12.1. All amounts are in real 1986 dollars. Crops listed in Table 12.3 which are not listed here had negative mean returns for the data period.

composed of the same number of products were then averaged to get the values in Figure 12.2. For twelve-product portfolios, for example, the average standard deviation was only 27 percent as large as the average standard deviation for one-product portfolios, meaning that at least 73 percent of original income risk in California agriculture is nonsystematic and can be diversified away.

Quadratic Programming's Volatile Results

To begin, a sample of portfolios was derived for the three California counties using a quadratic programming (QP) model for use later in illustrating the value of a simple alternative to QP analysis. Using crop mean and variance-covariance data, the QP model uses Equation 12.5 to estimate the optimal (i.e., minimum variance) portfolio, given a target return per acre and the constraint that $x_{i,j} \geq 0$. By repeating the calculations with different target returns, the expected value-variance frontier for the market can be developed.

Each portfolio in Tables 12.7 through 12.9 generates an arbitrarily selected higher target return than previous portfolios. Therefore, each of the portfolios labeled "A" has the lowest absolute levels of both return and risk for the group of products listed. Successive portfolios each produce more return, but have higher absolute levels of risk associated with them. As a result, low risk/return crops typically enter low-return portfolios, but are gradually replaced by higher-returning, riskier crops. This is the same micro process that leads to macro-level changes in cropping patterns described in Chapter 11.

The portfolios presented in Tables 12.7 through 12.9 demonstrate how volatile QP-derived crop rotations can be in terms of their scope (i.e., the number of crops included)[5] and their risk/return performance. For example, moving along the Yolo County efficient frontier from portfolio A to D in Table 12.9 involves shifting from a two-crop to a five-crop rotation and back again. This volatile composition does not facilitate analysis of the marginal effects of a one-crop change to an existing rotation—a common situation considered by farmers. Also, the relative return/risk performances of those portfolios shifts up and down, as indicated by the changes in the CV of the

Figure 12.2   **Diversification of Income Risk (Average of All California Counties)**

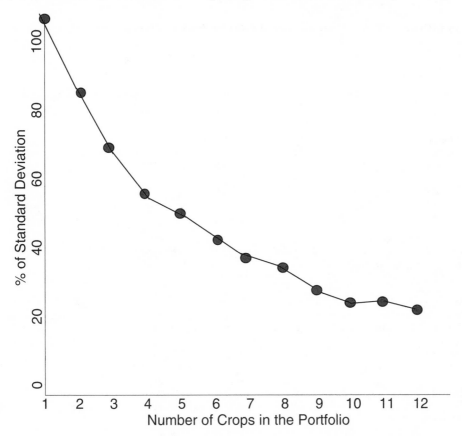

various portfolios. Although portfolios A through D in Table 12.9 are each "optimal" for the target return levels, they are not equal in their relative return/risk tradeoff.

A SIM approach to crop portfolio assessment facilitates marginal analysis of rotations and their return/risk tradeoff and, therefore, may provide a simple alternative to quadratic programming in some situations. If QP is used, a portfolio performance measure such as π_D can be applied as well, aiding in the portfolio selection process. Also, SIM techniques enable the scope of rotations to be manipulated directly during analysis, if desired.

Another reason commonly cited for using SIM as a substitute for QP methods is to reduce application difficulties caused by data requirements. Quadratic programming is data intensive and the crop rotations recommended by QP models are data sensitive—they might change if different temporal data are used (Tew, Musser, and Smith 1988). Yet, standard SIM methods also have problems with data sensitivity that require adjustments, as described next.

SIM Beta Instability

The finance literature has indicated that a security's beta should vary through time given changes in the micro and macro environments (Bos and Newbold 1984; Siegel 1995). Gempesaw et al.

Table 12.7

Sample Crop Portfolios on the Efficient Frontier, Fresno County

	Portfolio & Target Return/CV				
	A $850/38	B $1,250/28	C $1,650/27	D $1,950/32	
Trees and vines					
Apricots	.35	.295	.207	.012	
Grapes, raisin	.005	.0	.0	.0	
Grapes, table	.0	.0	.0	.0	
Grapes, wine	.205	.134	.0	.0	
Lemons	.175	.122	.056	.012	
Olives	.185	.048	.0	.0	
Oranges	.026	.126	.179	.067	
Peaches	.055	.137	.252	.508	
Plums	.0	.138	.306	.401	
	A $35/452	B $85/190	C $130/135	D $220/102	E $270/92
Field and horticultural crops					
Alfalfa hay	.0	.0	.0	.0	.0
Alfalfa seed	.405	.39	.364	.307	.23
Beans, dry	.595	.553	.52	.458	.412
Corn, field	.0	.0	.0	.0	.0
Cotton	.0	.0	.0	.0	.0
Lettuce	.0	.058	.116	.217	.262
Onions, dry	.0	.0	.0	.0	.0
Rice	.0	.0	.0	.0	.0
Silage	.0	.0	.0	.0	.0
Strawberries	.0	.0	.0	.0	.0
Sugar beets	.0	.0	.0	.018	.096
Tomatoes, fresh	.0	.0	.0	.0	.0

Note: The values listed under each portfolio letter represent the proportion of that portfolio allocated to the relevant crop with the sum equaling one (ignoring rounding). These portfolios are derived so as to generate the arbitrarily selected target returns listed. The CV for the portfolio is listed also.

(1988) raised the same issue in applying the SIM in agriculture. It is unlikely that the betas for individual crops are stable over the twenty-nine-year data period used here. However, it is expected that betas for portfolios of crops are increasingly stable as the portfolio becomes more diversified. By definition, a fully diversified portfolio always will have a beta of 1.0 regardless of what data period is used in its calculation. Therefore, the π_D procedure of using portfolio betas helps reduce data sensitivity.

To determine whether the relative measure of systematic risk is stationary over time, separate betas are estimated using data for each of the three sample counties from 1958–1986 and 1977–1986 and compared for equality based on a Chow test. This comparison for a range of partially diversified portfolios illustrates the effect of diversification on parameter stability. If β_p varies through time, its value in Equation 12.24 cannot be calculated using the entire data set; it must reflect only data considered relevant to the period being evaluated. The choice of relevant data is an empirical question; no general guidelines exist. Examples of approaches range from Blank's

Table 12.8

Sample Crop Portfolios on the Efficient Frontier, Imperial County

	Portfolio & Target Return/CV			
	A	B	C	D
	$538/67	$551/67	$557/84	$708/77
Crops				
Alfalfa hay	.0	.0	.0	.0
Alfalfa seed	.298	.30	.296	.016
Asparagus	.0	.0	.0	.0
Barley	.0	.0	.0	.0
Cantaloupes	.639	.506	.363	.984
Carrots	.0	.0	.0	.0
Cotton	.0	.0	.0	.0
Onions, dry	.0	.0	.0	.0
Oranges	.0	.0	.04	.0
Sugar beets	.063	.195	.301	.0

Note: The values listed under each portfolio letter represent the proportion of that portfolio allocated to the relevant crop with the sum equaling one (ignoring rounding). These portfolios are derived so as to generate the arbitrarily selected target returns listed. The CV for the portfolio is listed also.

(1990) use of a moving ten-year period to Gempesaw et al.'s (1988) use of all available data with a stochastic coefficients regression method.

Tables 12.10 through 12.12 present results for portfolios derived as examples only from the three sample counties. Of interest first are the two columns of betas. In those tables the columns

Table 12.9

Sample Crop Portfolios on the Efficient Frontier, Yolo County

	Portfolio & Target Return/CV			
	A	B	C	D
	$134/47	$158/100	$234/75	$275/66
Crops				
Alfalfa hay	.0	.0	.0	.0
Beans, dry	.0	.339	.168	.0
Corn, field	.0	.0	.0	.0
Grain sorghum	.0	.0	.0	.0
Pears	.0	.014	.0	.0
Rice	.0	.0	.0	.0
Saflower	.0	.0	.0	.0
Sugar beets	.0	.054	.005	.0
Tomatoes, processing	.048	.118	.281	.347
Wheat	.952	.475	.546	.653

Note: The values listed under each portfolio letter represent the proportion of that portfolio allocated to the relevant crop with the sum equaling one (ignoring rounding). These portfolios are derived so as to generate the arbitrarily selected target returns listed. The CV for the portfolio is listed also.

Table 12.10

Diversification Analysis of Crop Portfolios from Fresno County

Portfolio[a]	Mean Return	pi[b]	Beta[c] 29 yr	Beta[c] 10 yr	$\dfrac{\alpha}{\sigma(\varepsilon)}$ [d]	Ω_p	π_{Dp}
Tree & vine crops							
1. Plums	2,500	.822	5.00	6.46*	−0.03	71.14	14.48
2. Peaches	2,090	.868	3.93	4.86*	0.42	127.84	259.22
3. Lemons	1,896	.861	3.45	3.88*	1.14	141.30	245.94
4. Table grapes	1,758	.908	3.37	3.81*	5.24	140.34	270.88
5. Apricots	1,614	.950	3.15	3.10	16.24	156.94	310.03
6. Oranges	1,497	.957	2.90	2.83	22.49	165.80	294.99
7. Wine grapes	1,346	.964	2.63	2.47	9.07	164.45	252.31
8. Raisin grapes	1,204	.979	2.50	2.43	5.65	128.37	182.36
9. Olives	1,077	.995	2.28	2.31	9.24	119.64	150.68
Field & horticulture crops							
1. Tomatoes, fresh	5,280	.431	3.92	4.71*	1.63	171.41	−775.34
2. Strawberries	4,095	.363	2.02	3.36*	−6.54	365.45	187.92
3. Onions, dry	3,376	.440	1.52	2.38*	−11.44	746.50	1,027.63
4. Lettuce	2,747	.378	1.50	1.60	−7.23	336.66	−32.51
5. Cotton	2,249	.376	1.21	1.36	−7.74	364.56	−30.09
6. Sugar beets	1,912	.390	1.02	1.07	−8.36	454.18	65.55
7. Rice	1,665	.400	.88	.87	−8.88	538.49	96.96
8. Silage	1,475	.401	.78	.78	−8.86	606.46	85.43
9. Alfalfa hay	1,318	.397	.69	.68	−8.77	685.58	65.79
10. Corn, field	1,192	.397	.62	.60	−8.99	785.06	50.57
11. Alfalfa seed	1,087	.384	.55	.59	−9.12	888.06	21.60
12. Beans, dry	999	.380	.38	.51	−9.27	1,259.18	33.01

[a] The portfolio number indicates how many crops are included. The crops in a portfolio are those listed from 1 down to the portfolio number. All crops included are equally weighted in each portfolio.

[b] This is the correlation coefficient between the portfolio listed and the market portfolio for the county.

[c] These portfolio betas are calculated using data from 1958–86 and 1977–86, respectively. Asterisks indicate that the 10-year beta is significantly different than the 29-year beta according to a Chow test.

[d] This is the Treynor-Black index, as described in the text.

labeled "29-year" and "10-year," respectively, include each portfolio's beta calculated using data from 1958–1986 and 1977–1986. The two betas prove to be significantly different only for portfolios of up to 3 to 4 crops. This supports the hypothesis that betas for individual crops (i.e., one-crop portfolios) will vary through time and that increased diversification will create increasingly stable betas for portfolios. The implications of these results are that diversified portfolio betas are not sensitive to data used in their calculation (making their use less restrictive than crop betas), which means that they may better represent future risk levels than do measures using crop betas.

Previous studies have used varied methods to estimate the SIM betas for single crops. Collins and Barry (1986) and Turvey and Driver (1987) used ordinary least squares; Irwin, Forster, and Sherrick (1988) and Barry (1980) used the Cochrane-Orcutt approach to correct for autocorrelation; and Gempesaw et al. (1988) used the Prais-Winsten and stochastic coefficients regression methods. Blank (1990) used the Prais-Winsten generalization of the Cochrane-Orcutt procedure

Table 12.11

Diversification Analysis of Crop Portfolios from Imperial County

Portfolio[a]	Mean return	pi[b]	Beta[c] 29 yr	Beta[c] 10 yr	$\dfrac{\alpha}{\sigma(\varepsilon)}$ [d]	Ω_p	π_{Dp}
1. Sugar beets	819	.675	2.39	3.76*	−0.15	124.63	−652.67
2. Cantaloupes	769	.773	1.44	2.16*	0.34	124.83	0.11
3. Carrots	718	.894	2.18	2.29	0.38	−66.11	−169.84
4. Oranges	680	.924	1.47	1.82*	0.34	189.58	77.00
5. Onions, dry	638	.979	1.96	1.89	3.41	−49.35	−61.75
6. Cotton	591	.983	1.60	1.51	2.52	21.20	5.23
7. Asparagus	529	.999	1.47	1.49	4.11	−10.29	−5.32
8. Alfalfa seed	474	.999	1.27	1.26	3.14	−2.90	−1.16
9. Alfalfa hay	432	.999	1.12	1.11	2.43	16.15	1.58
10. Barley	396	1.0	1.0	1.0	—	0	0

[a] The portfolio number indicates how many crops are included. The crops in a portfolio are those listed from 1 down to the portfolio number. All crops included are equally weighted in each portfolio.

[b] This is the correlation coefficient between the portfolio listed and the market portfolio for the county made up of all crops listed in this table.

[c] These portfolio betas are calculated using data from 1958–86 and 1977–86, respectively. Asterisks indicate that the 10-year beta is significantly different than the 29-year beta according to a Chow test.

[d] This is the Treynor-Black index, as described in the text.

to estimate betas for crop portfolios rather than single crops. This chapter uses Blank's results, so betas reported here are not comparable to those reported by other authors.

Performance Measure Results

The first index assessed was the CML for the three sample counties. The three counties were chosen because they represent different geographical regions in the state. As a result, the CML for each county presents a different picture. The Yolo CML had a slope of 0.819. Imperial's CML had a slope of 0.726. Fresno County's data was separated into two product groups. Fresno's portfolios of field and horticulture crops had a CML with a slope of 1.975. Fresno tree and vine crops had a CML with a slope of 1.331. In general, these results indicate that Fresno County is the more profitable county of the three, in terms of its returns to risk. In other words, Fresno markets generally do not fluctuate over time as much as the markets in the two other counties, in relative terms. This partially explains why Fresno County has grown to be America's most productive agricultural county in terms of total sales revenues per year. However, these CML results do not assist in crop production decisions of individual farmers, thus other performance indexes are needed.

Performance results for the sample portfolios are also presented in Tables 12.10 through 12.12. Those results provide evidence of the weakness of the Treynor-Black (1972) index compared to Blank's indexes in evaluating the risk/return tradeoffs among crop portfolios. Using the Treynor-Black index to rank and select from among the groups of portfolios in Tables 12.10 through 12.12 often leads to greater levels of diversification than that indicated using π_D as the decision criterion. The Treynor-Black index assumes only a small percentage of assets in the market portfolio are held by the investor. As a result, it breaks down as a performance measure because it will have an

Table 12.12

Diversification Analysis of Crop Portfolios from Yolo County

Portfolio[a]	Mean return	pi[b]	Beta[c] 29 yr	Beta[c] 10 yr	$\frac{\alpha}{\sigma(\epsilon)}$ [d]	Ω_p	π_{Dp} 29 yr	π_{Dp} 10 yr
1. Tomatoes, process	582	.800	2.58	2.88*	1.04	43.83	5.70	−58.54
2. Sugar beets	408	.921	1.98	2.11*	0.95	66.86	52.57	30.53
3. Rice	339	.966	1.71	1.84*	1.27	78.96	52.45	33.06
4. Corn, field	291	.982	1.46	1.51	1.97	110.07	49.85	
5. Wheat	255	.986	1.19	1.26	3.16	274.94	54.96	
6. Alfalfa hay	225	.991	1.12	1.16	3.15	313.59	37.81	
7. Safflower	203	.987	1.02	1.07	2.33	901.78	28.38	
8. Beans, dry	184	.998	1.08	1.05	11.34	59.98	4.46	
9. Grain sorghum	168	1.000	1.00	1.00	—	0	0	

[a] The portfolio number indicates how many crops are included. The crops in a portfolio are those listed from 1 down to the portfolio number. All crops included are equally weighted in each portfolio.

[b] This is the correlation coefficient between the portfolio listed and the market portfolio for the county made up of all crops listed in this table.

[c] These portfolio betas are calculated using data from 1958–86 and 1977–86, respectively. Asterisks indicate that the 10-year beta is significantly different than the 29-year beta according to a Chow test.

[d] This is the Treynor-Black index, as described in the text.

increasingly small denominator and eventually become undefined as portfolios diversify to become more similar in composition to the market index portfolio. This means it is biased in favor of more diversified portfolios. Selecting the portfolio with the highest π_D from each group/county leads to product mixes with three to five crops only. The Ω index often agrees with the selection made by the π_D, but never indicates a less diversified portfolio is best in any case.

The Ω's in Tables 12.10 through 12.12 nearly all indicate positive abnormal performance. This is due to the market index portfolio being defined as including all profitable crops from a county, thus giving it the lowest return per acre of all portfolios, and only portfolios of the most profitable crops being evaluated. Portfolios of less profitable crops would be more likely to have negative Ω indexes.

The Ω index is very sensitive to beta (a portfolio's risk relative to the market index portfolio). Portfolios with adjusted betas near one have the highest Ω because the denominators in Equation 12.20 become very small. This can create situations such as that for Fresno field and horticultural crop portfolios, where there is a local maximum that is not the global maximum. The three-crop portfolio is a local maximum that may, in fact, be the best choice (as indicated using π_D) even though the ten-, eleven-, and twelve-crop portfolios have higher indexes. This situation illustrates the need for a more robust index when making cropping decisions.

The π_D performance measure is intended as a tool for ranking any number of portfolios based on their return/risk tradeoff. To demonstrate its robustness as an addition to standard SIM procedures, the index's application in California's Yolo County is considered. The last two columns of Table 12.12 present values for sample portfolios. The column of index values calculated with the entire 29-year data set leads to portfolios 5, 2, and 3 being ranked first, second, and third, respectively. However, portfolios 1 through 3 have betas that are unstable over time. As a result, new betas reflecting the most recent levels are calculated using the most recent 10 years of data.

Table 12.13

Returns to Some Traditional Crop Rotations in the Sample Counties

	Gross income	
Crop combinations[a]	Mean ($/acre)	CV
Fresno County		
A-A-A-SB	103	139
A-A-A-C-SB	134	122
A-A-A-C-C-SB	155	117
Imperial County		
A-A-A-C-C-C	222	126
A-A-A-C-C-B	175	121
A-A-A-C-C-SB	454	169
A-A-A-C-B-SB	252	120
Yolo County		
A-A-A-SB-W-W	113	104
A-A-A-T-SB-W	192	96
A-A-A-SB-T-SB	212	103

[a] Assumes equal proportions for each crop symbol in the rotation. Symbols are defined as: A = alfalfa, B = barley, C = cotton, SB = sugar beets, T = tomatoes, and W = wheat.

Source: Blank 1990. All returns are in real 1986 dollars. Means and CVs are calculated using data from 1958–86.

Substituting the 10-year π_D values for the 29-year values leads to a change in the relative rankings of these sample portfolios; portfolios 2 and 3 become ranked fifth and fourth, respectively. Also of interest, portfolio 1's π_D value becomes negative when shifting from the 29-year to the 10-year index, indicating that one-crop portfolio's return/risk performance was not good over the 10-year period.

To illustrate the usefulness of the π_D index as a rule-of-thumb substitute for more complicated methods of determining the best level of diversification, the results from Tables 12.10 through 12.12 are compared with quadratic programming model results presented in Tables 12.7 through 12.9. The number of crops in the QP portfolios generally conforms to the 3-to-5-product range found to be the best in the diversification analysis. Also, comparing the results for individual counties shows general agreement between the results using π_D and the programming model. This means that the best production and marketing strategy for California growers may be to produce only the 3-to-5 most profitable crops identified using historical data.

Finally, previous assessments of cropping decisions (e.g., Carter and Dean 1960; Harper et al. 1991; Ramirez and Somarriba 2000; Turvey, Driver, and Baker 1988) have identified and evaluated "traditional" cropping rotations within counties or regions. The analysis often focused on a representative farm consisting of some fixed total acreage. The rotations usually were evaluated as a unit over the number of years required to complete the cycle. That approach specifically recognizes the need to maintain soil quality by including crops such as alfalfa in rotations, despite their low level of profitability. Table 12.13 presents some traditional crop rotations from the three sample counties to facilitate comparison with portfolio results. Ignoring alfalfa, which is included for purposes of soil conditioning, the crops in traditional rotations are somewhat similar to low-returning portfolios listed in Tables 12.10 through 12.12. In general, the traditional rotations have lower return and higher risk levels than the efficient portfolios, as would be expected, because the traditional rotations evolved through a trial-and-error process. Of interest here is that the number of crops in the sample of traditional rotations (2 to 4) generally conforms to the range (3 to 5) recommended by the portfolio performance measures.

SUMMARY

The business risks faced by agricultural producers are both varied and significant (Just 2001). The objective of this chapter is to assist decision makers in their assessment of market opportunities by introducing topics on the risks involved with agricultural enterprises and how to measure those risks. The focus is on income risk and its management. In particular, the portfolio approach to risk management is described as a method of crop portfolio creation and selection.

The rewards to diversification are evaluated. Four performance measures are used in the analysis, including two indexes derived to measure agricultural production portfolio performance. The index measuring the returns to limited diversification is shown to be a robust measure of crop portfolio performance. It can be calculated easily with a computer spreadsheet using historical data. A cross section of results from three counties is presented as a case study of the risks facing crop producers in California, although the analysis techniques illustrated in the chapter can be applied to the crop selection decision in any location.

NOTES

Some of this chapter is a revised version of an article published by S. Blank as "Returns to Limited Crop Diversification," *Western Journal of Agricultural Economics* 15, no. 2 (1990): 204–212.

1. Portfolio variance equals the sum of all variances and covariances weighted by the proportions invested in each i and j crop (there are n^2 terms to be summed, thus the double summation, $\Sigma\Sigma$). Equation 12.5 could be rewritten in the shorter version on the second line because $\text{Cov}(R_i, R_i) = [\sigma(R_i)]^2$, the variance term in the longer version.

2. The "opportunity set" is made up of the points on the efficient frontier plotted in mean returns-variance space (Markowitz 1959). It represents all efficient portfolios available to an investor, from which the desired portfolio will be selected. In this chapter, the opportunity set consists of efficient crop and livestock portfolios that can be produced in a geographic market.

3. Both diversification costs and revenues are measured here in \$/acre so they can be compared directly with additional costs of production incurred due to lost economies of scale when additional crops are produced and marketed (i.e., the level of diversification is increased).

4. This means that marketing and production concerns are separated in this approach to crop selection. It is assumed that efforts to maintain soil quality must be ongoing, therefore crops included in traditional rotations for that purpose should be excluded from decisions concerning how to allocate land not undergoing conditioning. Next, a marketing view is taken in choosing the best portfolio of crops to produce on available acreages.

5. No application of a programming model with a constraint on the number of securities in the portfolio could be found in the literature. On the other hand, in a stock market study, Sutcliffe and Board (1988) constrained each security's portfolio proportion to be below a particular positive value, thereby forcing additional diversification.

REFERENCES

Antle, John M. 1987. "Econometric Estimation of Producers' Risk Attitudes." *American Journal of Agricultural Economics* 69: 509–522.

Bard, S., and P. Barry. 2001. "Assessing Farmers' Attitudes Toward Risk Using the 'Closing-In' Method." *Journal of Agricultural and Resource Economics* 26: 248–260.

Barry, Peter J. 1980. "Capital Asset Pricing and Farm Real Estate." *American Journal of Agricultural Economics* 62: 549–553.

Blank, Steven C. 1990. "Returns to Limited Crop Diversification." *Western Journal of Agricultural Economics* 15 (2): 204–212.

———. 1995. "The New Risk Environment in California Agriculture." *Agribusiness: An International Journal* 155–168.

Bos, T., and P. Newbold. 1984. "An Empirical Investigation of the Possibility of Stochastic Systematic Risk in the Market Model." *Journal of Business* 57: 35–41.

Bosch, D., and C. Johnson. 1992. "An Evaluation of Risk Management Strategies for Dairy Farms." *Southern Journal of Agricultural Economics* 24 (2): 173–182.

Burton, R., Jr., M. Crisostomo, P. Berends, K. Kelley, and O. Buller. 1996. "Risk/Return Analysis of Double-Cropping and Alternative Crop Rotations with and without Government Programs." *Review of Agricultural Economics* 18: 681–692.

Buschena, D., and D. Zilberman. 1994. "What Do We Know About Decision Making Under Risk and Where Do We Go from Here?" *Journal of Agricultural and Resource Economics* 19: 425–445.

Carter, H., and G. Dean. 1960. "Income, Price, and Yield Variability for Principal California Crops and Cropping Systems." *Hilgardia* 30: 175–218.

Collins, Robert A. 1988. "The Required Rate of Return for Publicly Held Agricultural Equity: An Arbitrage Pricing Theory." *Western Journal of Agricultural Economics* 13: 163–168.

Collins, R., and P. Barry. 1986. "Risk Analysis with Single-Index Portfolio Models: An Application to Farm Planning." *American Journal of Agricultural Economics* 68: 152–161.

Coyle, Barry T. 1999. "Risk Aversion and Yield Uncertainty in Duality Models of Production: A Mean-Variance Approach," *American Journal of Agricultural Economics* 81 (1999): 553–567.

Crisostomo, M., R. Burton, A. Featherstone, and K. Kelley. 1993. "A Risk Programming Analysis of Crop Rotations Including Double-Cropping." *Review of Agricultural Economics* 15: 443–461.

Featherstone, A., and C. Moss. 1990. "Quantifying Gains to Risk Diversification Using Certainty Equivalence in a Mean-Variance Model: An Application to Florida Citrus." *Southern Journal of Agricultural Economics* 22 (1): 191–197.

Feder, G., R. Just, and A. Schmitz. 1980. "Futures Markets and the Theory of the Firm Under Price Uncertainty." *Quarterly Journal of Economics* 95: 317–328.

Ford, B., and W. Musser. 1995. "A Comparison of Nominal and Real Historical Risk Measures." *Journal of Agricultural & Applied Economics* 27 (2): 669–685.

Gempesaw, C., A. Tambe, R. Nayga, and U. Toensmeyer. 1988. "The Single Index Market Model in Agriculture." *Northeastern Journal of Agricultural and Resource Economics* 17: 147–155.

Harper, J., J. Williams, R. Burton, Jr., and K. Kelley. 1991. "Effect of Risk Preferences on Incorporation of Double-Crop Soybeans into Traditional Rotations." *Review of Agricultural Economics* 13: 185–200.

Harwood, J., R. Heifner, K. Coble, J. Perry, and A. Somwaru. 1999. *Managing Risks in Farming: Concepts, Research, and Analysis.* Economic Research Service, U.S. Department of Agriculture, Agricultural Economics Report No. 774, March.

Held, L., and G. Helmers. 1991. "Impact of Machinery Ownership Costs on Risk Efficiency and Farm Organization." *Review of Agricultural Economics* 13: 85–98.

Hueth, B., and E. Ligon. 1999. "Producer Price Risk and Quality Measurement." *American Journal of Agricultural Economics* 81: 512–524.

Irwin, S., D. Forster, and B. Sherrick. 1988. "Returns to Farm Real Estate Revisited." *American Journal of Agricultural Economics* 70: 580–587.

Jacob, N., and R. Pettit. 1988. *Investments.* 2d ed. Homewood, IL: Richard Irwin.

Jensen, Michael C. 1968. "The Performance of Mutual Funds in the Period 1945–1964." *Journal of Finance* 23: 389–416.

Just, Richard E. 2001. "Addressing the Changing Nature of Uncertainty in Agriculture." *American Journal of Agricultural Economics* 83: 1131–1153.

Just, R., and R. Pope, eds. 2002. *A Comprehensive Assessment of the Role of Risk in U.S. Agriculture.* Norwell, MA: Kluwer Academic.

Karolyi, G. Andrew. 1992. "Predicting Risk: Some New Generalizations." *Management Science* 38: 57–74.

Lehmann, B., and D. Modest. 1987. "Mutual Fund Performance Evaluation: A Comparison of Benchmark Comparisons." *Journal of Finance* 42: 233–265.

Lence, S., and D. Hayes. 1995. "Land Allocation in the Presence of Estimation Risk." *Journal of Agricultural and Resource Economics* 20: 49–63.

Levy, Haim. 1992. "Stochastic Dominance and Expected Utility: Survey and Analysis." *Management Science* 38: 555–593.

MacMinn, Richard D. 1984. "A General Diversification Theorem: A Note." *Journal of Finance* 39: 541–550.

Mahul, Oliver. 2001. "Optimal Insurance Against Climatic Experience." *American Journal of Agricultural Economics* 83: 593–604.

Markowitz, H. 1959. *Portfolio Selection: Efficient Diversification of Investments.* New York: John Wiley & Sons.

Martin, Laura L. 1997. "Production Contracts, Risk Shifting, and Relative Performance Payments in the Pork Industry." *Journal of Agricultural & Applied Economics* 29 (2): 267–278.

McCarl, Bruce A. 1990. "Generalized Stochastic Dominance: An Empirical Examination." *Southern Journal of Agricultural Economics* 22 (1): 49–55.

McSweeny, W., D. Kenyon, and R. Kramer. 1987. "Uncertainty in Risk Programming." *American Journal of Agricultural Economics* 69: 87–96.

Meyer, J., and L. Robison. 1988. "Hedging Under Price Randomness." *American Journal of Agricultural Economics* 70: 268–272.

Moss, C., R. Weldon, and A. Featherstone. 1991. "A Simple Approach to Evaluating Risk Diversification Opportunities." *Journal of the American Society of Farm Managers and Rural Appraisers* 55: 20–4.

Nartea, G., and P. Barry. 1994. "Risk Efficiency and Cost Effects of Geographic Diversification." *Review of Agricultural Economics* 16 (3): 341–351.

Oviatt, B., and A. Bauerschmidt. 1991. "Business Risk and Return: A Test of Simultaneous Relationships." *Management Science* 37: 1405–1423.

Pennings, J., and P. Garcia. 2001. "Measuring Producers' Risk Preferences: A Global Risk-Attitude Construct." *American Journal of Agricultural Economics* 83: 993–1009.

Pyle, D., and S. Turnovsky. 1970. "Safety-First and Expected Utility Maximization in Mean-Standard Deviation Portfolio Analysis." *Review of Economics and Statistics* 52: 75–81.

Ramirez, O., and E. Somarriba. 2000. "Risk and Returns of Diversified Cropping Systems Under Nonnormal, Cross-, and Autocorrelated Commodity Price Structures." *Journal of Agricultural and Resource Economics* 25: 653–668.

Reid, D., and B. Tew. 1987. "An Evaluation of Expected Value and Expected Value-Variance Criteria in Achieving Risk Efficiency in Crop Selection." *Northeastern Journal of Agricultural and Resource Economics* 16: 93–101.

Robison, L., and P. Barry. 1987. *The Competitive Firm's Response to Risk.* New York: Macmillan.

Ruefli, T., and R. Wiggins. 1994. "When Mean Square Error Becomes Variance: A Comment on 'Business Risk and Return: A Test of Simultaneous Relationships.' " *Management Science* 40: 750–759.

Seale, J., Jr., and J. Shonkwiler. 1987. "Rationality, Price Risk, and Response." *Southern Journal of Agricultural Economics* 19: 111–118.

Sharpe, William F. 1963. "A Simplified Model for Portfolio Analysis." *Management Science* 2: 277–293.

Siegel, Andrew F. 1995. "Measuring Systematic Risk Using Implicit Beta." *Management Science* 41: 124–128.

Sutcliffe, C., and J. Board. 1988. "Forced Diversification." *Quarterly Review of Economics and Business* 28 (3): 43–52.

Tew, B., W. Musser, and S. Smith. 1988. "Using Non-Contemporaneous Data to Specify Risk Programming Models." *Northeastern Journal of Agricultural and Resource Economics* 17: 30–35.

Treynor, J., and F. Black. 1972. "Portfolio Selection Using Special Information, Under the Assumptions of the Diagonal Model, with Mean-Variance Portfolio Objectives, and Without Constraints." In *Mathematical Models in Investment and Finance,* ed. G. Szego and K. Shell, pp. 367–84. Amsterdam: North-Holland.

Turvey, C., and H. Driver. 1987. "Systematic and Nonsystematic Risks in Agriculture." *Canadian Journal of Agricultural Economics* 35: 387–401.

Turvey, C., H. Driver, and T. Baker. 1988. "Systematic and Nonsystematic Risk in Farm Portfolio Selection." *American Journal of Agricultural Economics* 70: 831–836.

Walker, M., and K. Lin. 1978. "Price, Yield, and Gross Revenue Variability for Selected Georgia Crops." *Southern Journal of Agricultural Economics* 10: 71–75.

Weimar, M., and A. Hallam. 1988. "Risk, Diversification, and Vegetables as an Alternative Crop for Midwestern Agriculture." *North Central Journal of Agricultural Economics* 10: 75–89.

CHAPTER 13

PORTFOLIO DECISION MAKING OF FARMLAND OWNERS AND TENANTS

"Having been tenant long to a rich Lord,
Not thriving, I resolved to be bold,
And make a suit unto him, to afford
A new small-rented lease, and cancel th' old."
—George Herbert (1593–1633), British poet

When a farmer owns farmland, his production decision-making process includes at least two investment decisions. He must decide how to "invest" that land, as well as how to invest his labor resource. Farmers that do not own land have a different decision perspective. For example, the cash leasing rate per acre is a potential income source for landowners, while it is a cost of doing business for nonowners. Thus, cash leasing rates influence land investment and other decisions of farmland owners and tenants.

The cash leasing rate per acre of agricultural land is expected to reflect the potential returns to land from use in crop production. Surprisingly, the relationship between cash leasing rates and production returns to land has not received much attention despite its implications concerning the willingness of both owners and tenants to lease land, as well as their selection of crops to be produced on that farmland.

Crop market opportunities available to landowners vary over time and space (Weimar and Hallam 1988; Walker and Lin 1978; French 1987). It is possible that a landowner's risk preference might not be satisfied by any of the returns currently expected from producing specific crops. In this case, a landowner may consider leasing land out to someone whose risk preference makes them willing to accept the returns available (Apland, Barnes, and Justus 1984; Chambers and Phipps 1988). The short-run equilibrium rental rate for farmland was shown by Chambers and Phipps (1988) to depend on the distributions of the current farmland stock, entrepreneurial ability, and market prices of crops. This dependence implies that when an owner chooses to lease out land, the tenant differs from that owner in terms of ability and/or price expectations held (Gustafson 1989). However, another hypothesis is that owners and tenants with identical abilities, price expectations, and risk attitudes will still make different cropping decisions due to differences in their land holding status.

The objective of this chapter is to evaluate the effects of land holding status on the cropping decisions of two groups of producers: farmland owners and tenants. Portfolio theory is used to explain the decision environment of each group.

Previous studies of producers in the United States have focused on some given set of enterprises and have used varied approaches to calculate returns to land. Barry (1980) calculated

268

a residual return to farmland based on the USDA's *Balance Sheet for the Farming Sector.* Dobbins et al. (1981), and Melichar (1984) each found a relatively constant relationship between farmland values and cash rents or land returns over the 1970s to 1980s. In a study considering land tenure effects, Ellinger and Barry (1987) found that both accounting rates of return and debt-to-asset ratios increase as the ratio of leased land to total land operated increases. Also, Vanvig and Hewlett (1990) found a relationship between ranch size, the percent of leased forage, and ranch selling prices. International studies have focused considerable attention on the economic incentives and entrepreneurial requirements of sharecropping (examples include Otsuka and Hayami 1988; Rao 1971; Stiglitz 1974). Those studies evaluated the relationship between risk preferences and market expectations of owners and tenants in this form of land tenancy (Otsuka and Hayami 1988). However, Blank (1993) was the first to deal directly with cash leasing and land holding status effects on the choice of crops produced on a parcel of land.

Portfolio theory is well suited to this situation because it facilitates describing landowners and tenants as investors facing the decision of how to allocate their land (and labor) assets so as to maximize utility (Robison and Barry 1987). That is the approach taken in the next section to outline cropping opportunities of landowners and tenants. In later sections the effects of leasing rate changes are evaluated and the returns to risk for each group are estimated in an example.

A PORTFOLIO MODEL OF CROPPING OPPORTUNITIES

A person deciding whether to produce crops in a particular market must first identify the opportunities available in that market. Those opportunities can be plotted on an expected return-variance (EV) graph to facilitate analysis.[1] This is done for a hypothetical market in Figure 13.1. The curved line labeled EV represents the opportunity set available to crop producers within some geographic market. Each point on the EV is a crop or portfolio of crops that is efficient in terms of its return/risk relationship. The location and shape of the EV is determined by the data used to calculate expected returns for all portfolios.

If no leasing is possible for whatever reason, only landowners can produce crops. Each person would choose to produce the portfolio represented by the point on the EV that is tangent to one of his or her indifference curves. This leads to different crop portfolios being produced by owners with different risk attitudes.

If a risk-free investment exists, borrowing and lending can occur and the opportunity set available to growers is altered. In this assessment of land allocation in crop production, a risk-free return (R_f) to land is defined as the return per acre from cash leasing it to others (as suggested by Collins and Barry 1986). During the period covered by a cash lease, the landowner is guaranteed a specific return per acre that will not vary (Barry et al. 2000; Bierlen and Parsch 1996). Such a risk-free return is available only if an active market exists for cash leases on land (Robison and Barry 1987). Lending occurs when land is leased out to others, borrowing occurs when land is leased in from others. Lending land is analogous to investing in a risk-free asset, which has a return of R_f, and is plotted as a point on the vertical axis of an EV graph. Borrowing land implies that a producer chooses to invest more than 100 percent of the amount of land owned in some crop portfolio ϕ that is expected to generate returns per acre exceeding the leasing rate. For a borrower, $E(R_\phi) - R_f > 0$.

Landowner Cropping Opportunities

When leasing is possible, the separation theorem indicates that all landowners who have the same returns expectations will produce the same crops, although the composition of their selected

Figure 13.1 Cropping Opportunities for Farmland Owners and Tenants

Gross returns

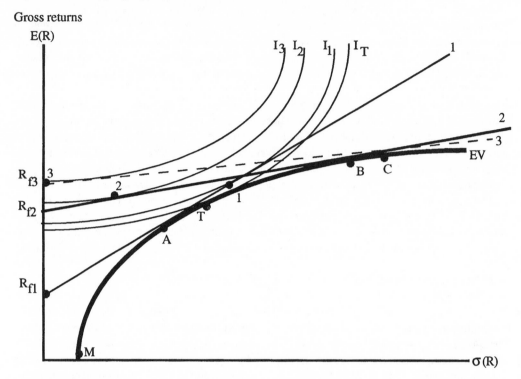

portfolios will still vary with their risk attitudes (Johnson 1967). Using the risk-free return, a single optimal risky portfolio and a landowner's cropping opportunities line (COL) can be identified. The COL for landowners is the capital market line (CML) concept from portfolio theory, which is described in Chapter 12. In this chapter, however, the CML concept is modified to fit the enterprise selection decision facing agricultural producers. As is shown later, the CML and COL are identical for landowners, but the COLs for landowners and tenants are quite different.

The COL represents the opportunity set available to landowners in a market (given some returns expectations). It is plotted as a straight line that passes through the point representing the risk-free return and is tangent to the EV. The COL dominates the EV at all points except where the two frontiers are tangent. The point of tangency represents the market's "optimal" portfolio, which has expected returns of $E(R_m)$. The optimal portfolio consists of the combination of crop (and/or livestock) enterprises that offers the best (i.e., most efficient) risk/return tradeoff given the producer's opportunities and risk attitudes. The portfolio that is actually selected by each owner is found at the point of tangency between this linear COL and an indifference curve for that person. The selected portfolio in this case is a mix of the market portfolio of crops and the risk-free asset and has expected returns of $E(R_\phi)$. The portions of the selected portfolio that are made up of land used in production and land leased out are determined by the producer's risk preferences, as reflected in his/her indifference curves.

For example, in Figure 13.1 the COL existing for landowners when leasing rates are the value R_{f1} is the line labeled "1," which is tangent to the EV at point A. If an owner's indifference curve is tangent to line 1 at point A, all of that person's land should be "invested" in the crops comprising the optimal portfolio represented by that point. If the indifference curve is tangent at some point to the left of A, the person will invest some land in producing portfolio A (the crops in the optimal portfolio) and the remaining land in the risk-free asset (by leasing that land out). Points on the COL to the right of A require an investment in portfolio A involving all of an owner's land and some land leased in. Thus, all land used for crop production by owners sharing the expectations represented by the EV will be planted to the same portfolio of crops in the same relative proportions. The only difference in composition of portfolios between owners will be the relative proportions of land each chooses to lease in or out. This result comes from the separation theorem, which suggests that the selection of the crop mix does not depend upon the decision maker's risk preferences, since it is constant along the COL. Instead, the amount of land leased in or out is the variable affected by risk preferences (see Johnson 1967; Turvey, Baker, and Weersink 1992 for further explanation of the separation theorem).

A landowner's profit function for holding his selected portfolio over some future period can be specified as

$$(13.1) \qquad E_o(\Pi_\phi) = E_o(GR_m)X_m + R_f X_f - OC$$

where Π_ϕ is net profit from selected crop portfolio ϕ, E_o is the owner's expectations operator, GR_m is gross returns from the market's optimal crop portfolio, R_f is the risk-free return from cash leasing out land, X_m is the proportion (or total number of units) of land planted in the market portfolio, X_f is the proportion (or total number of units) of land leased out (or leased in if negative), and OC is total fixed costs incurred in owning a parcel of land (including mortgage, property taxes, insurance, investments in improvements,[2] etc.), all expressed in per acre (or total dollar) terms. If X_m and X_f are expressed in terms of proportions (acres), they must sum to one (the total acres owned). The variance of returns for a portfolio held by a landowner is

$$(13.2) \qquad \sigma^2(\Pi_\phi) = X_m^2[\sigma^2(GR_m)]$$

where $\sigma^2(\Pi_\phi)$ and $\sigma^2(GR_m)$ are the variance in expected profits and gross returns of the selected and optimal market portfolios, respectively. The variance of the profit model is the variance of expected gross returns to the optimal portfolio component only because all other factors are known with certainty and, therefore, have zero variance.

In portfolio theory, utility maximization is assumed to be the objective. Therefore, the focus of decision making is the certainty equivalent of $E(\Pi_\phi)$, which Freund (1956) shows is

$$(13.3) \qquad E(U_\phi) = E(\Pi_\phi) - (\Lambda/2)\sigma^2(\Pi_\phi),$$

where U is utility and Λ is a risk-aversion parameter (equaling the slope of the indifference curve at the tangency point) that is positive for risk-averse hedgers.[3] The first-order conditions for Equation 13.3 give the utility-maximizing portfolio composition,

$$(13.4) \qquad X_m = \frac{E_o(GR_m) - R_f}{\Lambda \sigma^2(GR_m)},$$

subject to the constraint $X_m \geq 0$. Thus, Equation 13.4 shows what proportion (or total amount) of land owned should be used in the production of the market's optimal portfolio of crops. The proportion of land leased out or in (X_f in Equation 13.1) is $1 - X_m$.

Tenant Cropping Opportunities

Differences in the land holding status of owners and tenants alter the COL available to tenants and, therefore, the resulting cropping decisions. Tenants have no land to lend, so they can only borrow land. That means the COL available to tenants is a combination of the linear COL for owners and the curved EV. In Figure 13.1, for example, if line 1 is the COL for owners, the COL for tenants would be the segment of line 1 from point A to the right, plus the segment of the EV from points A to M.

The portfolios making up the EV are available to tenants as long as sufficient land is available to lease in. Portfolios on line 1 to the right of point A are also available only if land requirements can be met. Note that points on line 1 to the right of A represent the same combination of crops as in portfolio A, except that increasing total amounts of land are used as a grower moves further to the right on the line. This means portfolios on the EV, such as point C, require less land than portfolios on line 1 to the right of A.

A tenant would select a crop portfolio in the same manner as owners: the point of tangency between the COL and a person's indifference curve identifies the portfolio to be produced, if the prospective tenant chooses to undertake a lease. If the tangency point is at point A or to the right on line 1, the tenant will produce the same crops as a farmland owner with similar risk preferences— the optimal portfolio for that market. On the other hand, if a tenant's indifference curve is tangent to the COL somewhere to the left of point A, not having land to lease out means that the tenant's preferred portfolio on the COL is unavailable and he/she must select a portfolio on the EV, which is less risk efficient than points on line 1 to the left (i.e., line 1 dominates the EV in that it offers the same returns at lower levels of risk than available on the EV curve). Also, portfolios on the EV to the left of A are unique combinations of crops, not combinations of portfolio A and land leased out, as is the case for points to the left of A on line 1. This means that tenants and owners selecting portfolios to the left of A will be producing different crops.

A tenant's profit function for holding his selected portfolio over some future period can be specified as

$$(13.5) \qquad E_T(\Pi_\phi) = [E_T(GR_\phi)X_\phi] + [-X_\phi R_f]$$

where $E_T(GR_\phi)$ is the tenant's expected gross return from selected portfolio ϕ and X_ϕ is the amount of land in that portfolio. For tenants, the two X_ϕs must sum to zero, whether they are expressed in terms of portfolio proportions or acres, because no land is owned. When expressed as proportions, the weightings X_ϕ and $-X_\phi$ must be 1 and -1, since all land used is leased in and invested in crop portfolio ϕ. The variance of returns for a portfolio held by a tenant is $X_\phi^2[\sigma^2(\Pi_\phi)]$.

The focus of decision making by a utility-maximizing tenant is the certainty equivalent of $E_t(\Pi_\phi)$, which is expressed like Equation 13.3. This means that tenants face the same first-order conditions as owners and have a utility-maximizing portfolio composition,

$$(13.6) \qquad X_\phi = \frac{E_t(GR_\phi) - R_f}{\Lambda\sigma^2(\Pi_\phi)}$$

where $X_\phi \geq 0$. Equation 13.6 is similar to Equation 13.4 except that the optimal market portfolio is no longer the focus of production decisions, as it was for landowners; tenants produce portfolio ϕ.

EFFECTS OF CHANGES IN LEASING RATES

Comparing leasing rates to expected cropping returns leads to implications concerning the decision whether or not to produce and, if so, what crops to produce. For example, if the situation facing some individual landowners is $E_o(GR_m) < R_f$, those landowners would want to lease out all of their land to others and not engage in agricultural production. Demand for leased land in that case would depend on tenants' expected returns from production. On the other hand, if $E_o(GR_m) > R_f$, rational owners may not consider leasing out any of their land because higher returns are available to them from production of all combinations of efficient crop portfolios. Instead, landowners might want to lease in additional land.

Different cropping possibilities across time and spatial markets generate different levels of expected returns to land that, in turn, help explain land leasing rate differences between dates and locations. For landowners, gross returns from crop production are the alternative to leasing and earning the risk-free return. The higher the value of gross returns, the more incentive there is for owners to use their land for production rather than to lease it out to others. Demand for leased land depends on the expected value of net production profits to be earned by tenants. In a competitive market, if profit expectations are high, potential tenants may bid up leasing rates, reducing tenant profit expectations. Therefore, it is often necessary to specify a new COL to represent changing market opportunities available to landowners and tenants over time.

In this section, the effects of leasing rate changes on cropping decisions are discussed for landowners and tenants. To illustrate the effects of land holding status, as well, the remaining discussion will take the case of an owner and a tenant with exactly the same expectations concerning gross returns and with identical risk attitudes. It is hypothesized that leasing rates influence cropping decisions both directly and indirectly through other factors, as described below.

Direct Effects of Leasing Rate Changes

The first question to be addressed is what direct effects do changes in leasing rates have on cropping decisions of owners and tenants? To begin, it is assumed that a landowner and tenant each face a leasing rate of R_{f1}, making line 1 the relevant cropping opportunity line in Figure 13.1. The indifference curve I_1 reflects the risk attitudes of both people. Since I_1 is tangent to line 1 at point 1, the landowner and tenant would both select the same portfolio. Portfolio 1 requires that the landowner use all of his land and some additional land leased in for production of the crops in portfolio A (the market's optimal portfolio). The tenant would also produce the crops in portfolio A. (For now it is assumed that the tenant would be able to lease in the amount of acreage necessary to achieve the returns at point 1.)

If leasing rates increase to R_{f2}, cropping decisions of the owner change significantly. Line 2 in Figure 13.1 becomes the relevant COL for owners and it is tangent to the EV at point B. The owner's utility is increased, as indicated by the move from indifference curve I_1 to I_2. The new selected portfolio for the owner is at point 2. Portfolio 2 requires that the landowner use only part of his land for production of the crops in portfolio B (the new optimal portfolio), with the remaining acreage being leased out. The composition of portfolio B is clearly more risky than that of portfolio A. Hence, owners respond to increases in leasing rates by producing crops that are more risky, but they produce on fewer acres. As plotted, the difference between portfolios 1 and 2 is a slight reduction in expected returns and a large reduction in risk levels, resulting in an increase in the certainty equivalent (plotted at the intersection of the relevant indifference curve and the vertical axis). These results are summarized in the following proposition.

- PROPOSITION 13.1. *If cash leasing rates increase (decrease), landowners respond by producing a portfolio of crops that are more (less) risky, but they produce those crops on fewer (more) acres (i.e., a smaller [larger] proportion of acreage owned) and will lease out more (fewer) acres, yet they are better (worse) off because they will have a higher (lower) certainty equivalent return.*

The tenant will also change his cropping plans when leasing rates increase. If leasing rates increase to R_{f2}, the tenant's COL becomes the combination of line 2 in Figure 13.1 from point B to the right and the EV to the left of B. The tenant's utility is decreased, as indicated by the move from indifference curve I_1 to I_T (which is tangent to the EV at point T). The new selected portfolio for the tenant is at point T. The composition of portfolio T is clearly more risky than that of portfolio A although less risky than portfolio B. As plotted, the difference between selected portfolios I and T is a reduction in both expected returns and risk levels, resulting in a decrease in the certainty equivalent. Two propositions come from these results for tenants.

- PROPOSITION 13.2a. *If cash leasing rates increase, tenant farmers must produce a portfolio of crops that are more risky if they choose to remain in production, and their utility will drop, making them worse off.*
- PROPOSITION 13.2b. *If cash leasing rates decrease, tenant farmers may produce a portfolio of crops that are less risky and/or expand their operations, and their utility will increase, making them better off.*

Another difference between the new selected portfolios of the landowner and tenant is in their respective degrees of risk efficiency. Since the two decision makers are assumed here to have identical risk preferences, the tenant would also choose portfolio 2 if he could, but he is unable to do so because it requires leasing out land that he does not have. Due to differences in their ownership control over land, production efforts of the two people generate different portfolios: the owner produces crops in the optimal (risk-efficient) portfolio and the tenant produces his second-best alternative, which is the less efficient portfolio T. In this sense, the difference between the certainty equivalents of I_2 and I_T represents an opportunity cost (benefit) to tenants (owners).

- PROPOSITION 13.3. *In some circumstances, tenant farmers cannot select a crop portfolio available to landowners, forcing tenants to select a less risk-efficient portfolio and incur an opportunity cost equaling the difference in certainty equivalents of the two portfolios.*

If leasing rates increase further to R_{f3}, cropping decisions of the owner change again. Line 3 in Figure 13.1 becomes the relevant COL for owners and it is tangent to the EV at point C. The owner's utility is increased further, as indicated by the move from indifference curve I_2 to I_3. The new selected portfolio for the owner is at point 3. Portfolio 3 requires that the owner lease out all of his land. The composition of the optimal portfolio, C, is more risky than that of portfolio B and, considering the owner's risk preferences, C is too risky to produce given current leasing rates (which is why line 3 is dashed). As plotted, the difference between selected portfolios 2 and 3 is a relatively slight increase in expected returns and a total reduction in risk levels, resulting in another increase in the owner's certainty equivalent.

The tenant in this example will also cease production with leasing rates at this level. If leasing rates are R_{f3}, the tenant's COL becomes the combination of line 3 in Figure 13.1 from point C to the right, and the EV to the left of *C*. The selected portfolio for the tenant would remain at point *T*, but this is irrelevant because as plotted the expected gross return on portfolio *T* is less than the leasing rate, making production unprofitable and thus irrational for this person.

Effects of Risk Attitudes

The previous section assumed one set of risk preferences for a landowner and tenant; this section outlines how the cropping decisions might differ for two decision makers who were both more or less risk averse than the producers described in the analysis above. In particular, the issue addressed here is the possible effects of decision makers' risk attitudes on risk efficiency. Two propositions are derived from this analysis.

- PROPOSITION 13.4. *Being able to lease out land enables landowners to always select a risk-efficient crop portfolio.*
- PROPOSITION 13.5. *There is a positive relationship between tenants' degree of risk aversion, probabilities of being forced to select a risk-inefficient crop portfolio, and the opportunity cost that selection creates.*

For a landowner, being more or less risk averse would change his indifference curve and, hence, his choice of portfolios, but it would not change the risk efficiency of his selected portfolios. Landowners are always able to select a portfolio on the linear COL involving some efficient combination of the optimal portfolio and leasing (if leasing is possible). As is evident from Equation 13.4, a more (less) risk-averse owner would lease out a higher (lower) proportion of land than described earlier. Increasing values of Λ reduce the proportion of land used in production, thereby raising the amount of land to be leased out.

Across tenants, differences in risk aversion have more significance concerning efficiency of the selected portfolio. Tenants who are more risk averse are more likely to be forced to select a portfolio on the less risk-efficient EV segment of the COL. As can be seen in Equation 13.6, increasing the value of Λ (risk aversion) decreases a tenant's minimum desired level of returns, indicating that the point of tangency identifying the selected portfolio will move to the left. If it is to the left of the optimal portfolio, the tenant is on the EV segment and suffers an opportunity cost, as described earlier. Tenants who are less risk averse might avoid this problem but face another.

Credit Limit Effects

Tenants who are less risk averse are more likely to select a risk-efficient portfolio, but are also more likely to face lender resistance in the form of credit limits due to their higher "risk of ruin." Reducing the value of Λ (risk aversion) in Equation 13.6 increases the tenant's minimum desired level of returns, requiring greater amounts of leased-in land. At some point the tenant will not be able to obtain the desired amount of leased land (even if it is available) because his lender will not extend sufficient credit to do so.

Credit limits can have a significant affect on portfolio choice and its risk efficiency. This point can be illustrated using the case of an owner and tenant facing a COL like line 1 in Figure 13.1. Each grower would choose portfolio 1 if possible. If the owner needs to borrow additional funds to lease in land and expand production, he has the equity in his land to serve as collateral. The tenant, however, faces a much greater chance of being unable to borrow the full amount needed because he needs more funds (a tenant is leasing in *all* the land to be used in production, not just part of it like the owner) and has no equity in land to serve as collateral, hence, he may represent a more risky loan to the lender. If the tenant cannot borrow all the funds needed to produce the desired portfolio, he would find his new selected portfolio by moving to the left along his COL until the credit constraint was no longer binding. All opportunities on the COL to the right of the highest returning portfolio that can be funded are not available to the decision maker. This means for all growers credit constraints will, at some point, truncate the COL. For tenants, the lower their credit limits, the more likely they will be forced to select a portfolio on the less efficient EV portion of their COL. Also, it is important to note that *any* movement to the left on the COL due to credit limits reduces both expected and certainty equivalent returns. Such a reduction can be viewed as another opportunity cost (benefit) of lacking (possessing) land wealth.

- PROPOSITION 13.6. *Credit limits might force a farmer to select a less risky crop portfolio than desired, which, for a tenant, raises the probability of being forced to select a risk-inefficient crop portfolio and to incur the opportunity cost that selection creates.*

Profitability Considerations

The factor of leasing rates, R_f, is part of the profit functions for both owners and tenants (Equations 13.1 and 13.5, respectively), raising the question: Is the "profitability" of leasing rates considered when leasing decisions are made? This question must be answered separately for owners and tenants because they have different land acquisition costs. In this section, the "profitability" of a leasing rate is defined for owners in terms of whether it exceeds all fixed ownership costs (those included in variable *OC* in Equation 13.1). In other words, if leasing out land provides the owner with revenues (R_f) sufficient to cover all fixed costs (*OC*), the leasing rate is considered to be profitable: $R_f > OC$. For tenants, land acquisition costs are R_f, so "profitability" is positive if $GR_\phi > R_f$.

For owners, the answer to the question is "no." Whether leasing land out (which only owners are capable of doing) or in, leasing rate profitability is irrelevant to the decision; owners will produce on or lease out land based only on the interaction of their COL and risk preferences. This is true even if leasing out land is unprofitable (i.e., returns from leasing do not cover all fixed ownership costs). This result comes directly from the first-order conditions for owner utility maximization expressed in Equation 13.4. The only factors influencing the leasing decision of an owner are expected gross returns for the optimal portfolio, the variance of those returns, the opportunity cost of production (R_f), and the person's risk preference. Fixed costs of land acquisition, *OC,* are not in Equation 13.4.

For tenants, the answer to the question is "yes." When they lease land in (which is their only choice), gross returns to production represent the gross income received by tenants. These returns generate a net profit or loss when compared with the tenant's acquisition costs of that land—the leasing rates. Therefore, leasing rates are very relevant to the decision about leasing in land. Tenants will lease land in only if it is expected to generate a *net* profit. This result comes directly from the first-order conditions for tenant utility maximization expressed in Equation 13.6. The factors influencing the leasing decision in this case are expected net returns for the selected (rather than optimal) portfolio, the variance of those returns, and the person's risk preference.

Clearly, the difference between the cases of owners versus tenants facing a leasing decision is that owners consider the single optimal portfolio for the region and tenants focus their analysis on the selected portfolio, and leasing rates influence net returns of only the latter. This difference between groups is due to the fact that owners must consider their (unavoidable) fixed costs, which tenants do not have and, therefore, do not consider. In other words, owners are concerned about the gross profit from leasing while tenants are concerned about the net profit from leasing.

- PROPOSITION 13.7. *When making leasing decisions, tenants consider the "profitability" of leasing rates; landowners do not.*

The Decision to Produce Crops

The above discussion of profitability raises a question: At what point do owners and tenants decide to *not* produce? For owners this refers to the point at which they prefer to lease out all of their land. For tenants, deciding not to produce is equivalent to deciding not to lease in any land. Despite this difference in perspective, the answer to the question is the same for owners and tenants. Any potential grower will decide to not produce when the certainty equivalent of expected returns from the selected portfolio is less than or equal to the sum of all opportunity costs faced, as explained below.

As explained earlier, owners are concerned about the gross profits from leasing, therefore it is the certainty equivalent of expected gross returns that is relevant to their production decision. The opportunity costs incurred by owners involve both their land and labor assets. For a landowner, the foregone opportunity of investing land in crop production is the chance to collect cash lease payments, valued at R_f per acre. If a grower invests his own labor in crop production, he foregoes the opportunity to invest it off the farm, where it would be valued at the equivalent of $c_L L$ (the wage rate, c_L, times the quantity of labor "sold" off-farm, L, equals some average number of dollars per acre). Since both leasing out land and working for a wage off the farm are considered to be risk-free investments, it is clear why a necessary (although not sufficient) condition for crop production on the part of a landowner is

$$(13.7) \qquad\qquad E_o(U_\phi) \geq R_f + c_L L,$$

where $E_o(U_\phi)$ is the certainty equivalent of expected gross returns to selected portfolio ϕ and the factors on the right side are the opportunity costs.

Tenants are concerned about the net profits from leasing, therefore it is the certainty equivalent of expected net returns that is relevant to their production decision. The opportunity costs incurred by tenants involve only their labor assets since they own no land. If a potential tenant invests his labor in crop production, he foregoes the opportunity to invest it off the farm at a return of $c_L L$. Therefore, a necessary condition for crop production on the part of a tenant is

$$(13.8) \qquad\qquad E_T(U_\phi) \geq c_L L,$$

where $E_T(U_\phi)$ is the tenant's certainty equivalent of expected *net* returns to selected portfolio ϕ and the single opportunity cost is on the right side. This condition can be expressed as *gross* returns with the addition of the tenant's land acquisition costs, R_f, giving

$$E_T(U_\phi) \geq R_f + c_L L,$$

which is identical to Equation 13.7. This means that both owners and tenants, when facing a particular cropping opportunity, would reach the same conclusion about whether or not to produce.

- PROPOSITION 13.8. *A person's land holding status does not influence his or her decision about whether or not to produce an agricultural commodity, ceteris paribus.*

THE RETURNS TO RISK IN PRACTICE

The theoretical results presented in this chapter indicate that one aspect of the attractiveness of any cropping opportunity is reflected in the relationship between its returns and its risk. This relationship is expressed by the COL. Unfortunately, the optimal COL can be found in practice only if the EV frontier can be estimated, which requires data and sophisticated software that few potential growers possess. Yet, a simple trial-and-error method for ranking cropping opportunities is available that eliminates the need to derive an EV frontier. It involves calculating the slope coefficient of the COL created by any potential cropping opportunity. Each slope estimate can then serve as an index value that allows ranking of alternate opportunities, as described below.

The slope of the cropping opportunity line for landowners,

$$(13.9) \qquad \Delta_o COL \equiv \frac{E_o(GR_m) - R_f}{\sigma_m(\Pi_m)},$$

is literally the reward for bearing production risk, per unit of such risk, offered by the market in which the farmer is operating. The numerator is gross returns to production of the optimal portfolio in the market minus the opportunity cost of the land asset. The labor opportunity cost does not have to be included because it will not vary across cropping alternatives and, therefore, will not affect the relative rankings of those alternatives.

To measure a tenant's returns to risk in leasing, another index can be calculated,

$$(13.10) \qquad \Delta_T COL \equiv \frac{E_T(GR_\phi) - R_f}{\sigma_\phi(\Pi_\phi)},$$

where the numerator is net returns to production of the crop or portfolio being considered. Again, the labor opportunity cost does not have to be included because it will not affect the relative rankings of those alternatives.

The two indexes can be used by owners and tenants in selecting which crops to produce. Both indexes provide a measure of returns to risk for a single crop or portfolio that can be compared directly with values for other crops, facilitating cropping decisions.[4] Opportunities can be ranked from best to worst regarding the return/risk tradeoff expected in each market. Crops with the highest index values offer the best tradeoff, while crops with negative values should not be considered at all. Which crops are chosen depends on the grower's risk preferences, but the indexes can be useful inputs to that decision for all individuals.

To illustrate the relationship between crop production returns and cash leasing rates, returns to risk were calculated by Blank (1993) for crops grown in California's Imperial County. Table 13.1 summarizes his results from the annual data. The means and standard deviations for each crop were calculated from time series of "real" returns (1986 dollars) extending from 1958 through 1986. The third column in the table presents actual leasing rates adjusted from Reed and Horel (1980). The fourth column is the returns to risk from each crop for tenants. The weighted average value of $\Delta_o COL$ is expected to reflect the marketwide returns to risk for owners. Gross returns from the county's market portfolio, GR_m, are calculated using profitable crops weighted according to their portion of total acreage of profitable crops in the county.

Table 13.1

Gross Income, Leasing Rates, and Returns to Risk for Crops Grown Profitably in Imperial County ($/acre)

Crop	Gross income mean	Gross income std dev	Actual lease	$_T$COL	$_O$COL
Alfalfa hay	88.32	129.99	125	−.285	
Alfalfa seed	91.23	79.77	125	−.425	
Asparagus	159.53	715.41	150	.014	
Barley	73.01	78.32	100	−.346	
Cantaloupes	718.42	555.92	150	1.022	
Carrots	617.92	1,138.42	150	.411	
Cotton	354.88	469.68	125	.489	
Onions, dry	469.70	909.80	150	.352	
Oranges	565.91	703.87	150	.591	
Sugar beets	818.74	1,535.03	125	.452	
Weighted Market Average* (GR$_m$)	258.99	384.29	129		.338

Source: Ian (3).

Note: All amounts are in real   dollars.   rops gro n in the county but   hich had negative mean returns for the data periods are not listed here.

*These results are for all products listed   eighted according to each crop s percentage of total acreage.

Returns to risk for crops in Imperial County vary widely, as reported in Table 13.1. At one extreme there are three crops with negative values for Δ_TCOL. This means that only owners or overly optimistic tenants would choose to produce these crops. Since a negative Δ_TCOL indicates a net loss for a tenant, anyone producing alfalfa hay or seed or barley on leased land must be expecting returns far above the historical means for those products. Also, these three low-returning crops may be part of a selected portfolio because of their diversification effects when combined with more risky crops. On the other hand, all three of these crops could be produced by landowners as part of a rotation aimed at conditioning the soil. In this case, the owner might not be expecting to cover costs from the products themselves, but expects to improve future returns from other crops to be grown on the land after conditioning.

The seven crops with positive values for Δ_TCOL are easily ranked, but different selections will still be made across growers with different risk preferences. Cantaloupe has the highest value of Δ_TCOL for any single product, meaning that it offers the best return/risk tradeoff in the county market. As a result, it could be selected by tenants or owners as part of the preferred portfolio. Yet decision makers who value returns more heavily than they fear risk might favor adding sugar beets, the crop ranked highest by risk-neutral growers, to their portfolio. Sugar beets are the risk-neutral choice because they offer the highest mean returns. On the other end of the continuum, highly risk-averse growers are more likely to include cotton in their portfolios because it offers the lowest level of risk for the seven crops with positive returns to risk, as indicated by its standard deviation of returns.

Cotton results in Table 13.1 illustrate why the returns to risk index can be useful in making cropping selections. Of the seven crops offering positive net profits to tenants, cotton is ranked sixth in terms of mean income. This ranking, combined with cotton's low level of risk, might give the impression that only highly risk-averse growers should consider this crop. However, cotton's

Δ_7COL index ranks third in the county market, meaning that cotton may be a valuable portfolio component for both owners and tenants seeking a tradeoff between returns and risk. Without considering the index, this opportunity might have been overlooked.

SUMMARY AND CONCLUSIONS

This chapter uses portfolio theory to evaluate the effects of leasing rates on the cropping decisions of two groups of producers with different land holding status—farmland owners and tenants. From simple models of cropping opportunities available to each group it is found that differences in the factors considered when making crop selections do exist. The net effect of these differences is that tenants might not be able to choose the same risk-efficient crop portfolio that is always available to landowners.

Leasing rates are shown to have direct and indirect effects on cropping decisions of both groups of growers. It is shown that owners respond to increases in leasing rates by producing crops that are more risky, but they produce on fewer acres. Although tenants will also produce a riskier portfolio, they suffer a loss of utility from leasing rate increases while owners gain. Also, tenants who are more risk averse may suffer further because they are more likely to be forced to select a risk-inefficient portfolio. Credit limits are another factor that might force tenants to select a less efficient portfolio.

The "profitability" of leasing rates (as defined here) is shown to be irrelevant to owners deciding whether or not to produce, but it is the major criterion used by tenants making that decision. When facing a leasing decision, owners focus on the optimal portfolio and tenants focus on the selected portfolio, and leasing rates influence returns of only the latter. This difference between groups is due to the fact that owners must consider their (unavoidable) fixed costs, which tenants do not have and, therefore, do not consider.

Differences in land holding status also cause the two groups to focus on different data in decision making: owners make cropping decisions based on gross returns to risk, tenants use net returns to risk as the appropriate measure. The formulas used to empirically estimate these two indexes are shown to be nearly the same. Therefore, the decision-making processes of owners and tenants are virtually identical, but differences in land holding status will, ceteris paribus, generate results leading, on average, to lower returns and higher risk exposure for tenants.

NOTES

Some of this chapter is a revised version of an article published by S. Blank as "Effects of Farmland Cash Leasing Rates on Crop Selections of Owners and Tenants: A Portfolio Analysis," *Agricultural Finance Review* 53 (1993): 1–14.

1. Although expected utility maximization is the objective of decision making in portfolio theory, graphical EV analysis is used here because it simplifies the presentation of relevant economic concepts. Also, Freund (1956) showed that shifting from mathematical expressions in EV analysis to expected utility analysis is made easy by focusing on the certainty equivalent of expected returns. However, much literature argues that two-moment decision models are consistent with expected utility maximization only if the choice set or the agent's preferences are restricted (Levy 1974; Levy and Markowitz 1979). Yet Meyer (1987) noted that common restrictions, such as quadratic utility or normality assumptions, are not required for EV and utility maximization to be consistent. He showed that the location and scale condition, which fits many economic models (like the one here), is sufficient to ensure that an EV ranking of elements in a choice set is consistent with an expected utility maximization ranking of random variables.

2. Some land-improvement investment costs can be partially shared with tenants. For example, durable soil conservation investments can be partially covered in a share lease (Lichtenberg 2007).

3. Equation 13.3 is based on negative exponential utility and normality, although similar specifications can be derived using quadratic utility or other assumptions.

4. These indexes are very similar to the first-order conditions expressed in Equations 13.4 and 13.6. Whereas those conditions are to be maximized, it does not necessarily follow that a grower would select the cropping opportunity with the highest index; the indexes do not include the risk preference parameter, so it is not possible to judge how a person would view the return/risk tradeoff reflected in the index value.

REFERENCES

Apland, A., R. Barnes, and F. Justus. 1984. "The Farm Lease: An Analysis of Owner-Tenant and Landlord Preferences Under Risk." *American Journal of Agricultural Economics* 66: 376–384.

Barry, Peter J. 1980. "Capital Asset Pricing and Farm Real Estate." *American Journal of Agricultural Economics* 62: 549–553.

Barry, P., L. Moss, N. Sotomayor, and C. Escalante. 2000. "Lease Pricing for Farm Real Estate." *Review of Agricultural Economics* 22: 2–16.

Bierlen, R., and L. Parsch. 1996. "Tenant Satisfaction with Land Leases." *Review of Agricultural Economics* 18: 505–513.

Blank, Steven C. 1993. "Effects of Farmland Cash Leasing Rates on Crop Selections: A Portfolio Analysis." *Agricultural Finance Review* 53: 1–14.

Chambers, R., and T. Phipps. 1988. "Accumulation and Rental Behavior in the Market for Farmland." *Western Journal of Agricultural Economics* 13: 294–306.

Collins, R., and P. Barry. 1986. "Risk Analysis with Single-Index Portfolio Models: An Application to Farm Planning." *American Journal of Agricultural Economics* 68: 152–161.

Dobbins, C., T. Baker, L. Dunlap, J. Pheasant, and B. McCarl. 1981. "The Return to Land Ownership and Land Values: Is There an Economic Relationship?" Agriculture Experiment Station Bulletin, no. 311, Purdue University, February.

Ellinger, P., and P. Barry. 1987. "The Effects of Tenure Position on Farm Profitability and Solvency: An Application to Illinois Farms." *Agricultural Finance Review* 47: 106–118.

French, Ben C. 1987. "Farm Price Estimation When There Is Bargaining: The Case of Processed Fruit and Vegetables." *Western Journal of Agricultural Economics* 12: 17–26.

Freund, R. 1956. "The Introduction of Risk into a Programming Model." *Econometrica* 24: 253–263.

Gustafson, Cole R. 1989. "Controlling Farmland in the Red River Valley: A Stochastic Dominance Analysis of Alternative Means." *North Central Journal of Agricultural Economics* 11: 243–251.

Johnson, S. 1967. "A Re-examination of the Farm Diversification Problem." *Journal of Farm Economics* 49: 610–621.

Levy, Haim. 1974. "The Rationale of the Mean-Standard Deviation Analysis: Comment." *American Economic Review* 64: 434–441.

Levy, H., and H. Markowitz. 1979. "Approximating Expected Utility by a Function of Mean and Variance." *American Economic Review* 69: 308–317.

Lichtenberg, Erik. 2007. "Tenants, Landlords, and Soil Conservation." *American Journal of Agricultural Economics* 89 (2): 294–307.

Melichar, E. 1984. "A Financial Perspective on Agriculture." Federal Reserve Bulletin, no. 1: 1–13.

Meyer, Jack. 1987. "Two Moment Decision Models and Expected Utility Maximization." *American Economic Review* 77: 421–430.

Otsuka, K., and Y. Hayami. 1988. "Theories of Share Tenancy: A Critical Survey." *Economic Development and Cultural Change* (October): 31–68.

Rao, C. Hanumatha. 1971. "Uncertainty, Entrepreneurship, and Sharecropping in India." *Journal of Political Economy* 79 (May–June): 578–595.

Reed, A., and L. Horel. 1980. "Leasing Practices for California Agricultural Properties." Leaflet 2359, Division of Agricultural Sciences, University of California, various issues.

Robison, L., and P. Barry. 1987. *The Competitive Firm's Response to Risk,* Chapter 12. New York: Macmillan.

Stiglitz, Joseph. 1974. "Incentives and Risk Sharing in Sharecropping." *Review of Economic Studies* 41 (April): 219–255.

Turvey, C., T. Baker, and A. Weersink. 1992. "Farm Operating Risk and Cash Rent Determination." *Journal of Agricultural and Resource Economics* 17 (1): 186–194.

Vanvig, A., and J. Hewlett. 1990. "The Relationship of Ranch Size and Percent of Leased Forage and Ranch Selling Prices." *Journal of the American Society of Farm Managers and Rural Appraisers* 54 (2): 38–44.

Walker, M., and K. Lin. 1978. "Price, Yield, and Gross Revenue Variability for Selected Georgia Crops." *Southern Journal of Agricultural Economics* 10: 71–75.

Weimar, M., and A. Hallam. 1988. "Risk, Diversification, and Vegetables as an Alternative Crop for Midwestern Agriculture." *North Central Journal of Agricultural Economics* 10: 75–89.

CHAPTER 14

IS THE MARKET FAILING PRODUCERS WHO WISH TO MANAGE RISKS?

> *"Round up the usual suspects."*
> —Captain Renault, in *Casablanca*

The risk faced by agricultural producers is captured mostly by the variability of annual net income levels. This risk is a function of variability in output price, yield, input prices, and input quantities. Yet the financial tools available to manage some of this risk may be underutilized. For example, price risk tools (primarily forward cash contracting and hedging with futures or options) and yield risk tools (primarily crop insurance) are not widely used by producers in the United States. This is somewhat surprising considering that the expansive theoretical literature has long demonstrated that primary commodity producers stand to derive considerable risk-reduction benefit from hedging, forward contracting, and/or insuring. This raises the question, is the market failing to provide agricultural producers with effective risk management tools? If the answer to the question is "no," it indicates that producers are voluntarily accepting their level of risk exposure, implying that they might be less risk averse than assumed in most research. However, if the answer is "yes," it means that there are some attributes of the available risk management tools that conflict with the structure of agriculture and/or commodity markets. This would have significant policy implications, especially in light of the current trend toward placing responsibility for risk management on the producer and the market, rather than on government, as illustrated by changes enacted since the mid-1990s in federal crop insurance aimed at eliminating disaster aid programs.

This chapter adopts the Tew et al. (1985, p. 58) definition of "market failure" as "the underprovision of public goods by private market mechanisms." The question of market failure is addressed by comparing producers' demand for price and yield risk management tools with the actual tools available in a sample of California commodity markets. As such, the results here are a case study indicating the types of issues faced by producers anywhere when wanting to manage economic risks. It is expected that a market will provide tools that are designed to effectively manage the primary sources of risk faced by producers. Farm managers' needs for specific risk management tools are identified using both historical statistical data and data collected in a survey of producers.

The chapter begins with results of a survey of California farmers and ranchers concerning their perceptions regarding risk and their use of risk management tools. Next is a statistical assessment of the relative importance of price and yield risk in income volatility over time among a sample of agricultural products in California. This is followed by a brief discussion of market failure and policy implications.

283

SURVEY RESULTS REGARDING RISK NEEDS

Agricultural producers were surveyed concerning their risk needs. A mail survey with some follow-up interviews was used. Conducted by the author during 1993 across California, the survey generated 569 responses. Respondents were representative of the state's diverse agriculture because a stratified random sampling process assured that, as a whole, they covered a wide geographical and commodity base.

Following the example of previous studies (such as Patrick et al. 1985), several sources of risk were identified in the survey, falling into two general categories: production risks such as pests, drought, floods, freeze, and labor availability; and market risks such as output price, physical factor input cost, and labor cost. Producers were asked to rank the sources of risk in order of importance. The results of this ranking, presented in Table 14.1, reveal that production risk concerns are second to market risk among producers in California. Producers ranked output price and input costs as first and second, respectively, among their risk concerns. However, the significant number of responses received by each of the detailed types of risk listed in the table indicates the detail of producers' concerns; it is not just "price" or "yield" that concerns individual producers. This, in turn, indicates a need for varied and detailed risk tools.

The concern for output and input price risk expressed in the survey leads to expectations of high levels of use of price risk management tools. However, the data showed that a small minority of producers used each of the risk management tools that directly affect price: 23.4 percent used forward contracting and only 6.2 percent used hedging. Similarly, the rankings for the many sources of yield risk listed in Table 14.1 (disease, drought, etc.) make the low level of usage for crop insurance (24.4 percent) somewhat surprising. On the other hand, nearly half of all producers (47.6 percent) used the indirect risk management tool of diversification. These results can be interpreted as evidence indicating that the price and yield risk tools offered in the California market fail to meet the needs of most producers, so producers choose to "do it themselves" by using diversification. Diversification is a risk-reducing strategy requiring no use or knowledge of risk tools and their associated institutions (e.g., market brokers, insurance companies). Also, by definition, diversification is a risk strategy that involves actions on the part of individual producers that are tailored to their specific management needs.

ANALYSIS OF RISK SOURCES

To determine what producers' risk management needs are, the first task is to establish the relative importance of price and yield risk. This can be done by decomposing the variability of farm revenues to discover the percentages attributable to each primary source of variability. (Revenue, rather than net income, was used because data on input prices and use levels were not available.)

Revenue is a function, $R(P,Y,A)$, that equals the product of the three variables: $P \times Y \times A$; where R is revenue, P is unit price for a particular commodity, Y is the yield per acre, and A is the number of acres planted in that crop (all for a given year or season). The variance of revenue can be viewed in terms of the three components of revenue. Analysis of these components focuses on their relative weight, or contribution to the overall variability of a grower's revenue. (Statewide acreages over time are evaluated, making total acreage variation one source of systematic risk to individual growers.) The sections below explain how revenue decomposition is used to identify the greatest source of risk facing growers of specific crops in California.

Table 14.1

Sources of Risk (% of rank)

Sources of risk	1st	2nd	3rd	4th	5th	6th	7th	8th	Total no. of Observations
Disease	16.6	17.0	13.1	16.3	14.0	11.2	8.8	3.0	465
Drought	25.5	15.7	11.9	8.9	9.4	10.2	11.7	6.6	470
Floods	1.5	6.6	3.3	3.9	3.6	6.3	13.5	61.3	333
Freeze	19.9	16.8	8.9	7.6	7.8	11.2	14.8	13.0	447
Input price	12.5	21.3	21.1	13.6	14.9	9.7	4.6	2.2	445
Labor cost	8.9	12.4	13.5	13.1	15.7	16.9	11.3	8.2	451
Output price	32.0	25.9	14.6	11.1	7.1	4.4	2.9	1.9	478
Pests	12.4	17.9	20.4	14.3	17.2	8.8	5.9	3.2	476
Write-in responses:									
Other	35.6	15.6	13.3	17.8	6.7	2.2	2.2	6.7	45
Govt. Regulations	41.9	19.4	12.9	12.9	3.2	0.0	3.2	6.5	31
Competition/trade	66.7	0.0	0.0	33.3	0.0	0.0	0.0	0.0	3
Weather	47.2	25.0	13.9	8.3	5.6	0.0	0.0	0.0	36

Note: The first column lists a source of risk. The next eight columns list the percentage of respondents that ranked that source of risk as first most important, second, etc. The percentages in each row are calculated on the total number of responses received listed in the last column.

Statistical Treatment

The variance of a random variable (such as revenue) is defined as the expected value of the square of the difference between that random variable and its mean, or

$$(14.1) \qquad \sigma^2(R) = E([R - \mu_R]^2),$$

where E is the expectations operator and μ_R is the mean of revenue. To analyze the contributions of variability in price, yield, and acres to the variability in revenue, it is necessary to decompose the revenue variance term.

This is accomplished by replacing the random variable for revenue (R) with its function

$$(14.2) \qquad R \equiv P \times Y \times A$$

which yields

$$(14.3) \qquad \sigma^2(P \times Y \times A) = E\{[(P \times Y \times A) - E(P \times Y \times A)]^2\}.$$

All random variables (R, P, Y, and A) are observed for the same time period, therefore time subscripts are not shown here or in other equations. Decomposing the variance is the focus of the analysis, thus all three components of revenue (P, Y, and A) are allowed to vary.

The complete expression for the decomposition of the variance of a product of three random variables is both elaborate and ambiguous for the purposes of this analysis (see Bohrnstedt and Goldberger 1969). The actual variance term is composed of many terms that themselves consist of cross effects between varying orders of random variables. It is difficult to interpret the covariance between some pairs of random variables from the revenue function in Equation 14.2. For these reasons, an alternative method of decomposing the variance of revenue is needed. One method that lends to the separation and estimation of the direct and indirect effects of individual random variables on the variance of an identity is the log transformation. (Samples of other methods are illustrated in Burt and Finley 1968; Offutt and Blandford 1983; Hazell 1984; and Myers, Piggott, and Tomek 1990.) By taking logs, the data become stationary and the analysis becomes much simpler (by avoiding the Taylor series expansions that would be necessary if the data were not transformed). Applying the log transformation to the identity in Equation 14.2 yields

$$(14.4) \qquad ln[R(P,Y,A)] \equiv ln(P) + ln(Y) + ln(A).$$

Using Equation 14.4 and the definition of the variance from Equation 14.1 yields the following variance expression for the log transformation of revenue:

$$(14.5) \qquad \sigma^2\{ln[R(P,Y,A)]\} \equiv \sigma^2[ln(P)] + \sigma^2[ln(Y)] + \sigma^2[ln(A)] - 2\text{Cov}[ln(P),ln(Y)] \\ - 2\text{Cov}[ln(P),ln(A)] - 2\text{Cov}[ln(Y),ln(A)],$$

where Cov is the covariance of the indicated variables. The advantage of this approximation is that it consists of terms that are clearly direct effects of the variance of individual random variables (the first three terms of Equation 14.5) as well as interpretable indirect effects or covariance effects (the later three terms). The six terms in Equation 14.5 are those estimated in this chapter.

When using data spanning several time periods there may be a trend present that serves to distort the actual variance. This trend may be present in the actual revenue data or in any of the three components of the revenue function. One problem with trended economic time series is that the variance of the random variable increases with the level of that random variable. This nonstationarity invalidates the estimation of a single variance statistic for the series. The log transformation performed on the three components of revenue serves to correct for the effect of trend on the stationarity of the variance. Prior to applying the log transformation, the revenue components (price, yield, and acreage) are fitted and corrected for trend. This is a more direct approach to correcting for time trend and serves to stabilize both the variance and the mean of the random variables. Once detrended, the values for the direct and cross effects of the individual components of revenue may be expressed as a percentage of the total variance or as a percentage of total direct effects.

Estimation of Variance Decomposition

The revenue variance of a sample of twelve California crops was decomposed to establish the relative importance of price versus yield risk. Annual data from 1972–1991 was used (the data were reported in the *California Statistical Abstract*, California Agricultural Statistics Service, 1972–1993). The first step of the revenue decomposition process involves identifying and eliminating any time trends in the data for each crop. The three variables that comprise revenue are evaluated for any time trend using the following regression analysis of the variable of concern (V) plotted against time (t):

$$(14.6) \qquad V = \alpha + \beta t + \varepsilon.$$

For the purposes of this study, the t statistic for the estimate of the regression coefficient β is used as an indicator of the power of the relationship over time. Any regression yielding a t statistic significant at the 95 percent level indicates a trend.

The purpose of identifying a trend in the data is to obtain a measure of variance about the trend for that random variable. The desired outcome is to eliminate the effects of the trend on the variance of the random variable. One way to do this is to remove the trend from the original random variable and use the detrended random variable in calculating the (stationary) mean, variance, and covariances. With no trend present, the original random variable is used to calculate the mean, variance, and covariances in order to evaluate the variance decomposition formula described in Equation 14.5.

Next, the relative contribution of the individual components of the decomposed revenue variance can be evaluated in either of two ways. The first approach is to express each component as a proportion of the total variance of revenue. A more common approach is to express each component as a percentage of the total direct effects on variance. More explicitly, all terms in Equation 14.5 would be divided by the sum of the first three terms. This results in the sum of the first three percentages all being positive and summing to 100, while the remaining three percentages may take either sign and any value. The latter, more common approach is used here to generate the results in Table 14.2.

The values in Table 14.2 are estimates of the contributions of the direct variance terms and the covariance terms from Equation 14.5 as a percentage of the sum of the three direct variance terms. The columns $\sigma^2[ln(P)]$, $\sigma^2[ln(Y)]$, and $\sigma^2[ln(A)]$ are the direct variance contribution of price, yield, and acreage, respectively. The next three terms $\{(Cov[ln(P),ln(Y)],\ Cov[ln(P),ln(A)],\ Cov[ln(Y),ln(A)])\}$ refer to the covariance terms between price and yield, price and acreage, and yield and acreage, respectively. The column "Trend" indicates which random variables display significant time trends for the years 1972–1991.

The first term of importance is the contribution of price variation to the total variation in revenue. For eight of the twelve crops analyzed it is clear that price variation is dominant over variation in yield or acreage (as a percentage of total direct variation). Growers in California who produce any of these crops are experiencing price risk disproportionate to the other sources of risk in their revenue. This suggests there ought to be some grower demand for a price risk tool like hedging or forward contracting.

Two crops (peaches and wheat) exhibit a dominant contribution from yield variability to total revenue variation, and another crop (oranges) has yield variation nearly equal to its price variation. Growers of these crops may have a strong preference for a yield risk management tool such as crop insurance.

Only one crop exhibits a majority contribution from acreage variation, although a second crop has significant acreage variation. The percentage variation coefficient for processed tomatoes is high enough to allow neither price variation nor yield variation to dominate the share of total direct variation, although price variation appears to be more important. Rice acreage variation is also important as a possible indirect effect on price. These industries tend to be volatile in size, thus growers of crops like these may need varied pricing tools.

Larger positive values for the covariance terms represent higher correlation between the two random variables being considered. Large negative values for covariance between price and yield, like those estimated for almonds and oranges, indicate a competitive market in which the California industry is a sizable contributor. The other two columns of covariances have values that are generally insignificant.

Table 14.2

Estimated Revenue Variance Decomposition Percentages

Crop	$\sigma^2[ln(P)]$	$\sigma^2[ln(Y)]$	$\sigma^2[ln(A)]$	Cov[ln(P), ln(Y)]	Cov[ln(P), ln(A)]	Cov[ln(Y), ln(A)]	Trend
Alfalfa hay	85.7	3.8	10.5	3.1	−19.2	−1.0	P,Y,A
Almond	56.5	42.2	1.3	−34.1	3.6	−2.9	P,A
Cotton	85.5	4.4	10.1	−3.8	7.3	−1.7	P,Y
Grapes, table	59.1	35.4	5.5	−9.8	−13.0	−0.6	P,A
Lemons	56.8	40.2	2.9	−3.9	−3.6	−3.6	P,A
Lettuce	69.2	17.2	13.6	−17.2	−11.2	6.5	P,Y
Oranges	50.9	48.6	0.5	−40.2	−1.0	−0.5	P,Y,A
Peaches	32.2	51.9	15.8	4.4	4.9	14.8	P,Y,A
Pears	72.7	13.6	13.6	3.9	−3.2	−2.5	P,Y,A
Rice	56.1	3.1	40.8	−0.2	15.1	0.5	P,Y
Tomatoes, process	38.3	8.7	53.0	−5.5	26.4	−2.5	P,Y
Wheat	10.6	65.1	24.3	5.8	7.2	−0.7	P

Notes: P is price, Y is yield, A is acreage, R is revenue, σ^2 is variance, Cov is covariance. The variables listed in the last column are those testing positive for a trend.

General Remarks

Much can be learned from a variance decomposition. The dominance of a particular risk source within the revenue formula indicates a crop for which a specific type of risk management tool may be needed. In addition, relationships between the three variables may become evident because the covariance terms shed light on both direction and significance of correlation. If one can distinguish between endogenous and exogenous variables, then causality may be determined between pairs of variables as well. All of this lends insight to the decisions made by producers of certain crops, as well as suggesting remedies for lowering the variance of revenue.

As a group, these results indicate that producers' needs for risk management tools vary across commodities. Neither price nor yield risk is always dominant, and differences in the degree of importance between price and yield can be large (e.g., alfalfa has a wide difference, whereas oranges do not).

MARKETS FOR RISK MANAGEMENT TOOLS: FAILING, MISSING, OR INCOMPLETE?

With market failure defined as the underprovision of goods by market mechanisms, failure in the markets for commodity risk management tools appears to be common. However, the nature of the "failure" in specific commodity markets ought to be evaluated. If the failure to offer a tool to manage a particular risk is connected with uncertainty, there may be a case for government intervention because according to Layard and Walters (1978, p. 25), "for a free market to be efficient, there must be no market failure connected with uncertainty." If the failure is connected with risk, the market is operating efficiently and interventions could create inefficiencies (Radner 1970). Uncertainty is present when the probabilities of each possible outcome cannot be estimated objectively; risk is present when objective probabilities can be estimated for each possible outcome (Knight 1933; Robison and Barry 1987).

In general, two types of failure can be identified: "missing markets" and "incomplete markets." A missing market is one in which no exchange occurs between buyers and sellers. If this failure is connected with risk, there is no exchange because equilibrium exists at zero quantity, as illustrated in Panel A of Figure 14.1. The supply price is higher than the demand price at all non-negative quantities. To the extent that the market is connected with risk, the supply price is higher at all quantities by some amount equaling the seller's risk premium (Robison and Barry 1987). In such a case, the supply price facing consumers can be effectively lowered through the intervention of government or some other third party who is willing to pay suppliers some portion of the price for the tool. For example, federal subsidies to farmers are paid to insurers for selling crop insurance to farmers at discounted prices, thus increasing the market supply of insurance (shifting the supply schedule to the right) because subsidies compensate insurers for accepting the problems of moral hazard and adverse selection. At some level of intervention, a positive equilibrium quantity will occur. For example, in Panel B of Figure 14.1, a subsidy equaling P_s minus P_c per unit has shifted the supply schedule to the right so that equilibrium is found at quantity Q_c. The price per unit paid by consumers is P_c and the price received by suppliers is P_s. The total cost of the subsidy is the area of rectangle P_sABP_c. Also, an increase in demand can result in a positive equilibrium (Daly and Mayor 1980). For example, in Panel C of Figure 14.1, increased demand has shifted the schedule so that equilibrium is found at quantity Q_d. Therefore, markets connected with risk will be "missing" only as long as equilibrium quantities equal zero. Conversely, a market connected with uncertainty will not offer a risk tool because no positive equilibrium

Figure 14.1   **A Missing Market**

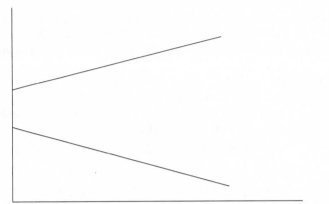

Panel A. Equilibrium equals zero quantity

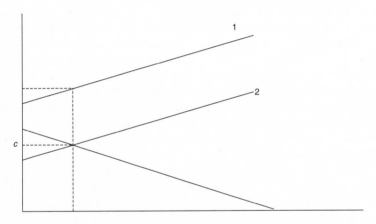

Panel B. Subsidy increases market supply

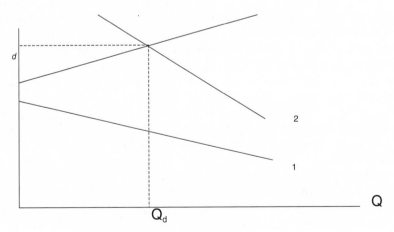

Panel C. Increased demand

quantity can be found. Whereas supply and demand schedules can be found under risk by using the probabilities from the relevant frequency distribution, no schedule can be calculated for supply or demand under uncertainty. Without some expectations regarding the frequency distribution, sellers or buyers cannot define their schedule. Therefore, a market with one or both schedules (supply, demand) undefined will always be "missing." In this chapter, a missing market for a risk tool is specified as one in which no tool is offered for managing a particular source of risk (i.e., price, yield, etc.) for a particular commodity.

An incomplete market, in this context, is one in which at least one tool exists for managing a particular source of risk in a commodity market, but that tool is not suitable for use by all producers. An unsuitable tool would not be used by a producer, even if the tool's price was zero. A tool is unsuitable for use by a producer if it is "incomplete" in addressing the source of risk faced by the individual; the tool is not expected to reduce risk exposure or to provide insurance against that exposure (Heaton and Lucas 1996). This type of market failure may be connected with either risk or uncertainty, but is more likely due to risk (Innes and Rausser 1989). If a tool exists that is of use to some, but not all, producers, then the relevant frequency distribution(s) must be known. The tool serves some portion of the distribution, but not all. This is a special case of a missing market for some segment of a known population that cannot be served economically.

RISK TOOLS IN COMMODITY MARKETS

A market can fail producers who wish to manage risks in either of two ways. Evidence of both types of failure is presented here as the results of two simple tests.

First, a market is "missing" if no tool is available for managing a producer's primary source of risk. California producers face missing markets for both price and yield risk management tools, as shown in Table 14.3. The columns state, respectively, whether or not futures contracts, cash forward contracts, and crop insurance are available to producers of the commodities considered in this study. Comparing the results in Tables 14.2 and 14.3 reveals that half of the crop markets (alfalfa hay, almonds, table grapes, lemons, lettuce, and pears) are missing a tool for the primary source of risk faced. In general, there are relatively few price risk management tools available even though price is the primary source of risk facing most producers in California. As a result, all of the missing markets lack *price* tools; the few markets requiring yield tools have insurance available. Interestingly, both futures and forward contracts are tools offered by *private* market participants, as opposed to the public source for federal crop insurance.

Are producers aware of, and concerned about, their price risk exposure? The answer to both questions is "yes," as indicated by the survey data shown in Table 14.4. The table presents a brief summary of producers' perceptions concerning price risk and actual levels of price risk faced by producers. The first column presents a measure of actual price risk: the coefficient of variation of historical prices. The second column, labeled "Price Not Stable," gives the percentage of producers of this commodity (where this is their primary commodity) who said their output price changes more than 25 percent between years. The fact that the data in the first two columns are positively correlated ($\rho = .63$) is evidence that producers are aware of their price risk exposure. The last column, labeled "High Price Risk," gives the percentage of producers of this commodity (their primary commodity) who ranked output price variability as their greatest source of risk. Strong concern for price risk is evident.

Table 14.3

Price and Yield Risk Management Situation for Selected Commodities in California

Commodity	Futures contracts available?	Forward contracts available?	Crop insurance available?
Alfalfa hay	Indirectly	No	Yes
Almonds	No	Some	Yes
Cotton	Yes	Some	Yes
Grapes, table	No	No	Yes
Lemons	No	No	Yes
Lettuce	No	Rare	No
Oranges	Indirectly	No	Yes
Peaches (fresh)	No	Rare	Yes
Pears (fresh)	No	No	Yes
Rice	Yes	No	Yes
Tomatoes, processing	No	Yes	Yes
Wheat	Yes	Rare	Yes
Feeder cattle	Yes	No	No
Fed cattle	Yes	No	No

Note: Crop insurance covering only yield variability is considered here. Revenue insurance is not considered.

Table 14.4

Producers' Perceptions of Price Risk for Selected Commodities

Commodity	CV (%)	Price not stable (%)	High price risk (%)
Alfalfa hay	12	19	48
Almonds	27	17	58
Cotton	10	35	37
Grapes, table	14	31	45
Lemons	42	100	33
Lettuce	49	82	64
Oranges	57	64	45
Peaches, fresh	47	33	44
Pears, fresh	45	10	40
Rice	12	0	33
Tomatoes, processing	6	0	43
Wheat	14	20	40
Feeder cattle	16	19*	45*
Fed cattle	12	*	*

Notes: CV is the coefficient of variation.
* The survey made no distinction between producers of fed and feeder cattle.

Table 14.5

Insurance by Commodity: Number of Growers Surveyed, Number Insured

Commodity	Number of growers	Number insured	Percent insured
Alfalfa	98	1	1.0
Almonds	87	40	46.0
Apples	19	1	5.3
Apricots	7	1	14.3
Barley	8	2	25.0
Beans	24	4	16.7
Cherries	6	1	16.7
Cotton	64	1	1.6
Figs	1	1	100.0
Grapes, raisin	22	16	72.7
Grapes, table	62	12	19.4
Grapes, wine	15	4	26.7
Lemons	12	1	8.3
Nectarines	9	2	22.2
Oranges	59	16	27.1
Peaches	24	1	4.2
Pears	18	1	5.6
Plums	18	7	38.9
Potatoes	10	1	10.0
Prunes	20	1	5.0
Sugar beets	24	3	12.5
Tomatoes	28	8	28.6
Walnuts	62	6	9.7
Wheat	53	9	17.0
Other fruit	21	1	4.7
Other vegetable	28	1	3.6

Note: The three columns present, respectively, the number of respondents in the survey who currently produce the crop listed, the number of those growers who are currently insured, and the percentage of respondents who are insured for that crop. The total number of growers exceeds the survey response because many growers produce two or more crops.

The second test identifies evidence of incomplete markets. It is expected that producers would use a tool to manage their most important source of risk if such a tool was available and reasonably priced. However, if usage levels for that tool are low, it indicates that the tool is ineffective. For example, based on producers' risk needs shown in Table 14.2, crop insurance should be used by growers of oranges, peaches, and wheat to manage their yield risk, but the data in Table 14.5 show that most of those growers are not insured. This means that despite the government subsidy reducing the price of federal crop insurance to growers, a majority of market participants believes the tool does not reduce their risk exposure sufficiently to justify purchasing it. (This may signal problems of risk pooling and/or risk spreading.)

The results in Table 14.5 are made easier to interpret by aggregating them into two categories of commodities: (1) tree and vine crops, versus (2) vegetable and field crops. Totaling the values from the three columns for these crop categories gives:

	Number of growers	Number insured	Percentage insured
Tree and vine crops	462	112	24.2
Vegetable and field crops	337	30	8.9

These summary results indicate that tree and vine crop producers are nearly three times more likely to be insured than are vegetable and field crop growers. To explain this result, one needs only to recognize that perennial crops requiring multiyear investments are being insured more often than are annual crops. Obviously, a larger investment is required for a perennial and that investment is "at risk" over a much longer period, meaning that there is a higher probability of suffering a loss with a perennial.

It is the low probability of suffering a yield loss large enough to trigger an insurance indemnity payment that makes federal crop insurance ineffective for most growers in California (Blank and McDonald 1996). Therefore, the markets for tools to manage the yield risk of many commodities are incomplete because a significant number of growers find the tools unsuitable and will never use them.

RISKY BUSINESS

Market failure is readily apparent in the markets for tools to manage risks related to commodities produced in California, and the same is true in other states. The markets for tools to manage price risk associated with particular commodities are often missing. All of the pricing tools available are provided through private market mechanisms. Yield risk management tools, which are usually offered through public market mechanisms, are incomplete.

These missing and incomplete markets are not all "market failures" of the sort that indicate inefficiencies that might justify government intervention. For example, crop insurance markets appear to be incomplete, indicating a market failure connected with risk (Miranda and Glauber 1997). In such a market, government intervention may create inefficiencies. On the other hand, markets for price risk management tools are often missing due to uncertainties about the effects of human behavior on prices. This implies that government interventions that create additional tools for price risk management might be justified. This partly explains why new "revenue insurance" policies are being developed by the USDA's Risk Management Agency.

If government intervention in agriculture is reduced, which was the general direction of recent agricultural policy before the 2002 farm bill, the effects on producers will vary across commodities. The decomposition of revenues from a sample of commodities showed that most producers' greatest needs for risk tools involve those that manage price variability. However, most government intervention in risk tool markets involves production levels. Therefore, reduced intervention (such as eliminating crop insurance subsidies) will have a greater effect on producers of crops for which yield risk is most important, such as wheat, corn, and soybeans grown in the Midwest. Since all price risk tools are offered by private markets, eliminating government support for agriculture may not eliminate producers' ability to manage price risk. These results indicate that policymakers ought to consider the relative importance of price and yield risk to each commodity affected by a proposed change in intervention levels. A preliminary consideration conducted by independent agricultural economists indicates that revenue insurance may grow to be very popular with producers of many commodities, thus possibly raising the overall effectiveness of government insurance efforts.

These results also partially explain why most producers use "do-it-yourself" risk management tools such as enterprise diversification. When markets fail to provide effective tools for managing risk, especially income risk, producers must develop alternative risk management plans that they can implement on their own. In the next chapter, the most commonly used tool is discussed: hedging with off-farm income. It is a "do-it-yourself" tool and a form of enterprise diversification that is proving to be both popular and necessary for agricultural producers.

APPENDIX: WHO USES PRICE RISK MANAGEMENT TOOLS?

Commodity producers stand to derive considerable price risk reduction benefit from hedging with either futures contracts or forward cash contracts, according to both theoretical and empirical research literature. The literature appears to contradict reality, however, because very few primary producers actually hedge. For example, a 1977 survey by the Commodity Futures Trading Commission (CFTC) found that only about 7 percent of U.S. grain farmers used futures, and many of those farmers were speculating rather than hedging. Only 20 percent of the farmers surveyed by the CFTC had ever used forward contracting. Little has changed in subsequent years. The 1993 mail survey conducted across California found that only 6 percent of respondents reported use of futures and 23 percent reported use of forward contracts. A much larger survey conducted in 2002 (discussed at the end of this appendix) found little change in the overall shares of producers in California using futures, options, and forward contracting (Lee and Blank 2004). Also, the CFTC survey found that farmers prefer forward contracting to direct hedging with futures contracts. Forward contracts are a substitute for futures contracts, as both provide an opportunity to reduce price risk. However, neither tool dominates the other as there are pros and cons of using one versus the other. Why do so few farmers hedge against price risk with either futures or forward contracts? This appendix uses survey data to explore the question further by investigating economic factors and firm characteristics that influence a producer's decision to hedge in California.

Data and Procedures

The 1993 California survey responses were used with probit regression analysis to derive models that best predict what type of producer will use either futures or forward contracts. For the hedging model, all observations had to correspond to producers whose main enterprise is traded on a futures market. Thus, only data from respondents whose main enterprise was either cattle, cotton, wheat, or rice were used when estimating the futures model, providing 114 observations. Data for all commodities were used to estimate the forward contracting probit model as forward contracts are widely available. Forward contracting only requires a two-party agreement, which can transpire at any time. Thus, forward contracts are always available despite their sometimes infrequent use. However, only 393 respondents included debt/asset information, thus the data set was constrained to those observations.

The following 15 variables were chosen to represent a producer's predisposition toward using risk management tools: operation size (acres, assets, total sales); experience (years farming, age, education); financial variables (off-farm income, debt/asset ratio); price fluctuation (perceived price risk, price stability, and input price risk); use of risk management tools (futures hedging, forward contracting); and knowledge of price risk management (storage of unpriced commodity as speculation, knowledge of futures markets).

The general format of the model to estimate the probability of a producer hedging with either futures or forward contracts follows the convention

(14.7)   Probability of Hedging $= \alpha + \beta X + \varepsilon$

where α denotes the intercept, X denotes the matrix of independent variables, β denotes the coefficient vector for the independent variables X, and ε is the random error term.

The following variables and their descriptions comprise the list of independent variables used in both the futures hedging and forward contracting models.

Acres = size of enterprise in acres.

Assets = total assets. This is a continuous variable measuring the farmer's reported assets in millions of dollars.

Assets² = total assets squared.

Knft = knowledge of futures markets. This is a dummy variable corresponding to an answer of yes (= 1) or no (= 0) to the question of whether or not the farmer is knowledgeable about the use of futures markets.

Off-farm = off-farm income. This is a cardinal variable representing the proportion of household income attributable to off-farm or nonagricultural sources.

OutPrSt = actual output price stability. The response to this question is measured in rank. The rank varies from 1 to 3, where 1 denotes the most stability and 3 denotes the most variability of historical prices.

OtPtRk = perceived output price fluctuation. This variable is of the same nature as *OutPrSt*, only it measures the importance of output price variation as a risk source relative to other risk sources.

Tsales = total gross sales for the operation. An ordinal ranking of the producer's total gross sales classification was obtained from the survey. The range for this variable is 1 to 6, where a classification of 1 represents the total gross sales bracket $0 to $25,000 and the classi- fication of 6 corresponds to the total gross sales bracket of $1,000,000 or more.

Store = storage as speculation. The question asks whether the respondent considers storage of an unpriced commodity to be speculation. This dummy variable takes on the value of 1 for a "yes" answer, and 0 for an answer of "no."

Age = age. This dummy variable has values of 1 indicating age 46 or older and 0 indicating age 45 or younger.

Futures Hedging Model Results

A small number of growers who indicated that they hedged using options were aggregated with those who hedged using futures markets. Certain producer characteristics elicited by the survey were expected to influence risk attitude. For example, the person's age was included in the regression model as a proxy for experience. The grower's assets were used as a measure of financial stability and size. One question asked whether or not the individual considers storage of an unpriced crop to be speculation; the correct answer to this question is "yes" and therefore the answer to this question is a good proxy for a farmer's awareness of the relationship between futures markets and price risk.

The objective is to determine which variables best characterize an individual who hedges with futures, and this can be measured by the significance of the coefficients and the prediction success table for the probit model. In several instances, more than one survey question may reasonably proxy a single determinant of an individual's preference toward risk and risk management (*Size* and *Assets,* for example). Therefore, a correction procedure was implemented to eliminate the spread of explanatory power across several variables that might proxy a similar characteristic.

Table 14.6 lists the futures hedging model regression results. Several variables significantly influence the probability that an individual will hedge. The *Asset* and *Assets-squared* variables are significant and have the correct sign. Assets are considered a measure of operation size, and the *Asset* variables better represent size than does acreage. Some smaller-acreage, higher-value, and more capital-intensive crops differ in financing from the larger-acreage, lower-value and less capital-intensive crops. It is expected that a producer's probability of using hedging could increase as his/her level of assets (financial size) rises, but that this increase is of decreasing magnitude as the level of assets continues to increase.

The variable signaling some knowledge of futures markets (*Knft*) was also significant. This indicates the importance of education or experience in risk management. It also suggests that training growers about hedging might increase the general level of use of this tool.

The output price stability variable (*OutPrSt*) measures the price stability of a grower's primary commodity. An alternative indicator of variability used in the preliminary model was the rank (relative importance) of output price variability among risk sources for each producer, *OtPtRk*. Although theory suggests that either variable (and certainly one of the two variables) could be statistically significant, the most significant variable had a *t*-ratio of only 1.46, which is not significant even at the 90 percent level.

A dummy variable indicating the use of forward contracting was also used in the final hedging model. The primary purpose of this variable was to indicate a predisposition toward the use of forward pricing tools as well as to provide some insight into the relationship between the use of different risk management tools. The estimated coefficient for *Forward* was both significant and positive. This suggests a correlation between the use of forward contracting and the use of hedging, as discussed later in this appendix.

The futures hedging model's predictions were fairly accurate. The model accurately identified individuals who do not hedge 95 percent of the time. The percentage of predicted hedgers who actually hedge was 78 percent. Therefore, the overall prediction success rate for the model was 83.3 percent.

Forward Contracting Model Results

The same attributes that influence a grower to hedge are expected to influence a grower's use of forward cash contracts. As with futures hedging, the underlying concern in forward contracting is managing price risk. The same general approach was taken with the forward contracting model as with the hedging model except that more observations were available. The final model, found in Table 14.7, lists the estimated coefficients and their associated *t*-ratios. Some notable differences exist between the models.

The forward contract model includes a number of significant variables representing individual producer attributes, operation attributes, and market attributes. The variables *Age* and *Store* embody the experience and knowledge of futures transactions for that person. The sign of the estimated coefficient for the *Age* variable was negative, signifying that older producers are less likely to use forward contracts than are younger producers. If age is considered a proxy only for knowledge of price risk management tools and the variability of prices in the primary crop, then the sign and significance of the coefficient on this variable contradict expectations. In fact, age

Table 14.6

Futures Hedging Model Estimation Results

Variable name	Coefficient	t statistic
Assets	0.00000019	2.82 (**)
Assets-squared	-0.154×10^{-14}	-1.90 (*)
Knft	0.9039	2.91 (**)
OutPrSt	0.3591	1.46
Forward	0.5470	1.80 (*)
Constant	-2.7090	-4.21 (**)

 ragg Uhler ^{2} 0. 0 n   .
 *   oef cient is statistically signi cant at the 0   level.
 **   oef cient is statistically signi cant at the   level.

Table 14.7

Forward Contract Model Estimation Results

Variable name	Coefficient	t statistic
Assets	-0.0744	-1.98 (**)
Assets–squared	0.0010	1.42
Acres	0.00004	1.64 (*)
Off–Farm	-0.2294	-1.66 (*)
OtPtRk	-0.0892	-2.30 (**)
Age	-0.1993	-2.30 (**)
TSales	0.2655	4.09 (**)
Hedge	0.9217	3.54 (**)
Store	0.2717	1.60
Constant	-0.9103	-1.98 (**)

 ragg Uhler ^{2} 0.3 n   3 3.
 *   oef cient is statistically signi cant at the 0   level.
 **   oef cient is statistically signi cant at the   level.

may represent many different grower perceptions and characteristics such as financial position (debt/assets), operator planning horizon, experience in crop diversification, or experience in marketing. Each of these qualities or perceptions may contribute to the significant negative sign on the estimated coefficient for the age variable.

The variables indicating the operation's size are *Acres, Asset, Assets-squared,* and *TSales* (total sales). The estimated coefficients for these variables have conflicting signs. While the coefficient on *Acres* was positive, supporting the notion that operations of larger physical size are more likely to forward contract, the negative coefficient for the *Asset* variable shows the contrary for financial size. One possible explanation for the conflict between these two similar variables is that tenant farmers, who have relatively few assets, may be forward contracting more often than owner operators. The coefficient on the *TSales* variable is positive and highly significant. This indicates a positive relationship between high total gross sales (income) and the propensity to forward contract.

The estimated coefficient for *Off-Farm* income is negative and significant, indicating a lower probability of using forward contracts if nonagricultural income is present. Small-scale operators, in particular, are more likely to have off-farm income. If total income is considered for the farmer, then diversifying income out of agriculture may have a stabilizing effect on the variability of total income from year to year, provided the alternative income source is relatively stable. The proportion of total income susceptible to the fluctuations in agriculture is smaller when income diversity is present. Hence, income diversity is its own form of risk management tool which, when used, could make forward contracting less attractive to that farmer.

The dummy variable indicating whether the grower is a futures hedger was highly significant and positive. As with the futures hedging model, where the variable for use of forward contracts was positive and significant, the result here signifies some correlation between applications of the two price risk management tools by a grower.

The overall prediction success ratio for the forward contract model was 84.7 percent. Thus, the two models performed about equally well.

Comparison of Hedging and Forward Contract Models

The indexes of operation size appear to have different effects for the two different models. The futures hedging model relies on the variables *Assets* and *Assets-squared* to represent an operation's financial size. The signs of the estimated coefficients of the quadratic form of the relationship indicate that the size of the operation contributes positively to an individual's decision to hedge, while displaying a decreasing marginal contribution to this decision. The forward contract model, on the other hand, estimates a negative coefficient for the *Assets* variable. This implies that the financial size of the operation has a negative effect on the propensity to forward contract. The squared component of the quadratic form is positive (although insignificant), thereby having the same decreasing marginal contribution (in the negative sense). These results imply that an operation's financial size (*Assets*) greatly affects an individual producer's choice among the two price risk management tools. This result suggests the price risk management tools are substitutes but differ in their suitability for use across operating scales. The large, fixed size of futures contracts may make them more suited to large-scale operations, while the flexible size of forward contracts makes them more attractive to small-scale operators.

The indices for knowledge and experience for the models were *Knft, Age,* and *Store*. The hedging model favored a producer's professed knowledge of futures markets (*Knft*). This result indicates that increased knowledge of futures and options markets should raise the level of participation in such markets. The experience and marketing knowledge evidenced by *Age* and *Store* in the forward contracting model are estimated to be better indexes for identifying producers who employ forward contracts, rather than futures.

Although three forms of price stability data were used in the initial model iterations for both price risk tools, the end results were somewhat different. In both final models an indicator for output price variability was significant. The difference between the two models lies with the form of output price risk. In the hedging model, the *OutPrSt* (output price stability) variable was preferred. This variable reflects historical output price fluctuations—an absolute measure of risk. The forward contracting model preferred the variable *OtPrRk* (output price risk), which is a rank of output price risk among several risk sources—a relative risk measure. This measure reflects risk perceptions rather than actual variation in output price. Therefore, a producer may observe high output price variability and yet be more concerned with other sources of risk. This implies that futures hedgers are reacting to short-term price fluctuations while forward contract users may be more risk averse and want to reduce price risk over the long-term.

Financial indicators of the operation appear only in the forward contract model. This implies that futures hedging as a price risk management tool is estimated to be independent of the status of finances in the operation. The forward contract model results indicate that off-farm income is a substitute for forward contracting and that income stability (high total sales) is a positive contributing factor to the use of forward contracts. However, the direction of causality is unclear. Additional research is needed to determine whether producers seek off-farm income because forward contracts are unavailable (or poorly suited to their needs), or if they seek forward contracts only when off-farm income is unavailable

Finally, it is clear by comparison of the estimated models that growers who already employ one of the two price risk management tools are more likely to employ the other than are growers who do not. This result may be considered an indication of a grower's knowledge of, or comfort level with, price risk management tools. A grower already using one price risk management tool (futures hedging or forward contracting) must be somewhat knowledgeable of the concepts and process and, therefore, is more likely to employ the other tool if deemed necessary. Although the tools serve similar purposes, there are differences between them that may influence the use of one tool over another in certain situations. Futures are flexible in allowing easy market entry and exit, but are unavailable for many commodities. On the other hand, forward contracts are fairly rigid in entry and exit while being available for many commodities.

Conclusions and Follow-Up

The 1993 survey of California farmers found that only 6 percent use futures and 23 percent use forward contracting to manage price risk. These findings imply that the theory of hedging may incorrectly predict the current usefulness of futures and forward contracts to farmers. The California survey results are consistent with a CFTC survey of U.S. grain farmers conducted in 1977. Farm size, degree of price instability, and a grower's knowledge of futures all have significant positive impacts on the likelihood of a farmer hedging with either futures or forward contracts.

Another survey of California producers was conducted in 2002 (Lee and Blank 2004). The project mailed questionnaires to over 35,000 farmers in the state who grew specialty crops (among other things). Over 15,000 responses were received. The data revealed that hedging with futures was available to only 3 percent of California producers (meaning that there were no futures markets for the commodities grown by 97 percent of farmers). Forward contracting was available to only 13 percent of respondents in 2002. Although this "self-reported" availability may understate the actual case somewhat, it clearly indicates that access to price risk tools has not significantly improved in at least a decade. What has increased is producers' willingness to use the tools when they are available. For futures hedging, 29 percent of respondents who said the tool was available reported using it regularly. For forward contracts, 68 percent of producers use the tool when it is available to them. This implies (1) that farmers are well aware of their price risk exposure and want to manage it, and (2) that farmers will use well-designed risk management tools if they are available. This is evident in the 2002 survey data for crop insurance, which shows that the expanded insurance programs of the past decade have raised the level of use of that tool from the 24.2 percent reported earlier in this chapter for tree crop growers to 53 percent, and from

8.9 percent to 31 percent for vegetable growers. Unfortunately, the poor level of availability for price risk tools indicates that the market is still failing producers.

NOTE

Some of this chapter is a revised version of an article published by S. Blank, C. Carter, and J. McDonald as "Is the Market Failing Agricultural Producers Who Wish to Manage Risks?" *Contemporary Economic Policy* 15, no. 3 (1997): 103–112.

REFERENCES

Blank, S., and J. McDonald. 1996. "Preferences for Crop Insurance When Farmers Are Diversified." *Agribusiness: An International Journal* 12: 583–592.

Bohrnstedt, G., and A. Goldberger. 1969. "On the Exact Covariance of Products of Random Variables." *American Statistical Association Journal* 64 (4): 1439–1442.

Burt, O., and R. Finley. 1968. "Statistical Analysis of Identities in Random Variables." *American Journal of Agricultural Economics* 50 (3): 734–744.

California Agricultural Statistics Service. *California Statistical Abstract,* for the years 1972–1993.

Daly, G., and T. Mayor. 1980. "Estimating the Value of a Missing Market: The Economics of Directory Assistance." *Journal of Law & Economics* 23 (1): 147–166.

Hazell, P. 1984. "Sources of Increased Instability in India and U.S. Cereal Production." *American Journal of Agricultural Economics* 66 (3): 302–311.

Heaton, J., and D. Lucas. 1996. "Evaluating the Effects of Incomplete Markets on Risk Sharing and Asset Pricing." *Journal of Political Economy* 104 (3): 443–487.

Innes, R., and G. Rausser. 1989. "Incomplete Markets and Government Agricultural Policy." *American Journal of Agricultural Economics* 71: 915–931.

Knight, F. 1933. *Risk, Uncertainty and Profit.* Boston: Houghton Mifflin.

Layard, P., and A. Walters. 1978. *Microeconomic Theory.* New York: McGraw-Hill

Lee, H., and S. Blank. 2004. *A Statistical Profile of Horticultural Crop Farm Industries in California.* Giannini Foundation Research Report 348, University of California, July.

Miranda, M., and J. Glauber. 1997. "Systematic Risk, Reinsurance, and the Failure of Crop Insurance Markets." *American Journal of Agricultural Economics* 79: 206–215.

Myers, R., R. Piggott, and W. Tomek. 1990. "Estimating Sources of Fluctuations in the Australian Wool Market: An Application of VAR Methods." *Australian Journal of Agricultural Economics* 34 (3): 242–262.

Offutt, S., and D. Blandford, 1983. *A Review of Empirical Techniques for the Analysis of Commodity Instability,* pp. 83–87. Ithaca: Cornell University Agricultural Economics Research.

Patrick, G., P. Wilson, P. Barry, W. Boggess, and D. Young. 1985. "Risk Perceptions and Management Responses: Producer-Generated Hypotheses for Risk Modeling." *Southern Journal of Agricultural Economics* 17 (2): 231–238.

Radner, R. 1970. "Problems in the Theory of Markets Under Uncertainty." *American Economic Review* 60 (3): 454–460.

Robison, L., and P. Barry. 1987. *The Competitive Firm's Response to Risk.* New York: Macmillan.

Tew, B., J. Broder, W. Musser, and T. Centner. 1985. "Market Failure in Multiphase Electric Power Development for Agricultural Irrigation." *Southern Journal of Agricultural Economics* 17 (2): 57–65.

CHAPTER 15

HEDGING WITH OFF-FARM INCOME

"Brother, can you spare a dime?"
—Popular song of the Great Depression

Off-farm income (OFI) earned by farm households plays at least two major roles in agriculture. In a macroeconomic role, OFI is a neglected index of a country's economic development. In a microeconomic role, OFI is one of the most important risk management tools available to farm households. The two roles are, of course, related in that the availability and level of use of risk management tools is directly related to a country's level of economic development. At the lowest levels of development, off-farm income opportunities are virtually nonexistent, but those opportunities increase as a country develops. At higher levels of development, countries have plentiful OFI opportunities available to farmers. The percentage of farmers earning OFI and the spatial spread of their off-farm activities across the country both go up with increased levels of economic development. At the highest level of development (as described in Chapter 5), the percentage of average "farm" household income coming from agricultural production is approximately zero, and there are few households earning a majority of their income from agricultural operations. The United States has not yet reached that level of economic development, but it is making progress.

As the U.S. economy has developed over the past century, the opportunities for off-farm income have expanded and created a tool for farm households to use in managing their income risk exposure. The role of OFI as a risk management tool received little attention until recently and, thus, is not widely understood. As a result, previous research on farm-level decision making is often flawed because it ignored OFI. Many forecasts of risk management behavior had poor empirical fits with observed behavior because the underlying theory omitted OFI. That misspecification became a significant source of "noise" in empirical data, leading analysts to overstate the expected level of use of other risk management tools. The noise obscured what is now becoming evident: OFI makes producers less sensitive to the details of other risk management tools and strategies, thus making it less likely that those other tools would be used.

Off-farm income derives some of its popularity as a risk management tool from the fact that it is a "do-it-yourself" tool that any farm household can implement with immediate effects. Like product diversification, OFI can be implemented by a producer without having to contract with others, as must be done with forward and futures contracts and insurance tools. OFI immediately raises a household's cash flows and, because the off-farm cash flows are usually steady across time, they reduce the variability of total household income (Mishra et al. 2002).

Off-farm income represents a high and generally increasing percentage of average farm operator household income in the United States (Mishra et al. 2002). As shown in Table 15.1, OFI accounted for about 95 percent of total farm household income in 2002, whereas it represented only 88 percent in 1998. This trend has been in place for decades (OFI represented about half

Table 15.1

U.S. Farm Income, 1998–2004

	1998	1999	2000	2001	2002	2003	2004
	$ billion						
Total cash receipts	195.8	187.6	192.1	200.1	195.0	216.6	241.2
Net farm income	42.9	46.8	47.9	50.6	36.6	59.5	82.5
Direct government payments	12.4	21.5	22.9	20.7	11.2	17.2	13.3
Adjusted production income*	30.5	25.3	25.0	29.9	25.4	42.3	69.2
	$ per farm operator household						
Net cash farm income	14,357	13,194	11,175	14,311	11,336	14,979	20,638
Earnings from farming	7,106	6,359	2,598	5,539	3,477	7,884	14,201
Off-farm earnings	52,628	57,988	59,349	58,578	62,284	60,713	67,279
Average farm household income**	59,734	64,347	61,947	64,117	65,761	68,597	81,480

Source: USDA (200 and earlier issues).

* This is calculated as net farm income minus direct government payments.

** This is the sum of earnings from farming and off farm earnings.

of farmers' income in 1964; Mishra et al. 2002), but has been more noticeable since the 1980s because real farm income has been trending downward since the 1970s. A long-used explanation for the increase in OFI of farm households is that rural economies have developed, thus making off-farm employment more available to farm families. Certainly, *availability* is a necessary condition, but it is not sufficient to explain why some farmers pursue OFI and others do not. A second explanation sometimes suggested is that farmers pursue OFI to replace lost income from farming operations that are becoming less profitable, thus implying that farmers focus on farm profit levels, possibly in a safety-first context, when making decisions about OFI. A third explanation has been proposed recently: that off-farm income represents a vehicle with which farm households can hedge against the variability in farm income. This view implies that risk (expressed as farm income variability) and farmers' risk attitudes are the factors driving the decision of whether or not to hedge. OFI is viewed as the obvious vehicle for hedging because labor is more flexible than land and physical capital, which are quasi-fixed in the short run.

The proposition of OFI as a hedging tool is consistent with the behavior of all types of American farmers. However, a strategy of risk management through diversifying labor allocations among on- and off-farm opportunities has wide-ranging implications for agricultural production and investment decisions, as summarized in the general proposition below.

- PROPOSITION 15.1. *Off-farm income is a management tool used to reduce financial (income) risk, enabling many farm households to stay in agriculture that could not do so without that income.*

Unfortunately, what has been overlooked in previous research on this topic is the effect of farm size on the decision to hedge with OFI. Farm size must be considered to provide a more complete understanding of the decision-making process of farm households that are allocating some of their labor to off-farm employment. Both the absolute *level* and *variability* of farm incomes are expected to increase with the size of farm. This means that different production and investment decisions might be made by producers who are identical in all respects except for the size of their farming operations. For example, very small-scale farms may not be capable of generating sufficient income to support a household, even if all household labor is allocated to farming, whereas large-scale farms might easily support families that have allocated most household labor off-farm.

The objective of this chapter is to evaluate the effects of off-farm income on the labor-allocation and cropping decisions of households across farm sizes in a hedging context. Portfolio theory is well suited to this effort because it facilitates describing farmers as investors facing the decision of how to allocate their labor (and other) assets so as to maximize utility (Robison and Barry 1987). Thus, a simple portfolio model is developed that identifies the optimal hedging position for farm households. Then, the effects of off-farm income opportunities are evaluated across farm sizes using the theoretical model. Finally, regression analysis is used to test hypotheses about the effects of farm size, a variable neglected in the literature.

SOME PERSPECTIVE

Returns from agriculture have been declining for a century (Schultz 1932; Tweeten 1969; Antle 1999; Mishra and Sandretto 2002). This creates a major source of default risk to farmers and provides an incentive to seek risk-reducing strategies. Unfortunately, the few business tools available for use in managing risks facing farmers (e.g., futures, options, crop insurance) all fail in some regard (Blank, Carter, and McDonald 1997). Conversely, the economic literature has shown that OFI can help with both parts of the problem: declining mean income and increasing income variability. For example, Mishra and Sandretto (2002) documented that real net farm income has been declining over the past fifty years, and that income variability has not diminished since the 1930s, on either an aggregate or per-farm basis. They also showed that OFI has contributed to significantly raising the level of farm household incomes, relative to nonfarm households, since the 1970s, and in reducing the variability of farm household incomes in recent years.

Much work has been done in evaluating the sources of farm income risk and its implications for farm household labor allocations (e.g., Findeis and Reddy 1987). Mishra and El-Osta (2001) evaluated the sources of variability in farm household income and found that farming is the primary source of variability in total income for farms participating in federal commodity programs, while the major source of income variability for nonparticipating households is income from off-farm sources. This indicates that the performance of the markets for a farm's commodity outputs plays a strong role in labor allocation decisions. Empirical results confirm that, as expected, variability in farm income and off-farm income have a positive and negative effect, respectively, on off-farm hours worked by farm operators (Mishra and Holthausen 2002).

Numerous studies have developed empirical estimates of the value of farm operators' time (e.g., El-Osta and Ahearn 1996; Blank 1999). When accounting for the opportunity cost of the farm owner-operator's time, Blank (1999) showed that average net returns to farmers are negative for all regions of the United States. This indicates that there are strong incentives to shift labor resources off the farm. This may partially explain the results of Goetz and Debertin (2001), who found counteracting effects from off-farm employment opportunities on the probability that a county would have a net loss in farm numbers. They concluded that off-farm employment could, in different local circumstances, lead to net farm losses or a stabilization in farm numbers within a county. This is consistent with other results. For example, Corsi and Findeis (2000) found evidence of labor state persistence for Pennsylvania farmers and spouses, thus indicating stability in labor market participation over time. Kwon, Orazem, and Otto (2006) found that Iowa farm couples adjust their off-farm labor supply in response to both permanent and transitory farm income shocks. Ahearn and El-Osta (1993) found off-farm work to be (1) a permanent way of life rather than a temporary situation, and (2) a way to supplement household income. Also, El-Osta, Bernat, and Ahearn (1995) found regional differences in off-farm employment. This result is likely due both to differences in economic development across regions and differences in the profitability of the commodities produced in various locations (Ngarambe, Goetz, and Debertin 1998). In total, these previous results lead to a hypothesis that farmers *want* to remain in agriculture and will do so if they can earn sufficient income from all sources to meet their financial obligations and, possibly, increase household wealth.

Although this chapter focuses on American farms, the results of international studies of OFI are consistent with domestic studies, implying that there is a consistent decision process for farmers in more-developed countries. In Canada, farming families depend upon employment in rural communities for family members who want to use their time more profitably (Jean 1996). This is due to the declining profitability of agriculture. Using census data from Israel, Kimhi and Lee (1996) found that a one-hour increase in farm labor supply causes a one-hour decrease in off-farm labor supply for men but not for women. Also, Kimhi (2000) concluded that part-time farming is a stable situation in Israel, not just a step on the way out of agriculture. However, off-farm employment levels vary over the life cycle and with levels of wealth (Ahituv and Kimhi 2002).

Income variability in agriculture has long been identified as a major source of risk in farm-level analyses (Held 1990). Hedging, as described by Peck (1975) and others, is a process with a goal of reducing income variability. It involves combining two or more sources of income that have low or negative levels of correlation in their variability over time so as to reduce the net level of variation in total household income. One such strategy is to combine nonfarm investments with farm production operations (e.g., Betubiza and Leatham 1994). Andersson, Ramamurtie, and Ramaswami (2003) provide a detailed theoretical model of this process and note the importance of household wealth in decision making. Pursuing OFI is a type of nonfarm investment of labor, thus it can be viewed as a hedging strategy for farm households.

When implementing a hedging strategy, a key factor is determining the "hedge ratio," or relative allocations in the two investments (Kawaller and Koch 1989). Since Kahl (1983) explained the process for determining the "optimal hedge ratio," much empirical research has applied it in various situations (e.g., Briys and Pieptea 1992).

Viceira (2001) showed one relationship between income variability and labor allocations in the nonfarm sector, noting that the analytical process involves choosing an optimal "portfolio." He showed that for nonfarm households, employment status (i.e., income and its stability) affects the level and composition of investments in risky assets. In this chapter, it is argued that the level and composition of a farmer's investment in producing risky agricultural enterprises (expressed as farm income and its variability) affect the household's off-farm income (i.e., employment) status. The decision process follows portfolio theory.

A PORTFOLIO MODEL OF OFF-FARM INCOME EFFECTS

Crop market opportunities available to farmers vary over time and space. It is possible that a farmer's financial obligations and/or risk preference will not be satisfied by any of the returns currently expected from producing specific crops. In this case, the farmer may consider "selling" some of the household's labor in some local market, rather than allocating it all to farming operations. The off-farm sales price of farm labor (i.e., the wage rate) was shown by El-Osta and Ahearn (1996) to depend on the current labor supply in the local market, local demand for particular skills, and the level of skills possessed by the individual job seeker (i.e., the human capital). Thus, the decision of whether to allocate some household labor to off-farm employment involves a comparison of the expected income from farming operations and the cost of foregoing off-farm opportunities.

A person deciding whether to produce crop and/or livestock enterprises in a particular market must first identify the opportunities available in that market. Those opportunities can be plotted on an expected return-variance (EV) graph to facilitate analysis.[1] This is done for a hypothetical market in Figure 15.1. The curved line labeled "EV" represents the opportunity set available to farmers within some geographic market. The curve is plotted with expected gross returns on the vertical axis and risk (in this case measured as the standard deviation of expected returns) on the horizontal axis. Each point on the EV is an enterprise or portfolio of enterprises that is efficient in terms of its return/ risk relationship, meaning that points on the EV curve have the highest available returns for the associated level of risk. The location and shape of the EV is determined by the data used to calculate expected returns for all portfolios. Therefore, each person may have a unique EV curve because of differences in production capabilities and expectations between people.

If no off-farm employment is available, for whatever reason, farmers can invest household labor only in the production of crops and/or livestock. Each person would choose to produce the portfolio represented by the point on the EV that is tangent to one of his or her indifference curves. This leads to different enterprise portfolios being produced by farmers with different risk attitudes.

If off-farm income is available, the opportunity set available to farmers is altered. In this chapter, a risk-free return (R_f) to labor is defined as the highest amount of money a farmer (or some other member of the household) could earn from working off-farm. That amount is the product of the hourly wage rate offered and the number of hours that can be worked (usually assumed to be "full-time," but it could be more if more than one member of the household is available to work). Such a risk-free return is available only if an active labor market exists for the skills a farmer possesses. Working only off-farm is analogous to investing entirely in a risk-free asset, which has a return of R_f, and is plotted as a point on the vertical axis of an EV graph.

When off-farm income is available, and under the assumption of efficient markets, the separation theorem indicates that all farmers who have the same returns expectations (represented by a single EV curve) and OFI opportunities will produce the same crops, although the composition of their selected portfolios will still vary with their risk attitudes (Johnson 1967). Using the risk-free return, a single optimal risky portfolio and a farmer's opportunity line (OL) can be identified. The OL represents the opportunity set available to farmers in a market (given some returns expectations). It is plotted as a straight line that passes through the point representing the risk-free return and is tangent to the EV. The OL dominates the EV at all points except where the two frontiers are tangent. The point of tangency represents the market's "optimal" portfolio, which has expected returns of $E(R_m)$. The particular portfolio selected by each farmer is found at the point of tangency between this linear OL and an indifference curve for that person. The selected portfolio in this case is a mix of the market portfolio of enterprises produced with the portion of labor allocated on-farm, and the risk-free asset amount earned as OFI, and has total expected returns of $E(R_i)$.

Figure 15.1 **Farm Labor Allocation and Production Decisions**

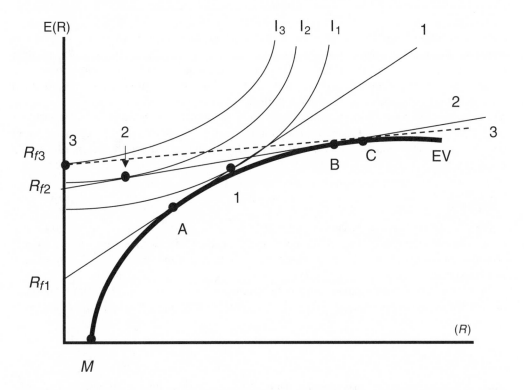

For example, in Figure 15.1 the OL existing for farmers when OFI opportunities have the value R_{f1} is the line labeled "1," which is tangent to the EV at point A. If a farmer's indifference curve is tangent to line 1 at point A, all of that household's labor should be "invested" in producing the crops comprising the optimal portfolio represented by that point. If the indifference curve is tangent at some point to the left of A, the household will invest some labor in producing portfolio A (the specific combination of crops in the optimal portfolio) and will invest the remaining labor in the risk-free asset by working off the farm. Points on the OL to the right of A require an investment in portfolio A involving all of a household's labor and some additional hired labor. Thus, all labor used for crop production by farmers sharing the expectations represented by the EV will be used to produce the same portfolio of enterprises in the same relative proportions. The only difference in composition of selected portfolios between farmers will be the relative proportions of available labor each chooses to use on- or off-farm (and the resulting difference in total agricultural output due to different input levels). This result comes from the separation theorem that suggests that the selection of the crop mix does not depend upon the decision maker's risk preferences, since it is constant along the OL. Instead, the amount of labor allocated on- or off-farm is the variable affected by risk preferences (see Johnson 1967 and Turvey, Baker, and Weersink 1992 for further explanation of the separation theorem). This is consistent with Viceira's (2001) results for labor allocations made in the nonfarm sector.

A farmer's profit function for holding his or her selected portfolio over some future period can be specified as

$$(15.1) \qquad E(R_i) = E(GR_m)X_m + R_f X_f - OC$$

where R_i is net profit (returns) from selected enterprise portfolio i, E is the farmer's expectations operator, GR_m is gross returns from the market's optimal enterprise portfolio, R_f is the risk-free return from off-farm employment, X_m is the proportion (or total number of units) of labor used to produce the market portfolio, X_f is the proportion (or total number of units) of labor sold (or hired if negative) off the farm, and OC is the total fixed costs incurred in owning a farm (including mortgage, property taxes, insurance, investments in improvements, etc.), expressed in per-acre (or total dollar) terms. If X_m and X_f are expressed in terms of proportions (hours), they must sum to one (the total hours available for the entire household). The variance of returns for a portfolio held by a farmer is

$$(15.2) \qquad \sigma^2_i = X^2_m[\sigma^2_m]$$

where σ^2_i and σ^2_m are the variance in expected returns of the selected and optimal portfolios, respectively. The variance of the profit model is the variance of expected returns to the optimal portfolio component only because all other factors are known with certainty and, therefore, have zero variance.

In portfolio theory, utility maximization is assumed to be the objective. Therefore, the focus of decision making is the certainty equivalent of $E(R_i)$, which Freund (1956) and others have shown is

$$(15.3) \qquad E(U_i) = E(R_i) - (\Lambda/2)(\sigma^2_i),$$

where U is utility and Λ is a risk-aversion parameter (equaling the slope of the indifference curve at the tangency point) that is positive for risk-averse hedgers.[2] The first-order conditions for Equation 15.3 give the utility-maximizing portfolio composition,

$$(15.4) \qquad X_m = \frac{E(GR_m) - R_f}{\Lambda \sigma^2_m}$$

subject to the constraint $X_m \geq 0$, and remembering that the proportion of labor sold or hired (X_f in Equation 15.1) is $100\% - X_m$. Thus, Equation 15.4 is analogous to the "optimal hedge ratio" for a household allocating its labor to farm and off-farm activities.

EFFECTS OF OFF-FARM INCOME LEVELS

Comparing OFI opportunities to expected production returns leads to implications concerning the decision whether or not to produce and, if so, what crop/livestock enterprises to produce. In general, if the situation facing some farmers is $E(R_m) < R_f$, those households would want to work "full-time" off-farm (but may choose to continue farming as a "leisure" activity; Blank 2002). On the other hand, if $E(R_m) > R_f$, some rational farmers might work full-time on-farm because higher returns are expected from production of efficient agricultural enterprise portfolios. However, most American farm households now allocate some labor to both farm and off-farm employment activities, indicating that differences between $E(R_m)$ and R_f are now small enough to be critical to the labor allocation decision.

Different cropping possibilities across time and spatial markets generate different levels of expected income that, in turn, help explain labor allocation differences between dates and locations. For farmers, returns from agricultural production are the alternative to working off the farm and earning the risk-free return. The higher the value of agricultural returns, the more incentive there is for farmers to produce crops rather than work for others. The reverse is also true. Therefore, it is often necessary to specify a new OL to represent changing market opportunities available to farmers over time and locations.

In this section, the effects of OFI levels on farmers' production and investment decisions are discussed. It is hypothesized that OFI affects cropping decisions both directly and indirectly through other factors, as described in the following subsections.

Direct Effects of Off-Farm Income Changes

The first question to be addressed is, "what direct effects do changes in off-farm income levels have on farmers' cropping decisions?" To begin, it is assumed that a farmer has the OFI opportunities reflected by R_{f1}, making line 1 the relevant OL in Figure 15.1. The indifference curve I_1 reflects the farmer's risk attitude. Since I_1 is tangent to line 1 at point 1, the farmer would select portfolio 1. Portfolio 1 requires that the farmer use all household labor and some additional hired labor for production of the crops in portfolio A (the optimal portfolio). Thus, X_m in Equation 15.4 is greater than one (or 100 percent) in this case.

If OFI opportunities increase to R_{f2}, cropping decisions of the farmer change significantly. Line 2 in Figure 15.1 becomes the relevant OL and it is tangent to the EV at point B. The farmer's utility is increased, as indicated by the move from indifference curve I_1 to I_2. The farmer's new selected portfolio is at point 2. Portfolio 2 requires that the farmer use only part of household labor for production of the crops in portfolio B (the new optimal portfolio), with the remaining labor being allocated off-farm ($1 > X_m > 0$). The composition of portfolio B is clearly more risky than that of portfolio A. As plotted, the difference between portfolios 1 and 2 is a slight reduction in expected returns and a large reduction in risk levels, resulting in an increase in the certainty equivalent (plotted at the intersection of the relevant indifference curve and the vertical axis). Hence, theoretically, farmers respond to increases in off-farm income levels by producing riskier crops, but they use lower labor inputs (and probably fewer acres). This means, for example, that a wheat farmer in Washington state might be more willing to shift some acreage into production of a specialty crop (such as a tree crop—e.g., apples, cherries) if some member of the household gains off-farm employment.

If available OFI levels increase further to R_{f3}, the farmer's cropping decisions change again. Line 3 in Figure 15.1 becomes the relevant OL and it is tangent to the EV at point C. The farmer's utility is increased further, as indicated by the move from indifference curve I_2 to I_3. The new selected portfolio is at point 3. Portfolio 3 requires that the farmer allocate all household labor off-farm ($X_m = 0$). The composition of the new optimal portfolio, C, is more risky than that of portfolio B and, considering the farmer's risk preferences, C is too risky to produce given current OFI opportunities (which is why line 3 is dashed). As plotted, the difference between selected portfolios 2 and 3 is a relatively slight increase in expected returns and a total reduction in risk levels, resulting in another increase in the farmer's certainty equivalent.

In sum, two results are derived from the analysis above. First, higher OFI opportunities lead to the production of more-risky crops and a "hedge ratio" involving more household labor being allocated off-farm. This can be seen by substituting higher values for R_f in Equation 15.4. This theoretical result is consistent with empirical results reported by Lee and Blank (2004). Their 2002 survey data show fruit/nut operations to be more risky and *much* smaller, on average, than vegetable operations. However, the attraction of tree crops is that they generate higher revenue per acre. Thus, it is not surprising that Lee and Blank (2004) report that the average portion of total household income coming from off-farm sources is higher for the more-risky operations: OFI is 64 percent of household income for fruit/nut producers, 42 percent for vegetable producers.

Finally, it is noted that farmers have some control over their OFI opportunities. A person's investments in their own human capital can raise their potential salary in off-farm markets. Much literature has documented that higher education and/or training can improve a person's skills, making him or her more valuable to potential employers. As explained above, higher OFI opportunities create incentives for farmers to produce higher-returning crops. Thus, a farmer's personal investments can lead directly and indirectly to higher returns from farming.

- PROPOSITION 15.2. *Opportunities to earn higher off-farm income are opportunity costs to agricultural producers that lead to more-risky crops being grown and more household labor being allocated off-farm.*
- PROPOSITION 15.3. *Human capital investments cause farm households to produce more-risky enterprises.*

Effects of Risk Attitudes

The previous subsection assumed one set of risk preferences for a farmer; this subsection outlines how the cropping decision might differ for producers who were more or less risk averse. In particular, the issues addressed here are what effect a decision maker's risk attitudes might have on risk efficiency and labor allocations over the life cycle.

Being more or less risk averse would change a farmer's indifference curve and, hence, his or her choice of portfolios, but it would not change the risk efficiency of his/her selected portfolios. Farmers are always able to select a portfolio on the linear OL involving some efficient combination of the optimal portfolio and off-farm income (if off-farm employment is available). As is evident from Equation 15.4, a more (less) risk-averse farmer would allocate a higher (lower) proportion of household labor off-farm than described earlier. Increasing values of Λ reduce the proportion of labor used in production, thereby raising the amount allocated off-farm. Of course, the reverse is also true.

Risk attitudes change over the life cycle, with people usually becoming much more risk-averse as they approach retirement (Viceira 2001). This is due to the decreasing amount of time a person has to recover from financial losses as they age. Such an increase in risk aversion means Λ in Equation 15.4 grows larger, indicating that the slope of a person's indifference curve at the point of tangency with the EV is steeper with age. In Figure 15.1 it is easily seen that increasingly steep indifference curves will be tangent to the EV at points moving closer to the vertical axis. This means that as a person approaches retirement, he/she will allocate more labor off-farm, if possible. This is consistent with the fact that off-farm income as a percentage of household income is highest among farms the U.S. Department of Agriculture's (USDA's) topology labels as "retirement" and other "residential farms." For example, "rural residence farms" account for about 63 percent of all farms in the United States and had an average net cash farm income of –$1,800 per farm over the 1996–2000 period. This means OFI represents over 100 percent of total household income for this group. Not surprisingly, in 2003 80 percent of the 851,000 farmers in this group worked full-time off-farm (USDA 2006).

In summary, the positive relationship between risk aversion and off-farm allocations of farm household labor has some implications for the structure of American agriculture. First, the increasing availability of off-farm employment has enabled many highly risk-averse farmers to at least partially remain in agriculture whereas they would have chosen to exit the industry if they faced a choice between full-time farming and full-time off-farm. Off-farm employment opportunities make part-time farming labor allocations possible for risk-averse people who would not be comfortable with the risk/return tradeoff offered by farming only. Second, with an aging farm labor force, the increasing risk aversion of farmers approaching retirement age will cause an increasing percentage of farm labor to be allocated off-farm, ceteris paribus. Finally, both of the implications noted above can, in the aggregate, lead farmers to be less responsive to markets for the commodities produced. It is expected that as the percentage of farm household income derived from farming operations declines, farmers may become less likely to make major changes to their operations (e.g., shift from producing one enterprise to producing another enterprise).

- PROPOSITION 15.4. *Risk aversion and the portion of farm household income earned off-farm are positively correlated, ceteris paribus.*

Effects of Farm Size

The two other variables on the right side of Equation 15.4, GR_m and σ_m^2, are both functions of farm size. A farmer's gross revenues from producing the optimal enterprise portfolio obviously are expected to increase when that portfolio is produced on more acres. The variance of those returns is also expected to increase as farm size increases. It is easily seen that higher values of GR_m in Equation 15.4 result in more labor being allocated on-farm while higher values for σ_m^2 encourage more labor to be allocated off-farm. Thus, in the simplest case, larger farm sizes can have either more or less household labor allocated off-farm, compared to decisions made by the same person when operating a smaller farm.

However, the simple case ignores economies of scale. One of the incentives for farmers to expand the size of their operations is the increased production and management efficiencies that lower production costs per unit, thus increasing profit margins. In other words, it is expected that economies of scale improve the return/risk tradeoff facing operators of increasingly larger farms. That means the value of X_m in Equation 15.4 is expected to grow as farm size grows. This theoretical result is consistent with observed behavior of American farmers: a smaller portion of household labor is allocated off-farm by farms of increasingly larger size (Lee and Blank 2004; Yee, Ahearn, and Huffman 2004).

This is illustrated graphically in Figure 15.2. There are three EV curves in the figure to represent three farms of different sizes, EV_1 being the smallest and EV_3 being the largest. The three curves are drawn so as to illustrate the two ideas mentioned above. First, the fact that returns and risk are positively correlated is shown by the position of each successive EV, from 1 to 3, being drawn above and to the right of previous curves. Second, the efficiency gains from larger-sized farms are shown by having larger farms able to earn higher returns at the same levels of risk as available to smaller farms. In other words, a vertical line from the x axis that intersects two or three of the EVs identifies portfolios (at the points of intersection with each of the EVs) that have identical levels of risk exposure, but have higher returns for larger farms. The effects of farm size on farm labor

Figure 15.2 **Off-Farm Income and Farm Size Effects**

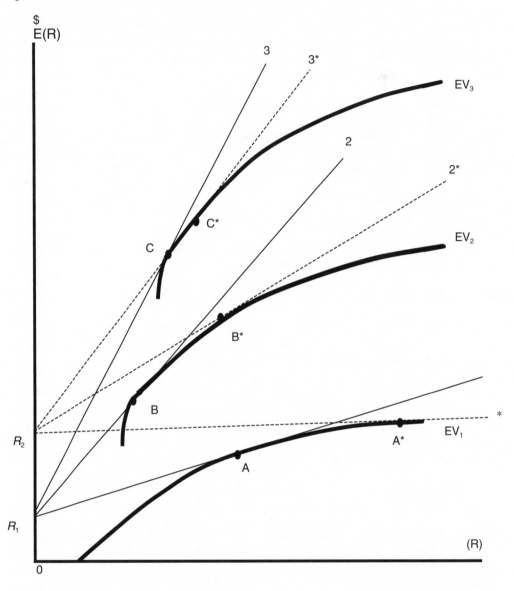

allocations are illustrated with three OLs drawn from a single off-farm income opportunity, R_1, tangent to the EVs to identify the optimal portfolio for each farm size at the points labeled A, B, and C. This shows how a single farmer would react if he or she were operating farms of different sizes. For example, given the OFI opportunity R_1, and assuming the farmer's indifference curve is tangent to OL_1 at point A, all household labor would be allocated on-farm to produce the enterprises in portfolio A. If that same farmer was operating the farms represented by EV_2 or EV_3, he or she would allocate increasing amounts of (hired) labor to producing portfolios B or C, respec-

Figure 15.3   **Average Farm Sales by Off-Farm Share of Household Income in California**

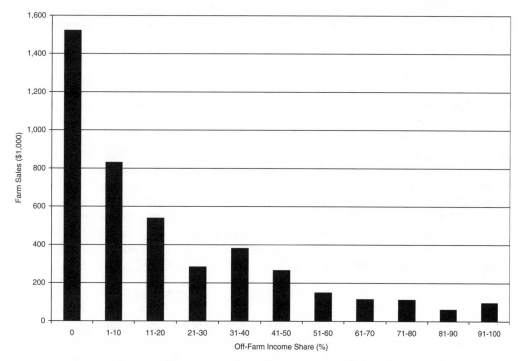

tively.[3] The amount of labor hired would be indicated by the point of tangency between OL_2 or OL_3 and one of that person's indifference curves (not shown in the figure).

Figure 15.2 also illustrates the theoretical result that increases in OFI opportunities cause farmers in the aggregate to produce riskier crops (as shown in Figure 15.1), but the scale of changes in production risk exposure and a farmer's reaction to it vary across farm sizes. For example, a change in OFI opportunities from R_1 to R_2 shifts the optimal portfolio from points A, B, and C to points A^*, B^*, and C^*, respectively. It is clear in Figure 15.2 that the new optimal portfolios are each more risky than the original portfolios, but the *amount* of increase in production risk exposure between the pairs of points (measured by the horizontal distance between the points, e.g., between A and A^*) is smaller with larger farm sizes. As a result, the points of tangency between the new opportunity lines (1*, 2* and 3*) and the farmer's indifference curves indicate much different hedge ratios across the farm sizes. If it is assumed that the tangency point for OL 1* is at R_2 on the vertical axis, all labor would be allocated off-farm by the farmer. That same person, however, would not allocate all labor off-farm if he or she were operating the farm represented by OL 2*. Finally, even less labor would go off-farm if the person were operating the largest farm.

- PROPOSITION 15.5. *Farm size and the portion of farm household income earned off-farm are negatively correlated, ceteris paribus.*

Proposition 15.5 is supported by data reported by Lee and Blank (2004), illustrated in Figure 15.3. The figure shows that farms in California with lower sales revenues from products grown earn a higher share of their total household income from off-farm sources than do farms with higher sales revenues. Substitution between farm and off-farm income is clearly apparent in the data. Lee and Blank (2004) show that sales revenues are positively correlated with other measures of farm size, such as total acreage, so it is expected that off-farm income as a portion of total household income is negatively correlated with all indicators of farm size.

EMPIRICAL ANALYSIS

The main hypothesis raised in the discussion above was tested empirically with farm household survey data. Specifically, the significance of OFI to household wealth was assessed across farm sizes. Wealth was the focus because studies have shown that wealth affects farmers' financial decision making and degree of risk aversion (e.g., Ahituv and Kimhi 2002; Andersson, Rama-murtie, and Ramaswami 2003). Wealth is the ultimate indicator of a household's well-being.

Off-farm income is expected to be important to a farm household because it is a source of wealth (Koenigstein and Lins 1990). Changes in wealth (measured by changes in a farmer's total equity) during a period of time ending at t are expected to consist of some function (j) of farm income ($FInc$) plus off-farm income ($OFInc$) plus capital gains (ΔK) minus consumption (Con). Thus, at the time that production and investment decisions must be made, t, the resulting expectations for changes in wealth are

$$(15.5) \qquad E_t(\Delta W_{t+1}) = f_j(FInc_t + OFInc_t + \Delta K_t - Con_t).$$

The components on the right-hand side of Equation 15.5 are themselves functions of other factors. For example, the capital variable (K) is a function of many other factors, including farm size. It can be expressed as the sum of the market values for all assets (farm real estate, non–real estate, and nonfarm assets) held by a person at time t. Those assets, such as farm real estate, may have market values based on factors such as expected farm income. Thus, a reduced form of Equation 15.5 can be estimated over time for farms of different sizes to determine whether OFI does, in fact, play a significant role.

Equation 15.5 was estimated using farm-level data from the U.S. Department of Agriculture's Agricultural Resource Management Survey (ARMS). It was estimated using repeated cross-sectional data from annual surveys for 1996–2004 over ten production regions: the Northeast, Lake States, Corn Belt, Northern Plains, Appalachia, Southeast, Delta, Southern Plains, Mountain, and Pacific.[4] Then, factors affecting the change in wealth were examined, given farm size and time effects. All production regions and all farms are included. This gives a total of 95,517 observations.

The rich data available in ARMS make this analysis possible. ARMS is a survey covering farms in the forty-eight contiguous states, conducted each year by the USDA, and designed to incorporate information from both a list of farmers producing selected commodities and a random sample of farmers based on area (USDA/ERS 2004). Since stratified sampling is used, inferences regarding the means of variables for states and regions are conducted using weighted observations. The USDA has an in-house jackknifing procedure that it believes is most appropriate when analyzing ARMS data (Dubman 2000; Kott 2005; Cohen, Xanthopoulos, and Jones 1988). The farm-level data are used in an innovative way. Nine annual ARMS surveys are linked to form a pooled time-series cross-section, assuming that the survey design for each year is comparable. Hence, using the annual ARMS data makes it possible to examine structural changes over time.

Incorporating the survey weights, and following the jackknifing procedure described in Kott (2005), assures that regression results are suitable for inference to the population in each of the regions analyzed. The USDA/NASS (2000) version of the delete-a-group jackknife divides the sample for each year into fifteen nearly equal and mutually exclusive parts. Fifteen estimates of the statistic, called "replicates," are created. One of the fifteen parts is eliminated in turn for each replicate estimate with replacement. The replicate and the full sample estimates are placed into the following basic jackknife formula:

$$(15.6) \qquad \text{Standard Error } (\beta) = \left\{ 14/15 \sum_{k=1}^{15} (\beta_k - \beta)^2 \right\}^{1/2}$$

where β is the full sample vector of coefficients from the SAS@ program results using the replicated data for the "base" run, and β_k is one of the fifteen vectors of regression coefficients for each of the jackknife samples. The t-statistics for each coefficient are simply computed by dividing the "base" run vector of coefficients by the vector of standard errors of the coefficients (Dubman 2000). Each reduced form equation was estimated with year and farm size fixed effects.

The farm-level data were assigned to three size categories, based on the USDA's farm typology groups (Hoppe and MacDonald 2001). Farm size 1 includes "limited resource," "retirement," and "residential" farms. These farms all have total sales of less than $250,000 per year (most have less than $100,000 per year) and the operators may report farming, a nonfarm occupation, or retirement as their major occupation. Hence, these are often referred to as "hobby farms" and are expected to be less responsive to agricultural markets than are farms that provide the primary source of income for a household. Farm size 2 includes typologies "farm/lower sales" and "farm/higher sales." Their total annual sales are less than $100,000 or less than $250,000, respectively, but farming is the operator's primary occupation, thus these operators are expected to be highly responsive to market opportunities. Farm size 3 covers the typologies "large family farms" and "very large farms" that have annual sales of $250,000 and more.

The nominal values of the monetary variables were deflated by the GDP implicit price deflator using the year 1996 as the base. Variables presented in Table 15.2 are in 1996 dollars.

It is clear in the results in Table 15.2 that size 1 households have focused some of their investment activities off the farm. Farm and nonfarm capital gains were both significant sources of wealth for small-sized farms. Medium- and large-sized farms derive wealth only from gains on their farm capital, which is most likely their land. Equation 15.5 was estimated with variables representing capital gains coming from both farm and nonfarm capital, although about 75 percent of farm household wealth is held in the form of farmland. Both capital components were highly significant when examining changes in farm wealth for farm size 1 (Table 15.2). Medium- and large-sized farms both derive wealth from gains on their farm capital only, which indicates that larger farms cannot afford to invest much money off-farm. Neither farm nor off-farm income was significant for any farm size, thus indicating that capital gains dwarf earned income. Therefore, wealth comes from capital, not income, for all farms. This result partially explains why farms that lose money each year on their production stay in agriculture: if their capital gains exceed their operating losses, the farm is increasing the wealth of its owners.

The 2002 Census of Agriculture (USDA 2004) reports that 53.3 percent of all farms generated a net loss for the year, although the average household earnings from farming activities for that year was $3,477 (Table 15.1). Mid-sized farms are likely to fall in the middle of the farm income distribution, which offers insufficient income to support a family, but those farms are not big enough to substitute much skilled hired labor for family labor that might work off the farm (as large-sized farms can do). This leads to the ironic conclusion that the households that need the

Table 15.2

Change in Wealth Estimation Results by Farm Size, 1996–2004

Variable	Farm size 1		Farm size 2		Farm size 3	
	Estimate	t value	Estimate	t value	Estimate	t value
FarmInc	−0.653	−0.92	−0.039	−1.31	−0.149	−1.08
NonFarmInc	0.009	0.11	0.077	1.54	−0.111	−0.72
ChngFarmCap	1.113	10.09*	1.018	40.74*	1.100	86.85*
ChngNFarmCap	0.318	20.09*	0.100	1.09	0.299	1.64
Consumption	0.516	1.01	−0.089	−1.21	0.313	0.89

Note : * denotes statistical signi cance at the   con dence level.
 arm si e   corresponds to limited resource retirement and residential farms. arm si e 2 corresponds
to farm lo er sales and farm higher sales. arm si e 3 are large family farms and very large farms.

income-risk-reducing effects of OFI the most (operators of mid-sized farms) are generally the least able to pursue OFI. The resulting higher risk exposure of mid-sized farms would make them more likely to be forced out of business over time, even compared to small-sized farms.[5]

ECONOMIES OF SCALE AND HOUSEHOLD OFF-FARM INCOME

Proposition 15.5 implies that there might be a negative relationship between economies of scale and the portion of a household's total income coming from off-farm sources. This hypothesis is based upon the idea that economies of scale are expected as farm size increases. In other words, larger farms are expected to achieve economies of scale in agricultural production that improve profit margins, thus creating an incentive to allocate more household labor on-farm than would be allocated by a smaller farm producing the same commodities. This hypothesis was evaluated using 2003 ARMS data, shown in Table 15.3. Average values for each region in the United States were calculated by farm size for two factors. The first factor is the average income per acre coming from agricultural production. The results are presented in the left side of the table. On the right side of Table 15.3 are the results showing the second factor: the average percentage of total household income coming from off-farm sources. It is clear that the data support the hypothesis: the correlation between the two factors is −0.83. The farm profit per acre increases with farm size across all regions, while larger farms earn a smaller portion of total household income from off-farm sources.

This simple assessment is not a complete test of the hypothesis, but it does make sense. Small farms have more incentive to invest household labor off-farm than do larger farms. This result is also consistent with the safety-first hypothesis of household labor allocation: labor is allocated first to the least risky source of income until sufficient income has been earned, and thereafter labor is allocated so as to maximize household utility. This means that until total income is sufficient to assure that the bills are paid, a household allocates its labor to the activity most likely to provide a positive return to labor. In most cases, the least risky income source is off-farm employment (assuming it is available). After the bills are paid, household labor is allocated to the activities that bring the most happiness (utility), adjusted for risk. Thus, for a person who wants to live and work in agriculture, the marginal return to (presumably less-desirable) off-farm employment goes down as total household income increases above the amount needed to pay the bills, enabling the person to allocate more time to his/her preferred vocation in agriculture. Therefore, OFI truly serves as

Table 15.3

Regional Averages by Farm Size, 2003

Region	Farm Income per acre ($)			OFI as % of total household income		
	Farm size 1	Size 2	Size 3	Farm size 1	Size 2	Size 3
Northeast	−97.59	8.55	117.29	112	97	36
Lake States	−20.22	44.46	74.26	104	74	31
Corn Belt	−9.69	34.42	68.52	102	74	30
Northern Plains	1.40	12.48	35.56	99	71	22
Appalachia	−28.39	30.18	166.97	105	88	25
Southeast	−26.15	42.73	184.33	105	86	30
Delta	−28.92	19.02	118.36	106	85	24
Southern Plains	−26.11	1.17	54.71	110	98	32
Mountain States	−9.35	5.58	22.41	107	76	24
Pacific	−62.62	25.31	115.10	109	81	21

Source: alculated from USDA A   S data.

a hedging tool in a safety-first context with generally smaller optimal hedge ratios expected for larger-sized farms.

SUMMARY AND POLICY IMPLICATIONS

This chapter uses portfolio theory to evaluate the effects of off-farm income levels on farmers' production and investment decisions. An "optimal hedge ratio" of farm household labor allocated on- and off-farm is derived from a simple model of hedging with off-farm income. It is found that off-farm income opportunities have direct and indirect effects on cropping decisions and farm household wealth.

Risk attitudes do not affect the composition of the "optimal portfolio" of agricultural enterprises, but risk aversion is positively related to the proportion of household labor allocated off-farm. This means the trend of the increasing average age of farm operators is partly responsible for the trend of increasing levels of off-farm income because people become more risk averse as they approach retirement age.

Farm size is shown to have significant effects on production and investment decisions through the improved return/risk tradeoff coming from economies of scale. As a result, large farm operators are expected to pursue fewer OFI opportunities than are small farm operators.

Taken together, the results from the simple model presented here have some significant theoretical implications for both U.S. agriculture and policy. First, hedging with OFI makes agriculture more risky in that the composition of enterprise portfolios produced by individuals with off-farm income is more risky than the portfolios of enterprises those people would produce if they did not have OFI. In other words, total output of "risky" crops increases with OFI. Second, hedging with OFI enables many risk-averse farmers to remain in agriculture longer than they would without OFI. Third, as OFI increases as a proportion of total household income, it facilitates hysteresis in that farmers become less likely to diversify or to use other risk-reducing strategies (Mishra and El-Osta 2002). This, in turn, makes markets less responsive and agricultural policies aimed at market operations less effective.

The empirical results provide evidence that OFI appears to affect farm household wealth, but possibly not in the way expected. The data in Table 15.1 show that OFI amounts are far larger, on average, than are annual farm income amounts. However, the results in Table 15.2 show that farms are not significantly aided by OFI, on average, in building wealth. This means that income, in absolute amounts, was small compared to capital gains. Therefore, the contribution of OFI to farm household efforts to build wealth may be indirect, rather than direct. OFI enables farm households to "pay the bills" while capital gains accumulate over time through the appreciation of farm capital—mostly farmland.

In summary, hedging with off-farm income is effective in reducing farm households' level of risk exposure, but the increase in its use makes clear that there is a need for new agricultural policy perspective. When a majority of farmers voluntarily stay in agriculture despite low or negative profits, production or investment policies based on profit-maximizing behavior by all farmers are obviously inappropriate. New policies must incorporate the wealth- and utility-maximizing perspectives of today's American farmers. For example, policies intending to stimulate investments in small "hobby" farms will be ineffective for the nation because there is little incentive for most of those households to expand their agricultural operations. However, policies that direct resources to mid- and large-sized farms and their potential for farm capital gains could generate the best production and investment results for American agriculture.

NOTES

Some of this chapter is a revised version of an article by S. Blank and K. Erickson published as "Agricultural Household Hedging with Off-Farm Income," *Western Economics Forum*, July 2007.

1. Although expected utility maximization is the objective of decision making in portfolio theory, graphical EV analysis is used here because it simplifies the presentation of relevant economic concepts. Also, Freund (1956) showed that shifting from mathematical expressions in EV analysis to expected utility analysis is made easy by focusing on the certainty equivalent of expected returns. However, much literature argues that two-moment decision models are consistent with expected utility maximization only if the choice set or the agent's preferences are restricted (Levy 1974; Levy and Markowitz 1979). Yet Meyer (1987) noted that common restrictions, such as quadratic utility or normality assumptions, are not required for EV and utility maximization to be consistent. He showed that the location and scale condition, which fits many economic models (like the one here), is sufficient to ensure that an EV ranking of elements in a choice set is consistent with an expected utility maximization ranking of random variables.

2. Equation 15.3 is based on negative exponential utility and normality, although similar specifications can be derived using quadratic utility or other assumptions.

3. Note that enterprise portfolios A, B and C are plotted to illustrate that increasing farm sizes have different return/risk tradeoffs. Moving from A to B is clearly an improvement because portfolio B offers both higher total returns and a lower level of risk. Conversely, moving from B to C is less obvious: portfolio C offers higher total returns but a higher level of risk. In this case, portfolio C is more efficient because it has a better return/risk tradeoff ratio than B.

4. The ARMS data, as a whole, are designed to give a representative "snapshot" of American agriculture each year, not a detailed assessment of any particular crop, state, or production region. Hence, this chapter is general in its focus and does not try to assess any particular group of households.

5. Many owners of financially stressed mid-sized farms may opt to reduce their scale of operations to "small-sized" farms, enabling them to shift some household labor off the farm rather than leaving farming entirely. Ironically, this shift could lead to much higher household income because of the significant contributions available from OFI, as indicated in Table 15.1. However, in regions with few

opportunities for OFI, households unable to maintain their mid-sized farms might have no choice but to exit agriculture entirely.

REFERENCES

Ahearn, C., and H. El-Osta. 1993. "The Role of Off-Farm Employment: Permanent or Transitional State?" Selected paper presented at the American Agricultural Economics Association annual meeting, Baltimore, MD, August.

Ahituv, A., and A. Kimhi. 2002. "Off-Farm Work and Capital Accumulation Decisions of Farmers over the Life-Cycle: The Role of Heterogeneity and State Dependence." *Journal of Development Economics* 68: 329–353.

Andersson, H., S. Ramamurtie, and B. Ramaswami. 2003. "Labor Income and Risky Investments: Can Part-Time Farmers Compete?" *Journal of Economic Behavior & Organization* 50: 477–493.

Antle, John M. 1999. "The New Economics of Agriculture." *American Journal of Agricultural Economics* 81: 993–1010.

Betubiza, E., and D. Leatham. 1994. "The Effects of Holding Nonfarm Related Financial Assets on Risk-Adjusted Farm Income." *Journal of Agricultural & Applied Economics* 26 (2): 565–579.

Blank, Emily C. 1999. "Returns to Farm Operators: An Analysis of Opportunity Costs." *Pennsylvania Economic Review* 8 (1): 18–31.

Blank, Steven C. 2002. "Is Agriculture a 'Way of Life' or a Business?" *Choices* 17 (Summer): 26–30.

Blank, S., C. Carter, and J. McDonald. 1997. "Is the Market Failing Agricultural Producers Who Wish to Manage Risks?" *Contemporary Economic Policy* 15: 103–112.

Briys, E., and D. Pieptea. 1992. "Optimal Hedging with Futures Contracts: The Case for Fixed Income Portfolios." *Journal of Futures Markets* 12: 693–703.

Cohen, S., J. Xanthopoulos, and G. Jones. 1988. "An Evaluation of Available Statistical Software Procedures Appropriate for the Regression Analysis of Complex Survey Data." *Journal of Official Statistics* 4: 17–34.

Corsi, A., and J. Findeis. 2000. "True State Dependence and Heterogeneity in Off-Farm Labour Participation." *European Review of Agricultural Economics* 27 (2): 127–151.

Dubman, R.W. 2000. *Variance Estimation with USDA's Farm Costs and Returns Surveys and Agricultural Resource Management Study Surveys*. Washington, DC: U.S. Department of Agriculture, Economic Research Service Staff Paper AGES 00–01.

El-Osta, H., and M. Ahern. 1996. "Estimating the Opportunity Cost of Unpaid Farm Labor for U.S. Farm Operators." USDA Economic Research Service, Technical Bulletin no. 1848, March.

El-Osta, H., A. Bernat, Jr., and M. Ahern. 1995. "Regional Differences in the Contribution of Off-Farm Work to Income Inequality." *Agricultural and Resource Economics Review* 24 (1): 1–14.

Findeis, J., and V. Reddy. 1987. "Decomposition of Income Distribution Among Farm Families." *Northeast Journal of Agricultural and Resource Economics* 16 (2): 165–173.

Freund, R. 1956. "The Introduction of Risk into a Programming Model." *Econometrica* 24: 253–263.

Goetz, S., and D. Debertin. 2001. "Why Farmers Quit: A County-Level Analysis." *American Journal of Agricultural Economics* 83 (4): 1010–1023.

Held, Larry J. 1990. "Evaluating Risk in Whole Farm Planning: Chance and Amount of Loss Versus Income Variability." *Journal of the American Society of Farm Managers and Rural Appraisers* 54 (1): 54–59.

Hoppe, R., and J. MacDonald. 2001. *America's Diverse Family Farms: Assorted Sizes, Types, and Situations*. ERS Agriculture Information Bulletin no. 769, at www.ers.usda.gov/publications/aib769.

Jean, Bruno. 1996. "Family Farming, Farm Labour and Rural Employment: Who Works Where? An International Comparison." *Canadian Journal of Agricultural Economics* 44 (4): 411–419.

Johnson, S. 1967. "A Re-examination of the Farm Diversification Problem." *Journal of Farm Economics* 49: 610–621.

Kahl, Kandice. 1983. "Determination of the Recommended Hedging Ratio." *American Journal of Agricultural Economics* 65: 603–605.

Kawaller, I., and T. Koch. 1989. "Yield Opportunities and Hedge Ratio Considerations with Fixed Income Cash-and-Carry Trades." *Journal of Futures Markets* 9: 539–545.

Kimhi, Ayal. 2000. "Is Part-Time Farming Really a Step in the Way Out of Agriculture?" *American Journal of Agricultural Economics* 82 (1): 38–48.

Kimhi, A., and M. Lee. 1996. "Off-Farm Work Decisions of Farm Couples: Estimating Structural Simultaneous Equations with Ordered Categorical Dependent Variables." *American Journal of Agricultural Economics* 78 (3): 687–698.

Koenigstein, K., and D. Lins. 1990. "Measuring Farm Sector Wealth and Income: Data Comparisons for Illinois Farms." *North Central Journal of Agricultural Economics* 12: 305–318.

Kott, P.S. 2005. *Using the Delete-a-Group Jackknife Variance Estimator in NASS Surveys.* U.S. Department of Agriculture, National Agricultural Statistics Service (USDA/NASS), NASS Research Report RD-98–01, Washington, DC.

Kwon, C-W., P. Orazem, and D. Otto. 2006. "Off-Farm Labor Supply Responses to Permanent and Transitory Farm Income." *Agricultural Economics* 34: 59–67.

Lee, H., and S. Blank. 2004. *A Statistical Profile of Horticultural Crop Farm Industries in California.* Giannini Foundation Research Report 348, University of California, July.

Levy, Haim. 1974. "The Rationale of the Mean-Standard Deviation Analysis: Comment." *American Economic Review* 64: 434–441.

Levy, H., and H. Markowitz. 1979. "Approximating Expected Utility by a Function of Mean and Variance." *American Economic Review* 69: 308–317.

Meyer, Jack. 1987. "Two Moment Decision Models and Expected Utility Maximization." *American Economic Review* 77: 421–430.

Mishra, A., and H. El-Osta. 2001. "A Temporal Comparison of Sources of Variability in Farm Household Income." *Agricultural Finance Review* 61 (2): 181–198.

———. 2002. "Risk Management Through Enterprise Diversification: A Farm-Level Analysis." Paper presented at the American Agricultural Economics Association annual meeting, Long Beach, California, July.

Mishra, A., H. El-Osta, M. Morehart, J. Johnson, and J. Hopkins. 2002. *Income, Wealth, and the Economic Well-Being of Farm Households.* USDA Economic Research Service, Agricultural Economic Report no. 812, July.

Mishra, A., and D. Holthausen. 2002. "Effect of Farm Income and Off-Farm Wage Variability on Off-Farm Labor Supply." *Agricultural and Resource Economics Review* 31 (2): 187–199.

Mishra, A., and C. Sandretto. 2002. "Stability of Farm Income and the Role of Nonfarm Income in U.S. Agriculture." *Review of Agricultural Economics* 24 (1): 208–221.

Ngarambe, O., S. Goetz, and D. Debertin. 1998. "Regional Economic Growth and Income Distribution: County-Level Evidence from the U.S. South." *Journal of Agricultural and Applied Economics* 30 (December): 325–337.

Peck, Anne. 1975. "Hedging and Income Stability: Concepts, Implications, and an Example." *American Journal of Agricultural Economics* 57: 410–419.

Robison, L., and P. Barry. 1987. *The Competitive Firm's Response to Risk.* New York: Macmillan.

Schultz, Theodore W. 1932. "Diminishing Returns in View of Progress in Agricultural Production." *Journal of Farm Economics* 14 (4): 640–649.

Turvey, C., T. Baker, and A. Weersink. 1992. "Farm Operating Risk and Cash Rent Determination." *Journal of Agricultural and Resource Economics* 17 (1): 186–194.

Tweeten, Luther G. 1969. "Theories Explaining the Persistence of Low Resource Returns in a Growing Farm Economy." *American Journal of Agricultural Economics* 51: 798–817.

U.S. Department of Agriculture. (USDA). 2004. *2002 Census of Agriculture.* Volume 1, Geographic Area Series Part 51, AC-02-A-51, National Agricultural Statistical Service, June.

———. 2006. "Farm Income and Costs: Farm Income Forecasts." Economic Research Service "Briefing Room," available at www.ers.usda.gov/Briefing/FarmIncome/data/Hh_t5.htm, August.

U.S. Department of Agriculture, Economic Research Service (USDA/ERS). Agricultural Resource Management Survey, Phase III, and Farm Costs and Returns Surveys for 1996 through 2004.

U.S. Department of Agriculture, National Agricultural Statistics Service (USDA/NASS). 2000. *Agricultural Prices, 1999 Summary.* Washington, DC, July.

Viceira, Luis M. 2001. "Optimal Portfolio Choice for Long-Horizon Investors with Nontradable Labor Income." *Journal of Finance* 56: 433–470.

Yee, J., M. Ahearn, and W. Huffman. 2004. "Links Among Farm Productivity, Off-Farm Work, and Farm Size in the Southeast." *Journal of Agricultural & Applied Economics* 36 (3): 591–603.

CHAPTER 16

COMMODITY MARKET EVOLUTION

"Now you see it, now you don't."
Statement often made by magicians.

One of the most common strategies used by American agricultural producers when faced with declining profits in a commodity market is to simply find another market that offers more profits. The effect of this strategy is to cause commodity markets to evolve over time. In the distant past, it was relatively easy for farmers to switch their production efforts out of one commodity and into another one that offered brighter prospects in the local market. If that failed, farmers could literally move to a new geographical market—a strategy used often as settlers moved west during the 1700s, 1800s, and early 1900s. In the modern era, characterized by a global agricultural market, some American farmers are still moving to new locations that offer profits, but those are now on different continents. Eastern Europe (especially Ukraine) and South America have become the new base of operations for a growing number of American farmers. For most producers, however, leaving the United States is not an option they are willing or able to consider.

Therefore, the modern market evolution process involves shifting production from one form of a single product to a new form. Farmers are pursuing higher profit margins by producing higher-quality forms of existing commodities. This strategy began many decades ago as agricultural research began to rapidly expand the number of plant varieties available. Near the end of the 1900s, a new version of this strategy emerged in the form of "organic" products.

At present, many people are asking, "can 'organics' save American agriculture?" Before that question can be answered, the numerous economic issues involved must be understood. Therefore, this chapter first explains this strategy and its economic processes in terms of how it affects commodity market evolution, then it summarizes the likely long-term implications for American farmers and ranchers.

PRODUCT QUALITY AND MARKET EVOLUTION

Organic agriculture essentially consists of a different production process from conventional methods, one that produces a commodity with some attributes that consumers consider "higher-quality" and thus more desirable than those of the current standard product form. Offermann and Nieberg (2002) answer the question "what is organic agriculture?" as follows: "Popularly known for renouncing the use of artificial fertilizers and pesticides, organic farming involves holistic production management systems emphasizing the use of management practices in preference to the use of off-farm inputs. This is accomplished by using, where possible, cultural, biological and mechanical methods in preference to synthetic materials."

The incentives for farmers to use organic methods are many (social, environmental, and economic), but higher prices received is one of the most important (Burton, Rigby, and Young 1999, 2003; Fairweather 1999; O'Riordan and Cobb 2001). Higher prices are received for organic commodities when consumers believe there is a quality premium available in an organic product's attributes (Boland and Schroeder 2002; Loureiro, McCluskey, and Mittelhammer 2001; Thompson and Kidwell 1998). The drawback to organic methods for farmers is that they often produce lower yields, raising unit costs (Lansink, Pietola, and Backman 2002; Tzouvelekas, Pantzios, and Fotopoulos 2001b). Therefore, increased profitability is not a certainty when shifting to organic production methods, and this inhibits some producers' willingness to make the shift (Lohr and Park 1992; Offermann and Nieberg 2000; Pietola and Lansink 2001; Tzouvelekas, Pantzios, and Fotopoulos 2001a). However, if a new market does reward early participants with profits, other farmers will be attracted to that market.

Agricultural product markets evolve over time as product attributes and consumer demand change. Small changes in demand or supply can create market "niches" that succeed or fail based on both the desirability of the product attribute differences and the profitability of serving the niche. Some niches disappear quickly, others grow and some become the market norm. For organic agriculture, there is some debate about "how big can the niche get?" (Klonsky and Tourte 1998). It has been hypothesized by some in the American organic industry that about 20 percent of total product sales is as big as an organic niche can, or should, get. Those people expecting the niche to remain a minority in the market think there is some constraint on consumer attitudes that prevents organic products from achieving general acceptance. For example, for some people, "organic" also means supporting local farmers and minimizing transport. To the extent that these concepts are embodied in the organic philosophy, it surely limits how large the sector could become, especially in cold climates. On the other hand, those people arguing that the niche *should* remain small to generate optimal economic results fear that general market acceptance will bring unfavorable changes to the industry, most notably lower output prices.

This chapter attempts to address the three- questions, "How big can, should, will organic markets get?" The first question is theoretical. It is shown how organic agriculture, in general, *can* become the norm in many American commodity markets. Then, the two other questions are addressed, noting that there is disagreement over the normative "should" question and much uncertainty about the positive/probabilistic "will" question. The chapter makes at least three contributions to the literature. First, a new theory is derived to explain the market evolution of products developed as a quality variant. The new theory is a composite of standard theories for different market structures and is modified for application to commodity markets. Another contribution is the chapter's review of the literature covering the many economic issues involved, noting differences necessary when dealing with agricultural commodities rather than branded products. Along the way, three general propositions are presented from which testable hypotheses can be drawn for future research. These propositions will contribute to the understanding of, and debate about, agricultural niche market evolution. Finally, some policy implications for organic markets are presented. This topic is important because the increasing pace of technological innovation is likely to make developing and pursuing quality variant markets an important new strategy for agricultural producers.

BACKGROUND

Organic agriculture in the United States has been receiving much attention since the government implemented standards for "organic" products in October 2002. Most reports highlight the rapid growth and bright prospects for the industry. For example, Dimitri and Greene (2002, p. 2) report that "once a niche product sold in a limited number of retail outlets, organic foods are currently sold in a wide variety of venues including farmers markets, natural product supermarkets, conventional supermarkets, and club stores. Since the early 1990s, certified organic acreage has increased as producers strive to meet increasing demand for organic agricultural and food products in the United States." In 2000, for the first time, more organic food was purchased in conventional supermarkets than in any other venue, plus organic products were sold in 73 percent of all conventional grocery stores (Dimitri and Greene 2002). Such market changes imply that organic products are on their way to widespread acceptance, which could lead to their becoming market norms. However, that conclusion is premature. The USDA (2002) reported that in 2001 certified organic acreage totaled 2.3 million, but that represents only 0.3 percent of the 828.0 million acres in American agriculture. Nevertheless, there is currently a rapid expansion of organic agriculture from a niche activity to nascent industry (Goodman 2000).

Across the European Union, the market for organic products is growing rapidly (Michelson et al. 1999) and producers in most countries are expanding output. Although, on average, the price of organic products is twice that of conventionally grown food, excess demand still exists within Europe (Sylvander and Le Floc'h Wadel 2000). For example, in the United Kingdom consumer demand is currently growing faster than supply despite the largest wave of farm conversions ever (Rigby, Young, and Burton 2001). Therefore, Europeans are optimistic about the prospects for organic agriculture.

GENERAL PROPOSITION

These rapid developments are certainly going to cause changes in the economic performance of organic markets in the future. To understand and anticipate those changes, a general theory is needed to explain the market evolution that can take a niche and make it a norm. This section outlines such an economic theory. The formal details are presented in the next section.

To begin, the theory proposed here, called the "Wheel of Commodity Marketing," follows the approach used in the "Wheel of Retailing" model of retail outlet evolution over time (described in Kohls and Uhl, 1980, p. 122). That approach is to focus on the basis for competition between firms over time as innovations create opportunities for market segmentation. The "Wheel of Retailing" describes a process that begins with stores competing using a low-price and low-service marketing strategy. Since all stores begin with low prices and customer service levels, they cannot afford to drop prices relative to their competition, so they compete with each other by gradually offering more services. If that method of differentiating itself succeeds in raising sales, a store continues to offer more services and pays for them by gradually raising prices. Over time, the entire category of store shifts to competition focusing on a marketing strategy of high quality, service, and prices as the outlet type matures. This shift in focus of competition between firms within an outlet category means that the original market segment (i.e., those customers preferring a low-price and low-service format) is not being served. This enables a new generation of firms to enter the market by offering a low-price and low-service option to customers, thus causing the "Wheel" to roll into a new market stage. For example, in the 1800s, "general stores" carrying many basic food products were the new innovation that began replacing specialty shops (e.g., butcher, baker, etc.). Then, in the early 1900s, came grocery stores with diverse food product lines, followed in the mid-to-late 1900s by supermarkets, and eventually "mega-stores" (*hypermarkets* in the European context). Each outlet type offered the lowest prices at the time of its development, but migrated up the Wheel toward higher prices and higher services with competition from similar outlets, thus leaving the low-price market segment vulnerable to capture by the next innovation. At any point in time, many forms of retail outlets may be operating in the market, but new entrants are most plentiful in the low-price segment and exits are more common in the high-price segment.

The "Wheel of Commodity Marketing" proposed here describes the transformation of a niche to the norm as involving similar economic processes to those observed in the retail case, although the focus of firm competition is reversed. The new "Wheel" begins turning when a technical and/or managerial innovation enables a firm to offer a higher-quality agricultural commodity at a price premium to a segment of the market. If sufficient numbers of consumers accept the new (organic) product to make it profitable for the producer to continue supplying it, other suppliers will be attracted. Initially all suppliers serving the niche will use a high-quality, high-price marketing strategy, so the focus of competition between them is on product quality. Over time, if consumer demand for the new product continues to make profits available to market participants, new suppliers will be attracted, thus total product supplies will increase. The increased number of suppliers makes it increasingly difficult for firms to differentiate their products. This causes the focus of competition between suppliers to shift from product attributes and quality to price. The "Wheel of Commodity Marketing" keeps turning as demand pushes the niche to become the norm, causing the growing number of suppliers to become price takers in the increasingly competitive market. In essence, consumer demand has turned what was a "high-quality" product into the new market standard that all suppliers must provide; the original standard product is no longer acceptable to consumers. Thus, all remaining suppliers of the new standard product are again faced with the low-price competitive market structure that existed at the beginning of the Wheel's cycle. A new cycle for the Wheel begins when another innovation enables a firm to pursue a new high-quality, high-price market segment. Again, as the Wheel turns, an old product is replaced by one offering new attributes and qualities, so competition is based on *quality* at first, but then on *price* as the number of firms offering the new product expands.

The "Wheel of Commodity Marketing," as applied to organic agriculture, is summarized in the following proposition.

- PROPOSITION 16.1. *Organic product marketing is characterized by a cycle that begins with a technical and/or managerial innovation that enables a firm to offer consumers a higher-quality product at a price above that in the standard market. Over time, a profitable niche attracts more suppliers, thus changing the market structure from a monopoly toward perfect competition, causing the focus of competition between firms to shift from quality to price. If consumers demand the higher-quality product, the niche will eventually become the norm, with a majority of sales being made in that category at prices near the competitive level of the original standard product.*

Many years may be required to observe this phenomenon, and it will not occur completely for most niches. Also, the evolution of organic markets is expected to require the "Wheel of Commodity Marketing" to keep turning with "new" organic products and/or methods being introduced, even if each niche becomes the market norm. This is similar to the way introduction of new plant varieties keeps pushing the market norm along over time. The economic theory behind this process is presented in the next section.

ECONOMICS OF THE MARKET EVOLUTION PROCESS

The model of market evolution presented below describes how a successful niche grows to be recognized as a market segment and, eventually, as the market norm while the market structure shifts from a monopoly to oligopoly and finally to a competitive market. This is possible in organic commodity markets partly because there are no significant barriers to entry for new producers.[1] The technology can be acquired and managerial innovations can be learned.

The market evolution process begins when a single firm is dissatisfied enough with the current market (usually because it does not offer enough profits) to seek some innovation with which it can capture some of the consumer surplus at the high end of the demand curve. In other words, the firm wants to get a higher price for its output. Pepall (1992) found that "first-mover firms" could be successful in achieving higher prices and profits if they identified a "special characteristic" or product attribute desired by consumers. Zucker and Anderson (1998) and Leoncini (2001) also noted that profitable market niches were identified by product attributes that could be the basis for product differentiation. However, Bastian et al. (1999) and Ilbery and Kneafsey (1999) showed that successful niches in food markets attract competitors and eventually become contested. Finally, Suryanata (2000) described how expansion of global competition has made it difficult for farmers to maintain premium values, even those from place-association, leaving producers caught in a "niche market treadmill" in that they continuously seek new potentials for high-value crops but are unable to maintain control of the market (and its profit margins) beyond their inventive stage.

Thus, the model here focuses on the behavior of firms using product quality to separate buyers into market niches. The literature is full of studies showing that there are quality variants for different classes of buyers (e.g., Kwoka 1992; Locay and Rodriguez 1992). It is well known that successful market segmentation may confer monopoly power to a firm through the ability to practice price discrimination (Nicholson 1998, pp. 578–579). What has received little attention is how a commodity market evolves over time when consumers recognize that some product innovation does offer more of the attributes that they judge to be of higher quality than the current market norm. That process is modeled in the following subsections.

Monopoly Stage

An innovative "first-mover firm" becomes a monopolist when it is the first to offer a higher-quality (organic) product in a local market. Graphically, the firm's situation is shown in Figure 16.1 (linear supply and demand functions are used for illustrative purposes). Panel A shows the single demand curve for the general product, indicating that consumers are not yet aware of the new version of the product. There are now two supply curves, one for the product created using conventional methods and another for the new, organic version. The position of the organic supply curve shows that costs per unit are much higher for the new product than those of the conventional product. However, the organic supply curve intersects the demand curve, so there are consumers willing to pay the higher prices necessary to make the new product profitable. The challenge to the farmer is to find a market outlet that reaches those consumers.

Panel B of Figure 16.1 shows the situation facing the first-mover firm. It is a price taker in the conventional product market. That means it could produce quantity Q_c^* and receive the conventional market price of P_c. On the other hand, since it is the only firm offering the new product (meaning that it represents the entire organic supply curve in Panel A), it can sell some small quantity of the organic product (Q_o) at the organic market price (P_o) by devoting some resources to producing and marketing the new product. The amount of resources that the firm will devote to producing and marketing the organic product determines the location of the supply curve, S_o. The allocation decision between conventional and organic production is made as follows.

To begin, how much consumers are willing to pay for quality (Θ) is given by the demand function $P_o(Q_o, \Theta)$ where $\partial P_o / \partial Q_o < 0, \partial P_o / \partial \Theta > 0$ and the quality of the organic product is

Figure 16.1   **The Initial Situation for a First-Mover Firm**

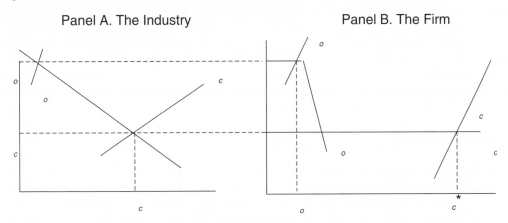

Panel A. The Industry   Panel B. The Firm

Note: c = conventional, o = organic

higher than the quality of the conventional product (or the organic product has some desirable attribute that is missing from the conventional product). If the costs of producing Q_o and Θ are given by $C_o(Q_o, \Theta)$, the first-mover firm will choose Q_o and Θ to maximize

(16.1) $$\pi = P_o(Q_o, \Theta)Q_o - C_o(Q_o, \Theta).$$

The first-order conditions are

(16.2) $$\frac{\partial \pi}{\partial Q_o} = P_o(Q_o, \Theta) + Q_o \frac{\partial P_o}{\partial Q_o} - C_Q = 0$$

(16.3) $$\frac{\partial \pi}{\partial \Theta} = Q_o \frac{\partial P_o}{\partial \Theta} - C_\Theta = 0.$$

As shown in Panel B, it is assumed that the firm's price and marginal revenue (MR) are flat (fixed) for the small quantity of new product the farmer can make available in the short run. In the small organic market outlet, such as a local farmer's market, a single price has to be offered to all customers, but that price is much higher than the average price received by the farmer in the conventional market. Also, the marginal revenue from this small amount of organic sales is assumed to be higher than those from the conventional market, so the farmer will provide Q_o first and then devote all remaining resources to supplying the conventional market outlet. Therefore, the firm can practice third-degree price discrimination by having a unique price in each of the two separate markets; however the farmer is still a price taker in the conventional market. Note in Panel B that the flat portion of the organic demand curve (D_o) extends to the right of the point of intersection with S_o, indicating that the market outlet had more customers than the farmer could supply at P_o.[2] This shows that the firm's organic output decision was to select the quantity at which marginal revenue equals marginal cost (MC) for that market. A monopolist practicing third-degree price discrimination makes output decisions for separated markets such that $MR = MC$ in each market.

As can be seen in Panel A of Figure 16.1, the price premium received for high-quality organic products peaks early in the life of a product or industry (Park and Lohr 1996; Thompson 1998, 2000). As the niche's supply grows larger and more consumers become aware of it, the market-clearing price decreases. Still, a significant premium over the conventional market price exists at this point in the market's evolution. At this point, there are two product supplies (as shown in Panel A) because the firm now differentiates its products. However, a single market demand persists because a majority of consumers do not perceive or distinguish between the higher-quality attributes of the new organic product versus the standard product.

Oligopoly Stage

As more consumers become aware of, and interested in, the new product's quality and/or attributes, the niche grows in size in two ways: more farmers adopt the organic technology to supply the expanding organic market, and the market becomes an oligopoly. First, the growth in demand may occur across a large geographic area creating spatial differentiation between firms as new suppliers enter the market in locations that had not been supplied previously. For organic products, outlets such as farmers' markets often emphasize freshness or other attributes that give nearby suppliers an advantage (Egan 2002). Local firms also have lower transportation costs than more distant suppliers. Thus, spatial differentiation makes it possible for relatively high-cost producers to become first-mover firms in local markets. This, in turn, makes the new product available to more consumers, helping to increase total consumer awareness of the product's attributes.

The second way the niche grows is when additional farmers decide to supply a market in which a first-mover firm is already operating. In this situation, two sorts of product differentiation occur. First, all firms within the single geographic market seek to differentiate the new (organic) product from the conventional product. The firms make this effort because product-differentiated oligopolies can benefit greatly by creating market power (Mazzeo 2002; Vickner and Davies 1999) and quality is a good basis for achieving differentiation (Giraud-Heraud, Soler, and Tanguy 1999). In other words, the firms strive to convince consumers that the new organic product is a higher-quality item so as to justify the organic price premium over the conventional product. Second, the firms try to differentiate themselves from one another.

At this early point in the market's evolution, consumers generally consider there to be only one "product group" for a specific commodity (e.g., carrots or lettuce or peaches, etc.) that includes both conventional and organic products.[3] Nevertheless, firms supplying the new organic product operate like a product-differentiated oligopoly with regards to their production and pricing behavior. A simple model of the behavior observed at this stage of the Wheel of Commodity Marketing follows.

To begin, assume there are m firms in the single product group and n of those are operating in the organic oligopoly within a geographic market (thus $m \geq n \geq 2$). Each of the n firms must decide how many resources to shift into (1) production of the organic product, and (2) differentiating its products. It is again assumed that all resources not used on the organic product will be directed into the conventional product. Organic production efforts of the ith firm result in quantity q_i, while resources used in their differentiation efforts are denoted as ϕ_i. The firm's total costs are $TC_i(q_i, \phi_i)$. There are $n + 1$ products in the product group at this point—one conventional product that is identical for all firms and n slightly different organic products, one for each of the firms operating in the oligopoly. That means there could be n different prices (denoted $P_1, \ldots, P_n$) for the organic products.[4] However, the price received by the ith firm depends on consumer demand for its product, which is a function of the quantity it produces, prices being charged by all other firms (P_j for $j \neq i$), and on that firm's and all other firms' efforts to differentiate their products ($\phi_j, j = 1, n$): $P_i = f(q_i, P_j, \phi_i, \phi_j)$, where $i \neq j$. This market is assumed to be normal in that $\partial f / \partial q_i \leq 0, \partial f / \partial P_j \geq 0, \partial f / \partial \phi_i \geq 0$, and $\partial f / \partial \phi_j \leq 0$.

The ith firm's profit is

(16.4)
$$\pi_i = P_i q_i - TC_i(q_i, \phi_i).$$

In the case where $\partial \phi_j / \partial q_i, \partial P_j / \partial q_i, \partial \phi_j / \partial \phi_i$, and $\partial P_j / \partial \phi_i$ are all zero, the first-order conditions are

(16.5)
$$\frac{\partial \pi_i}{\partial q_i} = P_i + q_i \frac{\partial P_i}{\partial q_i} - \frac{\partial TC_i}{\partial q_i} = 0$$

(16.6)
$$\frac{\partial \pi_i}{\partial \phi_i} = qi \frac{\partial P_i}{\partial \phi_i} - \frac{\partial TC_i}{\partial \phi_i} = 0.$$

These conditions state that production and differentiation activities should each be expanded to the point at which their marginal revenues equal marginal costs. The model in Equations 16.4 through 16.6 differs from the model in Equations 16.1 through 16.3 in two important ways. First, Equations 16.1 through 16.3 are for a single, first-mover firm while the second model is for multiple firms. Second, the key difference is the shift in competitive activities of firms. When a market has only a single supplier, that firm focuses on the costs of creating quality differences between its new product and the conventional product. When there are two or more firms supplying a higher-quality product to a market, each of those firms must focus on both the costs of creating quality differences in its product and the costs of informing consumers of those differences.

Previous empirical results show that this market structure influences the competitive behavior of firms. For example, Vickner and Davies (1999) found a higher degree of price collusion among brands within a market segment than they found between segments for conventional spaghetti. This implies that the differentiation efforts of organic firms are more often aimed at separating themselves from the conventional market rather than from each other. This is likely due to a goal of developing and maintaining an organic price premium that might be jeopardized if competition within the organic niche became too direct.

The long-run effect of firms' efforts to differentiate the organic product from the conventional version is to separate the single product group into two product groups that are now viewed as distinct by consumers. Figure 16.2 illustrates the changes that occur in a successful niche during the oligopoly stage of the Wheel of Commodity Marketing.

Panel A of Figure 16.2 shows the situation at the beginning of the stage as more resources are shifted into organic production. There is still only one demand curve because buyers view the quality variants as part of one quality distribution for a single product group. Current production and sales are skewed toward the right end of the demand distribution (lower quality) because that has been the competitive equilibrium in the market. However, as firms in the new organic niche begin to adjust their resource allocations in the expectation of increasing profits through sales in the niche, the supply curve of the conventional product, S_c, moves to the left and the organic supply curve, S_o, moves to the right.

At some point in time, the demand curve breaks into two separate quality distributions (market segments), as shown in Panel B of Figure 16.2. This means that many consumers have become

Figure 16.2   **Oligopoly Stage Changes in the Niche**

Panel A. Market with two segments   Panel B. Segments become two markets

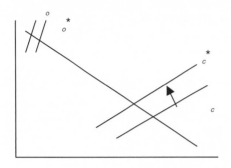 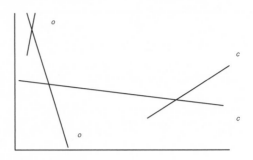

Note: c = conventional, o = organic

aware of information that changed their attitudes and now they make a distinction between the conventional and organic products based on each product's ability to satisfy their demand for specific quality attributes. This change in demand is the result of the information and education effects of firms' differentiation efforts.[5] In other words, a successful niche is one in which suppliers are able to convince sufficient numbers of consumers that there are attributes of the new product that are different from, and more desirable than, those of the conventional product. This distinction is often difficult to achieve because, as Lambert and Wilson (2003) note, agricultural markets may be inefficient in that signals do not adequately reflect product characteristics important to market participants. Governmental standards can complement the efforts of suppliers to differentiate organic from conventional products. Although some consumers may not trust governmental standards, other consumers will view governmental standards as those established by a disinterested third party at arm's length from firms in the industry. As such, standards transmit disinterested information whereas firms' efforts to promote their own products may be perceived by consumers as advertising with more persuasive than informational content. Thus, differentiation efforts have (at least partially) succeeded when a separate demand curve for an organic product, D_o, can be identified.

Which new distribution (i.e., demand function) is relevant to a firm's product depends on the product's degree of differentiation in the eyes of consumers. That assessment can be represented by a differentiation variable that ranges from zero to one ($0 \leq \Phi_i \leq 1$) in value. When $\Phi_i = 0$, a consumer sees no difference in product satisfaction between the ith firm's organic product and the market's conventional product. In this case, the two products are perfect substitutes for one another because the consumer perceives no difference between them and thus buys the lower-priced conventional product. When $\Phi_i = 1$, a consumer believes the ith firm's organic product fully provides the desirable attributes that the market's conventional product lacks. This prompts the consumer to pay a higher price, up to that which contains his/her full consumer surplus (CS) for the higher-quality product. In all other situations, $0 < \Phi_i < 1$, a consumer will weigh the degree of differentiation against the relationship between the ith firm's organic price premium and her/his consumer surplus for an organic product with all the desirable attributes, and will buy the organic product only when

(16.7) $$\Phi_i \geq (P_i - P_c)/CS.$$

$CS = P_{i*} - P_c$, and P_{i*} is the highest price an individual consumer would be willing to pay for the ith firm's organic product if it was fully differentiated.

Over time, successful organic niches develop a standard product due to actions by producers and consumers. This process gradually transforms the differentiated oligopoly into a homogeneous oligopoly that is quasi-competitive. Producers aid this process first by focusing their differentiation efforts primarily on product attributes (conventional versus organic), rather than on competing firms. This helps consumers learn about attributes without having a significant depressing effect on organic prices. As the market reveals which attribute-bundles (i.e., products) are the most desired, and profitable for suppliers, surviving firms migrate toward that product form. This means that the outputs of firms in the organic market become more alike in terms of product characteristics. The second influence leading to organic product standardization is consumers' desire for quality standards. This has taken the form of both farmer "certification" and the organic product standards issued by the U.S. government in October 2002. Consumers wanted both forms of information to reduce their uncertainty when making purchase decisions. The effects of these developments are, by definition, to standardize products in the market (Lohr 1998; Lohr and Park 1992), thus making it much more difficult for firms to differentiate their output from other firms' products.

The emergence of a standard, successful organic product reduces suppliers' ability to influence prices, thus making that market become quasi-competitive. This can happen more easily in the market for an agricultural commodity than for a value-added product or a manufactured good. As McClusky (2000) notes, organic commodities can have unobservable attributes of concern to consumers, thus making it more difficult to convince all consumers that real differences exist. As the range of product attributes narrows in the organic market, suppliers become (or at least behave like) price takers. This changes the model of the ith firm to the following.

The demand curve for the organic product shows that the price consumers, as a group, are willing to pay is a function of total quantities supplied by all n firms in the market:

(16.8) $$P = f(q_1 + q_2 + \ldots + q_n).$$

Each firm seeks to maximize its profits given the market price and its total costs of producing and marketing q_i. This is stated

(16.9) $$\pi_i = Pq_i - TC_i(q_i)$$

$$= f(q_1 + q_2 + \ldots + q_n)q_i - TC_i(q_i).$$

The first-order condition in this case becomes

(16.10) $$\frac{\partial \pi_i}{\partial q_i} = P - \frac{\partial TC_i(q_i)}{\partial q_i} = 0.$$

This condition states that each firm should produce the quantity for which its marginal costs equal the market price. The model in Equations 16.8 through 16.10 differs from the model in 16.4 through 16.6 in that differentiation activities are discontinued, indicating suppliers no longer believe those activities to be profitable. At this point in the Wheel of Commodity Marketing, firms begin behaving as price takers and the organic market moves toward a competitive outcome.

As the successful organic niche continues to attract consumers, more farmers become aware of it and shift resources to organic production in response to the higher expected profits offered by that market, as compared to the conventional market. Entry of new firms, however, helps transform the market from an oligopoly into an increasingly competitive structure.

Competitive Stage

The final stage of the Wheel of Commodity Marketing is characterized by change early and equilibrium late. The underlying factor driving the market at this stage is the spread of information. Consumers are increasingly aware of the new organic product and, in a successful niche, are shifting more of their purchases from the conventional product to the organic version. This increase in demand causes more farmers to become aware of, and pay attention to, the organic product, and, if it offers them a profit, to enter that market. Eventually, the niche becomes the norm when most consumers demand the quality attributes and farmers respond by shifting most resources into that technology.[6] This process is similar to what the famous economist Joseph Schumpeter called "creative destruction."

The rapid change occurring early in this stage is most noticeable on the supply side. The increased competition from farmers entering the organic market pushes supplies up and prices down. Conventional product supplies decrease over time as farmers leave that market in favor of the more profitable organic market. Also, the market price for the conventional product may decrease if consumers reassess their demand for it upon comparison with the new organic product. At this point in the market's evolution, consumers prefer the organic product's attributes, and supply increases cause its price to drop until the organic price is low enough to make it a "better buy" than the conventional commodity (which has lower quality). In general, the process leads to "fighting brands" and product line pruning (Johnson and Myatt 2003) resulting from the dissipation of profits as new suppliers enter the market (Rogerson 1987).

On the demand side of the market, consumers respond gradually to changes in information regarding the organic (higher-quality) product and to changes in prices and household income. Consumer response to product information is gradual because the sources of information change through time.[7] In the initial stages, product information is supplied almost exclusively by the firms themselves in the absence of clearly defined standards and certification. However, as the organic market matures, standards become more clearly defined and uniform, allowing consumers to distinguish clearly between organic and conventional versions of the same product.

As the supply curves for conventional and organic products shift rapidly, consumers will react to the resulting changes in market prices. Cross-price elasticities between organic and conventional food products measure the shifts in one product's market demand curve as the market price of the other product changes. Define the relevant uncompensated cross-price elasticities as $\varepsilon_j^{o,c} \equiv \partial ln Q_j^{org} / \partial ln P_j^{conv}$ and $\varepsilon_j^{c,o} \equiv \partial ln Q_j^{conv} / \partial ln P_j^{org}$ where j denotes the same food product differing only by organic (*org*) or conventional (*conv*) production methods. The aggregate quantity supplied of the jth organic product, Q_j^{org}, is the sum of all n firms' quantities supplied, $(q_1 + q_2 + \ldots + q_n)$, as in Equation 16.8.

- PROPOSITION 16.2a. *If $\varepsilon_i^{o,c}$ is positive in sign and "large" in magnitude, a given price increase for a conventional food product—or a given price decrease for an organic food product—will induce a "large" crossover or substitution of the organic for the conventional food, thereby shifting out the market demand curve for the organic food.*

This proposition suggests that as firms reallocate resources away from producing the conventional product and the aggregate supply schedule of the conventional product shifts back to the left, the resulting increase in conventional product price would drive consumers to buy relatively more organic products, thereby shifting out the demand curve for the organic product.

Another source of potential change in market demand curves is growth in household incomes. It is well documented that as household incomes grow through time owing to general economic growth, food consumption patterns change. The quantitative effects of growing household incomes on consumer choices of organic versus conventional products are measured by income (expenditure) elasticities. Define the income elasticity of the jth organic (conventional) product as $\eta_j^o \equiv \partial lnQ_j^{org}/\partial lnI$ ($\eta_j^c \equiv \partial lnQ_j^{conv}/\partial lnI$), where I denotes aggregate income. Gradual economic growth resulting in higher household incomes suggests the following:

- PROPOSITION 16.2b. *If income elasticities for organic products are large ($n_j^o > 1$), and income elasticities for conventional counterparts are smaller ($n_j^c < n_j^o$), market demands for organic foods will shift out more rapidly than market demands for conventional products as aggregate income rises.*

In heuristic terms, growth in household incomes allows consumers the possibility of substituting luxury (higher-quality) products for inferior (conventional) products. The results of economic prosperity in this case will lead to gradual but more pronounced shifts outward of the demand curve for the organic product than for the conventional product. This can be considered a "necessary condition" for an organic niche to become a market norm.

A third specific proposition can be derived about the role of demand in a niche market's evolution:

- PROPOSITION 16.2c. *Large own-price elasticities for organic food ($|\varepsilon_o| > 1$) will result in more market expansion for any given demand curve for organic foods. The effect of shifts out in the supply function for organic foods will result in more market expansion when own-price elasticities are large.*

Gradually, supply and demand shifts must make the organic segment larger than that for the original conventional product if the niche is to be successful in becoming the norm. At some point consumers quit buying the old commodity and buy only organic. This situation is illustrated in Figure 16.3. As illustrated, the two supply and demand curves have shifted such that market supply is entirely organic—the supply and demand curves for the conventional product still exist, but no longer intersect.

Changes in industry structure from the time that the first-mover firm establishes the organic niche until the early competitive stage can give the organic market a different supply function than that observed late in the competitive stage of the Wheel of Commodity Marketing. Specifically, long-run supply may be decreasing cost for the organic farming industry while it is a niche. There are two possible causes for this. First, a new niche may have no production and/or marketing infrastructure in place, but that infrastructure develops with the expansion of the successful niche, thus lowering firms' costs per unit as total supplies increase over time. Second, a niche is not a "perfectly contestable market" (Baumol 1982) because there is the chance of new, lower-cost firms entering the market as soon as they learn of the opportunity. When a niche grows large enough to become the norm, firms are obviously aware of the opportunity, so the market becomes perfectly contestable, as summarized in the following proposition:

Figure 16.3   **The Competitive Stage: The Old Market Gives Way to the New**

Organic niche becomes the market norm

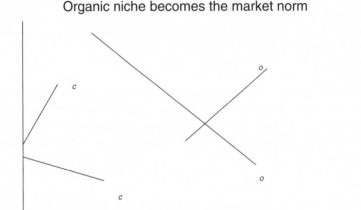

- PROPOSITION 16.3. *If a product's long-run supply elasticity is negative, its market is still only a small niche. When that market becomes perfectly contestable, its long-run supply elasticity is positive and the niche is moving toward becoming the norm.*

The key development during the competitive stage of the Wheel of Commodity Marketing is that the organic market becomes perfectly contestable. This process may develop quickly or slowly, but the increasingly standardized attributes of the organic product assure that it will happen. The lack of farm-level barriers to commodity market entry makes it relatively easy for new firms to pursue any profit opportunities that may be available. As Nicholson (1998, p. 602) notes, "even in the absence of price-taking behavior in markets with relatively few firms, perfect contestability provides an 'invisible hand' that guides market equilibrium to a competitive-type result."

Therefore, the new long-run equilibrium observed at the end of the Wheel of Commodity Marketing (shown in Figure 16.3) may be the intersection of the *original* demand curve with the new supply curve. The original demand curve for the conventional product is replaced with the organic (higher-quality) demand curve during the turning of the Wheel, but the location of the new curve will be different from the original only if the shift to a higher-quality product in that market has changed consumers' demand relative to their demand for other products (i.e., a substitution effect). The new supply curve might be to the left of the original if organic yields are lower than conventional "high-input" product yields. Thus, the new equilibrium price might be somewhat higher and/or the quantity somewhat lower than the original (Panel A of Figure 16.1) unless technological innovation occurs as growers shift to organic production, causing the supply curve to move to the right.

Finally, after the niche becomes the new norm, the distribution of production across the scale range of operators (small- to large-scale) may be back to the original, with the *distribution of profits* across firms also being close to the original. Both of these outcomes depend upon the nature of the technological changes that occurred during the turning of the Wheel. For example, if the changes shifted in favor of labor-saving or labor-improving methods and operators, suppliers structured accordingly will benefit, possibly becoming more numerous, while other suppliers may be forced out of the market. The *level* of profits for the product market and individual firms is ambiguous, compared to the original. Some firms may make more or less profit per acre than they did growing the conventional product, but individual outcomes and the market average cannot be predicted a priori, it is an empirical question.

HOW BIG *CAN* ORGANIC MARKETS GET?

The results presented above show that, in theory, organic niches *can* grow to become 100 percent of a commodity market. These results are consistent with Schumpeter's ideas about "creative destruction" in that they describe how new innovations can grow through a process of destroying existing market practices and structures by replacing them with improved market evolutions.

However, the *possibility* of an organic product becoming the norm in a market should not be interpreted as a forecast. The prescriptive *desirability* and descriptive *probability* of such a market evolution are separate questions. Those questions are dealt with in the following two sections.

HOW BIG *SHOULD* ORGANIC MARKETS GET? (AND WHAT ARE THE POLICY IMPLICATIONS?)

The answer to the first, normative question depends on the perspective taken. The optimal size from an innovative first-mover producer's point of view is a monopoly or oligopoly that maximizes producer surplus. From the perspective of consumers, the optimal size and structure is a competitive market that maximizes consumer surplus.

Social welfare concerns often motivate individuals to participate in organic markets. For example, Stagl (2002) found that many producers and consumers view local markets and initiatives as promising alternatives to an unsustainable global agro-industrial food production system. However, not all local areas are suitable for agricultural production (or have very limited production seasons for a small number of crops), thus some consumers *must* be served by large-scale suppliers located in other geographical areas. This conflict implies that (at least some) organic markets must grow large enough to achieve scale economies for total consumer surplus to be maximized. Also, McCluskey (2000) showed that some organic markets need to grow large enough to support some third-party monitoring system to assure consumer satisfaction necessary for market sustainability.

Individual firms pursuing sustainable profits can make significant progress if they take a strategic approach to developing niches that are compatible with the market structure in which they operate (Kemp, Schot, and Hoogma 1998; Pepall 1992). This may mean farmers need to pursue specialized value-added niches when other forms of product differentiation hold little promise (Brester 1999). Such local or regional markets might be small in absolute scale, but can be large enough to absorb all the output of some producers. There has been some informal discussion among organic farmers about how big their niche should be to enable them to maximize their profits. Estimates in the 10 to 20 percent of market share range have been suggested without any known empirical research support. Still, the very fact that some growers do *not* want their niche to become the norm indicates that they are aware of, and may have experienced, the narrowing profit margins that come from increased competition in market segments.

The U.S. government has already intervened in the debate by virtue of creating standards. Establishment of national standards reduces an individual firm's costs of differentiating its organic products from conventional products. To the extent that firms allocate fewer resources to production promotion, marketing costs are reduced and firm-specific product supply curves shift out, thereby shifting out the market supply of organic products. A second supply-side effect of the establishment of national standards regards the entry of new firms into the organic market. New firms will likely find it more attractive to begin producing organic products because the costs of differentiating those products in the eyes of consumers are now lower than before the existence of national standards. The effects of national standards both on existing firms in the market as well as on new entrants work in concert to increase the supply of organic products. To the extent that the land base on which organic and conventional production occurs is fixed or shrinking due to urban encroachment on agricultural lands, a shift to the right in the organic supply function will induce an inward shift in the conventional supply function because land must be converted from conventional to organic production.[8]

National standards also reduce the costs incurred by consumers in verifying product attributes. Once national standards become familiar, consumers can simply look for easily recognizable organic logos that assure them of organic status without having to read detailed labeling on packages. To the extent search and verification costs incurred by consumers are reduced, more consumers should be able to recognize and distinguish organic products, thereby making these products more easily substitutable for conventional counterparts. Also, to the extent most consumers purchase either the organic or the conventional version of a given food product, national standards may induce an increase in the demand for organic products and a concomitant decrease in the aggregate demand for conventional products.

Ultimately, the joint supply and demand impacts of national standards enhance the likelihood of moving the organic product market from niche to mainstream as supply and demand functions for organic products increase. This raises the question of *why* the government created the standards and might intervene in support of organic markets in the future. Some possible answers are proposed below.

To begin with, policy motives and justification may be environmental. As consumers become more familiar with organic production methods, there may be more interest in governmental support of organic farming and ranching. To the extent that organic production methods reduce use of agricultural chemical inputs, some consumers may argue that organic methods should be supported by the government because they reduce negative externalities associated with conventional production methods. Policymakers might be persuaded that instead of paying farmers to take land out of conventional production methods as is done with Conservation Reserve and Acreage Programs, a more desirable alternative is to keep land in production by encouraging conversion of land from conventional to organic farming practices, as is done in Europe.

Organic farmers and ranchers may also be joined by consumers and become more persuasive advocates for policy intervention, particularly as their numbers grow. If the movement from niche to norm begins to reduce farm gate prices for organic products, it is plausible that organic producers might begin to lobby for increased support of the organic industry in general. Although conversion of more land to organic methods from conventional practices would tend to further depress farm gate prices, organic producers might argue that without support (payments?) for land conversion, further expansion of the organic industry might not occur. In this case, both producers and consumers might be sufficiently persuasive to garner government support for the organic industry.

At present, with producers and consumers in conflict over the answer to the "should" question, the outcome becomes an empirical question. Each market will have its own answer.

HOW BIG *WILL* ORGANIC MARKETS GET?

This is also an empirical question. The answer depends on the interaction of demand and supply dynamics. Price elasticity, substitution between conventional and organic products, suppliers' ability to profit at prices offered, policy effects on demand and supply, and many more factors influence the answer for each niche.

In the next decade or two it is likely that organic markets will grow faster in Europe than in the United States. This is partly due to policies in Europe that encourage farmers to convert to organic methods (Lohr and Salomonsson 2000), although similar policies are beginning to appear in the United States (Greene and Kremen 2003). However, without government support the key to market growth in Europe and the United States is consumer willingness to pay price premiums for organic products (Dimitri and Greene 2002; Offermann and Nieberg 2002; Rigby, Young, and Burton 2001). Zanoli, Gambelli, and Vairo (2000) report the general assessment of a group of European experts concerning five possible scenarios for organic market development by 2010, noting that consumer acceptance is the deciding factor. However, wealthy consumers are more able and willing to pay for relatively "high-quality" (lower-yield) commodities. This means income elasticities for organic products will be key indicators of market potential, however the short history of organic markets has constrained the number of income elasticities estimated empirically. For examples from the United States, see Glaser and Thompson (1999, 2000) and Thompson and Glaser (2001); for a European example see Wier and Smed (2000).

Currently, markets for some organic products are progressing toward "norm" status in the United States, although only one has achieved that level of market penetration. The *Nutrition Business Journal* reported that in 2001 the organic share of the small but expanding market for nondairy beverages (juices, soymilk, and rice milk) was 62 percent of the total. Other organic market shares reported were much smaller (e.g., baby food, 4.5 percent; fresh juice, 3.9 percent; cereal, 2.9 percent; produce, 2.7 percent; frozen meals, 2.3 percent; dairy, 0.9 percent). However, research reported by Moran (2001) indicated that 46 percent of dairy beverages (a subset of the "dairy" category) were organic in 2000. Thus, it is too early to forecast which markets will continue progressing along the path outlined by the model; many organic segments could stall in their development and remain a niche or fail entirely.

Paucity of Data for Empirical Studies

For purposes of testing the hypotheses generated by the foregoing theory and predicting the magnitudes of organic market expansion, market-level observations on prices and quantities are necessary. For analysis of supply-side phenomena, a time series of price-quantity observations on organic and conventional products at the farm gate is required. Similarly, on the demand side, time series observations on prices and quantities at retail are necessary to identify shifts in organic and conventional demand. For organic and conventional products traded at wholesale levels, analogous time series would be necessary to analyze price transmission relationships between the farm gate and retail markets. Unfortunately, none of these series has been collected consistently for any extended period in the United States or elsewhere.

Only a handful of econometric analyses of supply and demand for organic products have been conducted owing to the paucity of secondary data. Park and Lohr (1996) employed weekly wholesale data on selected fresh vegetables to estimate demand and supply effects in a partial adjustment model. The time series they used was available only from September 1985 to December 1989 because the Organic Market News and Information Service shortly after ceased to collect observations on wholesale quantities. On the retail side, Glaser and Thompson (1999, 2000) and Thompson and Glaser (2001) assembled time series for selected organic and conventional products using national scanner data from supermarkets.[9] Although the scanner data afford a national perspective, they are very costly to purchase from scanner data companies. Also, assembly of useful time series from scanner data requires painstaking and time-consuming aggregation of products across hundreds of different bar codes.

Given the paucity of secondary data for empirical studies, the only plausible alternative for empirical analysis is to conduct case studies. Therefore, two case studies follow that document qualitatively the evolution of supply and demand phenomena, but they clearly cannot provide quantitative estimates of shifts in supply and demand curves.

Use of case studies means we must select particular organic products for analysis. Of course, the availability of market information and sparse data partially dictates this choice. Another criterion used for choosing the products analyzed was the level of processing required. The first organic products made available several decades ago were fresh fruits and vegetables requiring almost no processing other than washing, sorting, and packing. As organic markets have matured, food products embodying more processing have become available. Most fresh produce items are viewed by consumers as undifferentiated products whereas processed products are all branded and some consumers believe in the reputation effects conferred by brands.

Given the foregoing criteria, fresh pears and processed baby foods were selected for analysis in the case studies. Pears are differentiated by variety—Anjou and Bosc, for example—but there are few, if any, brands that might differentiate pears at retail markets. For a given variety of pear, organic and conventional pears would be virtually indistinguishable without labels indicating growing practices. Baby foods, by contrast, are prominently branded and their processed nature means there are dozens of different products available—juices, cereals, biscuits, fruits, vegetables, meats, and combinations in various sizes of containers and formats. These two products should provide readers with interesting contrasts between foods with minimal processing and foods with considerable processing, branding, and marketing.

Organic Commodities: The Case of Northwest Winter Pears[10]

In Washington State, organic pear production started in the late 1980s, at about the time the Alar scare caused a sudden shift to organic production in the apple sector. Organic pear production increased slowly during the 1990s. Then from 1999 to 2002 organic pear acreage more than tripled, from 456 to 1,771 acres (Figure 16.4). In addition, organic pear acreage was expected to continue increasing over the next ten years (Carman et al. 2003). In contrast, conventional pear acreage remained approximately steady during the 1988–2002 period.

The Pear Bureau estimated for the 2002–2003 production year that 81 percent of organic winter pears were of the Anjou variety, compared to that variety's 74 percent share of total production of all pears. Bosc and Bartlett varieties represent most of the remaining organic winter pear production.

A study conducted in 1992 (Seavert 1992) analyzed costs of production for both conventional and organic Anjou pears. Results showed that organic costs per acre exceeded conventional costs by $127 per acre (Table 16.1), or about 3.8 percent. Two-thirds of this cost difference was due to the machinery and materials used in the organic spray program. Costs for harvest labor were higher for the conventional production because the conventional yield is higher than organic yields. At that time the sales price per box was $9.22 for organic Anjou pears and $7.85 for conventional Anjou pears. Even with this $1.37 premium, the combination of a lower yield (393 boxes per acre compared to 723 boxes per acre) and higher costs of production resulted in organic production being less profitable than conventional production. This probably explains why organic acreage expanded slowly during that period.

Figure 16.4   **Evolution of Organic Pear Acreage in Washington State, 1988–2002**

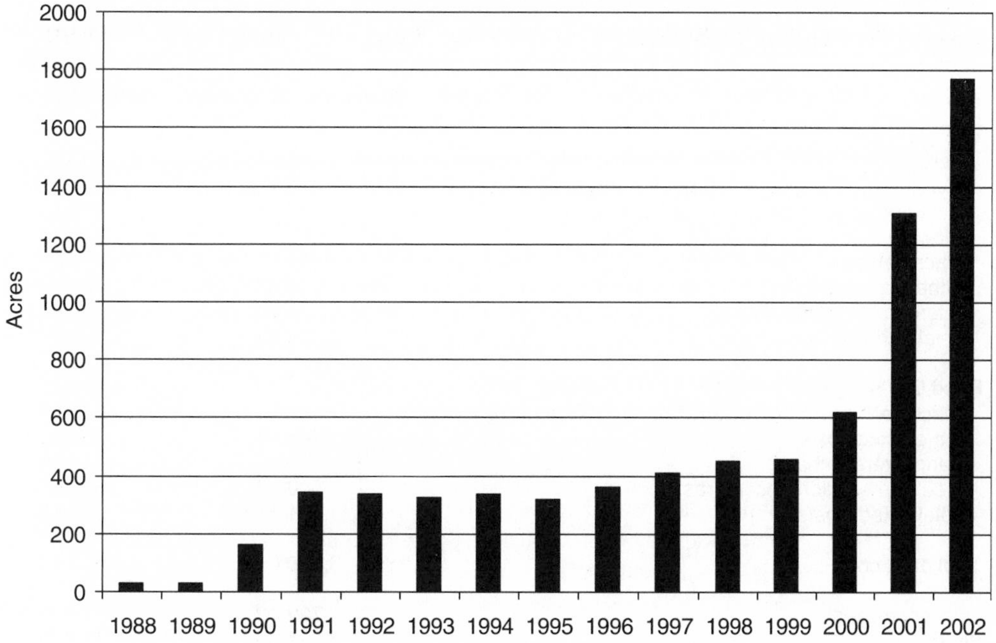

Source: Granatstein and Kirby (2002).

More recent surveys of growers indicate that organic production is still more expensive on a per-unit basis than conventional production. One large-scale organic pear producer interviewed in 1997 said organic pear production costs more because of labor-intensive tasks such as mowing, and more wear on equipment because of the greater number of applications of products such as insecticidal soaps (*Good Fruit Grower Magazine* 1997). However, the recent expansion in organic pear acreage may be explained by recent improvements in the relative profitability of organic pears due to the maintenance of a significant organic price premium, despite a declining trend in pear prices.

Granatstein and Kirby (2002) report organic pear prices from the Washington Grower's Clearinghouse Association, which began collecting organic pear prices in 1996. As shown in Table 16.2, organic Anjou pears sold in 1996 at prices more than twice the conventional price, that is, about $39 per box for organic Anjou compared to $18 per box for conventional Anjou. Since then, both conventional and organic prices have decreased, and the organic price premium has decreased as well. In 2002, organic Anjou pears still sold for about twice the conventional price, but the premium was just over $8 per box compared to about $20 per box in 1996.

Pear handlers expect organic pear prices to continue decreasing in the future, getting closer to the conventional price. Overproduction is mentioned in surveys as the reason for the price decrease. Also, handlers think that the pattern of prices is the same for conventional and organic pears. According to Carman et al. (2003), one survey respondent said that in the past conventional and organic price patterns were separated, but not anymore. Another handler mentioned

Table 16.1

D'Anjou Pear Enterprise Budget for a Conventional and an Organic Orchard in 1992

	Conventional ($/acre)	Organic ($/acre)
Variable Costs		
Fertilizer	62.78	30.40
Herbicide / Biological weed control (organic)	77.11	47.50
Spray program (conv: 7x, organic: 16x)	602.05	813.24
Mowing (conv: 4x, dandle mower, 2x)	23.67	18.26
Harvesting	532.16	475.89
Other variable costs	686.38	686.38
Interest: operating capital	24.80	25.90
Total Variable Costs	2,008.95	2,097.64
Fixed Costs		
Machine & equip depreciation, interest & housing	193.05	231.47
Other fixed costs	268.06	268.06
Land interest charge	350.00	350.00
Tree depreciation and interest	500.00	500.00
Total Fixed Costs	1,311.11	1,349.53
Total of all costs	3,320.06	3,447.17
Quantity (boxes)	723.18	393.38
$/box	7.85	9.22
Gross Income	5,677.00	3,628.58
Net projected returns	2,356.94	181.41

Source: lar Seavert ashington State University as reported in arman et al. (2003).

Table 16.2

Prices for Organic Pears in Washington State ($/44-pound box FOB)

Variety		1996	1997	1998	1999	2000	2001	2002
	Conventional	18.06	13.30	14.03	13.92	12.59	12.80	13.92
D'Anjou	Organic	38.67	24.50	30.20	25.73	24.64	15.00	22.34
	Premium	20.61	11.20	16.17	11.81	12.05	2.20	8.42
	Conventional	18.17	13.69	16.10	16.30	15.76	13.31	18.36
Bosc	Organic	41.04	41.48	37.57	34.73	24.81	15.82	27.65
	Premium	22.87	27.79	21.47	18.43	9.05	2.51	9.29
	Conventional	19.89	15.15	17.37	15.26	14.16	16.21	17.36
Bartlett	Organic	41.33	28.87	26.46	28.81	21.81	21.64	20.54
	Premium	21.44	13.72	9.09	13.55	7.65	5.43	3.18

Source: ranatstein and irby (2002).

that when the conventional price decreases it becomes difficult to sell organic pears without decreasing their price as well. Similarly, when the conventional price increases, the organic price also increases.

Clearly, the market for organic winter pears is still a niche. With only 3.8 percent of total pear acreage and 2.75 percent of total pear production, organic pears are far from becoming the market norm. However, they demonstrate the type of early potential that could lead to continued growth in market share. In particular, the maintenance of a price premium approximately equaling the conventional pear price during the recent expansion in output shows that (some) consumers are quite willing to pay for the perceived quality attributes. Also, the recent growth in organic pear acreage indicates that growers are expecting improved profitability from the niche.

Processed Organic Products: The Case of Baby Food

The market share of organic baby food grew significantly during the decade of the 1990s, achieving one of the highest market shares for processed organic food products. Market shares for various organic baby food products sold in mainstream supermarkets ranged from 2.3 percent for juices to 13.0 percent for dinners by 1999 (Thompson and Glaser 2001).[11] In contrast, most estimates of organic food sales resulted in total market shares of at most 1 to 2 percent. Baby foods present an interesting case to study because their market shares have grown much larger than those of most other organic food categories sold at retail.

The pioneers of the organic baby food firms were Arnold and Ronald Koos, who established Earth's Best in Vermont in 1987 (Grover 1991). Most of Earth's Best's initial sales were through health food stores (Harris 1997). At this incipient stage, organic baby food sales represented a niche market for several important reasons: Earth's Best was a relatively small firm offering a limited range of baby food products, which were not available in venues where the majority of the public bought its food. The giants of the conventional baby food industry—Gerber, Heinz, and Beech-Nut—literally dwarfed Earth's Best by selling a wide variety of conventional baby food products nationally in mainstream supermarkets. Gerber's total market share was a dominant 65 percent while Heinz (17.4 percent) and Beech-Nut (15.4 percent) accounted for virtually the rest of the baby food market (U. S. Court of Appeals for the District of Columbia 2001).[12] In 1991, Beech-Nut introduced a line of organic baby foods called Special Harvest. However, Beech-Nut's foray into the organic baby food market was short-lived: by April 1993, the line was discontinued (Quintanilla 1993).

During the first half of the 1990s, however, Earth's Best began making significant inroads into mainstream supermarkets. By 1996, organic baby foods were sold in as much as one-quarter of all supermarkets nationally (Thompson and Glaser 2001), whereas Heinz and Beech-Nut only had national all-commodity volume of 40 percent and 45 percent, respectively (U.S. District Court for the District of Columbia 2000).

In March 1996, H.J. Heinz Co. acquired Earth's Best through its acquisition of the Hain Food Group (Plank 1999). That acquisition represented one of the first times a large food corporation decided to pit organic products directly against its own conventional food products. Prior to that time, most food manufacturers worried that promotion of organic products might tarnish the reputation of their conventional products. However, the direct competition between organic and conventional product lines is likely mitigated because most shoppers do not know Heinz conventional baby foods and Earth's Best organic baby foods have the same parent company. In fact, Heinz has continued to let Hain Food Group (now Hain Celestial Group) market and promote Earth's Best products (*Wall Street Journal* 1998).

Table 16.3

Number of Baby Food Products by Brand, 2003

	Conventional			Organic	
	Gerber	Heinz	Beech-Nut	Earth's Best	Tender Harvest
First stage	13	10	17	6	6
Second stage	65	24	72	27	20
Third stage	39	27	29	7	7
Total	117	61	118	40	33

Source: erber ein eech ut and arth s est ebsites accessed ay 22 2003.

The emergence of Earth's Best as a serious, albeit miniscule, competitor in the baby food industry is surprising because for the last sixty years there has been virtually no market entry by firms to challenge Gerber, Heinz, and Beech-Nut (Federal Trade Commission 2000). However, after being acquired by Heinz, Earth's Best has had the advantage of more financial resources for market entry and promotion in mainstream supermarkets.

Shortly after Earth's Best's acquisition by Heinz, Gerber introduced its own line of organic baby foods in October 1997 under the Tender Harvest label (Groves 1997). The introduction of Tender Harvest represented a momentous change in the baby food industry whereby a company decided to market its organic and conventional baby foods side by side on store shelves with both products clearly labeled as belonging to the same manufacturer, namely Gerber.

The entry of a new firm, Gerber, and the acquisition of a "start-up" firm by a major food manufacturer, H.J. Heinz, has resulted in two noticeable phenomena in the organic baby food market: more types of organic baby food from which to choose over time, and a tendency for organic baby food price premiums to decline. When Earth's Best baby food was first introduced in 1988, its founders had to develop relationships with organic growers to assure supply of a small range of organic ingredients. Consequently, the range of baby foods initially marketed by Earth's Best was limited. Over time, however, new organic products have been introduced, widening the array of choices available to consumers (Earth's Best 2003).[13] Much of the growth in organic market share apparently occurred because a wider array of organic baby foods for babies of all ages has been developed. Nevertheless, the number of organic baby food products offered is still markedly smaller than the number of conventional items (see Table 16.3).

While the array of organic baby foods available in retail markets has grown, prices of organic baby foods relative to prices of conventional baby foods have declined. When Earth's Best first introduced its organic products in 1988, organic baby foods were about twice as expensive as their conventional counterparts (Thompson and Glaser 2001). By the early 1990s, price premiums for organic baby foods dropped to about 50–60 percent of conventional baby food prices. Not surprisingly, market shares of organic baby food began to grow as products became cheaper. With the entrance of Tender Harvest by Gerber in 1997, price premiums fell slightly more to about 50 percent for dinners, fruits, and vegetables while premiums for organic baby juices fell to 35 percent in 1999 (the last year for which Thompson and Glaser report results from national scanner data). The relative decline in prices of organic baby foods occurred while baby food prices in general rose when compared to the prices of all food consumed at home.

Product diversification and lower prices are consistent with an outward shift of the supply curve for organic baby food. On the demand side, the number of potential consumers—children from about 6 months to 2 years of age—declined from 1992 through 1997, the same period that witnessed considerable growth in the market share of organic baby foods. The aggregate quantity of organic baby food sold in supermarkets has expanded while relative prices of organic baby food at retail have tended to decline (May 2002). Although the number of major firms producing organic baby foods is small—just two—the number of conventional baby food manufacturers is also very small—only three. But apparently entry of major firms either through acquisition or through development of new product lines has stimulated market shares of organic baby foods while tending to lower retail prices of organic baby food relative to conventional prices.

TYING UP THE LOOSE ENDS

Agricultural market evolution depends upon the interaction of consumer demand for product attributes and farmers' ability to provide those attributes at a profit. In this chapter, a "Wheel of Commodity Marketing" is proposed to help explain this interaction. Within this context, organic agriculture is shown to be a logical response to wealthy consumers' desire for high-quality commodities. As a result, organic niches *can* grow to capture the majority of sales in a market in the United States, Japan, and Europe. However, it is too early in organic agriculture's history to develop empirical forecasts of which markets will grow from a niche to the norm. Until more organic products develop majority shares of market sales, empirical data will be unavailable for building forecasting models. Thus, two case studies are presented in this chapter. The cases provide empirical insights about the current status of the market evolution process described by the theory. In each of the cases the market is early in its development and illustrates supply and demand characteristics consistent with the oligopoly stage of the theory.

At this point in time, it is safe to forecast that one of the key factors in determining the future of organic market niches is the ability of producers to develop and implement organic technologies that reduce costs per unit to levels enabling them to earn a profit at prices near those of current conventional products. Most of the nonprice issues relating to organic products are slowly vanishing. Organic products are now available in most supermarkets and other popular venues. The real stumbling block to bigger market shares is the high relative price of organic products. If prices at retail could fall as low as conventional product prices, the organic market would assuredly expand by significant amounts and, due to the quality variant for organics, become the norm.

The probability of that happening is an unknown empirical question at this time, but it got higher after the new government "organic" standards were adopted in October 2002. Those standards will facilitate moving organic niches toward the norm because standards reduce differentiation between firms and encourage consumers to both try and adopt the product.

Thus, the answer to the big question is clear. Organic and other (quality) niches may become the norm, but they will not alter the long-run outcome: traditional American production agriculture as we know it today will disappear and be replaced with some new industry structure as commodity markets evolve. Some geographical niches will survive, like wine from California's Napa Valley, because consumers are willing to pay premiums for desired products from markets with some barriers to entry. However, there are few barriers to entry to most commodity markets, thus successful quality niches will eventually become competitive markets with no more profits available to American producers than are available in current markets. Ultimately, American consumers will benefit, but the current trend of decline will not change for independent American farmers and ranchers.

Finally, there is a great irony in the evolution of agricultural markets around the globe at present. As noted earlier, wealthy consumers are more able and willing to pay for relatively "high-quality" (lower-yield) commodities. Thus, the markets for organic products are likely to develop first in wealthy nations. Organic market development in less-developed countries will depend upon the distribution of income within those countries. Ironically, less-developed countries are moving *away* from traditional organic production methods in a necessary effort to increase output supplies by adopting modern, high-input methods. Thus, the production agriculture sectors of more-developed and less-developed countries are each trying to move in the direction of the other, and both groups are doing so in response to domestic consumer demand. Therefore, the presence, and prevalence, of organic agriculture in a country is becoming an indicator of that nation's level of economic development. Traditional organic production methods are prominent in the poorest countries; a shift from traditional organic to modern production methods signals a developing nation; and a shift from modern, high-output production methods to modern organic methods signals a wealthy nation. The long-run implication of this ironic shift in production focus is clear: agricultural markets evolve first to provide supplies adequate to feed the population, then they strive to lower consumer prices through continued expansion of output; once hunger is not an issue, improving the quality of output becomes the goal. This means future agricultural market evolution will be driven by quality variants.

NOTES

Some material in this chapter is a revised version of an article published by S. Blank and G. Thompson as "Can/Should/Will a Niche Become the Norm? Organic Agriculture's Short Past and Long Future," *Contemporary Economic Policy* 22, no. 4 (2004): 483–503.

1. In the short run there are some barriers that may constrain producers wishing to enter the organic market. For example, certification of farmland is a temporal barrier in that it takes three years to achieve "organic" status.

2. The scale of the figure is exaggerated to make it easier to see that S_o does not intersect D_o at the kink in D_o. This means that the firm underestimated the quantity of the organic product it could sell at P_o through the selected market outlet, or that it misjudged the yield it would get with the amount of resources used for organic production. Had the firm shifted enough resources into production of the new product to shift the supply schedule to the right such that it intersected the demand schedule at the kink, an optimal result would have occurred. This assumes that the profit per unit is higher for all organic sales until the last unit sold in each market, for which $MR = MC$, making $\pi = 0$.

3. "The outputs of a set of firms constitute a *product group* if the substitutability in demand among the products (as measured by the cross-price elasticity) is very high relative to the substitutability between those firms' outputs and other goods generally" (Nicholson 1998, p. 593).

4. It is likely that many of the organic products sold by the numerous suppliers are nearly identical and, therefore, might have similar prices.

5. Also, emerging certification of organic foods reinforces the distinction between conventional and organic products, a distinction of importance to lend credence to goods such as organic foods.

6. This raises an interesting question: Are consumer preferences stable? That is, are Φ constant over time? In the context of the figures, is the split in the demand curves from a single conventional to a conventional and organic curve just the result of the diffusion of information? Or do some consumers change their Φ_i as information, education, and certification become more prevalent? In some ways, the question does not really matter because the outcomes are, as econometricians say, observationally equivalent. On the other hand, some industry advocates might say that if education can increase consumers' Φ_i, more consumers will pay higher prices because of some "intrinsic" (ethical or moral) value. In that case, price differences between conventional and organic versions of a product might persist.

7. Food "scares" like Alar in apples or "mad cow" in beef can cause abrupt shifts in demand, but whether these abrupt shifts result in permanent change is not clear.

8. Land conversion from conventional to organic production is typically irreversible because conversion requires a three-year transitional period. Even though organic land could be used immediately for conventional production, this is unlikely to occur because in order to qualify anew as organic land, a costly new three-year transition period would be required.

9. Econometric estimates of consumer demand have been conducted in Denmark (Wier and Smed 2000; Hansen 2003). However, these studies use self-reported data from families tracked in a panel of Danish consumers.

10. This case draws heavily on material in a case presented by Carman et al. (2003). Interested readers should see that report for more details.

11. The market share reported in Thompson and Glaser (2001) is by volume. Organic baby food is appreciably more expensive per unit, so the value shares are higher than the volume shares. The data used by Thompson and Glaser (2001) only report sales from mainstream supermarkets. Club store, natural food supermarkets, convenience stores, health food stores, and other venues are not tracked in the scanner data they used.

12. In July 2000, the Federal Trade Commission sought a preliminary injunction against H.J. Heinz Company's proposed acquisition of Beech-Nut Nutrition Corporation because the merger would have resulted in two firms—Heinz and Gerber—controlling 98 percent of the U.S. baby food market.

13. The three largest baby food manufacturers divide products into three stages. The first stage consists of single ingredients pureed in small jars. These foods are designed to be among a baby's first solid foods. Second-stage foods usually combine more ingredients and come in larger jars. Third-stage baby foods are distinguished by more varied ingredients combined together with more chunks and texture for babies with some teeth.

REFERENCES

Bastian, C., D. Oakley-Simpson, D. McLeod, D. Menkhaus, D. Alsup, J. Ogden, and G. Whipple. 1999. "Niche Market Potential: The Case of the U.S. Craft Brewing Industry." *Review of Agricultural Economics* 21 (Fall–Winter): 552–562.

Baumol, William J. 1982. "Contestable Markets: An Uprising in the Theory of Industry Structure." *American Economic Review* 72: 1–19.

Beech-Nut. www.Beech-Nut.com/products/index.asp, accessed May 22, 2003.

Boland, M., and T. Schroeder. 2002. "Marginal Value Attributes for Natural and Organic Beef." *Journal of Agricultural & Applied Economics* 34 (1): 39–49.

Brester, Gary W. 1999. "Vertical Integration of Production Agriculture into Value-Added Niche Markets: The Case of Wheat Montana Farms and Bakery." *Review of Agricultural Economics* 21 (Spring–Summer): 276–285.

Burton, M., D. Rigby, and T. Young. 1999. "Analysis of the Determinants of Adoption of Organic Horticultural Techniques in the UK." *Journal of Agricultural Economics* 50 (January): 48–63.

———. 2003. "Modelling the Adoption of Organic Horticultural Technology in the UK Using Duration Analysis." *Australian Journal of Agricultural and Resource Economics* 47 (1): 29–54.

Carman, H., K. Klonsky, A. Beaujard, and M. Rodriguez. 2003. *Marketing Order Impact on the Organic Sector: Almonds, Kiwifruit and Winter Pears.* Information Series Report, Giannini Foundation of Agricultural Economics, University of California.

Dimitri, C., and C. Greene. 2002. "Recent Growth Patterns in the U.S. Organic Foods Market." U.S. Department of Agriculture, Economic Research Service, Agriculture Information Bulletin no. 777, September.

Earth's Best. www.earthsbest.com/products/all_prods.html, accessed May 22, 2003.

Egan, Timothy. 2002. "Growers and Shoppers Crowd Farmers' Markets." *New York Times Online,* September 29.

Fairweather, John R. 1999. "Understanding How Farmers Choose Between Organic and Conventional Production: Results from New Zealand and Policy Implications." *Agriculture and Human Values* 16 (March): 51–63.

Federal Trade Commission. 2000. "The FTC to Challenge Merger of Beech-Nut Nutrition Corp. and H.J. Heinz Co." www.ftc.gov/opa/2000/07/heinz.html, accessed May 21, 2003.

Gerber. www.gerber.com, accessed May 22, 2003.

Giraud-Heraud, E., L. Soler, and H. Tanguy. 1999. "Avoiding Double Marginalism in Agro-Food Chains." *European Review of Agricultural Economics* 26 (June): 179–198.

Glaser, L., and G. Thompson. 1999. "Demand for Organic and Conventional Frozen Vegetables." Selected paper presented at the Annual Meeting of the American Agricultural Economics Association, Nashville, Tennessee, August.

———. 2000. "Demand for Organic and Conventional Fluid Milk." Selected paper presented at the Annual Meeting of the Western Agricultural Economics Association, Vancouver, British Columbia, July.

Good Fruit Grower Magazine. 1997. "Most Organic Pears Are Grown in the Okanogan." August. Online. Available at www.goodfruit.com.

Goodman, David. 2000. "Organic and Conventional Agriculture: Materializing Discourse and Agro-ecological Managerialism." *Agriculture and Human Values* 17 (3): 215–219.

Granatstein, D., and E. Kirby. 2002. "Current Trends in Organic Tree Fruit Production." Center for Sustaining Agriculture and Natural Resources, Wenatchee, WA, September.

Greene, C., and A. Kremen. 2003. "U.S. Organic Farming in 2000–2001." U.S. Department of Agriculture, Economic Research Service, Agriculture Information Bulletin no. 780, February.

Grover, M.B. 1991. "Brown Rice for Babies." *Forbes,* March 18, p. 63.

Groves, Martha. 1997. "A Late Bloomer; Gerber at Last Feeds into Market Hungry for Organic Baby Food." *Los Angeles Times,* October 30, p. D4.

Hansen, Lars Gårn. 2003. "Organic Crowding Out? A Study of Danish Organic Food Demand." Institute for Local Government Studies (AKF), Copenhagen, November.

Harris, J. Michael. 1997. "Consumers Pay a Premium for Organic Baby Foods." *Food Review.* Economic Research Service, U.S. Department of Agriculture, Washington, DC, May–August, pp. 13–16.

H.J. Heinz and Company. http://www.heinzbaby.com/, accessed May 22, 2003.

Ilbery, B., and M. Kneafsey. 1999. "Niche Markets and Regional Specialty Food Products in Europe: Towards a Research Agenda." *Environment and Planning* 31 (December): 2207–2222.

Johnson, J., and D. Myatt. 2003. "Multiproduct Quality Competition: Fighting Brands and Product Line Pruning." *American Economic Review* 93 (3): 748–774.

Kemp, R., J. Schot, and R. Hoogma. 1998. "Regime Shifts to Sustainability Through Processes of Niche Formation: The Approach of Strategic Niche Management." *Technology Analysis and Strategic Management* 10 (June): 175–195.

Klonsky, K., and L. Tourte. 1998. "Organic Agricultural Production in the United States: Debates and Directions." *American Journal of Agricultural Economics* 80 (December): 1119–1124.

Kohls, R., and J. Uhl. 1980. *Marketing of Agricultural Products.* 5th ed. New York: Macmillan.

Kwoka, J.E. 1992. "Market Segmentation by Price-Quality Schedules: Some Evidence from Automobiles." *Journal of Business* 65 (October): 615–628.

Lambert, D., and W. Wilson. 2003. "Valuing Varieties with Imperfect Output Quality Measurement." *American Journal of Agricultural Economics* 85 (February): 95–107.

Lansink, A., K. Pietola, and S. Backman. 2002. "Efficiency and Productivity of Conventional and Organic Farms in Finland, 1994–1997." *European Review of Agricultural Economics* 29 (March): 51–65.

Leoncini, Riccardo. 2001. "Segmentation and Increasing Returns in the Evolutionary Dynamics of Competing Techniques." *Metroeconomica* 52 (May): 217–237.

Locay, L., and A. Rodriguez. 1992. "Price Discrimination in Competitive Markets." *Journal of Political Economy* 100 (October): 954–968.

Lohr, Luanne. 1998. "Implications of Organic Certification for Market Structure and Trade." *American Journal of Agricultural Economics* 80 (December): 1125–1129.

Lohr, L., and T. Park. 1992. "Certification and Supply Response in the Organic Lettuce Market." *Journal of Agricultural and Resource Economics* 17 (December): 253–265.

Lohr, L., and L. Salomonsson. 2000. "Conversion Subsidies for Organic Production: Results from Sweden and Lessons for the United States." *Agricultural Economics* 22 (March): 133–146.

Loureiro, M., J. McCluskey, and R. Mittelhammer. 2001. "Assessing Consumer Preferences for Organic, Eco-labeled, and Regular Apples." *Journal of Agricultural and Resource Economics* 26 (December): 404–416.

May, Thomas G. 2002. "Baby Foods Category Crawling Forward." *Natural Foods Merchandiser,* October.

Mazzeo, Michael S. 2002. "Competitive Outcomes in Product-Differentiated Oligopoly." *Review of Economics and Statistics* 84 (4): 716–728.

McCluskey, Jill J. 2000. "A Game Theoretic Approach to Organic Foods: An Analysis of Asymmetric Information and Policy." *Agricultural and Resource Economics Review* 29 (April): 1–9.

Michelson, J., U. Hamm, E. Wynen, and E. Roth. 1999. *The European Market for Organic Products: Growth and Development.* Organic Farming in Europe: Economics and Policy Series, vol. 7. Stuttgart: University of Hohenheim, Department of Farm Economics.

Moran, Michelle. 2001. "Natural Products Research Report: Organic & Soy Sales Lead Category." *Gourmet Retailer* (October): 72–79.

Nicholson, Walter. 1998. *Microeconomic Theory: Basic Principles and Extensions.* 7th ed. Fort Worth: Dryden Press.

Offermann, F., and H. Nieberg. 2000. *Economic Performance of Organic Farms in Europe.* Organic Farming in Europe: Economics and Policy Series, vol. 5. Stuttgart: University of Hohenheim, Department of Farm Economics.

———. 2002. "Does Organic Farming Have a Future in Europe?" *EuroChoices* 1 (2): 12–17.

O'Riordan, T., and D. Cobb. 2001. "Assessing the Consequences of Converting to Organic Agriculture." *Journal of Agricultural Economics* 52 (January): 22–35.

Park, T., and L. Lohr. 1996. "Supply and Demand Factors for Organic Produce." *American Journal of Agricultural Economics* 78 (August): 647–655.

Pepall, Lynne. 1992. "Strategic Product Choice and Niche Markets." *Journal of Economics and Management Strategy* 1 (Summer): 397–417.

Pietola, K., and A. Lansink. 2001. "Farmer Response to Policies Promoting Organic Farming Technologies in Finland." *European Review of Agricultural Economics* 28 (1): 1–15.

Plank, Dave. 1999. "Profitable or Perilous: Acquisition Can Take Many Paths." *Natural Foods Merchandiser,* August.

Qunitanilla, Carl. 1993. "Marketscan: Gerber Stumbles in a Shrinking Market." *Wall Street Journal,* July 6, p. B1.

Rigby, D., T. Young, and M. Burton. 2001. "The Development of and Prospects for Organic Farming in the UK." *Food Policy* 26 (December): 599–613.

Rogerson, William P. 1987. "The Dissipation of Profits by Brand Name Investment and Entry When Price Guarantees Quality." *Journal of Political Economy* 95: 797–809.

Seavert, Clark. "D'Anjou Pear Enterprise Budget for a Conventional and an Organic Orchard in 1992." Unpublished data, Washington State University.

Stagl, Sigrid. 2002. "Local Organic Food Markets: Potentials and Limitations for Contributing to Sustainable Development." *Empirica* 29 (2): 145–162.

Suryanata, Krisnawati. 2000. "Products from Paradise: The Social Construction of Hawaii Crops." *Agriculture and Human Values* 17 (June): 181–189.

Sylvander, B., and A. Le Floc'h Wadel. 2000. "Consumer Demand and Production of Organics in the EU." *AgBioForum* 3 (2–3): 97–106.

Thompson, Gary D. 1998. "Consumer Demand for Organic Foods: What We Know and What We Need to Know." *American Journal of Agricultural Economics* 80 (5): 1113–1118.

———. 2000. "International Consumer Demand for Organic Foods." *HortTechnology* 10 (4): 663–674.

Thompson, G., and L. Glaser. 2001. "National Demand for Organic and Conventional Baby Food." Paper presented at the Western Agricultural Economics Association Annual Meetings, Logan, Utah, July.

Thompson, G., and J. Kidwell. 1998. "Explaining the Choice of Organic Produce: Cosmetic Defects, Prices, and Consumer Preferences." *American Journal of Agricultural Economics* 80 (May): 277–287.

Tzouvelekas, V., C. Pantzios, and C. Fotopoulos. 2001a. "Economic Efficiency in Organic Farming: Evidence from Cotton Farms in Viotia, Greece." *Journal of Agricultural & Applied Economics* 33 (April): 35–48.

———. 2001b. "Technical Efficiency of Alternative Farming Systems: The Case of Greek Organic and Conventional Olive-Growing Farms." *Food Policy* 26 (December): 549–569.

U.S. Court of Appeals for the District of Columbia. 2000. *FTC v. H.J. Heinz Co.,* 116 F. Supp.2d 190. www.law.suffolk.edu/faculty/visit/patterson/antitrust/materials/heinz.html.

———. 2001. *Federal Trade Commission, Appellant v. H.J. Heinz and Milnot Holding Corporation, Appellees.* Appeal from the United States District Court for the District of Columbia (No. 00cv01688), decided April 27, 2001, on web at http://pacer.cadc.uscourts.gov/common/opinions/200104/00-5362.txt.

U.S. Department of Agriculture (USDA). 2002. "Organic Production." Economic Research Service "Data" on web at www.ers.usda.gov/Data/organic/, October.

Vickner, S., and S. Davies. 1999. "Estimating Market Power and Pricing Conduct in a Product-Differentiated Oligopoly: The Case of the Domestic Spaghetti Sauce Industry." *Journal of Agricultural & Applied Economics* 31 (April): 1–13.

Wall Street Journal. 1998. "Business Brief—H.J. Heinz Co.: Hain Food to Distribute Organic Baby-Food Line." May 28. p. 1.

Wier, M., and S. Smed. 2000. "Modeling Demand for Organic Foods." The 13th International Scientific IFOAM Conference, Basel, Switzerland, August.

Zanoli, R., D. Gambelli, and D. Vairo. 2000. *Organic Farming in Europe by 2010: Scenarios for the Future.* Organic Farming in Europe: Economics and Policy Series, vol. 8. Stuttgart: University of Hohenheim, Department of Farm Economics.

Zucker, D., and J. Anderson. 1998. "Implications of Choice Behavior and Preferences in Niche Markets." *Aquaculture Economics and Management* 2 (September): 61–70.

CHAPTER 17

REGIONAL AGRICULTURE AS A NATIONAL INDUSTRY

"Success is the ability to go from one failure to another with no loss of enthusiasm."
—Winston Churchill

Early chapters in this book show that profitability varies across locations, and that the competitiveness of an agricultural producer is now a function of that producer's comparative and absolute advantage in a commodity market. This subtle change from the traditional focus on a producer's comparative advantage only is due to shifts in how economic development works in this new era of global markets for agricultural products. This has huge implications for the future development of American agriculture. In essence, it means that each American commodity producer is in direct or indirect competition with producers of that commodity from all over the globe. This new market dynamic, in turn, means that only the most profitable producers will survive in the long run and those producers will be scattered across locations. Thus, it makes references to American agriculture as a "national" industry out-of-date and misleading. In reality, agriculture is a collection of local and regional industries; it is not national.

The realization that American agriculture is spread over a vast, heterogeneous landscape with different commodity specializations observed in different locations raises an obvious question that has received very little attention: *where* will agricultural production occur in the future? The answer, of course, is that economics will determine who survives—competitiveness comes down to comparative and absolute advantages. But the point to be made in this chapter is that survival is also a spatial question. People in different locations will react differently to changes brought about by economic development. Some will embrace change and others will resist it. These behavior patterns will combine with economic issues to alter American agriculture over the course of this century.

For example, there is an interesting irony in the current dialog about American agriculture: a growing number of people are discussing "localization" of food systems at the same time that most economists are acknowledging the trend of globalization of most agricultural commodity markets. One definition of localization involves developing a food system based on products produced within some nearby geographical market area and the exclusion of products originating outside the desired area. As it turns out, localization is both a negative reaction and a defensive response to globalization. Many of the arguments for localization are a blend of consumer concerns for food security and specialty groups' advocacy of environmental sustainability (e.g., Nabhan 2002). Proponents of localization also sometimes include commodity producers in geographic areas that are trying to use point-of-origin branding as part of a product differentiation campaign aimed at increasing the profitability of their local industry that is suffering from a loss of competitiveness in the globalized market (Hinrichs 2005). Unfortunately, this approach to defining "local" markets pits domestic producers against one another simply because they are located in different regions (DuPuis and Goodman 2005). For example, apple growers in Virginia may want consumers to "buy local," but that implies there may be something wrong with apples from New York, Washington, and other producing states. Thus, localization of this type will not succeed in combating globalization of commodity markets unless domestic consumers are convinced that there are sufficient quality attribute differences between products from different locations to justify any price differences.

A second definition of localization involves a characteristic of economic development: the geographic clustering of firms within a specific industry (Duranton and Overman 2005). In agriculture this occurs mostly due to site-specific comparative advantages based in the climate, soil type, or market infrastructure. This type of localization may, in fact, help local or regional agricultural industries reduce their costs through increased efficiencies, thus improving the competitiveness of those industries in their global markets. That is why this type of local clustering is observed even as "world-scale" food systems are being developed (Goodman 1997).

Finally, another factor influencing economic development across locations is the attributes of locations themselves. As Wu (2006) pointed out, the environmental amenities offered by a location strongly influence the demand for land uses such as residential and commercial development. Generally, environmental amenities raise the value of land, especially for residential use. Conversely, land used in agricultural production can be viewed as having either amenity or disamenity value to an area (Ready and Abdalla 2005). Some types of agriculture may be viewed favorably while other types may be viewed as a nuisance by nearby landowners. For American agriculture, this is an important part of the economic development process: where people want to live can clash with efficient development of agricultural production. When a clash occurs, agriculture usually loses. This is one source of the fragmentation of agricultural land being observed across the country.

Clearly, location questions need attention when trying to assess the future structure of American production agriculture. What may have been considered a national industry a few decades ago has already changed enough to make that type of reference in current policy debates wildly inaccurate. This chapter tries to update the level of understanding about how local factors will shape the development of this collection of regional industries.

SPATIAL AGRICULTURE

In the recent debate over the role that agriculture now plays and will continue to play in rural development, two issues remain largely unexplored. The first regards what factors are important to agricultural sector performance among places, and the second regards *where* conditions are expected to remain favorable for agricultural sector performance (or particular sectors of agriculture) in the future, given potential alternative uses for scarce resources such as land and water. This chapter explores these questions with a snapshot of the western United States in 2002 to emphasize the importance of "place" in examining agriculture's role in rural economies and their development.

Prevailing thoughts on agriculture's role in rural development have changed throughout the past fifty years (Ellis and Biggs 2001), reflecting the changes in attitudes and opinions as to what factors contribute the most to economic and social well-being in rural areas (Ashley and Maxwell 2001). Research in rural development has highlighted the importance of the noneconomic as well as the economic aspect in the overall well-being of rural communities (Deller et al. 2001;

Blank 2002). Additionally, recent trends in rural development have also emphasized urban-rural linkages (Weber 1998; Mishra and Sandretto 2002; Kimhi 2000) and socio-environmental sustainability factors in the overall well-being of America's farming communities (Lyson and Welsh 1993).

According to Blank (2005), the goal of any business, including rural agricultural producers, is to increase the wealth of the owners, and wealth is accumulated not only as net revenues from farm operations, but also as off-farm income and capital gains on assets invested in the operation. It has long been realized that on-farm income is only a part of the picture of rural economic development and rural sociological decision making (Mishra et al. 2002; Mishra and Sandretto 2002). In a broader community sense, people living in rural areas are not simply profit-maximizing producers of agricultural commodities, but rather, utility-maximizing households that make decisions that are financially, culturally, and lifestyle based (Brewster 1961; Blank 2005).

Rural producer households face the dual objectives of wealth accumulation and utility maximization, with the first being a subset of the second. In essence, net returns to agricultural production, asset appreciation, and off-farm income, as well as lifestyle preferences, all play a role in rural well-being and farm household decision making. While sociological factors and non-production-based income have been shown to be vitally important to rural well-being, and may increase in importance in the future, the effects of varying farm income from operations have been surprisingly absent in recent literature.

The revenue associated with the production of agricultural goods continues to be an economic base for many rural areas (Irz et al. 2001). It is estimated that one in five rural counties in the United States is dependent on agriculture for its economic base (Ghelfi and McGranahan 2004), and only real cash returns (not land appreciation) will benefit agriculturally enabled industries. Yet, land appreciation does affect wealth, and a wide array of evidence now suggests that natural amenities in rural areas have an important correlation with land values and the utility of rural households, which may represent the newest competitive threat to agricultural inputs (e.g., land and water). In short, agriculture will face many challenges in the coming decades (Blank 1998), and an understanding of the factors that contribute to the current production-based financial performance of the agricultural sector will be crucial information that should guide policy decisions and rural economic development strategies.

While previous studies have examined the importance of off-farm income and capital gains on assets such as land (Blank et al. 2004; Mishra et al. 2002), this chapter focuses primarily on the factors that contribute to on-farm net revenues of operations. Still, production-based gross revenues, off-farm income, and land valuation are not completely independent concepts. For example, urban encroachment is likely to provide greater opportunity for off-farm employment and will also yield higher asset valuation growth, thus making production income a less vital component of household wealth. The expected returns in these regions affected by these factors will influence the value of the land to agricultural producers through both real net cash returns and returns to investments in assets (namely land and water). Moreover, since some characteristics that make locations more desirable to agricultural producers (such as climate) may also make those locations more desirable to other industrial sectors and households, a complex set of market forces will shape the performance and long-term economic viability of farm enterprises.

This chapter looks conceptually at which factors contribute to financial performance, and hypothesizes why these characteristics exist where they do and what market forces might influence them in the future based on spatial patterns within maps illustrating differential levels of financial performance in the western United States. The primary research goal, then, is twofold: first, to determine what factors contribute to agricultural sector financial performance in the 413 counties of the western United States, and second, to explore why some locations perform better than others and where agriculture is most likely to persist in the face of continued threats from falling commodity prices and increasing production costs (including opportunity costs for fixed resources such as land). This is a regional economic question that must also consider the portfolio of agricultural enterprises, locational dynamics, urban dependence, climate, and heterogeneous land values.

LAND-USE EVOLUTION

According to the U.S. Department of Agriculture's (USDA's) Census of Agriculture (2007), total land in agriculture peaked in the United States in 1954 at around 1.2 billion acres, representing roughly 48 percent of the total land use in the United States. Since then, total land in agriculture has decreased steadily, reaching 938 million acres in 2002, or 39 percent of total land use. This represents a 22 percent reduction in the amount of land in agriculture over fifty years. Employment has seen an even greater reduction over the same time period. Labor is mobile and more adaptive than is land and can switch out of a sector much faster than can land. In 1950, 7.9 million of the total 65.5 million jobs in the United States were in agriculture, representing 12 percent of the total labor force. In 2002, 3.3 million of the total 166.7 million total U.S. jobs were in agricultural production, representing about 2 percent of the total labor force.

In order to discuss the factors that influence land-use evolution, it is useful to first examine what features are likely to be an attraction to agricultural producers and other households. This assessment is based on principles first introduced in the early 1800s by von Thunen that became the basis for economic gravity models (Anderson 1979). Gravity models have been used to describe the spatial distributions of shopping centers (Huff 1963), health care facilities (Gesler 1986; McGlashan and Blunden 1983; and Guptill 1975), trade flows (Tinbergen 1962; Bergstrand 1989; Oguledo and Macphee 1994), and migration (Hawking and Israel 1987; Karemera, Oguledo, and Davis 2000; Borjas 1989; and Zipf 1946).

Drawing from this seminal research on gravity models and applying it to agriculture, the analysis here starts by assuming that, given a homogeneous plane of featureless land, no producer would have any incentive to prefer any parcel of land over another. However, if one positive factor were allowed to vary (e.g., climate, so that higher-value crops or yields flourish), producers would be drawn to this new location and would be willing to pay more for this land. The arbitrage process would result in a market in which expected gains accruing to the producer would be equal to the additional cost of owning this land over the other land. This is the familiar marginal benefit equals marginal cost outcome. In short, land values would be bid up to the point where all the additional net revenue for producing in this higher revenue per acre area over the other locations would be capitalized into the value of the land and, all else equal, producers would not prefer the better location with the higher revenues and higher land cost to the other locations.

Similarly, a single factor (such as climate, employment opportunities, or natural amenities) might draw nonagricultural households to a given location. As in the case of agricultural producers, this will drive up the cost of the land with desirable characteristics to the point where the benefit of living in this desirable location will equal the cost of living there over the other locations. This is, of course, a reworking of the von Thunen rent gradient model with a gravity model framework.

Based on the principles first introduced by von Thunen and incorporating the recent concepts of agricultural competitiveness presented by Blank (1998), a hypothesis is constructed stating that all potential uses for land will be bid into land costs. This includes both agricultural and nonagricultural uses, thus agricultural land uses will be jointly determined by all potential land uses. Certain land may have a comparative advantage for high-value agricultural production, but it may also have a comparative advantage for even higher-value residential development. This even holds true if the option valuation perspective is considered because future returns are likely influenced by perceptions of future farm and nonfarm comparative advantages.

Blank (1998, 2001) predicted that as competition for land intensifies, agricultural production with low returns per unit of land will need to evolve into higher-returning production. As costs continue to rise, land will eventually need to move out of agriculture completely in order to be profitable. The hypothesis raised in this chapter is that, all else equal, land that has higher expected revenues per acre will be desirable to agricultural producers. This chapter empirically tests what factors relate favorably to net agricultural returns per acre in the western United States and thus predict what land should be highly desirable to producers. The theories of von Thunen predict that expected returns should be bid into land values, thus equilibrating the expected net returns per value of land. Using the same 2002 Census of Agriculture data, this study also empirically examines whether such an equilibrium more or less existed in 2002, albeit through aggregate, county-level measures that may mask some of the place-specific characteristics.

Agricultural producers are "attracted" to areas that might offer high returns on their investment in land and capital. In the initial "homogeneous plane" boundary condition, this would equate to net farm income per acre because all land would have the same attributes and therefore the same value. With the inclusion of differentially attractive forces, the net farm income per acre and the net farm income per value of land and capital would begin to diverge as land values in areas with greater potential for net farm income per acre were bid up through arbitrage, ceteris paribus. However, this theoretical result erroneously assumes that only agricultural producers are bidding on the land.

Amenity factors, including both natural amenities and cultural amenities, have been shown to draw households to a location (Roback 1988; Power 1996; Deller et al. 2005). These households, in turn, draw other sectors through the economic activity generated by the households and through sectors moving to the region to take advantage of the workforce willing to take a lower relative wage to live in this high-amenity area (Power 1996). Previous research has demonstrated that amenities in general (Rosen 1979; Roback 1988), and natural amenities specifically (Cragg and Kahn 1999; Shumway and Otterstrom 2001; Hunter, Boardman, and Saint Onge 2005), attract households. This has been empirically demonstrated by studies that have found people are willing to endure higher housing costs and lower wages to live in relatively high-amenity areas (Roback 1988).

Additionally, agricultural households may be driven to maximize expected net revenues and to maximize utility through the consumption of natural amenities. The fact that agricultural production can be both a way of life and a business (Blank 2002) means that both the "amenity" and "maximizing net revenue" forces may be acting on these households. This compound perspective somewhat complicates how this type of producer values land.

If the attraction of land to producers were completely independent of the attraction of land to households, then producers would bid up agricultural land values to the point where the total per-acre net revenue generated on the land would equal the total per-acre cost of owning and cultivating the land. Likewise, households would bid up land values to the amenity value level. It is possible, however, that the factors influencing the attractiveness of land to an agricultural producer are not completely independent of the factors influencing the amenity value the land has to households. In such cases, two different forces, guided by similar attractions, compete in the market for a parcel of land. This combined source of demand has driven much of the rural and exurban land planning and assessment debates and policy discussions over the past twenty years. The issue will be explored more fully later in this chapter.

The gravitational concept could play a role in explaining the differential performance among counties when considering land attributes, proximity to urban centers, and degree of natural amenities as factors that are important with respect to the desirability of land to agricultural producers and to households. Is there a way to draw some generalizable conclusions from inter-county financial performance analysis that would lend insight into what factors influence expected returns in agriculture? Can empirical evidence be garnered on how this one type of rural wealth generation (net farm production revenue) relates to the other components of rural household wealth and to characteristics of a given location? The analysis below tries to answer these questions by looking at Census of Agriculture data from 2002 to investigate what factors are contributing to financial returns in agriculture and whether the predictions of von Thunen and Blank, as well as those raised in this chapter, are supported in the counties of the western United States.

DATA AND METHODS

The hypotheses outlined above are tested using a gravity model. To provide some insight into the factors that might contribute to the "attractive mass" term in the gravity model, the cropping portfolios, livestock production, marketing strategies, and regional characteristics that contribute to agricultural sector performance are examined for counties of the eleven western contiguous states. It is assumed that every county has a portfolio of production strategies and natural characteristics that are employed to generate the highest agricultural sector returns.

The independent variables in this study fall into three main categories: (1) county agricultural sector production portfolios, (2) financial and marketing strategies employed in the county, and (3) county characteristics. The production portfolios were constructed as shares of (1) total crop acres in fruits, vegetables, corn, wheat, forage, and silage; and (2) the percentage of total revenues from livestock sales, dairy sales, and horticultural crop sales (Table 17.1). The financial and marketing strategies employed include revenues from goods marketed through cooperatives, revenues from custom agriculture, revenues from direct sales, average size of farm (to control for the magnitude of agricultural operations), and percentage of principal operators who work more than 200 days off-farm.[1] Other county characteristics include the degree of urban influence (shown in Figure 17.1), average temperature in January (to control for climatic effects), and a natural amenity rank index (shown in Figure 17.2).

All data for the counties' agricultural production portfolios and financial and marketing strategies were obtained from the USDA's 2002 Census of Agriculture. That included cross-sectional data on the total sales, net farm income of operations, total value of land and buildings in agriculture, and total acres in agriculture for the 413 counties of the 11 western U.S. states. The degree of urban influence, the average temperature in January, and a natural amenity rank index came from the USDA's Economic Research Service (2007).

To look at returns to portfolios, sales and net farm income data were adjusted by three factors to account for specific aspects of financial performance. Total sales were adjusted by acres in production to yield a total sales per acre measure of agricultural performance. For a more refined financial measure, net farm income data were adjusted by both total acres in agriculture and total value of land and buildings in agriculture to obtain net farm income per acre and net farm income per value of land and buildings. Each of these three measures provides some insight into agricultural sector performance and may be useful in examining the market force and economic activity differences among Western counties. From a finance perspective, total sales per acre

Table 17.1

Summary Statistics for County Portfolio Variables, 2002

Variable name	Description	Mean	Standard deviation
Orchards	Fraction of total agricultural acreage in fruit and nuts	0.038	0.103
Vegetables	Fraction of total agricultural acreage in vegetable production	0.026	0.077
Corn	Fraction of total agricultural acreage in corn	0.010	0.029
Wheat	Fraction of total agricultural acreage in wheat	0.077	0.114
Forage	Fraction of total agricultural acreage in forage crops	0.256	0.174
Silage	Fraction of total agricultural acreage in silage production	0.013	0.030
Horticulture	Fraction of total agricultural sales in horticultural specialty crops	0.096	0.198
Livestock	Fraction of total agricultural sales in livestock sales	0.543	0.316
Dairy	Fraction of total agricultural sales in dairy production	0.046	0.139
Direct sales	Fraction of total agricultural sales accounted for as direct sales	0.008	0.014
Off-farm income	Fraction of total agricultural operators in county who work more than 200 days off farm	0.353	0.083
Rural	Rural-urban continuum code (0 to 9, 0 being most urban)	6.036	2.786
Farm size	Average size of farms in county (acres)	1,655.485	2,226.322
Cooperatives	Fraction of total agricultural sales facilitated through coops	0.001	0.003
Custom	Fraction of total agricultural sales from custom agricultural services	0.007	0.007
January temp	Mean temperature for january (°F)	29.310	10.531
Nat. Amenity	Deviations from the mean natural amenity score (ranged from −3.82 to 11.17)	3.598	2.426

Note: The data are from the 413 counties in the 11 contiguous western states.

represents a gross sales turnover ratio or economic contribution to the economy, net farm income per acre represents net returns per unit of a fixed resource, and net farm income per value of land and buildings represents a proxy for rate of return on assets.

Census of Agriculture data are subject to nondisclosure issues when there are insufficient numbers of operators of a given type in a county to keep from divulging financial information about specific operators. Missing data are a particular problem in spatial econometrics due to the fact that it makes contiguous counties neighbors in instances where there are no missing data, but not neighbors in other variables where data are missing. To account for this, missing data were imputed in STATA using a regression of all the other independent variables. This method ensures that these imputed values add no more or less information to the regression than the other explanatory variables would predict. The most missing observations were found in the corn variable, where 35 of the 413 observations (8.47 percent) were subject to nondisclosure. A total of 3 percent of the observations of the independent variables needed to be imputed.

The decision to include government transfer payments to farmers in the measures of farm financial performance was somewhat difficult. Due to these payments, the current value of some

Figure 17.1   **Rural-Urban Continuum Index (lower numbers mean more urban influence)**

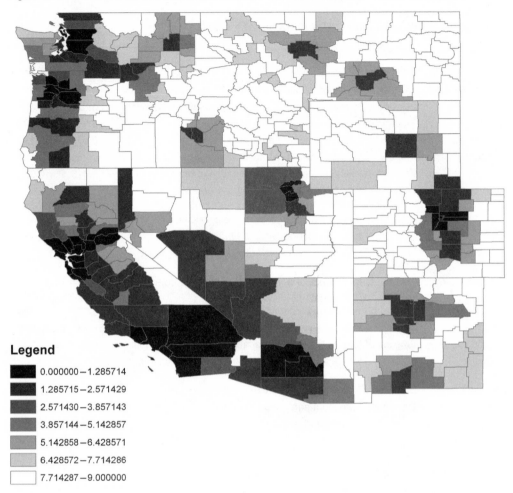

Legend
- 0.000000 – 1.285714
- 1.285715 – 2.571429
- 2.571430 – 3.857143
- 3.857144 – 5.142857
- 5.142858 – 6.428571
- 6.428572 – 7.714286
- 7.714287 – 9.000000

agricultural land is higher than it would otherwise be. Therefore, it was decided that government transfer payments must be included to accurately reflect the current market and policy forces shaping the operational and land investment decisions of agricultural enterprises.

This analysis is limited to the 413 counties in the 11 western states to provide a detailed case study of a regional agricultural sector. Sufficient climate, market, and demographic differences exist between the agricultural sectors in the eastern, southern, and western United States as to render a single relationship between explanatory variables and the measure of financial performance unrealistic. In fact, to explore whether structural differences exist between counties in coastal states and counties in interior states, the counties of California, Oregon, and Washington (the three states making up the USDA's Pacific region, as discussed in earlier chapters) were modeled separately, then compared with results from the other eight states (those states making up the USDA's Mountain region) as a seemingly unrelated regression estimate. A Chow test is used to test whether the underlying coefficients are the same between the two regions, and a short comparative analysis is performed.

Figure 17.2 **Natural Amenity Index**

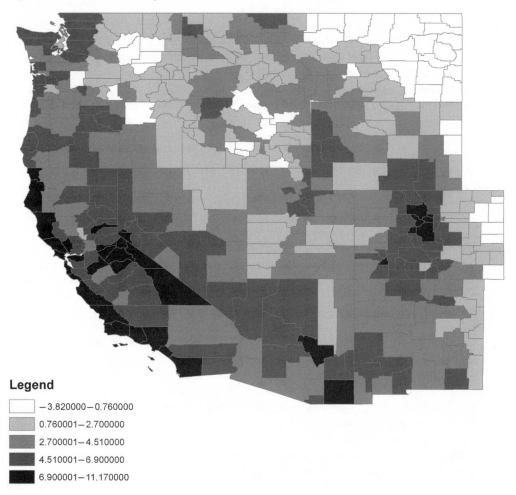

Legend

☐	−3.820000−0.760000
☐	0.760001−2.700000
☐	2.700001−4.510000
☐	4.510001−6.900000
☐	6.900001−11.170000

This analysis starts by assessing which variables were interrelated or, in short, how did some production enterprises and locational characteristics jointly influence financial performance. To further characterize the variables and their relationships, a principal component analysis (PCA) was conducted. PCA was first described by Pearson (1901) and independently by Hotelling (1933). The method is useful for describing the relationships between independent variables by assigning them to unique orthogonal eigenvectors with corresponding eigenvalues. The size of the eigenvalue relates to the percentage of variation in the data explained by the respective eigenvector.

It might be helpful to think of these eigenvectors as predictive combinations of variables. If silage and dairy production are found to move together in an eigenvector, then it is helpful to think of the two variables in tandem as a broader market force characterization rather than looking at the individual effects separately. From the principal components analysis, component scores are estimated for all observations (Jackson 1991). The fitted values are then incorporated into a rank restricted regression.

SPATIAL ECONOMETRIC MODELING

This study obviously focuses on a spatial question as each county exists in a specific place and each county is not independent from its neighbors. Spatial dependence negates the standard assumptions of ordinary least square regression analysis and can exhibit itself in two possible ways. First, a spatial error model arises when observations are related through common unmeasured variables that are correlated across space or through measurement errors that arise from the use of spatial units whose boundaries are not perfectly suited to the problem at hand. For example, county boundaries are somewhat arbitrary distinctions. Economic attributes, such as labor markets, and physical attributes, such as soil types, can cross over these boundaries. This introduces the possibility of correlation in the error between observations.

The second possible type of spatial dependence is seen in a spatial lag model. This occurs when a given attribute in one location has a direct effect on that attribute in another location. For example, if land prices increase in one county, land prices in nearby counties are likely to go up as well, even if there is less than a one-to-one corresponding change. It is also the case that spatial dependence is not unidirectional, as is autocorrelation in time series data. In time series data, observations from period $t-1$ can affect period t, but period t cannot affect period $t-1$. In spatial data, relationships are usually multidimensional. For example, Larimer County, Colorado, can affect the adjacent Weld County, Colorado, and vice versa. This makes the variance-covariance matrix full instead of only the upper triangular, as it is for time series. As a result, generalized least squares analysis is no longer the preferred solution to autocorrelation and different methods must be employed. A spatially dependent econometric model is generally estimated through maximum likelihood, although instrumental variable and generalized methods of moments estimators may also be employed.

The first step in constructing a spatial econometric model is to specify a weighting matrix that relates the observations to each other. There are a variety of possible weighting matrixes, with the majority falling into one of two main categories: distance-based weights and contiguity-based weights (Anselin 1990). Different weighting matrixes are often generated and the results of models estimated with each weighting are then compared to see which performs best (i.e., which maximizes the likelihood function). In this study, a variety of different weighting matrixes was constructed and incorporated into a maximum-likelihood regression. The first approach was to generate a spatial weights matrix using a first-order Rook contiguity weighting matrix. Alternatives constructed and incorporated into a maximum likelihood regression included a distance-based weighting matrix based on centers of counties, a "$k = 4$ nearest neighbors" weighting matrix based on the four nearest counties, and a second-order contiguity weighting matrix that included terms for both the counties that shared a common border and for the counties that were two counties away. Contiguity matrices allow for large and small counties to have their weights determined by the counties that surround them. Regardless of whether distance-based or contiguity-based measures are used, the spatial weights matrix is subject to some degree of arbitrariness. The contiguity-based spatial regression made more sense in this context and was found to maximize the likelihood function in all three regressions, thereby adding further credence to its selection as the appropriate spatial relationship. Thus, the results of the first-order contiguity-based method are discussed for this analysis.

The second step is to find the correct model specification. Using tests developed by Anselin et al. (1996), the residuals from a generalized least squares regression of the model with a spatially lagged dependent variable underwent simple and robust Lagrange multiplier (LM) tests for both the spatial lag and spatial error models.[2] The correct model specification depends on which robust LM test is significant.

RESULTS OF DATA STRUCTURE QUESTIONS

Two structural issues need to be addressed before financial performance can be evaluated. First is the question of whether the data are homogeneous across locations. Second is the question of whether the explanatory variables are independent of one another. The following two sections offer brief answers.

Chow Test for Structural Differences

A simple examination of the location of counties with the highest net farm income per acre, shown in Table 17.2, indicates that there seem to be some differences between the three states on the Pacific coast and the states of the Mountain region. Nineteen of the twenty counties listed in Table 17.2 are in the three states of the Pacific region, indicating that microclimate is probably the single most important explanation for differences across locations. Also, the twenty counties can all be characterized as areas where farming is irrigated and where there is little, if any, livestock production. Finally, three of the counties in California (Orange, San Mateo, and Los Angeles) are urban areas in which virtually the only agriculture is nursery operations. These results are consistent with the expectation of differences in enterprises across microclimates. The results of the Chow test for structural differences found significant differences among the two regions for total sales per acre and net farm income per acre, but not for net farm income per value of land and buildings. This third finding is interesting since controlling for differing land values should, and does appear to, "level the playing field" across counties. In other words, the result indicates that there has been a convergence of returns across the western United States, as indicated in earlier chapters of this book.

The Chow test results provide some insight into differences between the two regions, but for the analysis below, the results and discussion focus on the West as a whole. Yet, it is important to note that the point made at the beginning of this chapter is supported by the Chow test results: agriculture is a collection of local and regional industries; it is not national. The nature of the structural differences that exist between the Pacific and Mountain regions illustrate the point. Small regions of the United States must be considered independently if different place-based and market factors affect them uniquely. Production agriculture's survival is a location-specific question.

Principal Components Analysis

It is often the case in these types of cross-section studies that the largest two or three eigenvectors explain 80 percent of the variation. In this case it took nine vectors to account for 80 percent (see Table 17.3), probably due to varying factors that have some place-specific characteristics. This suggests that there is a very diverse set of market and place-based factors that influence farm financial performance. Five of the eigenvectors had values over one and are discussed below.

The first vector, for temperature, accounted for just over 20 percent of the variation of the independent variables. It was primarily associated with the average temperature in January and was strongly associated with fruits, vegetables, horticultural sales, natural amenities, and ruralness. The natural amenity index, ruralness index, and average temperature in January are correlated (which means they move together in the same eigenvector), indicating that larger cities in the western United States tend to be in warmer areas with higher natural amenities. It is not surprising that temperature, orchards, and vegetable production are also correlated because the production of these commodities is associated with mild winters.

Table 17.2

Counties with the Highest Net Farm Income per Acre, 2002

Rank	State–County	Net farm income ($/acre)
1	California–Santa Cruz	1,649
2	Arizona–Yuma	1,463
3	Washington–Mason	1,399
4	Washington–Skamania	1,183
5	California–Orange	1,076
6	California–San Mateo	911
7	California–Napa	737
8	California–Ventura	722
9	Washington–King	701
10	California–Los Angeles	691
11	Oregon–Multnomah	647
12	California–Monterey	640
13	California–San Diego	633
14	Oregon–Tilamook	632
15	Washington–Whatcom	558
16	Washington–Skagit	524
17	California–Imperial	403
18	Washington–Pierce	383
19	Oregon–Washington	379
20	California–Riverside	367
	Average	785
	Median	669
	Standard Deviation	378
	Population Mean	78
	Population Median	11
	Population Standard Deviation	199

Note: The sample population includes the 413 counties of the 11 western states.

For this analysis, it is helpful to think of the results for fruits, vegetables, and temperature in January as moving together in a unique eigenvector. Not surprisingly, this vector is also negatively related to forage, livestock sales, and average size of farms. This result raises the obvious hypothesis that intensive, high-value fruit and vegetable crop production[3] is negatively associated with low-value, extensive agriculture often characterized by ranches and large-scale field crop farms. A quantile map of vegetable production is presented in Figure 17.3.

The second vector, livestock, is strongly associated with livestock and forage and is negatively related to wheat, corn, and custom agriculture. It is postulated that livestock and forage are complementary activities and that livestock and field crops are competitors for land, and therefore would be negatively related.

The third vector, dairy, is most strongly associated with dairies, cooperatives, and silage and is negatively associated with horticultural sales, direct sales, and off-farm income. It makes sense that dairies, cooperatives, and silage would be associated with each other as dairies create a large derived demand for silage, and about 80 percent of the milk sold in the western United States is marketed through cooperatives.

Table 17.3

Principal Component Analysis

Variable	Temperature	Livestock	Dairy	Farm size	Corn	Component	Eigenvalue	Difference	Proportion	Cumulative
Orchards	0.3244	−0.2154	0.1044	−0.2467	−0.1717	Temperature	3.44428	1.12046	0.2026	0.2026
Vegetables	0.2895	−0.0601	−0.1075	−0.2484	0.1220	Livestock	2.32382	0.517694	0.1367	0.3393
Corn	−0.0085	−0.1280	0.1662	0.0870	0.5666	Dairy	1.80613	0.47467	0.1062	0.4455
Wheat	−0.1771	−0.4849	0.0207	0.2588	0.1179	Farm Size	1.33146	0.172847	0.0783	0.5239
Forage	−0.0909	0.4743	0.0785	0.0784	−0.2833	Corn	1.15861	0.199415	0.0682	0.5920
Silage	0.1260	0.1229	0.5426	0.1303	0.2862	Comp6	0.959197	0.0463909	0.0564	0.6484
Horticulture	0.2760	0.0897	−0.2481	0.3249	0.1391	Comp7	0.912806	0.08615	0.0537	0.7021
Direct sales	0.1529	0.1782	−0.2069	0.2424	−0.0523	Comp8	0.826656	0.0958336	0.0486	0.7508
Livestock	−0.2424	0.3987	0.2063	−0.1624	0.0224	Comp9	0.730823	0.0190871	0.0430	0.7938
Off-farm income	0.0497	0.2373	0.0356	0.4488	−0.0277	Comp10	0.711736	0.0644205	0.0419	0.8356
January temperature	0.4279	−0.0035	0.0309	−0.1073	0.1020	Comp11	0.647315	0.13485	0.0381	0.8737
Rural	−0.4251	0.0381	0.0093	−0.1383	−0.1119	Comp12	0.512465	0.0428762	0.0301	0.9038
Average size	−0.2461	−0.0241	−0.0202	−0.4439	0.2396	Comp13	0.469589	0.106848	0.0276	0.9315
Cooperative	0.1281	−0.2260	0.3454	−0.1302	−0.4242	Comp14	0.362741	0.024057	0.0213	0.9528
Custom	−0.0163	−0.2974	0.1682	0.2497	−0.4069	Comp15	0.338684	0.0904917	0.0199	0.9727
Dairy	0.1888	0.1456	0.5557	−0.0170	0.0369	Comp16	0.248192	0.0326967	0.0146	0.9873
Natural amenity	0.3434	0.2016	−0.2072	−0.2836	−0.0898	Comp17	0.215495		0.0127	1

Figure 17.3 **Share of Total Acres in Vegetable Production**

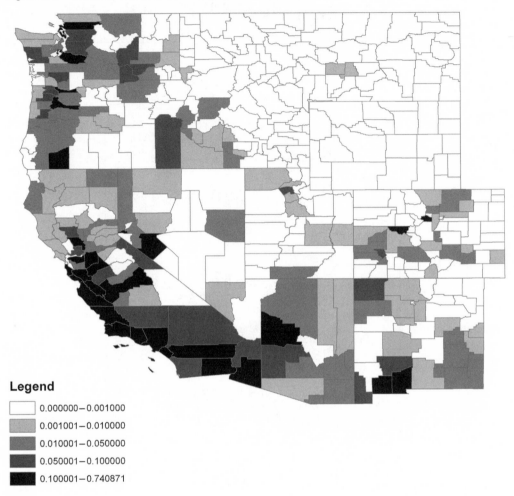

Legend

☐	0.000000 – 0.001000
▨	0.001001 – 0.010000
▨	0.010001 – 0.050000
▨	0.050001 – 0.100000
■	0.100001 – 0.740871

The fourth vector, referred to as the average size vector, most clearly demonstrates the negative relationship between the proportion of days worked off-farm and the average size of a farm. There is an understandable negative relationship between the size of an agricultural operation and the time it takes to manage it, so a larger farm would give the operator less time for off-farm employment. As a result, larger farms are less likely to be hobby farms and more likely to be the primary income source for the operator.

The fifth vector is primarily associated with field crops such as corn, wheat, silage, and size of farm. This component is referred to as the corn vector and is negatively related to custom agriculture, cooperatives, and fruit sales.

Due to moderate levels of multicollinearity, it may be appropriate to think of the explanatory variables in this model not simply as individual independent variables, but as contributing to unique orthogonal components or enterprise clusters. The results of the principal component analysis present a clear explanation for the five largest eigenvectors in the analysis, and regressions on the five largest principal components tell a similar story. Thus, it is advisable to keep in mind these five principal components and how they move together for the subsequent discussion of results.

RESULTS OF AGRICULTURAL SECTOR PERFORMANCE

One of the main goals of this chapter was to describe the components of agricultural sector performance and to determine what factors contribute to farm income by using different measures to evaluate performance. The factors that contribute to counties performing well in each of the three metrics used here varied somewhat among the three models, although total sales per acre and net farm income per acre were quite similar.[4] The full model results for all three regressions are presented in Table 17.4. Results for the spatial econometric maximum likelihood regressions of the three measures of financial performance on the fitted values from the five principal components with eigenvalues over one are presented in Table 17.5.

Total Sales Per Acre

The most simplistic way to look at the question of farm performance is to focus on average total sales per acre, which represents a gross sales turnover ratio and gross contribution to the county's economic base. The total sales per acre variable was derived by dividing total market value of goods sold by total land in farms. Although this variable does not measure profitability, it is important from a regional development perspective and points at areas where agriculture is generating a great deal of economic activity per unit of land (considered one of the truly fixed resources for any geopolitical area). Not surprisingly, this variable proved to be the most volatile measure of agricultural sector performance with a range of $2 per acre to over $30,000 per acre. The county with the highest average total sales per acre ($32,000) was Denver County, Colorado, a densely populated county with greenhouses but little farmland, which was shown to be an outlier. Even after removing the outlier, the range was still quite large. Figure 17.4 presents a quantile map that identifies the counties with the highest total sales per acre. There is a large concentration of high-performing counties in the Pacific region, as well as in the Southwest and in central Idaho.

Turning to econometric results, it is not surprising that fruits, vegetables, and horticultural sales shares contribute positively to average gross sales per acre. Fruits, vegetables, and horticultural specialties are high-value, high-input crops that generate a great deal of gross revenue per acre. The main areas of production for these crops tend to be in the Southwest and Pacific coast, where climate allows, and these crops are likely the primary drivers of higher-value sales per acre in those areas. After controlling for climate, the natural amenity index was found to be negatively related to total sales per acre.

In the regression on the fitted values of the principal components, the climate-fruit-vegetable component has a strong positive influence on this measure of financial performance. This is expected because warm-weather fruit and vegetable crops tend to be high-revenue operations. The dairy component is also significant and positive, indicating that dairies contribute favorably to total sales per acre in counties. The extensive agricultural operations component was found to relate negatively to total sales per acre. This, again, is consistent with the idea that lower-value crops are grown extensively with relatively high land usage. The first principal component is also strongly associated with urban influence, indicating that vegetable, orchard, and horticultural crops tend to be associated with urban proximity. These findings are consistent with Blank's (2001) hypothesis that agriculture is expected to evolve from low-returning extensive opera-

Table 17.4

Maximum Likelihood Regression Results

Variable	Total sales per acre	Net farm income per acre	Net farm income per value of land and buildings
Spatially lagged dependent variable	+++	+++	+++
Orchards	+++	+++	+
Vegetables	+++	+++	+++
Corn	0	0	+
Wheat	0	0	+
Forage	0	0	0
Silage	0	0	0
Horticulture	+++	0	—
Direct sales	-	—	—
Livestock	0	0	0
Off-farm income	0	0	0
January temperature	+	+	++
Rural	0	0	0
Average farm size	-	-	-
Cooperative	0	0	0
Custom	0	0	0
Dairy	+++	++	+++
Natural amenity	—	—	—-

Note: +++, ++, + denote positive significance at the 99%, 95%, and 90% confidence levels, respectively; 0 represents no significant relationship; and —,—, - denote negative significance at the 99%, 95%, and 90% confidence levels, respectively.

Table 17.5

Maximum Likelihood Spatial Regressions on Principal Components

Variable	Total sales per acre	Net farm income per acre	Net farm income per value of land and buildings
Spatially lagged dependent variable	+++	+++	+++
Temperature vector	+++	+++	+++
Livestock vector	0	0	0
Dairy vector	+++	+	+++
Average size vector	—	—-	0
Corn vector	0	0	++

Note: +++, ++, + denote positive significance at the 99%, 95%, and 90% confidence levels, respectively; 0 represents no significant relationship; and —,—, - denote negative significance at the 99%, 95%, and 90% confidence levels, respectively.

Figure 17.4   **Total Sales per Acre**

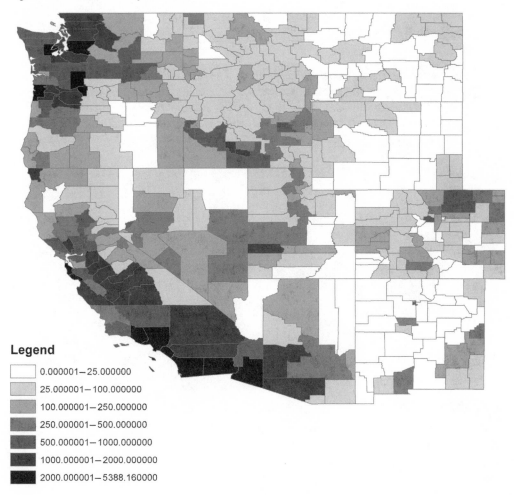

Legend

☐	0.000001−25.000000
	25.000001−100.000000
	100.000001−250.000000
	250.000001−500.000000
	500.000001−1000.000000
	1000.000001−2000.000000
	2000.000001−5388.160000

tions to high-value intensive operations as opportunity costs rise and it becomes necessary to generate greater revenue per acre to justify staying in agriculture. Or alternatively, it reinforces the idea that households are drawn to the same climatic amenities needed to produce many high-value crops.

Although it may provide insight into where agriculture might generate a great deal of economic activity in a local economy, total sales per acre does not account for production costs and, therefore, does not provide insight into overall financial viability of a given county's agricultural sector. Thus, the fact that far greater sales per acre are generated in areas where high-value production like horticultural and vegetable crops are grown is not terribly enlightening. This begs the question, then, can other measures of agricultural performance provide more insight into what factors are likely to contribute positively to agricultural sector profitability? Or will controlling for costs "level the playing field" across Western counties as the gravity model suggests?

Figure 17.5   **Net Farm Income per Acre**

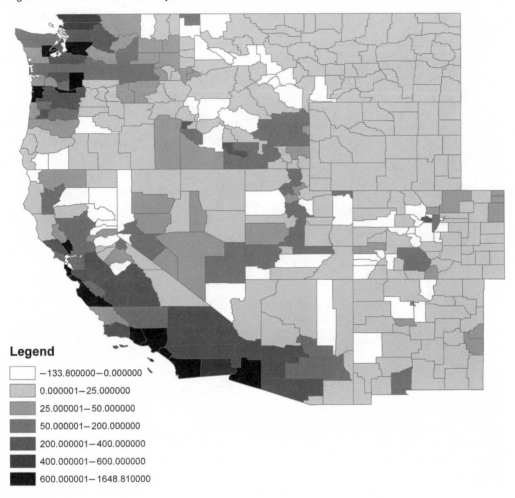

Legend

☐	−133.800000−0.000000
☐	0.000001−25.000000
☐	25.000001−50.000000
☐	50.000001−200.000000
☐	200.000001−400.000000
☐	400.000001−600.000000
☐	600.000001−1648.810000

Net Farm Income Per Acre

Average net farm income per acre is a very common (although simplistic) measure of agricultural performance that expresses net returns in terms of the primary input used for production. Net farm income per acre is calculated here by taking the total net farm income of operations and dividing by total land in farms for the county. This metric is superior to the original metric, sales per acre, because it nets out the direct costs of producing crops, but still may be biased toward high-value, intensive agriculture since it does not account for the value of the investment needed to create the income.

Table 17.2 lists the top performing counties in the West in net farm income per acre. Even netting out costs, there was still a wide range of returns per acre across the West, from negative $134 to over $1,600 per acre, with a mean of $78 and a median of $11. Figure 17.5 shows similar geographical patterns to those seen with total sales per acre. There is, however, a subtle shift toward the interior West relative to the total sales per acre graphic. Still, the highest-performing counties are concentrated among the Southwest and Pacific counties.

The results of the net farm income per acre regression are also similar to the total sales per acre regression but fewer variables were statistically significant (see Table 17.4). Again, positive effects were found for fruits, vegetables, and dairies. The natural amenity index was negatively related to net farm income per acre and was the opposite sign as average temperature in January. The spatially lagged dependent variable was positive and significant, suggesting some place-specific factor unrelated to climate or urban influence is influencing net income per acre and influencing multicounty regions rather than specific local places. The share of marketing receipts from direct sales shows up as a negative influence on profits, which is unexpected, but may be related to the scale of operations making direct sales.

Net Farm Income Per Value of Land and Buildings

The last, and maybe most interesting, metric of agricultural sector performance is net farm income per value of land and buildings. This is similar to a return on fixed assets or return on assets measure and was generated by taking net farm income of operations and dividing by estimated market value of land and buildings for a county. The distribution was expected to be tighter for this metric than for the previous metrics, as it puts county agricultural portfolios over a more common denominator. For example, in counties with more potential uses for land (e.g., housing development, industrial, or commercial use), land values should be bid up, so agricultural production would be more heavily weighted toward higher-value goods, and vice versa for more remote, rural areas. Figure 17.6 shows the distribution of average land values in the West. The gravity model leads to the hypothesis that potential profitability from all alternative uses of land are known, so any anticipated rents become capitalized into land prices.

The range for net farm income per value of land and buildings was between −4.6 percent and 31.9 percent with a mean of 2.8 percent and a standard deviation of 3.9 percent. These can be loosely interpreted as percentage returns to investment. Not surprisingly, land values are generally higher in urban and high-amenity areas. The correlation coefficient between average value of land and buildings and (1) ruralness is −.49, (2) share of sales from horticultural crops is .39, and (3) the natural amenity index is .37. These are the highest correlation coefficients seen between the average value of land and buildings and any of the independent variables in this study.

By accounting for value of land and buildings, the distribution of high-performing counties continues to move east and north from the original map of gross sales per acre (as shown in Figure 17.7). High returns are seen in areas where land values are low but returns to agricultural production are still substantial, such as in northeast Montana, southeast Idaho, southeast New Mexico, the San Luis Valley of Colorado, southwest Arizona, and eastern Washington.

The regression for net farm income per value of land and buildings shows some significant variables that were not seen in the previous regressions (see Table 17.4). Vegetables are still a significant factor.[5] Dairy continues to have a strong, positive influence on agricultural returns, indicating that agricultural products that have some locational dependence, a high degree of perishablilty, or import nonsubstitutability may compete well even in the face of increased land costs. The share of sales in horticultural enterprises now has a negative impact, probably due to the high cost of production assets (land and greenhouses) and, as in the case of Denver County, Colorado, the potential alternative uses for such land.

Interestingly, the fitted value for corn (in Table 17.4) and principal component corn vector (in Table 17.5) both show up as contributing positively to this measure of performance, probably due

Figure 17.6   **Average Value of Land and Buildings in Agriculture**

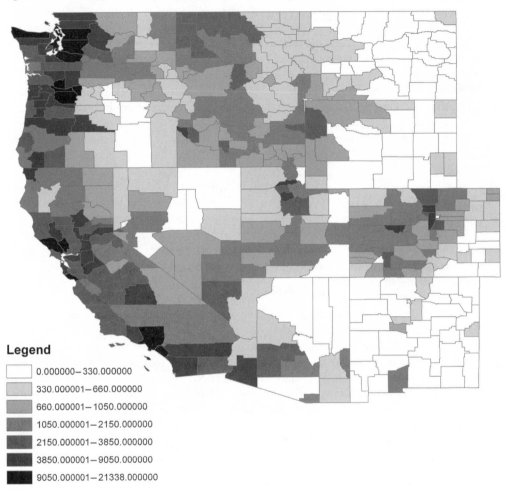

Legend

☐	0.000000–330.000000
☐	330.000001–660.000000
☐	660.000001–1050.000000
☐	1050.000001–2150.000000
☐	2150.000001–3850.000000
☐	3850.000001–9050.000000
☐	9050.000001–21338.000000

to the low land costs associated with many major corn production regions. After controlling for land prices, counties that grow extensive field crops such as corn compete relatively well. Government transfer payments are included in net farm income measures, so program crops such as wheat and corn may report profitability that is artificially high. However, in areas with little competition for land, program field crops do seem to contribute to financial performance in the agricultural sector through revenues and payments.

ECONOMIC IMPLICATIONS OF THE SPATIAL AUTOCORRELATION

The spatially lagged dependent variable in this analysis was consistently found to be positive and significant. Additionally, the spatial Lagrange multiplier tests were found to be significant for spatial lag dependence. This means that observations in this analysis (i.e., the counties) are not independent of each other and exhibit spatial dependence. In other words, the dependent variables

Figure 17.7   **Net Farm Income per Value of Land and Buildings**

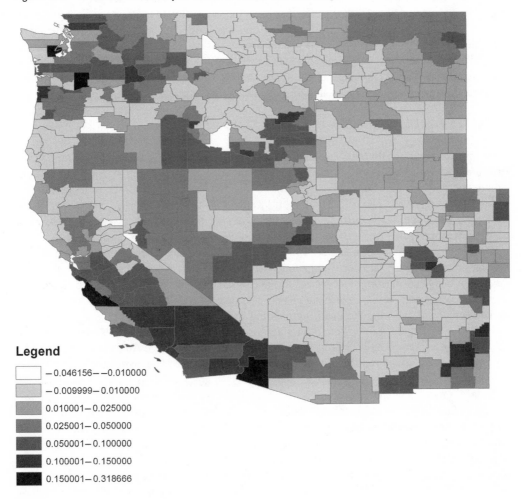

Legend

☐	−0.046156−−0.010000
▨	−0.009999−0.010000
▨	0.010001−0.025000
▨	0.025001−0.050000
▨	0.050001−0.100000
▨	0.100001−0.150000
▨	0.150001−0.318666

of counties could not be considered independent of neighboring counties. This result was expected, based on theory, and indicates the model is robust.

The likelihood dominance of the first-order Rook contiguity matrix indicates that the structure of the spatial dependence is best represented by the lagged dependent variable of the average of the surrounding counties that share a border. This means that the substance of the spatial dependence can be captured with just the first ring of surrounding counties, indicating a fairly simple spatial relationship.

The spatial dependence can occur due to economic factors such as spillover effects, agglomeration effects, spatial diffusion, and geopolitical effects. While it is beyond the scope of this chapter to determine the precise mechanism for the economic spatial dependence exhibited between counties in this dataset, the dependence was statistically significant.

In this case it is theorized that counties will not be independent of one another due to a variety of factors including agglomeration effects and spillover effects. Climate is already accounted for in the independent variables; however, factors such as transportation distance to processors and marketing infrastructure are not. An area may have the right climate to grow vegetables but, for whatever reason, the infrastructure to process and transport the crops is not present. Other theoretically likely causes of spatial dependence in this study include unmodeled agronomic characteristics such as common soil types among neighboring counties, similar water delivery infrastructure and availability among neighboring counties, and geopolitical spillover effects that occur between neighboring counties in the same state. Further investigation is left for future studies.

WHAT TYPES OF COUNTIES PERFORMED BEST?

The empirical portion of this chapter examines two important questions crucial to both farm sector structure and performance, and rural development fields. First, what are the "models" of agriculture that show the best financial performance as defined by enterprise mix, business strategies, and locational aspects? Then, subsequently, if locational factors are important (either in absolute terms or indirectly, through their influence on relative land values), what does this suggest about the need for more place-based agricultural and rural development policies and strategies?

One of the predictions that Blank (1998) posits is that locally determined agricultural production costs, including land costs, are going to continue to increase over the coming decades in the face of competition from other sectors for land, labor, capital, and inputs. This, coupled with decreasing commodity prices, which are increasingly determined on the world market, could lead to the decline and eventual end of the agricultural sector in America. Blank (1998) argues that one way for agriculture to compete is in enterprises that are relatively less exposed to global, downward price pressures. In the analysis here, dairy, silage, and shares of sales in cooperatives all consistently contributed positively to agricultural performance. This indicates that, even after accounting for the high production costs and relatively high land and building costs associated with dairy production, the vector associated with dairies demonstrates strong financial performance. A likely explanation is that the dairy industry enjoys a relatively high degree of "locality," so global competitive pressure may be lower with respect to dairy prices than with other industries. In short, dairy, silage, and cooperatives have some import nonsubstitutability and potential for value-added spillovers to them, which could translate to a relatively higher multiplier for communities.[6] This is important to combat the pressure of increasing local costs coupled with the global price pressure that Blank outlined. So, getting people to drink more milk might not only be good for our health, it also appears to be good for rural economic health, even though there continue to be environmental challenges to address as the West sees the development of larger dairies.

In keeping with another of Blank's (1998) conclusions, this analysis found that high-value crops usually generate more revenue and, when rising land and production costs necessitate higher returns per acre, production of fruits, vegetables, and horticultural crops is adopted. When opportunity costs increase, agricultural producers are forced to switch to higher-value production or move, a dynamic that could be explored with a longitudinal study of the same counties. It seems that nonagricultural factors are driving the agricultural sector to generate higher returns, or leading to longer-term shifts in agricultural production patterns. Conversely, in a low-land-value area with low opportunity costs, low-value and low-input crops are a rational investment and can generate high enough returns to the relatively modest investment in land to be considered viable. So, the future of agriculture is not as bleak as Blank might suggest for all geographical areas, at least not in the short or medium term, depending on urban development and other nonagricultural drivers of local economies.

There were some interesting findings for counties that performed well in this analysis. First of all, potato counties did well, which may be a function of 2002 being a good year in terms of potato yields and prices. For example, the San Luis Valley of Colorado is a persistent poverty region that grows a lot of potatoes, but it performed well in all the financial measures, which is not always the case.

After controlling for land values, it was again found that low-value crops such as corn are significant contributors to returns per value of land. This is an interesting finding, indicating that field crops are likely to be important sources of income in remote rural areas that do not face the land cost pressures seen in areas where vegetables and fruit crops are more likely to be grown. Moreover, the alternatives for other economic development enterprises may also be low, so agriculture will persist. New efforts to explore conservation and biofuel generation goals of the United States may play a role in increasing returns, as well as addressing broader rural development goals.

In keeping with this finding, some markedly different responses were found between the Mountain and Pacific regions in this analysis. Low-value agriculture still contributed positively for all three measures of performance in the Mountain region. There is little population pressure in much of the interior western and central United States, so land costs remain fairly low. As a result, the relatively low opportunity costs in these areas (expected given the lower "attracting masses" conceptualized in the gravity model) suggest that agriculture can be sustained in these locations. In short, Blank's (1998) conclusions seem to be playing out now in the Pacific region, but not yet in the Mountain region. More importantly, policies framed and implemented at the federal level may not be effective given these findings, as seemingly different market forces are affecting the viability of agriculture when comparing regions, states, and counties, thereby suggesting a need for more localized policy actions to support competitive agricultural sectors.

To a regional economist, these results are not necessarily a bad thing for agriculture or for rural economies. Higher-input, higher-revenue crops have the potential for higher multipliers that will spur more economic activity. As Blank's (1998) predictions play out, it is expected that areas facing population pressures and increased costs, specifically opportunity costs associated with escalating land values, would switch to higher-revenue crops or enterprises (such as the emerging bioenergy initiatives) to increase the average value of their crop portfolios. Agriculture would remain until land prices got so high as to make any type of agricultural production infeasible.

The problem that Blank (1998, 2001) and others have identified is the case of areas in which land suitable for high-value production is experiencing population pressure, thus making the cultivation of hinterland and exurban areas unprofitable. There is a real threat to agriculture in these regions. If the land taken out of agriculture for development is significantly better than the land remaining for production, and if American producers continue to see rising costs of land and production coupled with lower prices on the world market, then there is a danger of entirely losing agriculture in the American economic portfolio. This has been the impetus for the emergence of numerous land trusts. These trusts seek not only to preserve farmland, but also to target areas with greater urban influence, in an effort to maintain some open spaces and agricultural presence even when agricultural production cannot compete in the land market with commercial development. Not surprisingly, more of this type of activity is seen in coastal areas than in the interior of the country. This is to be expected given the relatively steep competition for land in coastal areas. In short, if there is underinvestment in public goods offered by farmland, there may be public and private policy and philanthropic solutions that will also mitigate the disappearance of agriculture in some parts of the United States. Subsequently, areas receiving the greatest attention from programs and policies to retain land in agricultural production are those in which the "competition" for land is the steepest between in-migrants who demand new housing and agricultural producers.

EVOLUTION OF THE AGRICULTURAL SECTOR
IN THE CONTEXT OF THE GRAVITY MODEL

Do the results of this empirical analysis provide any support for the predictions of the gravity model presented earlier? The gravity model predicted that attractive forces would draw agricultural producers to locations where they would have the greatest expected returns. One finding of this analysis is that, of all the characteristics of counties, mean temperature in January (Figure 17.8) was the most closely tied to expected returns. Thus, mean temperature in January might be the best proxy for the "attractive mass" term that creates an attractive force on agricultural producers because it is highly correlated with total sales per acre and net farm income per acre. The regressions consistently found that mean temperature in January related positively to all the measures of farm performance. Natural amenities related negatively to farm financial performance, after controlling for temperature. These results support the idea that locations with favorable climates for high-value agriculture, but that do not face the higher population pressure that comes from natural amenities, will enjoy relatively strong financial performance in their agricultural sectors.

The gravity model also predicted that areas with the highest expected returns would draw producers to that land. This would subsequently raise demand for land with desirable attributes, causing the value of that land to be bid up. The empirical results indicate that total sales per acre and net farm income per acre were positively correlated with average value of land and buildings, with correlation coefficients of .53 and .44, respectively. The model also predicted that, in equilibrium, average net farm income per value of land and buildings would be equal across all types of land. This is based on the idea that returns to a portfolio of commodities would be random, causing all counties to have similar returns to land since expected returns were bid into land values (leading to a homogeneous plane of returns per value of land).

Although this cross-sectional analysis did find a much more even distribution of returns across the counties using returns to land, it was far from a homogeneous plane and there were locations that performed statistically better in the specified model than others. One possible conclusion is that economic rents can still be obtained by locating in areas with higher returns on investment, but it is more likely that other forces are at play, including other industrial sectors and human utility and attachment to land. In other words, the American land market is not yet in equilibrium as the dynamic process of commodity market globalization continues.

It is very conceivable that some of the mass factors that contribute favorably to increased agricultural production returns may also contribute to increased amenity values. For example, expected returns of agricultural production is a function of the climate of the location, the cost of land at a given location is a function of expected returns and natural amenities, and the natural amenity index is a function of (among other things) climate. In looking at the correlations, temperature was positively correlated with all three measures of financial performance (although less so with net farm income per value of land and buildings). Also, natural amenities, although positively correlated with temperature, actually became negatively correlated with net farm income per value of land and buildings, thus confirming that agricultural production is in competition for land with housing development.

In fact, it was found that the residuals from the regression of natural amenities on mean temperature in January was a very strong predictor of high net farm income per value of land and

Figure 17.8 **Average Temperature in January**

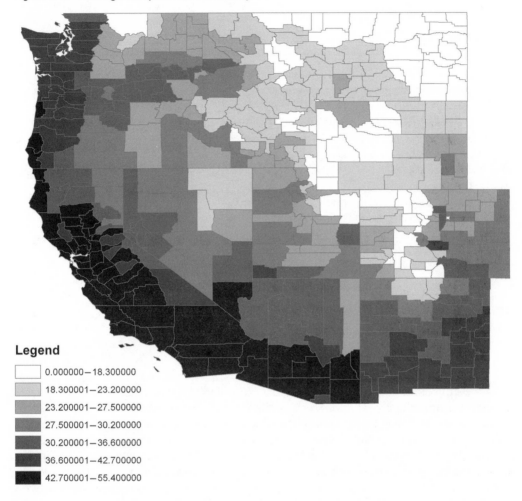

Legend

☐	0.000000 – 18.300000
▨	18.300001 – 23.200000
▨	23.200001 – 27.500000
▨	27.500001 – 30.200000
▨	30.200001 – 36.600000
▨	36.600001 – 42.700000
■	42.700001 – 55.400000

buildings, the most standardized measure of financial performance. The top-performing counties are clustered in the bottom right of Figure 17.9, representing counties with relatively high January temperatures and relatively low natural amenities. Conversely, counties that are clustered in the upper left of Figure 17.9 are counties with relatively high natural amenities and low temperatures in January.

If agriculture were the only demand agent for mild climate land, it would be expected that the Pacific region would be dominated by high-value agriculture and land prices would be bid up to where agriculture's expected marginal returns over other types of land are zero. In fact, a great deal of high-value agriculture is seen in the Pacific region and a disproportionately high concentration of counties with high net farm income per value of land and buildings is found in the Southwest and in the Northwest. This indicates that there is not yet equilibrium in expected returns on investment across the United States.

Figure 17.9   **Scatter Plot of Natural Amenity Index Against Average Temperature in January**

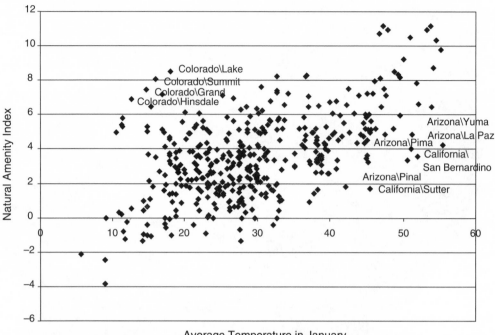

Average Temperature in January

However, counties that were in the top tier of net farm income per acre and have very favorable climates for agricultural production, such as Ventura and Santa Barbara counties on Southern California's coast, are no longer in the top tier for net farm income when expressed in terms of returns to the value of land and buildings. Households can generally outbid agricultural producers for desirable land, so agriculture is expected to be driven out of these counties despite their high agricultural income per acre. Likewise, northern California's Sutter County performs very well in the gravity model, yet it does not show up in the top echelon of profitable farm counties. Just north of Sacramento, the California state capital, Sutter County has a favorable climate for high-value agriculture, but a relatively low natural amenity index. The fact that it does not perform as well as counties like Yuma County, Arizona, is hypothesized to be due to the fact that Sutter County is a bedroom community for the state capital, which artificially increases household demand for land as people move to this region because of economic activity generated by the state capital. Therefore, this county is predicted to be well suited to high-value agriculture, but is less so due to artificially high land costs.

Overall, counties with a good climate but with little population pressure performed well. For example, Yuma County, Arizona, was in the top twenty for all three metrics and was number one in returns per value of land. In summary, those counties where high-value crops can be grown (especially off season) but which are not attractive to in-migrants do relatively well in generating agricultural returns. Not surprisingly, these counties may face other challenges, including absent landowners and more migrant labor, both of which contribute to leakages of economic activity out of the county. Clearly, agricultural producers face tradeoffs when deciding where they want to live and work.

LOOKING TO THE FUTURE

The empirical results in this chapter indicate that some regional agricultural industries will survive despite the general downsizing that earlier chapters show will continue to occur in the "national" production agriculture sector. As a result, there is no agricultural industry that is really national in scale. In general, American agriculture is shrinking back into being a collection of smaller, local and regional industries much like those that existed a century ago (although the scale of output is vastly expanded). The agricultural industries that will survive have climate and resource advantages in the production of commodities whose markets are not dominated by output from less-developed countries. These are markets in which less-developed countries are not able to produce a large enough supply to meet world demand, thus making it possible for low-cost local or regional domestic industries to survive. The spatial patterns of profitability in the results of this chapter show which western U.S. locations have been able to capture comparative advantages that still have some absolute advantages in the market for the commodities produced in those locations. Not surprisingly, those locations have warm climates that enable the cultivation of high-value fruit and vegetable crops, yet they do not have strong population pressures. Unfortunately, there are not many locations in the United States with those characteristics; much of the "Fruitful Rim" has rapidly expanding populations and the resulting growth in nonagricultural demand for land. In contrast, local industries that stand a chance of surviving include livestock grazing operations in low-population areas with cold climates unsuitable for farming and few natural amenities. For example, in many remote places in the mountains of the western United States, cattle operations may survive because the land has no viable alternative uses. In summary, the results in this chapter lead to the following proposition.

- PROPOSITION 17.1. *American production agriculture will eventually become small, regional niches with comparative and absolute advantages that enable them to serve a sizable enough market to make a reasonable return on investment.*

The results here have implications for the entire United States, not just the states analyzed. Most states in the American Southeast are part of the "Fruitful Rim" and are likely to see trends similar to those outlined here for the warm-climate areas of the West. This includes in-migration pushing land prices up and forcing agricultural producers out of business. In recent decades this adjustment has spurred concentration of agricultural operations in the Southeast, greatly decreasing farm numbers, but it has not yet pushed land and other input costs up to levels that greatly reduce average returns on investments. However, signs that returns are under pressure are increasing in the region.

The Midwest and Upper Midwest have relatively poor climates suitable for only grain and livestock production, like parts of the interior West, so similar trends are expected in those areas. In those regions, and even in the Corn Belt, livestock will be king and the grain industries will shrink to a size supported by livestock input demand. This means that domestic grain industries will be constrained by domestic population growth, which is what drives livestock consumption. The current high level of grain exports will virtually disappear because those sales will become unprofitable to American farmers. Grain commodities, in particular, are produced in many parts of the world, thus American farmers face the most global competition in those markets. Land prices in midwestern states therefore must remain low or even fall to give grain producers a reasonable chance of remaining competitive. This is unlikely in the long run, however, because lower land prices will increase in-migration. To the extent that both plants and people like warm climates, land prices will always threaten the disappearance of farming.

These trends indicate that a key to the future of American agriculture is land-use policy. If land-use tools such as zoning for agricultural use are not employed in many areas, especially those areas feeling pressures from nearby urbanization, agriculture will have no chance of surviving in the long term. Gradually, economic development will raise the opportunity costs of staying in agriculture and farm households will have to switch to alternatives, just as Blank (1998, 2001) hypothesized. Therefore, to a great extent, the future of American agriculture is a policy choice.

NOTES

Most of this chapter was written by Philip Watson and Dawn Thilmany. Steve Blank edited their paper, "Where and Why Agriculture Is Thriving: Lessons from an Analysis of Western Agricultural Financial Performance," into chapter form. The paper was drawn from Philip Watson's Ph.D. dissertation completed at Colorado State University.

1. The off-farm work factor competes with human capital inputs, but mitigates some financial risk and may relate to urban adjacency and agglomeration if labor markets are believed stronger in those areas.

2. The maximum likelihood function for both the spatial error and spatial lag model was first specified by Ord (1975) and it has yet to be improved upon (Anselin and Bera 1998).

3. The Census of Agriculture aggregation of vegetables can be somewhat problematic. For example, potatoes are considered vegetables, which is logical for marketing. Yet, from a production standpoint, potatoes are cultivated more like a field crop with extensive acreage, minimal cultural requirements during the growing season, and fully mechanized production. The dual nature of potatoes (as well as other crops, like onions) is reflected in the principal component analysis where vegetables also figure significantly into eigenvector five, which is primarily associated with field crops such as corn and wheat. A quantile map of vegetable production is presented in Figure 17.3.

4. This analysis is based on 2002 data, which may not be representative of all years. First, it was a strong year for potato yields and prices and counties that grow a large amount of potatoes tended to perform well in this analysis. Second, 2002 was a drought year across much of the West, which may have made it unrepresentative in terms of several agricultural enterprises. Yet overall, this model does well in predicting financial performance across counties, and illustrates the potential for further geographic diversity among western U.S. agricultural sectors.

5. This might be partly due to the strong performance in the potato sector in 2002 since counties with a concentration of potato production are strong performers in Figure 17.7.

6. Silage is a low-value input in dairy and livestock production. As such, it would *never* be economically viable to import or export, and draws its profitability from local livestock feeding operations. Cooperatives seek to increase the bargaining power of members, thus improving average profit margins. And, of course, milk prices are set through federal or state mechanisms that assure consumers of a plentiful milk supply by assuring dairy producers a strong return on their investment.

REFERENCES

Anderson, J. 1979. "A Theoretical Foundation for the Gravity Equation." *American Economic Review* 69: 106–116.

Anselin, L. 1990. "Some Robust Approaches to Testing and Estimation in Spatial Econometrics." *Regional Science and Urban Economics* 20: 1–17.

Anselin, L., and A. Bera. 1998. "Spatial Dependence in Linear Regression Models with an Introduction to Spatial Econometrics." In *Handbook of Applied Economic Statistics,* ed. A. Ullah and D. Giles. Berlin: Springer-Verlag.

Anselin, L., A. Bera, R. Florax, and M. Yoon. 1996. "Simple Diagnostic Tests for Spatial Dependence." *Regional Science and Urban Economics* 26: 77–104.

Ashley, C., and S. Maxwell. 2001. "Theme Issue: Rethinking Rural Development." *Development Policy Review* 19 (4): 395–425.

Bergstrand, J. 1989. "The Generalized Gravity Equation, Monopolistic Competition, and the Factor-Proportions Theory of International Trade." *Review of Economics and Statistics* 71: 143–153.

Blank, Steven C. 1998. *The End of Agriculture in the American Portfolio.* Westport, CT: Quorum Books.

———. 2001. "Producers Get Squeezed Up the Farming Food Chain: A Theory of Crop Portfolio Composition and Land Use." *Review of Agricultural Economics* 23 (2): 404–422.

———. 2002. "Is Agriculture a 'Way of Life' or a Business?" *Choices* 17 (2): 26–30.

———. 2005. "The Business of an Agricultural Way of Life." *Choices* 20 (2): 161–166.

Blank, S., K. Erickson, and C. Moss. 2005. "Profit Patterns Across American Agriculture." *Journal of Agricultural and Resource Economics* 30 (2): 205–230.

Blank, S., K. Erickson, C. Moss, and R. Nehring. 2004. "Agricultural Profits and Farm Household Wealth." *American Journal of Agricultural Economics* 86 (5): 1299–1307.

Borjas, G. 1989. "Immigrant and Emigrant Earnings: A Longitudinal Study." *Economic Inquiry* 27 (1): 21–37.

Brewster, J. 1961. "Society Values and Goals in Respect to Agriculture." In *Goals and Values in Agricultural Policy.* Ames: Iowa State University Press.

Cragg, M., and M. Kahn. 1999. "Climate Consumption and Climate Pricing from 1940–1990." *Regional Science and Urban Economics* 29 (4): 519–539.

Deller, S., D. Marcouiller, D. English, and V. Lledo. 2005. "Regional Economic Growth with a Focus on Amenities." In *Amenities and Rural Development: Theory, Methods and Public Policy,* ed. Gary Paul Green, Steven C. Deller, and David W. Marcouiller, pp. 129–152. Cheltenham, UK: Edward Elgar.

Deller, S, T. Tsai, D. Marcouiller, and D. English. 2001. "The Role of Amenities and Quality of Life in Rural Economic Growth." *American Journal of Agricultural Economics* 83 (2): 352–365.

DuPuis, M., and D. Goodman. 2005. "Should We Go 'Home' to Eat? Toward a Reflexive Politics of Localism." *Journal of Rural Studies* 21: 359–371.

Duranton, G., and H. Overman. 2005. "Testing for Localization Using Micro-Geographic Data." *Review of Economic Studies* 72: 1077–1106.

Ellis, F., and S. Biggs. 2001. "Evolving Themes in Rural Development, 1950s–2000s." *Development Policy Review,* 19 (4): 437–448.

Gesler, W. 1986. "The Use of Spatial Analysis in Medical Geography: A Review." *Social Science and Medicine* 23 (10): 963–973.

Ghelfi, L., and D. McGranahan. 2004. "One in Five Rural Counties Depends on Farming." *Amber Waves* 2 (3): 11.

Goodman, David. 1997. "World-Scale Processes and Agro-Food Systems: Critique and Research Needs." *Review of International Political Economy* 4 (4): 663–687.

Guptill, S. 1975. "The Spatial Availability of Physicians." *Proceedings of the Association of American Geographers* 7: 80–84.

Hawking, S., and W. Israel. 1987. *Three Hundred Years of Gravitation,* p. 6. Cambridge, UK: Cambridge University Press.

Hinrichs, C. Clare. 2005. "The Practice and Politics of Food System Localization." *Journal of Rural Studies* 21: 33–45.

Hotelling, H. 1933. "Analysis of a Complex of Statistical Variables into Principal Components." *Journal of Educational Psychology* 24: 417–441.

Huff, D. 1963. "A Probabilistic Analysis of Shopping Center Trade Areas." *Land Economics* 39: 81–90.

Hunter, L., J. Boardman, and J. Saint Onge. 2005. "The Association Between Natural Amenities, Rural Population Growth and Long-Term Residents' Economic Well-Being." *Rural Sociology* 70 (4): 452–469.

Irz, X., L. Lin, C. Thirtle, and S. Wiggins. 2001. "Agricultural Productivity Growth and Poverty Alleviation." *Development Policy Review* 19 (4): 449–466.

Jackson, J.E. 1991. *A User's Guide to Principal Components.* New York: Wiley.

Karemera, D., V. Oguledo, and B. Davis. 2000. "A Gravity Model Analysis of International Migration to North America." *Applied Economics* 32: 1745–1755.

Kimhi, A. 2000. "Is Part-Time Farming Really a Step in the Way Out of Agriculture?" *American Journal of Agricultural Economics* 82 (1): 38–48.

Lyson, T., and R. Welsh. 1993. "The Production Function, Crop Diversity, and the Debate Between Conventional and Sustainable Agriculture." *Rural Sociology* 58 (3): 424–439.

McGlashan, N., and J. Blunden. 1983. *Geographical Aspects of Health.* London: Academic Press.

Mishra, A., H. El-Osta, M. Morehart, J. Johnson, and J. Hopkins. 2002. *Income, Wealth, and the Economic Well-Being of Farm Households.* Washington DC: U.S. Department of Agriculture, Economic Research Service, Agricultural Economics Report 812.

Mishra, A.K., and C.L. Sandretto. 2002. "Stability of Farm Income and the Role of Nonfarm Income in U.S. Agriculture." *Review of Agricultural Economics* 24 (1): 208–221.

Nabhan, G. 2002. *Coming Home to Eat: The Pleasures and Politics of Local Foods.* New York: W.W. Norton.

Oguledo, V., and C. Macphee. 1994. "Gravity Model: A Reformulation and an Application to Discriminatory Trade Arrangements." *Applied Economics* 40: 315–337.

Ord, J. 1975. "Estimation Methods for Models of Spatial Interaction." *Journal of the American Statistical Association* 70: 120–126.

Pearson, K. 1901. "On Lines and Planes of Closest Fit to Systems of Points in Space." *Philosophical Magazine* 2: 559–572.

Power, T. 1996. *Lost Landscapes and Failed Economies: The Search for the Value of Place.* Washington, DC: Island Press.

Ready, R., and C. Abdalla. 2005. "The Amenity and Disamenity Impacts of Agriculture: Estimates from a Hedonic Pricing Model." *American Journal of Agricultural Economics* 87 (2): 314–326.

Roback, J. 1988. "Wages, Rents, and Amenities: Differences Among Workers and Regions." *Economic Inquiry* 26 (1): 23–41.

Rosen, S. 1979. "Wage-Based Indexes of Urban Quality of Life." In *Current Issues in Urban Economics,* ed. P. Mieszkowski and M. Straszheim, pp. 74–104. Baltimore, MD: Johns Hopkins University Press.

Shumway, M., and S. Otterstrom. 2001. "Spatial Patterns of Migration and Income Change in the Mountain West: The Dominance of Service Based, Amenity Rich Counties." *Professional Geographer* 53 (4): 493–501.

Tinbergen, Jan. 1962. *Shaping the World Economy: Suggestions for an International Economic Policy.* New York: Twentieth Century Fund.

United States Department of Agriculture (USDA). 2007. *Census of Agriculture,* on web at: http://www.agcensus.usda.gov/.

USDA Economic Research Service 2007. Briefing Rooms, on web at: http://www.ers.usda.gov/Briefing/.

Weber, Bruce. 1998. "Crossing the Next Meridian: The Economics of Rural-Urban Interdependence, Institutions, and Income Distribution in the American West." *Journal of Agricultural and Resource Economics* 23 (1): 1–11.

Wu, JunJie. 2006. "Environmental Amenities, Urban Sprawl, and Community Characteristics." *Journal of Environmental Economics and Management* 52 (2): 527–547.

Zipf, G. 1946. "The P1P2/D Hypothesis: On the Intercity Movement of Persons." *American Sociological Review* 2: 677–686.

PART V

AMERICAN AGRICULTURAL
POLICY QUESTIONS

CHAPTER 18

THE ROLE OF AMERICAN AGRIBUSINESS

"It was the best of times, it was the worst of times..."
—Charles Dickens, *A Tale of Two Cities*

The story of American agriculture is really a tale of two sectors, and one sector has a much brighter story than the other sector. This book has documented the fact that the farm and ranch production sector has been suffering its worst of times in recent decades. The agribusiness sector, on the other hand, continues to see the good times roll, and it may see the best of times in future decades as its control over the production sector expands.

The agribusiness sector includes those firms that provide inputs to, and handle outputs from, the production agriculture sector. If those firms are divided into two subsectors, it is easy to see that one group in particular has a prosperous future. Whereas the subgroup providing inputs to agricultural producers has limits on its profit potential because its market is shrinking with the declining production sector, the subgroup handling outputs from the production sector has the very best of times ahead.

Firms handling outputs from the production sector can look forward to improving profit totals because their market is growing and their control over their suppliers is increasing, thus giving them potential to improve their profit margins. For example, food processors are part of the American agribusiness sector and their prospects for future profitability are bright. Consumers have revealed strong preferences for value-added food products, thus giving processors some ability to manipulate demand so as to increase their average selling prices. This has historically given food manufacturers and other industries in the agribusiness sector higher profit margins, on average, than found in commodity production. A quick comparison shows the scale of the difference in profitability. Chapter 3 reports that American farmers and ranchers averaged about a 4 percent return over the 1960–2002 period. McLaughlin and Hawkes (1986) reported that retail grocery chain returns on assets averaged 4.2 to 6.9 percent during the 1965–1984 period. Schumacher and Boland (2005) found that retail firms averaged an 8.8 percent return on assets from 1981 to 2001. Also, they note that retail industry returns are consistently lower than the returns in the food processing industry, which averaged 11.4 percent for the 1981–2002 period. Thus, from farm gate to consumer, profit margins vary with the ability to add value. Higher profit margins, in turn, are an indicator of relative market power for an industry within a supply chain. This is apparent when comparing the American production agriculture sector to the U.S. food manufacturing industry. Census data for 2002 show that food manufacturing sales totaled $458.8 billion, more than double the total sales of crops and livestock for that year. Also, those sales, and the high degree of added value, were generated by only 27,915 food manufacturing firms with 1.5 million employees. Clearly, food manufacturing and the other industries in the agribusiness sector are large and powerful players in American agriculture.

Research trying to explain food manufacturers' ability to maintain relatively high profits has found that both product differentiation and industry structure were significant. For example, using data from 1954 to 1977, Rogers (1987, p. 248) found "the hypothesis that product differentiation is positively related to profit levels received statistical support." He also found a strengthening positive relationship between profit margins and four-firm concentration levels within the industry. Schumacher and Boland (2005) had similar results over the 1981–2001 period; however, they found that "the structure of the industry is more important than being a member of a diversified corporation" (p. 113).

Therefore, it is the relationship between industry structure and the agribusiness sector's increasing control over the supply of their inputs that is of most interest here. This chapter focuses on the control that the American agribusiness sector has, and will expand, over the production agriculture sector in the United States and over the globe. Evidence that this control already exists on an international scale comes from Acheampong (2000). She found that food processing firms in 11 industrialized countries, including the United States, had similar levels of profit performance, averaging about 20 percent return on equity from 1989 to 1995. This convergence of returns in food processing industries indicates the presence of a global market for food products. It is argued in this chapter that the U.S. agribusiness sector will lead the development of that global market by playing a central role in directing: (a) U.S. farm and ranch production output, (b) international commodity markets, (c) global food industries, and (d) technology and market development. The story begins down on the farm.

MARKET EVOLUTION AND THE RELATIONSHIP
BETWEEN AGRICULTURE AND AGRIBUSINESS

The structure, conduct, and performance of American agriculture are continually changing. This can be most easily seen in the agribusiness sector, where firms are becoming larger and more industrialized, causing industries to become more concentrated. This change in the agribusiness sector's structure is being driven partly by economies of scale. Conversely, the location-specific nature of agricultural production (which is driven by the comparative advantage of natural resources and microclimates) is likely to prevent that sector from becoming as concentrated as the agribusiness sector, thus the current imbalance in the bargaining positions of commodity sellers and buyers is expected to get worse in the future. The structural changes leading to concentration, in turn, are likely to change the conduct of commodity markets such that the economic performance of the two sectors will be affected, with the agribusiness sector expected to benefit at the expense of the production sector. This could have serious implications for American farmers, ranchers, and, possibly, consumers.

One of the ways this change in commodity market conduct is manifesting itself is through the increasing use of production and marketing contracts between agribusiness firms and farmers or ranchers. The trend of increasing contracting was slow to start, but has become more important over the last decade. The overall share of agricultural production value under contract in the U.S. has increased from 12 percent in 1969 to 39 percent in 2003 (MacDonald and Korb 2006). As shown in Figure 18.1, production and marketing contracts are two methods of vertical coordination. Thus, it has long been hypothesized that the use of these contracts, especially production contracts, is an indicator of industrialization in agriculture (e.g., Mighell and Jones 1963; Drabenstott 1995; Ahearn, Korb, and Banker 2005). However, the question of why different degrees of industrialization are found across agricultural markets has not been directly

Figure 18.1   **Methods of Vertical Coordination Along the Spectrum of Control**

Control offered to contractor or integrator			
Least			**Most**
|	|	|	|
Open production	Marketing contract	Production contract	Vertical integration

Source: Mighell and Jones (1963).

addressed. One of the reasons for this research void is that very little data are available at the beginning of a trend.

The general objective of the analysis in this chapter is to contribute to the understanding of the relationship between industry structure and production contracting. In this effort, two specific objectives are pursued. The first objective is to provide a base for future research. Given the limited amount of data available at this early stage in the trend toward increased use of production contracting, an explanation is proposed for what is driving that trend. Drawing from the literature, it is proposed here that there are unique structural constraints in each commodity market that determine the potential for production contracting.[1] It is conjectured that there is a positive relationship between the number of commercial uses applicable to a commodity and the number of buyers in that market, and hypotheses are tested on (1) the expected positive relationship between concentration in an agribusiness industry and the extent of production contracting for the relevant commodity, (2) the expected negative relationship between the portion of a commodity produced on contract and the number of products made from that commodity, and (3) the expected negative relationship between concentration and the number of products in a commodity industry. The origin of these conjectures is explained, then empirical data that are consistent with these hypotheses are presented from a small cross section of commodities.

The second specific objective is to evaluate whether there are farm-level economic explanations for the trend toward production contracting. The analysis explores significant differences between agricultural producers who enter into production contracts and those who remain independent. Thus, questions are raised here about whether the trend is being driven from the top down (i.e., by industry or market factors), from the bottom up (i.e., by farm-level factors), or a combination of the two. Based on the results, preliminary inferences are made on the future of production contracting in American agriculture—its potential for expansion as well as its fundamental limitations.

Vertical Coordination in Agriculture

This analysis focuses on production contracting, which is a form of vertical coordination between processors and producers. "Vertical coordination refers to the synchronization of successive stages of production and marketing, with respect to quantity, quality, and timing of product flows" (Martinez 2002). As shown in Figure 18.1, a production contract offers more control to a contractor than does a marketing contract, but both types of contracts offer only partial control compared to complete vertical integration achieved through common ownership of production and marketing activities at successive stages of the supply chain. A processor firm seeking complete control would prefer vertical integration over the partial control of contracts, ceteris paribus. However, farmers and ranchers prefer to be independent operators (Key 2005) ideally selling their commodities in spot markets, such as auctions.[2] Thus, the actual distribution of production being sold at different points between the two end points in Figure 18.1 may indicate (among other factors) the relative market power of market participants.

Contracts formed between agricultural producers and processors replace traditional spot markets (called "open production" in Figure 18.1) for all parties involved. According to results from the USDA's Agricultural Resource and Management Survey (ARMS), contract use is expanding in the United States. The total share of production value under contract has increased from 28.9 percent in 1991 to 39.1 percent in 2003. However, there are two different categories of agricultural contracts.

Under marketing contracts, prices, quantities, and delivery schedules are agreed upon before crops are harvested or livestock are delivered. Farmers and ranchers own their commodities throughout the entire stage of production and therefore they retain control over management decisions, including those related to inputs used in production. Katchova and Miranda (2004, p. 101) found that "personal and farm characteristics mostly affect the adoption decision rather than the quantity, frequency, and contract type decisions." Marketing contracts cover a greater share of crop production than livestock production, with 29.7 percent of total crop production value under marketing contracting compared to 13.7 percent of livestock production value in 2003. For all commodities produced in the United States, the total share of production value under marketing contracts has been about 21 percent since 1994 (MacDonald and Korb 2006).

Under production contracts, the commodity buyer sets input specifications and typically provides inputs such as veterinary services, feed, and young animals in the case of livestock. In some cases, the buyer owns the commodity being produced from the beginning of the contract period and has managerial control over the production process. In all cases, the producer provides technical and managerial inputs plus all labor and physical facilities needed to create the specified output. Additionally, the producer's payment is not agreed upon prior to the harvest but rather is determined at the end of the arrangement and is based on quantity and the degree to which the final product meets the buyer's specifications. Production contracts are much more prevalent among livestock commodities than they are among crops. In 2003 only 1.1 percent of total crop production value was under production contracts, compared to 33.7 percent for livestock. Furthermore, the share of total U.S. agricultural sales under production contracts increased from 10.6 percent in 1996 to about 18 percent in 2003, in contrast to the stable trend in marketing contracts (MacDonald and Korb 2006). Table 18.1 summarizes the share of production under contract by commodity and contract type for recent years.[3] Given that producers lose some of their autonomy under the terms of production contracts, their choosing these contracts over spot markets is somewhat surprising, thus justifying a quick review of producers' motivation.

Producer Motives for Production Contracting

Over the last five decades the literature has offered a fairly consistent list of motives for farmers and ranchers to choose contracting, but there has been no consistency in opinions on which motives are most important. Mighell and Jones (1963) identified four reasons for coordinating by nonmarket means: to increase efficiency, to obtain (or reduce the cost of) financing, to reduce uncertainty, and to gain market advantage. Ahearn, Korb, and Banker (2005) wrote that the two most commonly cited reasons for entering into contracts were risk management and minimization of production and/or transaction costs. These two reasons for contracting are essentially the same

Table 18.1

Share of Total Agricultural Sales by Commodity, Contract Type, and Year, 1991–2003

Item	1991–93	1994–95	1996–97	1998–2000	2001–02	2003
Commodities produced under marketing contract				Share of total sales (%)		
All commodities	17.0	21.2	21.5	20.4	19.7	21.7
Crops	22.8	24.0	21.1	22.5	24.7	29.7
Corn	10.2	13.8	12.9	12.6	14.7	13.8
Soybeans	9.6	9.8	13.2	9.7	9.5	13.6
Wheat	5.8	6.2	9.0	6.9	6.4	7.5
Sugar beets	88.5	83.7	74.6	83.1	95.8	95.1
Rice	19.7	25.2	25.8	30.5	38.6	51.8
Peanuts	45.2	58.3	34.2	44.9	27.9	53.3
Tobacco	0.3	0.6	0.3	1.9	52.6	54.8
Cotton	30.4	44.4	33.8	42.9	52.6	50.9
Fruit	n/a	61.0	54.3	63.3	60.1	67.2
Vegetables	n/a	45.3	32.3	27.3	31.5	36.4
Other crops	6.3	14.0	18.7	21.2	30.9	44.7
Livestock	11.6	18.2	22.0	18.4	14.5	13.7
Broilers	5.9	3.4	4.0	3.9	4.2	1.1
Hogs	n/a	2.4	2.7	9.1	6.1	6.8
Cattle	n/a	4.3	5.9	4.6	2.7	3.4
Other livestock	0.1	6.8	4.9	10.7	3.5	7.4
Dairy	33.6	56.7	58.0	53.4	48.0	50.5
Commodities produced under production contract				Share of total sales (%)		
All commodities	11.8	13.0	10.6	16.9	18.0	17.5
Crops	1.9	1.9	1.8	4.2	3.1	1.1
Vegetables	n/a	9.7	6.1	12.4	10.6	6.3
Livestock	21.1	24.7	22.9	29.6	33.8	33.7
Broilers	82.8	81.2	80.1	84.9	88.1	95.5
Hogs	n/a	28.7	47.3	76.3	78.1	84.8
Cattle	n/a	14.7	11.1	19.7	18.3	25.4
Other livestock	0.1	2.6	n/a	n/a	5.5	n/a
Dairy	0.2	0.2	0.1	0.2	0.7	0.6

Source :   acDonald and   orb (200) and the USDA s Agricultural   esource   anagement Survey for relevant years.

as the first three listed by Mighell and Jones (1963), with efficiency gains and financing being lumped under the production-transaction cost minimization umbrella. Some recent studies (e.g., Allen and Lueck 2003; Martinez 2002) have focused on the single explanation of transaction cost economics (Williamson 1979) and its emphasis on asset specificity as the driving force behind the decision to contract. For example, Lajili et al. (1997, p. 279) found that "the degree of asset specificity significantly influences farmers' choices of contractual arrangements." However, as pointed out by MacDonald, Ahearn, and Banker (2004, p. 745), "one weakness of transaction-cost analyses is that they typically don't nest market power and efficiency explanations. In Joskow's summary, they 'frequently ignore the possibility that there may be market power

motivations or market power consequences for these organizational arrangements as well.'"
Surprisingly, Mighell and Jones's (1963) fourth motive—to gain market advantage—has received the least research attention although it is argued here that it is the most likely explanation in American agriculture's current evolutionary state.

Gaining a market advantage may be easy in an industry like agriculture, which has imbalances in its structure (such as having many sellers and few buyers of a commodity). For example, Lanzillotti (1960) detailed how firms dealing with agriculture were already taking advantage of the production sector. He concluded that "leading firms possess considerable market power and are inclined to utilize such power to manage or administer their market situation" (pp. 1240–1241). The result of that market power imbalance was a significant difference in the profit margins of agribusiness firms and agricultural producers. In other words, gaining market power facilitates taking actions that improve a firm's profit margins, thus providing the strongest of incentives to seek bargaining power. As a result, it is surprising that relatively little empirical research was done to sort out the relationship between industry structure and market power. By 1986 the story was still unsettled, as reported by Schrader (1986, p. 1161):

> The relation of integration or nonmarket vertical coordination to market power has two interpretations. Integration and contract coordination are viewed by some as a means to enhance the integrator's market power. Others see market power on one side (or both sides) of a market as an incentive for vertical arrangements to capture gains from the side possessing market power or to achieve joint profit maximization.

The uncertainty was still apparent in 2005 when Ahearn, Korb, and Banker (2005) reported on the increasing concentration in agriculture and agribusiness and noted that "it is not obvious whether this concentration is the desirable result of cost efficiencies in production or the undesirable result of market power on the part of various players in the supply chain," citing the question raised by Williamson (1968). Thus, more research is needed into the influence of agricultural market structure on conduct such as contracting.

There is little literature dealing directly with the recent rise in production contracting. This is due partly to the scarcity of data on contracting (Ahearn, Korb, and Banker 2005). A review of the scant literature points to three possible explanations for the increased share of production under production contracts. These are risk aversion, the increase in processor concentration in U.S. agribusiness, and the increase in the total scale of agricultural production. While risk management is virtually undisputed in the literature as a catalyst for contracting in general, MacDonald et al. (2004) and Key (2004) stress that it should no longer be considered the sole motivating factor for farmers in choosing production contracts. The respective causal relationships between the increase in processor concentration and the increase in the scale of production with production contracting are less clear, but it is proposed here that concentration and size lead to market power that is used to expand contracting.

A defining characteristic of the ongoing transformation of U.S. agriculture may be the rise in concentration in the food manufacturing industry (Ollinger et al. 2005). According to data from the U.S. Department of Agriculture (USDA), the mean industry four-firm concentration ratio (CR4) in food manufacturing rose from 35 percent in 1982 to 46.1 percent in 1997.[4] The rate of increase in concentration for the meatpacking industry, in which there is also the highest degree of production contracting, significantly outpaced agriculture as a whole. The meatpacking CR4 increased from 29 percent to 57 percent over this time period. This trend continues in various processing industries. For example, the CR4 of U.S. beef packers was estimated at 86 percent in

Table 18.2

Commodity Usage and Industry Concentration

Commodity	Commodity usage index	CR4 1987 %	CR4 1992 %	CR4 1997 %	CR4 2002 %
Broilers	0.47	29	34	56	54
Hogs	0.52	20	25	64	68
Cattle	0.43	39	50	84	86
Dairy	0.80	21	22	21	30
Soybeans	0.18	71	71	75	95
Corn	0.19	74	73	80	69
Wheat	0.19	44	56	62	49
Oats	0.61	27	33	64	70
Barley	0.37	19	23	46	87
Rice	0.47	41	51	69	57
Cotton	0.40	18	19	20	26
Sugar beets	0.98	83	85	85	85
Peanuts	0.39	68	80	82	87
Tobacco	0.84	70	76	83	89

Note : The commodity usage inde is a buyer concentration inde calculated by the authors as a   er nd ahl type inde using then umber and share of the ma or product categories for each commodity.   is the concentration ratio reported by the U.S. ensus ureau for the ma or product category for the year indicated. The source for the   and for the data used in the usage inde calculations is the ensus ureau s
co o   c e   u

2002 and the CR4 for pork packers in 2002 was found to be 68 percent. The last four columns of Table 18.2 present CR4 data for a cross section of commodities over time.

Given that agricultural commodity producers have a strong preference for autonomy (Key 2005), the observed increase in processor concentration suggests that bargaining power on the part of farmers and ranchers is decreasing, thus fueling the trend in production contracting. This certainly appears to be the case in the hog industry, where producers who value autonomy less than they fear the risks of being without a contract eagerly adopt contracts (Davis and Gillespie 2007). However, there are exceptions to this argument. For example, the soybean processing industry saw an increase in concentration from 1982 to 2002, yet only a small portion of total soybean production is under any form of contract, as indicated in Table 18.1. The broiler industry has by far the largest share of production under production contract, yet among livestock commodities it has both the lowest CR4 and the slowest growth in concentration over the comparable time period.

Producer concentration is also on the rise in U.S. agriculture. According to USDA data, the percentage of farms in the United States with annual sales of $500,000 or more has increased from 2 percent in 1991 to 4.4 percent in 2001. More strikingly, these farms' share of total agricultural production increased over this period from 39 percent to 57.4 percent. Examining individual commodities, Rios and Gray (2005) determined that the share of industry total sales from farms with annual sales of $500,000 or higher increased from 10.9 percent to 77 percent for hogs from 1982 to 2002. Production contracting is relatively very high for hog production, even though the rate of growth in hog producer concentration significantly outpaced the equivalent numbers for commodities with low production contracting, such as wheat, corn, and soybeans. Just as increased processor concentration implies increased buyer bargaining power, increased producer concentration would normally suggest increased seller bargaining power. However, concentration of hog producers may be an outcome caused by the trend of processors offering contracts most often to larger producers only. Thus, the hog industry case indicates there are some commodity-specific factors influencing the level of production contracting and the direction of causality in that contracting (Key and McBride 2003).

Due largely to the location-specific nature of agricultural production, the food manufacturing sector is likely to consolidate faster than the commodity production sector. That is what happened in the United Kingdom (Duranton and Overman 2005). However, concentration in the U.S. manufacturing industry is not the primary determinant of the pattern of production contracting, particularly when considering the current trends in producer concentration. Clearly, many factors are significant, as noted below.

Key (2004) examined the supply side of agribusiness by evaluating the relationship between the scale of production and contracting. The scale of production, as measured by changes in the size and output of the largest farms by sector, was found to be directly correlated with the prevalence of contracting. Explanations offered by Key (2004) for this correlation included the usual stories of grower risk aversion and contractor transaction costs, as well as newer theoretical justifications such as asset specificity.

Finally, another possible determinant of contracting is the growth of production contracting itself. Recent research suggests that farmers in some commodity markets are turning to contracting out of necessity due to the incomplete markets created by other market participants' decisions to contract (Young and Burke 2001). Roberts and Key (2005) demonstrated that in some markets, farmers who choose to engage in production contracts could impose negative externalities on other farmers in the form of increased search and transaction costs. The farmers facing the externalities are induced to enter into contracts, which they would not have done otherwise, because contracts may represent the only available access to a buyer. This finding is consistent with the idea that spot markets have "tipping points" at which a market is thinned enough to induce all remaining participants to enter into contracts (MacDonald et al. 2004).

It is clear from the literature that questions remain regarding the primary determinants of production contracting in agriculture. Also, much is still unknown regarding the effects of contracting on producers, agribusiness, and consumers. Yet it is understood that contracting has played a large role in improving product consistency and traceability throughout the stages of food production (MacDonald et al. 2004). Furthermore, research has shown that contracting has a positive effect on farm productivity (Ahearn, Yee, and Huffman 2002; Key and McBride 2003; Morrison Paul, Nehring, and Banker 2004). There remain concerns over the effects on farmers who enter into contracts against their best interests (Roberts and Key 2005), and the managerial control imposed on farmers by the processors with whom they contract (Farm Foundation 2004). However, much of the rise in production contracting has occurred in just the past decade, suggesting that it could take years for the large-scale effects of production contracting to become evident in empirical analyses across a wide range of commodities.

Structural Constraints on the Development of Production Contracting

It is proposed here that the relationships between the extent of production contracting and both industry structure and market diversity can be represented as a continuum and that each commodity can be plotted at some point on that continuum. Shown in Figure 18.2, this continuum is based on the hypothesis that product attributes of each commodity influence the structure of the processing or manufacturing industries that can develop for that commodity and, in turn, the

Figure 18.2 **The Continuum Relating Contracting, Industry Structure, and Market Diversity**

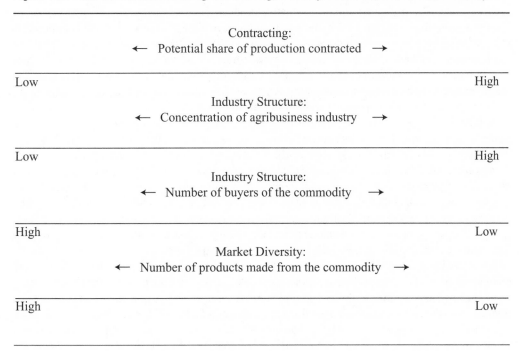

structure of those industries affects the extent of production contracting that will ultimately be seen at the farm and ranch level.

- PROPOSITION 18.1. *Each commodity falls on a particular point on the continuum representing the relationship between the extent of production contracting and both industry structure and market diversity.*

To explain the continuum and its underlying hypotheses, the discussion begins at the top of Figure 18.2. The top line of the four lines in the figure represents the range of possible shares of total production of a commodity that could be contracted. The ends of the line are labeled "low" and "high" (which could be labeled "zero" and "100 percent" in this case), thus the points along the line indicate that there is a continuous range of possibilities. The second of the four lines in Figure 18.2 represents the level of concentration in the agribusiness industry related to the commodity. The fact that the same ends of the second line are labeled "low" and "high" as is the case for the first line illustrates one of the main hypotheses of this analysis: there is a positive relationship between the (potential) level of production contracting and the level of concentration in the agribusiness industry that buys the commodity from producers.

The third line in Figure 18.2 represents the number of agribusiness firms buying a commodity. By definition, there is an inverse relationship between the number of firms in an industry and the level of concentration in that industry. Thus, the third line has labels of "low" and "high" at opposite ends relative to the first two lines. This illustrates the hypothesis of a negative relationship between the number of buyers available to producers of a commodity and the (potential) share of total sales of that commodity, which is production contracted.

The fourth line in Figure 18.2 represents the number of products made from the commodity. The physical attributes of a commodity determine how many different products can be made from it. Some commodities, such as wheat, can be made into a large number of products while other commodities, such as tobacco, can be processed into only a few products. It is expected that the more products derived from a commodity, the more firms there will be buying the commodity from producers, hence the positive relationship illustrated in the figure. Also, it is hypothesized that if there are a high number of products made from a commodity, producers will generally have more buyers to choose from, hence giving those producers more bargaining power. With that bargaining power, producers might be more likely to avoid production contracts, if possible. Thus, it is hypothesized that there is a negative relationship between the number of products made from a commodity and the share of that commodity's output that will be under production contract.

Each agricultural commodity has a unique set of physical attributes and a unique industry that has developed to process the commodity into various products, thus it is expected that each commodity would be plotted at a unique point along the continuum. In other words, it is proposed here that each commodity would fall on a single point along the continuum and, as a group, the array of commodities produced would be distributed along the continuum as determined by the composition of each industry. Each commodity would fall on the same horizontal point on each of the four lines making up the proposed continuum. So, for example, broilers are expected to be plotted far to the right on the horizontal lines of the continuum. A very low number of products are made from the livestock commodity, and the low number of buyers (i.e., broiler processing firms) means the agribusiness industry has a high degree of concentration, all leading to the expectation of a high share of broiler production (potentially) being under contract. Wheat, on the other hand, is expected to fall on a point far to the left on the continuum, while most other commodities will fall between these two examples.

Methods of Analysis

The analysis in this chapter, in general, is limited in its ability to test the ideas embedded in the contracting continuum presented in Figure 18.2. The evolutionary shift in market conduct that is creating the changes in production contracting is at such an early stage that data are very limited. Too little data means the conjectures derived here using induction can only be turned into propositions by preliminary analysis. Future testing, once adequate data are available, will be required for a thorough assessment of the hypotheses raised.

The two specific objectives of this preliminary analysis require very different methodologies. Strong-form tests of the hypotheses underlying the continuum shown in Figure 18.2 would require data from a large cross section of commodity markets but, as Ahearn, Korb, and Banker (2005) point out, the major rise in production contracting has occurred within the last decade, so data are scarce and hypothesis testing is difficult.[5] Therefore, this analysis uses three approaches to draw inferences on the future of production contracting in the United States. First, weak-form tests of the industry-level hypotheses underlying the continuum are conducted with the limited data available. Second, farm-level data across a small cross section of commodities are used for strong-form tests of differences between producers that production contract and producers that are independent operators (i.e., those producers of a commodity who do not participate in a production contract). Finally, two commodities are used as case studies to illustrate differences in the evolution of production contracting over time.

To begin, industry-level data are used to test three of the basic hypotheses underlying the continuum illustrated in Figure 18.2. Those hypotheses are (1) there is a positive relationship between the share of a commodity that is production contracted and the level of concentration in the agribusiness industry that buys the commodity from producers, (2) there is a negative relationship between the share of a commodity contracted and the number of products made from that commodity, and (3) there is a negative relationship between the number of products and the concentration of firms buying that commodity. Weak-form tests are conducted using simple regressions with data from the fourteen commodities listed in Table 18.2. These commodities represent a cross section of major crop and livestock industries for which significant amounts of contracting data are available.

The exact numbers of buyers in a market and products made from a commodity both vary over time and are subject to measurement error, therefore a proxy is used for this national analysis. A "commodity usage index" is derived here using the number of product categories processed from the commodity and the share of the commodity going into each of the categories. The usage index is a type of buyer concentration index calculated like a Herfindahl index. Normally, a Herfindahl index is a measure of the size of firms in relation to the industry and an indicator of the amount of competition among them. In this analysis, the commodity usage index is an inverse measure of the number and market share of products made from a commodity. The index is defined as the sum of the squares of the shares of the commodity going into each processed product category. As such, it can range from 0 (indicating there are a very large number of product categories) to 1 (indicating there is a single product). The index is expressed as

$$(18.1) \qquad\qquad H = \frac{1}{n} + nV$$

where n is the number of product categories and V is the variance of the shares (s) of the commodity going into each category, defined as

$$(18.2) \qquad\qquad V = \frac{\sum_{i=1}^{n}(s_i - 1/n)^2}{n}$$

If all product categories have equal shares (in which case $s_i = 1/n$ for all i), then V is zero and H equals $1/n$. If the number of product categories is held constant, then a higher variance due to a higher level of asymmetry between category shares will result in a higher index value.

The Commodity Usage Index for each commodity was calculated using data from the 2002 Economic Census conducted by the U.S. Department of Commerce (2006). As an example, the index for cotton was calculated as follows. First, the census listed cotton as having three categories of use; hence n was assumed to be 3. Those categories (proxying for separate firms) and their respective shares were "apparel" 0.247, "home furnishings" 0.545, and "industrial" 0.206 (these values are rounded, thus they do not total 1.0). Substituting 3 for n, and the three share amounts for s, into Equations 18.1 and 18.2 gives a Usage Index of 0.40 for cotton.

The second portion of this analysis uses farm-level survey data to test several hypotheses about the size, structure, and financial position of production operations. Producers who have production contracts are compared with those who remain independent. Based on the literature (e.g., Key 2004; Roberts and Key 2005; Morrison Paul, Nehring, and Banker 2004) it is hypothesized that farms entering into production contracts are likely to be larger than independents, significantly less diversified in terms of commodities produced, and facing increased risk, relative to the risk exposure of independents. Independent-sample t-tests of these and related hypotheses are conducted for a cross section of commodities. Using pooled farm-level data from the USDA's ARMS for the years 1996 through 2004 (USDA/ERS) gives a total of 95,517 observations.

Finally, two case studies are used to illustrate differences across commodity types. The relationship between production contractors and independents is expected to vary between livestock and crop operations. Given that the scale of production contracting is much smaller among crops than it is among livestock commodities (Table 18.1), the degree to which independents and contractors differ is expected to be less striking in crop industries. Therefore, case studies of hog producers and soybean farmers are presented to provide more detail in the implications drawn regarding the future structure of American agriculture.

Industry-level Results

All three of the hypotheses underlying the continuum shown in Figure 18.2 are supported by the limited cross-sectional data. Table 18.2 presents data on the number of products made from the commodity (proxied by the Commodity Usage Index) and the agribusiness industry's concentration, and Table 18.4 (to be discussed later) presents data on the share of the commodity under production contract. Simple regressions indicate that all three hypothesized relationships have the correct sign. To begin, the regression coefficient between the share of contracting and industry concentration is positive, but not significantly different from zero (the t-statistic is 1.56). This regression was estimated using only six commodities (broilers, hogs, cattle, corn, soybeans, and cotton) due to limited data on contracting for most commodities. Thus, this result is consistent with the hypothesis, but needs data from additional commodities to provide the degrees of freedom needed for a stronger test.

The second hypothesis suffers from the same contracting data limitation, but has stronger results. Using only the cross section of six commodities, the correlation between contracting share and the number of products made from the commodity ($r = 0.74$) is positive, which indicates a negative relationship between the two factors, as expected (due to way the Usage Index is calculated). A simple regression on those two variables generates a positive regression coefficient with a significant t-statistic of 2.91.

The third hypothesis was tested with the Usage Index and 2002 concentration data for the 14 commodities listed in Table 18.2. The simple regression coefficient was positive (due to the inverse nature of the Usage Index) and significant with a t-statistic of 6.01.

These three regression results are only weak-form tests because so few observations (i.e., commodities) are available at present. However, it is expected that as more commodities are studied and as more of the potential for production contracting materializes, the continuum relationships will strengthen and become more apparent in empirical data. In the meantime, the analysis focuses on the more plentiful farm-level data to detect factors influencing the decision to contract, and the effects of contracting on the structure of commodity industries.

Farm-level Results

The share of total sales under production contract varies greatly among commodities in the United States. The analysis examined fourteen major U.S. commodities for which adequate data were available and found that a continuum exists with regard to production contracting, ranging from

Table 18.3

Summary of Average Farm Results by Commodity, Production Contractors and Independents, 1996–2004 ARMS Data

Commodity	Number of producers surveyed	Total farm sales ($)	Total household income ($)	Off-farm share of income (%)
Broilers				
Contractors	4,065	909,943	71,003	58.2
Independents	648	626,224	190,669	23.3
Hogs				
Contractors	1,708	1,329,973	104,172	33.4
Independents	4,912	435,290	99,694	39.4
Cattle				
Contractors	426	2,839,963	158,876	21.4
Independents	49,740	395,561	86,188	53.0
Dairy				
Contractors	29	1,720,092	290,274	6.1
Independents	11,490	792,975	115,347	20.1
Soybeans				
Contractors	155	528,445	125,191	26.3
Independents	29,615	453,176	101,333	38.5
Corn				
Contractors	97	558,902	166,548	28.3
Independents	27,755	458,739	96,204	40.3
Wheat				
Contractors	27	604,476	197,309	16.9
Independents	21,762	470,876	98,457	39.0
Oats				
Contractors	5	1,920,000	600,606	5.3
Independents	2,642	301,005	64,276	49.9
Barley				
Contractors	5	524,552	173,746	7.9
Independents	3,443	447,324	80,039	39.8
Rice				
Contractors	2	655,090	91,331	13.7
Independents	2,310	557,600	151,577	26.3
Cotton				
Contractors	6	720,208	410,229	6.4
Independents	6,421	682,714	158,648	27.2
Sugar beets				
Contractors	46	1,510,000	2,810	980.1
Independents	1,459	772,418	96,235	29.3

virtually all production being under contract for broilers to no production contracting in the case of tobacco. This supports the idea that the nature of the commodities themselves may influence the potential share of production under contract. Also, previous research has found significant differences between producers who enter into production contracts and those that remain independent (Key 2004).

Patterns across both commodities and producers emerge from the survey data evaluated here. Table 18.3 provides farm-level descriptive statistics for twelve of the agricultural commodities examined in this study.[6] For all commodities, the producers operating under production contracts have higher average total sales than do the independents producing the same commodity. This result supports previous research (e.g., Key 2004), which found that production contracts, and contracting in general, are more prevalent among larger producers. The average total household income statistics in Table 18.3 tell a similar story. Average incomes are higher for contractors of most commodities; however, in the cases of broilers, sugar beets, and rice, production contractors have lower total household income than the independent producers, on average. In all three of these cases, the operations under production contract have significantly lower profit margins than independent operations, despite having significantly higher total sales.[7]

The difference in household incomes between contractors and independent producers of broilers is particularly interesting given that broilers have the highest level of contracting among all commodities. The hog market is second only to broilers in terms of the percentage of sales under production contracts. In the case of hog production, contractor total sales are triple those of independents, on average, yet contractors report total earnings only 4 percent higher than independents. Taken altogether, the average results from the two commodities with the greatest percentage of producers contracting suggest that production contractors in these industries are either receiving lower average prices than independent farmers for identical outputs, or that contractors may have higher average costs of production.

For nearly every other commodity in Table 18.3, the average total household income is higher for contractors than independents, and independents also earn a noticeably greater share of their income from off-farm sources. This suggests that when only a few producers are contracting, they tend to be large operations that specialize in the commodity and, as a result, are relatively more profitable than independent producers of the same commodity. This might be partly due to the stronger bargaining position of those large producers in an industry with little contracting going on. For example, cotton contractors, though very few in number, derive an exceptional amount of annual income ($410,229) from their total sales ($720,208). Independent cotton producers' profit margin on nearly the same sales is far lower. This result indicates that the terms of production contracts are financially beneficial to the handful of cotton producers (who may be offering a higher-quality product), which is not the case for producers of commodities for which production contracting is the market norm, like broilers.

Some of the commodities in Table 18.3 were evaluated in more detail to enable formal tests of hypotheses about differences in farm characteristics between production contractors and independent producers.[8] Table 18.4 presents various statistics, by commodity, and the results of independent-sample t-tests of differences in the reported average values for the two groups. Several patterns appear across the results, as described below.

The first hypothesis tested is that production contractors have a higher per farm output of the relevant commodity than do independent operators. The results are shown in the two rows labeled "sales of the commodity" in Table 18.4. The values are the annual average sales of only the commodity of interest, not total farm sales. For example, of the operators surveyed who produce broilers, those with contracts covering broiler production averaged $675,979 in broiler sales annually from 1996 to 2004. In contrast, independent broiler producers sold only $27,513 worth of the commodity annually, on average. For all of the commodities listed in Table 18.4, contractors produce significantly greater quantities per farm than do independents, on average. Also, in each case the t-test indicates that the difference in average sales is statistically significant, thus supporting the hypothesis. One implication of this result is that having a production contract may encourage operators to expand the scale of their output of the contracted commodity, although the direction of causality could be the reverse; producers who want to go large-scale adopt contracts to share risk, reduce transaction costs, and share managerial responsibilities.[9]

Table 18.4

Production Contracting in American Agriculture, Summary of Average Results per Farm, 1996–2004

	Commodity					
	Broilers	Hogs	Cattle	Corn	Soybeans	Cotton
Total number of producers surveyed	4,713	6,620	50,166	27,852	29,770	6,427
Farmers who Production Contract (%)	86.3	25.8	1.04	0.36	0.52	0.09
Contracting share of commodity sales (%)	95.5	78.7	18.6	0.77	1.44	0.12
Sales of the commodity, Contractors ($)	675,979***	753,164***	631,546***	201,558***	130,994***	373,125***
Sales of the commodity, Independents ($)	27,513	70,979	29,023	60,171	46,772	159,864
Total farm sales, Contractors ($)	909,943***	1,329,973***	2,839,963**	558,902**	528,445**	720,208
Total farm sales, Independence ($)	626,224	435,290	395,561	458,739	453,176	682,714
Commodity share of total sales, Contractors (%)	74.3***	56.6***	30.5***	36.3***	24.8	51.8***
Commodity share of total sales, Independents (%)	4.1	15.6	7.3	8.8	17.2	23.4
Total household income, Contractors ($)	71,003***	104,172	158,879***	166,548**	125,191*	410,229*
Total household income, Independents ($)	190,669	99,924	86,189	96,204	101,333	158,648
Off-farm share of income, Contractors (%)	58.2***	33.4	53.04***	28.3**	26.3*	6.4*
Off-farm share of income, Independents (%)	23.3	39.4	21.4	40.3	38.5	27.2
Farm net worth, Contractors ($)	698,145***	894,956	981,894	1,220,000*	1,010,000*	2,180,000*
Farm net worth, Independents ($)	899,987	940,565	975,049	939,469	882,686	922,669
Debt-to-Asset ratio, Contractors	0.26***	0.24***	0.31***	0.22	0.26**	0.08
Debt-to-Asset ratio, Independents	0.14	0.18	0.18	0.31	0.53	0.17

Data source the U.S. Department of Agriculture s Agricultural esource anagement Survey for the years through 200 .

*** ** * indicates a statistically signi cant difference bet een the mean values for producers ho contract versus independent producers at the and 0 con dence levels respectively.

The results in Table 18.4 lead to a second hypothesis—that producers with production contracts will be more specialized, or less diversified, in their commodity output. Diversification is a tool used by producers to reduce risks, so the implication is that having a production contract substitutes for diversification as a risk management tool. In Table 18.4, the commodity share of total sales is used as a measure of specialization. For all the commodities listed, contractors get a higher share of their total sales from the contracted commodity. As anticipated, livestock contractors are significantly less diversified than are independent producers. Moreover, as the percentage of producers engaged in production contracts increases among livestock commodities, the degree of diversification decreases. These results support the hypothesis, especially for livestock producers.

The limited data available here do not make it possible to directly test whether or not livestock producers are yielding net economic benefits from production contracts. However, the statistics in Table 18.4 show that among livestock commodities, average total income and average farm net worth for contractors decrease in both absolute terms and relative to independent producers as the share of production contracting increases and diversification decreases. Both broiler and cattle producers earn the majority of their total household income off the farm, in contrast to independents. The debt-to-asset ratio is a commonly used measure of producer's financial risk, and livestock contractors have a significantly higher ratio than do independent producers. In general, these results indicate that livestock operations using production contracts are larger, but less profitable, than independent operators and face slightly more financial risk. However, these observations vary inversely with the physical size of the animal involved, applying most strongly to broilers and to a lesser extent to hogs and then cattle.

Crop producers using production contracts are less diversified than are independents, on average, but the differences between the two categories of producers are smaller in the case of crops than they are between livestock producer categories. Also in contrast to the relationships governing livestock production, crop contractors typically have significantly greater household income and net worth than do independents, plus significantly smaller shares of income from off-farm sources. Finally, crop contractors have lower average debt-to-asset ratios than their independent counterparts.[10]

The most readily apparent difference between the livestock and crop commodity markets is that production contracting is a less popular choice among crop producers, as noted in the existing literature. Among all the crop commodities in Table 18.4, the percentage of farmers using production contracts is less than one.

Crop contractors produce significantly greater quantities of the commodities contracted than independents, as was true in livestock markets, but the average differences are considerably smaller in magnitude. Among crop contractors, commodity sales exceed those of independents by 55.5 percent on average, while the equivalent margin for livestock producers is 94.0 percent. In turn, crop contractors are more specialized than are independent crop producers, but crop contractors are more likely than livestock contractors to rely on some combination of contracting and diversification to manage risk.

Formal hypothesis testing on the financial net benefits of contracting is not possible with the limited data available, but the preliminary empirical results suggest that crop contractors reap greater benefits from production contracting than do livestock contractors. This may reflect the difference in producer bargaining power in livestock versus crop markets, with crop producers having more products made from their commodity, thus having more buyers available to them than do livestock producers. Risk, as measured by the debt-to-asset ratio, appears to be a significant motivating factor in favor of using production contracts in the case of livestock producers, but the same cannot be said for crop producers. Finally, these and other circumstances have changed across commodity markets over the past decade as markets have become increasingly concentrated, especially within the livestock sector. The brief case studies below illustrate some of the changes that have occurred over time, raising more hypotheses to be tested in the future as more data on production contracting become available.

Case Study Results

The hog industry has been the subject of much research on changes in livestock industry structure and the trend toward increased production contracting (e.g., Bessler and Akleman 1998; Key and McBride 2003; Martin 1997; Martinez 1999; Ollinger et al. 2005). Thus, it is used here to illustrate the relationship between livestock production contractors and independent producers. Table 18.5 reports similar descriptive statistics and *t*-tests as reported in Table 18.4, except that they are for the hog industry only and are calculated on an annual average basis.

The most important observation is that over the period from 1996 through 2004, the percentage of hog producers using production contracts has increased steadily. The share of total hog production under contract increased even more drastically, reaching 87 percent in 2004. As production contracting increased in scale, the diversification of the hog contractors decreased steadily, both in absolute terms and relative to independent hog producers. This means that the shift in hog industry structure toward most farm-level output being under production contract appears to have had the effect of substituting contracts for diversification as a risk management strategy for most hog producers. This may partly explain why production contractors had higher debt ratios than independents over most years. Although the data cannot answer the question of whether contractors have higher debts because they think that contracts reduce their financial risk exposure, or whether the higher debt ratios reflect the higher capital requirements of a larger, more specialized hog operation, it is expected that both explanations are partly accurate.

The financial performance data available contradict the hypothesis that contracts reduce producers' financial risk exposure. During most years in the 1996–2004 period, contractors and independent hog producers were statistically equivalent in terms of average net farm income. However, despite significantly higher sales of hogs and total farm sales, the average farm net worth of contractors has never significantly exceeded that of independents. Thus, production contracts have not led to higher wealth. Also, the fact that hog production contractors are steadily decreasing their share of off-farm income indicates that the larger scale of operations needed under contract has led to more specialized hog operations, leaving less time for off-farm income opportunities. This combined degree of household income specialization may give contract hog producers a *higher* degree of financial risk exposure than that faced by independent hog producers. This is apparent when comparing the standard deviations of the average net farm income over the nine years reported in Table 18.5: it is $48,260 for contractors and $15,016 for independent hog producers. Thus, the structural change that has led to increased production contracting has not significantly improved contractors' income, compared to independent operators, but it may have increased their exposure to income risk. Therefore, hog production contractors may be worse off financially, on average. This raises an interesting question: Do hog producers accept contracts because they think the productivity improvements found by Key and McBride (2003) will lead to improved profitability, or do they generally consent to the contract because they do not have the bargaining power to resist the demands of their buyers, as implied by Davis and Gillespie (2007)?

Table 18.5

Hog Production Contracting in American Agriculture, Summary of Average Annual Results per Farm

Year	1996	1997	1998	1999	2000
Total number of producers surveyed	569	1,058	674	735	595
Farmers who Production Contract (%)	7.96	15.13	16.81	21.28	26.87
Contracting share of commodity sales (%)	47.31	45.74	61.80	73.08	76.34
Sales of commodity: Contractors ($)	667,296***	385,033***	296,168***	584,245***	545,909***
Independents ($)	64,260	81,432	36,990	58,185	62,154
Commodity share of total sales: Contractors (%)	55.37***	23.62***	39.26***	42.65***	38.99***
Independents (%)	7.36	7.47	7.13	7.32	6.39
Net farm income: Contractors ($)	7,089***	98,667	61,455	68,493	61,071
Independents ($)	62,834	85,082	61,427	70,520	65,628
Off-farm share of income: Contractors (%)	83.40***	41.87	32.96*	35.91**	49.45
Independents (%)	46.82	43.98	45.77	47.17	50.85
Farm net worth: Contractors ($)	516,852***	787,605	412,594	725,796	760,218**
Independents ($)	771,825	706,556	800,034	849,652	918,803
Debt-to-Asset ratio: Contractors	0.38***	0.38	0.38***	0.26**	0.38**
Independents	0.25	0.48	0.26	0.19	0.20

Year	2001	2002	2003	2004
Total number of producers surveyed	542	856	1,103	2,196
Farmers who Production Contract (%)	29.36	28.14	32.10	37.25
Contracting share of commodity sales (%)	82.62	78.08	84.76	87.49
Sales of commodity: Contractors ($)	848,489***	592,636***	753,219***	1,063,133***
Independents ($)	74,169	65,156	64,032	90,207
Commodity share of total sales: Contractors (%)	53.36***	56.44***	50.89***	80.66***
Independents (%)	7.17	7.14	6.51	7.74
Net farm income: Contractors ($)	79,571	76,178	135,648***	176,125***
Independents ($)	93,272	68,443	99,817	93,482
Off-farm share of income: Contractors (%)	49.57	44.01	35.63*	35.47**
Independents (%)	40.45	54.32	43.39	42.73
Farm net worth: Contractors ($)	944,411	744,906***	919,205	1,070,000
Independents ($)	1,110,000	904,007	1,040,000	1,110,000
Debt-to-Asset ratio: Contractors	0.30***	0.31**	0.27**	0.23
Independents	0.18	0.23	0.19	0.47

Source: The U.S. Department of Agriculture s Agricultural esource anagement Survey for the years through 200 .

*** ** * indicates a statistically signi cant difference bet een the mean values for producers ho contract versus in dependent producers at the and 0 con dence levels respectively.

Soybeans are processed into a wide range of products, giving them the lowest usage index in Table 18.2. This means soybean producers may have the widest range of buyers available to them, giving growers more bargaining power than that held by producers of most other commodities. Conversely, soybeans have the highest level of CR4 concentration in Table 18.2. That difference in industry structure, compared to the hog industry, is believed to be responsible for the difference in the time series results presented in Table 18.6 compared to the results in Table 18.5. The soybean industry contrasts with the hog industry in that the percentage of soybean farmers who opt for production contracts is low and there was no discernible growth in contracting over the 1996–2004 period.

Across all years, soybean contractors are less diversified than independent growers, but the differences are smaller in magnitude than those found among hog producers and there is no discernible decrease in diversification over the time period. Also, in most years, contractors receive less off-farm income than do independents. Both of these results indicate that contractors might face more risk than do independents.

Facing more risk can be a logical choice if there is a reward for doing so. The financial performance results indicate that soybean production contractors may, in fact, be rewarded. The total household income and farm net worth are slightly higher for contractors, but there does not appear to be any pattern over time. The standard deviation of net farm income over the period is $110,488 for soybean contractors and $15,462 for independents, representing a clear difference in risk exposure. Therefore, it is possible that the very few soybean growers who are production contracting may be doing so because they think the higher financial rewards justify the higher level of income risk they face.

The sharpest contrast between the time series analyses for soybeans and hogs is the lack of consistency in the soybean results. There is no indication that the soybean industry is shifting toward conditions in which it may be more or less favorable for growers to enter into production contracts, while the hog industry has already grown to a point at which virtually only small-scale producers remain independent. These results are all consistent with the hypotheses underlying the contracting continuum proposed here.

Implications of the Contracting Results

This analysis proposes answers to some of the questions being raised about the trend of increasing use of production contracts in American agriculture. The answers are embodied in a proposed continuum of commodity contracting potential. The continuum draws its name from the fact that different commodities have different potential maximum shares of producer output that will fall under production contracts with buyers, thus individual commodities can be plotted at points along a horizontal continuum ranging from zero to 100 percent of output being contracted. It is argued here that the contracting potential for any commodity is related to the industry structure of the agribusinesses buying the raw farm output, and that structure is related to the number of products into which the commodity is processed. Since each commodity has a unique set of physical attributes, the number of products derived from it will be unique, thus leading to a unique industry structure and, ultimately, a specific potential for production contracting.

It is argued here that one factor in determining what share of output actually *is* production contracted is the relative amount of bargaining power held by commodity producers and their buyers. Research dating back to the 1960s shows that agribusiness firms use production contracts as a tool in vertical coordination of markets and, if possible, those firms will exert their bargaining power to improve their profitability. On the other side of the market, commodity producers prefer

Table 18.6

Soybean Production Contracting in American Agriculture, Summary of Average Annual Results per Farm

Year	1996	1997	1998	1999	2000
Total number of producers surveyed	1,733	4,404	2,164	2,776	2,820
Farmers who Production Contract (%)	0.52	0.52	1.07	0.62	0.75
Contracting share of commodity sales (%)	0.90	1.60	1.86	0.68	1.44
Sales of commodity: Contractors ($)	202,848***	94,549***	119,512***	56,709	84,030
Independents ($)	74,370	12,100	78,420	59,390	66,170
Commodity share of total sales: Contractors (%)	25.43***	17.55***	23.20***	20.34***	18.77***
Independents (%)	1.75	2.20	1.89	1.28	1.47
Net farm income: Contractors ($)	246,722***	166,717	25,844	82,284	56,982
Independents ($)	62,224	85,083	61,536	70,646	65,587
Off-farm share of income: Contractors (%)	23.59	24.73	31.55*	56.80	35.00
Independents (%)	47.06	44.01	45.65	46.74	50.86
Farm net worth: Contractors ($)	960,415	826,518	725,021	903,783	995,692
Independents ($)	769,947	707,351	798,008	847,826	916,511
Debt-to-Asset ratio: Contractors	0.27	0.24	0.17	0.23	0.20
Independents	0.25	0.48	0.21	0.33	0.20

	2001	2002	2003	2004
Total number of producers surveyed	2,277	3,974	4,867	4,908
Farmers who Production Contract (%)	0.49	0.10	0.41	0.55
Contracting share of commodity sales (%)	0.49	1.91	1.19	1.54
Sales of commodity: Contractors ($)	71,433	132,607***	135,957***	251,506***
Independents ($)	71,430	74,350	8,412	11,369
Commodity share of total sales: Contractors (%)	17.88***	17.88***	22.46***	42.21***
Independents (%)	1.40	1.40	1.88	2.39
Net farm income: Contractors ($)	23,476*	2,423*	312,903*	189,938**
Independents ($)	93,140	68,597	100,138	96,075
Off-farm share of income: Contractors (%)	49.11***	53.63***	18.72***	21.19**
Independents (%)	82.23	27.76	43.32	42.56
Farm net worth: Contractors ($)	613,739***	651,991	1,120,000	1,360,000
Independents ($)	1,110,000	901,418	1,030,000	1,110,000
Debt-to-Asset ratio: Contractors	0.33**	0.28	0.21	0.24
Independents	0.18	0.31	0.19	0.46

Source: The U.S. Department of Agriculture s Agricultural esource anagement Survey for the years   through 200 .
*** ** * indicates a statistically signi cant difference bet een the mean values for producers ho contract versus independent producers at the
and 0   con dence levels respectively.

to remain independent, as shown in recent research. Thus, the degree to which production contracting is used may depend on which side has more bargaining power. For example, in a market for a commodity like cotton, where producers have some bargaining power because there are many buyers needing the commodity, a few producers are willing to give up some of their independence only when they are rewarded financially. Thus, the first few cotton producers agreeing to production contracts expect benefits that exceed the costs. In other markets, such as for hogs, shifts in industry structure over time gave buyers (i.e., anyone buying hogs from a hog producer) more bargaining power, which led to higher shares of output being production contracted because some producers have access to no other types of buyer. Eventually, expanding use of production contracts make spot markets increasingly incomplete until they reach a "tipping point" beyond which producers are virtually forced to enter into contracts because of negative externalities imposed upon them by the thinning of the spot markets (Roberts and Key 2005). The broiler and hog markets each show signs of this being the case.

The preliminary empirical results here generally show that production contracts lead to production specialization which, in turn, may reduce off-farm income opportunities, both of which can increase the income risk of producers. This is an important observation because it contradicts one of the main arguments used to justify production contracting. Proponents of contracting and much of the theoretical literature have said that producers can use contracts to reduce risk, which is true. For the small cross section of commodities evaluated here, the reality is that contractors have higher sales totals and higher income variance than do independent producers, but not necessarily higher income levels, on average. In general, the empirical results of this analysis are consistent with the hypothesis that commodity producers with some bargaining power (e.g., cotton growers) may earn higher average incomes under production contracts than independent producers of the same commodity, but profitability falls for producers in other commodity markets (e.g., broilers) where buyers have relatively more bargaining power. Future research is needed on the causality of the relationships involved.[11]

It has been argued in the literature that buyer bargaining power increases with industrialization and that the potential for industrialization is influenced by a commodity's physical attributes (e.g., Sheldon 1996). In particular, it has been well established that livestock processing industries have scale economies that encourage continued industrialization and that the resulting industry concentration of the last few decades has facilitated increased use of production contracts in those markets (Ahearn, Korb, and Banker 2005; Bhuyan 2005; Drabenstott 1995; Key 2004; MacDonald and Korb 2006; Morrison Paul 2000). In crop industries, however, production contracting is rare in most markets, although marketing contracts cover a majority of output in some markets (MacDonald and Korb 2006). These differences across commodity types were apparent in the analysis here and raise questions for future research.

Looking to the future, the results of this preliminary analysis indicate that production contracting is likely to continue expanding to cover a higher share of total output for many commodities. This raises hypotheses to be considered when adequate data become available. For example, limited-use crops, like tobacco, are expected to eventually be dominated by production contracts. Also, some specialty crops, like strawberries, are already showing signs of moving in the same direction. This leads to one last implication of the contracting continuum: local and regional commodity industries are likely to experience increased use of production contracts. This development is expected because geographically concentrated production is susceptible to concentrated buying power, such as observed in the sugar beet industry (Bangsund and Leistritz 1998). This is an incentive for producers to form cooperatives or to use some other type of collective selling arrangements. However, cooperatives, bargaining associations, and similar selling arrangements employ a type of production contract with supplier-members. Therefore, all trends indicate that it may be increasingly difficult for producers to maintain their independence in the industrialized agriculture of America's future.

BLENDING AGRICULTURE AND AGRIBUSINESS FOR SUCCESS

> *"The significant problems we face cannot be solved at the same level of thinking we were at when we created them."*
> –Albert Einstein

Thus far, this chapter has presented a picture that is bright for the American agribusiness sector but bleak for the agricultural production sector. However, this is not the end of the story. Both sectors can survive in the future if industry participants take a slightly different perspective when viewing those in the other sector. It is argued in this section that blending American agriculture and agribusiness may be essential for success in the future (especially for the production sector) but, if accomplished, the resulting agrifood industry will play the leading role in the global market. In doing so, the new industry can create a truly "economically sustainable agriculture" in America, whereas none exists currently without policy interventions.

To begin, the concept of "blending" agricultural production and agribusiness is described. A blended industry, in the simplest sense, is one in which all participants understand and appreciate their mutual dependence on all other participants. No matter what form of vertical governance is used to blend firms into a coordinated system, the key point is that everyone in the system knows that it will fail without the contributions of each participant. Thus, everyone knows that their economic rewards depend in part on the performance of others in the system.

Existing examples of a blended industry include the horticulture-nursery and dairy-milk industries. In the first case, the horticultural participants are farmers producing plants that the nursery participants sell through wholesale and retail outlets. Without the plants, the nurseries have nothing to sell, and without the nurseries, the farmers have no market outlet. Each group needs the other. In the second case, dairy farmers produce raw milk that is processed, packaged, and distributed by the second group of participants. Again, each group needs the other. As a result, there is much communication and cooperation between the groups. The first group seeks to deliver a product that facilitates the input needs of the second group. That is possible because the second group carefully communicates its needs to the first group. In essence, the groups *try* to blend their activities into a seamless whole that has the best chance of successfully meeting the demands of consumers.

These two examples of a blended industry are similar in that the product's form is changed little in a vertical system that is "short" from top to bottom. In this short vertical system it is relatively easy for participants to both see how the other group contributes to the whole and communicate with each other. However, in the future, some blended industries will have to be very "tall" to serve their product markets, thus making it much more difficult for system participants to recognize and appreciate the contributions of all other participants. This is the challenge driving current market evolution.

The Current Situation

What is the current situation in the market evolutionary process shaping American agriculture and agribusiness? In simple terms, America is at a turning point between two eras in the relationship between its production agriculture sector and its agribusiness sector. The first era is not yet over, but will be soon. What will end the first era, and what will differentiate the second era from the first, is a simple change in the perspective of industry participants toward members of the other sector. At present, both sectors need the other, but they are in a "tug-o-war" when interacting, each seeking to maximize its own profits. This state of conflict is not sustainable.

Structural changes in American agricultural production are occurring in response to the increased globalization of commodity markets. Boehlje (1999, p. 1028) summarizes the changes by saying "production is changing from an industry dominated by family-based, small-scale, relatively independent firms to one of larger firms that are more tightly aligned across the production and distribution value chain." These changes are occurring against the wishes of many farmers and ranchers. As Key (2005) indicates, agricultural producers are very independent people, thus not eager to give up any control over their operations, if possible. Yet, that is what is happening at present, as explained earlier in this chapter. The agribusiness sector is using its market power to nudge producers into production and marketing contracts. As a result, there is lots of conflict in the interactions between the production and agribusiness sectors.

"Some would argue that the basic nature of competition has changed in all industries in recent years, especially in terms of the definition of a market" (Boehlje 1999, p. 1030). He adds, "worldwide sourcing and selling has changed the geographic boundaries of markets from regional or national to global." In response, "closer vertical coordination has occurred as the use of spot markets has declined, while production and marketing contracts, franchising, strategic alliances, joint ventures, and full vertical integration have increased" (Young and Hobbs 2002, p. 428).

This evolutionary change in markets for commodities makes it more difficult for independent farmers and ranchers to access buyers in a traditional negotiation, thus adding to the pressure on producers to align themselves with some new vertical coordination structure. Up to this point in time, most American producers have viewed these market changes as a threat. That perspective is understandable given the negative effects market changes have had thus far on producers' financial performance. However, that perspective could be the downfall of American agriculture.

If Nothing Changes Current Perspectives

What will happen if nothing changes the current perspectives of American agricultural producers and agribusiness managers? The conflict will continue, causing inconvenience to the agribusiness sector and virtually destroying the existing production sector. This unbalanced tale of two sectors is the logical, although unhappy, continuation of existing trends in American agriculture. The agribusiness sector will gradually win the tug-o-war in most commodity markets, thus continuing the trend of pushing reluctant agricultural producers into "supply chains" that will not be fully efficient because of the latent conflict in the relationships between chain participants. That conflict will continue to encourage American agribusiness managers to seek the lowest-cost suppliers of commodities, thus increasingly looking overseas as less-developed countries expand their agricultural output and willingly agree to be contract suppliers. The result would be a continued decline in the number of American farms as foreign competitors develop.

It is an unhappy fact that "producers are at a relative bargaining disadvantage, resulting in the well-known economic outcomes of an inefficient allocation of resources and a loss in social welfare" (Young and Hobbs 2002, p. 438). The source of producers' bargaining disadvantage is the difference in industry structures between the production and agribusiness sectors. Agribusiness industries are concentrated, with a few firms having significant influence on their markets, whereas producers are numerous and have no market influence individually because they each produce undifferentiated commodities. The traditional lack of coordination between producers of a commodity results in the allocation inefficiencies of having too much or too little output, relative to the needs of the agribusiness sector, in many years. Thus, the agribusiness sector has used its bargaining advantage to develop "supply chains" to reduce these inefficiencies. A "supply chain" is an integrated vertical system across different functions in the process required to create and deliver a product to the consumer. Such a system can be established using many types of governance structures. As described earlier in this chapter, production contracts are becoming more common as a tool agribusinesses use to establish a supply chain, even when producers are not eager to give up some control over their own operations.

The irony of the current situation is that if nothing changes current perspectives, the threat to producers of being forced to join a supply chain would be exceeded only by the threat of *not* being able to join a supply chain. As Young and Hobbs (2002, p. 432) conclude,

> some producers may have difficulty gaining entry to tightly coordinated supply chains. Entry may be difficult due to requirements for sophisticated production skills or the need for specialized equipment or capital. The inability of certain producers to gain entry to supply chains for these reasons would be a continuation of the forces that have prompted producers to exit from agriculture historically.

Why would a producer have to exit from agriculture if he or she cannot join a supply chain? The answer is that as more supply chains develop in the future, there will be fewer participants in traditional spot markets, causing those markets to erode and eventually disappear. In other words, spot markets are becoming thinner, which means they may be less likely to generate the competitive market prices needed to attract participants.

The threat to competitive markets posed by the development of supply chains raises the question of what constraints there might be to vertical integration. The answer is "none." No natural constraints will evolve from the changes in industry structure; agribusiness firms will continue to benefit from using their market power, so they will continue to push for expanded supply chains and other vertical control systems. No artificially imposed constraints will come from antitrust laws. For example, Sexton (2000) says that weak antitrust laws will not slow industrialization in agribusiness. He notes that "the main body of U.S. antitrust law is now about 100 years old and may well be rather ineffective in addressing the imbalance of power in today's agricultural sector" (p. 1101). Also a factor is the fact that antitrust enforcement has changed. Young and Hobbs (2002, p. 438) note that "the emphasis of antitrust investigations was whether or not entry was possible, neglecting benefits from possible gains in efficiency," but recently "acceptance of transaction cost economics moved the focus of the analysis used in antitrust investigations to the transactions the firm undertakes, with an understanding of how organizational variety arises to minimize transaction costs." This means antitrust regulators have apparently decided that the lower transaction costs coming from industrialization in the food manufacturing sector benefit consumers more than the possible costs incurred from structural changes that make it more difficult for agricultural producers to find a market for their output. Market access is also reduced by consolidation in food manufacturing industries, currently being driven by the economies of scale that increase profits when firms merge (Nguyen and Ollinger 2006). The fact that industrialization also makes it more difficult for new agribusiness firms to enter markets means that market access is not going to get better for farmers and ranchers.

Why and How the Current Situation Changes

Why will the current situation change even if nothing changes the current perspectives of those in the American agricultural sector? Profits and risk management will motivate the agribusiness sector to change the vertical market structure, using contracts and other governance methods, to create supply chains that give agribusiness firms a competitive advantage over domestic and foreign competitors (Boehlje 1999).

The traditional structure of American agriculture, with each sector operating separately as a collection of privately owned firms, exposed food manufacturing firms to risks that they have long sought to reduce or avoid entirely (Hayenga 1979). Those risks came first from the lack of certainty about whether agribusiness firms could acquire sufficient quantities of their commodity inputs on schedule. Once that problem was solved, the focus was on whether the quality of the commodities acquired was adequate to meet the demands of the food manufacturers' customers. To manage both sources of risk simultaneously, agribusiness firms found that they needed to control their supply chains, not just depend on commodity markets and "the invisible hand" of competition. Therefore, agribusinesses created the first supply chains using governance structures that gave them as much control over suppliers as possible. The first successes were small in scale, but the approach gained in popularity because it had positive effects on profit margins for virtually all types of agribusinesses that used the strategy.

Agricultural producers were quick to see the loss of control they suffered when participating in production contracts and, as a result, resisted the expansion of vertical integration as much as they could, given their lack of market power. However, farmers and ranchers quickly found it difficult to avoid agribusiness firms that were using the management strategy because nearly all firms adopted similar tactics. The tendency to converge in terms of management tactics employed has become an important characteristic of American agribusiness firms. When studying the management structure of agribusiness firms, Caswell (1987, p. 20) found that "larger firm size is related to looser forms of direct control but more extensive network influence" from managers in the industry. As a result, she concluded that the structure of management in American agribusiness firms "appears to encourage overall coordination in the sector," which means the future will have a more homogeneous agribusiness sector that is made up of firms following similar business strategies. The implication is that American agricultural producers will not be able to avoid what is becoming a standard agribusiness structure: the supply chain.

The next strategy tried by agricultural producers was to attempt to increase their market power to gain control over the chains in which they participate. Producer cooperatives are the most visible form of this strategy. Unfortunately, producers have some built-in disadvantages when competing with agribusiness firms. For example, Hendrikse and Bijman (2002) use incomplete contract theory to assess the optimal ownership structure in agrifood chains and find that farmers are at a disadvantage in seeking to control a chain, as indicated below.

> When the farmer's specific investment is high relative to the specific investment by the processor, farmer-ownership of the assets in the processing stage of the chain obtains the first-best solution. This is the classic farmer-owned marketing cooperative. However, if the investment by the processor (or retailer) becomes relatively more important for total chain value than the investment by the farmer, the cooperative may no longer be an efficient ownership structure. The current trend toward restructuring of cooperatives, particularly toward finding solutions for the lack of equity capital, may be an indication of the ineffi-

ciency of farmer-control over assets in the processing and marketing stages of the agrifood chain. (Hendrikse and Bijman 2002, pp. 114–115)

This means as supply chains become "taller" by adding more layers of processing and handling, the economics of control make it less likely that producer ownership will be the optimal arrangement. In essence, profit margin differences give the agribusiness sector an advantage, thus they will win in the long run if a state of conflict continues to exist between the sectors. However, Hendrikse and Bijman (2002, p. 114) also find that "each agent in a three-tier agrifood supply chain can make investments yielding a higher surplus if the agent collaborates with agents in the other tiers of the chain." Therefore, the future does not have to be bleak for all American farmers and ranchers.

How the Production Sector Can Survive

In the long run, the survival of most American farms and ranches may depend on their willingness to be a contract supplier to an agribusiness that is successfully meeting consumers' demands for specific product attributes. More specifically, for the American production agriculture sector to survive in a future that will be full of new foreign competitors with lower production costs, American producers will have to voluntarily blend with agribusiness in a "metasystem" aimed at improving the profits of each participant by improving the competitiveness of the U.S. agrifood firm versus foreign competitors. This strategy does not guarantee the survival of any particular firm or industry, but it is the only approach that adequately addresses the challenges faced by American agricultural producers and, thus, it offers a chance for prosperity.

The first challenge is the current state of conflict between producers and the agribusiness firms with which they deal. As long as farmers and ranchers view agribusiness as part of the problem rather than part of the solution, the conflict will continue and more producers will be forced to exit agriculture. On the other hand, if producers follow the old cliché, "if you can't beat 'em, join 'em," and replace the conflict with collaboration, they immediately raise their chances of survival. This is possible because market structures based on truly voluntary participation will be more successful in the long run because they eliminate internal conflict.

A metasystem is a state of collaboration that helps address the second challenge faced by American agricultural producers: foreign competition. By design, metasystems add value to commodities and differentiate them from the output of competitors. A metasystem is a special type of supply chain. As noted earlier, a "supply chain" is an integrated vertical system across different functions in the process required to create and deliver a product to the consumer. Most metasystems focus on quality management. Caswell, Bredahl, and Hooker (1998) say that food quality metasystems are strategies that affect any quality attribute involving food safety, nutrition, value, packaging, or process. They say "metasystems are implemented through metastandards, which most often define a process to be undertaken by a company to assure quality on an ongoing basis" (p. 549). Thus, a metasystem is an organized attempt to create and document quality differences in products. All firms in a metasystem willingly collaborate in this effort.

There are many benefits to participation in a metasystem. For example, according to Caswell, Bredahl, and Hooker (1998),

> in addition to affecting operation of the value chain, food quality metasystems are likely to confer significant marketing advantages on companies in selling to final consumers. These advantages come from selling a higher quality product and reliably being able to certify that

quality to consumers who are willing to pay more. These advantages may enter the company's profit performance through a higher price or lower transaction costs. (p. 552)

This ability to differentiate products based on higher quality attributes is a key weapon in the current conflict between American firms and the growing number of foreign competitors. As American producers lose the race to be the lowest-cost supplier of commodities, their salvation rests in being identified as the supplier of high-quality commodities as inputs to American agribusiness firms that create high-quality consumer products.

Metasystems are the future for the United States food industry. For example, Fouayzi, Caswell, and Hooker (2006) found that over 90 percent of fresh-cut produce firms have adopted a quality management system because, among other reasons, it facilitates trade between firms. With such a system, long-term contracts are more likely between firms within a supply chain, and transaction costs are reduced.

The ability to make long-term contracts holds great value for producers in many commodity markets. For example, it would help reduce the chances of being held up by processors—a major source of conflict in the current relationship between many producers and agribusiness. As Vukina and Leegomonchai (2006, p. 589) explain, when only short-term contracts are available, commodity producers can be held up by processors because

> growers' assets are a source of potentially appropriable quasi-rents in the sense that they have low salvage value outside the bilateral contractual relationship. This constitutes a hold-up problem that can manifest itself in two ways. First, . . . appropriable quasi-rents affect the level of investments. Being aware of the possibility that they may be held-up by processors, growers will cautiously invest in specific assets. [Second, after] facilities have been constructed, the processor may exploit his advantageous bargaining position by frequently requesting upgrades and technological improvements as conditions for contract renewal.

As a result of the holdup risk, producers underinvest in assets with specific uses (Castaneda 2006). A long-term contract reduces the risk of holdup and, in the process, reduces the state of conflict between producers and food manufacturing firms. The increased state of collaboration encourages producers to invest in more assets with specific uses, thus providing expanded output to agribusiness without those firms having to increase the number of contracts negotiated or supplier relationships maintained. This reduces transaction costs to all parties involved. The ability to sign long-term contracts also gives supply chain participants the ability to adopt many practices aimed at gaining a competitive advantage over other firms, such as time integration (Wilson and Thompson 2003) and other innovations. However, at present it is usually agribusiness firms resisting the move to long-term contracts (e.g., in the broiler industry), so they are apparently not yet willing to accept the advantages of long-term contracts and move to a full metasystem.

In total, the economics of supply chains and their effects on the structure of agriculture seem to be positive for agribusiness and consumers, so at this point in time there is no reason to think their growth will slow. Given this clear trend for agribusiness firms, agricultural producers need to decide sooner, rather than later, to join the team and enjoy the perks. Remaining in a state of conflict with agribusiness is a losing proposition. Unfortunately, the conflict may benefit agribusiness firms in some industries, so the path to integration will be bumpy.

The resistance of independent producers to joining a metasystem, or any other vertical market structure, is expected to continue for some time. To avoid dependence on an agribusiness, some farmers will continue to pursue the creation of their own supply chains, in the form of direct marketing to a niche market. In some places where large numbers of consumers are located close to talented farmers, niche markets will survive and generate adequate returns. In other places, potential niches are simply located too far from the farmer entrepreneur to enable the establishment of profitable operations. And finally, niches will fail in lots of places because the farmer did not realize that creating a supply chain meant that he would have to perform all the business and production functions himself. Sometimes when a producer talks about "eliminating the middleman," it is because that producer does not appreciate that agribusiness firms exist because they add value to commodities and it is the processed product that consumers want, not just the commodity that was used as an input in creating the final product. Supply chains create a synergy; the sum is (in) greater (demand) than the (demand for the) parts.

Finally, survival of the American agricultural production sector depends on the ability of farmers and ranchers to adjust to a new business structure. Metasystems and other supply chain structures are changing the theory of the firm. As early as 1992, Barry, Sonka, and Lajili (1992, p. 1219) observed that "the needs for farm-level product differentiation put pressure on open market relationships and may lead to vertical integration or contracting between key stages in the market system." Farm-level product differentiation often requires specialized equipment, creating asset specificity, and asset specificity and vertical coordination are considered to be positively related. "Greater asset specificity means greater transaction costs in redeployment, and a tendency toward more complex, long-term contracting and vertical integration" (Barry, Sonka, and Lajili 1992, p. 1221). Therefore, contracting continues to expand, as described earlier in this chapter, changing the nature of relationships between market participants. For example, production contracts (and other vertical integration tools) create an agency relationship. The agent (farmer) is expected to behave in concert with the objectives of the principals (buyers) so that these objectives can be optimally attained. This creates a situation in which "the manager's task now involves selecting the boundaries of the firm (defined by contractual and asset control relationships) along with the more traditional tasks" (Barry, Sonka, and Lajili 1992, p. 1223). In other words, American agricultural producers must decide the extent to which they are going to voluntarily blend their firm with others in a supply chain.

AMERICAN AGRIBUSINESS'S ROLE IN DIRECTING...

Whether or not American agricultural producers voluntarily join in the effort, the American agribusiness sector is going to continue leading the world in several regards. It is argued in the subsections below that the sector will directly influence agricultural industries across the globe. By doing so, American agribusiness will continue to influence economic development both directly and indirectly in many regions of the globe.

American Agricultural Production

The role of American agribusiness in directing American agricultural production has been discussed in much of this chapter. Yet there is still another aspect of the relationship between these two sectors that has enormous economic implications for the future evolution of American agriculture. That aspect can be labeled "location issues." As noted in the following proposition,

American agribusiness sector will influence *where* American agricultural production will survive, and vice versa.

- PROPOSITION 18.2. W*ithin a spatial market, producers and the agribusinesses serving them have a mutually dependent relationship that can be described as a feedback loop in which each group needs the other because both must maintain a critical mass in order for the market to survive.*

Standard economic theory usually leads to the belief that the production of commodities will occur in locations where the microclimate and natural resources are best suited to that commodity. In other words, agricultural production is expected to occur in locations that have a comparative advantage for those activities. Next, standard theory says that agribusinesses will locate their facilities either nearer to the source of their commodity inputs or nearer the buyers of the processed products made from the commodity, with the relative values and perishability of the inputs and outputs being the deciding factors (e.g., Clary, Dietrich, and Farris 1986; Diaz, Farris, and Litzenberg 1986; Dunn, Lee, and Thatch 1987; Henderson and McNamara 2000). Normally, storable commodities will have processing facilities located close to the source of the raw commodity because it is more economical to transport bulky commodities as little as possible, compared to the cost of transporting the higher-value (and less bulky) processed product. This means storable commodities can be produced far from consumers. Conversely, perishable commodities and their processing facilities need to be located as close as possible to consumers so as to minimize the risk of spoilage. In total, this standard view of location ties agricultural production and agribusiness together. However, in recent decades, technological changes and market evolution have created a new location factor that again ties together commodity production and food manufacturing industries. This new factor has been called "critical mass."

"The concept of a critical mass is based on the idea that economies of scale exist in both input and output businesses that are essential to agriculture. As production levels decline below a threshold, costs will rise, and support businesses will close or relocate" (Lynch and Carpenter 2002, p. 2). In simple terms, the critical mass problem of an agribusiness is based on the idea that a commodity processing facility needs at least some minimum volume of commodity inputs during a season or other time period to enable it to achieve operating economies of scale that are competitive with the facilities of rival firms. In turn, the critical mass problem for a commodity producer revolves around the availability of processing capacity sufficient to handle the producer's entire output in a timely manner. The mutually dependent nature of the problem facing commodity producers and processors in a spatial market can best be explained using an example.

Consider the case of tomatoes grown in California's Central Valley to be processed into ketchup, spaghetti sauce, and other products. The microclimate and natural resources of central California are perfectly suited to growing processing tomatoes, so long ago the Central Valley filled with tomato acreage and lots of processing plants. In the 1950s and 1960s, the tomatoes were harvested by hand and were highly perishable, thus processing plants had to be located within a relatively short truck ride of the fields. The length of that truck ride dictated each processing facility's size; each facility had to be only as big as needed to handle the output from the acreage of tomatoes within the area covered by the truck ride. Also, the technology used then meant that only a relatively small amount of tomatoes could be processed within a single plant during a time period. All of this meant that there were many small processing facilities spread across the valley. During the 1960s and 1970s the development of mechanical tomato harvesters led to adoption of new tomato varieties that were far less perishable. Those two technical innovations helped growers increase the total volume of output and the length of time the commodity could be stored. At first, the increased output of tomatoes coming from increased tomato acreage necessitated expansion of the processing capacity of agribusinesses, thus additional processing facilities were built. However, each new facility used current technological innovations, which, in general, were being driven by economies of scale. That caused the average size and capacity of each facility to grow. By the 1990s there were two problems facing tomato processors: there was excess tomato processing capacity in California, and some tomato producers were switching acreage to other, more profitable crops. The larger and more efficient processing plants found that they could serve a larger geographical area and this brought them into direct competition with firms in neighboring areas when trying to acquire sufficient local quantities of tomatoes to enable efficient and profitable plant operations (Durham, Sexton, and Song 1996). The competition between processing firms could not push up prices paid to farmers in the long run without reducing the profitability of the processing industry. Thus, the first outcome was that the least efficient (i.e., higher-cost) tomato processing plants were forced to close when they could not profitably purchase sufficient local supplies to maintain operations. Over time, profit squeezes pushed some farmers to shift acreage out of tomatoes and into other crops, while continued technical advances made some older processing facilities uncompetitive, forcing them to be closed. The ultimate outcome was a circular problem in which the loss of nearby tomato acreage raised costs to a local processing plant, thereby forcing that plant to close, which eliminated a buyer for some growers, pushing those farmers out of the tomato market. In summary, despite a comparative advantage in growing tomatoes, California was seeing tomato acreage in some locations decrease, causing some processing plants to close, adding to the pressure on local tomato growers when trying to find a profitable market.

The key concept in the critical mass question for agribusinesses is the "threshold level." In the tomato example above, the threshold was the number of acres of tomatoes needed to keep a processing plant operating at a profitable level. Efficient operation is a necessary, but not a sufficient, condition for profitability of a processing facility. Economies of scale mean that efficiency is usually improved with higher volumes of tomatoes being processed during a season, but as long as a processing plant is profitable, it can be kept open. However, if a processor cannot acquire adequate supplies of tomatoes to operate profitably (i.e., at or above the threshold level), the plant must be closed down.

The key concept in the critical mass question for commodity producers is market access. Loss of critical mass triggers the disappearance of firms (Roberts and Key 2005). In the tomato example, the loss of critical mass in local acreage triggers the disappearance of tomato buyers, thus reducing the market access of remaining tomato growers. If that loss of market access causes more growers to exit a market, a downward spiral can quickly develop. In this sense, critical mass has the same effects as "tipping points" in spot markets: once market volume drops below the threshold level, the structure of a market cannot sustain an adequate volume of transactions and the market disintegrates.

The "critical mass" problem is a special type of thin or incomplete market brought on by technological or structural change. Whereas a viable spatial market can exist before some technical innovation or structural change brought on by industrialization, after the technical or structural shock the market can become thin or incomplete. As noted by Ahearn, Korb, and Banker (2005, p. 348), "in an industrialized agriculture, producers are more likely to face incomplete markets because production of bulk commodities is replaced by production of specialized products." In the case of either thin or incomplete spot markets, producers have fewer choices, thus reducing the value of remaining a market participant. The outcome can be the complete disappearance of what had been a profitable market. This can happen in livestock markets, as well as crop markets. For example, Raper, Cheney, and Punjabi (2006) show that the 1998 closing of a hog processing plant in Detroit, Michigan, caused producers' relative price advantage to decline, becoming negative. That caused producers nearby to reduce or eliminate their hog production.

Finally, the critical mass problem can prevent a new market from developing. An example of this is the experience of farmers in northeastern California. During the 1990s and 2000s, farmers in the mountainous counties of this region sought to develop new commodity industries to replace their fading markets for traditional crops like potatoes. A county extension agent did some test plots and found that mint and wild rice could both grow well in the area. However, when that agent tried to get farmers to begin producing the crops, growers resisted the idea because there was no existing market for the crops in the region. So, the agent approached agribusinesses that processed those crops elsewhere, asking the companies to establish processing facilities in the area. The agribusinesses responded that it was too risky for them to invest in new processing facilities without assurances of being able to acquire adequate supplies to operate the processing plants profitably. When the agent brought that information back to farmers in the region, he found that the growers believed it was too risky to commit to contracts to supply a new commodity with which they had no production history. The result was that not enough acreage was committed by farmers to grow either crop, so the critical mass necessary for agribusinesses to establish processing facilities was never reached for either crop, and nothing happened. Had each side made the necessary investments, it is likely that both mint and wild rice would be grown and processed profitably in northeastern California, but instead the potential industries never materialized.

International Commodity Markets

The American agribusiness sector will play an important role in directing international commodity markets and, indirectly, foreign agricultural production through the weight of its global purchasing power. This future buying power does not come only from the volume of commodities that will be imported by American food manufacturing firms as inputs for domestic operations, but also from the commodity market participation of American-owned firms located in foreign countries. The new structure of global food markets is responsible for this change, which gives American agribusiness managers huge sway on nearly every continent.

To understand the role of American firms on foreign commodity markets, it is necessary to first realize that the composition of global trade shifted from bulk to nonbulk commodities during the 1980s and 1990s (Coyle et al. 1998). That shift reflects the change in market structure brought about because of the reduced cost of transporting commodities and the resulting expansion of processing activities in foreign countries. The reduction in transport cost, coming from technical innovations in transport and storage industries, enables food manufacturing to benefit from local comparative advantages held by firms in different locations, even if they are in different countries. As Hudson and Etheridge (2000, p. 1219) explain, "with the increasing 'globalization' of markets, industries are increasingly witnessing the sequential manufacturing of consumer products in several countries before reaching the final consumer." This means a raw commodity can be turned into a finished product by passing through the hands of several agribusiness firms, each performing the task for which it has a comparative advantage, thus leading to lower costs for the final product. In other words, international supply chains are forming. This means that commodities originating from many different countries could pass through the control of a single agribusiness firm that performs some specialized function as part of an international supply chain.

The result of such a structure is that international commodity markets are becoming linked through supply chains. Hudson and Etheridge (2000, p. 1219) conclude that "analysis of commodity markets as if they were disconnected from their downstream products may result in misleading or erroneous conclusions" regarding the competitiveness of a country's commodity producers. This means that commodity markets, and their production sectors, in countries across the globe are influenced by the agribusiness firms farther downstream in their supply chains.

American agribusiness firms recognized this emerging global linkage of production, commodity markets, and the food manufacturing sector long ago and have moved to gain influence in the developing international supply chains. They did so as part of an economic plan aimed at assuring Americans a plentiful supply of food while also assuring the firm a prosperous future. That story is in the next section.

Global Food Industries

American agribusinesses will continue expanding their role in directing global food industries because it is smart to do so. Being able to influence food industries around the globe gives American firms more market power, thus aiding them in accomplishing their two basic business goals: earning steady profits and maintaining steady supplies of food to American consumers. Obviously, America cannot be self-sufficient in all of the commodities we consume, thus food manufacturing firms must import some commodities. Also, the United States produces surpluses of some commodities that must be sold in export markets. Thus, American agribusiness firms need to participate in markets on a global scale. The ways that firms choose to go about participating in foreign markets varies but, as a whole, determines how market structures evolve. The choices being made by American agribusiness firms are leading to increased market power.

What business strategies are being used by American firms to enter and/or influence international commodity markets and global food industries? The answer depends, in part, on the structure of the agribusiness firm. For example, Buccola et al. (2001) found that food processing cooperatives have disadvantages in overseas markets compared to privately owned firms. As a result, "firms progress gradually from an 'experimental' to an 'active' to a 'committed' stage in international operations" (p. 123), based mostly on their amount of experience in foreign markets. Many firms use a portfolio of arrangements for each of their products. Buccola et al. (2001, p. 109) discuss several types of overseas business arrangements and order them from least to greatest involvement:

1. domestic sale to overseas trading company
2. sale through a foreign distributor
3. sale through a foreign broker
4. direct sale to overseas wholesaler or retailer
5. overseas co-venture and
6. foreign direct investment

Of these arrangements, the most important now and in the future is foreign direct investment (FDI). It involves becoming an owner of a firm operating in a foreign country. That means it is the most risky of the arrangements because it requires the largest investment, and that investment does not have the protection of the U.S. legal system. Nevertheless, FDI is growing because it is the strategy that offers American firms the most control over the foreign portion of their supply chain.

The economic goals being pursued by firms using FDI depend on the type of FDI being used. Hudson, Xia, and Yeboah (2005, p. 387) describe two types of foreign direct investment:

> [H]orizontal FDI is used when trade barriers, transport costs, etc., are high and the U.S. firm invests in production facilities at both home and abroad, with each production facility serving its local market. Vertical FDI, in contrast, is typically employed to take advantage of factor-cost differences.

Vertical FDI is "outsourcing" and horizontal FDI is "market expansion." Vertical FDI reduces domestic employment in production because "multinational firms move part or all of their domestic production to foreign countries where labor (and other) costs are lower." On the other hand, "horizontal FDI usually replicates production plants in foreign countries to serve customers in those countries and their neighboring regions" (Hudson, Xia, and Yeboah 2005, p. 388). Hudson, Xia, and Yeboah conclude that "FDI has become the leading means for U.S. processed food companies to participate in international markets" (p. 389). They agree with Solana-Rosillo and Abbott (1998) in concluding that American food manufacturers are using FDI as a market penetration strategy. Thus, its goal is most often market expansion, not outsourcing. With the expansion of a firm's market comes expansion of its influence and market power. Therefore, it can be argued that American firms are using FDI as a business strategy that may both raise their total profits (by expanding the number of markets in which they participate) and serve as a risk management tool (by giving them more control over activities in their international supply chain).

The volume of foreign direct investment grows and ebbs with market prospects. Marchant and Kumar (2005, p. 380) note that "global FDI grew from $24 billion in 1973 ... to a peak of $1,388 billion in 2000, before falling to $559 billion in 2003." *Where* investments are made also shifts over time. For example, Weatherspoon, Cacho, and Christy (2001) looked at foreign direct investment in the emerging markets of less-developed countries. They noted that "some food and agribusiness firms are choosing to serve their international clientele by establishing foreign production subsidiaries that they own completely" (p. 726). They observed that "the combination of opening economies, incentives, and firms seeking international markets have contributed to the dramatic increase in foreign direct investment in emerging markets," growing from about $10 billion to more than $180 billion from 1980 to 1998. Part of this expansion is explained by the higher average returns available in emerging markets compared to industrialized countries. In 1998, average returns were 15.3 percent in emerging markets versus 12.5 percent for all countries. Weatherspoon, Cacho, and Christy (2001) reported regional rates of return as 36.9 percent for Africa, 19.3 percent for Asia-Pacific, and 12.8 percent for Latin America and the Caribbean. Apparently, these average rates of return reflect the usual correlation with risk, because the amount of FDI going to the highest returning market, Africa, was the smallest during the 1980–1998 period (only about $1 billion in 1980 and $8 billion in 1998), indicating that Africa is judged to be the riskiest market.

Finally, it is worth noting that foreign direct investment by U.S. firms is playing a significant role in shifting global agribusiness industry structure and conduct. Gow and Swinnen (1998) described how FDI stimulated growth in the less-developed parts of Europe. The same can be said of FDI's role in international supply chains growing in all parts of the globe. One of the surprising ways this comes about is through the trade links it creates between countries. For example, empirical results presented by Marchant, Cornell, and Koo (2002, p. 300) "indicate a bidirectional complementary relationship between FDI in and exports to East Asian countries." This means that exports and FDI move in the same direction or, in the simplest terms, investments made by American agribusiness firms in firms across the globe stimulate the economies of both countries. For that reason, FDI will continue to grow, strengthening economic links between nations and adding fuel to the trend of convergence in returns across the globe.

Technological and Market Development

Last, but not least in importance, is the role of U.S. agribusiness in directing technological development in food manufacturing and the resulting effects on market development. The United States is the leader in both creating technological change and disseminating it to firms across the country and to firms in less-developed countries. The agribusiness sector plays a key role because (1) that sector is in the business of applying technology to commodities so as to add value, and (2) it is in contact with all other parts of the agrifood industry, thus having access to, and influence on, all the players from farmers to consumers.

In the United States, the food and kindred product (i.e., food manufacturing) industry has generated better profit levels than either the farming industry or the agricultural services industry (Konduru and Bjornson 2004). It has done so due mostly to the continued application of technological innovation. According to Konduru and Bjornson (2004, p. 761). "the profits in this industry are holding up, which may make food manufacturing attractive to investors." That is a key point: generating profits attracts investors, which are an essential input in economic development. In the United States, profits come from differentiation, which comes from innovation. In the American agribusiness sector, "there can be opportunity for any firm with an innovation or competitive advantage to be successful" (Konduru and Bjornson 2004, p. 761). Therefore, it is certain that continued investments will be made to continue expanding food markets in the United States.

Technical innovations developed by American agribusiness firms will also continue to be disseminated to firms in foreign countries, thus serving as a catalyst for economic growth through market development around the globe. The vehicles most often used for the dissemination of technical innovations to foreign firms are transfers through foreign direct investments and contacts (Bwalya 2006). For example, Makki and Somwaru (2004, p. 800) show that "FDI and trade contribute toward advancing economic growth in developing countries. There is a strong, positive interaction between FDI and trade. FDI is often the main channel through which advanced technology is transferred to developing countries." They also note that "FDI stimulates domestic investment" (p. 800). Gow and Swinnen (1998) provided interesting case studies of how the investment of both technology and capital can serve to stimulate growth in industries and their host locations, each having a multiplier effect on the regional and national economies. However, "the impact of FDI on [the] host economy is country-specific" (Zhang 2001, p. 185). Zhang (2001) suggested that although average inflows of FDI to less-developed countries increased during each decade since 1960, the economic effects vary with the economic structure of countries. Weatherspoon, Cacho, and Christy (2001) agree and describe how less-developed countries need a national strategy to leverage FDI to ensure positive results. This is important because, as Gemmell, Lloyd, and Mathew (2000) showed, the agricultural sector is a relatively large portion of a less-developed country's economy, and agriculture's growth determines the direction and speed of development possible in most other sectors of the national economy.

This brings us back to the beginning: the story of American agriculture is really a tale of two sectors, and one sector has a much brighter story than the other sector. The American agribusiness sector is going to remain a profitable, innovative segment of the U.S. economy. Part of the reason is that economies of scale and other structural factors have caused it to develop into a leader in the globalizing food industry. For the other sector, American agricultural producers, things look economically bleak because they are disadvantaged by the structure of the traditional markets for their undifferentiated output. The key question remaining is how long it will be before farmers and ranchers realize that America's agribusiness sector is not the source of their problems, but potentially the source of their solutions. Agribusinesses can offer producers profitable new markets to replace traditional choices that are losing their viability. When the American production and agribusiness sectors decide to quit being competitors in domestic commodity markets, and decide instead to collaborate as a formidable team to provide high-quality food products to global markets, the profitability and lifespan of both sectors will become brighter.

NOTES

Part of this chapter is based on a paper by S. Blank, R. Volpe III, and K. Erickson entitled "The Relationship Between Industry Structure and Production Contracting: Raising Questions at the Beginning of a Trend."

1. The "potential for production contracting" is defined as the share of total sales of a commodity that will be under production contract once the trend is complete in that all possible structural changes have occurred in commercial firms producing that commodity in the United States. In other words, the potential will be reached when a new equilibrium in contracting share is reached for a commodity. Each commodity has a unique potential.

2. Producers do not like selling in uncertain spot markets, but they prefer competitive spot markets to imperfectly competitive markets in which they are at a disadvantage relative to the buyers they face.

3. In this analysis, survey data are used in which the distinction between production and marketing contracts is made by survey respondents. The survey asks producers questions about both production and marketing contracts, but there is no way to know how those contract types are being interpreted. At this point in the trend of increasing contracting, the definitions of contract types are not standard.

4. CR4 is the concentration ratio measured using sales data from the four largest firms in the industry. It is the percentage of total industry sales revenues that are accounted for by the four largest firms. CR8 and CR20 are also used in some analyses.

5. A "strong-form" test is one that is conducted on adequate data using appropriate procedures that give results sufficient to support or reject the hypothesis. A "weak-form" test is conducted with limited data, thus limiting the power of its results. Weak-form test results that are inconsistent with a hypothesis may be used to reject that hypothesis, but weak-form results that are consistent with the hypothesis are a necessary, but not sufficient, condition to ultimately support the hypothesis.

6. Peanuts were dropped because there was only one contractor in the data; tobacco was omitted because, although a majority of total tobacco output is under contract, surveyed growers reported that they use marketing contracts rather than production contracts.

7. The profit margins are calculated simply as income from farm operations as a percentage of total farm sales. In order to save space, farm operation income is not presented in Table 18.3, but it can be calculated using the other data presented for each commodity and producer group. For example, total household income for sugar beet contractors is a small amount—approximately one-tenth of the amount earned from off-farm sources—because about nine-tenths of off-farm income is needed to cover the losses from farming operations, on average. Independent sugar beet growers, on the other hand, have strong profit levels, on average.

8. Some commodities in Table 18.3, such as rice, were not included in this analysis because the small number of farmers under production contracts made statistical tests difficult. Also, sufficient data were not available on the various farm-level variables to allow for the inclusion of sugar beets, despite the relatively high percentage of farmers using production contracts.

9. The risk-reducing character of production contracts may enable producers to comfortably expand their operations to achieve economies of scale. For example, Key and McBride (2003) found that for hog producers the use of production contracts is associated with a substantial increase in factor productivity, and represents a technological improvement over independent production.

10. The difference is significant only in the case of soybean producers because the small number of contracts in the other markets provide too few degrees of freedom for significant t-tests.

11. In individual cases, it is quite likely that having a production contract leads to production specialization, and in other cases, having specialized production leads to production contracting (to reduce risk).

REFERENCES

Acheampong, Yvonne J. 2000. "International Variation in Return on Equity in the Food and Beverage Industries." *Journal of Agricultural & Applied Economics* 32 (2): 383–392.

Ahearn, M., P. Korb, and D. Banker. 2005. "Industrialization and Contracting in U.S. Agriculture." *Journal of Agricultural & Applied Economics* 37 (2): 347–364.

Ahearn, M., J. Yee, and W. Huffman. 2002. "The Effect of Contracting and Consolidation on Farm Productivity." Paper presented at the Economics of Contracting in Agriculture Workshop, Annapolis, MD.

Allen, D., and D. Lueck. 2003. *The Nature of the Farm: Contracts, Risk, and Organization in Agriculture.* Cambridge, MA: MIT Press.

Bangsund, D., and F. Leistritz. 1998. *Economic Contribution of the Sugarbeet Industry to North Dakota and Minnesota.* USDA Economic Research Service, Agricultural Economics Report no. 395-S.

Barry, P., S. Sonka, and K. Lajili. 1992. "Vertical Coordination, Financial Structure, and the Changing Theory of the Firm." *American Journal of Agricultural Economics* 74 (5): 1219–1225.

Bessler, D., and D. Akleman. 1998. "Farm Prices, Retail Prices, and Directed Graphs: Results for Pork and Beef." *American Journal of Agricultural Economics* 80 (5): 1144–1149.

Bhuyan, S. 2005. "An Empirical Evaluation of Factors Determining Vertical Integration in U.S. Food Manufacturing Industries." *Agribusiness* 21 (3): 429–445.

Boehlje, Michael. 1999. "Structural Changes in the Agricultural Industries: How Do We Measure, Analyze and Understand Them?" *American Journal of Agricultural Economics* 81 (5): 1028–1041.

Buccola, S., C. Durham, M. Gopinath, and E. Henderson. 2001. "Food Manufacturing Cooperatives' Overseas Business Portfolios." *Journal of Agricultural and Resource Economics* 26 (1): 107–124.

Bwalya, Samuel M. 2006. "Foreign Direct Investment and Technology Spillovers: Evidence from Panel Data Analysis of Manufacturing Firms in Zambia." *Journal of Development Economics* 81: 514–526.

Castaneda, Marco A. 2006. "The Hold-up Problem in a Repeated Relationship." *International Journal of Industrial Organization* 24 (5): 953–970.

Caswell, Julie A. 1987. "Dominant Forms of Corporate Control in the U.S. Agribusiness Sector." *American Journal of Agricultural Economics* 69: 11–21.

Caswell, J., M. Bredahl, and N. Hooker. 1998. "How Quality Management Metasystems Are Affecting the Food Industry." *Review of Agricultural Economics* 20 (2): 547–557.

Clary, G., R. Dietrich, and D. Farris. 1986. "Effects of Increased Transportation Costs on Spatial Price Differences and Optimum Locations of Cattle Feeding and Slaughter." *Agribusiness: An International Journal* 2: 235–246.

Coyle, W., M. Gehlhar, T. Hertel, Z. Wang, and W. Yu. 1998. "Understanding the Determinants of Structural Change in World Food Markets." *American Journal of Agricultural Economics* 80 (5): 1051–1061.

Davis, C., and J. Gillespie. 2007. "Factors Affecting the Selection of Business Arrangements by U.S. Hog Farmers." *Review of Agricultural Economics* 29 (2): 331–348.

Diaz, J., D. Farris, and K. Litzenberg. 1986. "Alternative Fresh Beef Distribution Systems: A Form-Space Approach." *Agribusiness: An International Journal* 2: 199–214.

Drabenstott, Mark. 1995. "Agricultural Industrialization: Implications for Economic Development and Public Policy." *Journal of Agricultural & Applied Economics* 27 (1): 13–20.

Dunn, J., D. Lee, and D. Thatch. 1987. "The Effect of Transportation Rates on Interregional Competition in Agriculture: A General Case." *Agribusiness: An International Journal* 3: 393–402.

Duranton, G., and H. Overman. 2005. "Testing for Localization Using Micro-Geographic Data." *Review of Economic Studies* 72: 1077–1106.

Durham, C., R. Sexton, and J. Song. 1996. "Spatial Competition, Uniform Pricing, and Transportation Efficiency in the California Processing Tomato Industry." *American Journal of Agricultural Economics* 78 (1): 115–125.

Farm Foundation. 2004. *Production Contracts*. Oak Brook, IL.

Fouayzi, H., J. Caswell, and N. Hooker. 2006. "Motivations of Fresh-Cut Produce Firms to Implement Quality Management Systems." *Review of Agricultural Economics* 28 (1): 132–146.

Gemmell, N., T. Lloyd, and M. Mathew. 2000. "Agricultural Growth and Inter-Sectoral Linkages in a Developing Economy." *Journal of Agricultural Economics* 51 (3): 353–370.

Gow, H., and J. Swinnen. 1998. "How Foreign Direct Investment Has Stimulated Growth in the Central and Eastern European Agri-Food Sectors: Vertical Contracting and the Role of Private Enforcement Capital." Policy Research Group Working Paper no. 18, Department of Agricultural Economics, Katholieke Universiteit Leuven, Belgium, May.

Hayenga, Marvin L. 1979. "Risk Management in Imperfect Markets: Commodity Procurement Strategy in the Food Manufacturing Sector." *American Journal of Agricultural Economics* 61: 351–357.

Henderson, J., and K. McNamara. 2000. "The Location of Food Manufacturing Plant Investments in Corn Belt Counties." *Journal of Agricultural and Resource Economics* 25 (2): 680–697.

Hendrikse, G., and J. Bijman. 2002. "Ownership Structure in Agrifood Chains: The Marketing Cooperative." *American Journal of Agricultural Economics* 84 (1): 104–119.

Hudson, D. and D. Etheridge. 2000. "Competitiveness of Agricultural Commodities in the United States: Expanding Our View." *American Journal of Agricultural Economics* 82 (5): 1219–1223.

Hudson, D., T. Xia, and O. Yeboah. 2005. "Foreign Direct Investment and Domestic Industries: Market Expansion or Outsourcing?" *Review of Agricultural Economics* 27 (3): 387–393.

Joskow, P. 1989. "The Role of Transaction Cost Economics in Antitrust and Public Utility Regulatory Policies." *Journal of Law, Economics, and Organization* 7: 53–83.

Katchova, A., and M. Miranda. 2004. "Two-step Econometric Estimation of Farm Characteristics Affecting Marketing Contract Decisions." *American Journal of Agricultural Economics* 86 (1): 88–102.

Key, Nigel. 2004. "Agricultural Contracting and the Scale of Production." *Agricultural and Resource Economics Review* 33 (2): 255–271.

———. 2005. "How Much Do Farmers Value Their Independence?" *Agricultural Economics* 22: 117–26.

Key, N., and W. McBride. 2003. "Production Contracts and Productivity in the U.S. Hog Sector." *American Journal of Agricultural Economics* 85 (1): 121–133.

Konduru, S., and B. Bjornson. 2004. "Changing Factor Income Shares in Agri-Food Industries." *Journal of Agricultural & Applied Economics* 36 (3): 747–762.

Lajili, K., P. Barry, S. Sonka, and J. Mahoney. 1997. "Farmers' Preferences for Crop Contracts." *Journal of Agricultural and Resource Economics* 22 (2): 264–280.

Lanzillotti, Robert F. 1960. "The Superior Market Power of Food Processing and Agricultural Supply Firms—Its Relation to the Farm Problem." *Journal of Farm Economics* 42 (5): 1228–1247.

Lynch, L., and J. Carpenter. 2002. "Does the Farm Sector Have a Critical Mass?" Department of Agricultural and Resource Economics, University of Maryland, WP 02–14, July.

MacDonald, J., M. Ahearn, and D. Banker. 2004. "Organizational Economics in Agriculture Policy Analysis." *American Journal of Agricultural Economics* 86 (3): 744–749.

MacDonald, J., and P. Korb. 2006. *Agricultural Contracting Update: Contracts in 2003*. USDA Economic Research Service, Economic Information Bulletin no. 9, January.

MacDonald, J., J. Perry, M. Ahearn, D. Banker, W. Chambers, C. Dimitri, N. Key, K. Nelson, and L. Southard. 2004. *Contracts, Markets, and Prices: Organizing the Production and Use of*

Agricultural Commodities. USDA Economic Research Service, Agricultural Economic Report no. 837.

Makki, S., and A. Somwaru. 2004. "Impact of Foreign Direct Investment and Trade on Economic Growth: Evidence from Developing Countries." *American Journal of Agricultural Economics* 86 (3): 795–801.

Marchant, M., D. Cornell, and W. Koo. 2002. "International Trade and Foreign Direct Investment: Substitutes or Complements?" *Journal of Agricultural & Applied Economics* 34 (2): 289–302.

Marchant, M., and S. Kumar. 2005. "An Overview of U.S. Foreign Direct Investment and Out-sourcing." *Review of Agricultural Economics* 27 (3): 379–386.

Martin, Laura L. 1997. "Production Contracts, Risk Shifting, and Relative Performance Payments in the Pork Industry." *Journal of Agricultural & Applied Economics* 29 (2): 267–278.

Martinez, Steve W. 1999. *Vertical Coordination in the Pork and Broiler Industries: Implications for Pork and Chicken Products.* USDA Economic Research Service, Agricultural Economic Report no. 777.

———. 2002. *A Comparison of Vertical Coordination in the U.S. Poultry, Egg, and Pork Industries.* USDA Economic Research Service, Agriculture Information Bulletin no. 747– 05, May.

McLaughlin, E., and G. Hawkes. 1986. "Twenty Years of Change in the Structure, Costs, and Performance of Food Chains." *Agribusiness: An International Journal* 2: 103–118.

Mighell, R., and L. Jones. 1963. *Vertical Coordination in Agriculture.* USDA Economic Research Service, Agricultural Economic Report no. 19, February.

Morrison Paul, Catherine J. 2000. *Cost Economies and Market Power in U.S. Beef Packing.* Giannini Foundation Monograph no. 44, University of California, May.

Morrison Paul, C., R. Nehring, and D. Banker. 2004. "Productivity, Economies, and Efficiency in U.S. Agriculture: A Look at Contracts." *American Journal of Agricultural Economics* 86 (5): 1308–1314.

Nguyen, S., and M. Ollinger. 2006. "Mergers and Acquisitions and Productivity in the U.S. Meat Products Industries: Evidence from the Micro Data." *American Journal of Agricultural Economics* 88 (3): 606–616.

Ollinger, M., S. Nguyen, D. Blayney, W. Chambers, and K. Kelson. 2005. *Structural Change in the Meat, Poultry, Dairy, and Grain Processing Industries.* USDA Economic Research Service, Agricultural Economic Report no. 3.

Raper, K., L. Cheney, and M. Punjabi. 2006. "Regional Impacts of U.S. Hog Slaughter Plant Closing: The Thorn Apple Valley Case." *Review of Agricultural Economics* 28 (4): 531–542.

Rios, A.R., and A. Gray. 2005. "U.S. Agriculture: Commercial and Large Producer Concentration and Implications for Agribusiness Segments." Paper presented at the American Agricultural Economics Association Annual Meeting, Providence, Rhode Island.

Roberts, M., and N. Key. 2005. "Losing Under Contract: Transaction-Cost Externalities and Spot Market Disintegration." *Journal of Agricultural and Food Industrial Organization* 2 (2): 1–17.

Rogers, Richard T. 1987. "The Relationships Between Market Structure and Price-Cost Margins in U.S. Food Manufacturing, 1954 to 1977." *Agribusiness: An International Journal* 3: 241–252.

Schrader, Lee F. 1986. "Responses to Forces Shaping Agricultural Marketing: Contracting." *American Journal of Agricultural Economics* 68 (5): 1161–1166.

Schumacher, S., and M. Boland. 2005. "The Persistence of Profitability Among Firms in the Food Economy." *American Journal of Agricultural Economics* 87 (1): 103–115.

Sexton, Richard J. 2000. "Industrialization and Consolidation in the U.S. Food Sector: Implications for Competition and Welfare." *American Journal of Agricultural Economics* 82 (5): 1087–1104.

Sheldon, Ian M. 1996. "Contracting, Imperfect Information, and the Food System." *Review of Agricultural Economics* 18 (1): 7–19.

Solana-Rosillo, J., and P. Abbott. 1998. "International Entry Mode Decisions by Agribusiness Firms: Distribution and Market Power." *American Journal of Agricultural Economics* 80: 1080–1086.

U.S. Department of Agriculture, Economic Research Service (USDA/ERS). Agricultural Resource Management Survey, Phase III and Farm Costs and Returns Surveys for 1996 through 2004.

U.S. Department of Commerce. 2006. "Concentration Ratios: 2002." *2002 Economic Census,* EC02–31SR-1. Washington, DC: U.S. Census Bureau, May.

Vukina, T., and P. Leegomonchai. 2006. "Oligopsony Power, Asset Specificity, and Hold-Up: Evidence from the Broiler Industry." *American Journal of Agricultural Economics* 88 (3): 589–605.

Weatherspoon, D., J. Cacho, and R. Christy. 2001. "Linking Globalization, Economic Growth and Poverty: Impacts of Agribusiness Strategies on Sub-Saharan Africa." *American Journal of Agricultural Economics* 83 (3): 722–729.

Williamson, O. 1968. "Economics as an Antitrust Defense: The Welfare Tradeoffs." *American Economic Review* 58: 18–36.

———. 1979. "Transaction-Cost Economics: The Governance of Contractual Relations." *Journal of Law and Economics* 22 (1979): 233–262.

Wilson, P., and G. Thompson. 2003. "Time Integration: Agribusiness Structure for Competitive Advantage." *Review of Agricultural Economics* 25 (1): 30–43.

Young, H., and M. Burke. 2001. "Competition and Custom in Economic Contracts: A Case Study of Illinois Agriculture." *American Economic Review* 91 (3): 559–573.

Young, L., and J. Hobbs. 2002. "Vertical Linkages in Agri-Food Supply Chains: Changing Roles for Producers, Commodity Groups, and Government Policy." *Review of Agricultural Economics* 24 (2): 429–441.

Zhang, Kevin H. 2001. "Does Foreign Direct Investment Promote Economic Growth? Evidence from East Asia and Latin America." *Contemporary Economic Policy* 19 (2): 175–185.

CHAPTER 19

IS AGRICULTURE A "WAY OF LIFE"
OR A BUSINESS?

"The world is filled with willing people;
some willing to work, the rest willing to let them."
—Robert Frost

It seems as though every time American agricultural policy comes up for discussion—particularly in Washington, D.C.—someone proclaims the need to protect the "way of life" offered by "family farms." At various points in the discussion, family farms may also be referred to as "family businesses." In the language of the U.S. Department of Agriculture (USDA), those family farm businesses are sometimes referred to as "owner-operator households." The terminology gets a bit confusing at times, but one thing is clear: it is important to sort out the embedded issues in order to understand the conflicting forces beneath the current agricultural policy debate. As a start, we need an answer to a question: Is agriculture a way of life or a business?

This question cuts to the heart of agriculture and to agricultural policy. In policy debates, agricultural proponents have often used the "way of life" argument to support their claim that production agriculture, in general, and family farms, in particular, need to be protected in various ways—such as subsidization through direct and indirect government payments. That long-held position asserts that there is something special about agriculture that deserves to be preserved. However, an economically viable business does not need protection. Also, mature businesses that are economically viable are rarely the subject of policy debates. Thus, arguing that agriculture needs protection is equivalent to arguing that agriculture is not a viable business.

A LOOK AT THE RECORD

Certainly, agriculture was a business at some point in our past. As Cochrane (1993) details, agriculture was America's main industry early in the country's history. As the U.S. economy developed, other industries grew, but agriculture must have still been a profitable "business" into the twentieth century because it continued to attract resources, growing in numbers of firms until 1935 and in total acreage until 1954.

However, over the past half-century, agriculture has been shrinking in size, importance, and economic performance (Blank 2001). The economic development literature explains agriculture's decline by noting that "if resources are free to move, other things being equal, they will move in the direction of higher returns" (Mundlak 2000, p. 239). That type of profit-maximizing behavior is expected of a business, and agriculture has done a good job of moving human resources out of the sector over time. So why do agricultural producers stay where they get a return on equity averaging only about 1.5 percent recently, far below returns available elsewhere in our economy?

Clearly, agriculture is viewed as more than a business now. Many individuals in agriculture appear to be making an economic sacrifice to be there. Do people work in agriculture because it is a "better" lifestyle, or because an urban lifestyle is "worse"? The reverse migration from cities to small farms observed over the past decade suggests the first (Deller et al. 2001); the reluctance of farmers to leave agriculture suggests the second (Goetz and Debertin 1996, 2001; USDA 2000). The number of farms with annual sales of less than $10,000 has increased since 1992 as more Americans pursue a rural lifestyle. The reluctance of farmers to leave the industry is evidenced by their willingness to accept agriculture's low returns to production activities.

The debate over why farmers keep farming dates back many decades. Typical of the arguments are those Brewster (1961) and Martin and Jefferies (1966) advanced in the 1960s, and Ikerd (2000) more recently. Brewster (1961) hypothesized that farmers willingly accept lower returns than other investors because of the desirable lifestyle they derive from farming. Ikerd (2000) raises related issues with a religious fervor that includes a reference to the Dalai Lama.

Brewster's (1961) hypothesis implies that farmers are not sensitive to foregone opportunities off the farm. It explains why some farmers might exclude nonagricultural investments from their portfolio, limiting themselves to agricultural production opportunities. On the other hand, the fact that most farmers are part-timers indicates that farmers are indeed sensitive to off-farm opportunities and will pursue them if able (Mishra and Sandretto 2002). The USDA (2007) reports that for large family farms (those with annual sales of $250,000 to $499,999), "about 50 percent of the operator households reported that either the operator or the spouse did some off-farm work." This implies that farmers, like all investors, have a desire to build wealth, which is consistent with the view that producers see agriculture as a business.

Thus, farmers' behavior sends mixed signals: some seem to be pursuing a lifestyle while others act like business managers. It is also likely that many farmers are pursuing both lifestyle and business goals. We need to ask: "What is their objective?" Are farmers "profit maximizers" and wealth builders like businesses, or "utility maximizers" and happiness builders focused on a way of life?

PROFIT IS A KEY

A dictionary definition of "business" is "a commercial or industrial enterprise," and a definition of "commercial" is "designed for profit or for mass appeal." Clearly, profit is the key to answering the question. Also, the USDA has made it clear that profit performance is related to the structure of American agriculture. Thus, it is useful to assess the agricultural profit performance of farm owner-operators grouped according to size. "Commercial farms," defined by the USDA as those having annual sales of $250,000 or more, represented only 8.2 percent of U.S. farm businesses in 2002. They had average net cash income of $117,800 per farm, compared to their 1996–2000 average of $141,800. "Intermediate farms" (defined as those with sales below $250,000 yet whose operators report farming as their major occupation) represented 28.9 percent of farm businesses and had average net cash income of $7,200 in 2002, compared to their 1996–2000 average of $12,300. "Rural residence farms" accounted for the remaining 62.9 percent of farms in 2002 (that share increased to 68 percent by 2004) and had average net cash income per farm of –$2,800, compared to their -$1,800 average for 1996–2000 (USDA 2007).

Clearly, large commercial farms are building wealth through agricultural profits, so they are behaving like businesses. The average profit level for those farms is sufficient to support a family without off-farm income.

Intermediate farms are more ambiguous in their objectives. These operators report farming as their major occupation and they do make a profit (as calculated by the USDA), but the level of profits, on average, is not sufficient to support a family. Therefore, it is unclear whether these farmers are seeking to maximize their profits or their quality of life (i.e., utility).

Small-farm owners know they are losing money, on average, so it seems reasonable to assume they would quit farming if they were rational profit seekers. By not quitting, their behavior appears to indicate that their primary objective is not profits from farming. Thus, they appear to be "hobby" farmers that consider the time and labor spent in farming as *leisure*.

A dictionary definition of "hobby" is "a pursuit or interest engaged in for relaxation." A hobby is, therefore, a leisure activity with the primary objective of increasing a participant's happiness (utility), not his or her profit total. Hobbies have a cost that participants must pay to play. Anything taking time and money to play must be leisure with an *intrinsic value* equaling foregone wages and returns from capital invested, minus the expected financial result (loss).

Take, for example, a guy named Steve who likes to play golf. For Steve, golf is a favorite hobby that relaxes him by taking his mind off his for-profit activities (i.e., his job) for a while. The intrinsic value of golf is the total of Steve's foregone wages (the money he could earn during the time he spends golfing) plus capital costs (the gains foregone on the amount invested in golf equipment) and the direct costs of the greens fees and golf equipment he uses while playing. Although Steve has been known to win a few dollars in club tournaments, that total in any year has always been below his total direct costs of playing golf. Therefore, golf is not a business to him.

For hobby farmers, the same logic applies. A business seeks to increase the wealth of its owners by earning profits. For rural residence farms, owners' wealth is reduced by the operating losses incurred, on average, thus the objective is usually assumed to be lifestyle-oriented. Small-scale farmers voluntarily "pay to play," implying that leisure time spent pursuing a farming hobby (H) is not valued at $0, or at the opportunity cost of foregone wages (w), but at the difference of foregone wages plus gains on capital invested (k) and after-tax financial gains from farming (π). Thus, $H = (w + k - \pi)$. Yet, with profits expected to be *negative* for most small-scale farmers, the expected value of leisure exceeds wage rates and capital costs: $E(H) > w + k$, where k is the return on capital invested which is $(K)v$, K is the total dollars of capital invested, and v is the percentage rate of return on investment.

A simple decision rule can indicate whether a particular small or intermediate farm is a business or a lifestyle choice. In general, the rule is:

$$\text{if E(H)} \quad \begin{cases} < 0, \text{the farm is a business;} \\ > 0, \text{the farm is a lifestyle.} \end{cases}$$

In essence, if operating profits are expected to outweigh foregone gains, then H will be negative and the farm is operating like a business. When the foregone gains are expected to be greater than the profits earned, the farm is a hobby with utility maximization as its objective.

ANSWERING THE BIG QUESTION

Agriculture is both a way of life and a business. It is a way of life to, possibly, all participants, but it is a business to only some. Large-scale commercial farms clearly act like businesses. Many of those farm operators may also view their business as a desirable way of life. On the other hand, rural residence farms are hobbies that operators must subsidize with earnings from off-farm sources.

The scale of the voluntary subsidy by small-scale operators to their hobby farms now swamps the aggregate profit performance of larger farms in most years. As shown in Table 19.1, the average "earnings from farming" for all American farm households was very low in 2002 ($3,477 per household) because total losses from the large group of hobby farms almost equaled the total profits from commercial operations. Even in better years, such as 2004, average household earnings from farming fall far below the poverty line.

Finally, note that a hobby farmer's willingness to "pay to play" depends on his/her initial wealth, along with the cost of leisure. This means people will play when their lifestyle budget (which includes the total cost of hobbies) is met by income from normal nonagricultural sources. As shown in Table 19.1, an average "farmer" can afford to pursue a rural lifestyle because, although farming generates only $2,598–14,201 per year, average off-farm income of $53,000–67,000 is sufficient to support the operator and family as they enjoy their rural home.

The discussion thus far in this chapter implies that a majority of America's farms and ranches are "hobby farms" that represent a lifestyle choice more than a commercial business. However, this simple result begs for clarification. For example, there is no single agricultural lifestyle, so none of the many forms of the lifestyle is unique or "special" enough to justify preserving it at the cost of billions of dollars each year. Are farmers themselves willing to preserve their lifestyle by continuing to subsidize their production activities with off-farm income? To answer that question, the analysis is taken a step further by posing a second explanation for why farmers are willing to subsidize their family farms. It abandons the naive view often expressed by farm advocates that rural residents are only in it for the lifestyle. That gross underestimate of farm owner-operators' business savvy is replaced with a modern view of the big picture, which shows that all types of farm and ranch owners do have one thing in common.

THE NEVER-ENDING DEBATES

In policy debates, many things in agriculture are not what they seem. The "net farm income" totals reported by the U.S. Department of Agriculture overstate the profitability of agricultural production while they understate the profitability of being a farm owner-operator. The overstatement comes in the form of direct government transfers to agriculture that in some recent years have been about half the total net farm income reported by the Department of Agriculture (see Table 19.1). The understatement comes from the income data's focus on only farm and ranch production related activities, ignoring other sources of income. Of these two misrepresentations of American agriculture's big picture, the understatement is far more important. It leads to the perception that an agricultural way of life is one of poverty for most farmers, thus providing a justification for government support.

However, if things down on the farm are so bad, why do farmers stay in agriculture and why has the number of farms with annual sales of less than $10,000 *increased* since 1992 while total farm numbers continue to decline? As noted earlier, the reverse migration from cities to small farms observed over the past decade suggests that more Americans want to pursue a rural lifestyle (Deller et al. 2001). But is that all there is to it?

The debate over why farmers stay has been dominated by Brewster's (1961) hypothesis that farmers willingly accept lower returns than other investors because of the lifestyle benefits derived from farming. This view often leads to a mistaken interpretation of the fact that most farmers are part-timers. The misinterpretation usually made is that farmers seek off-farm income simply to enable them to pursue their lifestyle choice. However, a second possible explanation for why

Table 19.1

U.S. Farm Income, 1998–2004

	1998	1999	2000	2001	2002	2003	2004
	\$ billion						
Total cash receipts	195.8	187.6	192.1	200.1	195.0	216.6	241.2
Net farm income	42.9	46.8	47.9	50.6	36.6	59.5	82.5
Direct government payments	12.4	21.5	22.9	20.7	11.2	17.2	13.3
Adjusted production income*	30.5	25.3	25.0	29.9	25.4	42.3	69.2
	\$ per farm operator household						
Net cash farm income	14,357	13,194	11,175	14,311	11,336	14,979	20,638
Earnings from farming	7,106	6,359	2,598	5,539	3,477	7,884	14,201
Off-farm earnings	52,628	57,988	59,349	58,578	62,284	60,713	67,279
Average farm household income**	59,734	64,347	61,947	64,117	65,761	68,597	81,480

Source: USDA (2007 and earlier issues)

* This is calculated as net farm income minus direct government payments.

** This is the sum of "earnings from farming" and "off-farm earnings."

farmers stay is implied by the results of Blank et al. (2004), who found that farmers' wealth comes from capital gains, not production income. This leads to the following proposition.

- PROPOSITION 19.1. *Many owner-operators are real estate investors using off-farm income to help them stay on the farm until they choose to capture their capital gains.*

This proposition implies that farmers, like all investors, have a desire to build wealth, which is consistent with the view that owner-operators see agriculture as a business. In other words, the business of most farm owners enjoying an agricultural "way of life" is real estate.

WEALTH IS THE REAL KEY

A business has the objective of increasing the wealth of its owners. For most small- and mid-sized farms, owners' wealth is reduced by the production losses they incur most years, on average, thus they are often labeled as "hobby farms" (Mishra et al. 2002). However, as explained in Chapter 4, production income is only one source of wealth. Three types of income (i.e., economic gains) contribute to wealth: profits from farm output, off-farm income, and capital gains on assets. Total wealth (W) is usually expressed as equity at time t. Changes in wealth during a time period ending at t (ΔW_t) equal farm income ($FInc$) plus off-farm income ($OFInc$) plus capital gains (ΔK) minus consumption (Con), or

$$(19.1) \qquad \Delta W_t = FInc_t + OFInc_t + \Delta K_t - Con_t$$

Capital gains are simply the change in value of a farmer's capital from one period to the next (i.e., $K_t - K_{t-1}$). Capital gains are only realized if the asset is sold. However, lenders will usually loan a farmer up to some specific portion of the market value of assets, referred to as the *loan-to-value* ratio. Thus, some portion of unrealized capital gains can be immediately converted into cash and used to acquire other assets. In this regard, capital gains (even unrealized gains) immediately improve a farmer's ability to borrow and thus aid in financing a larger operation, which, presumably, will increase the growth in wealth.

So, how are agricultural producers doing in generating income to build wealth? The 2002 Census of Agriculture (USDA 2004) reported that 53.3 percent of all farms generated a net loss for the year, although the average household earnings from farming activities for that year were $3,477 (USDA 2007). Clearly, this amount is not sufficient to support a family (i.e., it does not exceed household consumption cost), so relying solely on this source of income would result in annual reductions in household wealth.

So, why continue to farm? Even though income from farming activities is low, on average, if it is still positive it helps operators cover (at least part of) their ownership costs. As an investment, farming has generated a positive return for American farmers. The first column of Table 19.2 shows the average return on assets (ROA) received by producers in the different regions of the country, plus the average for the United States, over the 1960–2002 period. It shows that over the long run American agriculture has generated a 3.04 percent average return on assets used in production activities. That provides some incentive to continue investing in the business.

What about capital gains? Farmland has historically represented about 75 percent of assets held by farm households (USDA 2000). Therefore, the ROA from capital gains reported in the second column of Table 19.2 are primarily from farm real estate. Agricultural land prices are the result of assessments of a parcel's value by both agricultural and nonagricultural markets (Drozd

Table 19.2

Average Rates of Return by Region, 1960–2002 (percent)

Region	ROA from current income	ROA from capital gains	Total ROA	St. dev. of total ROA	Total ROE	St. dev. of total ROE
Northeast	−0.03	2.56	2.54	3.65	2.24	4.38
Lake States	1.82	2.13	3.95	6.22	3.53	8.15
Corn Belt	3.13	1.06	4.18	7.83	3.86	9.57
Northern Plains	3.97	0.83	4.80	6.57	4.57	8.37
Appalachia	2.58	1.45	4.04	4.59	3.86	5.52
Southeast	5.50	1.92	7.42	4.48	7.90	5.50
Delta	4.62	−0.02	4.60	6.58	4.34	8.42
Southern Plains	1.87	0.71	2.58	4.92	2.27	5.88
Mountain	2.67	1.24	3.90	5.51	3.78	6.88
Pacific	5.41	0.97	6.39	4.95	6.84	6.57
Alaska & Hawaii	2.93	1.92	4.85	5.26	4.92	5.80
U.S. TOTAL	3.04	1.26	4.30	5.26	4.12	6.60

Note: "ROA" is the return on assets. "ROE" is the return on equity. "St. Dev." is the standard deviation of the time series.

and Johnson 2004; Plantinga, Lubowski, and Stavins 2002), and many of those factors are out of the control of the farm owner. Therefore, farmland values vary much more than do the values of other agricultural assets, but they have generated an average return on those assets of 1.26 percent annually for owners over the 1960–2002 period. The volatility of the two sources of returns is apparent in Figure 19.1. What is also apparent is that returns from capital gains have been higher than returns from current production income for most of the past decade. What is not apparent is the relative scale of the contributions to owner wealth that are made by capital gains.

As it turns out, capital gains have increased owner-operators' wealth more than have farming profits, on average, in many years. For example, in 2002 the Census of Agriculture found that the estimated market value of farm real estate was $1.145 trillion. Assuming that the long-run national average rate of return from capital gains of 1.26 percent (shown in Table 19.2) was earned on the real estate gives a conservative estimate of $14.4 billion for capital gains in agriculture for 2002. That total equals $6,777 in capital gains earned for the year by each of the 2,128,739 farms reported in the census. The actual capital gain rate reported for 2002 was 3.18 percent (USDA 2007), which gives an estimate for average capital gains of $17,078 per farm—nearly five times as much as the average amount of farm income per household for that year. Therefore, capital gains are relatively much more important in building farm owner-operator wealth, even though they look relatively minor as reported in Table 19.2. Also, the distribution of capital gains is likely to be weighted more heavily toward small, lifestyle farms (which are more often closer to cities) than to large, commercial farms (which are usually farther from urban areas). In other words, it is expected that small farms are earning above-average rates of capital gain, thus improving owner-operator wealth faster for lifestyle farms because of the "urban influence" on land values in their location (USDA 2000).

Finally, it should be clear that farm income must be augmented by off-farm income to cover the cost of living for most farm households. Even if capital gains could all be realized each year,

Figure 19.1   **U.S. Agriculture's Returns on Assets, 1960–2002**

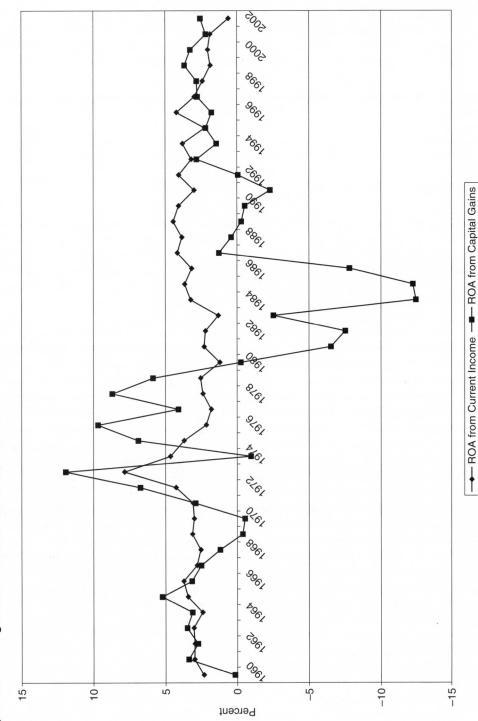

combining the long-run annual average of $6,777 in capital gains with the low average earnings from farm activities ($3,473 in 2002) gives an average farm household income of only $10,250 per year, which is far below the poverty line for a family of four. Therefore, off-farm income is a necessity for most farmers. Is this an indicator of poverty?

Apparently not. Farmers are doing better than the rest of us, on average. The average off-farm earnings of farm households in 2002 was $62,284, with lifestyle farms averaging much more than that and large farms averaging much less (USDA 2007). Combined with the $3,477 average earnings from farming activities, that gives a total income of $65,761, which was 13.7 percent higher than the U.S. average household income of $57,852 for that year. This means farm households may be building wealth faster than other American households, on average.

So, who wants to argue that the agricultural "way of life" needs government subsidies?

THE BUSINESS OF AN AGRICULTURAL "WAY OF LIFE"

Agriculture is a way of life to rural residents, but it is a business to all its investors, including absentee owners. Large-scale farms clearly act like profit-maximizing businesses. On the other hand, most smaller farms are lifestyle farms that provide owners with deductions to write off against their taxable earnings from off-farm sources while gaining wealth in the form of capital gains.[1] In other words, all farmers are pursuing both lifestyle and business goals. This can be more easily understood if we describe farm and ranch owner-operators as investors and wealth builders, just like all businesspeople.

A business that builds wealth primarily from capital gains is an investment firm. In many cases, a farm is a passive investment that does not interfere with the owner's ability to work off-farm. The census shows that 54.8 percent of all farmers reported working off-farm at some time during 2002, with the share being higher for small farms and lower for large farms, as expected. Even more telling is that 39.1 percent of farmers reported working off-farm 200 days or more during the year. That is virtually full-time employment! No wonder farmers earned more money per household *off-farm* during 2002 than the average American household earned in total. This indicates that farm owners are a talented group and are valued, on average, more highly than average Americans by the labor market. (Figure 19.2 shows that farm spouses often hold administrative or professional jobs off-farm.) Therefore, the business savvy of farmers should no longer be underestimated.

Many farmers are smart investors who have taken "moving to the suburbs" one step further and found wealth. The direction of causality in the migration from cities to small farms is unclear. Do the rising rural real estate values cause the migration, or does the migration raise farm real estate values? Or are both explanations working in a circular fashion?

Clearly, the answers vary across the country. For example, the regional results in Table 19.2 show that farms in the Northeast and Lake States derived a majority of their returns from capital gains, which outperformed returns from agricultural production as an investment over the long run. The reverse was true in the Delta region. Thus, the relative portions of "farms" in a region that might be called "investment firms" will differ across locations.

WHAT IS A "FARM"?

The discussion to this point has raised questions about whether all operations currently defined as "farms" by the American government truly deserve that label and the government support that comes with it. This chapter offers the proposition that many owner-operators are real estate investors using off-farm income to help them stay on the farm until they choose to capture their

Figure 19.2   **What Types of Jobs Are Held by Farm Household Members?**

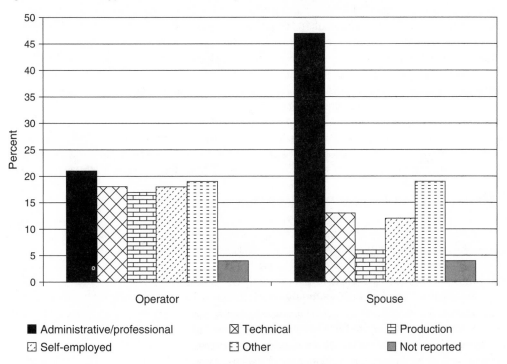

capital gains. If this description fits an operation, it can be argued that the household is more accurately portrayed as an investment firm, even if its members are enjoying an agricultural way of life. For those firms, the business motivating their rural way of life has little to do with real production agriculture.

"Real" farms and ranches make a real effort to support their household on earnings from agricultural activities. This means making household labor allocations with the primary objective of producing agricultural output, rather than viewing agriculture as the residual market for excess labor in the household. When more household labor is allocated off the farm than is allocated to agricultural activities, the operation is primarily a real estate investment firm, not a farm.

However, care must be taken when trying to distinguish between real farms and investment firms. Sometimes farmers act very much like investors in their business decisions, but they have very different motives. For example, it has often been observed that farmers reinvest most farm income into their operations. This raises the question, do farmers reinvest out of economic necessity, or are they making investments in expanding their farms to increase their long-run wealth derived from increased capital gains? It might appear that any investment made with capital gains in mind indicates that the person is not a real farmer. However, farm real estate investments play a very important role in the life of real farmers: providing current farmers with a "retirement nest egg." With no other source of income, most real farmers need to capture their farmland capital gains to be able to retire from the business that has been their life.

This became clear to city council members in Fresno, California, in 1990. Fresno, in the middle of the nation's most productive agricultural county, released a plan for its expected growth over the period of 1990 through 2015. When agricultural supporters noticed that the city, with a 1990 population of about 400,000, was expecting to become a metropolis of about a million people spread out over an additional 16,000 acres of prime farmland by 2015, they protested the loss of that valuable land resource. That raised a ruckus. One of the solutions suggested to avoid the loss of the farmland was to zone it for agricultural use only. That idea immediately caused the local farmers to protest. They did not want a zoning policy to prevent them from being able to sell their land near the growing town at its highest value—for urban development—because they needed to cash in the capital gains on their land to be able to retire.

Ultimately, differences in the nature of investments made in a farm will indicate whether the household is operating like a real farm or an investment firm. A farmer makes investments that raise the value of the operation as a "working farm." An investment firm makes investments that raise the real estate value of the operation. Some investments can raise both values.

POLICY QUESTIONS AND IMPLICATIONS

The results of this simple assessment of farmer objectives raise (at least) two policy questions. First, should agricultural producers be subsidized? Second, should government policy continue to facilitate "fragmentation" of agricultural land?

Farm policy has always claimed to have the goal of supporting agriculture because it is an important part of the American economy (Bonnen and Schweikhardt 1998). However, if agriculture is a "lifestyle" choice, it becomes impossible to justify government support. At present, about two-thirds of farms are "residential" in scale, lose money on average, and adversely affect commercial farmers by bidding up input prices and adding to total product supply, thus putting downward pressure on commodity prices. It does not make good business sense for the country to have taxpayers subsidize these activities any more than other hobbies. Yet current subsidies include income tax breaks, as well as direct government payments totaling billions of dollars each year (Table 19.1). The fact that most of that money goes to large farms adds fuel to the argument that much of agriculture is no longer economically viable.

According to the current logic in farm policy, Steve should be able to deduct the costs of pursuing his golfing hobby from his taxable income. Participating in hobby farms and hobby golf are both voluntary decisions made by individuals, knowing that their economic outcome will be a negative cash flow. However, the only way Steve can deduct his hobby is to call it a "business expense," as do corporate golfers when they entertain clients.

The lifestyle-driven reverse migration from cities to rural areas creates demand for small parcels, thus spurring farmland fragmentation. Fragmentation occurs when larger parcels are broken into smaller parcels. In the aggregate, this trend creates problems for the agriculture sector. As noted above, large commercial farms are more often profitable. This implies that agricultural income could be raised by consolidating small farms into large farms—the reverse of fragmentation. However, it is medium-sized farms that are more often consolidated into larger farms. Small-farm owners resist this resource reallocation by subsidizing their farms with off-farm income. Current policy facilitates fragmentation by being lifestyle-friendly. In essence, the subsidized lifestyle choices of rural residence farmers are helping to reduce the viability of commercial farms by breaking land into smaller parcels, making it more difficult for commercial farmers to find and afford farmland on which they can achieve production economies of scale.

Finally, another (of many) policy dilemma emerges: small farms fragment agricultural land, but are entry-level operations for many aspiring young farmers (Gale 1994) who may represent the future of American agriculture. Thus, size alone is not a sufficient base for policy decisions.

Many small-scale farmers have profit maximization as their objective and, therefore, may deserve assistance through policy efforts. However, "lifestyle" operations are no better investments for America than are any other hobbies.

Policies aimed at protecting an agricultural "way of life" are outdated and badly in need of replacement by programs that are based on an understanding of the true business objectives of those living in rural America. The country needs a modern definition of what constitutes a "farm" and an agricultural policy with differential treatment of farms across scale ranges with regard to policy benefits. Also, care must be taken in land-use policies so as not to hurt those people who have served the country as agricultural producers.

At present, at least 53 percent of farms lose money each year, on average, and focus much of their attention and household labor off-farm. This raises the question of whether those operations should be considered "farms" and receive agricultural policy benefits. It does not make sense to have taxpayers subsidize these real estate investors. Yet current subsidies include income tax breaks and direct government payments to farm owners totaling billions of dollars each year. The fact that a lot of money goes to large farms and/or absentee owners adds fuel to the argument that much of agricultural policy is no longer accomplishing its original goals of providing an economic "safety net" for those people producing our country's food supply.

Land-use policy now holds the future of American agriculture. The lifestyle-driven reverse migration from cities to rural areas has several economic impacts on American agriculture. It creates demand for agricultural parcels that can be developed, thus it increases the price of farmland in at least two ways (Drozd and Johnson 2004). First, farmland with potential for development serves two markets (rural and urban) and is valued at its "highest and best use," which is the urban value. Second, each time land leaves agriculture there is a new delineation of the urban fringe, causing an outward ripple in land prices reflecting the new pattern of development potential. This can raise the value of current farmers' retirement "nest egg," but can make it more difficult for new farmers to enter the profession. On the other hand, if land-use policy tries to keep land in agriculture through zoning, for example, it can hurt real farmers. Without the freedom to capture the development value of their farmland, many farmers will lose most of their expected retirement funds.

Thus, policymakers need to understand the composition of real farmers' wealth and the effects of any proposed legislation before undertaking a much-needed overhaul of agricultural programs. The country would be better served by investments in "real" farms rather than "lifestyle" operations housing real estate investment firms in rural locations.

The first questions that need to be faced during any agricultural policy overhaul include: Is agriculture a lifestyle worth preserving? At what cost? The country needs to make up its collective mind. Agriculture is a huge investment for the United States, and the industry's financial performance needs to be evaluated as the country decides agriculture's future role in America's portfolio.

NOTES

Some of the material in this chapter is an updated version of an article published by Steve Blank as "Is Agriculture a 'Way of Life' or a Business?" *Choices* 17, no. 3 (Summer 2002): 26–30. It won the American Agricultural Economics Association Award for Outstanding Article in *Choices* in 2003. Other material here is an updated version of an article published by Steve Blank as "The Business of an Agricultural 'Way of Life,'" *Choices* 20, no. 2 (2005): 161–166.

1. This helps farm owners in at least two ways. Capital gains are taxed at lower rates than is regular income. Thus, when one's lifestyle is called a(n unprofitable) business, taxable income can be reduced immediately and transformed into capital gains that are taxed less at a later date.

REFERENCES

Blank, Steven C. 2001. "The Challenge to Think Big as American Agriculture Shrinks." *Journal of Agricultural and Resource Economics* 26 (2): 309–325.

Blank, S., K. Erickson, C. Moss, and R. Nehring. 2004. "Agricultural Profits and Farm Household Wealth." *American Journal of Agricultural Economics* 86 (5): 1299–1307.

Bonnen, J., and D. Schweikhardt. 1998. "The Future of U.S. Agricultural Policy: Reflections on the Disappearance of the 'Farm Problem.' " *Review of Agricultural Economics* 20: 2–36.

Brewster, J. 1961. "Society Values and Goals in Respect to Agriculture." In *Goals and Values in Agricultural Policy,* pp. 114–137. Ames: Iowa State University Press.

Cochrane, W.W. 1993. *The Development of American Agriculture: A Historical Analysis.* 2d ed. Minneapolis: University of Minnesota Press.

Deller, S., T. Tsai, D. Marcouiller, and D. English. 2001. "The Role of Amenities and Quality of Life in Rural Economic Growth." *American Journal of Agricultural Economics* 83: 352–365.

Drozd, D., and B. Johnson. 2004. "Dynamics of a Rural Land Market Experiencing Farmland Conversion to Acreages: The Case of Saunders County, Nebraska." *Land Economics* 80 (2): 294–311.

Gale, H.F., Jr., 1994. "Longitudinal Analysis of Farm Size over the Farmer's Life Cycle." *Review of Agricultural Economics* 16: 113–123.

Goetz, S., and D. Debertin. 1996. "Rural Population Decline in the 1980s: Impacts of Farm Structure and Federal Farm Programs." *American Journal of Agricultural Economics* 78: 517–529.

———. 2001. "Why Farmers Quit: A County-Level Analysis." *American Journal of Agricultural Economics* 83: 1010–1023.

Ikerd, John. 2000. "The New American Farm." *Proceedings of the Oregon Horticultural Society,* vol. 91: January, pp. 90–100.

Martin, W., and G. Jefferies. 1966. "Relating Ranch Prices and Grazing Permit Values to Ranch Productivity." *Journal of Farm Economics* 48: 223–240.

Mishra, A., H. El-Osta, M. Morehart, J. Johnson, and J. Hopkins. 2002. *Income, Wealth, and the Economic Well-Being of Farm Households.* USDA Economic Research Service, Agricultural Economic Report no. 812, July.

Mishra, A., and C. Sandretto. 2002. "Stability of Farm Income and the Role of Nonfarm Income in U.S. Agriculture." *Review of Agricultural Economics* 24 (1): 208–221.

Mundlak, Y. 2000. *Agriculture and Economic Growth: Theory and Measurement.* Cambridge, MA: Harvard University Press.

Plantinga, A., R. Lubowski, and R. Stavins. 2002. "The Effects of Potential Land Development on Agricultural Land Prices." FEEM Working Paper no. 41.2002; KSG Working Paper no. RWP02–012, June. http://ssrn.com/abstract=305498.

U.S. Department of Agriculture. 2000. "Accumulated Farm Real Estate Value Will Help Farmers and Their Lenders Through Period of Declining Cash Receipts." *Agricultural Income and Finance: Situation and Outlook,* pp. 30–33. Economic Research Service AIS-74, February.

———. 2004. *2002 Census of Agriculture,* Volume 1, Geographic Area Series Part 51, AC-02-A-51, National Agricultural Statistical Service, June.

———. 2007. "Farm Income and Costs: Farm Sector Income." Economic Research Service "Briefing Room," on the web at http://www.ers.usda.gov/Briefing/FarmIncome/nationalestimates.htm, July 2007.

CHAPTER 20

THE ROLE OF AMERICAN AGRICULTURAL POLICY

"There is nothing more difficult to take in hand, more perilous to conduct or more uncertain in its success than to take the lead in the introduction of a new order of things."
—Machiavelli

The following was found on the Web page of an agricultural policy expert: "Never try to teach a pig to sing. It wastes your time and annoys the pig." Words to live by.

What does it mean? Is it some type of code for solving one of the great mysteries of our time? Possibly. Does the pig represent agriculture? And what about the singing—is it code for new skills or approaches? Possibly. Or is it all simply an empirical result from some misguided research? Possibly.

Agricultural policy is full of mysteries. One of the biggest mysteries centers on the question, "what has been the contribution of agricultural policy to the evolution of American agriculture?" Gardner (2000, p. 1073) found "no evidence that agricultural policies contributed to the growth of farm household incomes or the reduction of farm poverty." Wow, after over seventy years of government intervention in American agriculture you would think the industry might have benefited a bit. Maybe it has been government trying to teach a pig to sing, rather than considering what it could do to help people. Gardner's results show that people in agriculture, on average, have not benefited from agricultural policies, so the questions remain, "who has benefited from past policies, and why did the government choose to help them?" A logical follow-up question is, "where is government policy trying to take American agriculture?"

These and other questions are addressed briefly in this chapter as the story of American agriculture's evolution is summed up so as to indicate where it all leads in the future. The answers to the many questions involved are influenced both by what the people in American agriculture *want* to do and what the economics of the situation *enables* them to do. Also, there is more than one group in the agricultural sector, so agreement on the desired direction of agriculture is not likely. This is especially true when the economic rewards to one group are inversely related to the rewards of a second group, as is the case with the farm and ranch production group versus the agribusiness group. That dispute is often settled in favor of one group or the other when government wades into the battle. Thus, government policy plays a role that often shifts the economic balance in the battle over the direction of future efforts. However, government's role is confounded by the fact that it represents not just agriculture, but also consumers. Thus, policy is a wild card in the game of trying to assess the evolution of American agriculture and its contribution to global economic development.

WHICH FARMS RECEIVE GOVERNMENT PAYMENTS?

Government policies have many effects on agriculture, but some of the most direct come from payments to agricultural producers. Government payments to agriculture are transfers of taxpayers' money to some people involved in agricultural operations of some sort. This implies that the government believes the recipients of those transfers are doing something that benefits taxpayers in general. Thus, simple answers to the questions "who has benefited from past policies, and why did the government choose to help them?" come from an investigation of who has received government payments in the past and what it is that they provide that might justify the transfer of tax dollars. Therefore, this section offers a summary description of which farms received government payments during 2005. The source of the data is the Economic Research Service (ERS) of the U.S. Department of Agriculture and their report found on the Web (USDA/ERS 2007).[1]

To begin, some context is provided by indicating the total amount and types of government payments made to agriculture in 2005 compared to other recent years. Figure 20.1 provides this data for a decade. Two things are apparent in a quick scan of the figure. First, the total amount of payments varies over time. Second, the types of programs for which payments were made were fairly stable during the period. In general, there have been programs making fixed payments, payments based on commodity prices, payments for conservation programs, and a collection of miscellaneous payments. Payment totals for each of the four categories of programs were fairly normal in 2005 except that payments as a function of commodity prices were higher than normal. As a result, the total of payments for the year exceeded $24 billion.

That is a lot of money! In fact, $24 billion in government payments to agriculture represented over 10 percent of all cash receipts from American crop and livestock sales for the entire year of 2005. With that amount of taxpayer money to spread around, you would think that everyone in the production sector of American agriculture benefited. Not so.

According to the 2005 Agricultural Resource Management Survey, 42.7 percent of all farms received government payments in 2005. For farms that received a payment, the average payment per farm was $17,944. This payment represents, on average, 11.2 percent of a farm's gross cash income or 39.4 percent of its net cash income. About 34.7 percent of all farms received payments less than $25,000 in 2005, while 0.2 percent received payments of $150,000 or more. So, only some farmers are benefiting from government transfers, but the benefit is significant. Who are these farmers? The ERS report provides descriptive data by farm type, farm size, commodity specialization, and location. The report also provides comparisons between farms receiving payments and farms that did not receive payments during the year. In general, those comparisons show that the distribution of government payments is not random, implying that agricultural policy is playing favorites. For example, the gross cash income of farms receiving government payments averaged $160,774 in 2005, more than twice that of farms not receiving government payments. From this descriptive data emerge clues as to who it is that American agricultural policy favors in the race for survival. In turn, these clues indicate the direction in which government apparently wants the agricultural sector to evolve. Who have been the favored few?

The survey data grouped farm types using two different methods. The first method categorized farms based on the reported occupation of the primary operator, and the second method grouped farms by typology.

Only three occupation categories were used to group farms: "farming/ranching" (36.8 percent of total farms fell into this category), "something else" (42.7 percent of total), and "retired" (20.5 percent). Fifty-nine percent of farms receiving a government payment reported the primary operator's occupation as ranching/farming, and they received 81.6 percent of total payments. It is

435

Figure 20.1 **Government Payments, 1997–2007**

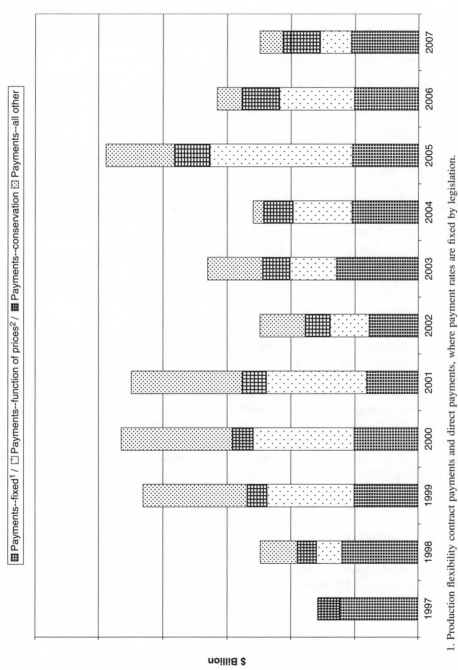

1. Production flexibility contract payments and direct payments, where payment rates are fixed by legislation.
2. Counter-cyclical payments, loan deficiency payments, marketing loan gains, and certificates exchange gains; where payment rates vary with market prices.
Source: The data for this figure are from the Economic Research Service web site.

Table 20.1

Distribution of Government Payments Among American Farms, 2005

Farm typology:	Percent of all farms* %	Percent of payment farms** %	Share of total payments %	Share of farms in category receiving payment %	Payments as % of net cash income on payment farms %	Average payment per payment farm $	Average payment per harvested acre on payment farms $
Limited-resources	11.6	9.5	2.4	35.0	565.1	4,569	128
Retirement	14.6	12.7	4.0	37.1	36.9	5,658	231
Residential/lifestyle	39.6	28.4	9.6	30.6	214.7	6,048	110
Farming occupation, lower-sales	17.9	20.5	8.1	48.8	58.1	7,117	74
Farming occupation, higher-sales	6.5	12.3	16.4	80.5	51.3	23,775	57
Large	4.0	7.9	20.9	83.7	41.0	47,640	57
Very large	3.3	5.6	31.4	72.2	25.5	100,122	66
Nonfamily	2.4	3.0	7.3	54.5	39.2	42,942	72
Total	100.0	100.0	100.0				

   *   ased on a total of 2 0   2 farms in the United States for 200 .
   ** ased on a total of   3 farms receiving payments in 200 .
   Source: USDA   S (200).

good to see that farmers and ranchers received most of the government payment dollars, but startling to realize that retired people were recipients of money aimed at the agricultural sector. Farms in the "retired" and "something else" categories benefited most from conservation payments. For the 35 percent of retirement farms that received payments in 2005, 22 percent of the farms' gross cash income came from payments. For the 20.3 percent of retirement farms that received conservation program payments, such payments accounted for 34.8 percent of their gross cash income. The average gross cash income of retirement farms that did not receive government payments was half that of retirement farms that did receive payments. So, some farmers can retire themselves and their land and still receive significant government payments. Sounds like a good deal for the lucky farm owners that get it, but it is difficult to see how consumers benefit from such a program.

The ERS uses a typology method with eight categories of farms, as shown in Table 20.1. The largest group receiving government payments was "residential/lifestyle" farms, which represented 28.4 percent of payment farms, and received 9.6 percent of total payments. "Very large" family farms accounted for 5.6 percent of farms that received payments, and they received 31.4 percent of total payments, by far the largest share of the money. For "retirement" farms, more than 56 percent of government payments were conservation payments. Limited-resources, retirement, and residential lifestyle farms (collectively called "rural residence farms" by the ERS) received larger payments from conservation programs than from the other programs. About 51 percent of the farms receiving government payments in 2005 were classified as rural residence farms. They received 16.0 percent of total government payments and 50.8 percent of conservation program payments. Again it appears that being small means being "green" for cash. The incentive to be green is clear when realizing that limited-resources and residential/lifestyle farms lost money, on average, in their farming operations (hence the large percentage of net cash income represented by government payments, shown in Table 20.1).

Thus far in reviewing the ERS data it appears that being a large-scale farm or ranch operation is not a deterrent to getting a government payment, which seems counterintuitive. It is normally expected that efforts to reduce poverty in agriculture would be directed toward smaller operations that are struggling to get established. However, as Gardner (2000) pointed out, American agricultural policy has not reduced rural poverty, hence some other goal must be driving government payment programs. As the ERS data show, many large-scale operations are pulling in big piles of taxpayer dollars. For example, 84.3 percent of the largest farm category (the 4 percent of operations with 2,000 acres or more) received government payments in 2005, while only 22.6 percent of the smallest category (the 51.3 percent of operations with less than 100 acres) received payments and more than 53 percent of their payments were from conservation programs. Since much of government payments are tied to either program acreage or program production, the magnitude of the payments is directly correlated to the number of acres operated. Hence, farms in the largest farm category received 31.9 percent of all payments.

Other measures of farm size confirm the hypothesis that being large increases your chances of receiving government payments. By value of annual sales, 63 percent of farms in the largest size category (those with $1,000,000 or more in annual sales) received government payments in 2005, compared to only 24.7 percent of farms in the smallest category (those with less than $10,000 in annual sales). By net cash farm income, the largest government payments were realized in the largest size category ($100,000 or more), and 76.8 percent of the farms in this category received payments. By operator household income, only 6.3 percent of farms fell into the largest size category ($200,000 or more), yet the largest average government payment was realized by this category, where 6.5 percent of payment farms received 24.0 percent of all government payments.

Wow, who are these large-scale operators that the government loves so much? A final look at the ERS data indicates a clear answer when using two different descriptors.

The first descriptive variable that points a finger straight at the big winners in the government's cash give-away is a farm's commodity specialization. The specialization is determined by the one commodity or group of commodities that makes up at least 50 percent of the farm's total value of production. The winners are clear. A higher share (all above 90 percent) of wheat, rice, corn, "other cash grain," soybean, and cotton farms received payments than other types of farms. These farms, which represented 23.6 percent of farms receiving payments, received 47.1 percent of total payments in 2005. The biggest group of winners is farms specializing in corn (9.7 percent of payment farms), which received 24 percent of all government payments in 2005. The average payment received by corn farms represented 17 percent of their gross cash income. Farms specializing in cotton received $90,886, on average, in 2005, by far the highest average payment of any farm type. Yet, this average payment represented only 16 percent of their gross cash income. The next highest payment was to rice farms, which received $74,041 on average. Together, cotton and rice farms represented 1.8 percent of the total payment farms and received 8.7 percent of all payments. One-third of wheat payment farms received disaster and emergency assistance payments in 2005. The $13,599 in average payments represented 39.2 percent of total government payments to those farms. However, the largest average disaster and emergency assistance payments ($51,415) were received by high-value crop farms. This payment represented 88.8 percent of the total payments received by the high-value crop type farms that received them. Only 13.4 percent of high-value crop farms received government payments in 2005, although more specialty crop producers are seeking government subsidies (Barrionuevo 2006).

The second descriptive variable is the location of farm and ranch operations receiving government payments. The commodities named above are produced primarily in certain parts of the country due to the comparative advantages of those places. In other words, large parts of the contiguous forty-eight states have agricultural commodity specializations. The USDA has identified nine "farm resource regions" based on the commodity specializations that are dictated by the natural resources in each location. It should not come as a shock to learn that most of the commodities receiving the bulk of government payments are grown in the American Midwest, made up mostly of three farm resource regions.[2] The Heartland region has the largest share of family farms. With 70.8 percent of these farms receiving payments, the Heartland also has the largest share of payment farms. These farms represent 33.2 percent of all farms receiving payments, and they received 39.8 percent of all payments in 2005. Also, 33 percent of farms in the Heartland received conservation program payments. In the Northern Great Plains, 43.1 percent of farms received conservation program payments. For those farms, conservation program payments contributed 42.5 percent of average government payments.

In sum, a large amount of taxpayer money is being given by the American government to owners of farms and ranches located in parts of the country that have natural resources poorly suited to producing much other than field crops that are in direct competition with foreign producers in the global markets for those commodities. A disproportionate share of the government payments are made to large-scale operations that have relatively high sales and income totals, thus the policy goal is clearly not to reduce poverty in the regions. The commodities receiving the biggest share of payments are all in global surplus, hence the policy goal cannot be to simply improve food security or diversity. Therefore, the question remains: now that we know who received government payments in the past, what is it that those farms provide that might justify the transfers of tax dollars?

A specific answer to that question is still a mystery, but some reasonable guesses can be derived from the general effects that U.S. agricultural policy has had over its three-quarters of a century lifespan. It is reasonable to guess that the aim of policymakers is to achieve some goal. Therefore, the process of trying to answer the question of what justified government transfers over the decades comes down to trying to assess what was accomplished, thus inferring what goals were being targeted by policymakers over time. With this framework in mind, two general goals are proposed here as possible explanations for the existence of agricultural policy.

To begin, the most likely original, long-term goal of agricultural policy was to stimulate a weak regional economy until it developed alternative sources of employment. This is an easy guess when considering that government intervention in agriculture essentially began during the Great Depression of the 1930s. With the economy of the entire Midwest depending upon agriculture at that time, and that industry being ravaged by the Dust Bowl weather patterns that were adding to the havoc of weak markets that were bankrupting many farmers and forcing them to move to California and other places in search of employment, it is easy to see why a national policy would be created to assist one industry. The truth is, it was not a national policy originally, but simply an economic development effort aimed at the nation's midsection. Government payments were made to midwestern farm owners to help them stay in business and to continue generating jobs for other people in the area directly and indirectly through the multiplier effects of those payments as the dollars rippled through the local and regional economy. That was the major contribution being made at that time by people in agriculture and, as such, was the primary justification for government payments to the agricultural sector.

It is proposed here that an attempt to make agricultural policy national in its scope came with the adoption of a relatively short-term secondary goal: to increase food supplies, thus lowering food costs. That goal could be used by government to justify to residents in other parts of the country why their tax dollars were being sent to farm owners in the Midwest. The story was reasonable during the 1930s and 1940s. After World War II, however, agriculture and the nation's economic fortunes changed. Agricultural production expanded and diversified in places like the West Coast and Southwest. It also developed what the USDA calls a "fruitful rim" of places growing high-value crops that greatly increased the profit potential of producers of those crops.

Today, both of the historical goals proposed here are essentially fulfilled, hence there is no longer a justification for further large-scale government interventions in American agriculture. Food supplies are in surplus and food costs in America are the lowest in the world compared to average incomes. The nation's economic development has expanded to the point where only 36.8 percent of farms surveyed by the USDA in 2005 reported "farming/ranching" as their primary occupation. In the Midwest the situation has changed to the point that it can now be argued that government payments to farm owners are serving as a *deterrent* to further economic development. Those payments are enabling many people to stay in agricultural production despite both their relative inefficiencies (indicated by high costs per unit of commodity output) and the market's signal that they are not needed. In other words, many people in agriculture (and especially in the Midwest) are now providing nothing but quantities of commodities that are in surplus, thus not needed, and that add to the downward pressure on market prices that harms all producers. Ironically, the country would probably be better off if people quit trying to stay in midwestern agriculture and reinvested their resources in some other industry—the opposite of the situation that existed in the 1930s. In the words of one farmer, "if the government would quit subsidizing bad farmers, life would be much better for good farmers." Also, if those "rural residence" farm owners would devote their productive efforts to something outside of agriculture (instead of investing their resources in something they are not very good at: agriculture), economic development of the region could expand. And, of course, if the transfers of taxpayer dollars to farmers were ended, the country could invest that money in more profitable industries.

WHERE IS AGRICULTURAL POLICY GOING?

The nature of American agriculture has changed such that new policies are needed along with a new focus that reflects the current realities facing the nation and, in the Midwest in particular, a new approach to investing our resources so as to promote continued economic development. Agriculture is now a very small part of the national economy and, as shown earlier in this book, it is a small part of state economies as well. As other sectors of the economy have grown, agriculture's relative impact has shrunk. However, the sparsely populated, land-expansive nature of agriculture in the Midwest has created several unique problems as the evolution of agriculture has played out there. As Monchuk et al. (2007, p. 17) note,

> the relative contribution of agriculture to the U.S. Midwest economy continues its century-long decline. The continuing development of ever-larger machinery, new biotech crops, and other labor-saving technologies has greatly decreased the need for people in rural areas that have traditionally depended on agriculture. The last century has brought significant changes to the U.S. Midwest. Many rural counties have come to grips with the reality that, given the current situation and the outlook for primary agricultural production, the future is not very attractive from a long-term growth perspective.

One result has been what Huang, Orazem, and Wohlgemuth (2002) called a "brain drain" from rural to urban areas. They said the pursuit of higher incomes, especially by young people, was the primary explanation for the exodus from the rural Midwest and from agricultural production. Unfortunately, these structural changes have significant implications for where "agricultural" policy needs to go. For example, one of Monchuk et al.'s conclusions is that

> the changing structure of the agricultural industry coupled with slow or no growth in nonfarm activities in many rural Midwest counties is responsible, at least in part, for the aging population. Counties with an older population experience slower or negative economic growth. This finding may create even greater challenges for rural counties as their tax bases erode further and their services continue declining unless state transfers maintain services which will place more burden on that state treasury, force state tax increases and further deter growth in counties. (2007, p. 37)

In other words, agricultural policy needs to become even more focused on economic development issues than it was during its formative years in the Depression era.

But let's not get ahead of the story. To understand where American agricultural policy is going, it is necessary to examine the many issues that current policy is trying to address. Those issues represent the government's current justification for intervention in agricultural markets.

To some extent, American agricultural policy gets its general focus from the issues facing agriculture around the world and, as would be expected, over time those issues change. For example, Pinstrup-Andersen (2002, p. 1201) summarized the current situation by saying "global food supplies per person are greater today than ever before. In fact, current global food supplies are sufficient to meet calorie requirements of all people, if the food were distributed according to needs." Thus, agricultural producers are doing a good job. He continued,

> per capita food supplies are projected to increase further over the next twenty years . . . thus, the world food problem now and in the foreseeable future is not one of global shortages. Instead, the world is currently faced with two main food-related challenges: widespread hunger and malnutrition and associated reduced but still significant population growth, and mismanagement of natural resources in food production. (2002, p. 1201)

This implies that policies ought to focus on (1) economic development to improve incomes so people can benefit from the plentiful food available, and (2) agricultural production methods that are both efficient and sustainable. Pinstrup-Andersen then discussed several key trends that influence policy, including increasing globalization:

> Current trends toward increasing globalization, including international trade liberalization, more integrated international capital markets, and a freer flow of labor, information, and technology are likely to continue. Globalization has benefited hundreds of millions of people but many others have been made worse off. . . . Effective food and agricultural policy and institutions are needed to complement and guide globalization to achieve sustainable economic growth, improved equity, and reduced poverty and hunger. (2002, p. 1203)

Therefore, trends pushing us toward global-scale production and marketing systems are creating increasing needs for global-scale policies. Pinstrup-Andersen concluded that the role of the public sector appears to be shrinking in many aspects of food security, while civil society and the private sector have taken on increasing importance. While such a shift may be appropriate, recent research and experience clearly show the importance of an effective public sector in many areas related to food security such as agricultural research to develop appropriate technology for small farmers, rural infrastructure, health care, education, development and enforcement of a legal system, and the creation of public goods in general. (2002, p. 1211)

So, globalizing commodity markets are making structural change necessary in American agriculture and in the policy guiding it. However, as Bonnen and Schweikhardt (1998) pointed out, structural changes in American agriculture raise questions about the nature and methods of policy interventions in the American agricultural sector. They accurately predicted in 1998 that the 1996 FAIR Act's shift in focus to "free market" mechanisms in agriculture would not last past 2002, when the Act expired. They noted that farm groups enjoy receiving government protection in some form, even though the industrial transformation of American agriculture raises questions about the justification for such protection. They pointed out that the "farm problem" has existed since the Civil War, and that it has been known since the early 1900s that

over the transformation from a low income, developing status to a developed, industrial economy, the rapid rise in farm productivity inevitably causes a nation to experience a secular decline in farm prices leading to great downward pressure on farm income. This decline in farm income creates political pressures to slow the process of structural change, or at least minimize its effects on farm welfare. (Bonnen and Schweikhardt 1998, p. 7)

They offer the following explanation:

In a high-income, developed nation, the farm sector is said to exhibit several endemic problems during its industrial transformation. These include:

1. instability of farm level prices and income,
2. low returns to factors of production over significant periods due to failure (inability?) to adjust productive capacity to demand,
3. growing vulnerability of the farm sector to macroeconomic events as the sector develops and becomes more integrated with the money (commercial) economy,
4. increasing vulnerability to international market events due to growing dependence on global markets and international trade,
5. the development (and recognition) of farm sector externalities such as environmental pollution, problems of water, soil and other resource conservation, and the sustainability of the resource base. (1998, p. 9)

They then proceed to show that each of those conditions is observed in American agriculture because the conditions are the predictable consequences of industrial maturity. Also, Bonnen and Schweikhardt (1998) conclude that many of those problems are not unique to agriculture, but are observed in other sectors of the economy as well. This means American agriculture's structure must continue to adjust, even though the necessary downsizing is painful to the individuals who are directly affected, and the only real justifications for government intervention in agriculture at this point are noneconomic issues.

There are no economic justifications?!? If there were, Gardner (2000) would not have reached his conclusions about the lack of policy impacts on farm household incomes or poverty levels. But what about the "safety net" that the government is supposedly holding below agriculture to prevent its fall into the economic abyss? A USDA report evaluated the "safety net" created by government policies and found that "the current set of farm safety net programs generally benefits farmers producing selected commodities, and the primary beneficiaries are larger farms" (Gundersen et al. 2000, p. 20). The report noted that "the current farm safety net may have appeal as a commercial or industrial policy." In other words, policies appear to be intended to shape the structure of the American production agriculture sector, not necessarily help all individuals in that sector. Key and Roberts (2006) provide support for this hypothesis. Using farm-level panel data from recent U.S. Agricultural Censuses, they examined how direct government payments influence the survival of farm businesses, paying particular attention to the differential effect of payments across farm-size categories. A Cox proportional hazards model was used to estimate the effect of government payments on the instantaneous probability of a farm business failure, controlling for farm and operator characteristics. Their results indicate that an increase in government payments has a small but statistically significant negative effect on the rate of business failure, and the magnitude of this effect increases with farm size. This means "government payments increase business survival rates proportionally more for larger farms. This result is probably attributable to the fact that government payments' share of farm household income increases with total sales" (Key and Roberts 2006, p. 391). Put bluntly, American agricultural policy has favored big farms over smaller operations and, thus, has influenced the structure of the industry. This may indicate that policies are trying to push the industry into making the structural adjustments believed to be necessary for improved global competitiveness, but it does not indicate that the policies can, as a group, be called a safety net. Ahearn, Yee, and Korb (2005) provide additional support for this interpretation. They found that "commodity payments reduced the number share of small farms, increased the share of large farms, and increased farm exits during 1982–96. This is consistent with the traditional view that farmers use commodity payments to expand their farms" (p. 1189).

So, if there are no economic justifications, what are the current issues being used to justify government intervention in American agriculture? Some of the most visible are discussed briefly in the four sections that follow.

Food Security and International Trade Issues

The issues of food security and international trade concerns are really one combined issue. When people raise "food security" as an argument for maintaining America's production agriculture at its maximum capacity, they are effectively saying, "I don't trust those foreigners to sell us the food we want." One version of the food security issue is the "food as a weapon" argument, which implies that some other countries will intentionally try to harm the United States by withholding food products at some time in the future. To believe this argument someone would have to completely misunderstand the realities of global commodity markets. Put bluntly, a country that tried to boycott commodity sales to the United States would hurt itself more than it hurt America: food is not a single commodity produced only by a few nations; it is a collection of hundreds of commodities with something being produced by every country, thus if one country cut off commodity sales to us, we would just buy commodities from another country. We would still be eating while the country trying to hurt us would suffer a significant economic loss of sales to the world's biggest customer. Therefore, the "food as weapon" argument makes no sense. The more likely version of the food security issue to face the United States in the future is the case of temporary global supply shortages of some commodity due to climate, disease, or other natural production problems. Such a scenario would be most easily dealt with in a free-trade world that enabled commodities to be efficiently traded between any nations. However, the current situation is still full of international trade barriers and disputes of many sorts that hinder the flow of commodities. This means that American agricultural policies still have a role to play during the slow transition toward global free trade of commodities.

As Reardon and Barrett (2000) pointed out, the three trends of agroindustrialization, globalization, and international development are all ongoing and interrelated. This means that the differences between countries in their stages of economic development will cause differences in their progress toward industrialization of their agricultural sectors, which will cause differences in their abilities to trade competitively in global commodity markets. As a result, each country will use policy tools to maximize its own development progress within the constraints imposed by the need to trade with other countries for commodities not produced domestically.

This raises the question: Can U.S. agricultural policy alter the outcome of economic development (i.e., continued downsizing in the American production agriculture sector)? It could, but in the long run it will not, because we have painted ourselves into the free trade corner. America needs free trade access to other countries' markets for our high-value nonagricultural products, so we must allow free trade of cheap imported food. The international pressures to do so are growing. For example, during the meetings of the World Trade Organization (WTO) in September 2003 there were protests by less-developed countries against more-developed nations' reluctance to lower protections and subsidies on agricultural commodities. The resulting lack of progress in agricultural talks stalled global agreements on trade. That result was too costly for too many nations, so in December 2005 the WTO agreed to eliminate agricultural export subsidies by 2013.

American policymakers have no choice in the long run but to give up agriculture so as to gain benefits for other sectors of our economy. U.S. subsidies to agriculture create surpluses of some commodities that end up being exported, creating a welfare loss to the United States—an outcome American taxpayers increasingly question. Our subsidized commodity exports are effectively a subsidy to foreign consumers and they harm foreign producers. Do other countries subsidize their agriculture? Of course, but the reasons and methods differ widely between the more-developed and less-developed parts of the world. Overall, the stronger economic arguments are on the side of less-developed countries.

This brings the current focus of American agricultural policy to dealing with incremental steps toward free trade. The same is true for other more-developed countries and regions, such as Japan and Western Europe. Each of these economic powerhouses is trying to adjust its domestic farm policies in response to current international economic realities. For example, Burfisher, Robinson, and Thierfelder (2002) reach several conclusions in an analysis of agricultural policies in the United States, European Union (EU), and Japan, including that "domestic agricultural policies are, to some extent, a response to market conditions created by distorting policies of other countries" (p. 780). As a result,

> multilateralism leads to a "softer landing" than unilateralism. In all three countries, domestic agricultural production contracts with unilateral reform. The adjustment is smaller when all three countries reform multilaterally, reflecting that each country's domestic policies are partly a response to subsidies in other countries. . . . This suggests that undertaking domestic reform in a multilateral context can reduce both the inefficiencies in one's own economy, as well as the world market distortions that provide a credible rationale for those domestic subsidies. (Burfisher, Robinson, and Thierfelder 2002, p. 780)

This means that as more-developed nations modernize their agricultural policies by reducing subsidies to production agriculture, domestic output will decline, raising the likely amount of food imports, but the efficiency of those national economies will improve. This clearly shows the link between a nation's agricultural competitiveness in international markets and its domestic policies. Truly free trade forces uncompetitive producers out of the market, while most government interventions in agricultural markets serve to keep some of those producers in operation.

Environmental Issues

There is an emerging environmental agenda that deals with the economics of sustainable agriculture. Among other things, it is leading to more habitat protection and conservation efforts that could actually help farmers by (1) restricting supply, (2) inducing innovation at a faster rate, and (3) giving them compensation payments for habitat and land retirement. At this point it is not clear in which direction environmental issues will push American agriculture. Agricultural landowners are split into the pragmatists (who will take compensation for habitat retirement) and the privatists (who do not want federal money because it will have too many strings), especially in the rural interior West. However, the data presented earlier on who has been receiving government payments indicates that less-competitive operators are quite willing to go "green" for greenbacks. Hence, it is expected that more policy tools will be used to expand the range of environmental programs.

At present, however, many of the new environmental programs are being offset by the net effects of other government programs for agriculture. As an example, Goodwin and Smith (2003, p. 201) found that "while the Conservation Reserve Program has reduced erosion an average of 1.02 tons per acre from 1982 to 1992, approximately half of this reduction has been offset by increased erosion resulting from government programs other than federally subsidized crop insurance." Thus, policymakers have not yet decided whether they are really ready to give up on traditional production-oriented programs and focus entirely on environmental issues. Another example of this hesitancy to go fully green is provided by Mapemba et al. (2007), who note that the 2002 Farm Bill permitted managed harvesting of biomass from Conservation Reserve Program land.

Another factor slowing expansion of environmental policies in American agriculture is the potential effect they can have on domestic producer competitiveness. Environmental issues are becoming increasingly important to the dairy industry, for example, because most new regulations add to operator costs. Yet, as environmental agendas grow in international policy debates, the effects on American producers can be either good or bad. This is illustrated in the study by Metcalfe (2002). He concluded that new environmental regulations for animal manure management would have minimal effects on hog producers in the United States and Canada, but more stringent regulations in the European Union could significantly reduce the competitiveness of producers there, thus benefiting pork producers in North America.

The current policy winds are blowing toward increased environmental programs and regulations in American agriculture. The reason the winds are likely to blow harder is that urban Americans are becoming increasingly concerned about the environment and its effects on both their food and lifestyles. Agriculture's response to this policy movement is discussed in depth later in this chapter.

Land Use and Other Resource Issues

Some policies aimed at environmental and other issues are having significant effects on the uses of land, water, and other productive resources in American agriculture. Also, the value of some resources, especially farmland, is influenced by many types of agricultural policies. Some of these effects are intentional, others unintentional.

Farmland is the most often regulated resource in agriculture. An entire group of federal, state, and local policies influences how owners can use this essential resource. The Conservation Reserve Program is just one example of policies aimed at eliminating the use of specific land parcels in agricultural production. Local zoning laws accomplish the same result near towns and cities all over the country. Ironically, many states and counties have regulations aimed at keeping land *in* agricultural production. In California, for example, farmland owners get a tax break on land they contract to keep in agricultural use for at least a decade. Also, private efforts, such as land trusts, pay farm owners for the development rights on their land just to assure that it remains rural. There are many economic questions arising from land-use policies. Some of those questions to be faced by policymakers in the relatively near future include (1) are land restrictions a deadweight loss or a transfer of wealth from agriculture to recreation? and (2) are the costs of land-use restrictions an acceptable transfer from taxpayers to agriculture?

The prices of farmland are significantly affected by policies on issues ranging from agricultural trade and openness, subsidies and tax regimes, and environmental considerations, to the definition and enforcement of water and other property rights. Since farmland values in the United States account for nearly 70 percent of total agricultural assets, they represent a significant component of the agricultural balance sheet. Accordingly, they significantly affect financial ratios measuring solvency, liquidity, and profitability. In addition, the linkage between sector solvency and farmland values may increase the coupling of farm program payments to production. Finally, the valuation of farmland has a significant effect on the estimation of productivity and competitiveness across regions and states. How do farmland prices affect the competitiveness and sustainability of American agriculture? Changes in farmland values impact the calculation of index numbers used to estimate changes in productivity and competitiveness. Rising farmland values increase farm sector solvency and thus improve lenders' portfolios too. Ironically, if farmland was valued lower, the current level of farm profits would look like a better return on assets, but the lower value would wipe out much of landowners' wealth. The contribution to this problem by agricultural policies was noted by Shaik, Helmers, and Atwood (2005). They found that "the share of agricultural land values generated by farm program payments increased up to as much as 30% to 40% of land values during the 1938–1980 period" and has since "declined to levels between 15% and 20%." This explains why it is difficult to reduce or eliminate farm payments: policies positively influence farmland values and the wealth of owners, thus eliminating government transfers would reduce the wealth of farmers and weaken the local economy in regions dominated by the production of "program crops."

Water is probably second only to land in terms of the amount of policy attention it receives, especially in the arid western states. With the relatively recent advent of water markets and other federal, state, and local allocation tools, it is no surprise that water can now be bottled and sold at prices higher than those of some fruit juices. Nevertheless, Rosegrant and Cai (2002) concluded that concerted policy efforts can mitigate the negative effects on agriculture of local water shortages. That debate will be long and heated.

Labor is one resource that is often affected unintentionally by agricultural policies. For example, Serra, Goodwin, and Featherstone (2005) evaluated Kansas farmers regarding the effects of the 1996 policy changes on household decisions to work off-farm. They concluded that the policy effects were mixed: the fixed, decoupled payments reduced the likelihood of off-farm work, but the riskier environment created by the policy reforms may have increased household desire to participate in nonfarm employment. Conversely, Ahearn, El-Osta, and Dewbre (2006) found that government payments, whether coupled or decoupled, have a negative effect on off-farm labor participation. Clearly, labor is a resource that is difficult for policymakers to manage, as indicated by a study by Boucher et al. (2007) showing that NAFTA and the Immigration Reform and Control Act of 1986 both were associated with an increase in migration to U.S. farm jobs from rural Mexico, contrary to expectations.

Other resource issues, such as air quality, will continue to grow in importance, assuring policy debates in the future (see Key and Kaplan 2007 as an example). As rural and urban interests collide, the supply of, and agriculture's access to, necessary resources will decline. That makes the policy debates to come ever more important to the future of the American production agriculture sector.

Efficiency Issues

Many policy debates of the past have focused on issues of efficiency in the structure and operation of America's production sector. Those debates will continue.

Policy effects on the structure of America's production agriculture vary from the sublime to the ridiculous. An example of the latter is provided by Schroeter, Azzeddine, and Aiken (2006), who note that nine midwestern states have laws that restrict the involvement of publicly held corporations in agriculture. They studied Nebraska's law against corporate ownership of feedlots to assess its effect on the evolution of the state's feedlot size distribution. As might be expected, fear of the big, bad corporate boogeyman has led to a competitive disadvantage for the state's feedlot industry because preventing corporate participation means preventing feedlot owners from accessing an important source of capital needed to grow to competitive scales of operation. In the cattle-feeding business, being small means being at a big cost disadvantage.

Policy effects on the operation of America's production sector have been wide-ranging and, for the most part, can be categorized as attempts to micromanage the many industries in the sector while "the left hand does not know what the right hand is doing."

In general, recent policy debates have swirled around the questions of whether or not to eliminate government interventions from agricultural commodity markets and what the effects of that action would be. Much of the focus in that debate has been on the 1996 farm bill. It was an attempt to reduce government's role in American agriculture by reducing subsidies to producers. As Key, Lubowski, and Roberts (2005, p. 1211) note, "in theory, lump-sum transfers are a way to redistribute wealth without distorting production decisions." They explain,

> the 1996 Federal Agricultural Improvement and Reform (FAIR) Act removed most price-contingent agricultural subsidies and replaced them with Production Flexibility Contracts—lump-sum payments with few ties to farmers' production decisions. The payments were envisioned as a way to maintain income transfers to agricultural interests while minimizing production distortions.

Key, Lubwoski, and Roberts conclude (2005, p. 1218) that "participation in domestic agricultural programs, including the mostly decoupled 1997 payment regime, had significant farm-level production effects." Their results show that "participants increased plantings of program crops considerably (38–59 percentage points) more than nonparticipants" (p. 1218). In another study, Lence and Hayes (2002, p. 335) generated results which "suggest that FAIR did not lead to significant increases in long-run price volatility or revenue volatility. The main impact of pre-FAIR, relative to the free-market regime, was to substitute government storage for private storage in a way that did little to support prices or to stabilize farm incomes." And, finally, Lamb and Henderson (2000) evaluated some of FAIR's effects on land values and found that lower government subsidies to corn producers were likely to reduce farmland values in the Corn Belt, especially in marginal production areas. This might explain why, after all the work to begin weaning agriculture from government subsidies, the direction of the 1996 farm bill was reversed by the 2002 farm bill.

In addition to debates over policies covering many commodities, there are many debates over a policy's effects on individual commodities, plus debates over a single attribute of a policy. For example, Chau and de Gorter (2005, p. 1181) evaluated policies related to American wheat and found that "whereas removal of decoupled payments can have a relatively large impact on the exit decisions of low-profit farm units, its aggregate output impact can remain quite limited so long as the output level of the marginal farm is relatively small." Goodwin and Mishra (2006) also assessed the effects of decoupled program payments and found that participants were not likely to expand acreage. Does all this sound like government micromanagement? When policy analysts have to go all the way down to farm-level operational decision making to assess a policy's effects, the answer is "yes."

A little micromanagement might not be so bad if the government policies did not conflict with one another. Unfortunately, the "left hand" and the "right hand" often move in opposite directions. In the 1990s the problem was not too bad, but it has gotten much worse since then. For example, in the 1990s, Atwood, Watts, and Baquet (1996) found that government price support programs and crop insurance were substitutes in reducing producer risk. A decade later, Gray et al. (2004) concluded that demand for crop revenue insurance was reduced by the high levels of government subsidies to agriculture. Thus, different government efforts to reduce farmers' risks conflict with each other.

In sum, these four issue areas of policy debate (food security, environmental, resource use, and efficiency) have all combined to push the likely future direction of American agricultural policy toward the subject driving policy debates in Western Europe:—"multifunctionality." Some American agricultural groups are already beginning to embrace this theme, so it is sure to grow. Therefore, some attention to this subject is needed.

MULTIFUNCTIONALITY

"Multifunctionality" is the new theme in European agricultural policy efforts and, in a slightly different form, it is beginning to appear in American policy debates as well. In the simplest of terms, multifunctionality refers to the existence of multiple commodity and noncommodity outputs that are jointly produced by agriculture. Also, the fact that markets for some of these noncommodity outputs do not exist or function poorly creates externalities leading to "market failure," which justifies government intervention. The argument for intervention is based to a great extent on the point that most, if not all, of the noncommodity outputs of agriculture are public goods. Cahill (2001, p. 36) noted that "food security, food safety, animal welfare, cultural and historic heritage values, environmental quality, landscape, biodiversity and rural development are just some of the outputs claimed to belong to the multifunctionality of the agricultural sector." In other words, multifunctionality embodies issues from all four of the topic areas described above as currently driving American agricultural policy.

Multifunctionality is not a European invention. It was first recognized at the international level in the Rio declaration on sustainable development in 1992, and later by the United Nation's Food and Agriculture Organization at its World Summit in 1996. Although the concept is most accepted in Europe, it underlies policy developments in many parts of the more-developed world. For example, Bennett, van Bueren, and Whitten (2004) found that Australian urban dwellers are willing to pay some positive amount to maintain rural populations because of the environmental stewardship function performed by rural residents. Despite common themes, perspectives of multifunctionality vary widely across countries. Paarlberg, Bredahl, and Lee (2002) described how some nations see multifunctionality as justifying subsidies to agricultural production, while others see it as disguised protection. They explained,

> in its general form, multifunctionality refers to services provided by agriculture beyond the marketed agricultural output and so a jointness with agricultural production is maintained . . . however, beyond that general definition, individual nations have more specific, yet varied ideas. Examples include specific benefits, such as flood control, avalanche protection, outdoor recreational activities, environmental protection, and food safety. (Paarlberg, Bredahl, and Lee 2002, p. 323)

They used a conceptual model to conclude that multifunctionality never justifies trade interventions, but it can justify production subsidies or taxes. Hence, the debate goes on.

The European Approach

In Europe, the debate over the role and value of noncommodity outputs of the agricultural sector goes back at least into the 1980s and continues today, as indicated by the study by Glebe (2007) that raised the question, "how legitimate are agri-environmental payments?" Answers to that and related questions vary even among European nations. It is generally agreed that France has the most positive support for policy measures aimed at preserving landscape and providing environmental goods. The French perspective includes both qualitative and quantitative assessments of the value of environmental goods produced by agriculture. One of the most interesting aspects of the quantitative data behind that policy perspective is its "investment" orientation. The story goes that the French government was assessing the significant contribution of the tourism industry to the national economy and, in the process, surveyed tourists to ask what it was that attracted them to France. Responses overwhelmingly included references to the beautiful countryside. The French government immediately realized that preserving the countryside had a relatively small cost for the nation to pay compared to the continued returns coming into the nation from tourism. In other words, paying French farmers to maintain the traditional look of the rural landscape yielded big dividends to the French economy, thus making the government program a good investment for the nation. Other European countries have different perspectives about the values of noncommodity outputs from agriculture, as well as different opinions about whether there are market failures for those outputs that justify government interventions.

For many Europeans, food security is more important than environmental protection efforts, so multifunctionality policy debates can be driven by either issue. Brunstad, Gaasland, and Vardal (2005) found that "without support, the levels of agricultural public goods such as food security and landscape preservation would fall short of demand in high-cost countries" in Europe. It is widely accepted in Europe, unlike the United States, that agriculture provides more than simple commodity outputs, so European policy debates have advanced to the stage of identifying which policy tools work best in directing agricultural producers in the desired direction. For example, Martins and Marques (2006) asked, "is agricultural policy promoting a new role for farmers?" They answered "yes," that new European policies are encouraging farmers to use environmental concerns when selecting production technologies. On the other hand, Havlik et al. (2005) assessed the joint production of environmental goods and agricultural commodities in Europe and concluded that "commodity-linked policy instruments are not suitable for the production of environmental goods even under uncertainty." Thus, European debates are ahead of those in the United States because environmental policy tools are receiving more attention in European capitals.

An American Option?

In the United States, a new approach to arguing for government support of farms and ranches is to claim that agricultural producers are "stewards of the land." This is much like the French approach, which acknowledges the concept of multifunctionality. The American version of the argument is that private efforts to preserve the environment should be compensated with public funds because of the public goods generated and, unlike the European view, most of those environmental efforts take land out of agricultural production. This is the basis for most American government conservation programs, however there are some recent exceptions. As Dobbs and Pretty (2004) note, recent policy initiatives in the United States often seek to establish steward-ship payments to farmers, similar to successful efforts in the United Kingdom. They describe the Conservation Security Program (CSP) as the most significant new program in the 2002 U.S. farm bill and observe that

> unlike the Conservation Reserve Program, which takes land out of conventional crop and livestock production in order to focus exclusively on environmental goods, the CSP is designed for *working lands*. The CSP constitutes an attempt to foster multifunctionality by leaving land in crop and livestock production and providing stewardship payments for the use of practices and systems intended to reduce negative environmental externalities or, conversely, increase positive ones. (Dobbs and Pretty 2004, p. 233)

Unfortunately, conflicting policies make it unlikely that multifunctionality programs will be widely successful in the United States in the near future. Dobbs and Pretty note that

> given the continuation of high price and income supports tied directly or indirectly to nar-row, intensive crop systems, it is likely to prove either difficult or very expensive to induce participation in whole-farm resource management plans that actually involve very much change in farmers' systems. (2004, p. 233)

However, Lambert, Sullivan, and Claasen (2007) note that among Conservation Reserve Program participants, there is a distinction between farm households using the program to ease out of farming and those using the program to augment production receipts. Based on this observation, they conclude that more conservation payments may be channeled to working farms in the future. This means multifunctionality programs may slowly grow as public acceptance of environmental public goods grows.

Eventually, multifunctionality is expected to become the central theme of American agricul-tural policy. This is because it is the most "sustainable" argument for government intervention in agriculture. Of the three general arguments for interventions that have some public support behind them currently—food security, economic development, and multifunctionality (in its "stewards of the land" form)—only multifunctionality will have support across America after the public learns the economics behind each argument. This will take a while, but it will happen. The fact that food commodities are in surplus globally is currently being discussed in the mass media, so people will get the message before long and the food security argument will fade away with barriers to free trade. Economic development tends to be a popular idea, but it has real effects only in local areas receiving the development efforts. That means Americans in urban areas will eventually vote to curtail the current lump-sum transfers to rural places. On the other hand, Americans are likely to follow the European path and embrace the multifunctionality approach to valuing an agricultural sector, which takes care of the environment while still using our nation's resources in a productive way. That "two for the price of one" type of policy sounds more efficient and like a much better investment, thus it will appeal to American taxpayers and voters.

This shift in focus of American agricultural policy will occur because all Americans are environmentalists. Of course, there are two kinds of environmentalists. The first type can be called "general environmentalists." A general environmentalist cares about environmental issues in general. Only some people fit this description, although the current discussion of global warming is showing that they are more numerous than previously thought. The second type of environmentalist can be called "personal environmentalists." A personal environmentalist cares about the environment in his or her personal space, thus everyone fits this description at some point. Therefore, we all are environmentalists, with the only difference being our range of sensitivity to environmental problems. A personal environmentalist will shout "not in my backyard!" and take action when an environmental problem comes too close to home, but a general environmentalist is willing to sacrifice something for a global solution. To capture both groups as supporters of agriculture, a policy shift is needed. The direction of the shift is summarized in the policy proposal below.

- Proposal 20.1. Agricultural Policy. *America needs to shift the focus of policy from viewing "agriculture as factory floor" to "agriculture as neighborhood." This change is needed because the farm factory is not always profitable, and taking the "neighborhood" view helps us realize that agriculture affects everyone.*

The proposal explicitly recognizes the key difference between agricultural production and production in many other industries: agriculture is "next door" to everyone's home in some sense. No other industry impacts as many people and their living space directly or indirectly as does agriculture. As noted in Chapter 9, most of the land surface of the world is being used in some form of agricultural production. Therefore, by definition, agriculture is the neighborhood in which all but a small percentage of people live. In the United States, we have demonstrated an increasing willingness to hire someone to take care of our yard work for us. Thus, our production agriculture sector can argue that taking care of the nation's "yard" is an important task worthy of compensation. When this public good is fully recognized by Americans, they will support the farmers and ranchers performing the task. Conversely, Americans are already tired of paying more than necessary for commodities, and especially for domestically produced commodities not consumed in America. This makes it clear that in the future, programs giving taxpayer dollars to producers of grain crops that are in surplus here and mostly exported are going to end. In other words, environmental programs are sustainable, commodity production programs are not; thus, only multifunctionality programs give agricultural producers a chance for public support in the long run.

AMERICAN AGRICULTURAL POLICY IN A GLOBAL MARKET

The first of (at least) two challenges facing American agricultural policymakers is to think big. America needs to take the long-run, global view that a more profitable resource allocation is an economic improvement, even when it hurts some of us. Policies can continue to assist America's agricultural producers in the short-run transition period, but policymakers cannot forget the big picture. In the end, comparative advantage does have an absolute limit, and in the big picture the lowest-cost commodity producers will often be in less-developed countries. In other words, to gain access to the global markets for the manufactured goods produced here, America will be forced to argue for free trade that, in the long run, means we will lose some of our production agriculture sector to foreign competitors. This shift in resources is an efficiency improvement to the country, even though it means many American agricultural producers will be forced out of their professions; consumers will benefit.

The second challenge facing American agricultural policymakers is to prepare U.S. agriculture for the transition from traditional agriculture to a modern food system while making it as painless as possible. Policymakers need to help guide producers toward the most profitable resource allocations in what will continue to be dynamic global markets. Traditional cropping choices will have to change in many areas and marketing issues will increasingly dictate production decisions. Vertical integration through strategic alliances will become a necessity, and financial diversification will become the norm. The smaller number of agricultural producers to be needed in the future will play even more important roles because they will be running much larger operations, on average, although their efforts will focus on fulfilling their contracts with agribusiness firms. The slow evolutionary transition period now under way will see many small-scale producers pushed out of agriculture if they cannot find another income source.

"Thinking big" requires an unselfish perspective as America addresses two policy questions. In these questions there are (at least) two challenges to the American production agriculture sector. The first question is: *Does America have an "obligation" to its agricultural producers?* The second question is: *Does America have an "obligation" to the world to manage and preserve our agricultural resources and capacity to meet long-run global needs?*

American farmers and ranchers deserve our help in dealing with the complicated issues embodied in these two policy questions. They also deserve the truth, so policymakers will have to work hard to be analysts of, not advocates for, agriculture. Policymakers must maintain their objectivity to best serve agriculture, America, and the world.

The two policy questions are difficult because they are also moral questions to be faced now and in the distant future. As summarized below, the questions can be stated as "What about us?" and "What about them?"

What About Us?

As commodity markets become global in scale, America's agricultural producers often wonder "what about us?" They wonder if the country will abandon them as their share of the market dwindles. Small-scale producers, in particular, often feel neglected by American agricultural policymakers. So, the question arises: *Does America have an "obligation" to its agricultural producers?*

Agricultural producers believe the answer is "yes" due to the many contributions of the production sector to America's well-being. Producers have not only fed the nation, but they also managed the majority of natural resources and fueled the development of the national economy. In return, producers want some sort of "safety net" from the government that will aid them in their efforts to develop a prosperous future. The nature of the government assistance desired by small farms was captured in 1998 by the policy recommendations of the USDA National Commission on Small Farms in its report, "A Time to Act." Those recommendations follow.

1. Recognize the importance and cultivate the strengths of small farms
2. Create a framework of support and responsibility for small farms
3. Promote, develop, and enforce fair, competitive, and open markets for small farms
4. Conduct appropriate outreach through partnerships to serve small farm and ranch operators
5. Establish future generations of farmers
6. Emphasize sustainable agriculture as a profitable, ecological, and socially sound strategy for small farms
7. Dedicate budget resources to strengthen the competitive position of small farms in American agriculture
8. Provide just and humane working conditions for all people engaged in agriculture

Similar ideas come from larger-scale producers as well. Some of these recommendations are already being carried out, some have been ignored by policymakers, and others are completely out of the control of American agricultural policy. Nevertheless, they show the range of issues worrying producers. In general, all producers believe they deserve "fair treatment" but have not always received it.

There is evidence that agricultural producers have not received much help from agricultural policy. However, the problem may have been the misguided farm policies used, not a case of government neglect. The result has been poor economic performance in many parts of rural America. For example, Fisher (2005) found that the share of people living in poverty is higher in rural America than it is in metropolitan areas. She asks whether there is something about rural places that leads to higher poverty rates, compared to nonrural places. That question is answered "no" by Partridge and Rickman (2007), who find that poor places can respond to the correct combination of policies. Partridge and Rickman (2007) found that in 494 of America's 3,000-plus counties, the poverty rate exceeded 20 percent in 1999 and, in 382 of those counties, the poverty rate was over 20 percent consistently for more than fifty years. Those counties are rural in nature. However, Partridge and Rickman (2007) note how jobs help reduce poverty, even in rural places. Agricultural production has not reduced rural poverty, despite policy interventions, thus economic development of rural areas needs nonagricultural policies. Farm policies focusing on commodity output and prices will not help the majority of farm households.

In summary, the types of assistance that will help agricultural producers most are those that promote the economic development of local communities. Assistance from policies that reward farmland owners for managing the rural resource base will also help, but are unlikely to be sufficient to support most families, thus those programs cannot be expected to go it alone, as is now the case. As noted by Dobbs and Pretty (2004), sustainable agriculture and conservation programs will be too expensive for the country. Yet, the benefits to the nation of those multifunctionality programs will be so great in the long run that they provide additional incentive for the government to undertake the community and economic development programs that can generate jobs offering the off-farm income necessary for many rural households to stay on the farm. The country needs its stewards of the land and those stewards need a fair household income to enable them to remain on the job.

What About Them?

Will Americans think about "them" (the people living elsewhere in the world, both at present and in the future) when making our agricultural policies in the future? Yes, the globalization of commodity markets forces us to be more aware of our place as neighbors to those people who will be producing some of our food. This raises some interesting dilemmas, especially with regard to what we do with our portion of the globe's natural resources. For example, at present, it appears that the world has sufficient resources that can be developed to meet food needs for the long run. But appearances can be deceiving. So the second question facing America is, "do we have an obligation to the world to preserve our agricultural capacity?" Our land might not all be needed to feed us, but it might be needed to feed others.

If America answers "yes," that we do have a global obligation, this creates a constraint on our economic development up the economic food chain. If we do not invest our land and other resources in their highest and best use, our economic growth will be slowed down. However, Americans are smart enough and selfish enough to realize that wasting a valuable resource, like our farmland, puts both us and "them" at risk. Thus, even if America answers "no" to any global food obligation, we will want our rural "neighborhood" available to us in the future, just in case we need it. That is what will motivate Americans to pay agricultural producers for their stewardship services in the future.

Another way of expressing the big question is, "what is the role and responsibility of U.S. agriculture in global food security?" In the long run, is not each country responsible for maintaining its own agricultural production capacity? Given the uncertainty behind global population and climate forecasts, and the risks associated with being incorrect in those long-run estimates, it would seem that agricultural resource management should be a big piece of future policy initiatives. In America, we have the wealth to consider such policies.

It was noted in Chapter 9 that land use is a national and local responsibility in the United States, thus we are well positioned to understand the problem and lead a global effort to establish policy initiatives at the international level. Maintaining global agricultural capacity may seem like an odd goal now as most more-developed nations are reducing their farmland totals, but such a complicated and expensive policy goal needs to be discussed now to begin the slow process of finding a way to arrive at international agreement on what (and where) the future's global agricultural sector will be.

The urgency of discussions on maintaining global capacity comes from the immediate implications of adopting such a policy goal. There is a fixed amount of "good" agricultural land, thus some thought ought to be given to its use. At present, land-use decisions in the United States are often made with only short-term economic perspectives. This often results in "good" land being taken out of agriculture permanently. A better, more responsible long-run approach would be to follow the example of a poor, small farmer. That farmer, with a very limited amount of land, would be keenly aware of the need to maximize output so as to feed his/her expanding family in the future. Therefore, that farmer would build his/her house on the poorest piece of his/her land so as to leave as much as possible of the good land for cultivation. The longer such policy decisions go without considering the national and global implications, the more likely it is that mistakes will be made.

WHERE IT ALL LEADS

Agricultural commodity groups in America often ask for government intervention when their product is no longer profitable. Yet, this book presents a brief explanation of why regional, and even national, markets may disappear as part of normal economic processes with no market failure involved. This implies that no government programs are justified by the usual economic argument in these cases. Thus, many of the existing government farm programs must be justified using some other argument. In the summary discussion below, it is argued that, in general, American farm programs were intended to be risk management tools, but have had few successes and a questionable price tag.

The story begins with the standardized nature of agricultural commodities. When products are undifferentiated between firms, supply and demand determines price and all suppliers are price takers.

Free trade of a commodity creates a price ceiling for all market participants. In other words, when trade is not affected by government intervention, all participants are limited in that the highest price they can receive for their output is the "market price"—they could receive a lower price, but they would not rationally ask for a lower price than that offered by the market. This means only firms that can at least break even, on average, when selling at the global market price will be able to survive in the market over the long run. Higher-cost suppliers are forced out of the market by the lack of profitability.

In the American Midwest, many farmers do not have alternatives to producing grain and livestock commodities; few nonagricultural options exist. This first became a problem when domestic free trade brought competitors from other American regions that squeezed mid-westerners out of most other commodities. Comparative advantage keeps them in those few grain-oriented enterprises that suit the climate and resources available. Unfortunately, the American Midwest is now losing its absolute advantage in global grain markets, which is aiding in the squeeze on the profitability of its grain-eating livestock. When the process began decades ago, the calls for government intervention began. Foreign free trade has the same effects as domestic free trade—production is shifted to different locations—but America's initial reaction was that it did not want to lose its agricultural sector, and so agricultural policy became a stalling tactic.

Government programs were created to keep America's production agriculture sector in business (Bonnen and Schweikhardt 1998). Many programs create price distortions that keep producers in the market longer. In effect, those programs raise the profitability of agriculture by paying farmers more than the global market price (although "price" is often not mentioned as the official problem). The drawback to such programs is that they create deadweight losses to the American economy. American taxpayers pay to keep resources in agriculture that might be more profitably invested in some other industry or, at the very least, invested in the production of some "nonprogram" commodity. These government supported bad investments "squeeze" the national economy.

The scale of government program costs has been quite significant in recent years, as shown in Figure 20.1. Direct government payments and other subsidies now support many farmers and some entire regions of the United States (see Egan 2001 for an example). As the American production agriculture sector slowly shrinks to a more competitive size, direct government payments seem to be getting more important. Those payments have been a larger portion of net farm income since the early 1980s. Since their peak in 1973, real agricultural sales and adjusted production income have both slowly trended down, but direct government payments have made net farm income fairly stable since 1984.

In general, it appears that government programs are a failed form of risk management tool because they were designed to reduce income risk for only a narrow group of agricultural producers. Overall, as Gardner (2000) and others have said, agricultural policies have not raised farm incomes or reduced poverty. This view raises the question: how long will taxpayers be willing to pay the "risk premium" to keep unprofitable American farmers in business? When those premiums are reduced or eliminated by policy changes, American agriculture will shrink much faster because producers will be forced to face the full effects of global competition in markets in which they are no longer the least-cost supplier. Yet, the more competitive producers that will remain in American agriculture will benefit financially and will probably become stronger competitors in global markets when the market-distorting effects of the many unprofitable American farms are gone.

In the opinion of most agricultural economists, government interventions in agricultural markets have been a failure in some sense, so the obvious solution is to let the markets run themselves. This can be accomplished by allowing the industrialization process to complete itself through the current trends in economic evolution. Such a "policy" decision will cause gradual changes with significant effects on the structure, conduct, and performance of the American agricultural sector. The eventual result will be that the agribusiness sector will direct virtually all large-scale commodity production as part of vertically integrated supply chains. Such a result will not be welcomed by many American farmers and ranchers, so they will fight it until they realize it represents a sustainable future for them.

Boehlje and Doering (2000) described industrialization as an inevitable direction for the future of American agriculture. They found that

> the economic benefits of the dual dimensions of industrialization of agriculture— implementation of a manufacturing approach to the food and industrial product production and distribution chain, and negotiated coordination among the stages in that chain—are expected to result in a much more industrialized agricultural sector. (p. 53)

In describing the industrialized future of agriculture, they said that

> industrialization of agriculture means the movement to larger scale production units that use standardized technology/management and are linked to the processor by either formal or informal arrangements. Size and standardization are important characteristics in lowering production costs and in producing products that fit processor specifications and meet consumers' needs for specific product attributes, as well as food safety concerns. Smaller operations not associated with an industrialized system will have increasing difficulty gaining the economies of size and the access to technology required to be competitive, except perhaps in niche markets. Access to input and product markets will be especially critical. (Boehlje and Doering 2000, pp. 53–54)

Therefore, as Boehlje and Doering (2000) pointed out, economics are pushing small operators out. This means in the future small farms' only hope for a positive cash flow is to go green for greenbacks. Small-scale operators may not be able to compete with large-scale farms and ranches in producing low-cost commodities, but they can participate in conservation efforts, thus their stewardship services have value.

The complete industrialization of commodity production will not happen soon, however, because agriculture knows how to "farm the system." This is evidenced by the fact that the industry has its own department in government with a cabinet-level secretary. That is a lot of power for an industry that contributes less than 1 percent of the nation's gross national product! How did this happen? A study by de Gorter and Tsur (1991) developed a model to explain why the farm sector has disproportionate amounts of influence on government policies that affect farmers. The study concluded that agricultural groups actively pursue politicians, offering financial and other support. Yes, agriculture knows how to harvest many things. However, the longer agricultural groups use their political power to slow the industrialization process, the

Exhibit 20.1

The Agricultural Food Chain of Economic Evolution

Early: land, labor emphasis
Middle: land, labor, capital
Modern: land, decreasing labor, capital, management
Current: decreasing land, decreasing labor, increasing capital, increasing management
Future: decreasing land, increasing capital, increasing management

longer it will be before a sustainable structure is developed for American farmers and ranchers. They need to recognize that vertically integrated supply chains are the only type of industry structure that can support producers of undifferentiated commodities in the global markets that are evolving. Yet producers are not the only ones that need to change their perspectives for industrialization to be completed. For example, Young and Hobbs (2002) said policy views must be updated to allow the modern supply chains, which may violate old anti-trust laws. The current anti-trust, anti-corporation view held by many in agriculture, especially in the Midwest, reflect the realities of nineteenth- and twentieth-century commodity markets, but those views will cripple America's ability to compete in the global markets of the twenty-first century. A new perspective is needed now.

Much attention has recently been focused on the global markets being created by economic development (e.g., Storm and Naastepad 2001) and the fact that the world is changing in response to those developments (e.g., Schaeffer 2003). It has become clear that there will be winners and losers as the changes run their course. Eventually, food consumers in many less-developed countries will be winners (Smil 2000), but small farms in America will be losers if they cannot find a (local?) niche market they can serve profitably or if they cannot contribute to some environmental program (Hazell 2005). All of these changes have been in progress for decades as economic development continues its steady march. They bring us to two last questions.

First, what is in store for agriculture, in general? Economic development at the global level will continue to move in the direction of more efficient use of the world's resources, subject to the short-run constraints that nations impose to give their agricultural sectors time to adjust. This has always been the case, but now we can see that the resources being emphasized in agriculture's economic development have changed over time. This idea is presented in Exhibit 20.1 as the "agricultural food chain." It shows that changes in agriculture over time are explained by changing resource emphases. This is a subset of the economic food chain idea that explains economic development, as discussed in Chapter 5. As shown in the exhibit, American production agriculture's current stage of development is de-emphasizing land and labor use because increasing use of capital and management is raising productivity more rapidly than demand for commodities is increasing. Some other more-developed countries are at the same stage in their agricultural development, while less-developed countries are emphasizing different resources. The poorest countries are still emphasizing land as they struggle to add capital. As capital is acquired, less emphasis on labor is observed and a modern agriculture sector develops. The addition of management in a modern sector enables technological innovation to reduce the need for land in responding to expanding food demands.

The differences in resources among countries of the world will increase pressure on countries to specialize their production in the commodities for which they have both a comparative and absolute advantage in global markets, and to trade for other commodities. This means there will be continued shifts in the location of specific commodities until, eventually, the major production regions of each commodity are found where the globe's resources best suit that commodity. This will be a very slow process because it is tied to the agricultural and economic development of virtually every country in the world. Yet, as free trade materializes, the economic incentives for these production shifts will increase. This process is a gradual movement toward a global equilibrium in commodity markets based on resource distributions. It seems almost impossible to imagine, but this equilibrium will eventually happen as the globalization process educates us all about each other, thus causing us to mature in our attitudes and behavior toward one another.

Finally, what is in store for American agriculture? In a nutshell, a difficult transition period that leads to a smaller, more competitive agricultural sector. Traditional agriculture—the type that existed in the nineteenth and early twentieth centuries—is ending as America transitions to an industrialized food sector led by what we now call "agribusiness." The agribusiness sector emerged during the late twentieth century as an important link between commodity producers and consumers. It added value to commodities and gave consumers a say in deciding what foods they were to eat and, as a result, it was richly rewarded (Schumacher and Boland 2005). Now the structure of the food system assures that the American agribusiness sector will be profitable while the commodity production sector will struggle until it integrates with agribusiness.

This book has tried to identify past and current trends in the commodity production sector so as to give some idea of where the sector is going in the future. Many of those trends are clear in their implications for the sector. However, the lesson of American agriculture's past is that policy can alter almost anything. Thus, the timing and exact path of economic evolution in American agriculture can never be predicted, but the direction of the path is fairly clear, as summarized below.

Traditional agriculture's life cycle is ending and a new industry structure is emerging that will eventually replace traditional markets for undifferentiated commodities with vertically integrated supply chains producing branded products. Traditional markets suited commodity producers during the nineteenth and early twentieth centuries when those markets were local or regional in nature, thus enabling farmers and ranchers to develop niches or occasionally exploit temporary supply shortages to earn positive profits. In the late twentieth century, however, technological advances began creating global markets for many commodities, causing those markets to approach the theoretical "perfect competition" model for undifferentiated commodities. In such markets, the expected profit is zero. Thus, the "profit squeeze" of the past few decades should not be surprising. It should also not be surprising that an industry with zero average profits will be forced to change. Unfortunately, given that the "competitive" production agriculture sector is faced by "oligopolistic/oligopsonistic" sectors selling it inputs and buying its output, it should not be surprising that the market power imbalance would lead to farmers and ranchers being forced to respond to the agribusiness sector. Global commodity markets are not very profitable, but value-adding supply chains can be highly profitable for all participants. So, American agriculture is currently transitioning from a traditional commodity sector into a (reluctant?) participant in a modern food system.

The pursuit of sustainable profits will continue to lead America through the current long, slow transition period in which farm and ranch numbers will decrease significantly and land use will be directed ever more closely by a system of local and global markets. Local niche markets will respond to Americans' desires for high-quality specialty products. Global markets will be run by agribusiness managers directing vertically integrated supply chains. In both local and global markets, metasystems will develop that focus on food quality.

The location of commodity production will shift in response to comparative advantages resulting in smaller, regional and local production industries, as described in Chapter 17. In the United States, this improved matching of resources means that some industries that currently have a global market orientation will fail and disappear, but some local markets that disappeared long ago will reappear. For example, in the Midwest many wheat farms will vanish under the pressure of global competition, but small fruit and vegetable niches may blossom. Iowa was an apple-producing region during the 1920s and may again be so, on a very small scale. The most likely changes are an expansion of fruit and vegetable crops in microclimates suitable for sustainable operations. Also, livestock grazing will continue to be a natural for mountainous parts of the country but, ironically, the future of grazing industries depends on the impacts of feed costs. Livestock operations could move closer to the Canadian border, on average, if feed supplies in the Midwest become smaller or more expensive. Imported Canadian wheat, barley, or oats, and Brazilian corn, could replace some domestic sources for livestock feed. This indicates the interrelated nature of many commodity markets.

The composition of America's agriculturally based output will continually change as farmers look for nonfood products that might raise demand for commodities. Corn for ethanol is a current example getting lots of attention (e.g., Vedenov, Duffield, and Wetzstein 2006). Corn farmers are building lots of ethanol processing plants in the hopes that the United States will develop an appetite for corn-burning cars. American ethanol output was estimated to be about 4 billion gallons in 2007, with projections for 2012 of about 7.5 billion gallons. These totals represent only 3 percent and 5–6 percent of the annual U.S. automobile fuel market for those respective years. Thus, there is no chance that America can go entirely to ethanol, which leaves it as a local niche market with lots of distribution problems. It also raises the problem that the higher domestic prices for corn due to demand from ethanol processors make it possible for Brazilian corn to be imported at lower total costs. It has long been known that the least-cost source for corn will likely be Brazil (Lee, Glauber, and Sumner 1994), thus making the current rush to ethanol a speculative bubble waiting to burst. For livestock producers the diversion of corn to ethanol is creating real problems. Higher corn prices depress the profits of feedlots, which then cannot afford to pay as much for the feeder cattle they purchase from ranchers. Thus, the government intervention in the corn market—setting goals for ethanol production—has serious cross effects for livestock producers. Such cross effects are a common problem with government policy (e.g., Blank and Ayer 1987) because policymakers apparently do not consider them before jumping in.

The future composition of America's agriculturally based output may or may not include ethanol, but it will include staples like dairy products, specialty crops, and new nonfood products like "farmaceuticals"—medical products made from agricultural commodities. America is very good at producing commodities and using technology to turn those commodities into products that consumers want. We are also relatively wealthy and willing to pay for high-quality food. Thus, once we get through the painful transition period in which we see many farmers and ranchers pushed out of business due to the profit squeeze created by competition in the evolving global commodity markets, American agriculture will settle into the new global equilibrium and will take the lead due to our innovative agribusiness leaders. The global food system that is developing will treat American consumers well. It will assure us of a safe and sustainable food supply. And American agricultural producers will contribute a wide array of products to the cornucopia.

The contribution of America's farmers and ranchers to our nation's economic development has been immense. Even though their current contribution is now dwarfed in value by the market value of other industries, agriculture's total contribution is invaluable because of the nature of it. It includes not just food, but environmental stewardship, strategic preservation of our agricultural capacity, lifestyle choices, and a link to our history. Less than 1 percent of Americans now live and work on farms and ranches, but most of us feel some pride in the sector's performance and our family's participation in it, no matter how long ago that participation occurred. We will always appreciate agriculture's contribution to our nation's development, even if our appreciation mostly goes unspoken.

NOTES

1. This section draws heavily from the report on 2005, which was published in 2007. Similar reports are published nearly every year, but the 2005 version was the most recent at the time this chapter was written. The year 2005 was typical with regard to both the types of payments made and the types of farms receiving payments. Thus, these data are presented as an example only.

2. The three farm resource regions making up most of the Midwest are the "Heartland," "Northern Great Plains," and "Prairie Gateway." The Heartland includes the western half of Ohio and Kentucky, all of Indiana, Illinois, and Iowa, all but the southwestern section of Missouri, plus southern Minnesota, and the eastern quarters of South Dakota and Nebraska. The Northern Great Plains includes a v-shaped swath starting in northeastern Colorado and spreading northeast to include northwestern Minnesota, and spreading northwest to include nearly half of Wyoming and Montana. All of North Dakota, most of South Dakota, and the northern third of Nebraska are in the Plains. The Prairie Gateway is a nearly rectangular region covering southern Nebraska, all of Kansas, the western two-thirds of both Oklahoma and Texas, plus the eastern halves of Colorado and New Mexico.

REFERENCES

Ahearn, M., H. El-Osta, and J. Dewbre. 2006. "The Impact of Coupled and Decoupled Government Subsidies on Off-Farm Labor Participation of U.S. Farm Operators." *American Journal of Agricultural Economics* 88 (2): 393–408.

Ahearn, M., J. Yee, and P. Korb. 2005. "Effects of Differing Farm Policies on Farm Structure and Dynamics." *American Journal of Agricultural Economics* 87 (5): 1182–1189.

Atwood, J., M. Watts, and A. Baquet. 1996. "An Explanation of the Effects of Price Supports and Federal Crop Insurance upon the Economic Growth, Capital Structure, and Financial Survival of Wheat Growers in the Northern High Plains." *American Journal of Agricultural Economics* 78: 212–224.

Barrionuevo, Alexei. 2006. "More Farmers Seek Subsidies as U.S. Eats Imported Produce." *New York Times,* December 3, pp. 1, 32.

Bennett, J., M. van Bueren, and S. Whitten. 2004. "Estimating Society's Willingness to Pay to Maintain Viable Rural Communities." *Australian Journal of Agricultural and Resource Economics* 48 (3): 487–512.

Blank, S., and H. Ayer. 1987. "Government Policy Cross Effects: The Cotton and Dairy Programs' Influence on Alfalfa Hay Markets." *Agribusiness: An International Journal* 3: 385–392.

Boehlje, M., and O. Doering. 2000. "Farm Policy in an Industrialized Agriculture." *Journal of Agribusiness* 18 (1): 53–60.

Bonnen, J., and D. Schweikhardt. 1998. "The Future of U.S. Agricultural Policy: Reflections on the Disappearance of the 'Farm Problem.'" *Review of Agricultural Economics* 20 (1): 2–36.

Boucher, S., A. Smith, E. Taylor, and A. Yunez-Naude. 2007. "Impacts of Policy Reforms on the Supply of Mexican Labor to U.S. Farms: New Evidence from Mexico." *Review of Agricultural Economics* 29 (1): 4–16.

Brunstad, R., I. Gaasland, and E. Vardal. 2005. "Multifunctionality of Agriculture: An Inquiry into the Complementarity Between Landscape Preservation and Food Security." *European Review of Agricultural Economics* 32 (4): 469–488.

Burfisher, M., S. Robinson, and K. Thierfelder. 2002. "The Global Impacts of Farm Policy Reforms in Organization for Economic Cooperation and Development Countries." *American Journal of Agricultural Economics* 84 (3): 774–781.

Cahill, Carmel. 2001. "The Multifunctionality of Agriculture: What Does It Mean?" *EuroChoices* 1 (Spring): 36–41.

Chau, N., and H. de Gorter. 2005. "Disentangling the Consequences of Direct Payment Schemes in Agriculture on Fixed Costs, Exit Decisions, and Output." *American Journal of Agricultural Economics* 87 (5): 1174–1181.

de Gorter, H., and Y. Tsur. 1991. "Explaining Price Policy Bias in Agriculture: The Calculus of Support-Maximizing Politicians." *American Journal of Agricultural Economics* 73 (5): 1244–1254.

Dobbs, T., and J. Pretty. 2004. "Agri-Environmental Stewardship Schemes and 'Multifunctionality.' " *Review of Agricultural Economics* 26 (2): 220–237.

Egan, Timothy. 2001. "Failing in Style." *Choices* 16 (1): 39–42.

Fisher, Monica. 2005. "On the Empirical Finding of a Higher Risk of Poverty in Rural Areas: Is Rural Residence Endogenous to Poverty?" *Journal of Agricultural and Resource Economics* 30 (2): 185–199.

Gardner, Bruce L. 2000. "Economic Growth and Low Incomes in Agriculture." *American Journal of Agricultural Economics* 82 (5): 1059–1074.

Glebe, Thilo. 2007. "The Environmental Impact of European Farming: How Legitimate Are Agri-Environmental Payments?" *Review of Agricultural Economics* 29 (1): 87–102.

Goodwin, B., and A. Mishra. 2006. "Are 'Decoupled' Farm Program Payments Really Decoupled? An Empirical Evaluation." *American Journal of Agricultural Economics* 88 (1): 73–89.

Goodwin, B., and V. Smith. 2003. "An Ex Post Evaluation of the Conservation Reserve, Federal Crop Insurance, and Other Government Programs: Program Participation and Soil Erosion." *Journal of Agricultural and Resource Economics* 28 (2): 201–216.

Gray, W., M. Boehlje, B. Gloy, and F. Young. 2004. "How U.S. Farm Programs and Crop Revenue Insurance Affect Returns to Farm Land." *Review of Agricultural Economics* 26 (2): 238–253.

Gundersen, C., M. Morehart, L. Whitener, L. Ghelfi, J. Johnson, K. Kassel, B. Kuhn, A. Mishra, S. Offutt, and L. Tiehen. 2000. *A Safety Net for Farm Households,* USDA Economic Research Service, Agricultural Economic Report no. 788, October.

Havlik, P., P. Veysset, J. Boisson, M. Lherm, and F. Jacquet. 2005. "Joint Production Under Uncertainty and Multifunctionality of Agriculture: Policy Considerations and Applied Analysis." *European Review of Agricultural Economics* 32 (4): 489–515.

Hazell, Peter. 2005. "Is There a Future for Small Farms?" *Reshaping Agriculture's Contributions to Society: Proceedings of the Twenty-fifth International Conference of Agricultural Economists,* pp. 93–101. International Association of Agricultural Economists, Durban, South Africa.

Huang, T., P. Orazem, and D. Wohlgemuth. 2002. "Rural Population Growth, 1950–1990: The Roles of Human Capital, Industry Structure, and Government Policy." *American Journal of Agricultural Economics* 84 (3): 615–627.

Key, N., and J. Kaplan. 2007. "Multiple Environmental Externalities and Manure Management Policy." *Journal of Agricultural and Resource Economics* 32 (1): 115–134.

Key, N., R. Lubowski, and M. Roberts. 2005. "Farm-level Production Effects from Participation in Government Commodity Programs: Did the 1996 Federal Agricultural Improvement and Reform Act Make a Difference?" *American Journal of Agricultural Economics* 87 (5): 1211–1219.

Key, N., and M. Roberts. 2006. "Government Payments and Farm Business Survival." *American Journal of Agricultural Economics* 88 (2): 382–392.

Lamb, R., and J. Henderson. 2000. "FAIR Act Implications for Land Values in the Corn Belt." *Review of Agricultural Economics* 22: 102–119.

Lambert, D., P. Sullivan, and R. Claasen. 2007. "Working Farm Participation and Acreage Enrollment in the Conservation Reserve Program." *Journal of Agricultural & Applied Economics* 39 (1): 151–169.

Lee, H., J. Glauber, and D. Sumner. 1994. "Increased Industrial Uses of Agricultural Commodities: Policy, Trade and Ethanol." *Contemporary Economic Policy* 12 (3): 22–32.

Lence, S., and D. Hayes. 2002. "U.S. Farm Policy and the Volatility of Commodity Prices and Farm Revenues." *American Journal of Agricultural Economics* 84 (2): 335–351.

Mapemba, L., F. Epplin, C. Taliaferro, and R. Huhnke. 2007. "Biorefinery Feedstock Production on Conservation Reserve Program Land." *Review of Agricultural Economics* 29 (2): 227–246.

Martins, M., and C. Marques. 2006. "Is Agricultural Policy Promoting a New Role for Farmers? A Case Study." *Journal of Policy Modeling* 28: 847–860.

Metcalfe, Mark R. 2002. "Environmental Regulation and Implications for Competitiveness in International Pork Trade." *Journal of Agricultural and Resource Economics* 27: 222–243.

Monchuk, D., J. Miranowski, D. Hayes, and B. Babcock. 2007. "An Analysis of Regional Economic Growth in the U.S. Midwest." *Review of Agricultural Economics* 29 (1): 17–39.

Paarlberg, P., M. Bredahl, and J. Lee. 2002. "Multifunctionality and Agricultural Trade Negotiations." *Review of Agricultural Economics* 24 (2): 322–335.

Partridge, M., and D. Rickman. 2007. "Persistant Pockets of Extreme American Poverty and Job Growth: Is There a Place-based Policy Role?" *Journal of Agricultural and Resource Economics* 32 (1): 201–224.

Pinstrup-Andersen, Per. 2002. "Food and Agricultural Policy for a Globalizing World: Preparing for the Future." *American Journal of Agricultural Economics* 84 (5): 1201–1214.

Reardon, T., and C. Barrett. 2000. "Agroindustrialization, Globalization, and International Development: An Overview of Issues, Patterns, and Determinants." *Agricultural Economics* 23 (3): 195–205.

Rosegrant, M., and X. Cai. 2002. "Water Constraints and Environmental Impacts of Agricultural Growth." *American Journal of Agricultural Economics* 84 (3): 832–838.

Schaeffer, Robert K. 2003. *Understanding Globalization: The Social Consequences of Political, Economic, and Environmental Change.* 2d ed. Lanham, MD: Rowman & Littlefield.

Schroeter, J., A. Azzeddine, and D. Aiken. 2006. "Anti-Corporate Farming Laws and Industry Structure: The Case of Cattle Feeding." *American Journal of Agricultural Economics* 88 (4): 1000–1014.

Schumacher, S., and M. Boland. 2005. "The Persistence of Profitability Among Firms in the Food Economy." *American Journal of Agricultural Economics* 87 (1): 103–115.

Serra, T., B. Goodwin, and A. Featherstone. 2005. "Agricultural Policy Reform and Off-Farm Labour Decisions." *Journal of Agricultural Economics* 56 (2): 271–285.

Shaik, S., G. Helmers, and J. Atwood. 2005. "The Evolution of Farm Programs and Their Contribution to Agricultural Land Values." *American Journal of Agricultural Economics* 87 (5): 1190–1197.

Smil, Vaclav. 2000. *Feeding the World: A Challenge for the Twenty-first Century.* Cambridge, MA: MIT Press.

Storm, S., and C. Naastepad, eds. 2001. *Globalization and Economic Development.* Northampton, MA: Edward Elgar.

U.S. Department of Agriculture, Economic Research Service (USDA/ERS). 2007. "Which Farms Receive Government Payments?" Available at www.ers.usda.gov/Briefing/FarmIncome/govtpay byfarmtype.htm, April.

Vedenov, D., J. Duffield, and M. Wetzstein. 2006. "Entry of Alternative Fuels in a Volatile U.S. Gasoline Market." *Journal of Agricultural and Resource Economics* 31 (1): 1–13.

Young, L., and J. Hobbs. 2002. "Vertical Linkages in Agri-Food Supply Chains: Changing Roles for Producers, Commodity Groups, and Government Policy." *Review of Agricultural Economics* 24 (2): 410–427.

GLOSSARY OF VARIABLES
AND MATHEMATICAL DEFINITIONS

LIST OF VARIABLE AND OTHER ABBREVIATIONS

A_i = total acreage devoted to commodity i

AC = average cost

C_i = total production costs per acre of crop i

C_t = total production costs of all commodities during period ending at time t

c_j = vector of unit costs of j variable inputs

c_L = wage rate for labor (on and off-farm)

cr_{ft} = firm's cumulative investment in human capital and productive resources through time t (cr_{ft} is some function of profits earned in all prior periods)

CEL = certainty equivalent line; the slope of an individual's CEL is $\Lambda/2$

CK_{ft} = cost of capital for firm f at time t

CL_t = basic cost of living during the period ending at time t

COL = cropping opportunity line

Con_t = consumption during a period ending at time t

$\mathrm{Cov}(R_i, R_j)$ = covariance in returns between products = $\rho_{ij}(\sigma\pi_i)(\sigma\pi_j)$

CV = coefficient of variation

D_t = dummy variable ($D_t = 1$ during a period of interest and 0 otherwise)

d = derivative

E = farm equity

$E(\bullet)$ = expected value of $(\bullet)$

e_t = error term at time t

FA = farm assets

f = firm, otherwise function symbol

G = potential increase in profits earned by an innovation that improves productivity

G_m = growth in management (technological progress)

GP_{ft} = government payments to farm f during period ending at time t

GR_m = gross returns from a market's optimal crop portfolio

$g(cr_{ft})$ = reflects the opportunities for improving productivity

K = costs per acre of owning a parcel of land

K_i = total ownership costs per acre of crop i

K_t = capital at time t

k_h = vector of unit costs of h capital inputs (land, improvements, equipment, etc.)

k = some critical value (such as $\Pi*$) in measuring a z-score

L = quantity of labor "sold" off-farm

MR = marginal revenue

m = number of nonagricultural investments in a farmer's total portfolio

m_f = innovation expertise of firm f ($m_f = m_{\max}$ for the most innovative firm)

$(m_f)g(cr_{ft})$ = probability of firm f improving its productivity in period t

n = number of commodities produced by the industry, or the number of crops in a farmer's crop portfolio

OC_t = total ownership costs of all commodities at time t

OFI = off-farm income

OK = opportunity costs

P_{it} = average unit price of commodity i at time t

PC_t = total production costs of all commodities during period ending at time t

$\Pr\{.\}$ = probability of event (.)

PV = present value

Q_{it} = quantity of commodity i produced at time t

QL = costs of voluntary expenses to raise the quality of life

R = total industry sales revenues

R_f = risk-free return to land from cash leasing it to others

R_i = revenue per acre from crop i

T_t = time trend dummy ($T_t = t$ during a period of interest and 0 otherwise)

TFP = total factor productivity

U = utility

v = nonagricultural investment, asset

$W(m)$ = distribution of m_f and $W(m_{max}) = 1$ by definition

w_i = weight of crop i in a farmer's crop portfolio

w_v = weight (% of asset values) of investment v in a farmer's total portfolio

X_m and X_f = proportion of land in the market portfolio, risk-free investment (i.e., cash leased)

x_{ij} = quantities of j variable inputs to be applied in the production of commodity i, or per acre

x_i and x_j = proportion of the portfolio in products i and j

Y_i = average yield per acre of commodity i

z = probability value in a statistical table for a normal distribution

z_{ih} = quantities of h capital inputs used in the production of commodity i, or per acre

α = regression intercept, a constant

β = regression coefficients to be estimated; also: beta is a standard measure used in finance to indicate the relationship between a product or portfolio i and the "market": a security's "systematic" risk relative to the market index

μ = arithmetic mean of a population or variable

ε = error term

ξ = elasticity

φ = market marginal land quality

Ω = Blank's index of expected risk/return tradeoff

Λ = risk-aversion parameter

λ_v = vector of exogenous factors affecting the profit of nonagricultural investment v

Γ = upper (acceptable) limit on $\Pr\{\Pi < \Pi*\}$ in Telser's criterion

Π = total industry profits (an income-random variable)

$\Pi*$ = income goal (i.e., the "disaster level" or the "safety threshold")

Π_ϕ = profit per acre from crop portfolio ϕ

π_{DP} = Blank's index of returns to limited diversification

π_i = profit per acre from crop i

π_v = profit (or ROI) of nonagricultural investment v and is a function of a vector of exogenous factors (λ_v)

ρ_{ij} = correlation between the returns from crops or portfolios i and j

σ_j = standard deviation of returns for state or region i

σ^2 = variance

$\sigma^2(\Pi_\phi)$ = risk defined as the historical variance of average profits per acre for portfolio ϕ

$\sigma^2(\pi_i)$ = risk defined as the historical variance of profits per acre for crop i

$\sigma^2(R_p) =$ variance in returns from portfolio p

$\sigma^2(\varepsilon_i) =$ portion of variance is "nonsystematic" or diversifiable risk

$\gamma =$ regression coefficients to be estimated

$(OC) =$ function, analogous to a risk premium (a minimum amount desired above the person's bare financial requirements)

ΔCML $=$ slope of the capital market line

ΔCOL $=$ slope of the cropping opportunity line, which is the CML for landowners, but not tenants

$\Delta(cr_{ft}) =$ change in cumulative investment during period t

MATHEMATICAL DEFINITIONS

The industry's revenue from all agricultural commodities ($i = 1, 2, \ldots, n$) at time t is

$$(2.2) \qquad R_t = \sum_{i=1}^{n} P_{it} Q_{it}$$

and the industry's profit from all n agricultural commodities at time t is

$$(2.3) \qquad \Pi_t = R_t - C_t - K_t,$$

where :
$$Q_{it} = Y_{it} A_{it},$$
$$C_t = \Sigma_i \Sigma_j c_{jt} x_{ijt}$$
$$K_t = \Sigma_i \Sigma_h k_{ht} z_{iht},$$

and $P_i, c_j, k_h > 0; Y_i, A_i, x_j, z_h \geq 0$.

Expected profit, for firm f at time t, is specified as

$$(2.4) \qquad E(\pi_{ft}) = E[R_{ft} - C_{ft} - K_{ft} + (m_f)g(cr_{ft})G - \Delta(cr_{ft})]$$

with G defined as

$G \equiv (R_{ft} - C_{ft} - K_{ft}) - (R_{ft}^* - C_{ft}^* - K_{ft}^*)$, where the asterisk indicates a value that would have existed for firm f in period t without the innovation.

$\Delta(cr_{ft}) = cr_{ft} - cr_{ft-1}$, and it is constrained to be ≥ 0.

A firm's expected sales revenues are

$$(2.5) \qquad E(R_{ft}) = R_{ft-1} + E[(m_f)g(cr_{ft})G + \Delta(cr_{ft})].$$

A general model to measure the slope of a given series, y_t, during some period is

$$(2.6) \qquad y_t = \alpha + \gamma y_{t-1} + \beta T_t = e_t$$

When both slopes and intercepts are to be measured, the model is

$$(2.7) \qquad y_t = \alpha + \gamma y_{t-1} + \beta_T T_t + \beta_D D_t + e_t$$

The general industry profit and sales equations estimated, respectively, are

(2.8) $$\Pi_t = \alpha + \gamma_1 \Pi_{t-1} + \gamma_2 (R_t/A_t) - \gamma_3 [\Delta(cr_t)] + \beta_T T_t + \beta_D D_t + e_t$$

(2.9) $$R_t = \alpha + \gamma_4 R_{t-1} + \gamma_5 (\Pi_t/R_t) + \gamma_6 [\Delta(cr_t)] + \beta_T T_t + \beta_D D_t + et.$$

Telser's criterion:

(3.9) and (11.3) $$\text{maximize}, E(\Pi)$$

subject to

(3.10) and (11.4) $$\Pr\{\Pi < \Pi*\} < \Gamma$$

The z for state or region i is calculated here as:

(3.11) $$z_i = \frac{E(R_i) - k}{\sigma_i}$$

The farm share of GSP and the "Location Quotient" (LQ):

(3.12) $$\text{farm share of GSP} = \frac{\text{farm GSP}_i}{\text{total GSP}_i}$$

(3.13) $$LQ = \frac{(\text{farm GSP}_i/\text{total GSP}_i)}{(\text{farm GNP}_{US}/\text{total GNP}_{US})}$$

The DuPont expansion for any time period is

(3.14) $$\frac{\Pi}{E} = \frac{R-C}{R} \frac{R}{FA} \frac{FA}{E}$$

Operating profit margin $= (R–C)/R$
Asset turnover ratio $= (R/FA)$
Leverage effect $= (FA/E)$

Wealth changes for the period ending at time t:

$$\Delta W_t = FInc_t + OFInc_t + \Delta K_t - Con_t.$$

Gross farm income:

$$FInc_t = R_t + GP_t - PC_t - OC_t$$

A simple model of the expected price of farmland:

$$E(LV_{ft}) = E(R_{ft} + GP_{ft} - CK_{ft} + PROD_{ft} + Den_{ft})$$

The expected profit for firm f at time t (an expansion of Equation 2.4):

$$E(\pi_{ft}) = E[R_{ft} + GP_{ft} - PC_{ft} - OC_{ft} + (m_f)g(cr_{ft})G - \Delta(cr_{ft})]$$

The growth in management (technical progress):

(8.7) $$G_m = G_q - e_{q,K}G_K - e_{q,L}G_L - e_{q,A}G_A.$$

Simple model of farmland value:

(9.1) $$\text{Land value} = f\left[\pi + PV\left(\sum_{i=1}^{n} E\pi_i w_i\right)\right],$$

$$\text{subject to :} \quad \sum_{i=1}^{n} w_i = 1.0.$$

Certainty equivalent of expected profits:

(11.1) $$E(U_\phi) = E(\Pi_\phi) - (\Lambda/2)(\sigma^2\Pi_\phi)$$

A farmer's return when the sole source of income is profits from production efforts:

(11.5) $$\Pi_\phi \equiv \sum_{i=1}^{n} w_i\pi_i$$

$$\text{where :} \quad \pi_i = R_i - C_i - K_i$$

$$R_i = P_iY_i$$
$$C_i = \Sigma_j\ c_jx_{ij}$$
$$K_i = \Sigma_h\ k_hZ_{ih}$$

and $\Sigma w_i = 1.0$; $P_i, c_j, k_h > 0; Y_i, x_j, z_h \geq 0$.

Risk for a portfolio containing three crops is:

$$\sigma^2(\Pi_\phi) = w_1^2\sigma^2(\pi_1) + w_2^2\sigma^2(\pi_2) + w_3^2\sigma^2(\pi_3) + 2w_1w_2\text{Cov}(\pi_1, \pi_2)$$
$$+ 2w_1w_3\text{Cov}(\pi_1, \pi_3) + 2w_2w_3\text{Cov}(\pi_2, \pi_3)$$
$$\text{where:} \quad \text{Cov} = \rho_{ij}(\sigma\pi_i)(\sigma\pi_j)$$
$$\rho_{ij} = \text{the correlation between the returns from crops } i \text{ and } j.$$

Crop category 1 (low-value annuals) includes crops with expected returns per acre ranging from a low of $E(\pi_{1L})$ to a high of $E(\pi_{1H})$, with an average of $E(\pi_{1A})$.

$$E(\pi_{1L}) < E(\pi_{2L}) < E(\pi_{3L}) < E(\pi_{4L}),$$

$$E(\pi_{1H}) < E(\pi_{2H}) < E(\pi_{3H}) < E(\pi_{4H}), \text{and}$$

$$E(\pi_{1A}) < E(\pi_{2A}) < E(\pi_{3A}) < E(\pi_{4A}).$$

Expected risk levels increase at higher stages of the Farming Food Chain, such that

$$E(\sigma^2\pi_{1A}) < E(\sigma^2\pi_{2A}) < E(\sigma^2\pi_{3A}) < E(\sigma^2\pi_{4A})$$

Certainty equivalent line (CEL) is the tangent line from the target/desired return, with a slope of $\Lambda/2$.

(11.6)
$$\Pi_{\phi'} \equiv \sum_{i=1}^{n} w_i\pi_i + \sum_{v=1}^{m} w_v\pi_v$$

where $\pi_v = f(\lambda_v)$ and $\sum w_i + \sum w_v = 1.0$.

The variance of returns to the portfolio in Equation 11.6 is

(11.7)
$$\sigma^2(\Pi_{\phi'}) \equiv \sum_{i=1}^{n}\sum_{v=1}^{m} Cov(\pi_i\pi_v)w_iw_v.$$

The designated minimum level of return is more fully described as:

$$\Pi* = \text{fixed financial obligations} + \text{lifestyle costs} + (\text{OC: opportunity costs}).$$

Necessary condition for crop production in the long-run on the part of a risk averse farmer is

(11.8)
$$E(U_{\phi}) > (\pi_f + c_LL + \pi_{vf}),$$

where the factors on the right side are the opportunity costs.

The expected average *returns* per acre at time t for each crop i is

(12.1)
$$E(R_{it}) = (PY)_{it} - C_{it}$$

Portfolio risk is measured using the full covariance model of returns for n products below:

(12.5)
$$\sigma^2(R_p) = \sum_{i=1}^{n} x_i^2[\sigma(R_i)]^2 + \sum_{i=1}^{n}\sum_{j=1}^{n} x_ix_jCov(R_i,R_j), i \neq j$$
$$= \sum_{i=1}^{n}\sum_{j=1}^{n} x_ix_jCov(R_i,R_j)$$

The expected return of a portfolio equals the sum of the weighted expected returns from the crops included in the portfolio:

$$E(R_p) = x_1 E(R_1) + x_2 E(R_2) + \ldots + x_n E(R_n)$$

(12.6)
$$= \sum_{i=1}^{n} x_i E(R_i)$$

In Chapter 12, gross income in rate-of-return form:

(12.7)
$$E(R_p) = \frac{(PY - C)_p}{C_p}.$$

(12.8)
$$\beta_i \equiv \frac{Cov(R_i, R_m)}{\sigma(R_m)^2}.$$

The slope of the capital market line (CML),

(12.9)
$$\Delta CML \equiv \frac{E(R_m) - R_f}{\sigma(R_m)},$$

is the reward for bearing risk, per unit of such risk, offered by the optimal portfolio.

The slope of the security market line (SML) is

(12.11)
$$E(R_m) - R_f$$

because the market portfolio has a beta of one by definition (beta used, not σ, for risk).

The slope of the cropping opportunity line for landowners, (tenants)

(13.9)
$$\Delta_o COL \equiv \frac{E_o(GR_m) - R_f}{\sigma_m(\Pi_m)},$$

is literally the reward for bearing production risk, per unit of such risk

(13.10)
$$\Delta_T COL \equiv \frac{E_T(GR_\phi) - R_f}{\sigma_\phi(\Pi_\phi)},$$

the zero-beta portfolio result:

(12.13)
$$E(R_z) = R_f,$$

The SIM most often used is

(12.14)
$$R_i = \alpha_i + \beta_i R_m + \varepsilon_i$$

The variance of returns for an enterprise is

(12.15)
$$\sigma^2(R_i) = [\beta_i \sigma(R_m)]^2 + \sigma^2(\varepsilon_i).$$

The β coefficient reflects the "systematic" risk from the market. The $\sigma^2(\varepsilon_i)$ portion of variance is "nonsystematic" or diversifiable risk that can be eliminated by diversifying totally.

Treynor-Black appraisal ratio:

(12.17)
$$\frac{\alpha}{\sigma(\varepsilon)}$$

from the temporal Jensen Performance Index equation,

(12.18)
$$R_{it} - R_{ft} = \alpha_i + \beta_i(R_{It} - R_{ft}) + \varepsilon_{it}.$$

(12.20)
$$\Omega_p \equiv \frac{E(R_p - R_m)}{\left[\left(\frac{\beta_p}{r_{pm}}\right) - 1\right]} - \left[E(R_m) - R_f\right].$$

By design, Blank's Ω_p tests whether portfolio p conforms to theoretical expectations concerning a market's risk/return tradeoff. If so, $\Omega_p = 0$; if not, it measures the deviations.

Blank's index of returns to limited diversification:

(12.24)
$$\pi_{Dp} \equiv R_p - R_f - 2\left(\frac{\beta_p}{r_{pm}}\right)\left[E(R_m) - R_f\right] + \beta_p\left[E(R_m) - R_f\right] - SC_p.$$

"Optimal hedge ratio" for a household allocating labor on and off-farm:

(15.4)
$$X_m = \frac{E(GR_m) - R_f}{\Lambda\sigma_m^2}$$

"Commodity Usage Index":

(18.1)
$$H = \frac{1}{n} + nV$$

where n is the number of product categories and V is the variance of the shares (s) of the commodity going into each category, defined as

(18.2)
$$V = \frac{\sum_{i=1}^{n}(s_i - 1/n)^2}{n}.$$

INDEX

470

ABOUT THE AUTHOR

Steven C. Blank is a Cooperative Extension economist in the Agricultural and Resource Economics Department at the University of California, Davis. He specializes in financial management, risk analysis, marketing, and management methods. After growing up around California agriculture, Dr. Blank completed a BA in business at California State University, Stanislaus, before attending the University of Massachusetts for an MBA and the University of Hawaii for an MS and Ph.D. in agricultural economics. He has worked in varied industry positions and has held faculty positions at California Polytechnic State University–San Luis Obispo, South Dakota State University, and the University of Arizona. His administrative experience includes serving UC Davis as Assistant Vice-Provost from 1996 to 2002. His international experience ranges from heading a research section of the Australian government for two years to various short research and consulting assignments around the world. He has authored or co-authored over 275 publications, including four books. His research and extension programs have both received awards from the American Agricultural Economics Association and the Western Agricultural Economics Association. He is a past president of the Western Agricultural Economics Association, and received that association's highest honor, the Distinguished Scholar Award, in 2007.